MW00479868

The Essence of the Old Testament:

A *Survey*

The Essence of the old Testament:

A *Survey*

Ed Hindson
Gary Yates
Editors

ACADEMIC

Nashville, Tennessee

To

Walter C. Kaiser Jr.

and

Eugene H. Merrill

*With gratitude for your scholarly research,
quality instruction, godly example, and evangelical spirit.*

Table of Contents

List of Maps

Abbreviations

ANET	*Ancient Near Eastern Texts Relating to the Old Testament*
AUSS	*Andrews University Seminary Studies*
BAR	*Biblical Archaeology Review*
BCOT	Baker Commentary on the Old Testament
BKC	*Bible Knowledge Commentary*
CBC	Cambridge Bible Commentary
DSB	The Daily Study Bible
EBC	*The Expositor's Bible Commentary*
FOTL	Forms of the Old Testament Literature
ICC	International Critical Commentary
ISBE	*International Standard Bible Encyclopedia*
ITC	International Theological Commentary
IVP	InterVarsity Press
JSOT	*Journal for the Study of the Old Testament*
JSOTSup	Journal for the Study of the Old Testament: Supplement Series
KJBC	*King James Bible Commentary*
NAC	New American Commentary
NCBC	New Century Bible Commentary
NT	New Testament
NICNT	New International Commentary on the New Testament
NICOT	New International Commentary on the Old Testament
NIGTC	New International Greek Testament Commentary
NIVAC	New International Application Commentary
OT	Old Testament
OTL	Old Testament Library
OTSB	Old Testament Study Bible
SJT	*Scottish Journal of Theology*
TOTC	Tyndale Old Testament Commentary
TWOT	*Theological Wordbook of the Old Testament*
VT	*Vetus Testamentum*
WBC	Word Biblical Commentary
WEC	Wycliffe Exegetical Commentary

Contributors

GENERAL EDITORS AND AUTHORS

Edward E. Hindson (Th.D., Trinity Graduate School); D. Min., Westminster Theological Seminary; D. Litt et Phil., University of South Africa; FIBA, Cambridge University, is the Dean of the School of Divinity and the Distinguished Professor of Religion and Biblical Studies at Liberty University.

Gary Yates (Th.M., Ph.D., Dallas Theological Seminary) is Associate Professor of Old Testament and Hebrew at Liberty Baptist Theological Seminary.

ASSOCIATE EDITORS, AUTHORS, AND CONTRIBUTORS

Alan Fuhr Jr. (Ph.D., Southeastern Baptist Theological Seminary) is Assistant Professor of Religion and Acting Chairman of the Department of Biblical Studies at Liberty University. *Wisdom Literature.*

Harvey Hartman (Th.D., Grace Theological Seminary) is Professor of Biblical Studies at Liberty University. *Editorial Assistance.*

Leo Percer (Ph.D., Baylor University) is Associate Professor of Biblical Studies and Director of the Ph.D. Program at Liberty Baptist Theological Seminary. *Editorial Assistance.*

Randall Price (Ph.D., University of Texas) is the Distinguished Professor of Judaic Studies and Director of the Center for Judaic Studies at Liberty University. *Archaeology and the Old Testament.*

Elmer Towns (D. Min., Fuller Theological Seminary) is the Distinguished Professor of Systematic Theology and the Vice President of Liberty University. *Ezra, Nehemiah, and Esther.*

Andrew Woods (Ph.D., Dallas Theological Seminary) is an Adjunct Professor of Biblical Studies at Liberty University. *Pentateuch and Historical Books.*

Preface

The Old Testament is made up of 39 books in the Protestant English Bible and comprises nearly three-fourths of the biblical text. Introducing the basic content of these books generally includes an examination of their authorship, background, message, theology, and application. Some surveys cover the content of the books with little attention to their cultural context or theological relevance. Others, especially technical introductions, spend a majority of their focus on critical questions of authorship and literary genre, almost to the exclusion of actually analyzing the message of the books themselves.

Our purpose is to provide a college-level textbook that is easily accessible, academically credible, and soundly conservative. We are committed to an evangelical view of the inspiration of the Bible. Therefore, we take seriously what the Old Testament says about such matters as the creation of the world, the origin of evil, God's plan of redemption, and the messianic prophecies. At the same time, we recognize the message of the Old Testament is anchored in the culture, values, and beliefs of the ancient world. Yet, we find its theology, poetry, wisdom, and prophecy transcend that world because it was inscribed by those who "spoke from God as they were moved by the Holy Spirit" (1 Pet 1:21, author's translation).

I (Ed) have taught Old Testament Survey to college freshmen at Liberty University for more than 30 years. I fully understand the challenge every professor faces in this regard. I have taught more than 50,000 students in the classroom and another 50,000 by distance learning. They come from every walk of life, majoring in everything from accounting to zoology—English, history, religion, journalism, philosophy, psychology, business, you name it. My goal has always been to challenge them academically, inspire them spiritually, and motivate them effectively to discover the great truths and wealth of wisdom in the pages of the Old Testament and apply it to their own lives.

Our intended readers are college and university students as well as laymen who want a better understanding of the Old Testament. Therefore, we have deliberately left many of the more technical discussions of authorship and genre to the seminary and graduate level introductions such as B&H's *The World and the Word* by Merrill, Rooker, and Gristanti, which we highly recommend. At the same time, we have included photos and maps to illustrate the Old Testament world for our readers. We have also included a feature we have not found in other surveys: "Hebrew Highlights." This is designed for non-Hebrew readers to acquaint them with the look, sound, and meaning of the original language.

In teaching Old Testament in the college and seminary settings for the past 12 years, I (Gary) have come to realize that students even from Christian backgrounds are increasingly unfamiliar with the basic message and stories of the Old Testament. We are hoping this survey will provide a good general overview of the entire Old Testament that will help students to see how the individual parts fit together as a whole. Students today are also confused as to how the Old Testament relates to the New Testament and to their Christian faith, so we have provided an explanation of the theological message of each Old Testament book as it relates to the whole canon of Scripture. I especially would like to thank the members of the Old Testament faculty at Dallas Theological Seminary who played a significant role in training me for my current ministry, particularly Drs. Robert Chisholm Jr. and Eugene Merrill and Prof. Donald Glenn.

I (Ed) want to express my gratitude to former professors who taught, mentored, and guided me along my own academic journey. I took my first undergraduate Old Testament surveys from Eugene Merrill and Norman Geisler. At the graduate level, I studied under such renowned evangelical scholars as Gleason Archer, Walter Kaiser, Kenneth Barker, Edward Young, John Whitcomb, and John Davis. Each one prepared me for the teaching career that I have enjoyed these many years. At the same time, they more than adequately prepared me for more critical challenges that I would face later in my studies abroad.

We also want to thank Dr. Gary Smith of Union University who served as the external editor for B&H and Michael Herbert, M. Div. of Liberty University, who served as the managing editor of the electronic file. There will always be new insights to gain, new views to analyze, and new criticisms to consider. But the basic message of the Old Testament will remain forever the same. It is a story of God's love for the world, His provision for His people, and His promises for their future. It is the essence of that story that we have endeavored to tell in the pages that follow. To God be the glory.

Ed Hindson and Gary Yates
Liberty University in Virginia

Chapter 1

INTRODUCTION
The Essence of the Old Testament

The Old Testament is a collection of 39 books that tell God's story. It is the story of His love for His people, not only the chosen people of Israel but all people worldwide. In the pages of these amazing books, one encounters a **plethora of humanity**: patriarchs, kings, queens, priests, merchants, farmers, warriors, women, children, prostitutes, saints and sinners, the godly and the ungodly. They are all there, each playing a significant role in God's story. Alec Motyer says they are "larger than life and yet intensely human, belonging to the distant past and yet portrayed with such vividness and relevance" that their stories come alive, just like people today.[1]

What is amazing about the Old Testament is the **stark reality** of these stories. This is not a collection of sanctified mythology that glosses over the faults of its heroes. Instead, the men and women of the Old Testament are portrayed as they really were, no holds barred. Philip Yancey observes, "In its pages you will find passionate stories of love and hate, blood-chilling stories of rape and dismemberment, matter-of-fact accounts of trafficking in slaves, honest tales of the high honor and cruel treachery of war."[2]

If you are unfamiliar with the contents of these 39 books, get prepared for some of the most exciting, challenging, and disturbing reading of your entire life. The **human drama** that encompasses the greater story of God's love will challenge your faith, blow your mind, and bless your soul. The personal narratives, national histories, passionate poetry, and predictive prophecies combine to weave the tapestry of the Old Testament. Jean-Pierre Isbouts notes that the principle thesis of the Hebrew Bible is the story of people who "were led, admonished, and ultimately saved by the power of one God, the creator of the universe, a Being passionately devoted to moral and social justice."[3]

THE CHARACTER OF GOD

The acts of God in the Hebrew Scriptures reveal the character of God. They portray Him not as an impersonal force but as a **personal Being** who sees each person's problems, hears their cries, is concerned about this sinful world, and, therefore, "comes down" to intervene in humanity's darkest hours. He walks in the garden, like a parent, calling: "Adam, where are you?" (Gen 3:9, author's translation). He appears to Moses in the burning bush, telling him that He is concerned about the Israelites' suffering, therefore, He has come down to rescue them (Exod 3:7–8). He stands at the foot of the bed of the boy Samuel, calling him by name, commissioning him to be His prophet (1 Sam 3:10). He requires those who claim His name to "act justly, to love faithfulness, and to walk humbly" with Him (Mic 6:8). He grieves over sin and condemns evil (Gen 6:6–8). Yet He extends grace and favor (Hb., *hen*) and shows loving-kindness (*chesed*) beyond anything that can be earned, merited, or deserved.

To the casual reader God's love seems to be extended to men like Abraham, Isaac, Jacob, and David. It also seems, at first glance, that His love is only for the people of Israel and no one else. But one need only read deeper into the pages of this incredible love story to discover that His love impacts the lives of the **women and foreigners** who intersect its pages. In these stories one will encounter Tamar, the Canaanite mother of Judah's sons (Gen 38:6); Asenath, Joseph's Egyptian wife, the mother of Ephraim and Manasseh (Gen 41:45–52); Jethro, the priest of Midian and his daughter Zipporah, Moses' Midianite wife (Exod 3:16–21); Rahab, the Canaanite harlot, who married into the messianic line (Josh 2:1; 5:25; Matt 1:5); as did the godly Moabite named Ruth, the great-grandmother of King David (Ruth 4:13–22); Bathsheba, David's mistress, then his wife and mother of Solomon (2 Sam 11:3–4,27; 12:24); Hiram, the king of Tyre, who supplied the materials to build the temple (1 Kgs 5:1–12); and Ebed-melech, an African Cushite who saved the prophet Jeremiah's life (Jer 38:7–13).

From the opening pages of the Old Testament in the book of Genesis to the last verse of Malachi, men and women, Israelites and foreigners are **encountering God**. His existence is assumed to be a self-evident reality. No attempt is made at an apologetic defense. The biblical text simply announces: "In the beginning God created the heavens and the earth" (Gen 1:1). He speaks creation into existence by fiat and pronounces it "good" (1:31). He creates human beings in His own image (Hb., *tselem*) and likeness (*demuth*) to have a relationship with Him and to rule the creation on His behalf (Gen 1:26–31).

THE PROMISE OF HOPE

But with the entrance of sin came spiritual and physical death, the corruption of the human race, and the long, difficult history of fallen humanity (Genesis 3). At every turn of the drama that follows in the ancient Hebrew text, God shows up. He makes the first sacrifice, sheds the first blood, and gives Eve the first prophetic promise of the Bible—the seed of the woman would ultimately crush the head of the serpent, Satan (Gen 3:15). No details were given, only a **word of hope for the distant future.** The fact that Eve assumed her firstborn son was probably that "seed' indicates she expected a literal human being to fulfill the promise.

But that was only the beginning. As the years rolled by and the reader turns the pages of the Old Testament Scriptures, the attentive person soon discovers that God is narrowing the field so that ultimately only **one Person** will fulfill this promise. He will not be any human being but a son of Abraham (Gen 12:1–3). He will not be a son of Ishmael but of Isaac (Gen 17:18–19). He will not be a son of Esau but of Jacob (Gen

25:23–26). He will not be a son of just any of Jacob's sons, but He must be a son of Judah (Gen 49:10). He will not descend from Jesse's older sons but from David, the youngest son (1 Sam 16:6–12). This process of elimination was designed ultimately to qualify only one person to fulfill the messianic prophetic destiny. It was not necessarily meant to represent rejection of the others as much as it was meant to reflect the sovereignty of God's divine selection.

Jesus believed He was the fulfillment of the Old Testament **promises**. Speaking to two of His own disciples, Jesus began "with Moses and all the Prophets" and "interpreted for them the things concerning Himself in all the Scriptures" (Luke 24:27). Jesus was so confident in the divine authority of the Old Testament that He quoted it to define Himself and His mission and to settle controversies with His critics (see Matt 22:15–45). He rebuked Satan by quoting from the book of Deuteronomy (see Matt 4:1–11). He even went so far as to affirm some of the most controversial passages in the Old Testament. He referred to Noah's flood as though He believed it actually occurred (Matt 24:37–39). He affirmed Moses, Daniel, and Isaiah as the authors of their own material (Matt 24:15). He talked about the miracles of Elijah and Elisha as though He really believed they happened (Luke 4:25–27). He even referred to Jonah's experience in the fish as a type of His own resurrection (Matt 2:39–41; 16:4).

On the cross Jesus quoted Ps 22:1, "My God, my God, why have You forsaken Me?" (Matt 27:46). In the face of His impending death, Jesus told Peter that "the Scriptures [must] be fulfilled that say it must happen this way" (Matt 26:54). In regard to His own future, Jesus said, "But I tell you, in the future you will see the Son of Man seated at the right hand of the Power and coming on the clouds of heaven," quoting Dan 7:13–14 (Matt 26:64). While He challenged the many misinterpretations of the Hebrew Scriptures prevalent in His day (e.g., Matt 5:21–22), nevertheless, Jesus affirmed the teachings of Scripture when rightly understood. Thus, He said, "Don't assume that I came to destroy the Law or the Prophets. I did not come to destroy but to fulfill. For I assure you: Until heaven and earth pass away, not the smallest letter or one stroke of a letter ["jot or tittle," KJV] will pass from the law until all things are accomplished" (Matt 5:17–18).

THE BIBLICAL MESSAGE

One cannot adequately understand the New Testament without the Old Testament. This is because the Hebrew Scriptures were the Bible of the earliest Christians. As God moved upon the authors of the Gospels, the Acts, the Letters, and the Revelation, they wrote assuming their readers were familiar with the Old Testament. Concepts and terms that appear throughout the New Testament Scriptures find their **antecedents** in the writings of the ancient Israelites. Terms like *covenant*, *law*, *grace*, *baptism*, *prophet*, *priest*, and *king* find their roots in the Old Testament. Concepts like justice, forgiveness, redemption, salvation, and sanctification were born in the Hebrew mind long before the days of the New Testament. Philip Yancey writes, "Our roots go deep in the Old Testament thinking in many ways—human rights, government, the treatment of neighbors, our understanding of God—we are already speaking and thinking Old Testament."[4]

Jesus Himself is often described by **Old Testament images**: Lamb of God, lion of Judah, promised Messiah, Immanuel, King of the Jews, Son of Man, and the good shepherd. The pages of the New Testament are filled with Old Testament names and terms:

Abraham	Matt 1:1	Israel	Matt 2:20
Ark of the Covenant	Rev 11:19	Jericho	Luke 19:1
Babylon	Rev 14:8	Jerusalem	Matt 2:1
Bethlehem	Matt 2:1	Jezebel	Rev 2:20
Canaanite	Matt 15:21	Joppa	Acts 9:43
Damascus	Acts 9:3	Lot's Wife	Luke 17:32
David	Matt 1:1	Melchizedek	Heb 5:6
Egypt	Matt 2:14	Moses	John 7:19
Elijah	Matt 11:14	Nineveh	Matt 12:41
Enoch	Heb 11:5	Passover	Mark 14:1
Euphrates	Rev 9:14	Pentecost	Acts 2:1
Gentiles	Luke 2:32	Sabbath	Matt 12:2
High Priest	Heb 3:1	Samaritans	Matt 10:5
Isaiah	Matt 3:3	Sodom	Matt 10:15

Even more important than the names and terms of the Old Testament is its **theology**, which is the foundation of New Testament doctrine. Concepts like sin, salvation, blood atonement, redemption, sacrifice, justification, and sanctification are all grounded in the theology of the Hebrew canon. Any person who examines the books of the Old Testament will discover a story of God's love for the world. It is a story that is as old as time itself. It opens with the words "in the beginning" (Gen 1:1) and carries us down the tunnel of time, through the halls of history, into the canyon of eternity.

In these pages God is at work calling people by name: Adam, Abram, Moses, and Samuel. His love, patience, anger, judgment, and forgiveness are evident again and again. As patriarchs, prophets, priests, and kings stumble on the path of life, God is there to rebuke, correct, and redeem a fallen world—all because of His great love.

Come with us on this incredible encounter with the Divine as we survey the essence of the books of the Old Testament one at a time.

For Further Reading

Arnold, Bill, and Bryan Beyer. *Encountering the Old Testament*. Grand Rapids: Baker, 2008.

Dillard, R., and T. Longman III, *An Introduction to the Old Testament*. Grand Rapids: Zondervan, 1994.

Geisler, Norman L. *A Popular Survey of the Old Testament*. Grand Rapids: Baker, 2007.

Harrison, R. K. *Introduction to the Old Testament*. Grand Rapids, Eerdmans, 1969.

Hill, A. E., and J. H. Walton, *A Survey of the Old Testament*. Grand Rapids: Zondervan, 2009.

Merrill, E., M. Rooker, and M. Grisanti, *The World and the Word: An Introduction to the Old Testament*. Nashville: B&H, 2011.

Motyer, Alec. *The Story of the Old Testament*. Grand Rapids: Baker, 2001.

ENDNOTES

1. Alec Motyer, *The Story of the Old Testament* (Grand Rapids: Baker, 2001), 8.

2. Philip Yancey, *The Bible Jesus Read* (Grand Rapids: Zondervan, 1999).

3. Jean-Pierre Isbouts, *The Biblical World: An Illustrated Atlas* (Washington, DC: National Geographic Society, 2007), 48.

4. Yancey, *The Bible Jesus Read*, 23.

Chapter 2

THE OLD TESTAMENT WORLD
Real People, Real Places

Religious literature in the nations around Israel was often written into a mythological vacuum. People and places, if they are mentioned at all, often never actually existed. This is not the case with the Old Testament. The Hebrew Scriptures weave a fascinating narrative about **real people** in **real places** in **real history**. At every turn of the page, these ancient texts in the Bible introduce the reader to fascinating people who actually existed in ancient times. The biblical story includes a myriad of ancient kings, cities, languages, cultures, and civilizations that form the tapestry of the biblical world.

R. K. Harrison, who taught at Wycliffe College at the University of Toronto noted: "Because the Hebrews drew to a large extent upon the contemporary cultural patterns of Near Eastern life, the history of the Israelites can best be understood by placing the narratives of the Old Testament against the background of what is known about the culture and archaeology of the period covered."[1] In doing so, one quickly discovers that it is possible to verify the presence of many of these cultural patterns in both the Old Testament and numerous ancient Near Eastern sources.

In the Old Testament one encounters a **variety of ancient people** who actually intersected with the biblical story. Roberta Harris comments: "The Near East has always been a region of extraordinary diversity of climate, terrain, and cultures. The land of the Bible, tiny in itself and yet in some ways the pivot of the whole region, is a microcosm of that diversity."[2] In God's providential wisdom, Israel was placed at the center of the Fertile Crescent in the middle of the cradle of civilization on the great land bridge between Asia and Africa. Here on what Jean-Pierre Isbouts calls the region that stretches from the "confluence of the Euphrates and Tigris Rivers . . . to the alluvial plains of Canaan and the rich Nile River delta" is the canvas on which the stories of the Bible unfold.[3]

PEOPLES OF THE MIDDLE EAST

Sumerians

The ancient inhabitants of **southern Iraq** (Mesopotamia) were known as Sumerians. Their population was centered in various cities located along the southern

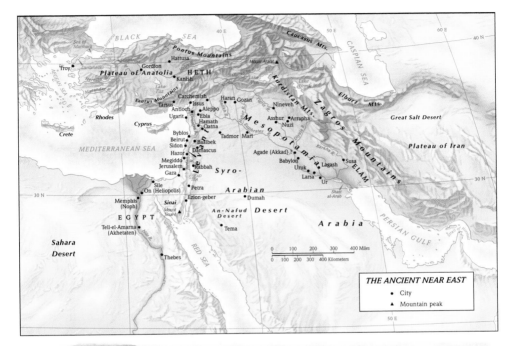

The excavations at Ur showing the palace foundations in the foreground with the ziggurat in the distance.

parts of the Tigris and Euphrates Rivers, the most significant of which were the cities of Ur, Eridu, Kish, Lagash, Nippur, and Uruk (biblical Erech). The culture, language, and literature of this society directly affected the entire Middle East.

The texts from ancient Erech (c. 3000 BC), attributed to the Sumerians, reflect a **non-Semitic language** which used a cuneiform (wedged-shaped) script later adopted by the Assyrians and Babylonians. Generally written with a stylus on clay tablets, the syllabetic script is preserved on thousands of clay tablets recovered by archaeologists. These tablets include everything from religious myths (stories of deities), economic texts (sales receipts), and political documents (explaining the relation of priests, kings, and administrators). Among the most well-known texts are the "Sumerian King List," which records incredibly long reigns, and the "Gilgamesh Epic," which includes the story of the great flood.

Excavations (1922–34) by Sir Leonard Woolley at Ur on the Euphrates River revealed an elaborate ancient culture reflected in gold and lapis lazuli decorated items, musical instruments, mosaic inlays on the "Standard of Ur," elaborate crowns, jewels, and bracelets. Designated by many as the city of Abraham's origin (Gen 11:27–31), Ur was one of the most developed cities of the ancient world, attested by the spectacular discoveries from the royal cemetery (c. 2500 BC). The ruins of the ziggurat (stepped pyramid) built by Ur-Nammu, founder of the prosperous Third Dynasty (c. 2150–2050 BC), are still visible at the site. The principal deity was Nanna (Semitic, Sin) who was also worshipped at Haran where Abraham later moved en route to Canaan.[4]

Babylonians

Babylon, which was built on the banks of the Euphrates, was one of the greatest cities of the ancient world. It eventually gave its name to the amalgamation of Akkadian Semites and Amorites who adopted the older Sumerian culture.[5] Flourishing under **Hammurabi** (1792–1750 BC), whose famous Law Code is well known, Babylon elevated Marduk as its chief deity. In antiquity the region was known as Chaldea, especially after the rise of the Chaldean dynasty in the Babylonian Empire of Nabopolassar (626–605 BC) and Nebuchadnezzar (605–562 BC).

The **city of Babylon** was surrounded by an intricate system of double walls that were decorated with enameled bricks displaying lions, dragons, and bulls arranged in alternate rows.[6] Visitors entered the city through the blue lapis-glazed Ishtar Gate. Paved roadways ran through the center of the city, leading to the palace-temple complex (*Esagila*), the famous "hanging

Hat and necklace from excavations at Ur, the original home of Abram.

gardens," and the 288-foot-high ziggurat (*Etemenanki*). A bridge over the Euphrates River connected the ancient capital to the new city on the west bank.

Nebuchadnezzar conquered the Assyrian Empire, Tyre, and Judah. Then he invaded Egypt, making Babylon the dominant power in the Middle East in the early sixth century. However, Bill Arnold notes that Nebuchadnezzar's inscriptional remains indicate that he prided himself more in his building activities than his military conquests.[7] During his 43-year reign, Nebuchadnezzar left his

Relief figure of a dragon from the façade of the Ishtar Gate at Babylon.

name on hundreds of bricks used in his massive building projects, giving ample testimony to his prideful assertion, "Is this not Babylon the Great that I have built by my vast power" (Dan 4:30).

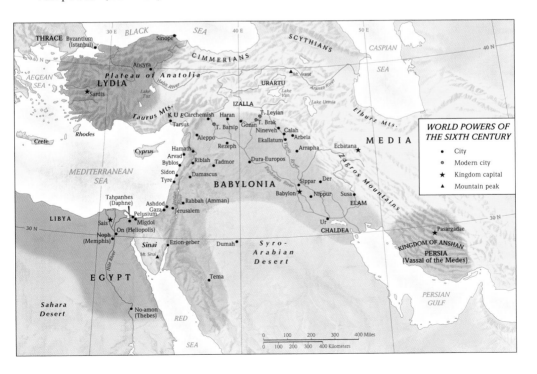

Assyrians

The ancient Assyrians occupied the upper Tigris Valley in northern Iraq (near the modern city of Mosul). The city of Ashur on the west bank of the Tigris River gave its name to the entire region. The city exalted the goddess Ishtar, whose symbol was a fish. Later **Nineveh**, on the east bank, became the capital and reached its zenith under Sennacherib (705–682 BC). The walls of his palace were decorated with reliefs of his conquests, including his siege of Lachish in Judah (Isa 37:8). The **violence** with which the Assyrians terrorized the ancient Middle East is clearly depicted on their monuments and in their written records. Ashurbanipal II (883–859 BC) boasted: "I stormed the mountain peaks. . . . I slaughtered them, with their blood I dyed the mountains red like wool." He bragged that he decapitated his enemy warriors and burned their children with fire.[8]

A relief from the palace of Ashurbanipal at Nineveh showing Assyrian soldiers subjecting captives to a series of tortures.

Sargon II (722–705 BC) conquered the city of Samaria in northern Israel, destroyed it, and took 27,290 captives who were deported to Assyria. His son, Sennacherib, attacked 46 cities in Judah and besieged Jerusalem in 701 BC. The Taylor Prism in the British Museum records his campaign against Hezekiah of Jerusalem. This attack and its subsequent failure are also recorded in 2 Kgs 18:13–19:37 and Isa 36:1–37:38. Sennacherib was later assassinated and replaced by his son Esarhaddon (681–669 BC) who built a new palace at Nineveh at Nebi-Yunus ("the hill of Jonah"). During his reign, Manasseh, the king of Judah, was taken captive for a few years (2 Chr 33:11). He was succeeded by Ashurbanipal in 669 BC. The last of the great Assyrian kings, he conquered Babylon, Elam, Tyre, and Thebes in Egypt (see Nah 3:8–10).

Ashurbanipal's massive **royal library** included tens of thousands of clay tablets, including an older collection originally assembled by Tiglath-pileser I (1115–1077 BC). The collection in the royal library included copies of the ancient Babylonian creation and flood epics. Despite Assyria's military and cultural success, in 612 BC the city of Nineveh was totally destroyed by a coalition of the Medes, plus the Babylonians under Nabopolassar and his son Nebuchadnezzar. Nineveh was leveled and was never rebuilt in fulfillment of the prophecies of Nahum and Zephaniah.

Cuneiform tablet and its envelope dealing with the sale of some land.

Persians

The Indo-European tribes of ancient Persia were closely related to the **Medes**. They arrived in the Iranian plateau in the second millennium BC in what today is modern Iran. The capital of the Medes was at Ecbatana on the major trade route from the Fertile Crescent to the Iranian plateau. Yamauchi notes that the names "Medes" (*Madaia*) and "Persians" (*Parsua*) first appear in the records of the Assyrian King Shalmaneser III (844–836 BC).[9] By the seventh century BC the united Median state allied with the Babylonians and helped overthrow the Assyrian capital at Nineveh in 612 BC.

The 40-year reign of Cyaxares (625–585 BC) marked the apex of Median power, which was eventually eclipsed by their **Persian allies** led by Cambyses I (600–559 BC) and Cyrus II (the Great) who ruled from 550 to 530 BC. In 550 BC Cyrus defeated his maternal grandfather, Astyages the Mede, at Pasargadae, where he later built his capital. After consolidating the Medes and Persians, under his rule Cyrus conquered Sardis in Asia Minor in 546 BC and Babylon in 539 BC. He did this by diverting the Euphrates River and taking the city without a battle. The account of the fall of Babylon in Daniel 5 corroborates the information in the *Nabonidus Chronicle* which indicates that Nabonidus (the last official King of Babylon) placed the city under his son and coregent Belshazzar several years before it fell.[10]

Cyrus later died in battle at age 70 in 530 BC and was succeeded by his son Cambyses II (530–522 BC) who conquered Egypt in 525 BC, extending the Persian Empire from Egypt to India. Darius I (522–486 BC) established a 1,700-mile courier service on the Royal Road that linked Susa to Sardis. He gave the inhabitants of Jerusalem permission to finish the second temple under the leadership of Zerubbabel (Ezra 5–6). He also moved his capital to **Persepolis** where he died in 486 BC, four years after the Greeks defeated the Persian army at the battle of Marathon in 490 BC. His son Xerxes I (485–465 BC), who is called Ahasuerus in Esth 1:1 and Ezra 4:6, destroyed most of Babylon, invaded Greece, and burned Athens. The next king, Artaxerxes I (464–424 BC), gave Ezra (458 BC) and Nehemiah (445 BC) permission to travel to Jerusalem to solidify the king's control of that part of his kingdom. The Persian Empire continued to flourish until it was conquered by Alexander the Great in 330 BC.

Hittites

The ancient Hittites were totally lost to history, except from biblical references (e.g., Genesis 23; Josh 1:4) causing many critical scholars to question their existence. However, archaeological excavations at Bogazkoy in Turkey in 1906 revealed the

Persepolis, the Persian royal retreat, built by Darius I and Xerxes I.

ancient Hittite capital of Hattusas and uncovered thousands of Hittite texts on clay tablets. The Hittites were Indo-Europeans who settled in **Asia Minor** circa 2000 BC. Their name derives from the earlier Hatti peoples, called the "children of Heth" (Gen 23:3 ASV). F. F. Bruce noted that with the spread of the Hittite Empire the designation "Hittites" was extended to the peoples and lands they conquered.[11]

The Hittite Empire was founded circa 1800 BC and reached its apex under Suppiluliumas I (c. 1380–1350 BC). During his reign the Hittites began smelting iron in what archaeologists designate as the early beginnings of the **Iron Age**. The Hittites continued to expand south until 1284 BC when Hattusilis III and Ramesses II of Egypt signed a treaty of peace. By 1180 BC the Hittite Empire collapsed and eventually disappeared from history. Of special interest to biblical scholars are the Hittite suzerain-vassal treaties that resemble the treaty form found in the book of Deuteronomy.[12]

Ancient Hittite Empire.

Arameans

The name Aram is derived from the grandson of Abraham's brother Nahor (Gen 22:21) and is identified in the Bible with the descendants of Shem (Gen 10:22). The Arameans were the inhabitants of the Fertile Crescent in Syria and upper Mesopotamia. Their language, known as **Aramaic**, became the major form of cultural communication in the region during the years of Babylonian and Persian dominance (600–330 BC). As early as Gen 25:20 and 31:20, Abraham's relatives Bethuel and Laban were called Arameans, as were the Israelite patriarchs (Deut 26:5).

Assyrian records depict the Arameans as large tribal groups of pastoral people living in towns and villages of ancient Syria. The cuneiform tablets from Ebla (2400–2250 BC) mention Aramean Damascus as one of Ebla's trading partners. Genesis 15:2 names Abraham's servant as " Eliezer of Damascus," indicating that the city was well established in patriarchal times. By the tenth century BC **Damascus** was the capital of the Aramean state and is frequently mentioned in the

The city wall of biblical Damascus.

biblical text of 1–2 Kings. W. T. Pitard notes, "The two nations had a close and complex relationship from the tenth through the eight centuries."[13]

Although the Israelite King David conquered Damascus (2 Sam 8:5), the city later regained power and influence under Ben Hadad I (900–860 BC), the probable "king of Aram" who fought against Ahab of Israel (1 Kgs 20:1–34; 22:29–36). Subsequent **Aramean kings** mentioned in the biblical record included Hazael (1 Kgs 19:15) and

These twin basalt column bases are a part of one of four Canaanite altars excavated at Beth-shean.

Rezin (2 Kgs 16:6). Later Damascus was conquered by the Assyrians and made a subsidiary city within the province of Hamath. Nevertheless, the influence of Aramean culture and the Aramaic language continued to have a significant influence in the Middle East, even until New Testament times.

Canaanites

The original inhabitants of the Syro-Palestinian coastlands, including southern Phoenicia, were the descendants of Canaan (Gen 10:15–18). The broad term Canaanites included the Jebusites, Amorites, Hivites, and Girgashites. They were a diverse group of people who were spread out from Sidon to Gaza (north to south) and from the Mediterranean coast to the Dead Sea (west to east). They were closely related to the **Amorites** of the hill country, called *Martu* by the Sumerians. The urbanization of Canaan began in the early Bronze Age II (2900–2700 BC). By the Late Bronze Age (1550–1200 BC) when the Israelites arrived, Canaan was a diverse population of various Canaanite and Amorite tribes. By then many walled Canaanite cities (e.g., Jericho and Hazor) were actual city-states ruled by local kings.

Keith Schoville identified the **Canaanite language** as one of the major branches of the Northwest Semitic family of languages.[14] The discovery of the Ebla tablets in 1976 in Syria indicated that the Eblaite language was Old Canaanite. The discovery of clay tablets at Ras Shamra (ancient Ugarit) in Syria in 1929 revealed numerous details about the Canaanite language, literature, and religion.[15] Canaanite deities included El (the supreme god), Asherah (his consort), Baal (storm god), Mot (god of the underworld), and Anat (sister of Baal). Canaanite religion included ecstatic utterances,

An overview of the ruins of Ugarit at Ras Shamra on the Syrian coast near the Orontes River.

emotional prayers, and temple prostitutes. Their religion personified and deified the forces of nature and became a constant distraction to the monotheism of the Israelites.

Phoenicians

The word *Phoenician* derives from the ancient Greek term for "purple," presumably referring to the purple dyes and cloths of these **ancient merchant people**. Phoenicia itself is roughly equivalent to modern Lebanon and stretches for 200 miles along the eastern Mediterranean coast. Protected by the heavily forested cedars of the Lebanon mountain range, ancient Phoenicia was often secluded by the boundaries of its natural setting. With natural resources of water and forests, the Phoenicians became expert sailors and traders. Their prosperous merchant empire stretched across the Mediterranean to the shores of Europe and North Africa. By the Iron Age (1200 BC), the Phoenicians were a dominant maritime force connecting East and West.

The Phoenician coastal cities of **Tyre**, **Sidon**, and **Byblos** were all active seaports when Wen-Amon of Egypt visited them circa 1075 BC.[16] The Bible records the commercial agreements of David and Solomon with Hiram I of Tyre (c. 1011–931 BC), contracting him to send cedar wood, carpenters, and stonemasons to build the palace of the house of David (2 Sam 5:11) and subsequently the temple of Yahweh (1 Chr 22:2–5). Solomon also cooperated with Hiram in establishing a seaport at Elath on the Red Sea so that their ships could reach the coasts of Africa and Arabia.[17] However, Hiram's successor Ethbaal attempted to further the alliance with Israel by giving his daughter Jezebel in marriage to the Israelite king Ahab (1 Kgs 16:31). This resulted in widespread Baal worship in Israel, which was vehemently opposed by the prophet

The harbor at Sidon in the modern state of Lebanon.

Elijah (1 Kgs 18:19). Jehu's slaughter of the children in Jezebel and Ahab's household (2 Kgs 10:1–11,17) ended Phoenician political influence in Israel.

Philistines

The Philistines were among the **Sea Peoples** who migrated across the Mediterranean from the Aegean in the second millennium BC. While small groups of Minoan traders may have reached Canaan by the time of the Patriarchs, the massive invasion of Mycenean-like Philistines came around 1200 BC. The impact of this Philistine migration is thoroughly documented in the books of Judges and Samuel, for they were often a threat to Israel in the stories of Samson, Samuel, Saul, and David. Their nation consisted of a **pentapolis** of these five cities: Ashdod, Ashkelon, Gaza, Gath, and Ekron. Philistine incursions into the interior are also recorded in the Bible at Beth-shean, Timnah, and Gerar.[18]

The Philistines developed a **distinctive type of pottery**, which included geometric designs and stylized birds, reminiscent of Aegean Mycenaean III pottery that the Philistines attempted to copy, probably in memory of their ancestral homeland. Also, like the Greeks, they buried their prominent dead in anthropoid clay coffins. Molded facial features on these coffins depict Europeans with feathered helmets.

Philistine pottery.

To date, archaeologists have found no Philistine inscriptions. A few words appear in the biblical text: *seren* ("lords"), *argaz* ("box" or "coffer"), and the names Achish and Goliath (*golyat*). Scholars assume the Philistine language was an Indo-European form of pre-Greek, which was later fully absorbed by the Semitic dialects of Canaanite and Hebrew. The challenge to a duel by champions, which Goliath issued to the Israelites (1 Sam 17:4–10), definitely reflects a **Greek**, rather than a Semitic, concept. Howard notes that the term "Philistine" appears 288 times in the Old Testament, clearly indicating that they played a significant role in Israelite history and society.[19] The Old Testament indicates that they worshiped **Dagon**, the grain god, and archaeological evidence indicates they also wor-

Philistine coffin displayed at the Hecht Museum, Israel.

shipped Baal and Asherah. Militarily, they dominated Israel for more than a century and succeeded in killing the Israelite king Saul (1 Samuel 31). But the Philistines were eventually conquered and subjugated by King David (2 Sam 5:17–25; 8:1–12).

Egyptians

The Hebrew designation for Egypt is *Mitsrayim*, referring to the great civilization along the banks of the **Nile River** in northwest Africa. Ancient Egypt was divided into *Upper* (southern) Egypt, from the Sudan to Memphis (near modern Cairo), and *Lower* (northern) Egypt, from the division of the Nile into the Delta and on to the Mediterranean coast. The ancient Egyptians spoke a Hamitic tongue mixed with Semitic elements. Old, Middle, and Late Egyptian were written in hieroglyphics (pictographs) and hieratic scripts. Religious texts and wisdom literature of the great sages like Imhotep

Procession of Philistine captives depicted on Egyptian monument at Madinet Habu.

and Amenemope record collections of shrewd maxims for wise conduct similar to the biblical proverbs.

Ancient Egyptian history is generally divided into the *Old Kingdom* (Dynasties 3–6) when the great pyramids were built (2700–2200 BC); the *Middle Kingdom* (Dynasties 11–12), which saw the golden age of Egypt's classical literature (2100–1750 BC); and the *New Kingdom* (Dynasties 18–20), which saw the rise of Egypt's imperial empire (1550–1069 BC) under powerful pharaohs like Thutmosis III, Sethos I, and Ramesses II. This period also witnessed the rise of Queen Hatshepsut, the she-king of Egypt (1508–1458 BC). It also paralleled the biblical account of the exodus.[20]

Queen Hatshepsut of Egypt.

The Egyptians were both intensely **religious and superstitious**. They believed the pharaoh was the divine incarnation of the god Horus. Major deities included Atum-Re of Heliopolis, Ptah of Memphis, Amon of Thebes, Isis, and Osiris. A strong belief in the afterlife caused the Egyptians to make elaborate provisions for funerals and burials which included mummification of dead bodies, elaborate tomb paintings, votive offerings, and provisions of items to be buried with the dead for use in the afterlife. The pyramids themselves were massive burial chambers attached to funerary temples.

The Fourth Dynasty pyramids at Giza. The pyramid of Menkaure with three subsidiary pyramids occupies the foreground, while the pyramids of Khephren and Kufu rise in the distance.

The biblical accounts that include references to Egypt clearly reflect **Egyptian culture**, including references to forced labor, brick making, grain storage, and even stories of escaped political prisoners and slaves. Later biblical references to interaction with the Egyptians include Solomon's marriage to an Egyptian princess (1 Kgs 3:1), the invasion of Judah by the Egyptian king Shishak (Sheshonq I) and his removal of Solomon's treasures (1 Kgs 14:25–26), plus the death of the Judean king Josiah at the hands of Neco II (2 Kgs 23:29) and the flight of Jewish refugees to Egypt following the Babylonian destruction of Judea in 586 BC (Jeremiah 43).

The Transjordan

The east bank of the Jordan River was home to the ancient people known as Ammonites, Moabites, and Edomites. The **Ammonites** inhabited the central region of the Transjordan plateau from the middle of the second millennium BC. Their capital was Rabbah-ammon (modern Amman, Jordan). The territory of Ammon in biblical times dropped 2,700 feet from the Jabbok River to the Jordan River in the Rift Valley (the Arabah) and was originally settled by seminomadic pastoralists. Initially, when the Israelites were beginning their conquest of Transjordan, they were told not to take the land of the Ammonites (Deut 2:19–21,37). The earliest records of hostilities between Israel and the Ammonites are recorded in Judg 3:12–14, where the Ammonites joined forces with Eglon, king of Moab, and in Judges 11, when an unnamed king of Ammon was confronted by Jephthah, the Israelite from Gilead. King Saul of Israel defeated the Ammonite king Nahash at Jabesh-gilead (1 Sam 11:1–11). David conquered Rabbah and seized the royal crown leaving the Ammonites under Israelite control for several years. Later the Ammonites were required to pay tribute to the Judean kings Uzziah and Jotham (2 Chr 26:8; 27:5).

The **Moabites** lived directly east of the Dead Sea, in the region south of the Ammonites, between the Brook Zered and the Arnon River. They worshiped the god Chemosh. Their kingdom flourished circa 1500–600 BC combining towns, villages, and nomadic groups. Moabites first appear in the biblical record as the descendants of Lot (Gen 19:37) and later are mentioned in Num 20:17 and 21:22, as opposing the Israelites en route to the Promised Land. The earliest nonbiblical references to *Moab* appear in two inscriptions at Karnak from the times of Ramesses II.[21] During the era of the judges, Eglon the king of Moab oppressed the Israelites and was assassinated by Ehud (Judg 3:12–20). Sometime later Ruth, a Moabitess, moved to Bethlehem and married the Israelite Boaz and became an ancestor of King David (Ruth 1–4). The most unique archaeological discovery related to the Moabites is the 34-line inscription, known as the Moabite Stone, which records the rebellion of the Moabite king Mesha against Israel after the death of King Omri (cf. 2 Kgs 3:4–5).

An eighteenth-century painting from Thebes of a nobleman hunting in the marshes.

The **Edomites** are identified in Gen 25:30 as the descendants of Jacob's brother Esau. They lived in the rugged red rocks of the Transjordan, southeast of the Dead Sea. Egyptian records from the fifteenth century BC refer to them as *Shashu*.[22] The seminomadic Edomites eventually settled in the cities of Bozrah and Petra along the Wadi Arabah which runs from the Dead Sea to the Red Sea at the Gulf of Aqabah. From their mountain fortresses (eagles' nests, Jer 49:16), the Edomites controlled the trade routes along the King's Highway.[23] They were conquered by Israel's king David who controlled their territory by building armed garrisons throughout the region. This allowed the Israelites to dominate the Edomites until they revolted against Jehoram of Judah circa 850 BC. Despite later incursions by the Assyrians and Babylonians, the Edomites survived, and the region was later designated *Idumaea* by the Hellenistic Greeks (331–165 BC). Eventually, the area was taken over by the Nabateans who carved a magnificent city out of the red rock cliffs at Petra. Their doom, however, was predicted by the prophet Obadiah, and the Edomites eventually disappeared from history, the abandoned city of Petra standing as mute testimony to this day.

Israel's neighbors.

THE LAND OF ISRAEL

At the center of the Old Testament story sits the land of Israel, home of the Hebrew people. The

The Moabite Stone found at Dibon. In the inscription, Mesha, king of Moab, gives thanks to Chemosh for delivering Moab out of the hands of Israel.

name *Israel* came from the new name given to the patriarch Jacob (Gen 32:28). Thus, in time, the 12 sons of Israel became the forefathers of the 12 tribes of Israel. After the Israelites' conquest of Canaan, they renamed the land after their ancient forefather. The **biblical borders** of Israel were stated as reaching *south* to the Negev wilderness, *north* to the border of Lebanon, *west* to the Great (Mediterranean) Sea, and *east* to the Euphrates River (Josh 1:3). Walter Kaiser points out: "The land on which the history of Israel and Judah was played out occupies about 9,500 square miles, an area the size of Vermont or the country of Belgium."[24] Altogether, Israel extended 150 miles from north to south and about 75 miles from east to west at its widest point. Yet, on this narrow tract of land, the successive armies of Egypt, Assyria, Babylon, Persia, Greece, and Rome marched in order to control the lands on both sides of the Jordan River.

The physical features of Israel include widely contrasting areas of beaches, farm lands, mountains, valleys, deserts, lakes, rivers and a salt sea. From the Galilee in the north to the Negev desert of the Great Rift Valley in the south, and from the Mediterranean Sea on the west to the Jordan River on the east the land was God's gift to the people of Israel.

The Plain of Sharon viewed from Aphek. The headwaters of the Yarkon River emerge from springs beside Tel Aphek.

The **coastal plain** (Sharon) runs from the Gaza strip north past modern Tel Aviv on toward the Plain of Acre, several miles north of Mount Carmel. The southern coastal plain was occupied by the Philistines during much of the Old Testament period. Seaports dotted the Mediterranean coast, including Gaza, Ashkelon, Joppa,

NATURAL REGIONS OF
ANCIENT ISRAEL
• City
○ City (uncertain location)
▲ Mountain peak

Sidon

Damascus

Mt. Hermon

Pharpar River

Tyre

Litani River

Dan

UPPER
GALILEE

Rosh HaNiqra
(Ladder of Tyre)

Hazor

Huleh
Basin

Mt. Meron ▲

N

Acco

Capernaum

Plain of Asher

Plain of
Acco

LOWER
GALILEE

Sea of
Galilee

BASHAN

Mt. Carmel ▲

Sepphoris

Cana

Nazareth

Yarmuk River

Dor

Plain of Dor

Kishon River

Jezreel Valley

▲ Mt. Tabor

Caesarea

Megiddo

N. Harod

Mt. Gilboa ▲

Beth-shan

Ramoth-gilead

MEDITERRANEAN
SEA

SAMARIA

Tirzah

Jordan River

G
I
L
E
A
D

Eastern Plateau

Plain of Sharon

Mt. Ebal ▲
Shechem

▲ Mt. Gerizim

Jabbok River

Joppa

N. Yarkon

Aphek

Shiloh

Jordan Rift

Rabbah (Amman)

N

Bethel

Mizpah

Western Mountains

Jericho

Jerusalem

Heshbon

Gezer

Medeba

Ashdod

Ekron

Gath

Shephelah

MISHOR

Ashkelon

Plain of Philistia

Coastal Plain

Wilderness of Judah

Hebron

Gaza

N. Besor

En-gedi

DEAD
SEA

Dibon

Arnon River

JUDAH

Beersheba

Arad

MOAB

Kir-hareseth

N

Negeb

W. el-Arish

Wilderness
of Zin

Tamar

A
r
a
b
a
h

EDOM

Eastern

Kadesh-barnea

Bozrah

S i n a i

Petra

and Dor. The fertile lands east of the sandy Philistine Plain were the "bread basket" of ancient Israel. Parallel to the farmlands of the Sharon Plain, the *Shephelah* separated the Philistine Plain from the Judean highlands.

The **central hill country** was settled by the tribes of Ephraim in the north and Judah in the south. The Judean hill country extended from Jerusalem south to the Negev desert. The central hill country extended north of Jerusalem to Mount Carmel and the Jezreel Valley. This was where the kingdoms of Judah (south) and Israel (north) developed, with capitals at Jerusalem and Samaria. Initially most Israelites lived in the hill country because the sovereignty of the Judean and Israelite kings was more easily maintained in the central hills.

To the north the Esdraelon and Jezreel valleys separated the hill country from **Galilee**, with its rugged hills and fertile valleys which surrounded the freshwater lake Gennesaret (Kinneroth), later called the Sea of Galilee. In this beautifully green area, rising almost 4,000 feet toward the Golan Heights, Jesus would launch His ministry in the days of the New Testament. North of the lake, the springs of Banias and Dan form the headwaters of the Jordan River.

The **Jordan Valley** is formed by the meandering curves of the Jordan River, which flows south from the Sea of Galilee through the *Arabah*, dropping from 700 feet below sea level to 1,300 feet below into the Dead Sea. The river itself is the physical life source of the valley, which today grows a rich crop of dates, figs, and tropical fruits.

Across the Jordan to the east are the **Transjordan Highlands**, today part of the nation of Jordan. In Old Testament times the northern region was known as Bashan and Gilead and was the home of the Israelite tribes of Reuben, Gad, and half of Manasseh.

A view of the Jezreel Valley viewed from near Megiddo.

From the Bashan plateau, the Yarmuk River empties into the Jordan bringing the melting snows of Mount Hermon from the Golan Heights.

In this incredible land called Israel, the story of the prophets, kings, and priests takes place. From the Golan Heights to the Gaza strip, from Galilee to the Dead Sea, from the cedars of Lebanon to the palms of Jericho, the men and women of the Bible lived their lives against the backdrop and on the stage of one of the most amazing places on earth. Here God called people to believe His message, follow His call, and live as citizens of His kingdom.

A view of the northwest portion of the Sea of Galilee at sunset.

For Further Reading

Aharoni, Yohanan, et al. *Carta Bible Atlas*. New York: Carta, 2002.

Bimson, John J. *Baker Encyclopedia of Bible Places*. Grand Rapids: Baker, 1995.

Brisco, Thomas V. *Holman Bible Atlas*. Nashville: B&H, 1998.

Harris, Roberta. *Exploring the World of Bible Lands*. London: Thames & Hudson, 1995.

Harrison, R. K. *Old Testament Times*. Grand Rapids: Baker, 2005.

Hoerth, A. J., G. Mattingly, and E. Yamauchi, eds. *Peoples of the Old Testament World*. Grand Rapids: Baker, 1994.

Isbouts, Jean-Pierre, *The Biblical World: An Illustrated Atlas*. Washington, DC: National Geographic, 2007.

Wiseman, Donald J., ed. *Peoples of Old Testament Times*. Oxford: Clarendon Press, 1973.

View of the southern end of the Dead Sea from Masada.

Study Questions

1. Who were the early inhabitants of Mesopotamia and how did their culture influence the world of the patriarchs?
2. Who were the Assyrians and why were they so greatly feared?
3. Why was the Hittite ability to make iron weapons so significant in the ancient world?
4. Which language emerged as the major form of communication in the Middle East between 600 and 330 BC.
5. Who were the original inhabitants of the Syro-Palestinian coastlands?
6. Who were the ancient merchants of the Middle East who sailed as far as Europe and North Africa?
7. Which group of "Sea Peoples" played a significant role in the history of Israel?
8. What are the major physical features of the land of Israel?

ENDNOTES

1. R. K. Harrison, *Old Testament Times* (Grand Rapids: Baker, 2005), 4.

2. Roberta Harris, *Exploring the World of the Bible Lands* (London: Thames & Hudson, 1995), 7.

3. Jean-Pierre Isbouts, *The Biblical World: An Illustrated Atlas* (Washington, DC: National Geographic Society, 2007).

4. See W. R. Bodine, "Sumerians," in ed. A. J. Hoerth, G. Mattingly, E. Yamauchi, *Peoples of the Old Testament World* (Grand Rapids: Baker, 1994), 19–42; G. Roux, *Ancient Iraq* (Baltimore: Penguin, 1992), 17–163.

5. D. J. Wiseman notes that Babylonia was the possible site of the garden of Eden (Gen 2:14) and the tower of Babel (Gen 11:1–9).

6. Ibid., 57.

7. Bill Arnold, "Babylonians," in Hoerth, Mattingly, and Yamauchi, *Peoples of the Old Testament World*, 63. See this excellent article for a detailed description of the history and archaeology of Babylon. Cf. also E. Yamauchi, "Babylon," in R. K. Harrison, *Major Cities of the Biblical World* (Nashville: Thomas Nelson, 1985), 32–48.

8. M. R. Wilson, "Nineveh," in Harrison, *Major Cities of the Biblical World*, 180–89.

9. E. Yamauchi, "Persians," in Hoerth, Mattingly, and Yamauchi, *Peoples of the Old Testament World*, 107–24. See also his *Persia and the Bible* (Grand Rapids: Baker, 1990).

10. P. A. Beaulieu, *The Reign of Nabonidus, King of Babylon 556–529 BC* (New Haven: Yale University Press, 1989).

11. F. F. Bruce, "Hittites," in *Baker's Encyclopedia of Bible Places* (Grand Rapids: Baker, 1995), 155–57.

12. H. A. Hoffner, "Hittites," in Hoerth, Mattingly, and Yamauchi, *Peoples of the Old Testament World*, 127–55.

13. W. T. Pitard, "Arameans," in Hoerth, Mattingly, and Yamauchi, *Peoples of the Old Testament World*, 216.

14.   Keith Schoville, "Canaanites and Amorites, in Hoerth, Mattingly, and Yamauchi, *Peoples of the Old Testament World*, 167.

15. A. Caquot and M. Sznycer, *Ugaritic Religion* (Leiden: E. J. Brill, 1980).

16. *ANET*, 25–29.

17. P. M. Bikai, "Rich and Glorious Traders of the Levant," *Archaeology* 43.2 (1990), 22–30.

18. See the excellent discussion by T. C. Mitchell, "Philistines," in *Baker Encyclopedia of Bible Places*, 248–51; E. Hindson, *The Philistines and the Old Testament* (Grand Rapids: Baker, 1972); D. M. Howard, "Philistines," in Hoerth, Mattingly, and Yamauchi, *Peoples of the Old Testament World*, 231–50.

19. Howard, "Philistines," in Hoerth, Mattingly, and Yamauchi, *Peoples of the Old Testament World*, 231.

20. For a detailed account of Egyptian history and culture, see K. A. Kitchen, "Egypt," in *Baker Encyclopedia of Bible Places*, 108–21; J. K. Hoffmeier, "Egyptians," in *Peoples of the Old Testament World*, 251–90.

21. J. R. Bartlett, *Edom and the Edomites* (Sheffield: JSOT Press, 1989), 77–80.

22. G. L. Mattingly, "Moabites," in Hoerth, Mattingly, and Yamauchi, *Peoples of the Old Testament World*, 317–33; J. F. A. Sawyer and D. J. A. Clines, *Midian, Moab and Edom* (Sheffield: JSOT Press, 1983), 9–17, 135–46.

23. K. G. Hoglund, "Edomites," in Hoerth, Mattingly, and Yamauchi, *Peoples of the Old Testament World*, 335–47, and J. A. Thompson, "Edom, Edomites," in *Baker Encyclopedia of Bible Places*, 106–7.

24. Walter C. Kaiser, *A History of Israel: From the Bronze Age through the Jewish Wars* (Nashville: B&H, 1998), 19.

Chapter 3

ARCHAEOLOGY AND THE OLD TESTAMENT
Digging Up the Past

Archaeology is a science that deals objectively with the data that comes from the **material culture** of past civilizations. Archaeologists dig up the remains of the past in order to clarify our present understanding of the ancient world. But archaeology faces a problem in the interpretation of what it uncovers due to the lack of information available to the archaeologist. Because much of the remains of the past was destroyed or no longer exists, the archaeologist begins with only a limited number of sites to excavate, and of these sites only a few will ever be completely excavated.

However, when archaeology takes into account the historical data provided by a **literary source,** it has an advantage in interpreting the limited data from the field. For example, a document like the Babylonian Chronicle provides unique correlation of ancient ruling figures and historical events only partially recovered through archaeological excavation. The Bible, as both a literary document and an archaeological artifact, provides the missing historical context for archaeological sites and discoveries in the biblical lands and assists in their proper interpretation.

Many people wrongly assume that the purpose of archaeology is to "prove" the Bible. However, as the Word of God, the Bible cannot be proved or disproved by archaeology anymore than God Himself is subject to the limited evidence of this world. The **proper use** of archaeology in relation to the Bible is to confirm, correct, clarify, and complement its theological message and fill in gaps in the modern understanding of ancient culture. Archaeology is *confirmatory* in that it provides a new assurance of the reality of the people and events described in the text. For example, at one time the Hittites (mentioned 47 times in the OT) were unknown outside the Bible. Then, in 1876 remains of the Hittite civilization were discovered at Boghazkoy (in modern Turkey) including more than 10,000 clay tablets chronicling their history. Archaeology is *corrective* through its provision of a wider corpus of Near Eastern language texts that can help us better understand the ancient languages of Hebrew and Aramaic used in writing the Old Testament. An archaeological discovery such as the Dead Sea Scrolls, which contained the oldest known copies of the Old Testament, aided scholars as well as translators in giving a more accurate knowledge of the biblical text. Archaeology also adds significant *clarification* to the background of the Old Testament by allowing the archaeologist to see the actual places where biblical events took place as well as images of some of the personalities mentioned in these events. Finally, archaeology is *complementary* to the witness of the Old Testament by corroborating and illustrating its theological message with greater detail by explaining its historical setting and material culture.

For students of the Old Testament, archaeology opens a window on the ancient past that permits them to connect with the world of the Bible, similar to its original participants. Through archaeology the Old Testament the material context becomes a world one can see and feel; therefore the reader is able to accept its message with a faith based on some additional facts.

ARCHAEOLOGICAL TIME LINE OF THE OLD TESTAMENT		
Name of Period	*Duration*	*Significant Biblical Events*
Postflood Early Bronze I–III	3000–2166 BC	Civilization reestablished throughout Fertile Crescent (urbanization, cities, agriculture, pottery, literacy)
Early Bronze IV	2166–2000 BC	Cities of the plain prominent in the Jordan Valley; Abram enters Canaan (2091 BC)
Middle Bronze	2000–1550 BC	Patriarchs in Canaan; Joseph in Egypt; Hebrew sojourn in Egypt
Late Bronze	1550–1200 BC	Moses delivers Hebrews in Exodus (1446 BC); Joshua enters Canaan and begins conquest (1406 BC); settlement of Hebrews in Canaan; judges begin to rule
Iron I	1200–900 BC	Philistine dominance in lowlands of Canaan; administration of Hebrew tribes under judges; establishment of united monarchy in Israel (c. 1000 BC); first temple built (960 BC); division of the nation into two kingdoms
Iron II	900–586 BC	Divided monarchy in Israel; fall of northern kingdom (721 BC), Assyrian monarch Sennacherib of Assyria invades Judah; destroys city of Lachish and threatens Jerusalem (701 BC); Babylonian monarch Nebuchadnezzar captures Jerusalem; destroys first temple and exiles population (605–586 BC)
Iron III/Persian	586–332 BC	Hebrews in captivity; fall of Babylon (539 BC); return of exiles to Judah; second temple built (538–515 BC); Alexander the Great conquers Persian empire (333 BC)

PRE-PATRIARCHAL PERIOD: CREATION AND FLOOD ACCOUNTS

The book of Genesis (chaps. 1–11) deals with the creation of the world and its destruction by a great flood and the new beginning of civilization with its global development and expansion. In the late nineteenth century archaeologists made discoveries of ancient Near Eastern **accounts** of creation and the flood.[1] One of these was a Mesopotamian account of creation from Ashurbanipal's library at Nineveh named *Enuma Elish*. Some of the parallels with the Genesis account are the watery chaos that is separated into heaven and earth (cf. Gen 1:1–2,6–10); light preexisting the creation of sun, moon, and stars (cf. Gen 1:3–5,14–18); and the prominence of the number seven (cf. Gen 2:2–3). A Babylonian account of creation and the flood, known as the *Atrahasis Epic*, adds other parallels: the gods ruling the heavens and earth (cf. Gen 1:1), making man from the clay of the earth mixed with blood (cf. Gen 2:7; 3:19; Lev 17:11), a flood is sent to destroy mankind (cf. Gen 6:13) with one man, Atrahasis, given advance warning of the flood and told to build a boat (cf. Gen 6:14) and load it with food, animals, and birds. After the boat lands, he offers a sacrifice to the gods with the chief god agreeing to continue mankind's existence (cf. Gen 8:20–22). In addition, an Old Babylonian flood account was also discovered in a document called the *Gilgamesh Epic*. This account gives more parallels in that Utnapishtim, the Babylonian "Noah," sent out a dove, a swallow, and finally a raven (cf. Gen 8:3–11); and when the raven did not return, he left the boat and offered a sacrifice to the gods (cf. Gen 8:12–22).

Even though these accounts were written down before the account recorded in Genesis, the biblical author Moses did not borrow from these stories. One reason for this is that the Near Eastern accounts are **highly mythological** in character while the biblical account reads as a realistic historical record. This can be seen from a comparison of certain elements in the parallel accounts such as the duration of the flood and the size and shape of the boat. In the pagan accounts the boat is not a seaworthy vessel, being described in one story as a cube. The Bible, by contrast, describes a rectangular

Gilgamesh Tablet.

vessel 450 feet long, 75 feet wide, and 45 feet high; dimensions that are imminently seaworthy. In comparing the ancient creation and flood stories to the Genesis record, Alexander Heidel notes the biblical accounts possesses a "depth and dignity unparalleled in any cosmogony known to us from Babylon or Assyria."[2] All of these accounts were likely based on the preserved knowledge of these common historical events, with the biblical author receiving his by divine revelation.

PATRIARCHAL PERIOD: ABRAHAM, ISAAC, AND JACOB

The early biblical period, often called the patriarchal period, is attested in the archaeological record of the **Middle Bronze Age**. The archaeological evidence for this period includes the Code of Hammurabi, Egyptian and Hittite texts, and thousands of clay tablets from the Amorite city of Mari (Tel Hariri), Nuzi (city of the biblical Horites), Tel Leilan, and Alalakh. In addition the Syrian site of Ebla (Tel Mardikh) has offered some comparative material in the form of law codes, legal and social contracts, and religious texts.[3]

Clay tablet found at Ebla, Syria.

Comparisons between these texts and the Bible show that the **proper names** recorded in this period are the same or similar, many having the same theophoric element (addition of words for God, such as *ya* or *'el*, see Ya'acob/Jacob and Rachel) as those appearing in the patriarchal narratives. Since names tend to be unique to a given time period, this evidence helps confirm the chronology of the patriarchs. In addition, laws that governed the patriarch's social behavior were based on the local customs of that time period, including specific inheritance laws reflected in the law code of Lipit-Ishtar (1870 BC).

The patriarchal narratives describe their seminomadic lifestyle. They frequently migrated between the lands of Canaan and Egypt. Evidence for this geographical migration pattern can be seen from the tomb mural of Beni-Hasan dating to around 1890 BC (during the patriarchial age). It portrays a parade of 37 Asiatics from the region of Shut (which includes the area of Sinai and southern Canaan) led by Abishai (their chief) coming to trade with the Egyptians. This discovery not only reveals the appearance of people like

View of the mud-brick arched gateway at Tel Dan from the time of the patriarchs.

the biblical patriarchs but also confirms that people from the area of Canaan came to Egypt during the general time and in the same manner as did Abraham and Sarah (Gen 12:10), Jacob and his sons (Gen 42:5; 43:11; 46:5–7), and Joseph (Genesis 37–50). Archaeological finds from this period have demonstrated that the biblical details are **historically accurate**, based on facts that could only be preserved by those who actually experienced the conditions at this time. Further, the recovery of the arched city gate of Laish (biblical Dan), dating from the time of the patriarchs, is one archaeological find that may correlate with an actual event connected with the biblical Abraham (Gen 14:14).

EXODUS: CONQUEST AND SETTLEMENT

The books of Exodus, Joshua, and Judges tell of a massive migration, warfare, and catastrophic conditions that affected the peoples of both Egypt and Canaan. While these are the kind of events that archaeology is usually able to verify, some factors reduce this possibility. For example, a proud people such as the Egyptians would hardly want to record a national defeat by foreign slaves. It is unlikely also that any inscriptional evidence will be found in Egypt of plagues being linked to the Hebrews. The Hebrews' migration (exodus) from Egypt and sojourn in the Sinai Desert was archaeologically invisible since virtually everything was used and nothing left behind as material evidence. Even if there were remains, the desert environment would destroy or cover what little was left. The archaeological record makes clear that the book of Exodus reflects the cultural settings of Egypt in the new kingdom era.[4]

A case for the historical nature of the exodus can be made from the Egyptian color of the Hebrew narrative (such as "birthstools," Exod 1:16 NKJV) and Egyptian loan words (such as the name of Moses, Exod 2:10); the description of Canaan as a "land flowing with milk and honey" which appears in the Egyptian *Tale of Sinuhe* and the *Annals* of Thutmosis III; the uniform use of the term *pharaoh* ("great house") for the king during the new kingdom (eighteenth dynasty, c. 1550–c. 1292 BC); the comparative Egyptian accounts of foreign (Semitic) slaves in Egypt (including their harsh treatment, use in building projects, and records of runaway slaves); an account of plagues similar to those mentioned in the Bible, such as in the Ipuwer Papyrus (thirteenth century BC); the importance of magic to the Egyptians (compare Moses' miracle in Exod 7:9–10); and the archaeological discovery of certain places such as Avaris

A painting from the tomb of Rekhmire at Thebes (c. 1450 BC) depicting the making of bricks in Egypt.

(Tell edh-Daba), Rameses (Pi-ramesse), Migdol (Tell Defari), and Succoth (Tell Masuta), mentioned in relation to the Hebrews.

Numerous ancient Near Eastern **law codes** have many parallels to the Ten Commandments and Mosaic law (Ur-Nammu Code, 2000 BC; Laws of Eshnunna, 1900 BC; Lipit Ishtar Code, 1870 BC; Code of Hammurabi, 1700 BC; Hittite Laws, 1500 BC). In addition, the Egyptian Stele of Merneptah (twelfth century BC) refers to the *'Apiru* (nomads, wanderers) as slaves and mentions for the first time *Israel* as a nation-state, indicating that the Hebrews had already immigrated to Canaan and developed to the status of a nation. While evidence is not conclusive, some scholars affirm that a probable reading of "Israel" in a hieroglyphic slab in the Egyptian Museum of Berlin may be even older.[5]

In the case of Joshua's conquest, only three cities were actually destroyed (Jericho, Ai, and Hazor) while others were occupied by the Hebrews. Although the history of the archaeology of Jericho (Tel es-Sultan) has multiple interpretations, it has, in the final analysis, revealed evidence in support of the details of the biblical text (Josh 6:3–24). This evidence includes fortification walls that collapsed outwardly (Josh 6:20), a layer of burned debris and ash three feet thick (Josh 6:24), storage jars full of grain indicating a short siege in the spring and unused by the invaders, just as the Bible describes (Josh 2:6; 3:15; 5:10; 6:17–19).[6] Many other Hebrew settlements among the Canaanites have been difficult to distinguish and are still a matter of debate.[7]

Millo Walls in the City of David.

MONARCHY: KINGS OF ISRAEL AND JUDAH

The Israelite monarchy peaked in the tenth century BC under King David and his son Solomon. Some scholars doubted the existence of **Jerusalem** as a royal fortified city at this time, but excavations at the tenth-century BC site of Khirbet Qeiyafa (biblical Neta'im), located on the outskirts of the tribal allotment of Judah (near the Elah Valley), revealed fortifications and a level of culture (based on the discovery of an archive). If such developments existed at a remote village, this would require the capital city of the region to be even more impressive, just as the Bible describes. Evidence for a tenth-century BC Jerusalem also has come from the excavations at the "City of David" and the structures associated with it: the Fortress of Zion (supported by a stone-stepped structure known as the Millo), a four-room Israelite house of Ahiel, and Warren's Shaft, a Canaanite structure possibly related to David's conquest of the city (2 Sam 5:8; 1 Chr 11:6).[8]

Excavations at the site of the Philistine city of Gath (Tel es-Safi) uncovered a ninth-century BC ostraca (inscribed potsherd) in Proto-Canaanite. One of the Philistine names in this text was the etymological equivalent of "Goliath" and supports the reliability of the use of this name in the earlier biblical account of David's battle with Goliath of Gath (1 Samuel 17). Archaeological support for the existence

of **David** was discovered on a victory stele unearthed at Tel Dan, a northern Israelite city from the ninth–eighth centuries BC located in the present-day Golan Heights. On this stele is recorded the defeat of the Judean king Ahaziahu by the Israelite king Jehoram the son of Ahab (2 Kgs 8:7–15; 9:6–10), about 150 years after the time of King David. The defeated king is identified as being from "the house of David." This military declaration by an enemy of Israel clearly reveals that the term "house of David" was commonly used to describe the Davidic dynasty.[9]

Excavations have also revealed the chariot cities of Hazor, Megiddo, and Gezer that were fortified by **Solomon** (1 Kgs 9:15,19).[10] While no remains of the famous first temple built by Solomon were found, related structures such as a Solomonic fortification line that includes a city gate and a royal structure with a tower 18

Replica of Tel Dan "House of David" inscription.

feet high were discovered on the southern side of the Temple Mount. The particular design of the Solomonic temple, as given in the Bible (1 Kgs 6:2–17), was derived from the style of the long-room temple common in Syria from the second millennium BC. The best example of this is the Neo-Hittite temple at 'Ain Dara (Syria). Several other ancient Near Eastern parallels also exist, including the tenth/ninth century BC Neo-Hittite temple at Tel Tayinat (Turkey).[11]

When the monarchy divided, the Israelite king Jeroboam built a **rival sanctuary** to the legitimate Jerusalem temple on the high place at Dan (1 Kgs 12:31). Excavations at this site uncovered the ninth-century BC city gate and the sanctuary site including a square platform 60 by 62 feet on the northwest side of the site, a flight of five ashlar steps to a raised platform on which the golden calves were once installed, remains of a large horned altar for burnt offerings, and the cultic precincts where priests prepared offerings.

The archaeological record for the **divided monarchy** is extensive with entire books devoted to archaeological commentary on the books of the Bible that cover this period.[12] Archaeological evidence includes the Moabite Stone (846 BC) which names Mesha the king of Syria and Omri the king of Israel (2 Kings 3) and the black obelisk of Shalmaneser III (841 BC) which visually depicts Jehu, king of Israel (2 Kings 9–10). Bullae (clay seals) and other kinds of stone seals were found with the names of these biblical rulers: Jeroboam II, king of Israel (c. 796–780 BC); Hoshea, king of Israel (c. 730–721 BC); Azariah (Uzziah), king of Judah (c. 788–737 BC); Jotham, king of Judah (c. 749–734 BC); Ahaz, king of Judah (c. 741–726 BC); numerous seals

Details of the black obelisk of Shalmaneser III that records his campaign into the southern Levant in 841 BC. Jehu, the Israelite king, is depicted bowing down.

and a signet ring of Hezekiah, king of Judah (c. 727–698 BC); Manasseh, king of Judah (c. 698–643 BC); and Jehoahaz, king of Judah (c. 609 BC). In addition, one bulla contained the name (and fingerprint) of Baruch, the secretary of the prophet Jeremiah who penned the words of the biblical text.[13]

The end of the biblical period is also well attested in the archaeological record. The attack by the Assyrian king Sennacherib on Judea in 701 BC (including the assault against King Hezekiah of Jerusalem, 2 Kgs 18:13–19:37; 2 Chr 32:1–23; Isaiah 36–37) was preserved on official court annals recorded on several six-sided **clay prisms** inscribed in Assyrian cuneiform: the Taylor Prism, the Nimrud Prism, and the Oriental Institute Prism. These record the name of Hezekiah and give details concerning Sennacherib's capture of Judean cities, including the burning of Lachish (2 Chr 32:9), an event preserved in great detail on a 90-foot-long panel from Sennacherib's palace at Nineveh. Sennacherib's assassination, as recorded in the Bible (2 Kgs 19:36–37; 2 Chr 32:21; Isa 37:37–38), is also recorded in the Babylonian Chronicles, cuneiform tablets that also detail the Babylonian siege of the first temple. One of these tablets gives a ration list for King Jehoiachin of Judah who was taken to Babylon during the siege (Jer 52:31–33).

EXILIC AND POSTEXILIC ERA

Archaeological excavations at **Nineveh and Babylon** in modern-day Iraq reveal extensive evidence of the capitals of ancient Assyria, Babylon, and Persia.[14] These cities were totally destroyed and were never rebuilt in fulfillment of the predictions of the

The altar and worship area established by Jeroboam I at Dan.

Hebrew prophets. Bricks discovered in Babylon bear the name of Nebuchadnezzar and indicate that he actually rebuilt the city (Daniel 1–4). The Nabonidus Chronicle affirms that Nabonidus installed his son Belshazzar as his coregent, leaving him in control of Babylon (Daniel 5). A decree of Cyrus the Great (Isa 44:28), similar to that recorded in the Bible concerning the return of the Jews to Jerusalem to rebuild the temple (Ezra 1:2,7–11; Isa 41:25; 44:26–45:6) was given in the Cyrus Cylinder found in the ruins of Babylon in 1879. Altogether these artifacts support the general historicity of the biblical text.

The Nabonidus Chronicle, an ancient Babylonian document on display in the British Museum.

For Further Reading

Avi-Yonah, Michael. *Encyclopedia of Archaeological Excavations in the Holy Land,* 4 vols. Jerusalem: Israel Exploration Society, 1976.

Kerrigan, Michael. *The Ancients in Their Own Words: Ancient Writing from Tomb Hieroglyphs to Roman Graffiti.* New York: Fall River Press/Amber Books, 2009.

Kitchen, Kenneth, A. *On the Reliability of the Old Testament.* Grand Rapids, MI: William B. Eerdmans, 2003.

McCarter, P. Kyle, Jr. *Ancient Inscriptions: Voices from the Biblical World.* Washington, DC: Biblical Archaeology Society, 1996.

Millard, Alan. *Illustrated Wonders and Discoveries of the Bible.* Nashville: Thomas Nelson, 1997.

Price, Randall. *The Stones Cry Out: How Archaeology Confirms the Truth of the Bible.* Eugene, OR: Harvest House Publishers, 1996.

Study Question

1. Describe the proper uses of archaeological data.
2. What is the significance of ancient creation and flood stories?
3. In what way do archaeological discoveries help confirm the historical accuracy of the biblical accounts?
4 What is the significance of the Tel Dan inscription?
5. Which ancient monuments make specific reference to Israelite Kings?
6. Whose existence is affirmed by the Nabonidus Chronicle?

ENDNOTES

1. See J. B. Pritchard, ed., *The Ancient Near East: An Anthology of Texts and Pictures* (Princeton: Princeton University Press, 1958), 28–86.

2. Alexander Heidel, *The Babylonian Genesis* (Chicago: University of Chicago Press, 1962), 139–40.

3. See D. W. Thomas, ed., *Documents from Old Testament Times* (New York: Harper & Row, 1965); Cyrus Gordon, *Forgotten Scripts* (New York: Basic Books, 1982); Paolo Matthiae, *Ebla: An Empire Rediscovered* (Garden City, NY: Doubleday, 1981).

4. K. A. Kitchen, *On the Reliability of the Old Testament* (Grand Rapids: Eerdmans, 2003), 241–312; James Hoffmeier, *Ancient Israel in Sinai: The Authenticity of the Wilderness Tradition* (New York: Oxford University Press, 2005).

5. Hershel Shanks, "When Did Ancient Israel Begin?" *BAR* 38, no. 1 (January/February 2012): 59–62, 67.

6. Bryant Wood, "Did the Israelites Conquer Jericho?" *BAR* 16 (March/April, 1990): 44–57. He defends the 1400 BC date for the conquest based on pottery fragments, stratigraphy, scarab data, and carbon 14 dating.

7. V. Fritz, "Israelites & Canaanites: You Can Tell Them Apart," *BAR* 28, no. 4 (July/August 2002): 28–31, 63; A. Rainey, "Shasu or Habiru?" *BAR* 34, no. 6 (November/December 2008): 45–50, 84.

8. "Jerusalem," in M. Avi-Yonah, ed. *Encyclopedia of Archaeological Excavations in the Holy Land* (Jerusalem: Israel Exploration Society, 1976), 2:579– 647; S. Weksler-Bodlah, et al., "Layers of Ancient Jerusalem," *BAR* 38 (January/February 2012): 36–47.

9. A. Rainey, "The House of David," *BAR* 20, no. 6 (1994): 68–69.

10. E. M. Blaiklock and R. K. Harrison, eds., *New International Dictionary of Biblical Archaeology* (Grand Rapids: Zondervan, 1983), 212, 230, 308–9.

11. Randall Price, *The Stones Cry Out* (Eugene, OR: Harvest House, 1996), 180–86.

12. Cf. Gonzalo Baez-Camargo, *Archaeological Commentary on the Bible* (Garden City, NY: Doubleday, 1984); G. Cornfield, *Archaeology of the Bible: Book by Book* (San Francisco: Harper & Row, 1976).

13. Price, *The Stones Cry Out*, 235–37.

14. Andre Parrot, *Nineveh and the Old Testament* (New York: Philosophical Library, 1955) and *Babylon and the Old Testament* (New York: Philosophical Library, 1956); Joan Oates, *Babylon* (London: Thames & Hudson, 1979).

Chapter 4

THE CANON AND TEXT OF THE OLD TESTAMENT
Where Did It Come From?

God revealed His word to ancient Israel over a thousand-year period (c. 1400–400 BC), and then scribes copied the biblical scrolls and manuscripts for more than a millennium after that. The process by which the Old Testament books came to be recognized as the Word of God and the history of how these books were preserved and handed down through the generations enhances our confidence in the credibility of the Old Testament as inspired Scripture (2 Tim 3:16).

WHAT BOOKS BELONG IN THE OLD TESTAMENT?

The **canon of Scripture** refers to the list of books recognized as divinely inspired and authoritative for faith and practice. Our word *canon* is derived from the Hebrew *qaneh* and the Greek *kanon*, meaning a "reed" or a "measuring stick." The term came to mean the standard by which a written work was measured for inclusion in a certain body of literature. The books of the Bible are not inspired because humans gave them canonical status. Rather, the books were recognized as canonical

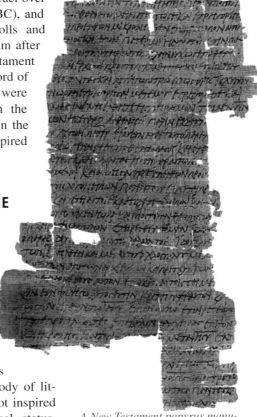

A New Testament papyrus manuscript of the Gospel of Matthew.

by humans because they were inspired by God. As Wegner explains, the books of the Old Testament "did not receive their authority because they were placed in the canon; rather they were recognized by the nation of Israel as having divine authority and were therefore included in the canon."[1] The community of faith did not create the Scriptures; rather, the Scriptures helped to create the community of faith by giving form and substance to its identity and system of beliefs.

The order and arrangement of the **Hebrew canon** is different from that of our English Bibles. The Hebrew canon consists of three major sections, the Law (*Torah*), the Prophets (*Nevi'im*), and the Writings (*Kethuvim*). Collectively they are referred to as the Tanak (an acrostic built on the first letters of these three divisions—TNK).

THE HEBREW CANON			
Law	*Prophets*		*Writings*
Genesis	*Former Prophets*	*Latter Prophets*	Psalms
Exodus	Joshua	Isaiah	Job
Leviticus	Judges	Jeremiah	Proverbs
Numbers	1 and 2 Samuel	Ezekiel	Ruth
Deuteronomy	1 and 2 Kings	Minor Prophets	Song of Songs
		(Book of the 12)	Ecclesiastes
			Lamentations
			Esther
			Daniel
			Ezra
			Nehemiah
			Chronicles

The **Septuagint** (LXX), the Greek translation of the Old Testament, first employed the **fourfold division** of the Old Testament into Pentateuch, Historical Books, Poetical Books, and Prophetic Books that is used in the English Bible. The inclusion of historical books within the prophetic section of the Hebrew canon reflects their authorship by the prophets. Daniel appears in the Writings rather than the Prophets because Daniel was not called to the office of prophet even though he functioned as a prophet from time to time. Chronicles at the end of the canon provides a summary of the entire Old Testament story from Adam to Israel's return from exile though it was written from a priestly perspective. The Roman Catholic canon of the Old Testament includes seven apocryphal books (Tobit, Judith, Wisdom of Solomon, Ecclesiasticus or Sirach, Baruch, Letter of Jeremiah, and 1 and 2 Maccabees) written during the Intertestamental period, as well as additional materials for the books of Esther and Daniel.[2] The Eastern Orthodox Church also recognized these works as canonical, as well as four additional compositions (1 Esdras, Psalm 151, 3 and 4 Maccabees, and the Prayer of Manasseh).

HOW WERE THE OLD TESTAMENT BOOKS SELECTED?

When Moses came down from Mount Sinai with the commandments God gave him, the people of Israel immediately recognized their **divine authority** and promised to obey them as the words of the Lord (Exod 24:3–8). The writings of Moses were stored at the central sanctuary because of their special status as inspired Scripture (Exod 25:16,21; Deut 10:1–2; 31:24–26). In Deut 18:15–22, the Lord promised to raise up a prophet "like Moses" to speak for subsequent generations. Thus, the pronouncements of the messengers of God would also be recognized as possessing authority. The prophet Samuel wrote down laws of kingship that were deposited before the Lord when the monarchy was established in Israel (1 Sam 10:25). David's extensive writings came to be recognized as inspired Scripture because the Spirit of God spoke through him (2 Sam 23:1–2), and the words of the prophets came to be placed alongside the Torah in the Hebrew Scriptures because of the self-authenticating message. Histories, psalms, and wisdom writings recognized as coming from others speaking with a prophetic voice were also similarly respected and preserved.

Jewish sofer copying Hebrew Scripture.

WHEN WAS THE PROCESS COMPLETED?

Jewish tradition affirmed that prophecy ceased in Israel c. 400 BC after the ministry of Malachi. First Maccabees 9:27 states, "So there was great distress in Israel, such as had not been since the time that the prophets ceased to appear among them." Baruch 85:3 makes a similar claim, and the Jewish Talmud states that the Holy Spirit departed from Israel after the prophets Haggai, Zechariah, and Malachi in the **early postexilic period**. While some questions remained regarding some of the "writings" that were already included in Scripture (e.g., Esther) even at Jamnia in AD 90, the evidence suggests that the Hebrew canon was essentially completed and fixed by 200 BC. All of the canonical books of the Old Testament, except for Esther, appear among the copies of the Dead Sea Scrolls (250 BC–AD 70).[3] In the second-century BC, the prologue to the apocryphal book Ben Sirach (or Ecclesiasticus) testifies to the existence of a threefold canon by making reference to the "law," "prophecies," and "the rest of the books." Philo, the Jewish philosopher (c. 20 BC–AD 50), also reflects awareness of a three-part canon in his writings as did Jesus in Luke 24:44 c. AD 32. In the first century AD, the apocryphal work of 2 Esdras (14:45–58) refers to 24 books and the Jewish historian Josephus (*Against Apion* 1.7–8) to 22 books that correspond to the 39 books of the Hebrew canon.

A Torah scroll being held in its wooden case at a celebration in Jerusalem.

HOW DOES THE NEW TESTAMENT VIEW THE OLD TESTAMENT?

Jesus and the apostles accepted the inspiration of the Old Testament Scriptures and often referred to or quoted them as **authoritative**. According to Jesus, the words written by the human authors of Scripture were the "command of God" and "God's word" (Mark 7:8–13; cf. Matt 19:4–5). As God's Word every part of the Old Testament would be accomplished and fulfilled (Matt 5:17–18; 26:54,56; Luke 24:27,44; John 7:38), and nothing it stated could be voided or annulled (Luke 16:17; John 10:35). Jesus described the Old Testament canon as extending from Genesis to Chronicles when speaking of the murders of Abel and the prophet Zechariah in Matt 23:34–35 and Luke 11:49–51 (cf. Gen 4:8 and 2 Chr 24:20–22).

WHY IS THE APOCRYPHA EXCLUDED?

Though the Roman Catholic and Eastern Orthodox Churches accept the books of the Apocrypha as canonical Scripture, these books **never claim** to be the Word of God. They were written after the time when the Jews believed God stopped speaking through His prophets. Philo frequently quoted from the Old Testament Scriptures but never referred to the apocryphal works. Josephus stated, "From Artaxerxes to our own times a complete history has been written, but has not been deemed worthy of equal credit with the earlier record, because of the failure of the exact succession of the prophets" (*Against Apion* 1.41). Jude 14–15 quotes from the pseudepigraphal book of 1 Enoch, but this work was never accepted as canonical by either Jews or Christians.[4] This referencing of a reliable tradition in 1 Enoch does not confer authoritative status to the entire work. In fact, New Testament writers even occasionally quoted from secular sources to prove a point (see 1 Cor 15:33; Titus 1:12).

Despite their historical and religious value, the apocryphal books are not on par with the books of the Hebrew Bible. Historical inaccuracies (locating Nebuchadnezzar at Nineveh instead of Babylon) and theological errors (prayers for the dead) are not in harmony with the perspective of inspired Scripture.

The earliest known Christian list of the Old Testament books is found in a letter from Melito, the bishop of Sardis (c. AD 170). This list included all of the books of the traditional Jewish canon except Esther and omitted all of the apocryphal materials. The lists of Origen in the third century and Athanasius in the fourth century also included only the Hebrew Scriptures with the exception of Baruch and the Letter of Jeremiah. Even Jerome's Latin Vulgate (AD 382–405) relegated the apocryphal books to a **secondary status**. Early English Bibles, including the original 1611 King James Version, included the Apocrypha; but this practice was later discontinued. Christians can learn much from the apocryphal books about early Jewish history and religious beliefs, but the reasons for their rejection as canonical Scripture far outweigh the reasons for their acceptance.

HOW RELIABLE ARE THE OLD TESTAMENT DOCUMENTS?

Though the earliest parts of the Old Testament were written c. 1400 BC, the earliest **existing Hebrew manuscripts** for the Old Testament are the more than 200 biblical manuscripts found at Qumran among the Dead Sea Scrolls, dating from roughly 250 BC to AD 70. Prior to the discovery of the Dead Sea Scrolls in 1947, the earliest previous extant Hebrew manuscripts of the Old Testament dated 800–1000 years after the time of Christ. The earliest complete copy of the Old Testament is Codex Leningrad, dating to near AD 1000.

Despite these significant chronological gaps between the original manuscripts and the earliest documents, one can have confidence that the original message of the Hebrew Bible was faithfully preserved throughout its long and complicated **transmission process**. The recognition of the authoritative status of the Old Testament books at the beginning of the inscripturation process meant that the biblical scrolls and manuscripts were carefully copied and handed down from one generation to the next. The writings of Moses were stored at the central sanctuary (see Exod 25:16,21; Deut 10:1–2; 31:24–26), and Moses warned the people that they were not to add to or subtract from the words he received from the Lord (Deut 12:32). Scribal practices in the ancient Near East demonstrate the care and precision taken by members of that craft in copying important political and religious texts. Israelite scribes who had a special reverence for the Scriptures as the Word of God were careful when copying the biblical manuscripts.

As the earliest existing Hebrew manuscripts, the **Dead Sea Scrolls** are an important witness to the textual integrity of the OT. Many of the biblical scrolls found at Qumran reflect a text that closely resembles the later Masoretic Text (MT), the textual tradition represented in the Hebrew Bible today. The close similarity of the Isaiah Scroll (1QIsa[b]) found at Qumran to later Masoretic manuscripts of Isaiah reflects how carefully the scribes copied the text.

After the close of the OT canon (c. 300 BC) and the **standardization** of the Hebrew text (first century AD), meticulous and careful scribal practices ensured that the received text of the OT was handed down unchanged. A special group of scribes called the Masoretes (500–1000 AD) played a vital role in the transmission and preservation

Dead Sea Scroll fragment.

of the OT text. The Masoretes developed a system for writing vowel letters in the Hebrew Bible as a means of preserving the correct vocalization of the text. Prior to their work the Hebrew text contained only consonantal letters, with a few consonants being used to represent certain vowels. The Masoretes added a system of accenting to facilitate the correct reading of the text and added a detailed set of marginal notations dealing with textual problems and the proper reading of the text. The Masoretes also meticulously counted the letters, words, and verses in the text. For example, the final

Masorah at the end of Deuteronomy notes that there are 400,945 letters and 97,856 words in the Torah and that the middle word in the Torah is found in Lev 10:16.

Other important **manuscript witnesses** to the Hebrew text include the Samaritan Pentateuch, the Greek Septuagint, Aramaic Targums, Syriac Peshitta, and the Latin Vulgate. The Samaritans accepted only the first five books of Moses as authoritative Scripture and had their own version of the Pentateuch. The earliest manuscripts of the Samaritan Pentateuch date from roughly 1100 AD, but these manuscripts are believed to reflect a text that dates to 200–100 BC. The Septuagint (LXX) is the Greek translation of the OT dating from 250–100 BC that was necessitated by the spread of Greek language following the conquests of Alexander the Great and the large number of *diaspora* Jews living outside the land of Israel. The LXX was especially important to Christians because nearly 70 percent of the OT quotations in the NT follow the readings of the LXX, which became the OT of the Christian church. The Aramaic Targums composed prior to the Christian era are another important textual witness for the OT. Aramaic became the language of the Jews living in Babylonian and Persian exile so it is not surprising that parts of Daniel and Ezra were written in Aramaic.

The study of **textual criticism** is the science that enables scholars to determine and establish the most plausible wording of the original text. The number of textual variants due to handwritten mistakes that affect the meaning of the text are relatively few, and none of these variants change any major OT teaching or Christian doctrine.[5] Rather than undermining a person's confidence in the Scriptures, the textual criticism and transmission history of the Bible enables everyone to see how accurately the Bible today reflects what God originally communicated to His people in His Word. By contrast, no other documents from the ancient world were as accurately copied, preserved, and transmitted as the Old Testament Scriptures.

For Further Reading

Beckwith, Roger. *The Old Testament Canon of the New Testament Church: And Its Background in Early Judaism.* Grand Rapids: Eerdmans, 1985.

Brotzman, Ellis R. *Old Testament Textual Criticism: A Practical Introduction.* Grand Rapids: Baker, 1994.

Kaiser, Walter C., Jr. *The Old Testament Documents: Are They Reliable and Relevant?* Downers Grove, IL: IVP, 2001.

Merrill, Eugene H., "The Canonicity of the Old Testament," and Mark F. Rooker, "The Transmission and Textual Criticism of the Bible." In Eugene H. Merrill, Mark F. Rooker, and Michael A. Grisanti, *The World and the Word: An Introduction to the Old Testament.* Nashville: B&H, 2011.

Wegner, Paul D. *A Student's Guide to Textual Criticism of the Bible: Its History, Methods and Results.* Downers Grove, IL: IVP, 2006.

Study Questions

1. What does the term "canon" mean in relation to biblical books?
2. What is the threefold division of the Hebrew Bible?
3. What is the Greek translation of the Old Testament called?
4. Why were the Apocryphal books excluded from the Protestant canon?
5. What is the function and purpose of textual criticism?
6. How reliable are the Old Testament documents?

ENDNOTES

1. Paul D. Wegner, *The Journey from Texts to Translations: The Origin and Development of the Bible* (Grand Rapids: Baker Academic, 1999), 101.

2. The word *Apocrypha* means "hidden books" and was first used with reference to these works by Jerome c. AD 400. The exact meaning of this term when applied to these books is unclear but implies their biblical authority was doubtful. Thus, they are not included in Protestant versions of the Bible.

3. In the 24-book canon, the Minor Prophets are a single book ("The Book of the 12"), and 1–2 Samuel, 1–2 Kings, 1–2 Chronicles, and Ezra-Nehemiah are viewed as one book each. Josephus arrived at a total of 22 books by also viewing Judges-Ruth and Jeremiah-Lamentations as single books.

4. The word *pseudepigrapha* refers to works falsely attributed to biblical characters or events. Scores of these works appeared in Jewish and Christian circles in the intertestamental and early Christian eras but were never accepted as authoritative Scripture.

5. Mark. F. Rooker, "The Transmission and Textual Criticism of the Bible," in Eugene H. Merrill, Mark F. Rooker, and Michael A. Grisanti, *The World and the Word: An Introduction to the Old Testament* (Nashville: B&H, 2011), 109.

Chapter 5

THE PENTATEUCH

The first five books of the Bible, known as the Torah ("Law") or the Pentateuch ("five scrolls"), form the **first literary unit** of the Hebrew Scriptures. They tell the story of God's dealings with both the human race in general and the Hebrew race in particular. In so doing these chapters trace the actions of God in history from the creation of the world until the death of Moses. For both Jews and Christians, these books are the source of theological truth, biblical morality, and ethical behavior that laid the foundation of Western civilization.

Moses Segal of the Hebrew University in Jerusalem stated: "The Pentateuch is also great literature, rich in noble prose, and grand poetry, matchless in its variegated contents of story and legislation, of narrative and description, of instruction and exhortation."[1] These books take the reader back through the tunnel of time to the beginning of human existence and introduce the **ultimate questions**: Who are we? Where did we come from? Why are we here? They describe the first steps of the human journey to find God.

The five books of the Pentateuch are collectively known as the **Torah**, the Hebrew word for "law" or "teaching." As such, they establish the foundation for a biblical theology of the entire canon of Scripture. Without these books people would have little understanding of the rest of the Bible, for in them is found the reason for the call of Abraham and the election of Israel as God's response to the predicament of the fallen world. These books introduce the following concepts:

The Gezer Calendar is believed to be one of the oldest Hebrew inscriptions found to date. The inscription is on a limestone tablet and dates from 925 BC.

- Genesis: The Beginning
- Exodus: Exit from Egypt
- Leviticus: Way of Holiness
- Numbers: Wilderness Journey
- Deuteronomy: Covenant Renewal

Each book, in turn, **introduces** the one that follows it. Genesis concludes with Israel in Egypt. Exodus describes Israel's liberation from Egypt and the trek to Mount Sinai. Leviticus describes the religious system of worship that was given at Sinai. Numbers picks up the story of the journey from Sinai to Canaan. Finally, Deuteronomy provides instructions for the new generation, born in the wilderness, as they prepare to enter Canaan in fulfillment of God's promises that began in Genesis.

Both Jewish and Christian traditions have affirmed the **Mosaic authorship** of the Pentateuch, ascribing it to the prophet, lawgiver, and founder of the nation of Israel. This is the unanimous testimony of the Old and New Testament authors, ancient Jewish rabbis, and the early church fathers, medieval Catholic scholars, and Protestant reformers. However questions about the authorship of the Pentateuch raised in the seventeenth century by the Jewish philosopher Benedict Spinoza and in the eighteenth century by French medical professor Jean Astruc eventually led German scholars to formulate the theory that multiple authors of various documents were eventually edited together to form the Pentateuch. Known as the Documentary Hypothesis, the theory is now regarded as virtual fact by many critical scholars.

Proponents of the **Documentary Hypothesis** rely on various pieces of internal factors such as differing literary styles, differing names for God (*Elohim; Yahweh*), couplets (repeated stories), and editorial insertions (14:14; 36:31; 47:11). They often argue that writing and monotheism were unknown during the time of Moses. The Documentary Hypothesis was given its classical articulation by Julius Wellhausen (1876–83), who argued that anonymous editors compiled the Pentateuch long after Moses from the four documents: J (Yahwist, 850 BC), E (Elohist 750 BC), D (Deuteronomist, 621 BC) and P (Priestly Code, 525 BC).[2]

The Samaritan Pentateuch at Nablus. Samaritans consider only the Pentateuch as canonical Scripture.

Despite the widespread acceptance of the Documentary Hypothesis, several reasons cause it to be **suspect**. First, it is contradicted by the traditional view of the Jews and the early church. Second, the Pentateuch itself declares Moses to be the author (Exod 17:14; 24:4,7; 34:27; Num 33:1–2; Deut 1:8; 31:9). Third, the rest of the Old Testament presupposes Mosaic authorship of the Pentateuch (Josh 1:7–8; 8:32,34;

22:5; 1 Kgs 2:3; 2 Kgs 13:23; 14:6; 21:8; 1 Chr 1:1; Ezra 6:18; Dan 9:11–13; Mal 4:4). Fourth, the New Testament designates Moses as the author of the Pentateuch (Matt 19:4–8; Mark 7:10; 12:26; Luke 16:29–31; 20:37; 24:27; John 5:46–47; 7:19,23; Acts 15:1; Rom 10:5,19). Fifth, the Pentateuch reflects a thematic literary unity that implies a single author. Sixth, the author writes as an eyewitness to much of the Pentateuch's content, which would be impossible for a writer long after the events (Exod 15:27; Num 2:1–31; 11:7–8). Seventh, the writer demonstrates a familiarity with Egyptian culture and geography, which would be unlikely for a later Judean writer (Gen 13:10; 16:1–3; 33:18; 39:4; 40:9–11; 41:40,43). However, Moses' Egyptian education would have certainly qualified him to write the Torah. In addition, archaeologists have discovered multiple written languages existed long before the time of Moses.

The Documentary Hypothesis is built on **unfounded assumptions and evidence**. The documents that the theory relies upon have never been discovered. There is no archaeological evidence nor extrabiblical historical proof that such documents (J, E, D, P) ever existed. To the contrary, archeological discoveries from nearby ancient Near Eastern countries in the period of Abram and Moses contain similar laws and customs. These finds rebut the documentary presupposition that some material in the Pentateuch is historically impossible or represents life at a much later period. After careful analysis of the theory, Moses Segal of Hebrew University rejected it because of "the absurd lengths to which it carries the analysis of the text, breaking up homogenous passages, and even single verses, into smaller fragments."[3]

Conservative evangelical scholars recognize that certain small elements of the Pentateuch were probably added later, such as the account of Moses' death and burial (Deuteronomy 34), but they believe Moses was the **substantial author** of the Pentateuch. He probably used ancient patriarchal records (*toledoth*) to compile the early chapters of Genesis so he should be considered the primary editor, arranger, and author of this material as is affirmed by the biblical record.[4]

For Further Reading

Cassuto, Umberto. *The Documentary Hypothesis.* Jerusalem: Magnes Press, 1961.

Clines, D. J. A. *The Theme of the Pentateuch.* JSOTSup 10. Sheffield: JSOT Press, 1999.

Garrett, Duane. *Rethinking Genesis: The Sources and Authorship of the First Book of the Pentateuch.* Grand Rapids: Baker, 1991.

Hamilton, Victor. *Handbook on the Pentateuch.* Grand Rapids: Baker, 2009.

Livingston, G. Herbert. *The Pentateuch in Its Cultural Environment.* Grand Rapids: Baker, 1987.

Millard, Alan, and Donald J. Wiseman, *Essays on the Patriarchal Narratives.* Winona Lake, IN: Eisenbrauns, 1983.

Sailhamer, John. *The Pentateuch as Narrative.* Grand Rapids: Zondervan, 1992.

Segal, Moses. *The Pentateuch.* Jerusalem: Magnes Press, 1967.

ENDNOTES

1. M. H. Segal, *The Pentateuch* (Jerusalem: Magnes Press, 1967), xi.

2. For a discussion of the historical development of the Documentary Hypothesis, see Bill Arnold and Bryan Beyer, *Encountering the Old Testament: A Christian Survey* (Grand Rapids: Baker, 1999), 68–75.

3. Segal, *The Pentateuch*, xii. For a classic refutation, see U. Cassuto, *The Documentary Hypotheses* (Jerusalem: Magnes Press, 1961), and D. Garrett, *Rethinking Genesis* (Grand Rapids: Baker, 1991).

4. Eugene H. Merrill, Mark F. Rooker, and Michael A. Grisanti, *The World and the Word* (Nashville: B&H, 2011), 169.

Chapter 6

GENESIS
The Beginning

Genesis is the book of beginnings. It tells the story of the beginning of the human race in general and the beginning of the Hebrew race in particular. The Hebrew Bible titles the book *bere'shith* ("in the beginning") after the first word in the Hebrew text. The pages of Genesis introduce the basics of the biblical message. God is introduced as an absolute personal being who cares about His creation and the human struggle of the fallen world. The pages of this incredible book describe the beginning of the cosmos (1:1), the natural world (1:2–25), the human race (1:26–28), marriage (2:22–24), sin (3:1–7), sacrifice (3:21), salvation (3:15), family (4:1–15), civilization (4:16–21), government (9:1–6), covenant (15:1–5), and faith (15:6).

This mountain in modern Turkey may be part of the mountains of Ararat where Noah's ark came to rest after the flood.

In one sense Genesis is the **story of God**. He speaks, creates, calls, blesses, promises, and visits His creation to intervene personally in the lives of His people. On the other hand, Genesis is the story of the men and women who are the forerunners of future generations. Genesis uniquely tells the story of the lives and challenges of people like Adam and Eve, Cain and Abel, Noah's family, Abraham and Sarah, Isaac and Rebekah, Jacob's wives, and his 12 sons. Unlike ancient mythological literature, Genesis shows its heroes as they really were, giving a realistic glimpse of human nature in the ancient world.

The book of Genesis is an anonymous work that was traditionally attributed to Moses until the eighteenth century. Proponents of the Documentary Hypothesis argue that Genesis, like the rest of the Pentateuch, is the result of various, often conflicting, documents which were edited, redacted, and conflated into their present form many centuries after Moses' time. Some biblical critics even deny that there was ever a historical Moses. Despite the popular acceptance of the critical view, conservative scholars still hold to the **Mosaic authorship** of Genesis.[1] His Egyptian education, as the adopted son of Pharaoh's daughter, provided him with the skills to compose this book. While Moses probably used sources, like ancient patriarchal family records (Gen 5:1), he, rather than some later figure, was the ultimate author, compiler, and editor of the Genesis record.

BACKGROUND

The book of Genesis involves **three basic settings**. Genesis 1–11 recounts the ancient history of the world from creation until the birth of Terah (c. 2296 BC) and takes place in the *Fertile Crescent*. Genesis 12–36 unfolds between the birth of Terah (2296 BC) and Joseph's arrival in Egypt (1899 BC) and takes place mostly in *Canaan*. Genesis 37–50 fits between Joseph's arrival in Egypt (1899 BC) and the death of Joseph (1806 BC) and takes place mostly in *Egypt*. Many conservative scholars date the patriarchs as follows:

PATRIARCH	DATE
Abraham	2166–1991 BC
Isaac	2066–1886 BC
Jacob	2006–1859 BC
Joseph	1916–1806 BC

A key structural marker used throughout the book is the **10 *toledoth***, which means, "the records of" (Gen 2:4; 5:1; 6:9; 10:1; 11:10; 25:12,19; 36:1,9; 37:2). This repetition yields the following literary outline after the introduction to the generations (1:1–2:3):

1. Records of the heavens and earth (2:4–4:26)
2. Records of descendants of Adam (5:1–6:8)

3. Records of Noah (6:9–9:29)
4. Records of the sons of Noah (10:1–11:9)
5. Records of Shem (11:10–26)
6. Records of Terah (11:27–25:11)
7. Records of Ishmael (25:12–18)
8. Records of Isaac (25:19–35:29)
9. Records of Esau (36:1–37:1)
10. Records of Jacob (37:2–50:26)

Thus, *toledoth* introduces a section rather than concludes it. *Toledoth* says this is what became of someone. Each *toledoth* starts out broadly and then narrows to a person, line, or a special group of interest within that given section.[2]

However, the outline followed here is a thematic one focusing on primeval (Gen 1–11:9) and patriarchal history (Gen 11:10–50:26) as the **two key divisions** in the book. These two sections can also be categorized as the beginning of the human race and the beginning of the Hebrew race. The four key events of primeval history include creation (chaps. 1–2), fall (chaps. 3–5), flood (chaps. 6–9), and dispersion of the nations (10:1–11:9). The four key people of patriarchal history include Abraham (11:10–25:11), Isaac (25:12–26:35), Jacob (chaps. 27–36), and Joseph (chaps. 37–50).

Outline[3]

I. Primeval History (Genesis 1–11:9)
   A. Creation (Genesis 1–2)
   B. Fall (Genesis 3–5)
   C. Flood (Genesis 6–9)
   D. Nations (Genesis 10:1–11:9)
II. Patriarchal History (Genesis 11:10–50:26)
   A. Abraham (Genesis 11:10–25:11)
   B. Isaac (Genesis 25:12–26:35)
   C. Jacob (Genesis 27–36)
   D. Joseph (Genesis 37–50)

MESSAGE

Genesis provided Israel with an explanation of her place in the history of the world. In Genesis, Moses explains how God's original plan for creation was marred by sin and how Israel was set aside for the special purpose of mediating God's redemptive blessings to the world. As a **divine history** of the world, Genesis covers more time than any other biblical book.

Genesis also emphasizes the importance of the Abrahamic covenant, which gave Israel a right to the land (Gen 12:1–3; 15:18–21). Because they would soon have to take the land by fighting the Canaanites, Israel was in need of understanding that it was God's will for the nation to remove and exterminate them (Gen 9:25; 15:16). Thus, the book was intended to cause Moses' generation to trust God by better understanding their past heritage, present purpose, and future destiny as they anticipated entrance into the Promised Land.

I. Primeval History (Genesis 1–11:9)

The book's opening prologue (chaps. 1–11) explains to Israel her purpose by tracing **God's redemptive program** and messianic lineage from Eden to Abraham. This section explains the terrible progress of sin and the reason God's redemptive program was necessary. Thus, it is the foundation of the biblical worldview, and without this part the rest would be somewhat incomprehensible.

Eastern Wall of Doura Europa and the Euphrates River, which is one of the rivers mentioned in connection with the garden of Eden.

A. Creation (Genesis 1–2)

The first two chapters of Genesis describe God's original work of creation. From the opening verse, Gen 1:1 assumes the existence of God (*Elohim*) and the fact of creation. Knowledge of the **original creation** would also help the nation comprehend how sin negatively impacted the wonderful world God created. Knowledge of God's six days of work and one day of rest would help Israel understand the foundation of their workweek (Exod 20:8–11) and Sabbath rest as the sign of the Mosaic covenant.

Hebrew Highlight

Create. Hebrew בּרא **(bara).** The Hebrew word bara', both active and passive, always conveys the idea of "create." With God as its subject, it appears 48 times in the Hebrew Bible, 21 of which are found in Genesis. The subject of this verb is never man. It suggests creating something new (Jer 31:22). Bara', used in Gen 1:1, expresses initial creation. God is said to create sea creatures (Gen 1:21), heavenly bodies (Isa 40:26), wind (Amos 4:13), a clean heart (Ps 51:10), words of praise (Isa 57:19), and new heavens and a new earth (Isa 65:17). God alone is the One who creates, and He does so as an expression of His own sovereign will.

The fact that man is the pinnacle of God's creative work is evident from his designation as God's image bearer (Gen 1:26–27). Man and woman were given the role of theocratic administrators who would corule God's creation on His behalf (Gen 1:28; 2:8–20). Man's stewardship over this creation (2:15) as well as the presence of the tree of life, and the tree of the knowledge of good and evil (2:9,17) would remind Moses' audience that they too had the responsibility of obedience in order to experience God's blessings (Leviticus 26; Deuteronomy 28).

Chapter 1 summarizes the creation of the world, and chapter 2 scrutinized it in greater detail. Dutch scholar G. C. Aalders observes the creation is one of **absolute beginning** and not a transformation of a preexistent one. He states, "The words 'In the beginning' must be taken in their absolute sense . . . although the alternative interpretation is linguistically possible, it does not reflect common Hebrew usage."[4] The biblical description of creation is *ex nihilo* (from nothing) by the power of God's spoken word ("then God said," 1:3,6,9,11,14,20,24,26,29), though 2:7 indicates that man was made from the dust of the ground. Thus, the original creation appears to be instantaneous, having an appearance of age and living things (plants and animals) reproducing "according to their kinds" (1:12,21,24,25). Reformed scholar O. T. Allis believes, "The account of creation is definitely theistic. . . . God is distinct from both man and nature. He is the Creator of both. All things owe their existence to His almighty fiat."[5]

The opening verses of Genesis clearly refute:

Atheism	There is no God.
Pantheism	All is God.
Polytheism	Many gods exist.
Materialism	Matter is eternal.
Humanism	Man is the measure.
Naturalism	Nature is ultimate.

The Genesis account of creation also contradicts **secular evolution**, which theorizes that all life, including humans, evolved over billions of years from lower life forms by natural processes. Theories of origins that accommodate evolution (gap theory, day=age theory, revelatory day theory, theistic evolution, etc.) have all generally proven inadequate explanations of the obvious contrast between the biblical account of creation and general evolutionary theory. The results of the naturalistic evolutionary hypothesis have left a spiritual void that "erases all moral and ethical accountability and ultimately abandons all hope for humanity."[6]

B. Fall (Genesis 3–5)

The major crisis for the newly created world comes in chap. 3 with the fall of **Adam and Eve** into sin. This resulted in their expulsion from the garden of Eden because of their sinful acts of rebellion against God. Their descendants followed in the rebellious ways of their parents, resulting in what would become the beginning of the continuing story of human depravity and its terrible consequences. Spiritual death and human suffering came immediately as the result of their sin and eventually led to their physical death (3:3,19). As a result, the apostle Paul observes, "death reigned" because of Adam's sin (Rom 5:14). Thus, the one biblical doctrine for which there is no lack of empirical evidence is the depravity of the human race.

While the immediate consequences of human sin brought guilt, shame, fear, and broken communication with the Creator (Gen 3:7–13), God graciously confronted Adam and Eve asking, "Where are you?" (3:9) and "What is this you have done?" (3:13). After pronouncing the penalty for their sin, God provided for their redemption by clothing their inadequacy (3:21) and predicting their ultimate salvation by the "seed" of the woman who would "crush" (NIV) the head of the serpent (3:15). This promise of the annihilator of the wicked instigator by the promise of a human conqueror was the **first prophecy** of the Bible. It has often been called the *proto-evangelium* or what Aalders called "the gospel announced by God Himself to our first parents."[7] No time frame is indicated, but the biblical reader sees the first ray of hope to enlighten the human predicament.

Most importantly, the *protoevangelium* (Gen 3:15) made clear that one day God would send one who would defeat God's enemy. This would eventually allow for the restoration of everything to God's original design and restore man's position as theocratic administrator.[8] Thus, the information presented in Genesis 1–3 would help Israel understand why redemption was necessary. Putting this together with Gen 12:1–3 would help the reader understand why the nation was singled out for the special purpose of mediating God's redemptive blessings. Such blessings would ultimately restore God's original intent in creation that was lost in the fall.

The **genealogy from Adam to Noah** traces the line from which God's blessing (Gen 3:15) would eventually come (Gen 4:25–5:32) and contrasts it with the ungodly line of Cain (Gen 4:17–24). The repetition of death in Genesis 5 testifies to the reality of the curse (Gen 3:19). The fact that people still retained the image of God even in their fallen condition (Gen 5:1; 9:6) reveals humanity's dignity and why God wanted to restore His relationship with mankind after the curse. Moreover, Enoch's translation (Gen 5:24) as well as Lamech's description of Noah as the "comforter" (Gen 5:29 NIV) provided hope that the reality of the curse would one day be done away with.[9] In the meantime Genesis traces the destiny of the godly line of Seth versus the ungodly line of Cain.

A reproduction of tablet 11 of the Gilgamesh Epic describing the Babylonian account of a great flood.

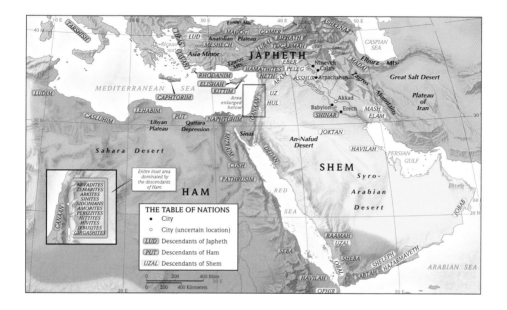

C. Flood (Genesis 6–9)

The growing power of sin approached epic proportions as the human race became involved in perpetual wickedness (Gen 6:1–7), so God moved to destroy humanity through the flood. Because Noah was a righteous and blameless man who walked with God (6:9), God safely preserved him and his family in the ark while the world was flooded. The **global extent** of the flood is indicated by the fact that all of the high mountains were covered (7:19), all land living things perished (7:21), the flood lasted 371 days, and the ark was of great size (1,400,000 cubic feet). It is also evident from extrabiblical and New Testament testimony (1 Pet 3:3–7) and the use of unique terms for the deluge (Hb. *mabbul*, and Gk. *kataklusmos*).[10]

God's intent to restore creation is seen in His provision of the **Noahic covenant** following the flood (Gen 8:20–9:17). The creation of human government with the power of capital punishment would serve as a deterrent preventing humanity from regressing back to the level of violence exhibited in the antediluvian world. God's desire to restore creation is also seen in His command to Noah to subdue creation and His promise, as signified by the rainbow, never to destroy the race again by a flood of water. However, despite God's provision of the Noahic covenant, man's sinful nature remained perverse even after the flood (Gen 8:21). This is illustrated in Noah's drunkenness, the sin of

A ziggurat dating to the Babylonian period (605–550 BC).

Ham, and the subsequent curse of Canaan (Gen 9:18–28). Thus, God's chosen servant Noah failed to live as a beacon of light in this new world after the flood.

D. Nations (Genesis 10:1–11:9)

The subsequent **dispersion of the nations** at the tower of Babel (Gen 10:1–11:9) indicates that obedience results in blessing and disobedience results in scattering. Unfortunately, such scattering would recur many times throughout Israel's history (Leviticus 26; Deuteronomy 28). The confusion of languages that resulted continued unabated until the day of Pentecost in Acts 2. The scattering of the nations following the incident at Babel ("gate of God") set the stage for the calling and selection of Abraham.

II. Patriarchal History (Genesis 11:10–50:26)

The rest of the book of Genesis focuses the reader's attention on patriarchal history (Gen 11:10–50:26). Moses' goal in this section is to connect **God's redemptive purposes** in chaps. 1–11 to later generations in order to give the exodus generation an incentive to cooperate with God's covenant purposes. From this point onward, Genesis focuses on four great patriarchs: Abraham, Isaac, Jacob, and Joseph, although Judah actually emerged as the ancestor of the messianic line.

A. Abraham (Genesis 11:10–25:11)

God's redemptive promises are now focused on one individual, Abraham. Initially called Abram ("great father"), Abraham would become the "father of a multitude," including Isaac, the son of promise. Thus, Moses is careful to trace the Hebrew line

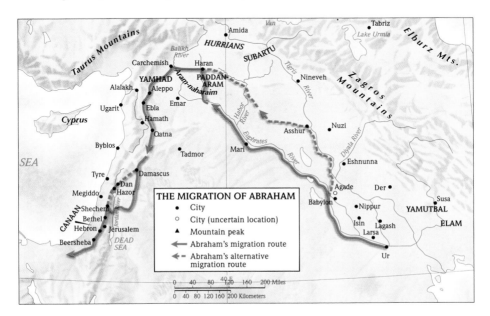

from Noah's son Shem to Abram's father Terah (Gen 11:10–26). In Gen 12:2–3,7 the promises from Gen 3:15 are restated in the form of the **Abrahamic promises**. According to these promises, God would give land, seed, and blessing to Abram's descendants; and through these descendants the entire world would be blessed. The seed aspect of these blessings specifically amplifies the unconditional promise of a seed who would defeat the forces of evil in Gen 3:15.

Contrary to God's command to separate from his family (Gen 12:1), Abram instead took Lot (Gen 12:4) on the journey to Canaan and stopped in **Haran** in Padan-aram (Syria) for some time. After finally moving to Canaan, Abram eventually went to Egypt (Gen 12:10), where he lied to Pharaoh about Sarai being his sister and was rebuked by the pagan king. The resulting plagues that came upon Pharaoh would remind Moses' readers of what happened in their time as well.

In Genesis 13, Abram separated from Lot and fulfilled God's original plan of complete separation of his father's household (Gen 12:1). Thus, the **land promises** were restated after this separation occurred. In Genesis 14, Abram refused to take tribute from the king of Sodom and maintained his independence from the wicked Sodomites (Gen 13:13; 14:21–24). Abram's blessing instead came from the king-priest Melchizedek who was a prototype of Christ (cf. Gen 14:18–20; Heb 7:22–28).

Genesis 15 formally confirmed the **Abrahamic covenant** as a formal covenant relationship with Abram. Thus, the initial expectation of hope in Gen 3:15 is now explained in the form of an official ancient Near Eastern treaty between God and Abram. Such a treaty normally called for both parties in agreement to pass through rows of severed animal pieces. This ritual signified that a similar fate suffered by these severed animals would fall upon the breaching party if he failed to meet his obligations under the treaty. However, the unconditional nature of this treaty was seen in the fact that Abram was asleep while God alone passed through the animal pieces (Gen 15:12,17). Thus, the fulfillment of the treaty was totally dependent on God rather than on the performance of Abram or his descendants. With total faith in God's promises, Abram "believed the LORD," and God credited him with righteousness (15:6; see Rom 4:3; 9:22; Gal 3:6; Jas 2:23).

Despite God's promise that Abraham would have a son from his "own body" (15:4), barren Sarai insisted that Hagar, their Egyptian slave, should serve as a surrogate mother (16:1–3). As a result, Hagar became the mother of **Ishmael** ("God hears"), the ancestor of the Arab peoples. Twice God showed His grace toward Ishmael by sparing his life (16:7–15; 21:14–21) and

Bab Edh Dhra is believed by many archaeologists to be ancient Sodom and/or Gomorrah.

promising to make him a "great nation." God's selection of Isaac by a miraculous birth to Abraham and Sarah in their old age was a deliberate reflection of His divine will (18:9–15). To reflect the great lineage that would come from this line, Abram's name was changed to Abraham ("father of multitudes") and Sarai's name was changed to Sarah ("princess").

The birth of **Isaac** ("laughter") caused Sarah to laugh with God, instead of laughing at Him (cf. 18:12–15; 21:6–7). Years later God tested Abraham's faith in this promise by telling him to sacrifice Isaac on Mount Moriah (22:1–16). Despite the command Abraham's faith was expressed by telling the servants "we'll come back to you" (22:5). At the most dramatic moment of the patriarchal narrative, "the Angel of the LORD" called Abraham to stop (22:11–12).[11] He had passed the test of faith, and God provided the ram instead. Therefore, Abraham named the place "The LORD Will Provide" (Hb. *yahweh yir'eh*; Jehovah Jireh, KJV).

B. Isaac (Genesis 25:12–26:35)

Genesis 25:12–18 distinguishes Isaac's line from the line of Ishmael. Because the covenant was given to Isaac, Ishmael's descendants had no legitimate claim to the Promised Land. The rest of chap. 25 clarifies that the line would continue through Isaac's youngest son Jacob rather than through his oldest son Esau. The **divine election** of Jacob over Esau is evidenced through the prophecy that the older would serve the younger (Gen 25:23). Esau's character weakness is evident in his despising his birthright and selling it to Jacob (Gen 25:27–34) and his rebellious marriages to Hittite women (Gen 26:34–35). The Abrahamic covenant was reconfirmed to Isaac (Gen 26:1–5,23–25) with promises of personal blessing and protection (Gen 26:12–16).

C. Jacob (Genesis 27–36)

The theme of **deception** recurs throughout the story of Jacob's life. The patriarch Jacob moves to the forefront in Genesis 27–36. Despite the fact that Jacob deceived Isaac and cheated Esau out of the blessing of the firstborn (Gen 27:1–40), the Abrahamic covenant was reconfirmed to Jacob in the next chapter (Gen 28:10–17). This repetition of God's everlasting promises emphasizes the unconditional nature of the covenant. Jacob escaped from Esau's rage for stealing his blessing (Gen 27:41–45) by journeying north to his mother's ancestral home in Haran (28:10) where he eventually married

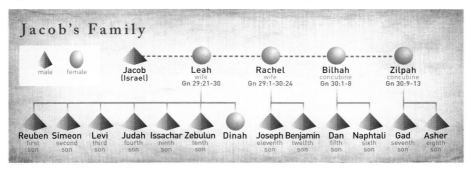

Leah and Rachel, the daughters of Laban, his mother's brother (29:1–29). In route to Haran, Jacob stopped at Luz where he encountered God in the dream of the angelic stairway. Believing it to be the "gate of heaven," he renamed it Bethel ("house of God"), and vowed that the Lord (*Yahweh*) would be his God (28:16–21).

Jacob's marriages to Leah and Rachel are carefully traced because through these marriages (and their maidservants) would come 12 sons who would become the **12 tribes of Israel** (Gen 29–30:24). The 14 years Jacob served Laban in order to marry Rachel were necessary in order to mold Jacob's character. Only as Jacob the deceiver encountered the deception of Laban could this flaw in his character be rectified. Even though Jacob was deceived into marrying Leah, she would become the mother of Judah and perpetuate the messianic line of Christ (Matt 1:1–2).

After residing about 20 years in Haran, God told Jacob to leave and **return to Bethel** (35:1). This decision became the turning point of Jacob's life as he finally returned to the Promised Land. So dramatic was his desire to please the Lord that he insisted his family "get rid of the foreign gods" they had accumulated (35:2). Upon returning to Bethel, he called on the "God of Bethel" (*el bethel*), indicating his full intention to serve the Lord. As a result, God changed his name from Jacob to Israel (35:10), setting the stage for the rest of the story.

The Jabbok River.

D. Joseph (Genesis 37:1–50:26)

Genesis 37–50 focuses on Joseph as the human instrument God would use to relocate the nation in Egypt. God's selection of the younger brother to accomplish His will reveals a pattern (Isaac over Ishmael, Jacob over Esau, Judah and Joseph over Reuben, Ephraim over Manasseh) throughout the book, indicating that God is not limited by human preferences or traditional customs. God revealed His purpose for Joseph in a dream. When he shared the dream with his brothers, they became envious and sold him as a **slave into Egypt** (Genesis 37), setting the stage for their own descendants' future enslavement in Egypt.

Despite his brother's evil intentions and subsequent deception of their father Jacob, Genesis 39–41 records the circumstances by which Joseph was promoted to second in command over all of Egypt as a grand vizer to Pharaoh (probably Sesostris III).[12] **Joseph's exaltation** is attributed to his faithfulness to God in both Potiphar's household and in prison (Gen 39:2–5,21–23; 40:8; 41:16). In Gen 42:1–47:26, Jacob's descendants finally settled in Egypt. Judah's willingness to become a substitute for Benjamin erases the hostility between Joseph and his brothers and resulted in all the brothers being reunited (Genesis 45) and bringing their father Jacob to Egypt (Genesis 46). The family eventually settled in Goshen in the delta region, where they maintained their distinctiveness as God's special nation (Genesis 47).

Genesis 48–50 concludes with Jacob blessing Joseph's sons (Gen 48:8–22), **Jacob's prophetic blessings** pronounced upon the tribes (Gen 49:1–28), Jacob's burial in Canaan (Gen 50:1–14), Joseph's prediction that the nation would return to Canaan (Gen 50:24), and the oath by the sons of Israel that they would bury Joseph's bones in Canaan (Gen 50:25). Of particular significance regarding the guarantee of future covenant blessing was the prediction that the Messiah would come from Judah (Gen 49:10; Matt 1:2,6). Genesis 49:10 is messianic in that it teaches that the ruler's staff would remain in Judah "until the one comes to whom it belongs" (the meaning of

The step-pyramid of King Djoser (Zoser) of the Third Dynasty located at Saqqara.

Shiloh).[13] While Judah received the messianic promise, Joseph was given a double blessing through the adoption of his sons, Ephraim and Manasseh, as "sons of Israel," each becoming future tribes of Israel.

In Genesis God set in motion His **redemptive program** that would bring forth the Messiah who would one day restore God's original design for creation (Gen 3:15). To accomplish this goal, God created and preserved an elect nation that would one day bring forth the long-awaited Messiah from the tribe of Judah (Gen 49:10). The foundation of this new nation was the Abrahamic covenant. This covenant, which is described (Genesis 15) and traced throughout the book of Genesis, would later be confirmed to the exodus generation (Exod 6:2–8). Thus, the author sets the stage for the story of the exodus that follows.

The mosque of the patriarchs at Hebron built over the traditional site of the Cave of Machpelah.

THEOLOGICAL SIGNIFICANCE

Genesis begins with the act of creation and ends with the words, "in a coffin in Egypt" (50:26). In between the author lays the **foundation** of all biblical theology. The opening verse of the Bible assumes, rather than attempting to prove, the existence of God and the fact of creation by His sovereign will and spoken word (Genesis 1). Genesis defines human beings as a unique and distinct creation made in the image of God (1:26) and given a mandate to rule God's creation (1:28). However, Adam's sin brought death and disorder to the creation and often resulted in divine judgment

(1:24; 6:5–7; 11:8). As the world turned away from God, He turned to one man, calling Abraham to believe, trust, and follow Him (Gen 12:1–3), promising to make of his descendants a "great nation" through which He would bless all peoples. The election of Israel was confirmed by the Abrahamic covenant (15:1–6) and reaffirmed to his descendants Isaac, Jacob, and Jacob's 12 sons—the forefathers of the nation of Israel. Paul House observes, "Genesis acts a foundational prelude to Israel's greatest defining moment (Sinai) and Israel's immediate future (the conquest of Canaan)."[14]

For Further Reading

Arnold, Bill. *Genesis*. New York: Cambridge University Press, 2009.
Davis, John J. *Paradise to Prison: Studies in Genesis*. Grand Rapids: Baker, 1975.
Hamilton, Victor. *Genesis*, 2 vols. NICOT. Grand Rapids: Eerdmans, 1990, 1995.
Mathews, Kenneth. *Genesis 1:1–11:26* and *Genesis 11:27–50:26*. NAC 1A, 1B. Nashville: B&H, 1996, 2005.
Morris, Henry M. *The Genesis Record: A Scientific and Devotional Commentary on the Book of Beginnings*. Grand Rapids: Baker, 1976.
Ross, Allen. *Creation and Blessing: A Guide to the Study and Exposition of Genesis*. Grand Rapids: Baker, 1996.

Study Questions

1. In what way are human beings uniquely created by God?
2. How does the fallen nature of humanity affect our relationship to God?
3. How does the biblical description of the flood (Genesis 6–9) indicate its extent?
4. In what way is Abraham's faith an example to us today?
5. What can we learn about the importance of character and personal integrity from the contrasting stories of Jacob and Joseph?

ENDNOTES

1. See the extensive discussion and references in E. H. Merrill, M. Rooker, and M. A. Grisanti, *The World and the Word: An Introduction to the Old Testament* (Nashville: B&H Academic, 2011), 136–73. They view Moses as the substantial and predominant author, with minor editorial insertions such as the reference to Dan in Gen 14:14. Others, like W. S. LaSor, D. A. Hubbard, and F. W. Bush (*Old Testament Survey: The Message, Form, and Background of the Old Testament* [Grand Rapids: Eerdmans, 1996], 8–13), view the book as being shaped by "inspired authors, editors, and tradition bearers of God's chosen people."

2. Allen Ross, *Creation and Blessing: A Guide to the Study and Exposition of Genesis* (Grand Rapids: Baker, 1996), 72–73.

3. The outline follows Bruce Wilkinson and Kenneth Boa, *Talk thru the Bible* (Nashville: B&H, 2002), 5–7.

4. G. C. Aalders, *Genesis*, Bible Student's Commentary (Grand Rapids: Zondervan, 1981), 1:51.

5. O. T. Allis, *God Spoke by Moses* (Philadelphia: P&R, 1977), 12.

6. John MacArthur, *The Battle for the Beginning* (Nashville: Thomas Nelson, 2001), 15.

7. Aalders, *Genesis*, 108.

8. Some hold that Eve's mistaken belief that she had begotten the Messiah (4:1) and Lamech's belief that Noah would ameliorate the curse (3:17; 5:29) indicate that they understood Gen 3:15 in messianic terms. Arnold Fruchtenbaum, *Messianic Christology* (Tustin, CA: Ariel, 1998), 14–17.

9. Allen Ross, *Creation and Blessing: A Guide to the Study and Exposition of Genesis* (Grand Rapids: Baker, 1996), 174.

10. See John Whitcomb and Henry Morris, *The Genesis Flood* (Philadelphia: P&R, 1961); Henry Morris, *The Genesis Record* (Grand Rapids: Baker, 1976), 163–244.

11. "The Angel of the Lord" is a *theophany* (appearance of God in human form) and is most likely a preincarnate appearance of Christ in the Old Testament (Gen 18:1; 22:11; Josh 5:13–15; Judg 6:11–16; 13:3). See James Borland, *Christ in the Old Testament* (Chicago: Moody Press, 1978).

12. On the conservative view of the chronology, see John J. Davis, *Paradise to Prison: Studies in Genesis* (Grand Rapids: Baker, 1975), 266–67.

13. Ross, *Creation and Blessing*, 703. Judah was selected for this honor because Reuben, Simeon, and Levi were disqualified.

14. Paul R. House, *Old Testament Theology* (Downers Grove, IL: IVP, 1998), 58; cf. also E. Merrill, "A Theology of the Pentateuch," in *A Biblical Theology of the Old Testament*, ed. Roy Zuck (Chicago: Moody Press, 1991), 30.

Chapter 7

EXODUS
Exit from Egypt

The book of Exodus tells a dramatic tale of faith, hope, and love. It is also a story of betrayal, slavery, emancipation, and liberation. Its images are so powerful they are quoted more than 120 times in the Hebrew Bible. Exodus is the story of the Israelites' exit from bondage in Egypt. It is a narrative account of the history of the descendants of Jacob (Israel) from the death of Joseph in c. 1806 BC (Exod 1:1–7) until the construction of the tabernacle in the wilderness in 1446 BC (Exod 40:17). The account includes the years of Israel's bondage and servitude in Egypt, the call of Moses, the confrontation with Pharaoh, the dramatic events of the exodus, and Israel's arrival at Mount Sinai to receive the law from Jehovah (Yahweh) God.

Exodus is also the story of God's love for His people. Yahweh is not an aloof, inactive, functionless deity. He sees, hears, observes, and cares about the struggles

The smallest of the three pyramids at Giza, built by Mycerinus (Menkaure).

of His people (Exod 3:7). He is an intensely involved, vitally concerned, moral being who demands that His creatures reflect His moral attributes. Jewish scholar Nahum Sarna observes: "History, therefore, is the arena of divine activity. . . . The nation is the product of God's providence, conditioned by human response to His demands."[1] The God who revealed Himself to the patriarchs is the same God who revealed Himself to Moses and called him to lead the people in the exodus. The time had come to fulfill God's promise to Abraham (Gen 15:13) in an incredible display of His covenant faithfulness.

The Hebrew title of the book is *ve'alleh shemoth* ("and these are the names"), which comes from the book's opening words. The English title, Exodus, comes from the LXX Greek title, *Exodos*. Interestingly, the same Greek word as used in the LXX title is also used in Luke 9:31 and 1 Pet. 1:15 to depict "departing, going out" to death.

BACKGROUND

People have vigorously debated the **Mosaic authorship** of the book of Exodus, but several lines of evidence point to Moses as the book's author. First, the book is interconnected with Genesis. Exodus's first words seem to pick up where Gen 50:26 left off. Furthermore, Exod 1:1–7 bears resemblance to Gen 46:8–27 in describing Jacob's family that came to Egypt. Thus, if it is accepted that Moses authored Genesis, then it is likely that Moses authored Exodus. Second, the book of Exodus itself claims that Moses spoke and recorded some of the book's content (Exod 17:14; 24:4,7; 34:27). Third, the rest of the Old Testament claims Moses as the book's author (Josh 8:31; Mal 4:4). Fourth, the New Testament indicates that Moses wrote Exodus (Mark 7:10; 12:26; Luke 2:22–23; 20:37; John 1:45; 5:46–47; 7:19,22–23; Rom 10:5). Fifth, extrabiblical material, including the Dead Sea Scrolls (CD 5:1–2; 7:6,8–9; 1 QS 5:15) and the *Babylonian Talmud* (*Baba Bathra* 14b–15a), indicates that Moses authored the book.

The details of the exodus account clearly reflect an **Egyptian**

The famous Sphinx of Giza, built by Chephren (Khafre), measuring 240 feet from front to back.

cultural background, which included the enslavement of foreigners as brick makers, the common use of midwives to deliver babies, the use of birth stools, snake charming by priestly magicians, worship of calf deities such as Apis, the veneration of the Nile River, the reference to the king as Pharaoh ("Great House"), and the occupation of the Egyptian delta by Semites.[2] The covenant structure and pattern of the Israelite legal system reflected in Exodus clearly indicates a firsthand knowledge of scribal methods, international treaties, and legal terminology typical of the mid-second millennium BC. Kitchen argues convincingly that the content of Exodus can hardly reflect the work of a "runaway rabble of brick-making slaves."[3] Rather, he suggests it is clearly the work of a Hebrew leader who was experienced with the life of the Egyptian court and had a traditional Semitic social background, just as Moses is described in the book of Exodus.

DATE OF THE EXODUS

The date of the book is contingent upon how one dates the exodus event. Hill and Walton correctly observe, "Pinpointing the date of the exodus constitutes one of the major chronological problems of Old Testament study."[4] The significance of the exodus date in turn affects the date of the conquest of Canaan, the length of the Judges period, and the credibility of various chronological references in the Old Testament (Judg 11:26; 1 Kgs 6:1). Those holding to the early date (1446 BC) for the exodus identify Thutmosis III (1504–1450 BC) as the pharaoh of the oppression and Amenhotep II (1450–1425 BC) as the pharaoh of the exodus. Those preferring the late date (1290 BC) view Ramesses I (1320–1318 BC) and Seti I (1318–1304 BC) as the pharaohs of the oppression and Ramesses II (1304–1237 BC) as the pharaoh of the exodus.

Arguments for the **early date** (1446 BC) are generally based on the following observations:[5] (1) First Kings 6:1 states the exodus occurred 480 years prior to King Solomon's fourth year (966 BC), dating the exodus as 1446 BC. (2) Jephthah, in c. 1100 BC, claimed Israel had occupied Canaan for 300 years (Judg 11:26). Adding 40 years for the wilderness journey puts the

The Merneptah Stele that contains the first mention of Israel.

date of the exodus between 1446 and 1400 BC. (3) The Merneptah Stele (c. 1220 BC) refers to "Israel" as an already established people in the land in the record of Ramesses II's son. This hardly allows time for the exodus, wilderness wandering, conquest, and settlement of Canaan by the Israelites. (4) The Amarna Tablets (c. 1400 BC) refer to a period of chaos in Canaan, which could equate with the Israelite conquest. (5) The Dream Stele of Thutmosis IV, who followed Amenhotep II, indicates he was not the firstborn legal heir to the throne, the eldest son having died.

Arguments for the **late date** of the exodus are generally as follows: (1) The biblical years are reinterpreted as symbolic (480 years = 12 generations) or exaggerated generalizations (e.g., Jephthah's 300 years). (2) No extrabiblical references to "Israel" have been found prior to the Merneptah Stele (c. 1220 BC). (3) Archaeological evidence seems to be lacking for a fifteenth-century BC conquest at some sites in Canaan. (4) The Israelites helped build the cities of Pithom and Rameses (Exod 1:11), which were completed by Ramesses II. (5) Overlapping judgeships in Judges may account for tabulating a shorter period of time for the conquest, settlement, and judges era.

The temple of Ramesses II at Abu-Simbel. The four colossal statues depict the king wearing the double crown signifying his role as ruler over all of Egypt.

The major weakness of the late date view is that it totally discards any literal reading of the biblical chronology in favor of highly debatable and inconclusive archaeological data. It is entirely likely that future excavations will continue to clarify this picture. In the meantime **minimalist critics** discount the entire story of the exodus and conquest as Jewish mythology, making any date for the exodus irrelevant for them. Those who take the biblical account at face value have offered a more than adequate defense of their position.[6] The basic laws and religious rituals of Israel were probably shaped over time, but they had to have a beginning at some point in history. Suggesting there never was a Moses involved in the foundation of the nation of Israel would be like arguing there never was a George Washington involved in the founding of America.

Thus, assuming Mosaic authorship and the early date of the exodus, the book was likely written anytime between the two years after the exodus (1444 BC) and Moses' death (1406 BC). The earlier end of this spectrum seems more appropriate since the events described occurred then.

The recipients of the book were the generation of Hebrews who experienced the exodus from Egypt and the covenant at Sinai (17:14; 24:4; 34:27–28) and the subsequent generation that was born in the wilderness.

ROUTE OF THE EXODUS

Scholars have advanced **three theories** as possible explanations for the route of the exodus. First, the *northern theory* places Mount Sinai in the northwestern area of the Sinai. In its favor is the fact that Moses requested a three-day journey (Exod 3:18) and that the northern route is the shortest journey to Kadesh Barnea. However, this theory fails since it keeps Israel close to Egyptian territory, does not consider the 10-day journey between Kadesh and Mount Sinai (Deut 1:2), and does not acknowledge that God led Israel away from the Philistines fortresses along the coast (Exod 13:17).

Second, the *central theory* places Mount Sinai in Arabia (at Jabel-Al Lawz), beyond the gulf of Aqabah, east of the Sinai Peninsula. This view has several ingredients in its favor, such as Paul's indication that Sinai was in Arabia (Gal 4:25), the existence of an active volcano in the area reminiscent of Exod 19:16–25, and the association of Arabia with the Midianites (Exod 3:1; 18:1). However, several reasons have made scholars reticent to embrace this view. Among them are the beliefs that the events of Exod 19:16–25 have more in common with a theophanic divine manifestation rather than a volcanic eruption and that Moses is also related to the Kenites who were a nomadic Midianite clan prevalent in the Sinai region (Judg 1:16; 4:11). Also, it is virtually impossible to reach the crossing point into Arabia in 11 days.[7]

Third, the *southern theory* places Mount Sinai on the southern tip of the Sinai Peninsula. This theory takes into consideration the general direction of the movement of the nation after leaving Egypt. The Lord led Israel from Ramses to Succoth, then from Succoth to Etham on the outskirts of the wilderness (Exod 13:20). After Israel camped at Pi-hahiroth (14:2), she then entered the wilderness of Shur in the northwest of the Sinai Peninsula (Exod 15:22; Num 33:8). It is also worth noting that Christian tradition dating back to the fourth century AD has associated Jebel Musa or Mount Horeb with the same Mount Sinai where Moses received the covenant. Whichever of these three views the interpreter holds, dogmatism should be avoided since new archaeological discoveries are constantly being made adding new light to the subject.[8]

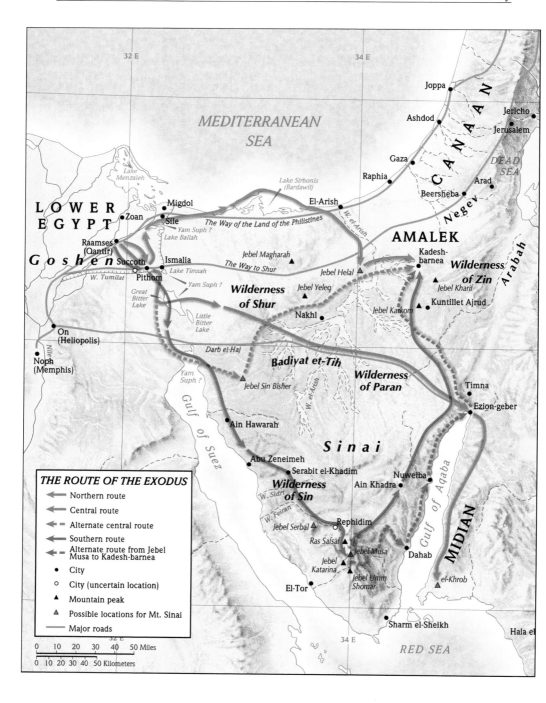

THE ROUTE OF THE EXODUS

Northern route
Central route
Alternate central route
Southern route
Alternate route from Jebel Musa to Kadesh-barnea
• City
○ City (uncertain location)
▲ Mountain peak
△ Possible locations for Mt. Sinai
Major roads

0 10 20 30 40 50 Miles
0 10 20 30 40 50 Kilometers

MESSAGE

The book of Exodus focuses on **Moses' life** which can be divided into three 40-year time periods. They include the period from his birth and his rearing as a prince of Egypt (Acts 7:23), the time he spent in Midian as a shepherd (Exod 7:7), and the time he spent as leader of the exodus in the wilderness (Acts 7:36). The book of Exodus covers the first two of these periods and introduces the third period. Exodus also uses three dominant **genres**. The first type is narrative. The second type is psalm or hymn, found in the song of Moses (Exodus 15), which probably represents the first psalm in the entire Old Testament. The third type is law (Exodus 20–24). Most agree that the Decalogue (20:1–17) represents *apodictic* law while the book of the covenant (20:22–23:33) represents *casuistic* law. Apodictic law involves affirmative or prohibitive statements while casuistic law is couched in "if . . . then" language in an attempt to cover various hypothetical situations.

Outline

I. Exodus from Egyptian Bondage (Exodus 1–18)
  A. Redemption (Exodus 1:1–12:30)
  B. Liberation (Exodus 12:31–15:21)
  C. Preservation (Exodus 15:22–18:27)
II. Instruction for the Redeemed Nation (Exodus 19–40)
  A. Offer of the Covenant (Exodus 19)
  B. Covenant Text (Exodus 20–23)
  C. Covenant Ratification Ceremony (Exodus 24)
  D. Tabernacle of Worship (Exodus 25–40)

I. Exodus from Egyptian Bondage (Exodus 1–18)

The first half of the book involves **God's redemption** of His elect nation Israel from Egyptian servitude (chaps. 1–18). God accomplished this feat in the following three phases: redemption (1:1–12:30), liberation (12:31–15:21), and preservation (15:22–18:27). Moses begins by providing information concerning why redemption was necessary (1:1–22).

A. Redemption (Exodus 1:1–12:30)

After Jacob's descendants migrated into Egypt, the Israelites began to experience numerical growth (1:1–7) as promised by the Abrahamic covenant (Gen 13:16).[9] Following Joseph's death, a Pharaoh arose who did not know Joseph.[10] Threatened by the growing Jewish population, he **subjugated the Hebrew race** (1:8–14). Another attempt to reduce Israel's population was through the practice of infanticide (1:15–22).

The next major section (1:8–12:30) focuses on the **human instrument** God used to accomplish Israel's redemption from Egypt (chaps. 2–4). The book records Moses' supernatural guidance to Pharaoh's household and the rearing he received there (2:1–10). Some believe Moses got his name from the word "mose" found in Thutmosis as a

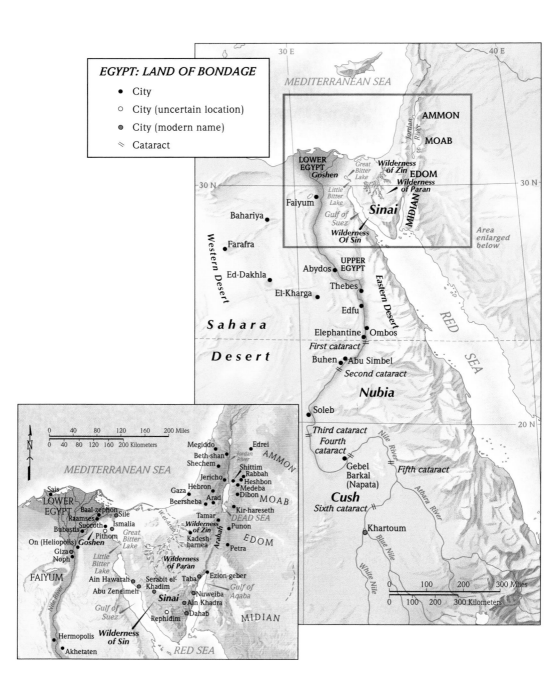

EGYPT: LAND OF BONDAGE

- • City
- ○ City (uncertain location)
- ◉ City (modern name)
- ≋ Cataract

potential future pharaoh. However, according to 2:10, his name comes from the fact that the princess drew him from the water. In Hebrew his name means "to draw forth," and in Egyptian it means "son of the water."[11] If Thutmosis I was in power when Moses was born, it is possible that Hatshepsut, or someone like her, was the princess who took him as her son. Hatshepsut, the royal widow of Thutmosis II, ruled as pharaoh without a male heir from 1504 to 1482 BC.

However, as Moses grew into adulthood, his spiritual immaturity became apparent through his rash decision to kill an Egyptian. In preparation for His task as deliverer, it was necessary for God to train His servant an additional 40 years in the **wilderness of Midian**, the place he would later lead the Israelites for 40 years. Thus, Moses' flight from Pharaoh was just one more step in the divine plan that would eventually lead to the fulfillment of His covenant promises

Sunrise over the Nile from Minia.

to Israel (2:23–25; Gen 15:16). The Midianites were a confederacy of seminomadic tribes stretching from the Sinai Peninsula up through the Syro-Arabian desert. Genesis 25:2 traces their lineage back to Abraham through Keturah. Moses' father-in-law Jethro (3:1), also called Ruel (2:18), was the priest of Midian.

The turning point in the first phase of the book came when Moses encountered God at the **burning bush** (3:1–10). The Lord told Moses He was concerned about His people and therefore He announced, "I have come down to rescue them" (3:8) adding, "I am sending you to . . . lead My people out of Egypt" (3:10). Overwhelmed with the magnitude of the task, Moses offered God five reasons why he was not the man for the job. However, God answered each objection (3:11–4:13) with the promise of miraculous manifestations in Egypt (4:1–9). In the process God revealed Himself as "I AM WHO I AM" (3:14). "The term I AM is the first person form of the Hebrew verb *hayah*, 'to be.' The name implies that God is the Self-Existent One."[12] The name was written as YHVH (יהוה) and is generally vocalized as Yahweh (KJV, Jehovah). The divine name is so sacred to the Jews that they do not pronounce it, generally substituting *ha shem* ("the name") or *'adonai* (Lord).

The book moves on to discuss the actual **redemption of the nation** (5:1–12:30). In this section the author shows how God redeemed Israel by demonstrating His sovereignty over the Egyptian pantheon that was holding the nation in bondage. Yahweh's request to release His firstborn son, Israel, eventually resulted in the death of the firstborn Egyptians in the tenth plague. Moses' first encounter with Pharaoh explains why a miraculous display of God's power over the Egyptian pantheon would be necessary. Both Pharaoh and God were claiming sovereignty over Israel. After Moses made the initial request (5:1–3), Pharaoh responded with stubbornness and even increased

Israel's workload (5:14–19). The prediction of God's hardening of Pharaoh (4:21) represents a divine judgment against someone who was already self-hardened. Exodus shows Pharaoh repeatedly hardening his own heart (7:13,22; 8:15,19,32; 9:7). Not until the sixth plague did God harden Pharaoh's heart (9:12).

The **10 plagues** that God poured out on Egypt were designed to discredit the forces of nature the Egyptians worshipped (7:14–12:31). Through this process God showed that His claim to sovereignty over Israel was superior to the claim of sovereignty asserted by Pharaoh. The plagues increased in intensity until Pharaoh's self-will was broken through the death of his firstborn. The end result of the plagues was the liberation of Israel from the illegitimate control of Pharaoh to the legitimate jurisdiction of Yahweh. Some deny the miraculous nature of these plagues, instead attributing them to the normal flood cycle of the Nile. However, the miraculous nature of the plagues is seen in how Moses knew about them beforehand (8:10; 9:5,29), their instantaneous appearance, their instantaneous termination, their description as "signs and wonders" (7:3), their intensification, their timing, their accomplishment of a moral purpose (11:1), the response they invoked from the Egyptian sorcerers (7:22; 8:18–19), and how the last seven plagues did not affect the Hebrews living in Goshen (9:6).

Given the context of the story, the 10 plagues were intended to show Yahweh's superiority over the **gods of Egypt.** Possible parallels include:

PLAGUE	EGYPTIAN DEITY	REFERENCE
1. Water to Blood	Osiris, Hapi, Khnum	Exod 7:14–25
2. Frogs	Heqt, frog deity	Exod 8:1–15
3. Mosquitoes	Seb	Exod 8:16–19
4. Flies	Kephra and Uatchit	Exod 8:20–32
5. Cattle	Typhon and Imhotep	Exod 9:1–7
6. Boils	Hathor and Apis	Exod 9:8–12
7. Hail	Serapis and Isis	Exod 9:13–35
8. Locusts	Seth, protector of crops	Exod 10:1–20
9. Darkness	Ra, sun deity	Exod 10:21–29
10. Death of Firstborn	Ptah, god of life	Exod 11:1–12:36

The climax to the account of the plagues was the **Passover** (12:1–4). During the tenth plague the "death angel" passed over Egypt, claiming the lives of the firstborn, including Pharaoh's son. To escape this plague, the Israelites were instructed to slaughter an unblemished lamb, spread its blood on their doorposts, roast the lamb, and eat it along with unleavened bread and bitter herbs. This meal (*pesach*) was the prelude to the exodus. Their faith became the basis of the nation's redemption from Egypt. Thus, God mandated that Israel celebrate the Passover Feast throughout the generations in commemoration of this important event (12:1–14). Because Israel was to leave Egypt immediately and because it took time for bread to rise, the Hebrews were to remove the leaven from their households. Thus, God also mandated that Israel celebrate the Feast of Unleavened Bread (*matstsoth*) throughout the generations to commemorate the speed in which redeemed Israel left Egypt (12:15–20). Jesus shed His blood for our redemption at the time of Passover (John 19:14), fulfilling John the Baptist's statement, "Here is the Lamb of God, who takes away the sin of the world!" (John 1:29).[13]

B. Liberation (Exodus 12:31–15:21)

After Pharaoh finally gave Israel permission to leave Egypt (12:31–36), the redeemed nation journeyed from Rameses to Succoth (12:37–42). This was the first major move of the nation after 430 years of bondage in Egypt (12:40). The Lord instructed Israel regarding the **consecration of the firstborn** once they arrived in Canaan (13:1–16). The dedication of the firstborn symbolized God's redemption of His own firstborn son, the nation of Israel (4:22–23). Thus, both the Passover Feast as well as the ceremony involving the consecration of the firstborn served as signs testifying to the special status of God's redeemed nation.

Although the nation was redeemed, her liberation was not yet totally complete as evidenced by Pharaoh's pursuing army (14:3–14). However, God accomplished the nation's complete liberation from Egypt by allowing Israel miraculously to pass through the **Red Sea** (14:15–22) and by drowning the pursuing Egyptian army (14:23– 31). The nation then celebrated its liberation by singing the famous *Song of the Sea* (15:1–21).

Ancient Egyptian mummy case.

C. Preservation (Exodus 15:22–18:27)

Now that Israel's redemption (1:1–12:30) and liberation from Egypt (12:31–15:21) were accomplished, the book of Exodus focuses on Israel's miraculous preservation in the wilderness (15:22–18:27). God's **miraculous provisions** included guidance to the oasis at Elim (15:22–27) and the provision of manna (Hb. *man hu'*, "what is it?") to feed the people. Despite these provisions, this section (15:22–18:27) routinely characterizes the nation as grumbling, unbelieving, and disobedient. Although they were elect (4:22–23) and redeemed (12:21–30), they still needed further guidance regarding how to live the sanctified life. Such guidance was provided in the Mosaic covenant (chaps. 19–40).

II. Instruction for the Redeemed Nation (Exodus 19–40)

At this point in the book, God is the sovereign who has control over the nation of Israel. Several questions logically follow. How is this newly redeemed nation to conduct itself toward God, toward one another, and toward the rest of the world? These questions are answered through the provision of the **Mosaic covenant** (chaps. 19–40). The Mosaic covenant explains how the nation was to be organized under God's kingship. This covenant was not given to redeem people. The nation was already elect (4:22–23), redeemed (12:21–30), and walking by faith (14:31). Rather, the covenant taught them how redeemed people are to live in this world.

Jebel Musa, the traditional site of Mount Sinai, in the southern Sinai Peninsula.

A. Offer of the Covenant (Exodus 19)

After Israel traveled from Rephidim to the foot of Mount Sinai (19:1–2), God explained that Israel would become a **holy nation** and a **kingdom of priests** if they accepted the covenant and adhered to its terms (19:3–6). Thus, the Mosaic covenant offered the nation the opportunity to be the vessel through which God would transmit His redemptive purposes to the rest of mankind. After Israel accepted God's offer of the covenant (19:7–8), the nation then consecrated itself to God (19:9–15) as God manifested Himself to Moses on Mount Sinai (19:16–25) in preparation for giving the covenant text (chaps. 20–23).

B. Covenant Text (Exodus 20–23)

The covenant text (chaps. 20–23) spells out the obligations Israel must meet to allow the suzerain (God) to bless the vassal (Israel). The covenant text consists of the Decalogue (Ten Commandments, 20:1–21) and the book of the covenant (20:22–23:33). The Decalogue is the foundational covenant text while the book of the covenant spells out how the Decalogue is to be applied in the everyday life of the nation.

The first four of the **Ten Commandments** pertain to the individual's relationship to God while the remaining six pertain to how members of the community are to relate to one another. The book of the covenant (20:22–23:33) explains how the Decalogue is applied in daily life in the areas of idolatry (20:22–26), slavery (21:1–11), bodily injuries (21:12–36), property rights (22:1–17), moral and civil obligations (22:18–23:9), Sabbath and feasts (23:10–19), and the impending conquest (23:20–33). If Israel obeyed the covenant stipulations and maintained her relationship with God, she would then become distinct among the nations and would experience the covenant blessings.

Ten Commandments (Exodus 20:1–17)

Responsibilities to maintain their relationship with God

1. "No other gods" vs. polytheism
2. "Do not make an idol" vs. idolatry
3. "Do not misuse the name" vs. profanity
4. "Remember the Sabbath" vs. secularism

Responsibilities to maintain their relationship with other people

5. "Honor your father and mother" vs. rebellion
6. "Do not murder" vs. murder
7. "Do not commit adultery" vs. adultery
8. "Do not steal" vs. theft
9. "False testimony" vs. lying
10. "Do not covet" vs. materialism

C. Covenant Ratification Ceremony (Exodus 24)

The various items spoken of in this chapter, such as duplicate copies of the covenant text (24:3–4,12), the vassal's verbal commitment to follow the terms of the covenant (24:3), the sprinkling of the altar with blood (24:4–8), and the meal between the covenant parties (24:9–11) are all germane to ancient Near East covenant ratification ceremonies.[14]

D. Tabernacle of Worship (Exodus 25–40)

The construction of the **tabernacle** (*mishkan*) represented how God was to dwell among His people and how the nation's fellowship with God was to be restored after sin. The Tabernacle was to be created according to exact divine specifications since it was the place where God would dwell among His people (25:8). The ark of the covenant and mercy seat represented His presence (25:1–22), the table of bread represented His provision (25:23–30), and the lampstand represented His guidance (25:31–40; 27:20–21; 30:22–33).

Of paramount significance was the existence of the **veil** separating the holy place from the most holy place (26:31–35). This veil represented the barrier between holy

God and sinful man (Matt 27:51). The bronze altar where the animal sacrifices were to be offered (27:1–8) illustrated that there was a great divide between God and man. People could only come to a holy God through the atoning work of a sacrifice rather than through their own meritorious works. The single doorway indicated that there was only one way into God's presence, not many ways. The description of the priesthood (chaps. 28–29) explained how certain elements were necessary before any person could approach God. The existence of the laver (30:17–21) communicated that a person must be cleansed both physically and spiritually before approaching God.

The altar of incense helped people understand the importance of worship and prayer (30:1–10,34–38). The annual half-shekel tax to be paid for the purpose of

Reconstruction of the Israelite tabernacle and its court. The court was formed by curtains attached to erect poles. In front of the tent was placed the altar of burnt offerings and the laver. The tabernacle was always erected to face the east, so this view is from the northeast.

supporting the tabernacle activity reminded the people that worship of Yahweh was obligatory rather than voluntary (30:11–16). The concluding exhortation to keep the Sabbath (31:12–17) connected the tabernacle description to the Mosaic covenant. God gave Moses the covenant tablets at the conclusion of His tabernacle instructions (31:18). Thus, the tabernacle instructions represented the part of the Mosaic covenant that taught the redeemed nation how to worship God, how God would dwell among them, and how the nation's fellowship with God could be restored when they sinned.

Hebrew Highlight

Dwelling. Hebrew מִשְׁכָּן (*mishkan*). The Hebrew word translated "taberna-cle" (Exod 26:1) is *mishkan*, meaning "dwelling" or "residence" and comes from the root word *shakan*, "to dwell." The "tents" or "dwellings" can refer to human dwellings (Num 16:24) or the divine dwelling place (Ps 43:3). The term is used 58 times in Exodus. The tabernacle as constructed in Exodus was the special place where God dwelt among His people. God's presence with His people in the tabernacle (chaps. 25–40) is comparable to Christ's presence with believers in the New Testament. Through the use of the Greek verb *skenoo*, John used the tabernacle as an analogy for Christ's incarnation (John 1:14). In other words, in His incarnation Christ dwelt or "tabernacled" among men.

The events of the next three chapters (32–34) represent a **threat** to the covenant. Aaron led the people in a repudiation of the first two commandments (32:1–10). Because of the covenant's bilateral nature, the sinful behavior of the Hebrews jeopardized the covenant. This event sets the stage for the eventual giving of the new covenant where God promises that such rebellion will be curtailed since He will write His laws on the hearts of His people (Jer 31:31–34). However, after Moses interceded for (32:11–14,30–35), confronted (32:15–24), and purified the nation (32:25–29), the people repented (33:1–6), and consequently the nation was spared from divine wrath and total annihilation (32:10).

The instructions for building of the tabernacle (35:1–39:31) and inspecting it (39:32–43) were given to Moses. Upon noting that the tabernacle was built according to the precise divine instructions, it was then erected (40:1–33) and indwelt by God (40:34–38). The presence of **God's glory** (*kabod*) represented His personal presence with His people. In conclusion God emancipated Israel (chaps. 1–18) from Egyptian servitude by redeeming (1:1–12:30), liberating (12:31–15:21), and preserving (15:22–18:27) His elect nation. The Mosaic covenant (chaps. 19–24) taught redeemed Israel how they were to relate to God, one another, and the rest of the world as His special kingdom of priests. The tabernacle instructions and construction (chaps. 25–40) explained to the redeemed nation how they were to worship God, who now dwelt among them.

THEOLOGICAL SIGNIFICANCE

The book of Exodus is foundational to both Jewish and Christian theology. Arnold and Beyer state, "The exodus as a salvation event was the formative beginning of the nation of Israel historically and theologically."[15] It illustrates how God is the **Redeemer** from injustice, sin, and oppression and thus serves as a paradigm for all future redemption. Exodus teaches us that God is sovereign over His creation and that human beings cannot ultimately defy His will or limit His purposes. As the great **Liberator**, Yahweh sets His people free to worship and serve Him. He is also the source of the Judeo-Christian ethical system, which is summarized in the Ten Commandments. Jesus affirmed the validity of the law (Matt 22:36–40) and claimed that He had come to fulfill it (Matt 5:17). He even referred to His "departure" or death on the cross as an *exodus* (Luke 9:31).

For Further Reading

Cassuto, Umberto. *A Commentary on the Book of Exodus.* Jerusalem: Magnes Press, 1967.

Davis, John J. *Moses and the Gods of Egypt.* Grand Rapids: Baker, 1998.

Hannah, John D. "Exodus." In *BKC.* Colorado Springs, CO: Chariot Victor, 1983.

Kaiser, Walter C., Jr. "Exodus." In *EBC.* Grand Rapids: Zondervan, 2008.

Motyer, Alec. *The Message of Exodus.* Downers Grove, IL: IVP, 2005.

Sarna, Nahum. *Exploring Exodus.* New York: Schocken Books, 1986.

Study Questions

1. How did God use Moses' background to prepare him to confront the pharaoh of Egypt?
2. What is the significance of the divine name I AM?
3. How does the Passover prefigure Christ's death for us?
4. How do the Ten Commandments form the basis of the Judeo-Christian ethic?
5. How does the tabernacle symbolically picture our relationship to God?
6. What is God teaching you about the importance of worship?

ENDNOTES

1. Nahum Sarna, *Exploring Exodus* (New York: Schocken Books, 1986), 1.

2. Randall Price, *The Stones Cry Out* (Eugene, OR: Harvest House, 1997), 125–40; K. A. Kitchen, *On the Reliability of the Old Testament* (Grand Rapids: Eerdmans, 2003), 241–312.

3. Kitchen, *Reliability,* 295.

4. Andrew E. Hill and John H. Walton, *A Survey of the Old Testament* (Grand Rapids: Zondervan, 1991), 105.

5. Ibid., see charts 106–7.

6. See detailed discussions cf. J. M. Miller and J. H. Hayes, *A History of Ancient Israel and Judah* (Philadelphia: Westminster Press, 1986); contra, Bryant Wood, "Did the Israelites Conquer Jericho?" *BAR* (September-October 1990), 45–69; William Dever, "How to Tell an Israelite from a Canaanite," *Recent Archaeology in the Land of Israel*, ed. H. Shanks (Washington, DC: Biblical Archaeology Society, 1985), 35–41.

7. Gordon Franz, "Is Mount Sinai in Saudi Arabia?" *Bible and Spade* 13 (4):101–13.

8. For example, see Lennart Möller, *The Exodus Case* (Copenhagen: Scandinavia, 2002).

9. Genesis 46:26 says that 66 people entered Egypt while Exod 1:5 places the number at 70. However, the Genesis text omits Joseph, Joseph's two sons Ephraim and Manasseh, and Jacob (see Gen 46:27). While the LXX, Acts 7:14, and a Qumran document list the number at 75, this number probably includes Joseph's three grandsons and two great-grandsons who are mentioned in Numbers 26 (see Gen 46:26 in the LXX where these names are added); Gleason L. Archer, *A Survey of Old Testament Introduction* (Chicago: Moody, 1996), 238.

10. Joseph died at the end of the Twelfth Dynasty. The decline of the Twelfth Dynasty led to the chaotic reign of the Asiatic Hyksos. Later, native Egyptians overthrew the Hyksos. These events ushered in the Eighteenth Dynasty of the New Kingdom period. This regime oppressed Israel. Its founder, Ahmose I (1570–1546), oppressed the chosen people since he viewed them as pro-Hyksos agents. Charles Dyer and Gene Merrill, *Old Testament Explorer: Discovering the Essence, Background, and Meaning of Every Book in the Old Testament* (Nashville: Thomas Nelson, 2001), 43–44.

11. Archer, *A Survey of Old Testament Introduction*, 236–37; Kitchen, *Reliability*, 297, believes the name is of Hebrew origin but was vocalized *Masu* in Egyptian. Sarna, *Exploring Exodus*, 33, believes the name was Egyptian in origin.

12. J. Carl Laney, *Answers to Tough Questions from Every Book of the Bible: A Survey of Problem Passages and Issues* (Eugene, OR: Wipf & Stock, 2010), 30.

13. See Brant Pitre, *Jesus and the Jewish Roots of the Eucharist* (Garden City, NY: Doubleday, 2011).

14. For a comparison with the six elements of the contemporary Hittite suzerain-vassal treaty structure with the mosaic covenant, see M. Kline, *Treaty of the Great King* (Grand Rapids: Eerdmans, 1963).

15. Bill Arnold and Bryan Beyer, *Encountering the Old Testament* (Grand Rapids: Baker, 1999), 111.

Chapter 8

LEVITICUS
Way of Holiness

Holiness and cleanliness are the major themes of the book of Leviticus, which is the worship guide for both priests and laymen in Israel. It describes the way laymen need to approach the Holy One, how the priests were to assist in this process, and how all the people were to demonstrate personal holiness. Gordon Wenham states: "Holiness characterizes God himself and all that belongs to him . . . holiness is intrinsic to God's character."[1] Thus, He commands, "Be holy, for I am holy (Lev 11:44–45; 19:2; 20:26, author's translation).

God is depicted as the Holy One who is ever present in the daily lives of His people. Perhaps that is what causes so many people to shy away from this book. How can anyone possibly live up to the standard of holiness which God requires? Yet it is clear that holiness is a state of grace to which true believers are called by God and enabled by God to attain. For the Old Testament believers it meant placing their faith in the commands, rituals, and sacrifices of God. The blood atonement of animal sacrifices was necessary because "without the shedding of blood there is no forgiveness" (Heb 9:22). The word "blood" appears 88 times in Leviticus, reminding God's people of the seriousness of sin and pointing ahead to the ultimate sacrifice of Christ (Acts 20:28; Rom 5:9; Rev 7:14).

The purpose of the book of Leviticus is to teach Israel how they are to walk in **practical holiness** with God, which was necessary because of Israel's status as God's elect (Exod 4:22–23), redeemed (Exodus 12), regenerated (Exod 14:31), and holy nation. A people of such exalted spiritual status needed to know how their daily behavior should conform to their status as holy people. They needed

The Stele of Hammurabi containing the famous Law Code of Hammurabi (about 1750 BC).

to learn about practical sanctification so they could satisfy their obligations under the Mosaic covenant and thus fulfill their mandate to be a kingdom of priests (Exod 19:5–6). The failure to fulfill this mandate brought the indictment of the prophets against the people of Israel and caused them to lose the glory of the Lord (Ezekiel 8–11).

BACKGROUND

The book of Leviticus picks up where Exodus left off. God revealed the contents of Leviticus to Moses after the renewal of the Mosaic covenant (Exodus 32–34) and His indwelling of the tabernacle (Exod 40:34–38). Because the events of the book transpired after the arrival at Sinai but before the nation departed from Sinai, no geographical movement is represented in the book of Leviticus. All of the allotted events took place while the nation was **encamped at Sinai**. Leviticus was written at Sinai initially to the generation that experienced the Exodus.

The Hebrew title of the book is *wayyiqra'* "and he called," derives from the first word of the book. The Jews entitled the book "The Law of the Priests" and "The Law of the Offerings" after its subject matter.[2] The LXX entitled it *Leuitikon*, which means "that which pertains to the Levites," and so the English title. Leviticus is a book about the priestly offering and religious festivals of the Jewish people.

AUTHOR

Although the book of Leviticus is an anonymous work, several lines of evidence point to Moses as the book's author. First, the book repeatedly reiterates how God imparted the law to Moses (1:1; 27:34). This concept appears 56 times in the 27 chapters of Leviticus. If it is assumed Moses wrote down the revelation he received from God as he did for the book of Exodus (Exod 17:14), then Moses is an obvious candidate for the authorship of Leviticus. Second, Leviticus is interconnected with the rest of the Pentateuch. The conjunction "and" in Lev 1:1 indicates that it is to be read in harmony with the book of Exodus. This interrelationship is buttressed upon remembering that the formulas "the LORD also spoke to Moses" (Exod 31:1; Lev 1:1) and "Moses did everything just as the LORD had commanded" (Exod 40:16; Lev 8:13) is used in both books. Thus, Leviticus is the sequel to Exodus. Harrison also notes the connection between the two books when he says, "Leviticus enlarges upon matters involving the ordering of worship at the divine sanctuary that are mentioned only briefly in Exodus."[3]

Despite the critical view that Leviticus was written by the "priestly source" (P), in the postexilic era, Leviticus must be a preexilic work since Ezekiel made extensive use of its legislation. Assuming Mosaic authorship and an early date for the exodus, Leviticus was likely written sometime after the erection of the tabernacle (1445 BC) and before Moses' death (1406 BC). External evidence confirms this early date. "The Ras Shamra Tablets (c. 1500–1300 BC), found along the Syrian coast, demonstrate that the antiquity of the Levitical system of trespass offering extends back to the time of Moses."[4] Hill and Walton note several parallels to ritual participation and animal sacrifices among Near Eastern peoples of the same era.[5]

Outline

I. Way to the Holy One: Sacrifice (Leviticus 1–10)
  A. Laws of Sacrifices (Leviticus 1–7)
  B. Laws of Priesthood (Leviticus 8–10)
II. Way of Holiness: Sanctification (Leviticus 11–27)
  A. Laws of Purity (Leviticus 11–15)
  B. Day of Atonement (Leviticus 16)
  C. Holiness Code (Leviticus 17–27)

MESSAGE

The message of Leviticus is that the nation could achieve **progressive sanctification** and thus become distinct from the surrounding nations through daily access to God via the sacrifices (chaps. 1–10) and through obedience (chaps. 11–27). Thus, the book places great emphasis on holiness (Hb. *qodesh*), which is used 87 times in the book. The book also stresses sanctification. The word *sanctify* is found 17 times in the book. Leviticus also emphasizes sacrifice and worship. This emphasis is evident in the various feast days mandating when and under what circumstances the nation must appear before the Lord to worship Him (Leviticus 23).

I. Way to the Holy One: Sacrifice (Leviticus 1–10)

In the first major section of the book (chaps. 1–10), Moses explains that sacrifices are essential for the Israelites to maintain daily access to God and thereby experience practical sanctification. Because God graciously accepts an innocent animal substitute as a payment for the penalty of sin, the nation can continue to experience daily fellowship with God if they will repent and confess their sin.

A. Laws of Sacrifices (Leviticus 1–7)

Moses outlines the **five sacrifices** that guarantee ongoing fellowship with God (chaps. 1–7). Before explaining how the priests are to administer these sacrifices (6:8–7:38), Moses first shows how they are beneficial to national Israel (1:1–6:7). The first three sacrifices were voluntary (1:1–3:17) and were a sweet savor to the Lord (1:9,13,17; 2:9; 3:5,16). In other words, those who are already in fellowship with God offer them to please God. The first sacrifice, known as the *burnt offering*, was given for the purpose of making atonement for sins in general (1:1–17). The second sacrifice was known as the meal or the *grain offering*. It was offered as a general thanksgiving for the harvest (2:1–16). The third sacrifice was known as the fellowship or *peace offering*. It was given for the purpose of expressing thanksgiving and celebration regarding the reconciliation or peace that existed between the worshipper and God (3:1–17).

SACRIFICIAL SYSTEM			
Name	Reference	Elements	Significance
Burnt Offering	Leviticus 1; 6:8–13	Bull, ram, male goat, male dove, or young pigeon without blemish. (Always male animals, but species of animal varied according to individual's economic status.)	Voluntary. Signifies propitiation for sin and complete surrender, devotion, and commitment to God.
Grain Offering. Also called Meal or Tribute Offering	Leviticus 2; 6:14–23	Grain, flour, or bread (always unleavened) made with olive oil and salt; or incense.	Voluntary. Signifies thanksgiving for firstfruits.
Fellowship Offering. Also called Peace Offering, which includes: (1) Thank Offering, (2) Vow Offering, and (3) Freewill Offering	Leviticus 3; 7:11–36; 22:17–30; 27	Any animal without blemish. (Species of animal varied according to individual's economic status.) (1) Can be grain offering.	Voluntary. Symbolizes fellowship with God. (1) Signifies thankfulness for a specific blessing; (2) offers a ritual expression of a vow; and (3) symbolizes general thankfulness (to be brought to one of three required religious services).
Sin Offering	Leviticus 4:1–5:13; 6:24–30; 12:6–8	Male or female animal without blemish—as follows: bull for high priest or congregation; male goat for king; female goat or lamb for common person; dove or pigeon for slightly poor; tenth of an ephah of flour for the very poor.	Mandatory. Made by one who had sinned unintentionally or was unclean in order to attain purification.
Guilt Offering	Leviticus 5:14–6:7; 7:1–6; 14:12–18	Ram or lamb without blemish.	Mandatory. Made by a person who had either deprived another of his rights or had desecrated something holy. Made by lepers for purification.

The final two sacrifices (4:1–6:7) were compulsory and were issued for the purpose of restoring broken fellowship between the sinner and God. Thus, these sacrifices were no longer merely "sweet aroma" sacrifices for those already in fellowship with God. The first of these sacrifices was known as the *sin offering* (4:1–5:13). It was issued for the purpose of making **atonement** for specific sins, such as those committed by a priest (4:1–12), the nation (4:13–21), a ruler (4:22–26), an individual (4:27–35), and the inadvertent sinner (5:1–13).

The second offering was known as the trespass or *guilt offering* (5:4–6:7). It was designed to atone for sin as well as to make restitution for particular sins. Atonement involved offering a ram without defect. **Restitution** occurred with a monetary payment for the sin. The amount of the payment consisted of the priest's valuation of the sin plus 20 percent. This restitution was to be paid not only for sins committed against the Lord (5:15–16) but also for sins that defrauded a fellow Israelite (6:5). This offering not only forgave the offender for specific sins, but it also reminded him that sin has ongoing temporal consequences even after God has forgiven it.[6]

B. Laws of Priesthood (Leviticus 8–10)

Because of the priests' importance in leading the nation into practical sanctification and fellowship with God through the proper administration of the sacrifices, the next three chapters (chaps. 8–10) are devoted to discussing the **priesthood**. Specifically, these chapters cover the priests' consecration (chap. 8), commencement (chap. 9), and condemnation (chap. 10). While Exodus 28–29 explains how the priests were to be selected, anointed, and outfitted for their ministry, Leviticus 8–9 essentially provides the fulfillment of these instructions. After Israel assembled (8:1–5), the consecration of the priests is seen in their clean and proper clothing (8:6–9), their anointing (8:10–13), and by the various offerings that were issued on their behalf (8:14–36). Having received these instructions, the priests were consecrated and blessed (chap. 9), but Aaron's two sons (Nadab and Abihu) did not treat God as holy, so God put them to death (10:1–7).

II. Way of Holiness: Sanctification (Leviticus 11–27)

The laws of sanctification were intended to mark Israel as a unique people who were "**separated**" from the practices of their pagan neighbors. To accomplish this purpose, the laws of Leviticus designate everything as either "holy" or "common"; and common things, in turn, were considered either "clean" or "unclean." Clean things became "holy" when they were sanctified, and "holy" things, when defiled, could become either common or polluted. Thus, the laws of purity were related to the entire concept of sanctification.

A. Laws of Purity (Leviticus 11–15)

Moses continues to expound on the theme of Israel's progressive sanctification through fellowship with God by commanding the nation to embrace the clean and to reject the unclean (chaps. 11–15). Although at first glance many of these distinctions

Plate of pure gold
with inscription:
"HOLY TO THE LORD."
Ex 28:36

Turban or mitre
Ex 28:36-38

The shoulder straps for
the breastplate capped
with two onyx stones
bearing the names of
Israel's twelve sons, six on
each, in order of their birth
Ex 28:9-10

Twelve gemstones,
each bearing a name of
one of the twelve tribes
Ex 28:17-21

Sash
Ex 28:4,39,40

Ephod, woven and
reflecting the colors of
the sanctuary
Ex 28:5-15,31

Fringe composed of
alternating pomegranates
and gold bells; the pomegranates
are woven from blue, purple,
and scarlet yarn
Ex 28:33-35

Artist's rendering of the high priest's garments (28:1–38).

seem related to hygienic concerns, their overriding purpose was to **distinguish Israel** as set apart from the pagan practices of her Canaanite neighbors in regard to the food they ate (chap. 11), their contact with blood (chap. 12), and bodily diseases, imperfections, and discharges (chaps. 13–15). Thus, as Israel followed the commands given in these chapters, she would find herself progressing toward sanctification through fellowship with God and thus distinct from the surrounding nations.[7] The basic principles of holiness and cleanness were related to wholeness and completeness; thus everything presented at the tabernacle had to be physically perfect and without blemish. Even priests and worshippers were required to "wash" in a *mikveh* in the days of the temple (Lev 14:8).

B. Day of Atonement (Leviticus 16)

The Day of Atonement (*yom kippur*) is the **holiest day** on the Hebrew calendar. It occurs 10 days after the Feast of Trumpets, following the "days of awe."[8] In Leviticus 16 it represents the high point in the unit dealing with the sacrifices (chaps. 1–17). On this special day the properly attired high priest (Aaron) would enter into the holy place. First, a bull was slaughtered for Aaron's sins. Then two goats were selected to be used for the different purposes of propitiation and expatiation. The first goat was killed

A mikveh (Jewish ritual bath used for purification) at Masada.

and its blood was sprinkled on the mercy seat on the ark of the covenant in the most holy place. This event represented the only time during the year when Aaron could enter the most holy place. After the sins of the nation were symbolically transferred to the second goat (the "scapegoat"), it was then released into the wilderness to symbolize the removal of sin. Through this annual ritual the collective indebtedness for sin that Israel had accumulated during the previous year was atoned and removed from the congregation.

C. Holiness Code (Leviticus 17–27)

In the final section Moses encourages national sanctification and distinctiveness through **obedience** (chaps. 17–27). In this section the theme of obedience expands the reader's personal responsibility for sanctification. Moses explains how Israel is to be distinct from their pagan neighbors by adhering to God's instruction concerning the proper treatment of blood (chap. 17) and by rejecting the perverse sexual standards of the pagans (chap. 18). After calling Israel to a lifestyle that was different from the Egyptians and the Canaanites (18:1–5), Moses expounds on Yahweh's requirement that Israel abstain from all kinds of incestuous relationships (18:6–18) and immoral behaviors (18:19–23). Moses concludes this chapter by explaining that if the Israelites imitate the Canaanite sexual practices, then they too would run the risk of being evicted from the land, just as the Canaanites would soon be evicted (18:24–29).

Next Moses focuses on how Israel should exhibit holy behavior toward God and man (chap. 19). He points out that a proper understanding of God's holy character furnishes a natural incentive for obeying both the horizontal (man to man) and vertical (man to God) aspects of the Decalogue (19:1–4). Loving another from the heart just as strongly as one already loves himself also furnishes an impetus for following the horizontal components of the Decalogue (19:17–18). With these two stimuli in mind, Moses explains how these incentives should alter behavior in differing areas of life (19:5–36). Moses concludes the chapter by reminding the people of **God's character** as the ultimate incentive for holy living (19:37). Thus, God demanded sanctified obedience from the priests (chaps. 21–22) as well as from the laity (chaps. 18–20). The principles of moral and social behavior in this section form the foundation for Judeo-Christian ethics.

PRIESTS IN THE OLD TESTAMENT *(Listed alphabetically)*		
Name	*Reference*	*Identification*
Aaron	Exodus 28–29	Older brother of Moses; first high priest of Israel
Abiathar	1 Sam 22:20–23; 2 Sam 20:25	Son of Ahimelech who escaped the slayings at Nob
Abihu	See Nadab and Abihu	
Ahimelech	1 Samuel 21–22	Led a priestly community at Nob; killed by Saul for befriending David
Amariah	2 Chr 19:11	High priest during the reign of Jehoshaphat
Amaziah	Amos 7:10–17	Evil priest of Bethel; confronted Amos the prophet
Azariah	2 Chr 26:16–20	High priest who stood against Uzziah when the ruler began to act as a prophet
Eleazar and Ithamar	Lev 10:6; Num 20:26	Godly sons of Aaron; Eleazar—Israel's second high priest
Eli	1 Samuel 1–4	Descendant of Ithamar; raised Samuel at Shiloh
Eliashib	Neh 3:1; 13:4–5	High priest during the reign of Josiah
Elishama and Jehoram	2 Chr 17:7–9	Teaching priests during the reign of Jehoshaphat

	PRIESTS IN THE OLD TESTAMENT (continued) _(Listed alphabetically)_	
NAME	_REFERENCE_	_IDENTIFICATION_
Ezra	Ezra 7–10; Nehemiah 8	Scribe, teacher, and priest during the rebuilding of Jerusalem
Hilkiah	2 Kings 22–23	High priest during the reign of Josiah
Hophni and Phinehas	1 Sam 2:12–36	Evil sons of Eli
Ithamar	See Eleazar and Ithamar	
Jahaziel	2 Chr 20:14–17	Levite who assured Jehoshaphat of deliverance from an enemy
Jehoiada	2 Kings 11–12	High priest who saved Joash from Queen Athaliah's purge
Jehoram	See Elishama and Jehoram	
Joshua	Hag 1:1,12; Zechariah 3	First high priest after the Babylonian captivity
Nadab and Abihu	Lev 10:1–2	Evil sons of Aaron
Pashhur	Jer 20:1–6	False priest who persecuted the prophet Jeremiah
Phinehas	(1) Num 25:7–13 (2) See Hophni and Phinehas	(1) Son of Eleazar; Israel's third high priest whose zeal for pure worship stopped a plague
Shelemiah	Neh 13:13	Priest during the time of Nehemiah; was in charge of administrating storehouses
Uriah	2 Kings 16:10–16	Priest who built pagan altar for evil King Ahaz
Zadok	2 Samuel 15; 1 Kings 1	High priest during the reign of David and Solomon

The nation could experience sanctified obedience by appearing before the Lord regularly to worship (the Sabbath) and celebrate various feasts that would remind them of their covenant relationship with Him (chap. 23). Moses began by enumerating Israel's **seven religious feasts**. They include Passover and Unleavened Bread (23:4–8), Firstfruits (23:9–14), Pentecost (23:15–22), Trumpets (23:23–25), Atonement (23:26–32), and Booths or Tabernacles (23:33–35).

The first four feasts took place in the spring. Passover (*pesach*) remembered the nation's redemption from Egypt. Unleavened Bread (*matstsoth*) commemorated the nation's separation from Egypt. Firstfruits (*bikkurim*) praised God for the firstfruits of the harvest in expectation for the full harvest. Pentecost (*shavu`oth*) involved the marking of the wheat harvest as well as thankfulness for the harvest. Uniquely, these spring feasts were fulfilled with the death and resurrection of Christ and the baptism of the Holy Spirit on the day of Pentecost (Acts 2).

The fall feasts began with Trumpets (*rosh hashanah*) celebrating the beginning of the New Year. Atonement (*yom kippur*) dealt with annual covering of national sin. Tabernacles (*succoth*) remembered God's provision throughout the wilderness wanderings from Egypt to Canaan.[9]

JEWISH FEASTS AND FESTIVALS				
NAME	*MONTH*	*DATE*	*REFERENCE*	*SIGNIFICANCE*
Passover	Nisan	(Mar./Apr.): 14–21	Exod 12:2–20; Lev 23:5	Commemorates God's deliverance of Israel out of Egypt.
Festival of Unleavened Bread	Nisan	(Mar./Apr.): 15–21	Lev 23:6–8	Commemorates God's deliverance of Israel out of Egypt. Includes a Day of Firstfruits for the barley harvest.
Festival of Harvest, or Weeks (Pentecost)	Sivan	(May/June): 6 (seven weeks after Passover)	Exod 23:16; 34:22; Lev 23:15–21	Commemorates the giving of the law at Mount Sinai. Includes a Day of Firstfruits for the wheat harvest.
Festival of Trumpets (Rosh Hashanah)	Tishri	(Sept./Oct.): 1	Lev 23:23–25; Num 29:1–6	Day of the blowing of the trumpets to signal the beginning of the civil new year.
Day of Atonement (Yom Kippur)	Tishri	(Sept./Oct.): 10	Exod 30:10; Lev 3:26–33	On this day the high priest makes atonement for the nation's sin. Also a day of fasting.
Festival of Booths, or Tabernacles (Sukkot)	Tishri	(Sept./Oct.): 15–21	Lev 23:33–43; Num 29:12–39; Deut 16:13	Commemorates the 40 years of wilderness wandering.

JEWISH FEASTS AND FESTIVALS (continued)				
Name	*Month*	*Date*	*Reference*	*Significance*
Festival of Dedication, or Festival of Lights (Hanukkah)	Kislev and Tebeth	(Nov./Dec.): 25–30; and Tebeth (Dec./ Jan.): 1–2	John 10:22	Commemorates the purification of the temple by Judas Maccabaeus in 164 BC
Feast of Purim, or Esther	Adar	(Feb./Mar.): 14	Esther 9	Commemorates the deliverance of the Jewish people in the days of Esther.

Israel was also expected to continue to practice sanctified obedience after arriving in Canaan (chaps. 25–26). Israel could honor God in the land by honoring His **Sabbath-rest principle**. Just as God called the people to have a weekly Sabbath (23:1–3), He also called upon them to have a yearly Sabbath (25:1–7) every seventh year. The seriousness in which God takes this principle is evidenced from the fact that the duration of the 70-year captivity in Babylon was based on the number of times Israel neglected this yearly Sabbath rest, which was to take place on every seventh year (Lev 26:35; 2 Chr 36:21; Jer 25:11; 29:10; Dan 9:2). Not only could Israel experience sanctification through obedience by honoring God's Sabbath principle on a weekly and yearly basis, but they were also to honor it on a 49-year basis by allowing the fiftieth year or the Jubilee Year to be a year of rest (25:8–55).

In order to provide an incentive for sanctification through obedience once inside the land, Moses next explains the law of **blessings and curses** (26). After reminding his readers of the covenant (26:1–3), Moses explains that obedience is the condition for blessing. He then enumerates the physical, material, and national blessings that will transpire when Israel obeys the terms of the covenant (26:4–13; Deut 28:1–14). Moses then enumerates the physical, material, and national curses for disobedience (26:14–39; Deut 28:15–68).

In the final section of the book (17–27), Moses has assembled a wide variety of material explaining how Israel could experience sanctification by conforming their **daily lives** to God's revealed will. While the book of Exodus explained how Israel received its calling to be a kingdom of priests (Exod 19:5–6), the book of Leviticus explains how Israel is to live out this priestly calling. According to Leviticus, the nation could only fulfill this high calling when they lived as a holy people and thereby became distinct from the surrounding Gentile nations. Such progressive sanctification was possible as the nation used the sacrificial system and thus enjoyed unhindered access to God after repenting and confessing their sins (chaps. 1–16). Such sanctification was also possible as the nation obeyed God's revealed will (chaps. 17–27).

THEOLOGICAL SIGNIFICANCE

The **holiness of God** is the dominant theological theme of Leviticus. God is pictured as an ever-present personal holy God who demands holiness from those who want to have a covenant relationship with Him. People, animals, and even plants are to be "holy" unto the Lord (Lev 11:44–45; 19:24), as are the priests, Levites, and the tabernacle equipment (Lev 21:6; 29:36; 40:9). Years later the prophet Zechariah (14:20–21) predicts a time when even the pots and pans in Jerusalem will be "holy to the LORD." Holiness will characterize the future kingdom of the Messiah (Isa 66:20–21), and the New Jerusalem will become the Holy City (Rev 21:2). The New Testament writers connect the theme of holiness to New Testament believers. Peter quotes the Levitical injunction when he writes, "But, as the One who called you is holy, you also are to be holy in all your conduct; for it is written, Be holy, because I am holy" (1 Pet 1:15–16). Paul adds, "I urge you to present your bodies as a living sacrifice, holy and pleasing to God" (Rom 12:1). The New Testament builds on the Old Testament principle of the necessity of an atoning sacrifice to eradicate the effects of human sin, infirmity, and depravity. Only the sacrificial atonement of the sinless Son of God is sufficient to cleanse us from sin and unrighteousness (1 John 1:7).

Hebrew Highlight

Holy. Hebrew קֹדֶשׁ (qodesh). The noun often functions adjectivally as "holy," "sacred," "dedicated," or "sanctified." It appears 92 times in Leviticus to refer to that which is devoted to the Lord in the sphere of the sacred. It can also designate a "holy place," or "sanctuary" (Lev 16:16). Occurring twice in a row it is used as a superlative, "most holy place," or "holy of holies" (Exod 26:34). Singular uses indicate "holiness" (Exod 15:11). Plurals can signify "holy things" (Lev 5:15). Holiness is associated with God's glory and commands respect with restrictions because God is holy and separated from sin. Therefore, holy things and holy people are set apart and consecrated for God's purposes.

For Further Reading

Gane, Roy. *Leviticus-Numbers*. NIVAC. Grand Rapids: Zondervan, 2004.

Harrison, R. K. *Leviticus: An Introduction and Commentary*. TOTC. Downers Grove, IL: IVP, 1980.

Lindsey, F. Duane "Leviticus." In *BKC*. Colorado Springs, CO: Chariot Victor, 1983.

Rooker, Mark F. *Leviticus*. NAC 3A. Nashville, TN: B&H, 2000.

Ross, Allen. *Holiness to the Lord: A Guide to the Exposition of the Book of Leviticus*. Grand Rapids: Baker, 2002.

Wenham, Gordon J. *The Book of Leviticus*. NICOT. Grand Rapids: Eerdmans, 1979.

Study Questions

1. How does Leviticus serve as a worship guide for the Jewish people?
2. Why is holiness important, and how does it distinguish God's character and His people?
3. How do the blood sacrifices prefigure the death of Christ?
4. How does the "Holiness Code" form the basis of the Judeo-Christian ethical system?
5. To what degree is personal holiness important to Christian believers today, and how can it be attained and maintained?

ENDNOTES

1. Gordon J. Wenham, *The Book of Leviticus*, NICOT (Grand Rapids: Eerdmans, 1979), 22.

2. R. K. Harrison, *Leviticus*, TOTC (Downers Grove, IL: IVP, 1980), 13.

3. Ibid., 13–14.

4. Norman L. Geisler, *A Popular Survey of the Old Testament* (Grand Rapids: Baker Academic, 1996), 65.

5. Andrew E. Hill and John H. Walton, *A Survey of the Old Testament* (Grand Rapids: Zondervan, 1991), 120–24.

6. For some of the more specific and nuanced differences between these sacrifices, see J. Barton Payne, *Encyclopedia of Biblical Prophecy: The Complete Guide to Scriptural Predictions and Their Fulfillment* (New York: Harper & Row, 1973), 193; Hill and Walton, *A Survey of the Old Testament*, 125; *Nelson's Complete Book of Charts and Maps* (Nashville: Thomas Nelson, 1996), 44–45.

7. Later revelation makes clear that these laws are no longer binding upon the church (Ps 147:19–20; Mark 7:19; Acts 10:11–16).

8. For details see K. Howard and M. Rosenthal, *The Feasts of the Lord* (Orlando: Zion's Hope, 1991), 119–33.

9. For the differences between these feasts, see Terry C. Hulbert, "The Eschatological Significance of Israel's Annual Feasts" (Th.D. diss., Dallas Theological Seminary, 1965); H. Wayne House and Randall Price, *Charts of Bible Prophecy* (Grand Rapids: Zondervan, 2003), 105; Hill and Walton, *A Survey of the Old Testament,* 127; *Nelson's Complete Book of Charts and Maps*, 43, 46–47.

Chapter 9

NUMBERS
Wilderness Journey

The book of Numbers tells the story of the wilderness journey which began at Mount Sinai. It serves as a **travel diary** of the Israelites after the exodus. After the giving of the law, the Lord instructed Moses to number the army of Israel. Every male 20 years and older was qualified to serve in the army of the Lord of hosts. Then God surrounded His dwelling place, the tabernacle, with an inner circle of priests and their assistants to safeguard it from ritual impurity. The rest of the Israelites encircled the Levites, camping under the banner of their respective tribes.[1] The census was designed to reorganize Israel into a **military camp** in preparation for the conquest of the Promised Land. The tribal lists began with Reuben, Jacob's firstborn, and followed the birth order of the sons based on their mother's status. Sons of Leah came first, Rachel's offspring next, and the children of the concubines last. The priestly tribe of Levi was exempt from military service and, according to Jewish tradition, exempt from the judgment that fell upon that generation as well (Num 26:64).

The story of the wilderness journey began with celebration and preparation at Mount Sinai. But it quickly turned to disappointment and failure as the people **turned back** at Kadesh Barnea and wandered in the desert for nearly 40 years until the disobedient generation of adults perished in the wilderness. By the end of the story, the new generation, born in the wilderness, remobilized and proceeded to Moab in preparation to finally enter the Promised Land.

The Wadi Rum in southern Jordan in what would have been the northern part of ancient Midian. This photo was taken from the top of a sand dune well over 100 feet tall.

The Hebrew title of the book (*bemidbar*) is taken from words in the opening verse, meaning "in the wilderness" (1:1). The LXX entitles the book *arithmoi* ("numbers") after the **two censuses** recorded in chaps. 1 and 26 and other numerical data. The English title is derived from the English translation of the LXX title.

BACKGROUND

Numerous lines of evidence point to Moses as the author of the book of Numbers. First, the opening words of the book are "and the LORD spoke to Moses" (1:1). This phrase occurs more than 80 times throughout the book. The book refers to itself as the statutes God gave to Moses (36:13). The book also refers to Moses' writing activity in relation to the book (33:1–2). Numbers appears in the middle of the Pentateuch and is therefore interconnected with it as it provides the transition from Exodus-Leviticus to Deuteronomy, which contain self-claims of Mosaic authorship (Exod 17:14; 19:7; 24:4; Deut 1:1; 31:24). This belief is reaffirmed by the New Testament, which assumes Mosaic authorship over the entire Pentateuch (Matt 8:4; 19:8; Luke 24:44; John 1:45; 5:46–47; Rom 10:5).[2] The events recorded in Numbers took place over a period of 38 years and nine months (Num 1:1; Deut 1:3) presumably between 1444 BC and 1406 BC. Numbers covers the time period in between the covenant setting at Sinai (Exodus-Leviticus) and Israel's preconquest setting on the plains of Moab (Deuteronomy). Thus, it covers most of the time that elapsed in between the giving of the law and the conquest. The book of Numbers represents that unique period of time in Israel's history after the nation received the land promises and before the fulfillment of these promises. The book describes the first generation's **pilgrimage to Canaan** and failure to obtain the benefits of God's promises due to unbelief. In a practical sense Numbers speaks to us today about the importance of obedience in our spiritual journey.

Moses challenged his readers to understand that because the first generation was elected (Exod 4:22–23), redeemed (Exodus 12), regenerated (Exodus 14:31), a recipient of the covenant (Exodus 19–40), sanctified (Leviticus), and blessed (Numbers 1–10), they had everything they needed to enter the land. Yet because of unbelief and disobedience (Numbers 13–14), they forfeited the blessings of living in the land. Moses' goal in presenting this information was to urge the second generation not to make the same mistake. Interestingly, Scripture often uses the failure of the first generation as a basis for exhorting subsequent generations to trust and obey God (Pss 78:40–55; 95:8–11; 1 Corinthians 10; Hebrews 3–4).

MESSAGE

Numbers tells the story of the initial success and **ultimate failure** of the exodus generation. The Israelite males who experienced the miraculous deliverance of the exodus from Egypt succumbed to doubt, fear, and unbelief. Having left the bondage of Egypt, they turned back in unbelief at Kadesh Barnea and wandered in the Sinai wilderness. By contrast the generation of Israelites who were born in the wilderness made the commitment to trust the Lord and move on by faith.

The **structure** of the book comes from chaps. 1 and 26, which represent the different census for the first and second generations respectively. Chapters 13 and 14 mark a transition away from the prominence of the first generation and refocus on the second generation. The first *faithless* generation failed to follow God in the wilderness (1:1–25:18), but the second *faithful* generation willingly followed God into the Promised Land (26:1–36:13). The primary genre of the book is narrative. However, Dyer and Merrill note the many subgenres displayed in the book, including census lists, travel procedures, regulations for the priests and the Levites, sacrifice and ritual instructions, inheritance rights, prophetic oracles, and poetry.[3]

Outline

I. First Generation (Numbers 1–25)
  A. Preparation of the First Generation at Sinai (Numbers 1–10)
  B. Failure of the First Generation (Numbers 11–25)
II. Second Generation (Numbers 26–36)
  A. Reorganization of Israel on the Plains of Moab (Numbers 26–30)
  B. Preparation for Conquest of the Land (Numbers 31–36)

I. First Generation (Numbers 1–25)

A. Preparation of the First Generation at Sinai (Numbers 1–10)

In the first major section of the book, Moses remembers the **numerous blessings** God gave to the first generation (chaps. 1–10). They had everything they needed to succeed in the conquest of Canaan but failed because of their own unbelief and disobedience. The second generation, which was similarly blessed, learned that the only thing standing in the way of their success was their own unbelief. These blessings are divided into those pertaining to the organization of Israel (chaps. 1–4) and those related to the nation's sanctification (chaps. 5–10). The section dealing with the ordering of the tribes begins with a census of the tribes (chap. 1) for purpose of military organization and their arrangement around the tabernacle (chap. 2). The large numbers (603,550 men) tabulated in the census have caused many to question whether these numbers are to be understood literally. Various solutions have proposed an adjustment to these numbers, but it is not reasonable to assume they were misstated all six times (Exod 12:37; 38:26; Num 1:46; 2:32; 11:21; 26:51). Exodus records the rapid growth of Israel's population (Exod 1:7–12), and a miraculous preservation of such a large population fits with Exodus's theme of glorifying God on account of His miracles (Exod 7:5).[4]

The next section (chaps. 3–4) records a census of the Levites so they could be organized into various clans. Not only were these clans arranged in different positions around the tabernacle (chap. 3), but they also were given various responsibilities over the tabernacle (chap. 4). While all priests are Levites, not all Levites are priests.

A priest had not only to be a Levite, but he also had to be a descendant of Aaron. Only the priests had the privilege of administering the sacrifices while the nonpriest Levites were considered the priests' helpers.

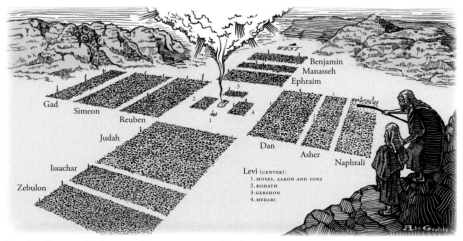

The Lord prescribed a specific arrangement for the Israelites to camp in the wilderness around the tent of meeting.

Not only does Numbers describe the external order of the first generation (chaps. 1–4) but also its internal order through **sanctification** (chaps. 5–10). Four areas of spiritual blessing are emphasized. First, the people were to be sanctified by separation from those who were leprous, who had a bodily discharge, and who had contact with a corpse (5:1–4) so that the camp would not be defiled and God could dwell among them. Second, the people were sanctified through the *Nazirite vow*, allowing them the opportunity to devote themselves to God for a season (6:1–21). Later Samuel, Samson, and John the Baptist took the Nazirite vow. People could also be sanctified through the *Aaronic blessing* assuring them of God's continued grace upon them (6:22–27).[5] Third, they were sanctified through worship (7:1–9:14), reflected in the offerings that were presented at the dedication of the tabernacle (chap. 7), Aaron's arrangement of the lamps within the tabernacle (8:1–4), the dedication of the Levites (8:5–26), and through their celebration of their second Passover (9:1–14). Ultimately, the Israelites were sanctified through divine guidance (9:15–10:36). The nation was guided by the cloud above the tabernacle (9:15–23) and by the two silver trumpets (10:1–10). The trumpet blasts signaled the beginning of the new month as well as the annual festivals. Today Jewish congregations sing Num 10:35 ("arise Adonai") as the scrolls are lifted in the Torah processional.[6]

Upon departing for the Wilderness of Paran (10:11–13), the Israelites were given divine guidance in the pillar of cloud by day and the pillar of fire by night (10:33–36). In sum the nation was sanctified through separation (chap. 5), vows (chap. 6), worship (7:1–9:14), and guidance (9:15–10:36). They had everything they needed to conquer

Canaan. Furthermore, their journey from Sinai to Kadesh Barnea was a mere 11 days (Deut 1:2).

B. Failure of the First Generation (Numbers 11–25)

Unfortunately, unbelief resulted in the first generation's **disqualification** from the blessings of Canaan. Chapters 11–12 foreshadow the climactic failure that transpired at Kadesh Barnea (chaps. 13–14). Their unbelief and disobedience were indicated as the people complained at Taberah (11:1–3) and murmured about God's provision of food (11:4–9). Moses' failure is also apparent as he complained about the immense burden of leading the Israelites (11:10–15). However, God graciously provided leadership support for Moses (11:16–30) and quail for the people to eat. Rather than being grateful, the "mixed multitude" (11:4 NKJV) continued to complain again and again. Their unbelief and disobedience were so pervasive that Moses' own family challenged his divinely given authority (12:1–16). Disgruntled over Moses' marriage and ministerial supremacy, Moses' brother Aaron and sister Miriam rose up against him at Hazeroth. The divine judgment upon Miriam came in the form of leprosy, though Moses' gracious intercession led to her healing. After encamping in the wilderness of Paran (12:16), the nation finally arrived at Kadesh Barnea where the rebellion now reached its apex (chaps. 13–14).

South end of the Wilderness of Paran where Israel wandered.

Racial Prejudice

Miriam and Aaron's objection was motivated by jealousy and prejudice. **Moses' "Cushite wife"** (KJV, Ethiopian) may possibly refer to Zipporah (cf. Hab 3:7, which uses "Midianite" and "Cushite" interchangeably) or a second wife of African descent (the normal Hebrew usage of "Cushite") assuming Zipporah had died. However one interprets this text, it is clear that God defended Moses in this decision. Miriam's leprosy (extreme whiteness) was the opposite of the complexion of Moses' wife. While God called the Israelites into a unique covenant with Him, He did not exclude others from the opportunity of His blessings. Isaac married Rebekah, an Aramean; Jacob married Rachel and Leah, Aramean sisters; Judah fathered twins by Tamar, a Canaanite; and Joseph married Asenath, an Egyptian. All these women later became mothers of the various tribes of Israelites. A thorough reading of the Pentateuch makes clear that the Abrahamic covenant was spiritual rather than racial.

Moses selected 12 men, one from each ancestral tribe, to scout out the land of Canaan in advance. After the spies returned with a negative report (chap. 13), Israel lapsed into unbelief and rebelled against God's command to take Canaan (14:1–10). Their desire to return to Egypt and to kill Moses and Aaron showed both a rejection of what God accomplished for them and a rejection of God's divinely chosen leaders. Although Moses' gracious intercession once again spared the first generation from immediate extinction (14:11–19), God **permanently disinherited** them from the land blessings (14:20–38). Only Joshua and Caleb, the two faithful spies, plus all those who were under 20 years of age were exempt from responsibility. The nation's rebellion was further revealed in the way they later attempted to take the land without God's permission, resulting in their subsequent defeat at Hormah (14:39–45). The determination of the age of 20 and above as the basis of God's

The Kadesh Barnea region viewed from the ancient tel.

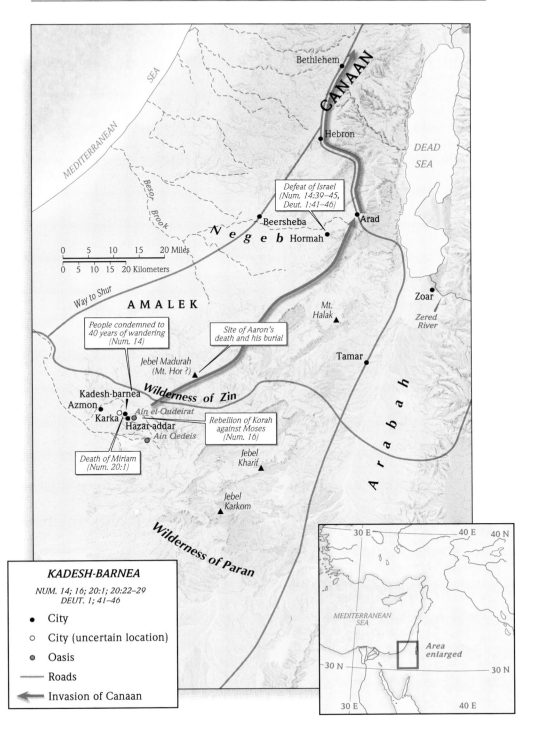

Bethlehem

CANAAN

Hebron

DEAD SEA

Defeat of Israel
(Num. 14:39–45,
Deut. 1:41–46)

Arad

N e g e b Beersheba Hormah

Zoar

Zered River

Mt. Halak

Way to Shur

A M A L E K

Tamar

People condemned to
40 years of wandering
(Num. 14)

Site of Aaron's
death and his burial

A r a b a h

Jebel Madurah
(Mt. Hor ?)

Kadesh-barnea

Azmon

Karka Ain el-Qudeirat

Hazar-addar *Ain Qedeis*

Wilderness of Zin

Rebellion of Korah
against Moses
(Num. 16)

Death of Miriam
(Num. 20:1)

Jebel Kharif

Jebel Karkom

Wilderness of Paran

MEDITERRANEAN SEA

Besor Brook

KADESH-BARNEA

NUM. 14; 16; 20:1; 20:22–29
DEUT. 1; 41–46

- ● City
- ○ City (uncertain location)
- ◉ Oasis
- — Roads
- ← Invasion of Canaan

30 E   40 E   40 N

MEDITERRANEAN SEA

Area enlarged

30 N   30 N

30 E   40 E

judgment was based on the age of accountability and responsibility for military service (Num 1:3).

This is the turning point of the wilderness journey. What began so well ended in total failure as the majority of the Israelites turned back in unbelief. At this point the fate of the first generation was sealed. The exodus generation would not be the conquest generation. What originally was an 11-day journey into Canaan (Deut 1:2) now became a **40-year sojourn** of continual wandering in the wilderness (15:1–20:13). The Israelites spent an additional 38 years in the wilderness because of unbelief.

The events surrounding the **rebellion** of Korah, Abiram and Dathan are recorded next (chap. 16). This rebellion represented a further challenge to Moses and Aaron's priestly authority. These rebellious acts were met with severe repercussions. First, the earth opened and swallowed the instigators while fire consumed the others. Second, a severe plague broke out that resulted in 14,700 deaths. These accounts remind one of the challenges of leadership as well as the high price of disobedience

God performed the miracle of the **budding rod** in order to confirm Aaron's priestly authority (chap. 17). Thus, contrary to the ambitions of Korah, Aaron represented God's selection as the nation's high priest. The placing of Aaron's staff near the ark of the covenant (17:10) served as an ongoing reminder of God's attitude toward those who rebel against His established leaders. This is followed by the ceremony of the **red heifer sacrifice** and the mixture of its ashes in a ritual of cleansing (chap. 19). This procedure to cleanse the priesthood was done to encourage the second generation to honor the priesthood once inside the land. It also demonstrated that the covenant and the priesthood were still available to the second generation, regardless of the rebellion waged against it by the first generation. The author of Hebrews (9:13–14; 13:11) compares the sacrificing of the red heifer outside the camp with the fact that Christ was crucified outside the walls of Jerusalem.

Numbers 20:1 represents a key **chronological marker** in the book. It is the first month of the fortieth year after the exodus event (20:1,22–29; 33:38). At this point Israel had wandered in the wilderness for 38 years, three months, and 10 days. But the book of Numbers reports almost nothing about these 38 years which intervened between their first departure from Kadesh Barnea (14:25) and their second (20:22). However, the story of Moses' own failure (20:1–13) is included for the benefit of the second generation. Moses' actions (striking the rock instead of speaking) revealed his failure to trust and obey God. His disobedience disqualified him from entering the Promised Land. Thus, the theme of disinheritance (chaps. 13–14; 20:1–13) recurs several times in this section. The nation's rebellion against Moses (20:2–5) at Meribah is included as a similar negative example of unbelief and mistrust. Aaron's death at Mount Hor, just east of Kadesh Barnea (20:22–29) conveys the same lesson. Aaron's sin at Meribah disqualified him from his Canaan inheritance. This forfeiture was symbolized in Aaron's clothes being stripped off of him and given to his successor Eleazar. All of these accounts provide a realistic picture of the consequences of unbelief. It seems highly unlikely that a later generation of Israelites would have simply written these stories in such a negative manner.[7]

The Israelites' brief success against the king of Arad (21:3) was followed by failure when the people rebelled against Moses as they traveled along Edom's eastern border. God responded by sending serpents to destroy the people. Moses' intercession and God's grace through the provision of the **bronze serpent** prevented the entire generation from being destroyed (21:4–9). The Gospel of John refers to the lifting up of the bronze serpent in the wilderness as something comparable to the lifting up of the Son of Man (John 3:14).

Israel then traveled around Edom's eastern border and entered the territory of Moab east of Jericho (21:10–20). This area is still known today as Wadi Musa (Arabic for the "Valley of Moses"). The nation then experienced two more victories over the Amorite king Sihon (21:21–32) and Og, the king of Bashan (21:33–

Jebel Harun (Mount Hor) with Aaron's tomb on top of the mountain.

35). The arrival at Moab (chaps. 22–25) introduces the **Balaam oracles** (chaps. 22–24), which indicate that God's purposes for the nation as expressed in the Abrahamic covenant cannot be thwarted despite the first generation's failure. Balaam was a *Baru* or sorcerer who specialized in manipulating and receiving information from various ancient Near East deities through incantation and divination. Although hired by Balak ("the Destroyer"), the Moabite king, to curse Israel, Balaam could only bless the covenanted nation and curse her adversaries through seven oracles (chaps. 23–24), which emphasize God's blessing upon Israel.[8]

The first Balaam oracle (23:1–12) explained God's irrevocable blessings upon Israel. The second oracle (23:13–26) claims that the source of Israel's blessing was her unique relationship to Yahweh. The third oracle (23:27–24:14) extolled Israel's beauty. The fourth oracle (24:15–19) explained that a future messianic deliverer (Gen 49:10) would spring forth from Israel. The "star" that would rise out of Jacob is understood as a messianic prediction by both Jewish and Christian scholars. The final three oracles (24:20–25) explained that God would curse those who cursed Israel, including the Amalekites, Israel's first foes in the wilderness (Exodus 17).

II. Second Generation (Numbers 26–36)

The second half of the book of Numbers (chaps. 26–36) shifts the reader's attention to the second generation's hopes for a better future. The story line in Numbers clearly indicates that God will bypass one generation if necessary and move on to the next generation. Ironically, the exodus generation failed for the most part, despite witnessing God's miracles. By contrast the **wilderness generation**, who witnessed so much turmoil and disobedience from their elders, became the generation that conquered the Promised Land. This indicates that miracles alone do not change people; only God can truly change the heart.

A. Reorganization of Israel on the Plains of Moab (Numbers 26–30)

The second generation's blessings (chaps. 26–36) included Israel's political blessings (chaps. 26–27). These involved another census for purposes of military conquest and inheritance rights (chap. 26), the divine decree that daughters with no surviving brothers had a right to inherit land from their fathers (27:1–11), the selection of **Joshua** as the **new leader** (27:12–23), and various blessings that will follow if the nations keeps the covenant (28–30).

B. Preparation for Conquest of the Land (Numbers 31–36)

A second set of blessings pertains to preparation for the conquest of Canaan (chaps. 31–36). This section includes exhortations for covenant faithfulness and begins with the defeat of the Midianites (chap. 31). This section also mentions the settlement of Gad, Reuben, and half of Manasseh in the **Transjordan** (chap. 32). Fortunately, these eastern tribes pledged to help the other tribes conquer the land of Canaan. The rehearsal of Israel's journeys from Egypt to Moab (33:1–49) would encourage the second generation since this historical survey reveals God's continued faithfulness in spite of the first generation's repeated failures.

A key exhortation for covenant faithfulness is found in the command to **slay the Canaanites** (33:50–56). Here, Moses warned that if the nation did not do this then the Canaanites would repeatedly trouble them. The pattern of the remainder of the Old Testament bears out the validity of this concern. Another divine blessing given to the second generation involves the demarcation of the borders of Canaan that they will eventually possess (34:1–12).

This section also explains the selection of leaders responsible for apportioning the land (34:13–39) as well as the establishment of **Levitical cities** (35:1–8) and **cities of refuge** (35:9–34) in Canaan. The Levitical cities allowed the Levites to live among the people throughout the land. The cities of refuge allowed justice to be exacted against murders and also prevented innocent blood from being spilled due to vigilantism, thereby keeping the land free from spiritual pollution (35:33–34). Finally, each tribe was blessed with the ability to preserve land as in the case of Zelophehad's daughters (chap. 36). Those women, who had no surviving brothers, inherited property from their fathers but were required to marry men of their own choice from their tribe. Thus, Moses reminded the second generation of their blessings and their opportunity to trust

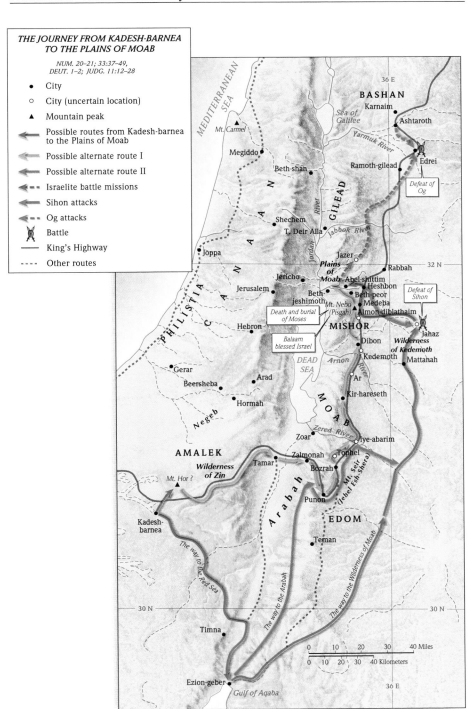

THE JOURNEY FROM KADESH-BARNEA
TO THE PLAINS OF MOAB

NUM. 20–21; 33:37–49,
DEUT. 1–2; JUDG. 11:12–28

• City

○ City (uncertain location)

▲ Mountain peak

← Possible routes from Kadesh-barnea
to the Plains of Moab

← Possible alternate route I

← Possible alternate route II

◄--- Israelite battle missions

← Sihon attacks

◄--- Og attacks

⚔ Battle

— King's Highway

---- Other routes

God. Their covenant faithfulness would be the key to their success in conquering the land of Canaan.

In conclusion, Moses emphasized the need for faith and obedience by the second generation by reminding them that the first generation was blessed (chaps. 1–10) yet disinherited solely due to disobedience (chaps. 11–25). The second generation was challenged to remain faithful to the Lord so they could receive their inheritance in the Promised Land (chaps. 26–36). As the second generation honored the Mosaic covenant, they would see the promises of the Abrahamic covenant fulfilled within their own lifetime. Thus, the new generation, born in the wilderness, would accomplish what the exodus generation failed to do. The apostle Paul used these stories as "examples" for his readers as well (1 Cor 10:1–13).

THEOLOGICAL SIGNIFICANCE

Numbers is replete with many rich theological themes. They include God's holiness, man's sinfulness, the necessity of covenant obedience, and the consequences of covenant disobedience. God's faithfulness to the Abrahamic covenant is clearly displayed despite Israel's faithlessness to the Mosaic covenant. The patience and mercy of God, the visual presence of God manifested through the ark and the tabernacle, and God's divine providence are contrasted to the disobedience and unfaithfulness of the exodus generation. The book of Numbers also provides a practical insight into the depravity of human nature and the necessity of divine intervention in a fallen world.

Hebrew Highlight

Number. Hebrew פָּקַד (*paqad*). The root of the Hebrew word *paqad* occurs in all Semitic languages and comes from the concept of "paying attention" to details. It is used to refer to "counting" (1 Sam 11:8), "recording" (Exod 38:21), "taking note" (Jer 15:15), "appointing" (Num 1:50), "depositing" (Jer 36:20), or "entrusting" (Lev 6:4). As used in the book of Numbers, *paqad* indicates the significance of the censuses taken and their attention to detail in counting the men in the Israelite army. The leadership of the nation and its families were dependent on God's use of these men to defeat Israel's enemies so that the Promised Land could be occupied.

For Further Reading

Allen, Ronald B. "Numbers." In *EBC*. Grand Rapids: Zondervan, 1990.
Cole, R. Dennis. *Numbers*, NAC 3B. Nashville: B&H, 2000.
Feinberg, Jeffrey. *Walk Numbers!* Baltimore: Lederer Books, 2002.
Merrill, Eugene H. "Numbers." In *BKC*. Colorado Springs, CO: Chariot Victor, 1983.
Wenham, Gordon J. *Numbers*. TOTC. Downers Grove, IL: IVP, 1981.

Study Questions

---

1. In what way does the book of Numbers function as a travel diary?
2. What was the significance of age 20 as an age of accountability for Israelite men?
3. What lessons about racial discrimination can be learned from the incident involving Moses' wife?
4. Why was the failure of the Israelites at Kadesh Barnea so decisive?
5. How did the establishment of cities of refuge insure social justice in Israel?
6. What does the book of Numbers teach us about our walk with God?

ENDNOTES

1. For a messianic perspective, see J. E. Feinberg, *Walk Numbers!* (Baltimore: Lederer Books, 2002), 13 ff.

2. Cf. Raymond B. Dillard and Tremper Longman III, *An Introduction to the Old Testament* (Grand Rapids: Zondervan, 1994), 83; Merrill, "Numbers," in *BKC* (Colorado Springs, CO: Chariot Victor, 1983), 215; Gordon J. Wenham, *Numbers*, TOTC (Downers Grove, IL: IVP, 1981), 4:15–16; R. K. Harrison, *Introduction to the Old Testament* (Peabody, MA: Hendrickson, 2004), 615–16.

3. Charles Dyer and Eugene Merrill, *The Old Testament Explorer: Discovering the Essence, Background, and Meaning of Every Book in the Old Testament* (Nashville: Thomas Nelson, 2001), 96.

4. J. Carl Laney, *Answers to Tough Questions* (Kregel: Grand Rapids, 1997), 43–44.

5. A partial copy of the Aaronic blessing written in *paleo* Hebrew was discovered in 1979 in the Hinnom Valley in Jerusalem inscribed on two silver scrolls. These are the oldest copies of a biblical text ever found to date. Their existence clearly indicates the antiquity of the text of Numbers. Cf. details in Merrill, Rooker, and Grisanti, *The World and the Word: An Introduction to the Old Testament* (Nashville: B&H Academic , 2011), 232–34.

6. See details in Feinberg, *Walk Numbers!* 57.

7. Liberal scholars persist in segmenting the book into various unrelated documents, which they believe were edited to produce the current form of the book as late as the fourth century BC. Contra this approach, see Brevard Childs, *Introduction to the Old Testament as Scripture* (Philadelphia: Fortress Press, 1979), 199 ff.; James Hoffmeier, *Ancient Israel in Sinai: The Evidence for the Authenticity of the Wilderness Tradition* (New York: Oxford University Press, 2005), 153–59.

8. The beginning of each oracle is discernible through the repetition of the formula "he took up his discourse and said" (23:7,18; 24:3,15,20,21,23 NASB). Balaam is routinely held up in Scripture in a negative light and an object of universal condemnation (Num 31:7–8,15–16; Deut 23:3–6; Josh 13:22; 24:9–10; Neh 13:1–3; Mic 6:5; 1 Pet 2:15–16; Jude 11; Rev 2:14). The Deir Alla inscription found in Jordan in 1967, dating from 800 BC, also refers to Balaam as a divine seer.

Chapter 10

DEUTERONOMY
Covenant Renewal

The book of Deuteronomy is the **final book** of the Law, and it completes the Torah scrolls. It contains Moses' three speeches to the new generation of Israelites who were about to enter the Promised Land. The book ends with the Song of Moses (chap. 32), the blessing of Moses (chap. 33), and the transition of leadership to Joshua (chap. 34). The book begins in Hebrew with the title *'elleh haddebarim*, "these are the words." However, the LXX title, *Deuteronomion*, is the source of the English title Deuteronomy, which is often taken to mean the "second law," when in reality it is actually an expansion of the original law given at Mount Sinai.

AUTHOR

Various lines of evidence point to Moses as the primary author of the book. Deuteronomy contains roughly 40 references indicating **Moses** is the author who spoke the words and recorded them in this book (Deut 1:5,9; 4:44; 5:1; 27:1; 29:1–2; 31:1,9,22,24; 30; 33:1,36). The rest of the Old Testament frequently claims Moses as the book's author (Josh 1:7–8; Judg 1:20; 3:4; 1 Kgs 2:3; 2 Kgs 14:6; 18:6; 2 Chr 25:4; Ezra 3:2; Neh 1:7; Ps 103:7; Dan 9:11; Mal 4:4). Christ specifically referred to Moses as the author of Deuteronomy (Matt 19:7; Mark 7:10; 10:3–5), and New Testament speakers and writers routinely referred to Moses as the book's author (Matt 22:24; Mark 12:19; Luke 20:28; Acts 3:22–23; 7:37–38; Rom 10:19; 1 Cor 9:9; Heb 10:28). Therefore, Jewish and Christian tradition presumed Mosaic authorship until the eighteenth century when

Hittite covenant treaty. The Hittite treaties were similar to God's covenant with Israel.

de Wette, following Spinoza, theorized that Deuteronomy was written much later than Moses and suggested it was actually the lost "Book of the Law," which was conveniently "discovered" in the days of Josiah in 622 BC (2 Chr 34:14–33).[1]

The preamble (1:1–5), the record of Moses' death (chap. 34), and various other sections (2:10–12,20–23; 3:13b–14) were probably written by someone other than Moses. However, these **additions** notwithstanding, Moses still was responsible for composing the bulk of the book. Also, some contend that Deuteronomy was not written during the time of Moses since it contains prophecies of dispersion and regathering that happened much later in Israel's history (4:25–31; 28:20–68; 29:22–28; 30:1–10; 32:23–43). However, this objection represents nothing more than an antisupernatural bias against predictive prophecy and begs the question by denying that Moses anticipated the issues that would face the new nation in the years ahead.[2] Conservative scholars reject these views because little evidence supports the critical view. It has been observed: "No ancient texts have been found" and "no contemporary corroboration unearthed" which substantiate the critical view.[3]

The view of Canaan from Mount Nebo.

BACKGROUND

The book was probably written around 1406 BC, at the end of the wilderness wanderings and on the eve of the conquest of Canaan (4:44–49; 34:1–4). These events transpired at least 40 years after the exodus from Egypt (Num 14:33–34; Deut 2:7, 14; Josh 5:6). Most of the book was written just before Moses' death, which occurred when he reached the age of 120 (Deut 31:2). Because Moses spent 40 years in Egypt (Acts 7:23), 40 years in Midian (Exod 7:7), and led the nation for an additional 40 years in the wilderness (Acts 7:36), his death occurred roughly 40 years after the exodus.

The book of Deuteronomy covers the **70-day period** between the inauguration of the book's events, which began on the first day of the eleventh month of the fortieth year after the exodus from Egypt (Deut 1:3), and the crossing of the Jordan, which transpired on the tenth day of the first month of the forty-first year after the exodus from Egypt (Josh 4:19). The context of the entire book occurred as the nation was encamped on the plains of Moab prior to entering Canaan (Deut 1:1,5; 29:1; Josh 1:2). The contents of the book were spoken on the plains of Moab east of Jordan across from Jericho (Num 36:13; Deut 1:1,5; 29:1; Josh 1:2). The audience consisted of the second generation that emerged from the wilderness wanderings as they awaited the Canaan conquest.

Outline

I. Past: Review of Israel's History (Deuteronomy 1–4)
II. Present: Record of Israel's Laws (Deuteronomy 5–26)
   A. Principles of the Covenant (Deuteronomy 5–11)
   B. Priorities of the Covenant (Deuteronomy 12–25)
   C. Practice of the Covenant (Deuteronomy 26)
III. Future: Revelation of Israel's Destiny (Deuteronomy 27–34)
   A. Ratification of the Covenant (Deuteronomy 27–30)
   B. Preparation of the Community (Deuteronomy 31–34)

MESSAGE

Deuteronomy was written to invoke covenant renewal on the part of the **second generation** so they could enter Canaan, conquer the Canaanites, and experience prosperity and peace in the land. To accomplish this goal, Moses reviewed God's past acts on Israel's behalf (1–4:40), instructed the second generation to honor the Mosaic covenant (4:41–26:19), and explained what God would do for Israel (chaps. 27–34). In this third category Moses promised that God would bless or curse Israel based on their obedience and disobedience (chaps. 27–28), ultimately restore Israel (chaps. 29–30), and would provide the nation with a new leader (chaps. 31–34). Moses persuasively argued that his audience must "'hear' (50 times) and 'do,' 'keep,' 'observe' (177 times) God's commands out of a heart of 'love' (21 times)."[4] Moses wrote to offer future guidance to the nation. This goal is evident in 17:14–23 where Moses addresses the nation's future kings. He also wrote to furnish a historical bridge linking Israel of the wilderness wanderings to Israel in Canaan. This connected the giving of the law at Sinai with the application of the law in Canaan.

Deuteronomy is **sermonic** and follows a threefold division. The first sermon, found in chaps. 1–4, is retrospective and historical. It seeks to get Israel to remember what God did for her by reciting God's saving acts on her behalf. The second sermon, found in chaps. 5–26, is introspective, emotional, and legal. It calls for Israel to love God with all their heart, to reverence Him, and serve Him. Moses explains what God expects Israel to do through the exposition of the principles of His covenant law. The third sermon, found in chaps. 27–34, is prospective and prophetic. It invokes hope by explaining what God will do for Israel and by providing a final summation of the covenant demands.

The book contains some narrative material, and it also includes legal material. However, the book is largely sermonic and persuasive since it represents an exposition of the law (1:5). The entire structure of the book can be compared to a **suzerain vassal treaty** since it contains the six parts found in a fifteenth-thirteenth century BC Hittite treaty. These six divisions are: preamble (1:1–5), historical prologue surveying "the past relationship between the parties" (1:6–4:40), stipulations or covenant obligations (4:41–26:19), "storage and public reading instructions" (27:2–3; 31:9,24,26), covenant deity witnesses (31–32; 32:1), and curses and blessings showing how the suzerain will respond to the vassal's compliance with the treaty terms (27–30).[5] The fact that Deuteronomy is found in this format reinforces its central purpose of invoking covenant renewal by reminding the second generation of the importance of the covenant. Various subgenres represented in the book include travel itineraries, exhortations, hymns, and poetry.[6]

Deuteronomy contains several **unique features**. First, the book contains almost 200 references to the land as the Israelites prepare to conquer and possess the Promised Land. Second, the book is frequently quoted throughout Scripture: 356 times in the Old Testament and about 80 times in the New Testament. Deuteronomy is used extensively by Christ, not only to validate His messiahship and summarize the law, but also to rebut Satan (Matt 4:4,7,10; Deut 6:16,13; 8:3). While other books of the Pentateuch reveal new law, Deuteronomy helps the reader have a deeper appreciation for

The Kadesh Treaty between the Hittites and Egyptians is the earliest example in existence of a written political treaty.

existing covenant law. Although the book contains legal material, it is unlike Leviticus in the sense that it is for the benefit of the laity rather than the priests. Uniquely, Deuteronomy instructs not just the immediate audience but also the future leaders of Israel and serves as Moses' farewell address to the nation. Thus, Deuteronomy represents his last will and testament.

I. Past: Review of Israel's History (Deuteronomy 1–4)

In Moses' **first sermon** (1:1–4:41), he sought to invoke covenant renewal on the part of the second generation, who were born in the wilderness, by reminding them of what God did for Israel. He reminded them of the discipline that was imposed on the first generation with the hope that the second generation would not repeat the same mistakes, but would instead honor God's covenant. Moses explained God's saving acts on Israel's behalf so that the second generation would be confident that God would also intervene on their behalf as they enter Canaan. Moses then traced Israel's journey from Sinai to Kadesh (1:6–18) and then from Kadesh to Moab (2:1–23). Included in this section are God's commands for Israel not to disturb the Edomites (2:1–7), Moabites (2:8–15), and the Ammonites (2:16–23) since He gave land inheritance to each of these groups.

Moses also emphasized the conquest of the Transjordan. Through covenant obedience Israel defeated Sihon (2:24–37) and Og (3:1–11), and Moses permitted two and a half tribes to settle East of the Jordan (3:12–20). He completed this historical review by reminding the second generation of his own disinheritance (3:21–29). Moses included this information as an example of the cost of covenant disloyalty. He ended this historical review by exhorting the new generation to obey the covenant (4:1–40).

II. Present: Record of Israel's Laws (Deuteronomy 5–26)

Moses now transitions away from what God did for Israel and instead moves toward Israel's obligations to God in the covenant relationship (chaps. 5–26). Moses accomplishes this goal by expounding on how the Decalogue was applicable to daily life in Canaan. Moses wanted this information to create an appetite for covenant renewal and obedience on the part of the second generation as they learned how the Decalogue was relevant to the impending conquest of Canaan and life in the Promised Land.

A. Principles of the Covenant (Deuteronomy 5–11)

In the first major section (chaps. 5–11) of his **second sermon** (chaps. 5–26), Moses articulates the covenant law (chap. 5) as well as its essence (chap. 6) and application (chaps. 7–11) in view of the impending Canaan conquest. Before showing how the covenant is applicable to the new generation in Canaan, Moses recalled how God summoned Israel to Horeb or Sinai (5:1–5) and gave the nation the Ten Commandments (5:6–21). Moses remembered how the people responded with an attitude of reverence and receptivity (5:22–27) and how God further exhorted them toward obedience (5:28–33).

A Jewish man near the western Temple Mount wall in Jerusalem with a phylactery tied to the upper left arm with the remainder of the doublestrap descending down the arm in a tightly drawn spiral fashion, symbolizing the pain suffered under Egyptian bondage.

Moses expounded on the essence of the covenant relationship. It is to love and obey the Lord. He unfolded the essence of the covenant in the form of the **Shema**

(6:4–5). This principle involves loving God with all one's heart and the totality of one's being, and teaching the covenant to one's children (6:6–9). This statement of faith and practice is the core of Judaism to this day. It emphasizes that the religion of the Old Testament was a matter of the heart. It was not merely a series of rituals and regulations but a matter of spiritual devotion to the one true God. As a result of their devotion, God promised to give the Israelites the land of Canaan as a gift of His grace (9:1–6).

Hebrew Highlight

Listen. Hebrew שָׁמַע (*shema*) The Hebrew word *shema* is translated as "listen" or "hear." It appears more than 1,000 times in the Hebrew Bible conveying the idea of "perceiving" or "understanding." This word captures the **essence** of the book of Deuteronomy, which emphasizes the need for the second generation to listen to the Mosaic covenant so they might succeed in the Promised Land. *Shema* is used in Deut 6:4–9 to emphasize the need for the Israelites to perceive Yahweh's unity as well as the significance of loving Him and revering His law. As believers, we too must carefully listen to God's Word so that we might understand what it means to become the type of people He has called us to be as we apply His truth to our lives.

B. Priorities of the Covenant (Deuteronomy 12–25)

In the second major section (chaps. 12–25) of Moses' second sermon (4:41–26:19), Moses applied each of the Ten Commandments to a variety of **specific situations**. This section is developed in the form of case laws applied to a variety of scenarios the second generation will likely encounter in daily life in Canaan.

Moses began by explaining the laws arising from the first four commandments to honor the Lord (chap. 12). Moses explained the necessity of destroying the Canaanite places of worship (12:1–4), worshipping Yahweh only in a centralized location (12:5–14), not imitating pagan religious practices (12:29–32), not following false prophets or those making graven images (chap. 13), not profaning God's name with unclean food (chap. 14), not abusing the poor and enslaved (chap. 15), and not forgetting to celebrate the three main feasts (16:1–17).

Moses next explained the laws arising from the fifth through tenth commandments to honor one's parents, judges, and Levites (16:18–18:22) and to protect the innocent by forbidding revenge murder (19:1–22:4), to avoid adultery (22:5–23:18), theft (23:19–24:7), lying (24:8–25:4), and coveting (25:5–19). Thus, Moses explained the intent of the Ten Commandments as an inward motivation toward godly behavior in the civil, social, and ceremonial life of Israel.

C. Practice of the Covenant (Deuteronomy 26)

In the third section (chap. 26) of his second major sermon, Moses exhorted his audience to **remember the covenant**. As the nation offers its firstfruits (26:1–11) and the third year tithe to the Lord (26:12–15), she will be able to remember how God has blessed the nation through the covenant. Israel will also be prepared to honor the covenant when they understand that their blessings are attached to their adherence to the covenant terms (26:16–19). In conclusion, all of the major sections of Moses' second major sermon (4:41–26:19) are dedicated to the theme of invoking covenant renewal on the part of the second generation. Moses has not only called attention to the Decalogue, but he has also discussed its essence, implications (chaps. 5–11), and applicability to life in Canaan (12–25).

III. Future: Revelation of Israel's Destiny (Deuteronomy 27–34)

In the **third major sermon** (chaps. 27–34), Moses continues with his theme of covenant renewal by forecasting Israel's future destiny, calling upon the new generation to ratify the covenant (chaps. 27–28) and receive the promises of the land covenant (chaps. 29–30). He concludes the final sermon with a statement about the transition of leadership to the next generation.

A. Ratification of the Covenant (Deuteronomy 27–30)

Moses began this part of the sermon by discussing the **covenant renewal ceremony** that is to take place in Shechem after the second generation enters Canaan. After an altar is built (27:1–8) and the nation is exhorted to obey (27:9–10), half of the tribes are to go up to Mount Gerizim to represent the covenant blessings for obedience. The other half of the tribes are to journey to Mount Ebal to represent the covenant curses for disobedience (27:11–13). This procedure is

The south side of Mount Gerizim, which rises above the valley below. Moses told the people that on Mount Gerizim Joshua would place half the tribes of Israel and pronounce God's blessing.

to be followed by the recitation of curses for particular sins (27:14–26). Moses then outlined the blessings (28:1–14) and curses (28:15–68) the nation would experience for obedience and disobedience. These curses grow in intensity until they culminate in deportation. When taken as a whole, they spell out the history of the nation in advance.

Moses then announced the **promises** of the land covenant (chaps. 29–30). Just as the Lord was faithful to the nation in the past (29:2–8), this faithfulness will continue based on what He promised to do when they arrive in the Promised Land. The Abrahamic covenant promised to give his descendants the land unconditionally, but the Mosaic land covenant reminded them they would only be blessed conditionally when they lived in obedience to God's laws. Although the nation would experience curses as a result of disobedience to the Mosaic covenant (29:16–29), God would ultimately restore the nation spiritually and politically to the land promised to the patriarchs (30:1–10).

B. Preparation of the Community (Deuteronomy 31–34)

Moses concluded his third sermon with transitionary information explaining that the new leadership under Joshua will guide the second generation in its conquest of Canaan (chaps. 31–34). Moses also predicted the apostasy that Israel's future generations would exhibit (31:14–22), insisting that the covenant text should be stored in the ark of the covenant (31:24–29). The previously introduced themes of apostasy and restoration are given further treatment in the Song of Moses (32:1–43), which exhorts the second generation to covenant faithfulness (32:44–47).

The events surrounding the **death of Moses** (32:48–34:12) were probably written by Joshua. They serve as a final reminder to the second generation to honor God's covenant and follow this new leader. Despite Moses' uniqueness as a servant of God (34:10–12), he was denied his inheritance in Canaan. Joshua replaced Moses as the leader of the second generation (34:9), and Moses died (32:48–52; 34:5–8) having only seen Canaan from a distance (34:1–4). His burial by God was in an unmarked grave on Mount Nebo.

Mount Nebo and the Jordan Valley. Mount Nebo is where Moses was buried.

THEOLOGICAL SIGNIFICANCE

Throughout the book of Deuteronomy, Moses weaved his material together for the purpose of fostering an attitude of **covenant renewal** in the hearts of the second generation of Israelites. He conveyed this theme in three powerful sermons. First, Moses argued that covenant obedience to God's will is justified on account of God's past acts on Israel's behalf (1:1–4:40). Second, Moses explained how the second generation is to love, revere, serve, and obey God; this is what it means to keep the covenant (4:41–26:19). Third, Moses used what God promised to do for Israel as an additional incentive for covenant obedience (chaps. 27–34).

The theology of Deuteronomy emphasizes the giving of the law as an act of God's grace to enable Israel to establish a covenant community of spiritual righteousness and social justice. In the process the book portrays history as theology. It is "God in action," as Hill and Walton so aptly express it.[7] The history of Israel and the prophecies of her future make evident that God's electing grace was poured out to the people of Israel.

The most direct Christological reference in the book is the prediction that God would one day raise up a **prophet** like Moses (Deut 18:15–18). This prediction of the coming prophet provoked people to ask John the Baptist, "Are you the Prophet?" (John 1:21). "No," he replied, "He is the One coming after me" (John 1:27), pointing to Jesus as the Lamb of God (John 1:29). Thus, Jesus fulfilled the law as the ultimate sacrifice for our sins. Furthermore, Moses, like Christ, was a redeemer (Exod 3:10), mediator (Exod 20:18–21), and intercessor (Exod 32:7–35). Also, Moses was like Christ since he fulfilled the three offices of prophet (Exod 34:10–12), priest (Exod 32:31–35), and king (Exod 33:4–5). As great as Moses was, he was only a shadow of the One to come, but he did appear as one of the two witnesses at Christ's transfiguration (Matt 17:1–3).

For Further Reading

Craigie, Peter C. *The Book of Deuteronomy.* NICOT. Grand Rapids: Eerdmans, 1976.

Deere, Jack S. "Deuteronomy." In *BKC.* Colorado Springs, CO: Chariot Victor, 1983.

Kline, Meredith. *Treaty of the Great King.* Grand Rapids: Eerdmans, 1963.

Merrill, Eugene H. *Deuteronomy.* NAC 4. Nashville: B&H, 1994.

Thompson, J. A. *Deuteronomy: An Introduction and Commentary.* TOTC. Downers Grove, IL: IVP, 1974.

Study Questions

1. Why was it important for Moses to review the law for the new generation of Israelites?
2. How does Deuteronomy parallel suzerain vassal treaties of the ancient Near East?
3. In what way does Deuteronomy read like a series of case laws?
4. Why are the blessings and curses included?
5. What is the significance of the prediction of the coming prophet?

ENDNOTES

1. See Eugene H. Merrill, Mark Rooker, and Michael A. Grisanti, *The World and the Word: An Introduction to the Old Testament* (Nashville: B&H Academic, 2011), 252–57. Cf. M. Noth, *The Deuteronomistic History* (Sheffield: JSOT Press, 1981) and A. F. Campbell and M. A. O'Brien, *Unfolding the Deuteronomistic History* (Minneapolis: Fortress Press, 2000).

2. Cf. Jack S. Deere, "Deuteronomy," in *BKC* (Colorado Springs, CO: Chariot Victor, 1983), 259–60; and Andrew E. Hill and John H. Walton, *A Survey of the Old Testament* (Grand Rapids: Zondervan, 1991), 164–66.

3. Merrill, Rooker and Grisanti, *The World and the Word*, 255.

4. Bruce Wilkinson and Kenneth Boa, *Talk Thru the Bible* (Nashville: Thomas Nelson, 2002), 38.

5. John H. Walton, *Chronological and Background Charts of the Old Testament*, rev. and exp. ed. (Grand Rapids: Zondervan, 1994), 86.

6. Charles Dyer and Gene Merrill, *The Old Testament Explorer: Discovering the Essence, Background, and Meaning of Every Book in the Old Testament* (Nashville: Thomas Nelson, 2001), 129.

7. Hill and Walton, *A Survey of the Old Testament*, 176.

Chapter 11

THE HISTORICAL BOOKS

The books from Joshua to Esther tell the story of God's sovereign actions in dealing with the nation of Israel from the conquest to the dispersion. Each book focuses on the key people, events, cycles, and patterns in its stories. While these books describe what humans did throughout the history of Israel, they also tell the story of the God who works in history to accomplish His divine purposes.

The historical books comprise one-third of the Old Testament and serve as the continuation of the **story of Israel** after the era of the patriarchs and the exodus. The book of Joshua opens with the death of Moses and then transitions to Joshua's leading the tribes of Israel to cross the Jordan River and enter the Promised Land. The book of Judges serves as a transition from the success of the conquest to the difficulties of the settlement of the tribes. The books of Samuel, Kings, and Chronicles trace the history of the kings of Israel through the stages of unity, division, and collapse, resulting in the deportation of Israel into Assyrian and Judah into Babylonian captivity.

The story of **Israel's survival** after the exile is told in the books of Ezra, Nehemiah, and Esther. The first two record the account of the Jews who returned to Jerusalem after the Babylonian deportation. Esther tells the story of the protection and survival of the Jews of the Diaspora, who did not return to their homeland but remained dispersed throughout the Persian Empire.

DIVINE PERSPECTIVE

Biblical history is written from a perspective of **theological interpretation**. By contrast, secular Western history is generally written in a naturalistic style that records facts and interprets them as arbitrary events that are the results of social, political, or economic factors. Hill and Walton observe: "Cause and effect in the world of the ancient Near East is viewed almost entirely in supernatural terms."[1] Thus, the style of the Old Testament historical books is typical of the era from which they originate.

The **Hebrew canon** includes the historical books of Joshua, Judges, Samuel, and Kings under the heading "Former Prophets" in the section called *Nevi'im* because some thought they were written by the prophets Samuel and Jeremiah. Historical books that were put in the section of "Writings" (*Ketuvim*) of the canon include Ezra,

Nehemiah, and Chronicles, books thought to be written by Ezra, plus the book of Esther, which was recorded by the "men of the great assembly."[2]

CRITICAL CONCERNS

Critical scholars have raised numerous questions about the **historical accuracy** of many technical details in these narratives: miraculous events (e.g., the sun standing still, Josh 10:1–15), exaggerated emphases (e.g., Samson's exploits, Judg 15:16), large numbers (e.g. Gideon's foes, Judg 8:10), the accuracy of dates (e.g., 300 years from the conquest to Jephthah, Judg 11:26) and even the general accuracy of the biblical accounts of the exodus, conquest, settlement, and the kingships of David and Solomon.[3] Minimalist critical scholars tend to reject the historicity of all these people and events and consider many archaeological finds as having little significance on proving the historical accuracy of the biblical record (e.g., the "house of David" reference in the Tell Dan inscription).[4] Therefore, they interpret the individual accounts of major events (e.g., exodus, conquest, judges, kings) as *ideographic* accounts that are colored by the author's limited religious and political perspective (e.g., Judean interpretation of northern Israel's kings).

Most critical scholars today tend to view the Old Testament historical books as a series of independent literary units woven together by various editors with revisions and additions by redactors during the exilic period. They view the final form of these books as a "**Deuteronomistic history**," designed to reinforce the theology of the book of Deuteronomy as the determining theological ideology in the history of Israel. What remains unproven in their approach is whether these books were rewritten to recast their recorded events to fit a theology of Deuteronomy (curses and blessings) or whether they were originally written to express such a viewpoint as inspired Scripture in the first place.

Walter Kaiser points out that there is currently no consensus among critical scholars in regard to any plausible reconstruction of the history of Israel. He counters many of their objections by pointing out that miracles in the historical accounts are not arbitrary explanations but a network of **divine interventions** that determined the course of events. He also argues that lack of documentation does not prove that certain events never occurred. Several people mentioned in the Bible have only recently been attested in nonbiblical sources (e.g., Belshazzar, Jehoiachin). Even debatable archaeological sites (Jericho, Ai) may yet be clarified by future excavations.[5]

BIBLICAL SOURCES

The **twelve books** that comprise the Historical Books of the Old Testament provide a rich treasure of information about Israel's leaders: judges, kings, priests, and prophets. They also open up a window into the daily lives of the people: their culture, their customs, beliefs, practices, successes, and failures. Because of the information recorded in these books, there is more known about life in ancient Israel than any of her Middle Eastern neighbors. Leon Wood observes: "Israel was one of the smallest countries of the pre-Christian era, but her history has had a major impact on the world."[6]

The Historical Books cover a period of nearly 1,000 years from Joshua's conquest of Canaan (c. 1405 BC) until the Persian period in the days of Ezra and Nehemiah (c. 430 BC). The biblical record defines the following **periods of Israel's history**:

PERIODS OF ISRAEL'S HISTORY	
1405–1390 BC	Conquest of Canaan (Joshua)
1390–1050 BC	Settlement of the Tribes (Judges)
1050–1010 BC	Kingship of Saul (1 Samuel)
1010–970 BC	Kingship of David (2 Samuel)
970–931 BC	Kingship of Solomon (1 Kings 1–11)
931–586 BC	Kings of Israel and Judah (Kings and Chronicles)
605–535 BC	Babylonian Captivity (Kings and Chronicles)
486–464 BC	Dispersion of the Jews (Esther)
458–430 BC	Return from Exile (Ezra and Nehemiah)

The **precise dating** of many Old Testament historical events cannot be determined by any permanent fixed point of reference, but events that intersect with well-known ancient Near Eastern kings (e.g., Sennacherib's attack on Hezekiah in Jerusalem in 701 BC) make precise dating possible. Other dates in the biblical books are often limited to the number of years a particular king ruled (e.g., "the eleventh year of Joram," 2 Kgs 9:29). Longer periods of time are indicated (e.g., 430 years in Egypt, Exod 12:40; or 480 years from the exodus to the fourth year of Solomon's reign, 1 Kgs 6:1); but sometimes no beginning or ending dates are given. The resolution to this challenge, writes Eugene Merrill, is "the discovery of datable events of ancient Near Eastern history to which those of the OT can be associated. These consist primarily of astronomical phenomena that can be precisely pinpointed and chronological texts that make reference to them. When these are integrated, a consistent and virtually certain chronological framework emerges for the OT historical books."[7]

The **themes** of the Historical Books revolve around God's activity in calling, choosing, punishing, redeeming, and using the nation of Israel as His covenant people to accomplish His global purposes. In this regard these books not only tell the story of the nation and people of Israel but the greater story of God's redeeming grace for all people (e.g., Rahab the Canaanite, Ruth the Moabite, Naaman the Syrian). In each book the covenant promises of God are expressed in terms of divine blessing, judgment, forgiveness, restoration, and preservation.

THEMES OF THE HISTORICAL BOOKS	
Joshua	The Conquest
Judges	The Struggle
Ruth	Ray of Hope
1–2 Samuel	Kings and Prophets
1–2 Kings	Kings of Israel and Judah
1–2 Chronicles	Priestly Perspective
Ezra	Rebuilding the Temple
Nehemiah	Rebuilding the Wall
Esther	Rescuing the People

Written mostly as narrative prose, with a few outbursts of poetic expression (e.g., Song of Deborah and Barak, Judges 5), the Historical Books transport the reader down the corridor of time through nearly a millennium of human encounters with divine providence. The Lord Yahweh Himself intervenes in Israel's national life to preserve the promises and fulfill the prophecies of His covenant with them time and time again.

For Further Reading

Chisholm, Robert B., Jr. *Interpreting the Historical Books: An Exegetical Handbook*. Grand Rapids: Kregel, 2006.

Davis, John J., and John Whitcomb. *A History of Israel from Conquest to Exile*. Grand Rapids: Baker, 1971.

Hamilton, Victor. *Handbook of the Historical Books*. Grand Rapids: Baker, 2001.

Howard, David M., Jr. *Introduction to the Old Testament Historical Books*. Chicago: Moody Press, 1993.

Kaiser, Walter C., Jr. *A History of Israel*. Nashville: B&H, 1998.

Merrill, Eugene. *Kingdom of Priests: A History of Old Testament Israel*. Grand Rapids: Baker, 1987.

Walton, John. *Ancient Near Eastern Thought and the Old Testament*. Grand Rapids: Baker, 1987.

Wood, Leon. *A Survey of Israel's History*. Grand Rapids: Zondervan, 1977.

ENDNOTES

1. Andrew Hill and John Walton, *A Survey of the Old Testament* (Grand Rapids: Zondervan, 2009), 208.

2. Talmud (*Baba Bathra*, 14b–15a).

3. For examples, cf. Albrecht Alt, *Essays in Old Testament History and Religion* (New York: Harper & Row, 1966); Martin Noth, *The History of Israel* (New York: Harper & Row, 1960); John Bright, *A History of Israel* (Philadelphia: Westminster, 1981); J. A. Soggin, *A History of Israel* (London: SCM, 1985); John Hayes and Maxwell Miller, eds., *Israelite and Judean History* (Philadelphia: Westminster, 1977).

4. See Baruch Halpern, "Erasing History: The Minimalist Assault on Ancient History," *Bible Review* 11, no. 6 (1995):26–35, 47.

5. Walter Kaiser, *A History of Israel* (Nashville: B&H, 1998), 1–15.

6. Leon Wood, *A Survey of Israel's History* (Grand Rapids: Zondervan, 1977), 18.

7. Eugene H. Merrill, Mark Rooker, and Michael A. Grisanti, *The World and the Word: An Introduction to the Old Testament* (Nashville: B&H, 2011), 275. For a detailed discussion, see E. H. Merrill, *An Historical Survey of the Old Testament* (Grand Rapids: Baker, 1991), 97–100.

Chapter 12

JOSHUA
The Conquest

The book of Joshua tells the story of the conquest and settlement of the **Promised Land** under the leadership of Joshua (*yehoshua'*, "the LORD is salvation"). The LXX title is rendered *Iēsous*, which is also the Greek spelling of the name Jesus (savior). Thus, Joshua is depicted as a savior or deliverer of the Israelites. He is the representative of Yahweh and the human instrument of the fulfillment of His divine promises to the children of Israel.

The conquest was the **fulfillment of God's prophecy** to Abraham that his descendants would possess the land of Canaan after 400 years of slavery and oppression (Gen 15:12–15). While the book of Joshua opens the section of the Historical Books in the English Bible, it was the first book of the Former Prophets in the section of the Prophets (*Nevi'im*) in the Hebrew Bible. Marten Woudstra explains: "The intent of the Former Prophets is to present an interpretive (prophetical) history of God's dealings with his covenant people Israel."[1]

Like the other historical books, Joshua is an **anonymous work**. Despite its anonymity, several lines of evidence point to Joshua as the book's author. The Babylonian Talmud (*Baba Bathra* 14b) names Joshua as the author. The book itself portrays Joshua's involvement in various writing projects (8:32; 18:8–9; 24:26). The events spoken of in the book are narrated from the perspective of an eyewitness. Moreover, the writer sometimes uses the first-person plural pronouns "we" (5:1 NIV) and "us" (5:6 NIV) when describing the events of the book. Other indications of a fifteenth- to thirteenth-century BC composition include the employment of ancient names of Canaanite peoples, deities, and cities (3:10; 13:4–6; 15:9,13–14) and the fact that the covenant renewal ceremony (chap. 24) reflects Hittite suzerain vassal treaty structures from that era.[2]

BACKGROUND

Because the events of the book are narrated from the **perspective of an eyewitness**, how one dates the book is contingent upon how one dates the exodus and the conquest of Canaan. While many date the exodus in 1290 BC and the conquest in 1250 BC, it seems better to date the exodus in 1446 BC and the conquest in 1406 BC. According to 1 Kgs 6:1, the exodus happened 480 years earlier than the inauguration of the building of the temple, which took place in the fourth year of Solomon's reign in 966 BC. Thus, the exodus took place in c. 1446 BC. Because of the existence of an additional 40-year period between the exodus and the entrance into Canaan (Exod 16:35; Num 14:34–35), the beginning of the conquest took place in 1406 BC.

Also, Caleb indicates that he was 40 years old at the time of the Kadesh Barnea failure (Josh 14:7) and 85 at the conclusion of the conquest (Josh 14:10). Thus, 45 years elapsed between the Kadesh Barnea incident and the completion of the conquest. Because Israel wandered in the desert for roughly 38 years before entering Canaan (Num 10:11; 20:1,22–29; 33:38; Deut 1:3; Josh 4:19), the conquest must have taken about **seven years**. This figure is not surprising in light of Josh 11:18, which indicates that the conquest took some time. All things considered, the conquest probably began in 1406 BC and was completed around 1399 BC. Thus the first half of the book of Joshua (chaps. 1–14) depicting the conquest transpired from 1406 BC to 1399 BC, while the last half (chaps. 15–24) took place between 1399 and 1374 BC.[3]

The oasis of Jericho taken from atop the Old Testament tel Jericho.

Furthermore, archaeological evidence indicates support for the **early date** for the conquest. The excavations of Jericho, Ai, and Hazor have led to a vigorous debate about the date of the destruction of various Canaanite cities during Israel's conquest of Canaan.[4] Both Jericho and Hazor clearly show evidence of being burned in the fifteenth century BC, which fits with the early date for the exodus. References to Joshua's death (24:24) and the elders that outlived him (24:31) indicate that these final notations were added by another inspired writer, perhaps Phinehas (24:33).

The place of writing is **Canaan** since Israel was in this land at the time of the book's closing. Joshua addresses the second generation that emerged from the wilderness to experience the conquest. At the end of the initial conquest, much land remained to be conquered (13:1). Thus, Joshua wrote to the second generation of Israelites to exhort them to continue to conquer the land as well as honor God's covenant so that their descendants would continue to stay in the land. Whereas the older generation failed to trust God fully in the wilderness (Numbers 14), the younger generation, born in the wilderness, fully committed themselves to God and followed Joshua's leadership in conquering the Promised Land.

The Jordan River near Jericho.

The structure of the book of Joshua contains **three major sections**: the conquest of Canaan (chaps. 1–12), the division of Canaan (chaps. 13–22), and the conditions necessary for remaining and prospering in Canaan (chaps. 22–24). The conquest section (chaps. 1–12) can be further divided according to the various campaigns waged by Joshua against the Canaanites. Among them are the central campaign (5:13–9:27), the southern campaign (chap. 10), and the northern campaign (chap. 11).

Outline

I. Conquest of Canaan (Joshua 1–12)
   A. Preparation of the People (Joshua 1–5)
   B. Progression of the Conquest (Joshua 6–12)
      1. Central Campaign (Joshua 6–9)
      2. Southern Campaign (Joshua 10)
      3. Northern Campaign (Joshua 11–12)
II. Division of Canaan (Joshua 13–21)
   A. Unconquered Land (Josh 13:1–7)
   B. East Bank Tribes (Josh 13:8–33)
   C. West Bank Tribes (Joshua 14–19)
   D. Designated Cities (Joshua 20–21)

MESSAGE

I. Conquest of Canaan (Joshua 1–12)

The first major section of the book describes Israel's conquest of Canaan (chaps. 1–12). This section can be divided into the following **two parts**: preparations for the conquest (chaps. 1–5) and the actual conquest itself (chaps. 6–12). Joshua meticulously records all of this information not only to show God's faithfulness to the promises given in the Abrahamic covenant but also to demonstrate that the second generation will consistently have victory over their enemies when they honor the Mosaic covenant. These patterns would serve as a valuable model for continued prosperity in the future.

A. Preparation of the People (Joshua 1–5)

The opening chapters of Joshua (chaps. 1–5) emphasize the importance of **spiritual preparation** for the people of Israel. Before the author deals with the actual account of the conquest, he introduces several key elements that will be essential for Israel's military success against such overwhelming odds. These preparations will include meditating on the Word of God and reciting its principles (1:7–9); challenging the people to total obedience (1:16–18); sending out two spies to identify their options (2:1–24); miraculously crossing the Jordan River on dry ground (3:1–17); setting up the memorial stones as a testimony to future generations (4:1–24); establishing the battle camp at Gilgal (4:20); circumcising the men who were not circumcised in the wilderness (5:2–9); and celebrating the Passover (5:11–12).

While Joshua prepared to attack Jericho, the major Canaanite fortress city in the Jordan Valley, he encountered the theophanic "commander of the LORD's army" (5:12–15). The **divine nature** of this person is evident in His command to Joshua to remove his shoes because he is standing on holy ground. Just as Moses met God at the burning bush (Exod 3:1–6) and removed his shoes, so now Joshua has a similar experience confirming that God was calling him to lead the Israelites to victory, just as Moses led them in the exodus. Both men have a divine encounter and experience a miraculous water crossing which affirmed their leadership to the people of Israel.

B. Progression of the Conquest (Joshua 6–12)

1. Central Campaign (Joshua 6–9). The central campaign was built on a "divide and conquer" theory that drove a wedge between northern and southern Canaan, thus

Hebrew Highlight

Devote. Hebrew חרם (chêrem). The basic meaning is the exclusion of an object and its irrevocable surrender to God (Lev 27:28). The term first appears in Num 21:2–3 where the Israelites vow to "utterly destroy" the Canaanites (NKJV). The noun form chêrem is found in Josh 6:17 meaning "to place under the ban" or "devoted to destruction." God's command to Joshua to annihilate and eradicate Jericho meant the entire city was placed under the divine ban and devoted to God for destruction. Many people today balk at God's command to Joshua to destroy the Canaanites. However, the Canaanites were not innocent victims but rather were involved in gross depravity (Leviticus 18; 19:26,31; Deut 9:4–5; 12:31; 18:9–11; 2 Kgs 23:10). God had already extended patience to the Amorites (Gen 15:13–16), but they and the Canaanites ignored God's warnings.

inhibiting these two entities from forming an alliance. This strategy allowed Israel to defeat each of them separately. Jericho was the first Canaanite city Israel conquered in her central geographic thrust. The **fall of Jericho** resulted from Joshua's obedience to follow the plan of the "commander of the LORD's army." When he spoke, the Lord (Yahweh) spoke (6:2), telling Joshua to circle the city every day for six days and then seven times on the seventh day. When they were finished, they were to shout and blow the trumpets (shofars), then the walls would fall. Joshua includes this event so that his audience will understand that national victory does not come through military strength alone but through covenant obedience (6:21,24,26). Joshua also records how Rahab and her household were saved from genocide that was imposed on all of the inhabitants of Jericho (6:22–23,25). Joshua includes this story as an example of God's grace, showing his readers how they too could experience divine protection if they honor God's covenant.

The nation's subsequent defeat at Ai (chap. 7) is included to show how individual **covenant disobedience** (6:19; 7:1,11,15) damages the success of the entire community. Things quickly turned around for Israel when they did away with Achan, the covenant transgressor (8:1–29), and finally experienced victory at Ai. The covenant renewal ceremony at Shechem (8:30–35) reinforced the nation's need for continual obedience to the covenant (Exod 20:25; Deuteronomy 27; Josh 8:35).

This section also includes the story of Israel's treaty with the **deceptive Gibeonites** (chap. 9) as Joshua fails to pray about his decision and gives his word to their deceptive representatives (9:1–14). Thus, both the defeat at Ai (chap. 7) and the treaty with the Gibeonites (chap. 9) contribute to the book's literary purpose of emphasizing the necessity of covenant obedience.

2. Southern Campaign (Joshua 10). In the southern campaign the king of Jerusalem became fearful of Israel due to the nation's resounding victories at Jericho and Ai. Thus, he persuaded the **southern coalition** (Hebron, Jarmuth, Lachish, and Eglon) to attack the Gibeonites, thereby drawing Israel into open conflict (10:1–5). However, God's blessing was upon Israel, evidenced by His confounding of the enemy by the hailstorm He sent to defeat them, and by the miraculous extension of the day that allowed Israel time to route the enemy.[5] Joshua eventually captured the five fleeing kings, publicly executed them, and conquered the southern territory (10:16–43). Throughout these events the writer consistently calls attention to how Israel honored her treaty with the Gibeonites and manifested covenant obedience (10:28–30,33,35,37).

3. *Northern Campaign (Joshua 11–12).* After some time Joshua advanced against the gathering northern Canaanite coalition to fight them at Merom (11:1–5) and handily defeated them with a surprise attack, routing their forces and destroying **Hazor**, the major Canaanite fortress city in the north (11:6–11). The chapter concludes with a summation of the northern campaign emphasizing Israel's obedience to the Mosaic covenant as the key to her victories (11:16–23). The summary of Israel's conquests in chap. 12 is provided for the same reason. This chapter lists Israel's conquests of 31 individual city-states in Transjordan (12:1–6) and Canaan (12:7–24). Despite Joshua's initial successes, the next chapter reminds the reader that a great deal of the land remains to be possessed.

List of 31 Cities Conquered		
• Jericho	• Arad	• Shimron-meron
• Ai	• Libnah	• Achshaph
• Jerusalem	• Adullam	• Taanach
• Hebron	• Makkedah	• Megiddo
• Jarmuth	• Bethel	• Kedesh
• Lachish	• Tappuah	• Jokneam in Carmel
• Eglon	• Hepher	• Dor in
• Gezer	• Aphek	Naphath-dor
• Debir	• Lasharon	• Goiim in Gilgal
• Geder	• Madon	• Tirzah
• Hormah	• Hazor	

II. Division of Canaan (Joshua 13–21)

A. Unconquered Land (Joshua 13:1–7)

At this point the author inserts a list of **unconquered regions** that still remained independent of Israelite control (13:1–6). These included pockets of Philistines, Geshurites, Canaanites, Amorites, and Phoenicians (Sidonians of Lebanon). These will be left for future generations to deal with as is described in Judg 1:1–3:6. These areas were not completely absorbed until the time of David and Solomon many years later.

B. East Bank Tribes (Joshua 13:8–33)

Joshua begins this section by reviewing the settlement of the **Transjordan tribes** (13:8–33). Now that the Transjordan tribes fulfilled their obligations in helping liberate Canaan, the soldiers from these tribes were released from military obligation and allowed to return home. These tribes included Reuben (13:15–23), Gad (13:24–28), and half of Manasseh (13:29–31). Much of this area was later known as Gilead (Josh 22:9; Judg 10:8). However, the author later records the crisis that occurred when the eastern tribes erected a large altar on the frontier at the Jordan River (Josh 22:9–12).

Overview of the excavations at Tel el-Qedah (ancient Hazor) north of the Sea of Galilee.

C. West Bank Tribes (Joshua 14–19)

The decision to **divide the land by lot** (14:1–5) shows that Israel's gains came about through compliance with the covenant since Moses originally mandated division by lot as the method to be used when apportioning the land among the tribes (Num 26:55; 33:54; 34:13). Caleb's proclamation of God's faithfulness in finally awarding him what was originally promised is included to show God's faithfulness to the Abrahamic covenant and to His faithful servant Caleb. Caleb's desire to drive out the Canaanites is also included as a positive example for Joshua's readers to follow. Thus, all of the material in chaps. 13 and 14 is included to stimulate Joshua's readers toward further covenant obedience.

The designation of **Judah's borders** (15:1–12) as well as the inheritance of the various clans within Judah (15:20–63) once again shows God's covenant faithfulness. Caleb's decision to conquer Hebron and drive the Canaanites out of his territory

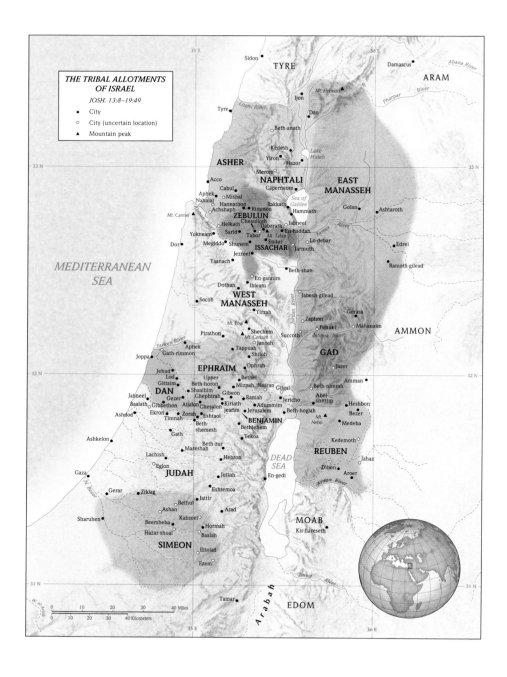

THE TRIBAL ALLOTMENTS
OF ISRAEL
JOSH. 13:8–19:49
• City
○ City (uncertain location)
▲ Mountain peak

also serves as a positive example of covenant obedience that the next generation is to imitate (15:13–19). However, Judah's failure to drive the Jebusites from Jerusalem (15:63) left the city under Jebusite control until the time of David (2 Samuel 5).

Joseph's inheritance (chaps. 16–17), which included the inheritances of both Ephraim (chap. 16) and west Manasseh (chap. 17), is included to show God's faithfulness to Joseph through Jacob's promise to him in his patriarchal blessing (Gen 48:10–22). However, the failure of Ephraim (16:10) and Manasseh (17:12–13) to drive the Canaanites from their territory (16:10) serves as a negative example to challenge Joshua's readers to continue the effort to remove them. The same challenge to keep the covenant and remove God's enemies was given at the tabernacle in Shiloh (18:1) to Benjamin (18:11–28), Simeon (19:1–9), Zebulun (19:10–16), Issachar (19:17–23), Asher (19:24–31), Naphtali (19:32–39), and Dan (19:40–48). Shiloh would serve as the nation's religious headquarters for the next 300 years. Correspondingly, the tribe of Levi was to serve as the nation's priests and was given no territorial allotment.

D. Designated Cities (Joshua 20–21)

More examples of God's faithfulness to His covenant promises are given through the establishment of the promised **cities of refuge** (chap. 20) and the **Levitical cities** (21:1–42). Because these items were also promised in the Mosaic covenant (Numbers 35; Deut 4:41–43; 19:1–13), they serve as further testimony to Joshua's readers of the blessings that could be received through covenant obedience. Joshua concludes this major section of his book on the division of the land (chaps. 13–21) with a comprehensive statement regarding God's faithfulness to the promises He gave to the second generation (21:43–45).

III. Conclusion of Joshua's Ministry (Joshua 22–24)

Now that Joshua has described the conquest (chaps. 1–12) and division of Canaan (chaps. 13–21), he transitions into the third and final section of his book where he assembles material showing the **second generation** how they can remain in the land as well as experience prosperity in the land (chaps. 22–24).

A. Dispute about the Altar (Joshua 22)

Joshua begins this final section by recounting how the soldiers from the Transjordan tribes, after being given permission to return home, built an altar in the Jordan Valley, potentially rivaling Shiloh as the central sanctuary (chap. 22). The establishment of such an altar represented a potential covenant violation since the Mosaic covenant mandated a single centralized sanctuary (Deut 12:1–7). Fortunately the situation was resolved amicably since the motivation for the altar was to establish **unity** between the eastern and western tribes rather than to set up a rival system of worship. Thus, the altar was called *Ed*, which means "witness." In other words, the altar was a witness to the unity between the eastern and western tribes, which were united in their devotion to the Lord.

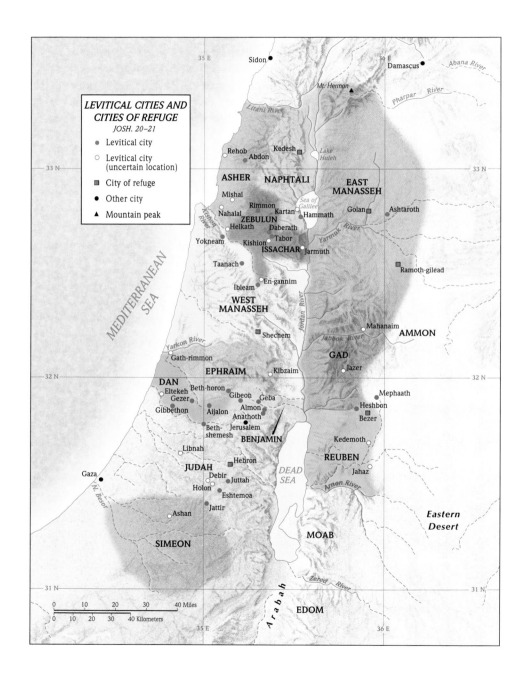

LEVITICAL CITIES AND
CITIES OF REFUGE
JOSH. 20–21

- Levitical city
○ Levitical city
   (uncertain location)
■ City of refuge
● Other city
▲ Mountain peak

B. Joshua's Final Sermon (Joshua 23)

Joshua's **farewell address** to the nation's leaders attributes the nation's past blessings to its covenant fidelity (23:1–12). He also explained that the future curses Israel will experience will be due to the nation's covenant infidelity (23:13–16). The main danger will be the threat of idolatry, which represents an attack on the foundation of the covenant itself since the first two commandments in the Decalogue prohibit idolatry. The message to the second generation is clear. They will remain in Canaan and prosper in the land only when they comply with the Mosaic covenant.

C. Covenant Renewal at Shechem (Joshua 24:1–28)

Joshua concludes the book by recording the second covenant renewal ceremony at Shechem. After assembling the leaders to Shechem (24:1), Joshua summarized the history of Israel from her election to the conquest (24:2–13), reviewed the covenant terms (24:14–24), and encouraged covenant's preservation (24:25–28).[6] The book of Joshua contains two covenant renewal ceremonies (8:30–35; 24). Because the first of these ceremonies took place toward the beginning of the conquest and the last of these ceremonies took place after the land was conquered and divided, they serve as **brackets** for this section of the book. Such bracketing shows that everything God has done for the nation and will continue to do on her behalf is based on Israel's response to the Mosaic covenant. Thus, the nation's entire future is inextricably bound to her response to the Lord Yahweh. Thus, Joshua challenges the people with the options of worshipping the gods the patriarchs rejected "beyond the river," the gods of the Egyptians from whom they escaped, or the gods of the Amorites whom they had conquered (24:14–15). "No!" the people insisted, "We will worship the LORD" (24:21, author's translation).

Standing stones at Gezer dating to about 1500 BC and reminiscent of the 12 stones that Israel set up on the west bank of the Jordan.

D. Deaths of Joshua and Eleazar (Joshua 24:29–33)

Not only does this section record the deaths of Joshua (24:29–30) and Eleazar the high priest (24:33), but it also records information regarding the **burial of Joseph's bones** in Shechem (24:32). This detail is included to emphasize Israel's faithfulness to Joseph's request to bury his mummified remains in the Promised Land (Gen 50:29).

THEOLOGICAL SIGNIFICANCE

Joshua emphasizes **God's faithfulness** to both the Abrahamic and Mosaic covenants. God's faithfulness to these covenants is seen in His unilateral actions in support of Israel by restraining the Jordan (3:14–17), destroying the walls surrounding Jericho (6:20), sending a hailstorm on Israel's enemies (10:11), and extending the day so Israel could gain victory over her enemies (10:13–14). God's faithfulness is accentuated in that He provides victory in spite of the death of His choice servant Moses and in spite of overwhelming odds.

The book also teaches the importance of **covenant obedience** as the key to God's blessings. The reader is drawn to the focus on key spiritual disciplines that are essential for spiritual formation—prayer, meditation, faith, and courage are highlighted as keys to Joshua's success. The underlying theology of the book reminds the reader that spiritual discipline is the key to victorious living. Vigilance must be consistent so that today's success might not turn into tomorrow's defeat.

For Further Reading

Campbell, Donald K. "Joshua." In BKC. Colorado Springs, CO: Chariot Victor, 1983.

Constable, Thomas L. "A Theology of Joshua, Judges, and Ruth." In *A Biblical Theology of the Old Testament*. Edited by Roy B. Zuck and Eugene H. Merrill. Chicago: Moody, 1991.

Hess, Richard. *Joshua: An Introduction and Commentary*. TOTC. Downers Grove, IL: IVP, 1996.

Howard, David M., Jr. *Joshua*. NAC 5. Nashville: B&H, 2002.

Madvig, Donald H. "Joshua." In EBC. Grand Rapids: Zondervan, 1992, 239–371.

Woudstra, Marten. *The Book of Joshua*. NICOT. Grand Rapids: Eerdmans, 1981.

Study Questions

1. What spiritual preparations were made by the Israelites before they attempted to conquer the cities of Canaan?
2. How do we know the "Commander of the Lord's army" was a divine being?
3. Why was Achan's sin a transgression punishable by death?
4. How did Joshua divide the land of Canaan in order to conquer it?
5. How did the conquest fulfill God's covenant promises to Abraham's descendants?
6. What principles for victorious living can we learn from Joshua's example?

ENDNOTES

1. Marten Woudstra, *The Book of Joshua*, NICOT (Grand Rapids: Eerdmans, 1981), 3.

2. Richard Hess, *Joshua: An Introduction and Commentary*, TOTC (Downers Grove, IL: IVP, 1996), 26–31.

3. For detailed discussion of the dating of Joshua, cf. Woudstra, *The Book of Joshua*, 5–25; K. A. Kitchen, *Ancient Orient and Old Testament* (Downers Grove, IL: IVP, 1966), 90–102; Y. Kaufmann, *The Biblical Account of the Conquest of Palestine* (Jerusalem: Magnes Press, 1953); Bryant Wood, "The Biblical Date for the Exodus Is 1446 BC: A Response to James Hoffmeir," *JETS* 50, no. 2 (June 2007): 249–58.

4. Cf. details in E. M. Blaiklock and R. K. Harrison, *New International Dictionary of Biblical Archaeology* (Grand Rapids: Zondervan, 1983), 258–61; K. Schoville, *Biblical Archaeology in Focus* (Grand Rapids: Baker, 1978), J. J. Bimson, *Redating the Exodus and Conquest* (Sheffield: University of Sheffield, 1978), 115–45.

5. For a discussion of the various interpretations of Joshua's long day, see J. Carl Laney, *Answers to Tough Questions: A Survey of Problem Passages and Issues from Every Book of the Bible* (Grand Rapids: Kregel, 1997), 60–61.

6. The structure of this covenant renewal ceremony contains the relevant sections of a fifteenth-thirteenth century BC suzerain vassal Hittite treaty. See John H. Walton, *Chronological and Background Charts of the Old Testament*, rev. and exp. ed. (Grand Rapids: Zondervan, 1994), 86; Meredith Kline, *Treaty of the Great King* (Grand Rapids: Eerdmans, 1963).

Chapter 13

JUDGES
The Struggle

The book of Judges introduces us to the long years of Israel's struggle to maintain control of the Promised Land from the death of Joshua until the rise of the kings. After Joshua's death, a loose **tribal confederacy** emerged with various military heroes empowered by the Spirit of God to bring deliverance from their common enemies. The main body of the story revolves around six cycles of apostasy, distress, and deliverance. God intervenes time and again to rescue the struggling Israelites from military oppression, spiritual depression, and ethnic annihilation.

Mount Tabor, located a few miles southeast of Nazareth.

The **covenant violations** of Israel's first generations born in the land are exposed as the cause of her constant struggle for survival. The temptations of idolatry, immorality, and religious syncretism left the tribes divided, confused, and in a constant state of conflict. The repeated phrases, "There was no king in Israel," and, "Everyone did what was right in his own eyes," remind the reader that the theocracy was in jeopardy without a strong central leader to maintain justice, stability, and order.

The book of Judges derives its title from the Latin *Liber Judicum*. The Hebrew title is *shophetim*. The verbal form describes the activity of the various deliverers whom God used despite their personal challenges, oddities, or inadequacies. Ehud is left-handed, Deborah is a woman, Barak was reluctant, Gideon was afraid, Jephthah was an outcast, and Samson was a Nazirite. Nevertheless, the book of Hebrews lists many of these judges (Gideon, Barak, Samson, Jephthah) as heroes of the faith (Heb 11:32). The real key to their success was the empowerment of the Spirit of God (3:10; 6:34; 11:29; 13:6,25; 15:14) who enabled them to accomplish great feats.

Many believe the books of Judges and Ruth originally formed one document in the Hebrew Bible. They deal with events following Joshua's death (c. 1380 BC) and continue until the reference to David in Ruth 4:17,22, but they were written from a **prophetic viewpoint** following the days of the judges (cf. 17:6; 18:1; 19:1; 21:25, "In those days there was no king in Israel") and prior to David's conquest of Jerusalem, since it was still held by the Jebusites according to the author in 1:21. While the author is not indicated by the text, Jewish tradition has ascribed it to Samuel the prophet since he was the major spiritual figure of the time of the judges. The critical view, which would attribute the authorship of this book to a Deuteronomistic recension based on mythological hero sagas, must be rejected in light of the many historical details which may only be attributed to the time of the judges themselves.[1]

If **Samuel** the prophet was the author, or editor, of Judges, its composition would date from circa 1050–1000 BC. The chronological material in the book has been subject to a great deal of discussion and widely variant dating. British evangelical scholarship has tended to follow the late date for the exodus and, therefore, dates Othniel at 1200 BC,

Hebrew Highlight

Judge. Hebrew שֹׁפֵט (*shophet*). The word for a judge (*shopet*) is closely related to the verb *shaphat*, "to judge," and also to *mishpat*, "justice." The biblical concept of judgment includes the administration of justice. Thus, there is no justice without judgment and no proper judgment without justice. The two are interconnected; therefore the judge was to maintain justice as well as settle legal disputes. In the book of Judges, the Hebrew word *shofet* is used once in reference to Yahweh (11:27), six times in reference to those who "delivered" Israel under the empowerment of God's Spirit (2:18; 3:9; 13:25; 14:6,19; 15:14), and seven times in relation to those "judges" who served as administrators (4:4; 12:8–9,11,13–14; 15:20). Throughout the book of Judges, the Spirit-empowered "judges" functioned as the "deliverers" of Israel as God judged the hearts of His people in response to their prayers (2:16–19).

while conservative American scholars date him at circa 1350 BC.[2] The latter approach takes the biblical data regarding these dates as exact rather than general figures. In Judg 11:26 Jephthah referred to a period of 300 years between the conquest and his own time, which correlates with the figures supplied in the text by subtracting the 18-year Ammonite oppression with which he was contemporary. The total number of years mentioned in Judges is 410 years. However, a simple adding of numbers may not be the key to the chronology of this period, for there probably were **overlapping judgeships** functioning at the same time but in different locations. Many commentators believe that the 20 years of Samson's judgeship should be included within the Philistine oppression, which was finally broken by Samuel at Ebenezer (1 Samuel 7). Jephthah's reference (11:26) to 300 years from Joshua (1406 BC) to himself (1105 BC) coincides with the statement in 1 Kgs 6:1 regarding 480 years from the exodus (1446 BC) to the fourth year of Solomon's reign (966 BC). The biblical data supports the early date for the exodus.

CYCLE	ENEMY	PERIOD OF SERVITUDE	JUDGE	PERIOD OF REST
First 3:7–11	Mesopotamia	8 Years (1381–1373 BC)	Othniel	40 years (1373–1334 BC)
Second 3:12–31	Moab	18 years (1334–1316 BC)	Ehud	80 years (1316–1237 BC)
Third 4:1–5:31	Canaanites	20 years (1257–1237 BC)	Deborah and Barak	40 years (1191–1151 BC)
Fourth 6:1–8:32	Midianites	7 years (1198–1191 BC)	Gideon	40 years (1149–1105 BC)
Fifth 10:6–12:15	Ammonites (in east)	18 years (1105–1087 BC)	Jephthah	29 years (1087–1058 BC)
Sixth 13:1–16:31	Philistines (in west)	40 years	Samson	20 years (1069–1049 BC)

BACKGROUND

The events recorded in the book of Judges occurred during one of the most **turbulent and transitional times** in the history of the ancient Near East. In Egypt the confusion of the Amarna period followed the conquest and settlement of Canaan. Assuming the early date for the Exodus, the first judges were contemporary with the powerful pharaohs of the nineteenth dynasty while the later judges were contemporary with the period of confusion which followed. Meanwhile, to the north, the kingdom of Mitanni fell to the Hittites circa 1370 BC. Further west, the great Minaon and Mycenean empires also collapsed; and a period of mass migrations (people movements) followed, ultimately bringing the Bronze Age culture to an end and introducing the Iron Age. The Israelite disadvantage in regard to iron weapons and chariots is mentioned several times throughout the book of Judges.

Both the Canaanites and the Israelites were pressured by the invasion of the Sea Peoples (Philistines) who gained firm control of the coastal area of southern Canaan. Throughout Judges and the early chapters of 1–2 Samuel, the Philistines were the major threat to Israel's survival. To the south and east, the nomadic tribes had begun to settle into the Transjordanian kingdoms of Moab, Ammon, and Edom. This **discordant milieu** is the setting of the book of Judges. Thus, God had ample sources to draw upon as a means to discipline the sins of Israel. However, the sovereign hand of God, and not just political chaos, ruled over the events of men during this time.

Outline

I. Reason for the Judges (Judges 1–2)
II. Rule of the Judges (Judges 3–16)
   A. First Cycle: Othniel Versus Cushan (Judges 3:1–11)
   B. Second Cycle: Ehud Versus Eglon (Judges 3:12–31)
   C. Third Cycle: Deborah and Barak Versus the Canaanites (Judges 4:1–5:31)
   D. Fourth Cycle: Gideon Versus the Midianites (Judges 6:1–10:5)
   E. Fifth Cycle: Jephthah Versus the Ammonites (Judges 10:6–12:15)
   F. Sixth Cycle: Samson Versus the Philistines (Judges 13:1–16:31)
III. Ruin of the Judges (Judges 17–21)
   A. Idolatry (Judges 17–18)
   B. Immortality (Judges 19–21)

MESSAGE

Most of the biblical judges were **heroes or deliverers** more than legal arbiters. They were raised up by God and empowered to execute the judgment of God upon Israel's enemies. The sovereignty of God over His people is seen in these accounts as God, the ultimate Judge (11:27), judges Israel for her sins, brings oppressors against her, and raises up judges to deliver her from oppression when she repents.

I. Reason for the Judges (Judges 1–2)

The period of the judges followed the death of Joshua (1:1) when Israel was left with no central ruler. While the book of Joshua represents the apex of victory for the Israelite tribes, the book of Judges tells the story of their **struggle** to maintain control of the land. While the conquest of the land was relatively quick and decisive, the settlement of the tribal territories was slow and cumbersome. Many pockets of resistance remained, and the Israelites eventually settled on a policy coexistence rather than conquest.

Initial resistance came from the Canaanites, the aboriginal tribal inhabitants of the region.[3] They were a loosely confederated settlement of various city-states, related to the Amorites, Perizzites, and Jebusites. Their religion was essentially a nature cult based on a pantheon of deities led by the gods El, Baal, and the goddess Asherah (also called Ashtar). The first chapter includes a catalog of **unoccupied territories** that remained after the initial conquest (1:27–36). The second chapter explains the reasons for this failure and the rebuke by the angel of the Lord at Bochim ("weepers," 2:1–5).[4] The author concludes this section noting the cycles of apostasy, oppression, distress, and deliverance that would follow because they would continue to sin and God would continue to "raise up judges" to deliver them (2:16).

The Valley of Jezreel as viewed from the top of the Megiddo tel.

II. Rule of the Judges (Judges 3–16)

The **six cycles** of the judges include years of oppression, deliverance, and rest, punctuated by interludes that discuss minor judges and the usurper Abimelech (chaps. 9–10). Each cycle portrays a downward spiral which includes Barak's reluctance, Deborah's insistence, Gideon's cowardice, Jephthah's foolish vow, and Samson's immoral relationship with foreign women. The recurring theme in these chapters is Israel's apostasy which is displayed in her covenant violations of idolatry and immorality. This was reflected in the moral and spiritual weakness of the time in which lying, stealing, adultery, and murder were often condoned.

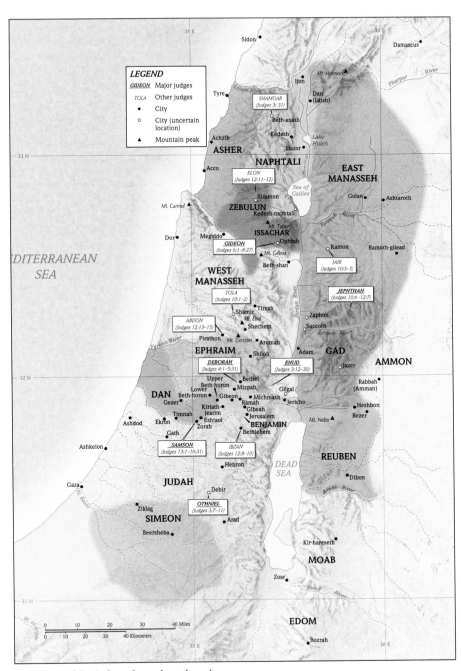

Locations of the judges throughout Israel.

A. First Cycle: Othniel Versus Cushan (Judges 3:1–11)

The author introduces this section listing those nations that continued to harass Israel, culminating by the invasion of Cushan-rishathaim ("Cushan the doubly wicked") from Aram Naharaim (KJV, "Mesopotamia"), the area of northeastern Syria. After an eight-year oppression, the Lord raised up Othniel of the tribe of Judah to defeat him because the "Spirit of the Lord" came upon him. The description of the **Spirit-empowered judges** is repeated seven times emphasizing the real source of their power (3:10; 6:34; 11:29; 13:25; 14:6,19; 15:14). Othniel's victory was followed by 40 years of peaceful rest (3:11).

B. Second Cycle: Ehud Versus Eglon (Judges 3:12–31)

The second recorded invasion was led by Eglon the king of Moab and a confederacy of Moabites, Ammonites, and Amalekites (3:13). They recaptured a rebuilt Jericho, the "City of Palms," and used it as a base against Israel for 18 years (3:14). Eventually, God "raised up" Ehud, a **left-handed Benjamite**, who assassinated Eglon with a dagger hidden on his right hip and led an attack that drove the Moabites back across the Jordan River (3:26–30). The chapter ends with a brief reference to Shamgar, son of Anath, who slew 600 Philistines (probably a lifetime total) with an ox goad (3:31).

C. Third Cycle: Deborah and Barak Versus the Canaanites (Judges 4:1–5:31)

By the third cycle of the judges, Israel had lost control of the northern region to the Canaanites at Hazor. **Sisera** was the commander of a Canaanite army that included 900 iron chariots, and he used it to oppress the Israelites in that area for 20 years.[5] God spoke to Deborah, who was serving as a judge at that time, to summon Barak to challenge the northern tribes to confront the Canaanites at Wadi Kishon in the Jezreel Valley. When Barak refused to go unless Deborah accompanied him, she told him that the credit for the victory would go to a woman (4:9).

Barak's troops took the high ground at Mount Tabor and attacked the Canaanites in the valley below. Deborah and Barak's victory song indicates the "river Kishon swept them away" (5:21), implying a flash flood that bogged the chariots in the swampy ground and caused Sisera to abandon his chariot and flee to the tent of a woman named Jael. She killed the unsuspecting commander with a tent peg and a mallet (4:21) thus fulfilling Deborah's earlier prediction. The entire account emphasizes the **lack of male leadership** in Israel at that time.

D. Fourth Cycle: Gideon Versus the Midianites (Judges 6:1–10:5)

The story of Israel's leadership crisis continued with the raiding attack of the Midianites and their Arab Bedouin allies. Things were so bad the Israelites hid in the mountain clefts while swarms of armed desert bandits pillaged the land for seven years. At that time the angel of the Lord called Gideon from the tribe of Manasseh to lead a resistance. **Fearful and reluctant**, Gideon went from hiding in a winepress to making excuses and putting out fleeces. The spiritual weakness of Israel was indicated by the fact that Gideon's own father had a Baal altar on the family farm which Gideon finally tore down. After this the Spirit of the Lord came upon Gideon, so he blew a trumpet (shofar) and rallied 32,000 men to go against the Midianite and Amalekite raiders.

Fearful himself, Gideon was told to let all those who were afraid go home, and two-thirds of his "army" of volunteers left. When God thinned his numbers down to only 300 men at the **spring of Harod** ("trembling"), Gideon had to be reassured of success by overhearing the dream of the barley cake (7:9–15). During the night he equipped his men with trumpets, pitchers, and torches and surprised the unsuspecting raiders. The enemy was thrown into confusion so the Israelites won an incredible victory by daybreak (7:16–23).[6]

However, Gideon's success was followed by the tragic story of **Abimelech** ("My father is king"), his son by a concubine (8:31). After Gideon's death Abimelech rallied his mother's relatives in an attempt to become a king at Shechem. Rebuked by Jotham's parable of the trees (9:7–15), which depicted him as a bramble bush, Abimelech was eventually killed when a woman threw a piece of millstone down on his head while he was attacking the tower at Thebez (9:50–55).

The Harod Spring at Ainharaod at the foot of the Gilboa mountain range. This is where Gideon gathered his men before fighting the Midianites.

E. Fifth Cycle: Jephthah Versus the Ammonites (Judges 10:6–12:15)

When the Ammonites in Transjordan attacked the Israelites in Gilead, the elders in desperation called the outcast Jephthah from the land of Tob (11:3) to lead Israel in battle. When Jephthah's negotiations with the Ammonites failed, he made a **vow** to the Lord Yahweh that "whatever" came out of his house to greet him upon his return from battle "will belong to the LORD, and I will offer it as a burnt offering" (11:31). When his daughter, not an animal, came out first, he was devastated. Scholars have long debated whether he actually sacrificed his own daughter or dedicated her to a lifetime of virginity, never to marry and carry on his family line (11:34–40).[7] Either way she bewailed her "virginity," and he grieved that he would have no descendants.

The rugged hill country of Gilead.

F. Sixth Cycle: Samson Versus the Philistines (Judges 13:1–16:31)

The final cycle involved Samson from the tribe of Dan. By this time the tribe of Dan had already abandoned their God-given territory in the land of the Philistines, leaving Samson's family and a few others in a displaced persons "camp" (13:25). The uniqueness of Samson was the **Nazirite vow** which was imposed on him from birth (13:5; cf. Num 6:2–12). Tragically, Samson ultimately violated all three stipulations of the vow, touching the "unclean" dead lion (14:8–9), participating in a "drinking feast" (Hb. *mishteh*, 14:10), and finally having his head shaved (16:19). Even his initial victory over 1,000 Philistines was accomplished with an "unclean" jawbone of a dead animal (15:15).

Samson's life story revolved around **three women**, presumably all Philistines: (1) the woman of Timnah, whom he attempted to marry (14:1–15:6); (2) the prostitute at Gaza (16:1–3); and (3) Delilah of the Valley of Sorek (16:4–20). Despite his gift of physical strength given by the power of the Spirit, Samson's inability to conquer his own passions ultimately led to his demise. The deadly lover's game he played with Delilah eventually caused him to reveal the truth about the Nazirite vow (16:17). She immediately exposed his secret to the five lords (*seren*) of the Philistines who each paid her 1,100 pieces of silver (16:5). Captured and blinded, Samson was imprisoned at Gaza (16:21). Despite his hair beginning to grow, his power did not return until he finally "called out" to the Lord, who empowered him one last time to pull down the pillars of the pagan temple and kill more Philistines by his death than in his life (16:30).

Regardless, the final cycle of the judges ends with Samson crushed beneath the rubble and Israel still without a leader.[8]

A Philistine coffin made of pottery clay.

III. Ruin of the Judges (Judges 17–21)

The final chapters of Judges (chaps. 17–21) are actually an **appendix** added to the end of the book to emphasize just how bad things really were in Israel in the time of the Judges. They are not in chronological order. Religious compromise led to moral corruption that ultimately resulted in a civil war. These closing chapters reveal that morality was "upside down" during the era of the judges. Throughout this section the author emphasizes "there was no king in Israel" and chaos reigned because "everyone did whatever he wanted" (17:6; 18:1; 19:1; 21:25).

A. Idolatry (Judges 17–18)

Micah was an Israelite from Ephraim who maintained a shrine of various "household idols" (17:5) so he bribed a Levite from Bethlehem to be his own personal priest (17:13). In the meantime the tribe of Dan was migrating north, fleeing from the Philistines, when they happened upon Micah's house, stole his idols, and talked the Levite into going with them. The **apostate tribe of Dan** not only abandoned its God-given inheritance but forsook the Lord as well.[9] The Danites attacked the city of Laish and renamed it Dan (18:28–31), making it not only Israel's most northern city but also a place infamous for its pagan practices (1 Kgs 11:29).

B. Immorality (Judges 19–21)

The closing chapters of Judges tell the sad story of immorality, moral confusion, and a civil war between the tribes of Israel and the **tribe of Benjamin**. The story is about a Levite traveling with his concubine from Bethlehem to Gibeah in Benjamin. During an overnight stay at Gibeah, the concubine was raped and killed by the men of the town so the Levite dismembered her corpse in an attempt to arouse the other tribes against the Benjamites who refused to deal with the evil men of Gibeah. The end result was a brutal civil war that annihilated all but 600 men of Benjamin. Had the tribe of Benjamin been exterminated, there never would have been a King Saul, Esther, Mordecai, or the apostle Paul. The book of Judges ends leaving the reader realizing again that "there was no king in Israel" (21:25). Thus, the stage of divine revelation was set for the books that follow. Despite the dark days of the judges, a ray of hope was about to shine.

THEOLOGICAL SIGNIFICANCE

By routinely attributing Israel's depravity to the lack of a king (17:6; 18:1; 19:1; 21:25), the author showed that Israel could never fulfill her divinely intended design as long as she lived under judges. The book demonstrates that the Israelites were incapable of adhering to the law of Moses since "everyone did whatever he wanted" (21:25, author's translation). Because a judge could only partially and imperfectly administer Torah (legislative function), execute justice (executive function), and condemn lawbreakers (judicial function), a king was needed who could more effectively fulfill all three roles. The stories in Judges also show that not just any king could effectively govern the nation but rather a king who honored **God's covenant**. By tracing the various cycles of bondage and deliverance, the author shows that Israel's external condition was inextricably linked to her spiritual condition. The moral and civil disasters Israel experienced were a direct result of her spiritual disobedience. Yet, even then, when the people repented, God graciously judged the intent of their hearts and "raised up judges" to deliver them (2:16).

For Further Reading

Block, Daniel I. *Judges, Ruth*. NAC 7. Nashville: B&H, 1999.
Cundall, A. E., and Leon Morris. *Judges and Ruth*. TOTC. Downers Grove, IL: IVP, 1968.
Hindson, Edward E. "Judges." In *KJBC*. Nashville: Thomas Nelson, 1999.
Lindsey, F. Duane. "Judges." In *BKC*. Colorado Springs, CO: Chariot Victor, 1983.
Wood, Leon. *The Distressing Days of the Judges*. Grand Rapids: Zondervan, 1975.
Younger, K. Lawson. *Judges, Ruth*. NIVAC. Grand Rapids: Zondervan, 2002.

Study Questions

1. What was Israel's major struggle for survival during the era of the judges?
2. In what way does God function as the ultimate Judge?
3. How did God use Israel's enemies to get their attention to spiritual matters?
4. What were some of the unusual characteristics of the judges that God overcame in using them?
5. How did the process of religious compromise lead to moral corruption and civil catastrophe in Judges?
6. What lessons can we learn from this process in relation to our lives and our society today?

ENDNOTES

1. For a detailed discussion of the authorship questions related to the book of Judges, see R. K. Harrison, *Introduction to the Old Testament* (Grand Rapids, MI: Eerdmans, 1969), 680–94.

2. Cf. E. Hindson, "Judges," in *KJBC* (Nashville: Thomas Nelson, 1999), 225.

3. See A. R. Millard, "Canaanites," in D. J. Wiseman, ed., *Peoples of Old Testament Times* (Oxford: Clarendon Press, 1973), 29–52; and E. Anati, *Palestine Before the Hebrews* (New York: Knopf, 1963).

4. K. A. Kitchen, *Ancient Orient and Old Testament* (Downers Grove, IL: IVP, 1966), 19–64, refutes critical scholars who attempt to explain such names as mere aetiological traditions.

5. Sisera served under "Jabin . . . who reigned in Hazor" (4:2) probably a dynastic title of the ruler of a rebuilt Hazor (cf. Josh 11:1–11), although Kitchen, *Ancient Orient and Old Testament*, 68, suggests otherwise. Cf. also Y. Yadin, *Hazor* (Jerusalem: Steinmatzky, 1970).

6. See Chaim Herzog and M. Gichon, *Battles of the Bible* (New York: Random House, 1978), 54–62.

7. Those favoring the view that he actually sacrificed his daughter point to the general spiritual confusion of the time, noting that the sinful Israelites did occasionally make such sacrifices (2 Chr 28:3). They also note that this was the oldest known view among Jewish commentators. Those favoring the view that she was not actually sacrificed point to the fact that human sacrifice violated Mosaic law (Lev 18:21; 20:2–5) and that Jephthah was filled with the Spirit when he made the vow (11:29). They also point out the use of the *waw* ("and") in 11:31 is indefinite and can be translated "or," implying that he had a choice of either making a sacrifice "or" a dedicated offering.

8. For details, see Hindson, "Judges," 263–71.

9. The apostasy of Dan may be the reason it is the only tribe of Israel not named in the book of Revelation (cf. Rev 7:4–8).

Chapter 14

RUTH
Ray of Hope

The book of Ruth is one of the great love stories of all time. It is a **romantic drama** of a destitute young Moabite widow who marries a wealthy and compassionate Israelite named Boaz. Like the book of Esther, it is named for the woman who is the main character. Historically, Ruth is the "lynchpin of the covenant" and provides an essential key to the transition from the judges to the kings of Israel.[1] Theologically, the story of Ruth and Boaz illustrates the biblical concept of redemption.

In spite of her humble origin, Ruth plays an important role in the history of the Old Testament as the great grandmother of King David (Ruth 4:18) and an ancestress in the line of Jesus of Nazareth. Set in the dark days of the judges (1:1), Ruth is a **ray of light and hope** for Israel's future. As a Gentile who marries a Hebrew from Bethlehem, she pictures the love of God for both Hebrews and Gentiles. God's promise to Abraham that He would bless all nations begins to come to fruition through Boaz and Ruth, and it will eventually result in the birth of the Messiah. Indeed, the Christmas story has its beginning in Ruth's journey to Bethlehem where her personal and spiritual destiny was fulfilled.

BACKGROUND

The Hebrew title of the book is a possible Moabite modification of the Hebrew word *reuit*, meaning "friendship." Although the book is anonymous, Jewish tradition claims that Samuel was the author. Also, Dyer and Merrill suggest, "The attachment of the Book of Ruth to the Book of Judges in the twenty-two-book arrangement of the Hebrew Bible implies common authorship or compilation of the two books."[2] Others contend that the writer could not be Samuel since the book mentions David (4:17,22) and Samuel died (1 Sam 25:1) before David's inauguration (2 Samuel 2; 5). E. J. Young believes the absence of Solomon or later Judean kings in the closing genealogy indicates that the book was written no later than the time of David.[3] However, the story itself definitely occurred much earlier and reflects **archaic forms** of rustic Hebrew poetry and morphology.

View of Bethlehem with Herodium in the background.

Many argue that the book was written in the Solomonic era since the Jewish custom regarding the exchanging of the sandals had to be explained (4:7).[4] However, because Solomon is not mentioned in the concluding genealogy, it seems better to conclude that the book was written in the early part of the kingdom era before Solomon's rise to power. The main story was likely written in the period of the judges or the earliest part of the kingdom era while Saul was still ruling. If this was the case, the genealogy (4:18–22) was probably appended to the book by another inspired writer in the time of David.

The reader must grasp at least four elements in order to understand fully the message of the book of Ruth. First, the Moabites were the **descendants of Lot** (Gen 19:30–38) who lived northeast of the Dead Sea. Because they worshipped Chemosh and opposed Israel's entrance into Canaan (Numbers 22–25), they were banned from entrance into Israel's public worship assembly (Deut 23:3–6). The Moabites engaged in numerous battles with Israel throughout biblical history (Judg 3:12–30; 1 Sam 14:47; 2 Sam 8:11–12; 2 Kgs 3:4–27) so the relationship was not friendly.

Second, the **right** of **redemption** (Lev 25:25–28) gave the next of kin (Hb., *go'el*) the responsibility of buying back property that was sold because of foreclosure due to poverty. The logic of this provision was to keep the property within the family. Because of Naomi's impoverished condition upon returning from Moab, she was powerless to regain her lost Bethlehem property unless she had help from a kinsman redeemer.

Third, under the principle of **Levirate marriage** (Deut 25:5–10), the next of kin of a deceased man was to marry his widow and produce an offspring in order to prevent the deceased man's lineage and name from dying out.[5] Because Naomi was too old to reproduce a child, her daughter-in-law Ruth continued the family name by marrying the kinsman redeemer Boaz and giving birth to a son Obed.

Fourth, according to Deut 23:3, a **Moabite**, or any of his descendants up to the tenth generation, could not gain entrance into Israel's public assembly. How then could Ruth become a Jewish proselyte (1:16–17) since she was from Moab? One possible resolution is by noting that Ruth was a Moabite woman (1:22) so some hypothesize that the prohibition of Deut 23:3 applied only to Moabite men. What is more evident in the 10-generation genealogy is the affirmation of David's right to rule as king as a descendant of the illegitimate birth of Perez 10 generations earlier (cf. Deut 23:2; Gen 38:1–30).

Outline[6]

I. Love's Resolve: Ruth's Determination (Ruth 1)
II. Love's Response: Ruth's Devotion (Ruth 2)
III. Love's Request: Boaz's Decision (Ruth 3)
IV. Love's Reward: Family's Destiny (Ruth 4)

MESSAGE

The book of Ruth reads like a **four-act play**. An announcer sets the stage by explaining the background of the story. A Jewish family left Bethlehem for Moab where everything went wrong. As the curtain rises on the drama, three men have died, and three desperate women are widowed. Each chapter of the book is set in a different location: (1) the plains of Moab, (2) the fields of Bethlehem, (3) the threshing floor, (4) the city gate of Bethlehem. The drama reaches its climax with Ruth's bold proposal and Boaz's clever response to redeem the Gentile bride into the family of Israel.

In times of national infidelity, God sovereignly used the faithfulness of an **unlikely candidate** named Ruth to change the course of history. She was a female, Gentile, pagan, poverty stricken, widowed, and a Moabitess. Ruth broke with her own pagan background (Gen 19:30–38; Deut 23:3–6) to embrace the people of Israel and their God. But in spite of this, God used her to perpetuate the Davidic and messianic lineage. As a result of God's covenant promise to bless obedience (Deut 28:1–14) as well as bless all who bless Israel (Gen 12:3), God blessed Ruth by giving her a new husband, a son, and a privileged genealogical position.

I. Love's Resolve: Ruth's Determination (Ruth 1)

As the curtain rises on the drama, the first chapter describes the **journey of Elimelech's family to Moab**, which sets the stage for the rest of the story. It explains how Naomi became an impoverished widow and how Ruth attached herself to Naomi. The fact that this story took place during the era of the judges and the nation was experiencing a famine due to the pouring out of the covenant curses (1:1) reveals this general pattern of covenant unfaithfulness. This pattern is also seen in how Elimelech's family journeyed to Moab, which had a notorious background (Gen 19:30–38) and was a known oppressor of Israel (Numbers 22–25). The marriages of Mahlon and Chilion to Moabite women represented a blatant rejection of the covenant (Deut 23:3). Also, the sudden deaths of Elimelech, Mahlon ("sick"), and Chilion ("pining") may be the outworking of covenant curses imposed for disobedience (Deut 28:15–68). In other words, a Jewish reader would be shocked at the family's decision to abandon their God-given inheritance by moving to a Gentile nation.

Woman gathering grain.

However, against this negative backdrop of covenant infidelity (1:1–5) and Naomi's dire circumstances (1:6–14), the writer inserts a note of optimism and hope. He records **Ruth's positive example** of not wanting to leave Naomi's side (1:15–18). Ruth's willingness to break with her own pagan background in order to embrace the people of Israel and their God is highlighted at this point because it explains God's willingness both to use and to reward her. The positive example of Ruth ("friendship") is contrasted with the decision of Orpah ("neck, stubbornness") to return to her Moabite home and gods.

Despite receiving a warm welcome from her fellow countrymen upon returning to Bethlehem of Judah from Moab, Naomi ("pleasantness") asks that they call her *Mara* ("bitterness"). Not yet comprehending God's plan, she sees her situation as bleak since God has deprived her of her husband, sons, and property, plus her family line is on the verge of extinction. This information is included to reveal Naomi's desperate need for a **kinsman redeemer**.

Hebrew Highlight

Redeemer. Hebrew גֹּאֵל (go'el). *The* notion of *go'el* or redemption is replete throughout this book. Various forms of the Hebrew words *ga'al* ("redeem") and its derivatives are used 20 times in the book. The word *go'el* ("one who redeems" or "close relative") is found 13 times in the book, mostly in reference to Boaz, whose temporal work of redemption can be compared to Christ's eternal work of redemption. Boaz redeemed or purchased Ruth and Naomi from poverty and eradication of the family lineage, while Christ's sacrificial work on our behalf purchases us from the bondage of sin. Ruth had to trust in the work of her redeemer Boaz in order to experience blessing, and so we too must trust in Christ's redemptive work on the cross in order to experience the blessing of redemption and liberation from the consequences of sin.

II. Love's Response: Ruth's Devotion (Ruth 2)

Ruth's devotion to Naomi and her decision to forsake Moab for the people of Israel and their God allowed God to use Ruth strategically in order to further His covenant purposes. The second chapter records Ruth's **providential meeting** with her future husband and kinsman redeemer Boaz ("in him is strength"). Ruth's commitment to Naomi is seen in her desire to glean from among the grain (Lev 19:9–10) on behalf of her mother-in-law (2:1–7). "Gleaning" meant picking up the scraps as one followed the "reapers" in the harvest. The sovereign guidance of God in guiding Ruth to the field of Boaz is found in the statement "and she happened to come to the portion of the field belonging to Boaz" (2:3 NASB).

Upon learning of Ruth's identity as the Moabite who clung to Naomi, Boaz did everything within his power to assist her. For example, he instructs Ruth to remain on his property during the harvest and even blesses her with **special privileges** (2:8–17). By protecting and providing for Ruth, Boaz already sensed his special responsibility to his relative Naomi. When Ruth told Naomi of the day's happenings, Naomi recognized Boaz's identity as their redeemer and told her daughter-in-law to continue to glean from his field throughout the remainder of the barley season (2:18–23). In sum, the events of chap. 2 are included to explain how God used the commitment of Ruth to the people and faith of Israel to sovereignly guide her to a kinsman redeemer who was a Davidic ancestor.

III. Love's Request: Boaz's Decision (Ruth 3)

Chapter 3 records the steps leading to the eventual marital union between Boaz and Ruth. Naomi recognized that while she was too poor to buy back her Bethlehem property and too old to have children to perpetuate her family's name, Boaz as the kinsman redeemer could rectify both of these situations by marrying her daughter-in-law Ruth. Because Boaz took no further steps in this regard, Naomi hatched a plan whereby Ruth would **propose marriage**. This plan involved Ruth's sleeping at Boaz's feet and uncovering them, thereby symbolically communicating her interest in marriage (3:1–5).[7]

Ruth's devotion to Naomi is further verified through her willingness to execute this plan (3:6–13). This series of events gives the writer further opportunity to highlight Ruth's spirituality by recording Boaz's comments extolling **Ruth's virtuous character** (3:10–11). The author wants the reader to understand that because of Ruth's decision to embrace the people of Israel and their God, He will use Ruth not only for the short-term purpose of bringing fullness to Naomi's life but also for the long-term purpose of completing the Davidic and messianic lineage. The revelation of a **nearer kinsman** having a first right of refusal and Boaz's age (perhaps 20 years her senior) may explain his initial hesitation. But he expressed his joy at her request ("May the LORD bless you, my daughter" (3:10) and signified his intent by giving grain to Ruth to take back to her mother-in-law. Upon returning to Naomi, she counseled her daughter-in-law to have patience as she waited to see if Boaz would act as her kinsman redeemer (3:14–18). Older and wiser, Naomi assured Ruth that Boaz "won't rest unless he resolves this today" (3:18).

IV. Love's Reward: Family's Destiny (Ruth 4)

The marriage between Boaz and Ruth is finalized in the book's fourth chapter. The chapter begins with the nearest kinsman's decision not to marry Ruth (4:1–7). Boaz invited the kinsman to sit with him and the other elders in the city gate to transact business. Upon recognizing that his responsibility would include not only buying back Naomi's property but also marrying Naomi's foreign daughter-in-law Ruth, the **nearest kinsman declined** to exercise his rights and duties as kinsman redeemer. He was concerned that taking on this new responsibility would somehow jeopardize his own family inheritance. The nearest kinsman's decision to relinquish his claim over Naomi's estate and Ruth was then finalized through the symbolic gesture of the removal of his sandal (4:6–7).

The nearest kinsman's decision not to exercise his rights freed Boaz to become Ruth's husband. This marriage reversed the prior emptiness Ruth had experienced due to the death of her husband Mahlon. The fact that this marriage would be significant for purposes of perpetuating an important lineage is alluded to through the witnesses' utterance of a blessing upon the new couple. Here they prayed that the newlyweds would be prolific like Rachel and Leah who begat Israel's tribes. **Obed's birth** reversed Naomi's prior emptiness and bitterness as she was given the fulfilling position of acting as the child's nurse. Through Ruth and Boaz Elimelech's lineage was perpetuated. According to 4:17, Obed's birth also preserved the line that led to David. Since Ruth had replaced Naomi's bitterness and emptiness with fullness, Naomi's neighbors appropriately proclaimed that Ruth was worth more to Naomi than seven sons.

Since Boaz was not only the kinsman redeemer but also the one carrying the **Davidic lineage**, Ruth's marriage to Boaz permanently enshrined her in both David's and the Messiah's genealogy. As a female, Gentile, pagan, poverty stricken, and formerly widowed Moabitess, Ruth was unqualified for such a position, but God's grace (Hb. *hen*) brought her into the family of Israel. Interestingly, Ruth is not the only unqualified person mentioned in this genealogy. Perez (4:18) was also the product of the incestuous union between Judah and Tamar (Gen 38:1–30). Salmon, the son of Rahab the harlot (Matt 1:5), is also mentioned in the genealogy (4:20). In each case God's grace was extended to a Gentile woman, indicating His desire to bring the blessing of Abraham to all people—Hebrews and Gentiles alike.

Kinsman Redeemer

Under the requirement of redemption of the land, the closest relative of the deceased was obligated to buy back the deceased's property if it was lost due to poverty or foreclosure so that it could remain within the family (Lev 25:25–28). Under the requirement of **Levirate marriage**, the closest relative of the deceased was also to marry the deceased's wife so that the name of the deceased would not die out (Deut 25:5–10). This meant the husband's family was responsible for his widowed wife's care. Some of Boaz's actions can be compared to Christ's. The kinsman redeemer was to be the next of kin to qualify to perform the work of redemption (Deut 25:5,7–10; Ruth 2:20). Christ became a member of the human race to qualify to become humanity's redeemer (John 1:1,14; Rom 1:2; Gal 4:4; Phil 2:5–8; 1 Tim 2:15; Heb 2:14,16–17; 10:51). The kinsman redeemer had to have the means to pay the purchase price for the land (Ruth 2:1); Christ also paid the expensive price associated with redeeming lost humanity (1 Cor 6:20; 1 Pet 1:18–19). And just as Boaz was willing to be the redeemer (Ruth 3:11), Christ was similarly willing to redeem humanity (Matt 20:28; Mark 10:45; John 10:15–18; Heb 10:7; 1 John 3:16). Just as Boaz took Ruth as a Gentile bride whom he financially enriched, Christ also took a Gentile bride (the church) that He spiritually enriches.

THEOLOGICAL SIGNIFICANCE

Several important theological themes recur throughout the book of Ruth. One dominant theme is *hesed*, which means "loving-kindness" or "covenant loyalty." It is used in regard to both God (1:8; 2:20) and Ruth (3:10). The book deals with **God's faithfulness** to His own covenants. God's faithfulness to the seed of the Abrahamic covenant (Gen 15:4–5) is evidenced through the preservation of the Davidic and messianic lines (4:18–22). God's promise to bless the Gentiles (Gen 12:3) is seen in

His blessing of Ruth the Moabitess. The curses for disobedience associated with the Mosaic covenant (Deut 28:15–68) are seen in the famine Israel was experiencing at the time. However, the blessing for obedience associated with the Mosaic covenant (Deut 28:1–14) is seen in the way God blessed Ruth for honoring His covenant people.

Second, **God's sovereignty** is displayed throughout the book (1:6; 2:3,12; 4:6,13). God is seen working behind the scenes in furtherance of His covenant purposes in the dark era of the judges. God responds to the prayers of His people. Petitions of blessing are recorded from Naomi (1:9; 2:19–20), Boaz (2:4; 3:10), and the people of Israel (2:4; 4:11–12,14–15). The book also demonstrates God's grace as He not only blesses Ruth who was a citizen of Israel's foreign enemy, but He also allows Boaz to become the kinsman redeemer although he was not the closest relative (3:12).

One of the unique characteristics of Ruth is the **redeemer motif** which appears more than 20 times in the book. The redeemer (Hb. *Go'el*) needed to be a relative who could potentially redeem (*ga'al*) a family member from slavery, widowhood, or being orphaned. The story of redemption in Ruth presents the clearest example of how this concept was carried out in ancient Hebrew culture. It provides a beautiful picture of God's redeeming a Gentile bride as an act of love and grace.

For Further Reading

Block, Daniel I. *Judges, Ruth.* NAC 6. Nashville: B&H, 1999.
Cundall, A. E., and Leon Morris. *Judges and Ruth.* TOTC. Downers Grove, IL: IVP, 1968.
Hindson, Edward E. "Ruth." In *KJBC.* Nashville: Thomas Nelson, 1999.
Hubbard, R. L. *The Book of Ruth.* NICOT. Grand Rapids: Eerdmans, 1988.
Reed, John W. "Ruth." In *BKC.* Colorado Springs: CO: Chariot Victor, 1983.
Younger, K. L. *Judges, Ruth.* NIVAC. Grand Rapids: Zondervan, 2002.

Study Questions

1. Why did Naomi ("pleasant") insist on being called Mara ("bitter")?
2. How did Boaz show grace (favor) to Ruth?
3. What advice did Naomi give Ruth regarding Boaz?
4. What is the significance of the 10-generation genealogy at the end of the book?
5. How does Boaz's role as kinsman redeemer prefigure Christ's relationship to believers today?
6. How does God's providential provision for Ruth encourage you to trust God with your future?

ENDNOTES

1. Andrew E. Hill and John H. Walton, *A Survey of the Old Testament*, 3rd ed. (Grand Rapids: Zondervan, 2009), 250.

2. Charles H. Dyer and Eugene H. Merrill, *Old Testament Explorer*, Swindoll Leadership Library, ed. Charles R. Swindoll and Roy B. Zuck (Nashville: Word Publishing, 2001), 197.

3. E. J. Young, *Introduction to the Old Testament* (Grand Rapids: Eerdmans, 1960), 358.

4. John W. Reed, "Ruth," in *BKC*, ed. John F. Walvoord and Roy B. Zuck (Colorado Springs: CO: Chariot Victor, 1983), 415.

5 See detailed discussion in Donald Leggett, *The Levirate and Goel Institutions in the Old Testament with Special Attention to the Book of Ruth* (Cherry Hill, NJ: Mack Publishing, 1974).

6. Based on Norman L. Geisler, *A Popular Survey of the Old Testament* (Grand Rapids: Baker, 1996), 108.

7. In biblical times a position at someone's feet represented a place of submission (Josh 10:24–25; Ps 110:1). In this context such submission implies the submission associated with the marital relationship. Furthermore, the request for coverage (3:9) represented a request for security (Ezek 16:8). Once again this context indicates that this request was actually a petition for the security of marriage. J. Carl Laney, *Answers to Tough Questions: A Survey of Problem Passages and Issues from Every Book of the Bible* (Grand Rapids: Kregel, 1997), 68.

Chapter 15

1–2 SAMUEL
Kings and Prophets

The books of 1–2 Samuel form the **transition** from the era of the judges to that of the kings. They introduce a series of contrasts between good and evil judges and kings and their interaction with the prophets of God. As 1 Samuel opens, the era of the judges is still in the forefront, but it is fading fast. Gone are the military heroes of the previous book. The leadership of Israel rests upon the undisciplined and elderly Eli, the high priest of the tabernacle at Shiloh and one of the last of the minor judges (1 Sam 4:18). Throughout the early chapters of 1 Samuel, the author draws a sharp contrast between Eli and his ungodly sons and the godly prophet Samuel. By the middle of the book (chaps. 15–16), the same kind of contrast is drawn between Saul and David, Israel's first kings.

In 2 Samuel, the narrative shifts to the **reign of David** as he rises above Saul's son Ish-bosheth to become the king, first of Judah and then of all the tribes of Israel (5:1–4). The book records David's wars of conquest including the capture of Jerusalem and the relocation of the ark of the covenant to the City of David (chap. 6). But the author also records David's failures: his adultery with Bathsheba (chap. 11), Absalom's rebellion (chaps. 15–18), Sheba's revolt (chap. 20), and the disastrous census (chap. 24). Like all the prophetic writers, the author presents a portrait of his historical figures as they are analyzed from the perspective of their faithfulness to God's covenant.

The name *Samuel* means "the name of God," "His name is God," or "asked of God." The Massoretes originally considered both 1 and 2 Samuel as one book. The LXX calls 1–2 Samuel and 1–2 Kings "First, Second, Third, and Fourth Kingdoms." The content of each of the books is generally the same as 1–2 Samuel and 1–2 Kings. Each of these books was included in the section of the "**Former Prophets**" in the Hebrew Bible because it was believed that they were written by the prophets, whereas 1–2 Chronicles was placed in the "writings" (*kethuvim*) because they were written by priests.

The books of 1–2 Samuel are **anonymous** works. They were most likely named in honor of Samuel who authored other works (1 Sam 10:25; 1 Chr 29:29) and was the head of a group of prophets (1 Sam 10:5; 19:20). However, Samuel could not be the author of all of the books' contents since the book records his death (1 Sam 25:1) and events after his death (2 Sam 1–24). *Baba Bathra* 15a asserts that the prophets Nathan and Gad wrote the rest of the material (cf. 1 Chr 29:29). These books were probably written circa 960 BC after the death of David in 971 BC and during the reign of Solomon (cf. 2 Chr 9:29).[1]

BACKGROUND

The dates of the reigns of **Israel's three kings** of the united kingdom must be kept in mind when determining the scope of 1–2 Samuel. Saul reigned from around 1051 to 1011 BC (Acts 13:21). David reigned from 1011 to 971 BC (2 Sam 2:11; 5:4–5). Solomon reigned from 971 to 931 BC (1 Kgs 11:42). Moreover, 1 Samuel begins where the judgeship of Samson left off (Judg 16:31). Thus, 1 Samuel begins with the

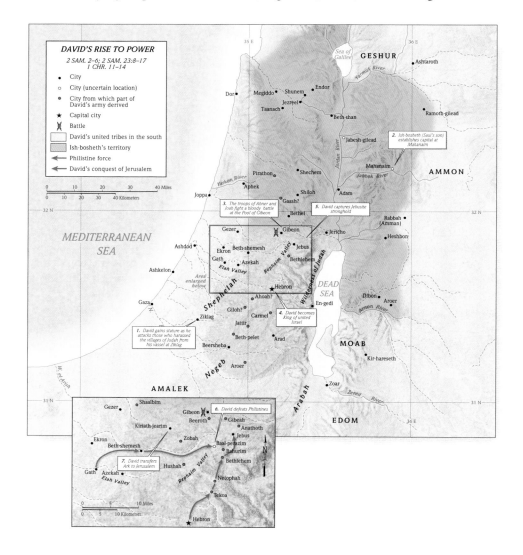

birth of Samuel and extends until Saul's death. Because Samuel, who was born around the same time as Samson, had sons who were old enough to be judges before the reign of Saul (8:1–4), Samuel's birth could be around 1121 BC.[2] Thus, 1 Samuel covers the 110 year period of time between the birth of Samuel (1121 BC) and the death of Saul (1011 BC). Second Samuel covers the 40 years of David's reign (1011–971 BC).

Most of the major world empires (Egypt, Assyria, Babylon) were in a state of weakness during this time. The **Philistines** were the major enemies oppressing Israel when the events of 1 Samuel transpired. Known as the "Sea Peoples," the Philistines migrated across the Mediterranean in massive numbers during the time of the judges, taking the coastal plains during this time and pushing Israel into the hill country.[3] Due to their monopoly on the use of iron (1 Sam 13:19–22), the Philistines enjoyed a strategic advantage over Israel. The Philistines' aggressive military behavior during this time made Israel long for a king who would fight their battles for them (1 Samuel 8).

OUTLINE

First and Second Samuel follow a **fourfold structure**. First, the house of Samuel is exalted while the house of priest-judge Eli is abased (chaps. 1–7). Second, the book records the conflicts in the Samuel and Saul narrative (chaps. 8–15). Third, the struggle between David and Saul is recorded (chaps. 16–31). Fourth, 2 Samuel records the reign of David. First Samuel 1–7 records the decline of the theocratic administration under the judges. Chapters 8–31 record the rise of the theocratic administration under the monarchy. In this last section Samuel represents the final judge, the "kingmaker" of Israel's first two kings. Second Samuel 1–24 records the reign of King David.

Outline

   I. Transition from Eli to Samuel (1 Samuel 1–7)
      A. Samuel's Birth (1 Samuel 1:1–2:10)
      B. Samuel Contrasted with Eli (1 Samuel 2:11–3:21)
      C. Soldiers Take the Ark of the Covenant (1 Samuel 4:1–7:2)
      D. Samuel's Judgeship (1 Samuel 7:3–17)
  II. Samuel and Saul Narrative (1 Samuel 8–15)
      A. Saul's Selection (1 Samuel 8–11)
      B. Samuel's Warning (1 Samuel 12)
      C. Saul's Rejection (1 Samuel 13–15)
 III. Transition from Saul to David (1 Samuel 16–31)
      A. Anointed by Samuel (1 Samuel 16–17)
      B. Attacked by Saul (1 Samuel 18–31)
 IV. Reign of David (2 Samuel 1–24)
      A. David's Faith (2 Samuel 1–10)
      B. David's Faults (2 Samuel 11–12)
      C. David's Foes (2 Samuel 13–20)
      D. David's Fame (2 Samuel 21–24)

MESSAGE

In 1 Samuel, God transitions His covenanted nation away from the failing theocratic administration under the tribal judges and toward the theocratic administration through the united monarchy. By showing the deficiencies of the final phase of the judges' era (1–7), 1 Samuel is an **apologetic for the new monarchy**, which God graciously establishes for His people in spite of their sin. The book also highlights the inferiority of Saul in comparison to David (16–31) whose rule was yet to be inaugurated. The promises to David anticipate the coming of David's greater son who will rule in perfect obedience to God's covenant (Gen 49:10; Deut 17:14–20; 2 Sam 7:12–16; Ps 89:36–37; Isa 7:14; 9:6–7). Therefore, 1 Samuel is the first biblical book in the English Bible to use the term "anointed one" or *messiah* (2:10).

Hebrew Highlight

Anointed. Hebrew מָשִׁיחַ (*mashiach*). The Hebrew word m*ashiach* is translated "anointed one" or "messiah." First Samuel 2:10 represents one of the early biblical references to this term. The word *mashiach* is used in reference to those who were specially **empowered by God's Spirit** to accomplish a significant task. For example, the word *mashiach* was applied to patriarchs (Ps 105:15), priests (Lev 4:3,5,16), and Hebrew (2 Sam 1:14,16; 22:51) as well as Gentile kings (Isa 45:1). The Old Testament ritual of anointing a person with oil was used to recognize their calling to a special task. Thus, prophets (1 Kgs 19:16), priests (Exod 29:7), and kings (2 Sam 1:14) were "anointed." Eventually *mashiach* was used in reference to the coming Messiah (Ps 2:2; Dan 9:25–26). The Greek counterpart of this Hebrew name is *christos*. This title was applied to Jesus as "the Christ" in recognition of His special task of delivering His people from their sin and ultimately ushering in the long-awaited kingdom (Matt 16:16–17; Rom 1:1; 3:24). The title *christos* carried over into the church age as those who belong to Jesus were later called "Christians" (Acts 11:26).

The message of 1–2 Samuel also highlights the **role of the prophets** in relation to the kings. Samuel and Nathan confront the sins of Saul and David and call them to repentance (1 Samuel 13; 15; 2 Samuel 12). Whereas Saul makes excuses for his mistakes, David genuinely repents saying, "I have sinned." These stories set the stage for future accounts of prophets (e.g., Elijah, Elisha, Isaiah, Jeremiah) confronting the errant kings of Israel and Judah.

I. Transition from Eli to Samuel (1 Samuel 1–7)

God used Samuel to anoint Israel's first two kings thereby transitioning the nation away from the judges' era and into the monarchy. Thus, the writer shows the **preeminence of Samuel** over the existing regime as represented by the household of judge-priest Eli. The writer shows this preeminence in the first three chapters where he highlights the interchange between Samuel and the house of Eli.

A. Samuel's Birth (1 Samuel 1:1–2:10)

The spirituality of Samuel's lineage is seen in **Hannah's prayer** for a child after being provoked by her rival (1:1–8), her vow to dedicate her child to the Lord (1:9–18), the providential birth of the child (1:19–23), her faithfulness to her vow (1:24–28), and her praise to God (2:1–10). Thus, Hannah's praise to God emphasizes the sovereignty of God as well as His promotion of those whose hearts are right before Him (cf. Luke 1:46–55). Chapter 2 focuses on the wickedness of Eli's sons, Hophni and Phinehas, emphasizing the spiritual failure of this judge and his sons.

B. Samuel Contrasted with Eli (1 Samuel 2:11–3:21)

The third chapter begins by mentioning the **rarity of visions** in those days (3:1) presumably due to the general failure of the judges and the wickedness of Eli's household. God was not speaking because no one was listening. Consequently, instead of revealing His plans to the existing judge-priest Eli, God discloses His plans to the boy Samuel. The tender picture of God standing at the foot of his bed and calling the child by name shows the compassion of God for one person and His rejection of another. The message to Samuel was that God will bypass a disobedient generation and call a new generation to follow Him. God reveals that He will destroy Eli's household (3:12–14) and confirms Samuel as the divine spokesperson (3:17–21).

Shiloh, about 30 miles north of Jerusalem, was Israel's religious center for over a century, after the conquest of Israel.

C. Soldiers Take the Ark of the Covenant (1 Samuel 4:1–7:2)

The next major section of the book records the **journeys of the ark** (chaps. 4–7). The author includes this to demonstrate the superiority of God and shows that Israel's oppressed status had nothing to do with any failure on God's part. Rather it was due to Israel's own covenant disobedience. The book's fourth chapter discusses Israel's loss of the ark and the resulting consequences (4:1b–22). Israel's defeat by the Philistines soldiers (4:1–4) and the loss of the ark ushered in the destruction of Eli's household, thereby fulfilling the predictions of Samuel (4:11–22). Not only did Eli die (4:18), but so did his sons (4:11b) and his daughter-in-law while she was giving birth to Ichabod ("no glory") (4:19–22). For the Israelites, losing the ark meant a total disconnection from God's presence and the mosaic covenant.[4] But the loss was only temporary, for soon the Philistines returned the ark (6:1–16) because God severely punished the Philistines and their god Dagan while the ark was in Philistine territory (5:1–12). In the meantime God was raising up Samuel in the midst of the vacuum created by the destruction of Eli's household.

D. Samuel's Judgeship (1 Samuel 7:3–17)

The failure of the judges' era is illustrated in the rebellious ways of Eli and his sons, which are set in contrast to the **successful judgeship** of Samuel (7:3–17). Samuel successfully led the people spiritually in the covenant renewal ceremony at Mizpah (7:3–6). He also successfully led the people politically by gaining victory over the Philistines (7:7–14). The chapter concludes by noting the various cities included in Samuel's circuit (7:15–17). Because all of these cities are located in the territory of Benjamin and since Saul was also from Benjamin, their inclusion links this larger unit involving Israel's final days under the judges (chaps. 1–7) to the following Samuel and Saul narrative (chaps. 8–15).

II. Samuel and Saul Narrative (1 Samuel 8–15)

The writer's emphasis on the failure of the judges' era in the book's first seven chapters shows the **necessity of the coming monarchy**. The failure of even Samuel's sons shows the inadequacy of divine rule through the family of judges (8:1–5). However, 1 Samuel is not simply an apology for the monarchy. It is more specifically an apology for the kingship of David and his dynastic successors by showing that God will only rule in the era of the monarchy through an elect, obedient king. The writer communicates this point by recording the disastrous kingship of Saul (chaps. 8–15).

A. Saul's Selection (1 Samuel 8–11)

As Samuel aged, the people of Israel insisted they select a king "like all the other nations" (8:5, author's translation). The events surrounding the selection of Saul for king (9:1–10:16) demonstrate that he was the **people's choice**, more than God's choice for a king. The people seemed to focus on Saul's outward appearance (9:2) rather than his heart (16:7). Even the events of Saul's coronation (10:17–27) reveal God's displeasure. Samuel indicated that the people had rejected God (10:19) in requesting a king.

However, Saul's resounding victory over Nahash the Ammonite who threatened to gouge out the eyes of the people of Jabesh-gilead solidified Saul's authority as Israel's first king in the eyes of the people. Thus, the nation rallied around their new leader at Gilgal (chap. 11).

B. Samuel's Warning (1 Samuel 12)

Samuel's subsequent warning against national covenant unfaithfulness (chap. 12) demonstrated that God's vision for Israel's king was vastly different from the vision the people espoused. **Samuel's warning** accompanied by thunder and rain threatened the wheat harvest. In great fear the people cried out: "We have added to all our sins the evil of requesting a king for ourselves" (12:19). Thus, the author skillfully shows that Israel's request for a king was ill motivated and ill timed. Saul was from the tribe of Benjamin, not Judah, the promised messianic tribe (Gen 49:10). God's timing was also awaiting a descendant from the tenth generation of Judah's son Perez (cf. Ruth 4:18–22), but the people did not yet understand this.

C. Saul's Rejection (1 Samuel 13–15)

Despite Saul's strong beginning (chap. 11) and being warned by Samuel to honor the Mosaic covenant (chap. 12), Saul's poor choices caused his kingdom to **deteriorate rapidly** (chaps. 13–15). For example, his usurpation of priestly functions while awaiting Samuel to offer the sacrifices at Gilgal before the battle with the Philistines (chap. 13) caused God to vow that He would remove the kingdom from Saul (13:14; 16:7). In addition, Saul's desire for vengeance against the Philistines, coupled with his insensitivity toward the physical needs of his men, caused him to make a rash vow that

Valley of Elah where David killed the Philistine, Goliath.

almost cost the life of his own son Jonathan (chap. 14). Finally, Saul's disobedience (chap. 15) in following the divine command of exterminating the Amalekites (Exod 17:8–16) caused Yahweh to reject him as king (15:23). Samuel's confrontation with Saul over his sin (chaps. 13, 15) emphasizes the ministry of the prophet as a covenant enforcer.

III. Transition from Saul to David (1 Samuel 16–31)

This theme of David's election over Saul is the dominant theme in the book's final and longest section (16–31), known as the **David and Saul narrative**. It describes a transition from the house of Saul to the house of David, indicating David's superior character in contrast to Saul's inferior character.

A. Anointed by Samuel (1 Samuel 16–17)

The events surrounding David's selection and anointing (16:1–13) make clear that he was **God's choice** to become the next king of Israel. As a Bethlehemite (16:1), David was from the tribe of Judah and, therefore, in line with the messianic promise. Samuel's anointing of David, as well as the Spirit's empowerment of him (16:13), made clear that David represented God's choice as king. In contrast to David, the Spirit departed from Saul, and demonic forces oppressed him.

God's selection of David receives further confirmation through David's resounding **victory over Goliath** of Gath in the valley of Elah (17). In contrast to Saul, who began his tenure as king hiding by the baggage (10:22), David left his own baggage to take on Goliath (17:22). In fact, David's boldness in contrast to Saul's fear is brought out routinely in this chapter. That God brought the victory through David rather than through Saul is evidenced by the fact that David refused to use Saul's armor (17:38–40). David rises to the Philistine's challenge of a "battle by champions" by separating himself from Saul, standing alone with God and winning a dramatic victory because he believed that "the battle is the LORD's" (17:47).

B. Attacked by Saul (1 Samuel 18–31)

This section begins with a description of the friendship and covenant between David and Jonathan (18:1–5). This friendship is significant since God will later use Jonathan to protect His elect king from Saul's pursuit. The chapter records the upward ascent of David and the **downward spiral** of Saul (18:6–16). While David's popularity accelerates (18:7), Saul is depicted as jealous, demonically tormented, and capable of murdering David. Despite Saul's attempt to have him killed in battle, David enjoyed military success, the acclaim of the people, and the loyalty of two

View of the tel of ancient Gath, home of Goliath the Philistine, and where David fled from Saul's relentless pursuit.

members of Saul's own family, Jonathan and his sister Michal, whom David eventually married (18:17–30). As Saul's jealous and murderous rage intensified (19:6), God supernaturally protected David through the work of Jonathan (19:1–10; 20) and Michal (19:11–17), Saul's own children.

The next several chapters record **David's exile** (chaps. 21–30). God continued to protect and bless David since he represents the elected king destined for the throne. These narratives also emphasize the contrast between his character and that of Saul. The theme of preservation is evident as David continues to escape Saul's pursuit of him in the wilderness of Judah near the Dead Sea caves (22:1–2; 24:1–3). David's character is also highlighted as he refuses to kill Saul, showing his respect for the office of king and the significance of God's anointing. This is especially seen in the incident at the cave of En Gedi when David humiliates Saul but refuses to kill him. As a consequence Saul acknowledges that one day David will be king (24:20).

Samuel's death (25:1) reminds the reader that a prominent character from the old era has passed, but before long another leader of Israel would follow. Saul's debased character became even more transparent through his consultation with the witch at Endor (chap. 28). Not only was this action a hypocritical violation against Saul's own national ban prohibiting mediums, but it also constituted a gross covenant violation (Leviticus 18; Deut 18:9–14). The need to seek the guidance of such a medium furnished another sign of God's rejection of Saul because the Lord would no longer speak to him directly (28:15). Another confirmation that David was God's choice as the future king of Israel happened when the revived Samuel promised that the kingdom would be torn away from Saul and given to David (28:17).

The hills around En Gedi where David hid from Saul.

The final two chapters (chaps. 30–31) form an **epilogue** by paving the way for David's future position of authority as Israel's king. God's favor upon the elect heir is evident through his preservation in the wilderness (30:11–12) as well as through his ability to recover everything the Amalekites stole from Ziklag. Whereas God no longer spoke to Saul, the Lord continued to speak to David (30:8). Tragically for Saul, David was driven away by the king's own paranoia, and he was not present to assist him in his final and disastrous battle with the Philistines at Mount Gilboa. This battle resulted in Israel's defeat, Saul's wounding and suicide, and Jonathan's death (chap. 31).

IV. Reign of David (2 Samuel 1–24)

The book of 2 Samuel follows a **fourfold division**. The first section exemplifies David's triumphs (chaps. 1–10). The second section emphasizes David's transgression (chaps. 11–12). The third section highlights David's troubles (chaps. 13–20). The fourth section represents six nonchronological appendices dealing with the greatness of the Davidic covenant and kingdom (chaps. 21–24).

A. David's Faith (2 Samuel 1–10)

The book's first 10 chapters begin by emphasizing David's political victories. They describe how David, the elect king, consolidates and unifies the entire nation under his authority. The high point of David's triumphs in this unit is the reception of

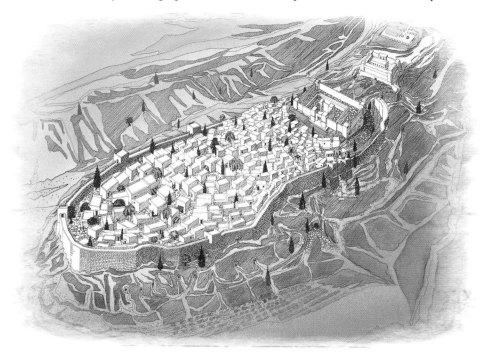

Reconstruction of David's Jerusalem.

the **Davidic covenant** (chap. 7). The covenant's unconditional nature and conditional blessing (7:14) sets the tone for the remainder of the book.

After receiving word concerning **Saul's death** (1:1–10), David disposed of the man who took credit for killing Saul (1:11–16). David is presented in a positive light as one who is still concerned with proper treatment of the Lord's anointed (1 Samuel 24; 26). Because of this concern, David lamented the deaths of Saul and Jonathan (1:17–27). Eventually, David was anointed king of Judah at Hebron at age 30 (2:1–4). In the meantime Saul's son Ish-bosheth was raised to power over the 10 northern tribes of Israel (2:8–10), but he was eventually assassinated by two of his own men, whom David later executed for their evil deed (4:1–12). Afterward, the elders of the northern tribes came to Hebron and anointed David king over all Israel (5:1–4).

Further evidences of David's upward political ascent include his **capture of Jerusalem** from the Jebusites (5:7–10; Judg 1:8,21), his alliance with Hiram, king of Tyre (5:11–12), his many children which were a sign of covenant blessing (5:13–16), his defeat of the Philistines (5:17–25), and his decision to move the ark of the covenant to Jerusalem (chap. 6). This is followed by the confirmation of the Davidic covenant (chap. 7) and David's military victories over Philistia, Moab, Zobah, Aram, and Edom (chap. 8). Thus, David extended Israel's borders from Egypt to the Euphrates in partial fulfillment of what was originally promised to Abraham (Gen 15:18). David established justice and righteousness, installed trusted public officials, and incorporated foreign territories into the land of Israel. As vassals these nations had to pay tribute to the Israelite government. During this prosperous season in David's life, the Lord helped David with victory wherever he went (8:6,14).

The Davidic Covenant

David achieved spiritual victory by receiving the Davidic covenant (2 Samuel 7; Psalm 89). Although David wanted to build a house (temple) for God, God instead promised to build a house (dynasty) for David. In this covenant God **unconditionally promised** David fame (7:9), land (7:10), rest (7:11), seed (7:12), a kingdom (7:13), a throne (7:13), a house (7:16), and the eternality of all these promises (7:16). Christ is most clearly predicted in 1–2 Samuel through the giving of the Davidic covenant (2 Samuel 7). The same three promises of an eternal kingdom, throne, and seed are later given to Christ (Luke 1:32–33). The promise of a permanent dynasty is fulfilled in Christ, the "son of David" (Matt 21:9; 22:45), who will sit upon the throne of David (see Isa 9:7; Luke 1:32). Unlike the other Davidic kings, only Christ will perfectly fulfill the covenant's righteous requirements and bring the true kingdom of heaven to earth in His millennial reign.

B. David's Faults (2 Samuel 11–12)

David's **covenant violations** take place in the book's pivotal eleventh chapter. They involve adultery (11:1–3) and murder (11:14–27) as well as a host of deceptive acts committed in an attempt to cover up these sins. The incident involving Bathsheba occurred while David remained in the palace and the troops were fighting across the Jordan against the Ammonites (11:1–3). Having been attracted by Bathsheba's beauty, David sent for her, slept with her, and she became pregnant. Attempting to cover this up, David made arrangements for her husband's death and then married her.

God sent the **prophet Nathan** to confront David's sin with the judicial parable about the rich man who stole a poor man's sheep (12:1–4). Infuriated by the story, David unwittingly pronounced judgment upon himself and his household. Nathan announced that David was the rich man and that God's judgment would fall on David's household. This meant that the child born out of wedlock would die (12:15–22), as would David's sons Amnon (13:28–33) and Absalom (18:14–15). As a result of Absalom's rebellion, David's concubines would be kidnapped. But worse than all, David's sins caused his enemies to blaspheme the Lord. The subsequent birth of Solomon ("peace"), also called Jedidiah ("loved by the Lord"), to David and Bathsheba indicated that David's sins had not nullified what was promised to him in the covenant. Although David suffered the consequences of his sins, his genuine repentance (see Psalm 51) brought God's forgiveness and restoration.

C. David's Foes (2 Samuel 13–20)

The next section (chaps 13–20) describes the **outworking of the curses** that Nathan predicted would come upon David and his family. It depicts both trouble in David's immediate family (chaps. 13–18) and trouble within the nation (chaps. 19–20). Tamar's rape by her half brother Amnon and his execution by her brother Absalom eventually led to Absalom's ill-fated rebellion and death. Nevertheless, in spite of all of the covenant discipline that was inflicted upon David and his family, God was faithful to preserve the Davidic dynasty and fulfill His original promises to David.

The Davidic covenant's **unconditional nature** allowed David to believe that in spite of Absalom's rebellion he would eventually be returned to the throne. Thus, David instructed Zadok to return the ark to Jerusalem instead of having it accompany him into exile (15:25). David's optimism is also seen in how he expressed confidence that the curses uttered against him by Shimei would one day be turned into blessing (16:12). David's restoration finally came after the failed revolts of Absalom (chaps. 16–18) and Sheba (chaps. 19–20).

D. David's Fame (2 Samuel 21–24)

The author concludes with six nonchronological **appendixes** extolling the preeminence of the Davidic covenant (chaps. 21–24). Each appendix brings out a different facet of David's covenant obedience. He vindicated the Gibeonites against whom Saul had sinned (21:1–9), properly buried the bones of Saul and Jonathan (21:10–14), defeated the Philistines (21:19–22), sang a song of thanksgiving (chap. 22), and gave his farewell words expressing his confidence in the "everlasting covenant" (23:1–7). The author concludes with a list of David's warriors (23:8–39), the military census, and resulting plague, which stopped at the threshing floor of Araunah in Jerusalem (24:1–17). David obeyed God in purchasing the threshing floor "set up an altar to the LORD," and on this site Solomon would later build the temple (24:18–25). Thus, the book ends with Israel strategically positioned to build the temple during Solomon's reign.

THEOLOGICAL SIGNIFICANCE

Numerous theological themes recur throughout 1–2 Samuel to support the basic teachings of **covenant fidelity**. The sovereignty of God is displayed as God unilaterally transitions from one form of theocracy to the next and raises a lowly shepherd to the pinnacle of power. Robert Bergen observes that Samuel's "narrative tapestry is woven around the theological threads of the Torah," which he lists as: covenant, land, divine presence, and obedience to God.[5] The books of 1–2 Samuel also explain the offices of both the prophet and the king and their interconnection with each other. The prophet rises above judges, priests, and kings as the spokesman for God. The "seer" (*roeh*) becomes the "prophet" (*nabi*) who sees what is in the mind of God and announces it to the people of God, calling them to repentance and faith. From the end of the era of the judges to the beginning of the era of the kings, the author makes clear that the Lord Yahweh alone is the ultimate king of Israel (1 Sam 8:6–7). Thus, human kings will only prosper as they obey Him and keep His covenant.

For Further Reading

Arnold, Bill. *1 and 2 Samuel*. NIVAC. Grand Rapids: Zondervan, 2003.
Bergen, Robert. *1, 2 Samuel*. NAC 7. Nashville: B&H, 1996.
Gordon, Robert. *I and II Samuel: A Commentary*. Grand Rapids: Zondervan, 1986.
Merrill, Eugene H. "1 and 2 Samuel." In *BKC*. Colorado Springs, CO: Chariot Victor, 1983, 431–82.
Vannoy, J. Robert. *1–2 Samuel*. CBC. Carol Stream, IL: Tyndale House, 2009.
Youngblood, Ronald F. "1, 2 Samuel." In *EBC*. Grand Rapids: Zondervan, 1992.

Study Questions

1. In what way did Samuel represent the transition from the judges to the kings?
2. Why was Israel's initial request for a king wrongly motivated?
3. What are some of the obvious contrasts between Saul and David?
4. How does the Davidic covenant point to its ultimate fulfillment in Jesus Christ?
5. What lessons can we learn from 1–2 Samuel about the importance of obedience to God's Word?

ENDNOTES

1. Cf. Ronald F. Youngblood, "1, 2 Samuel," in *EBC* (Grand Rapids: Zondervan, 1992), 3:554; Eugene H. Merrill, "1 and 2 Samuel," in *BKC* (Colorado Springs, CO: Chariot Victor, 1983), 431.

2. E. H. Merrill, *Kingdom of Priests* (Grand Rapids: Baker, 1987), 149, dates the birth of Samuel to 1121. On p. 179 he dates the birth of Samson to 1123 BC.

3. E. E. Hindson, *The Philistines and the Old Testament* (Grand Rapids: Baker, 1972); T. Dothan, *The Philistines and Their Material Culture* (Jerusalem: Israel Exploration Society, 1983).

4. See details in Marten Woudstra, *The Ark of the Covenant from Conquest to Kingship* (Philadelphia: P&R, 1965).

5. Robert Bergen, *1, 2 Samuel*, NAC 7 (Nashville: B&H, 1996), 43.

Chapter 16

1–2 KINGS
Kings of Israel and Judah

The books of 1 and 2 Kings tell the story of the kings of Israel (northern kingdom) and Judah (southern kingdom) from the time of David until the Babylonian captivity some 400 years later. Written from the **perspective of the prophets**, the book of Kings (Hb. *melakim*) was undoubtedly one book in its original form. Patterson and Austel observe, "Thematically the continuity of Elijah narrative (1 Kings 17–2 Kings 2), itself part of the prophetic section dominating 1 Kgs 16:29–2 Kgs 9:37, and the recurring phrase 'to this day' (1 Kgs 8:8; 9:13; 10:12; 2 Kgs 2:22; 10:27; 14:7; 16:6; 17:23,34,41; 21:15) clearly indicate that the two books of Kings form a single literary unit."[1]

Although the book is an anonymous work, several pieces of evidence point to **Jeremiah** as the book's author or final editor. First, Jewish tradition (*Baba Bathra* 15a) cites Jeremiah as the author. Second, similarities of style can be detected between the books of Jeremiah and Kings (Jeremiah 40–44; 52; 2 Kgs 24:18–25:30). Third, both books speak of God's righteous judgment upon apostasy, idolatry, and immorality. Fourth, because the phrase "to this day" is used repeatedly throughout the book (1 Kgs 8:8; 9:13; 10:12; 12:19; 2 Kgs 2:22; 10:27; 14:7; 16:6; 17:23,34,41; 21:15), the book was obviously written prior to the Babylonian exile and therefore would fit the general time period of Jeremiah's ministry, with the exception of the reference to the release of Jehoiachin (2 Kgs 25:27–30), which was probably added in 560 BC after Jeremiah's death.

The book of Kings makes use of several theological and historical **source materials**. Examples include Solomon's proverbs (1 Kgs 4:32), official court records (2 Kgs 18:18), Isaiah 36–39 (2 Kings 18–20), the Book of the Acts of Solomon (1 Kgs 11:41), the Book of the Chronicles of the Kings of Israel (14:19; 15:31; 16:5,14,20,27), and the Book of the Chronicles of the Kings of Judah (14:29; 15:7,23; 22:45). Jeremiah probably would have had access to these records since he descended from the priestly line of Abiathar. Since Jeremiah used Baruch as his scribe (Jer 36:4), it is also possible that Baruch helped compile and complete this inspired record.

BACKGROUND

If Jeremiah wrote his book throughout his ministry, then the **intended recipients** would be the people of Judah before the exile in 586 BC and afterward. Since the final form of the book was completed after 560 BC, Jeremiah's prophecy (see Dan 9:1–3) and this book were written for the benefit of the Jews of the Babylonian captivity and the dispersion. Throughout the prophet's history of the kings of Israel and Judah, numerous references to foreign powers are interwoven in the account. Egypt, Syria, Assyria, and Babylon play major roles in Israel's history.

Because the book begins with the end of David's reign and the beginning of Solomon's reign (971 BC) and ends with the release of Jehoiachin (560 BC), the book's events transpired over a **411-year period**. Key events that transpired within this time period include David's death, Solomon's inauguration (971 BC), Solomon's death, Rehoboam's enthronement, the division of the kingdom (931 BC), Jehu's accession and purge of both the northern and southern kingdoms (841 BC), the Assyrian captivity (722 BC), Sennacherib's threatening of Hezekiah resulting in God judging Assyria (701 BC), and the three deportations to Babylon (605, 597, 586 BC).

The book of Kings follows a **threefold structure**. The first part consists of the united kingdom under Solomon (1 Kings 1–11). These events take place between 971 and 931 BC. The second part consists of the divided kingdom from the time of the north-south division until the Assyrian dispersion of the northern kingdom (1 Kings 12–2 Kings 17). This tragic historical period unfolded between 931 and 722 BC. The third part consists of the remaining years of the southern kingdom of Judah, from the time of the Assyrian dispersion until the Babylonian conquest (2 Kings 18–25). This section of Kings reports key events between 722 and 586 BC.

KINGS OF ISRAEL[2]				
King	Scripture	Years of reign	Dates of reign (Thiele)[3]	Prophet
Jeroboam I	1 Kgs 11:26–14:20	22	931–910	Ahijah
Nadab	1 Kgs 15:25–28	2	910–909	
Baasha	1 Kgs 15:27–16:7	24	909–886	Jehu
Elah	1 Kgs 16:6–14	2	886–885	
Zimri	1 Kgs 6:9–20	7 days	885	
Omri	1 Kgs 6:15–28	12	885–874	
Ahab	1 Kgs 16:28–22:40	22	874–853	Elijah, Elisha
Ahaziah	1 Kgs 22:40–2 Kgs 1:18	2	853–852	Elijah, Elisha
Joram	2 Kgs 1:17–9:26	12	852–841	Elisha
Jehu	2 Kgs 9:1–10:36	28	841–814	Elisha
Jehoahaz	2 Kgs 13:1–9	17	814–798	Elisha

KINGS OF ISRAEL[2] (Continued)				
King	Scripture	Years of reign	Dates of reign (Thiele)[3]	Prophet
Jehoash	2 Kgs 13:10–14:16	16	798–782	Elisha
Jeroboam II	2 Kgs 14:23–29	41	793–753	Jonah, Amos
Zechariah	2 Kgs 14:29–15:12	6 months	753–752	Hosea
Shallum	2 Kgs 15:10–15	1 months	752	Hosea
Menahem	2 Kgs 15:14–22	10	752–742	Hosea
Pekahiah	2 Kgs 15:22–26	2	742–740	Hosea
Pekah	2 Kgs 15:25–31	20	752–732	Hosea, Obed
Hoshea	2 Kgs 15:30–17:6	9	732–722	Hosea

KINGS OF JUDAH[4]				
King	Scripture	Years of reign	Dates of reign (Thiele)	Prophet
Rehoboam	1 Kgs 11:42–14:31	17	931–913	Shemiah
Abijam	1 Kgs 14:31–15:8	3	913–911	Iddo
Asa	1 Kgs 15:8–24	41	911–870	Azariah
Jehoshaphat	1 Kgs 22:41–50	25	870–848	Jahaziel
Jehoram	2 Kgs 8:16–24	8	848–841	Obadiah
Ahaziah	2 Kgs 8:24–9:29	1	841	
Athlaiah	2 Kgs 11:1–20	6	841–835	
Joash	2 Kgs 11:1–12:21	40	835–796	Joel
Amaziah	2 Kgs 14:1–20	29	796–767	Unnamed prophets
Uzziah	2 Kgs 14:21; 15:1–7	52	767–740	Isaiah
Jotham	2 Kgs 15:32–38	16	740–732	Isaiah, Micah
Ahaz	2 Kgs 16:1–20	16	732–716	Isaiah, Micah
Hezekiah	2 Kgs 18:1–20:21	29	716–687	Isaiah, Micah
Manasseh	2 Kgs 21:1–18	55	687–642	Nahum
Amon	2 Kgs 21:19–26	2	642–640	

KINGS OF JUDAH[4] (Continued)				
King	Scripture	Years of reign	Dates of reign (Thiele)	Prophet
Josiah	2 Kgs 21:26–23:30	31	640–608	Jeremiah, Zephaniah, Huldah
Jehoahaz	2 Kgs 23:30–33	3 months	608	Jeremiah
Jehoiakim	2 Kgs 23:34–24:5	11	608–597	Jeremiah, Habakkuk, Daniel
Jehoiachin	2 Kgs 24:6–16; 25:27–30	3 months	597	Jeremiah, Daniel
Zedekiah	2 Kgs 24:17–25:7	11	597–586	Jeremiah, Daniel, Ezekiel

Problems remain concerning how to fit all of the kings of the divided era into the time frame from (931–586 BC) and how to **synchronize** the reigns of the kings of Judah and the kings of Israel. Edwin Thiele has proposed resolving these problems by acknowledging various methods used by the northern and southern kingdoms to calculate accession years and co-regencies for the various kings.[5]

The book of Kings refers to many surrounding **foreign nations** and their rulers who are well attested in various extrabiblical historical references. These are captured on the following chart.[6]

REALM	RULER	REFERENCE
Egyptian	Unnamed Pharaoh	1 Kgs 3:1
	Shishak [945–924]	1 Kgs 11:40
	So or Osorkon [726–715]	2 Kgs 17:4
	Neco [609–594]	2 Kgs 23:29–35
Arameans	Rezon [940–915]	1 Kgs 11:23–25; 15:18
	Tabrimmon [915–900]	1 Kgs 15:18
	Ben-Hadad I [900–860]	1 Kgs 15:18,20
	Ben-Hadad II [860–841]	1 Kings 20
	Hazael [841–806]	2 Kgs 8:15
	Ben-Hadad III [806–770]	2 Kgs 13:3
	Rezin [750–732]	2 Kgs 15:37
Phoenicians	Ethbaal [874–853]	1 Kgs 16:31

REALM	RULER	REFERENCE
Edomites	Hadad [?]	1 Kgs 11:14–22
Moabites	Mesha [853–841]	2 Kgs 3:4ff.
Assyrians	Tiglath-pileser III [745–727]	2 Kgs 15:19–22
	Shalmaneser V [727–722]	2 Kgs 17:3–6
	Sargon II [721–705]	Isa 20:1; 2 Kgs 18:17
	Sennacherib [704–681]	2 Kings 18–19
Babylonians	Merodach-baladan II [703]	2 Kgs 20:12–13
	Nebuchadnezzar [604–562]	2 Kings 24–25
	Evil-Merodach [562–560]	2 Kgs 25:27–30

Outline

I. United Kingdom under Solomon (1 Kings 1–11)
II. The Divided Kingdom: Until the Assyrian Invasion (1 Kings 12–2 Kings 17)
III. The Southern Kingdom: Until the Babylonian Captivity (2 Kings 18–25)

The tripartite building at Megiddo, a building dating from the period of King Solomon, 970–930 BC.

MESSAGE

The kings, as the nation's representatives, are evaluated from a **covenant perspective** by the prophetic author. Thus, the book traces the glory of the United Kingdom under Solomon, its eventual division, and how the kings of the divided kingdoms led the people into increasing apostasy and idolatry culminating in the Assyrian and Babylonian captivities. Despite this downward pattern, the writer also makes clear that God has a glorious future in store for Judah on account of her elect status. These truths are recorded so that the exiles, in light of their history, would be encouraged and repent of their sin (1 Kgs 8:33–34) so God could restore them back to the Promised Land.

"The kingdom was established in First Samuel and consolidated in Second Samuel. First Kings records its division and decline, and Second Kings its destruction and deterioration."[7] Although the book of Kings represents a single book, it is still likely that the writer composed the different parts of the book, known as 1 and 2 Kings, with different purposes based on the **themes** emphasized in each section. These contrasting themes are represented on the following chart.[8]

1 KINGS	2 KINGS
Opens with David, king of Israel	Closes with Nebuchadnezzar, King of Babylon
Solomon's glory	Zedekiah's shame
The temple built and consecrated	The temple violated and destroyed
Begins with blessing for obedience	Ends with judgment for disobedience
The growth of apostasy	The consequences of apostasy
The united kingdom is divided	The two kingdoms destroyed
Kings' failure	Consequences of the failure of the kings
Elijah predominant	Elisha predominant
The Lord's patience	The Lord's judgment
Concludes with a note of despair	Conclusion with a note of hope

The book of Kings represents the outworking of both covenant discipline and God's unconditional covenant promises to Judah. The book mentions several prophets thereby explaining how the **ministry of the prophets** began to develop in the era of the kings. The book also shows how the kings functioned as the people's representatives. Thus, their covenant rebellion negatively impacted the entire nation and was consistently confronted by God's true prophets.

Each king is identified with a consistent formula which includes an introduction (name, age at accession, and patriarchal or matriarchal reference), accession, covenant evaluation, historical record, capital city (Jerusalem or Samaria), and concluding reference (death, burial, duration of reign, and successor). By contrast, the prophets generally appear on the scene without formal introduction in times of national crises.

I. United Kingdom under Solomon (1 Kings 1–11)

In the book of Kings, the various kings of the nation are evaluated by the Mosaic (Deuteronomy 28) and Davidic (2 Sam 7:14–16) covenants so that the exiles will learn from this history and be deterred from future covenant disobedience. The book's first major section (chaps. 1–11) puts Solomon under **covenant inspection** and begins by explaining the transfer of the kingdom from David to Solomon (1:1–2:12).

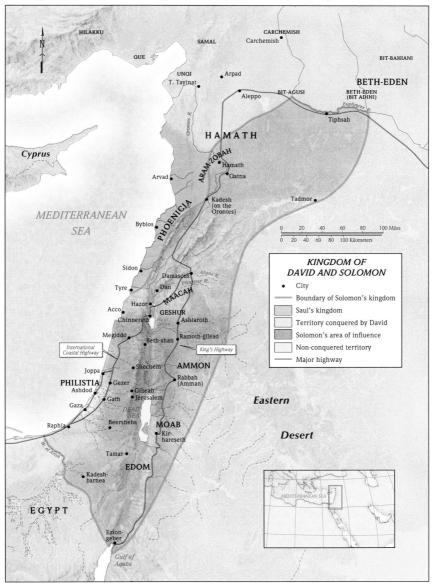

Solomon began on the right track as he followed David's exhortation and purged the nation of those who posed a threat to Solomon's power and the covenant (2:13–46). Solomon's **covenant obedience** led to his successful consolidation of the nation, "So the kingdom was established in Solomon's hand" (2:46b). Solomon's blessings for his covenant obedience included wisdom (chap. 3) and prosperity (chap. 4), resulting in international fame (4:34). So prosperous was Solomon that God expanded Israel's borders to the degree originally promised in the Abrahamic covenant (4:21; Gen 15:18–21) and reaffirmed to Joshua (Josh 1:3–4).

Because the temple represented the presence of God among His people, the pinnacle of Solomon's career was his **construction and dedication of the temple** (chaps. 5–8). This section shows that covenant obedience invites God's presence. This conveys to the exiles that similar covenant obedience on their part will return God's presence to their nation. However, because the nation will later experience idolatry and destruction despite the presence of the temple, this theme is also included to rectify a misconception among the exiles that the temple would act as a "good luck charm" warding off covenant curses in spite of national covenant disobedience.

Solomon prepared to build the temple (chap. 5) by contracting with Hiram, the king of Tyre, for building materials (5:1–12), workers, and administrators needed to accomplish this all-important task (5:13–18). Following these preparations, Solomon oversaw the construction of the temple from the fourth to the eleventh years of his reign (chaps. 6–7). The connection between Solomon's covenant obedience and the **presence of God** is brought out clearly in the dedication of the temple (chap. 8). God's glory residing on the ark of the covenant in the Most Holy Place assured the people of Israel that God was with them.

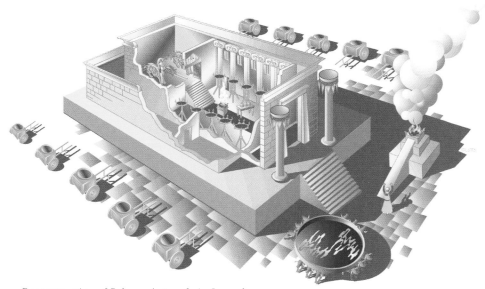

Reconstruction of Solomon's temple in Jerusalem.

Unfortunately, Solomon lost most of God's blessings in the duration of one short chapter due to **covenant disobedience** (chap. 11). This transitional chapter is included to explain to the exiles that covenant curses follow covenant rebellion. Solomon's proliferation of wives (11:1–8) turned him away from wholeheartedly following the Lord. The disintegration of Solomon's empire was immediately felt as those Solomon once ruled over began to break away (11:14–40).

II. The Divided Kingdom: Until the Assyrian Invasion (1 Kings 12–2 Kings 17)

This section begins with the **division of the kingdom** (12:1–24). Rehoboam listened to the inexperienced advice of the younger men, rather than the older men, concerning Jeroboam's request for tax relief. This rash decision alienated Jeroboam and the 10 northern tribes, thereby causing them to secede from Judah, rejecting the Holy City, the temple, and the Davidic line. In order to further draw the connection between the north's eventual defeat at the hands of the Assyrians in 722 BC and her covenant violations, the writer calls attention to Jeroboam's wicked rule over Israel (12:25–14:20). Most problematic was his creation of an alternative system of worship in an attempt to prevent northerners from returning to the Jerusalem temple. He also introduced golden calf worship and appointed non-Levitical priests, thus leading the northern kingdom into apostasy from Dan to Bethel.

The writer mentions the reigns of a series of **wicked northern rulers** (15:25–16:28) leading up to Ahab (16:29–34), skillfully using each of these reigns to solidify, in the minds of the exilic readers, the connection between covenant disobedience and covenant curses. The major focus of the next section is on the wicked practices of King Ahab and his Phoenician wife Jezebel (chaps. 16–22). The writer notes how Ahab's marriage to Jezebel encouraged him toward promoting Baal worship throughout the north, Baalism in a rival temple in Samaria, and the construction of numerous other centers of paganism throughout Israel.

The inclusion of the **Elijah narratives** (1 Kings 17–2 Kgs 2:11) is designed to express the courage of the prophets and expose the evil of the northern kings. These chapters demonstrate just how evil the kings of the north were. Second, they show the callousness of the nation since Elijah's miraculous ministry proved insufficient in returning the nation to covenant faithfulness. They also serve as a polemic revealing the supremacy of Yahweh over Baal in the confrontation between Elijah, the lone prophet of God, and the 450 prophets of Baal on Mount Carmel (chap. 18).

The **polemical nature** of the Elijah narratives is evident in the following contrasts: although Baal claimed the ability to control the rain, God demonstrated His supremacy over Baal as Elijah, whose name means "Yahweh is God," commanded a drought (17:1–7). While Baal guaranteed agricultural productivity, God demonstrated His supremacy as the true giver of grain and oil (17:8–16). While Baal claimed jurisdiction over life and death, Yahweh showed His supremacy by raising the dead (17:17–24). While Baal claimed to control lightning and fire, God again showed His supremacy as Elijah called fire from heaven (18:1–40). While Baal as the storm god claimed the ability to control the rain, God again demonstrated His supremacy over Baal as Elijah prayed for an end to the drought (18:41–46).[9]

The book of 1 Kings next records the **call of Elisha** to succeed Elijah as Israel's next great prophet (19:16–21). In the closing chapters the young prophet is trained to take over the spiritual leadership of Israel at a time when the kings no longer follow the Lord. First Kings ends with a comparison of the reigns of Jehoshaphat in the south and Ahaziah in the north (22:41–53). Jehoshaphat was the second of Judah's eight good kings. He removed idolatry, developed the trading industry, expelled the Sodomites, and made peace with the northern kingdom. However, he was only a partial reformer (22:43) because his major blunder was to make an alliance with Ahab (22:41–50). In contrast to Jehoshaphat's partially good reign in the south, Ahaziah's reign in the

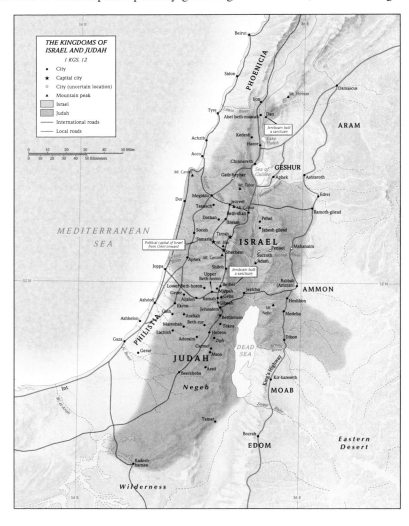

north was completely wicked as he followed in the wicked footsteps of his father Ahab (22:51–53).

The book of 2 Kings begins in the midst of Ahaziah's reign and continues the theme of covenant curses upon those who rejected the true worship of Yahweh. Second Kings then transitions away from the Elijah narratives (1 Kgs 17:1–2 Kings 1) and into the **Elisha narratives** (2 Kgs 2:1–8:15). The transition is made through Elijah's giving Elisha the double portion of the Spirit and Elijah's rapture into heaven in a chariot of fire (2:1–18). The inauguration of Elisha's ministry (2:19–25) continued to show Yahweh's supremacy over Baal. Elisha purified the bitter water at Jericho making it drinkable and brought about the defeat of Mesha, king of Moab, through his miraculous provision of water in the desert of Edom. Altogether the text refers to Elisha performing twice as many miracles as Elijah. Though less spectacular by some standards, these miracles were effective in demonstrating Yahweh's supremacy over life, death, and agricultural productivity (4:1–6:7).

The miraculous healing of leprous **Naaman** of Aram (Syria) shows Yahweh's supremacy and grace to all people, even those outside the covenant community. The story of Naaman is also included as a point of contrast to the rebellious northern kingdom. While Israel failed to respond to Elisha's miraculous ministry, a Gentile did respond to the suggestion of a young Hebrew girl by doing what seemed foolish (5:13). He was so spiritually receptive that he even wanted to erect an altar in his own country in order to worship Yahweh there. His reaction stands in contrast to Gehazi, Elisha's Hebrew servant, who sought to profit from this miracle. Consequently, Gehazi became white as snow with leprosy while Naaman was healed of leprosy.

A potential bright spot emerges in the north through the **reign of Jehu** (chaps. 9–10).[10] After he is anointed as king by Elisha (9:1–10) and accepted as king by his peers (9:11–13), he proceeds to fulfill numerous of Elijah's prophecies by killing Jehoram of Israel, Ahaziah of Judah, and Jezebel (9:14–37). Jehu also kills Ahab's 70 sons and Ahaziah's 42 relatives (10:1–14). Then Jehu aligned himself with Jehonadab who completed the eradication of Ahab's house (10:15–17). Jehu also eradicated all of Israel's Baal worshippers (10:18–28). However, these improvements only represented partial reforms since Jehu permitted some false religion in the land of Israel (10:29–31). Because of this covenant violation, the nation suffered the covenant consequence of the gradual occupation of the Transjordan territories by Israel's hostile neighbors (10:32–36).

The reign of **Jeroboam II** in the north (14:23–29) imitated the same sinful pattern as Jeroboam I (14:24). However, his reign experienced territorial expansion into areas consistent with what was spoken through the prophet Jonah (14:25). Such expansion was something God unilaterally brought to pass due to the unconditional promises given in the Abrahamic covenant (14:27). Thus, the wicked behavior of Jeroboam II could not cancel the Abrahamic covenant, but it also could not bring God's continued blessing on the nation. The northern kingdom lasted as long as it did solely because of God's grace and His honoring of the Abrahamic covenant and not because of covenant fidelity on the part of Israel's kings.

The brief rule of the other kings from the north mentioned in the following chapters is also included to illustrate the familiar principle that **covenant disobedience** leads to discipline. Zechariah's disobedience led to his assassination at the hands of Shallum (10:30; 15:8–12). Because of Shallum's covenant violation of assassinating Zechariah, he in turn was assassinated by Menahem (15:10–15). Due to Menahem's wickedness associated with his brutality and the promotion of idolatry, he suffered the penalty of having to pay tribute to the Assyrian king Pul or Tiglath-pileser III (2 Kgs 15:19–20). This all set the stage for the final Assyrian deportation in 722 BC.

The writer again highlights covenant consequences in the reign of **Hoshea**, who was **Israel's last king** (17:1–6). When Hoshea refused to pay tribute to the Assyrian king Shalmaneser V and instead opted to seek refuge with So (Osorkon), the king of Egypt, Shalmaneser V invaded Israel and attacked Samaria. At some point in the three-year siege of Samaria, Shalmaneser died, so his son Sargon II completed the conquest of Israel in 722 BC and deported the people to Halah and Habor on the Gozan River and in some cities of the Medes.

To help his readers understand the fate of the northern kingdom, the writer provides three reasons for the **north's downfall** (17:7–17): (1) They followed other gods (17:7–12). (2) They rejected the ministries of the prophets who sought to enforce the covenant (17:13–14). (3) They rejected the covenant itself (17:15–17). The end result was the Assyrian captivity (17:18). Sadly, Judah failed to learn from the consequences suffered from the northern kingdom since she too would experience captivity at the hands of the Babylonians in 586 BC (17:19–23).

After the deportation the Hebrews remaining in the land were mixed in with deportees from other nations who were moved into the northern region to establish an **Assyrian colony**. Some Hebrew priests were forced to teach alongside unbelieving teachers who taught the new immigrants the Assyrians brought into the land. Thus, a syncretistic form of Judaism emerged pulling the people in the former land of Israel even farther away from the covenant. The writer includes this information with the hope that his audience will not embrace such syncretism so they can be restored to a place of covenant blessing (17:24–41).

III. Southern Kingdom: Until the Babylonian Captivity (2 Kings 18–25)

The third and final major section in the book depicts **Judah's final days** as the remaining Hebrew kingdom (chaps. 18–25). This section also shows the exiles how Judah's rebellion led to her captivity. It would also encourage the exiles by reminding them of God's grace since the southern kingdom lasted 140 years beyond the northern kingdom's destruction.

The **reforms of Hezekiah** (18:1–12) allow him to be categorized as one of Judah's best kings. When Assyria under Sennacherib invaded Judah (18:13–37), God miraculously spared Judah (chap. 19) on the basis of what He had promised in the Davidic covenant (19:34). This victory was a major turning point in Judah's survival. While the northern kingdom had fallen to Assyria in 722 BC, Judah survived the Assyrian threat in 701 BC and enjoyed nearly a century of divine protection until the Babylonian invasion in 605 BC.

Unfortunately, **Manasseh's reign** (21:1–18) was so wicked and violent that he sealed Judah's fate. Thus, his reign caused God to predict inevitable judgment and captivity. Therefore, the exiles should suffer from no misconceptions concerning why the events of 586 BC transpired. Amon governed like Manasseh (21:19–26); and as a result of his covenant rebellion, he experienced the consequences of assassination by some conspirators.

Josiah represents the last godly king of Judah (chaps. 22–23). Josiah began his reign with an extensive temple renovation (22:1–7), which allowed him to discover a copy of the neglected law of Moses (22:8–20). The fact that the law was not readily accessible prior to Josiah's day reveals how neglectful Judah was during the reign of Manasseh. The rediscovery of the covenant law caused Josiah to lead the nation in covenant renewal (23:1–3) and reform (23:4–25). However, because Judah's covenant rebellion had already gone too far, these reforms were too little and too late to avert inevitable judgment (22:14–20; 23:26–27). In fact, Josiah's premature death at the hands of Pharaoh Neco foreshadows such imminent judgment (23:28–30). The writer includes the reign of Josiah to explain to his readers why conditions in Judah deteriorated so quickly after Josiah's death.

The history of the southern kingdom concludes with the reigns of **Josiah's sons**, who illustrate that covenant rebellion brings unavoidable covenant discipline. Jehoahaz was imprisoned by Pharaoh Neco, and Judah was subjected to paying a tribute to the Egyptian king (23:31–33). Because of Jehoiakim's (23:34–24:7) covenant violations (23:37), bands of Chaldeans, Arameans, Moabites, and Ammonites came against him (24:2). As a consequence, Judah became a vassal of Babylon resulting in the first deportation in 605 BC. Because of Jehoiachin's covenant violations (24:8–16), the second deportation to Babylon in 597 BC transpired (24:10). Finally, Zedekiah (24:17–25:7) rebelled against Babylon and rejected the warnings of the prophet Jeremiah. As a result, Babylon launched its final siege against Jerusalem. Zedekiah was personally captured, deported, imprisoned, and blinded after trying to escape from King Nebuchadnezzar of Babylon.

The closing verses record the **destruction of Jerusalem** in 586 BC (25:8–17), the third deportation (25:18–21), and a brief description about the life of those who remained in Judah under their puppet governor Gedeliah (25:22–26). However, by recording King Jehoiachin's release from prison and exaltation in the thirty-seventh year of the exile (25:27–30), the book ends on a note of optimism that God will still fulfill the Davidic covenant. The future is kept alive by God's divine intervention to spare the Davidic line, thus maintaining the promise of the messianic hope. As a whole, the book of Kings evaluates the nation's royal representatives from a covenant perspective. These evaluative criteria are embedded in each narrative as it traces the story from the glory of the united kingdom under Solomon, its eventual division, and how the kings of the divided kingdom led the people into increasing idolatry culminating in the Assyrian and Babylonian captivities. Despite this downward pattern, from time to time the writer makes clear that God still has a glorious future in store for Judah because of God's covenant promises to the people of Israel.

THEOLOGICAL SIGNIFICANCE

The history of Israel's kings is recorded and explained from the **prophetic perspective**. The author continually notes the interaction between the prophets and the kings. When the kings listen to the message of God's servants the prophets, they make the right decisions and experience the blessings of God. When the leaders reject the prophet's inspired message, the entire nation suffers. Thus, everything ultimately rises or falls spiritually, socially, militarily, and politically because of leadership. As God's anointed leaders, the kings are held accountable to maintain the standards of God's covenant. Failure to do so ultimately brought the curses of the covenant on both Israel and Judah (Deut 28:15–68).

For Further Reading

Constable, Thomas L. "1 Kings" and "2 Kings." In *BKC*. Colorado Springs, CO: Chariot Victor, 1983.

House, Paul, R. *1, 2 Kings*. NAC 8. Nashville: B&H, 1995.

Patterson, R. D., and Hermann J. Austel. "1 & 2 Kings." In *EBC*. Grand Rapids: Zondervan, 1988.

Thiele, Edwin R. *Chronology of the Hebrew Kings*. Grand Rapids: Zondervan, 1977.

Wiseman, Donald J. *First and Second Kings*. TOTC. Downers Grove, IL: IVP, 1993.

Wood, Leon. *Israel's United Monarchy*. Grand Rapids: Baker, 1979.

Study Questions

1. How does 1–2 Kings express the perspective of the prophets in dealing with the kings of Israel and Judah?
2. What was King Solomon's crowning achievement?
3. How did God use Elijah and Elisha in the lives of the kings?
4. Why did God allow Assyria and Babylon to conquer Israel and Judah?
5. What lessons can we learn about the use and abuse of power and authority from these stories?

ENDNOTES

1. R. D. Patterson and Hermann J. Austel, "1 & 2 Kings," in *EBC (NIV): 1 & 2 Kings, 1 & 2 Chronicles, Ezra, Nehemiah, Esther, Job*, ed. F. E. Gaebelein (Grand Rapids: Zondervan, 1988), 4:4. The Latin Vulgate title, "Third and Fourth Kings," is followed in most Roman Catholic versions.

2. Chart by Andrew Woods.

3. Edwin R. Thiele, *Chronology of the Hebrew Kings* (Grand Rapids: Zondervan, 1977).

4. Chart by Andrew Woods.

5. Edwin R. Thiele, "Chronology of the Last Kings of Judah," *Journal of Near Eastern Studies* 3 (1944): 137–286; idem, *Chronology of the Hebrew Kings*.

6. Based on chart in Andrew E. Hill and John H. Walton, *A Survey of the Old Testament* (Grand Rapids: Zondervan, 1991), 205.

7. Bruce Wilkinson and Kenneth Boa, *Talk Thru the Bible* (Nashville: Thomas Nelson, 2002), 94.

8. Ibid., 94. Copyright ©2002 Thomas Nelson. Reprinted by permission. All rights reserved.

9. See Leah Bronner, *The Stories of Elijah and Elisha as Polemics Against Baal Worship* (Leiden: E. J. Brill, 1968).

10. Shalmaneser III of Assyria (859–824 BC) erected a monument known as the Black Obelisk (see p. 35) on which he recorded his various military victories. The monument portrays Jehu paying tribute to Shalmaneser III. This obelisk is useful in dating Jehu's accession and the duration of his reign (843–841 BC). *Nelson's Complete Book of Bible Maps and Charts* (Nashville: Thomas Nelson, 1996), 131–32.

Chapter 17

1–2 CHRONICLES
Priestly Perspective

The books of 1–2 Chronicles tell the story of Israel's history in a **parallel account** to the books of 1–2 Samuel and 1–2 Kings. While many of the details are similar, the chronicler includes specific items that were especially of interest to the priestly community. His major focus is the temple, its worship leaders, and religious services.

The Hebrew title is *Divre Hayyamim*, which means "the words of the days." This phrase is like saying an account of the events of the times. This title was adopted since it communicates the book's content: the events which happened in the days of the Davidic kings of Judah. The LXX entitles the book *paraleipomenon*, which means "of things omitted." Thus, the LXX title suggests the erroneous notion that Chronicles exists for the purpose of filling in missing details not found in Samuel or Kings.[1] Jerome's Latin Vulgate entitles the book *Chronicorum Liber* or "the Book of Chronicles." Thus, the English title "Chronicles" was first introduced by the Vulgate. Through the use of this title, Jerome was referring to "a chronicle of the whole divine history."[2]

Because Chronicles is an **anonymous work**, most scholars refer to the author as "the Chronicler." Most also agree that both books were written by the same author on account of tradition as well as commonality in style, flavor, viewpoint, themes, and literary patterns. Tradition supports the notion that Ezra and Nehemiah were the book's authors. According to the Babylonian Talmud, "Ezra wrote the book that bears his name [that is, Ezra-Nehemiah] and the genealogies of the Book of Chronicles up to his own time. . . . Who then finished it [the book of Chronicles]? Nehemiah the son of Hachaliah (*Baba Bathra* 15a)."[3] The writer displays the style and interest of a Levitical scribe. The writer consistently acknowledges his sources, focuses on the temple priesthood, and traces the line of David through Judah. Such a description fits Ezra who was also a Levitical scribe (Ezra 7:1–6).

Both the books of Chronicles and Ezra focus on items that are significant from a **priestly perspective**. These items include genealogical lists, rituals, obedience to the law, temple worship, and the priesthood. The emphasis on the restoration of temple worship not only dominates Chronicles, but it also dominates the first half of Ezra. Interestingly, the opening and conclusion of the two books are nearly identical (2 Chr 36:22–23; Ezra 1:1–3a). According to the Apocryphal book of 2 Maccabees, Nehemiah compiled a library with the sources necessary for his contemporary Ezra to compose Chronicles (2 Macc 2:13–15).[4]

BACKGROUND

Chronicles covers the **history of the world** from a Jewish perspective. It was written after 538 BC since it concludes with Cyrus's first year and his first decree after conquering Babylon (2 Chr 36:22–23). If Ezra is the book's primary author, then it cannot be written after 445 BC since that is the date of the last recorded event of his life (Neh 8:1–12). If tradition is accurate and Nehemiah is a contributing author, then the book was not written after 432 BC since this is the date of the last recorded event of his life (Neh 13:6). However, Zerubbabel's genealogy pushes the book even later since it records individuals who must have lived well into postexilic times (1 Chr 3:17–24); therefore, the final version may date as late as 400 BC.[5]

The recipients of the book were without a Davidic king and currently under **Persian domination**. Questions in their minds would no doubt be whether God was going to fulfill the Davidic covenant and if they still were connected to this covenant? Furthermore, these beleaguered returnees saw their own rebuilt temple as paltry in comparison to the former grandeur of Solomon's temple (Ezra 3:12; Hag 2:3). Thus, they were in desperate need of encouragement after the 70 years of captivity had expired.[6]

Outline

I. Genealogies: From Adam to Zerubbabel (1 Chronicles 1–9)
   A. Adam to Jacob (1 Chronicles 1)
   B. Judah to Zerubbabel's Grandsons (1 Chronicles 2–3)
   C. The Twelve Tribes (1 Chronicles 4–9)
II. David's Reign: Preparation for the Temple (1 Chronicles 10–29)
   A. David's Ascension (1 Chronicles 10–12)
   B. David Brings the Ark to Jerusalem (1 Chronicles 13–16)
   C. Davidic Covenant (1 Chronicles 17–20)
   D. David's Temple Preparations (1 Chronicles 21–29)
III. Solomon's Reign: Building the Temple (2 Chronicles 1–9)
   A. Solomon's Wisdom (2 Chronicles 1)
   B. Solomon's Temple (2 Chronicles 2–7)
   C. Solomon's Prosperous Reign (2 Chronicles 8–9)
IV. Judah's Kings: Apostasy and Decline (2 Chronicles 10–36)
   A. Division of the Kingdom (2 Chronicles 10–13)
   B. Kings of Judah (2 Chronicles 14–36)

MESSAGE

In order to exhort the Jewish returnees to unite and resume temple worship, the writer reminds them of their genealogical connection with God's past purposes in general and with the Davidic covenant in particular (1 Chronicles 1–9). To this end the writer also features David's priority of pursuing temple worship (1 Chronicles 10–29), Solomon's priority in building the temple (2 Chronicles 1–9), and the revivals and reforms of those southern kings who pursued true worship of God as well as the apostasy of those southern kings who did not (2 Chronicles 10–36). Rather than continuing the history begun in Samuel and Kings, the author of Chronicles writes a **parallel history** to reveal the primacy of national worship. The distinctive purposes behind Samuel and Kings in comparison to the purposes behind Chronicles are captured on the following chart.[7]

SAMUEL AND KINGS	CHRONICLES
Divided kingdom	Southern kingdom only
Political history	Religious history
Prophetic authorship	Priestly authorship
Prophetical perspective	Levitical perspective
Moral concerns	Spiritual concerns
Written soon after the events	Written long after the events
Negative view	Positive view
Covenant rebellion and judgment	Hope for the future
Man's failings	God's faithfulness
Kings and prophets	Temple and priests
Throne	Temple
Inclusion of kings' sins	Omission of kings' sins
Disobedience	Revival and reform
Many wars	Fewer wars
National history	Davidic line
Classified with the Former Prophets	Classified with the writings
Excludes genealogies	Includes genealogies

I. Genealogies: From Adam to Zerubbabel (1 Chronicles 1–9)

In the book's first major section (chaps. 1–9), the writer establishes the genealogical ancestry of the returnees to stimulate them toward resuming faithful worship in the rebuilt temple. He shows the returnees their genealogical connection to **God's redemptive purposes** in general and the Davidic covenant in particular. Knowledge of their Davidic lineage would have encouraged the returnees since they may have questioned their relationship to the Davidic Covenant because they had no present reigning Davidic king.

A. Adam to Jacob (1 Chronicles 1)

The writer begins this section by tracing the genealogical connection between **Adam and Israel** (chap. 1). First, he notes the connection between the first man Adam and the first Hebrew Abraham (1:1–27). He traces Adam to Shem (1:1–4; Gen 4:25–26) and Shem to Abraham (1:24–27; Gen 5:1–32; 11:10–26) probably because of the promises given to Shem (Gen 9:26). Second, he notes the connection between Abraham and Jacob, who was later called Israel (1:28–54). The Chronicler makes this linkage clear by calling the latter Israel rather than Jacob (1:34). Thus, the writer motivates the returnees to remember their spiritual and national heritage by skillfully connecting God's agenda for them all the way back to God's purposes in creation.

B. Judah to Zerubbabel's Grandsons (1 Chronicles 2–3)

The author next notes the genealogical link between **Jacob's son Judah** and the returnees (chaps. 2–3). He shows how Jacob is connected to David (chap. 2) and how David through Solomon is connected to Zerubbabel's descendants (chap. 3). The returnees connection to Judah is significant since the prophesied Messiah would come from that tribe (Gen 49:10). Thus, the returnees should remember their great forefathers and remain true to God's purposes for His people since they are genealogically connected to them and the Davidic line.

C. The Twelve Tribes (1 Chronicles 4–9)

Next the writer focuses on the genealogies of all of Israel's 12 tribes (chaps. 4–8). He records all of the tribes in order to show the **solidarity of the nation**. Although all of the tribes are mentioned, this section seems to focus mostly on Benjamin, Judah, and Levi. Benjamin and Judah merit special attention since most of the postexilic community came from these two tribes. Levi also warrants special attention because of the role the priests play in temple worship.

The chronicler next records the genealogies of the **Transjordan tribes** (chap. 5). Thus, the writer mentions Reuben (5:1–10), Gad (5:11–17), and East Manasseh (5:23–26). Next, the chronicler devotes an entire chapter to the **tribe of Levi** (chap. 6). Such disproportionate treatment is explainable in terms of Levi's prominent role in temple worship by clarifying the roles the priests and the Levites play in temple worship. The **tribe of Benjamin** is mentioned last (chap. 8). The tribes of Judah and Benjamin bracket this genealogical summary (chap. 4–8) because they epitomize God's elective purposes through Judah (Gen 49:10).

II. David's Reign: Preparation for the Temple (1 Chronicles 10–29)

In the book's second major section (chaps. 10–29), the author traces **David's prosperous reign** and his priority of pursuing genuine worship. The author records these events so that his audience will learn from his positive example and resume temple worship. Thus, many of the sinful and negative events surrounding David's life in the books of Samuel are omitted. The writer deems these as inconsistent with his primary purpose of promoting a resumption of temple worship among the returnees.

A. David's Ascension (1 Chronicles 10–12)

The Chronicler begins this section by briefly mentioning **Saul's death** (chap. 10) in order to transition from Saul as the nation's first king to the writer's primary focus, David the king after God's heart. David's flight from Saul (1 Samuel 16–31) as well as Saul's reign (1 Samuel 8–15) are omitted so the writer can move directly to David. However, despite the scant space the Chronicler devotes to Saul's reign, he does mention that religious apostasy was the cause of Saul's death (10:13–14). The writer notes how "all" the nation gathered as "all" the elders came to anoint David as king at Hebron (11:1–3).

The greatness of David is further seen in the diversity of groups that unified and rallied behind him when he assumed the throne (chap. 12). Even Saul's tribe of Benjamin followed David (12:1–7,16–18). Other Israelite groups that rallied behind David's cause include the Gadites (12:8–15), Manasseh (12:19–22), Simeon, Levi, Ephraim, Issachar, Zebulun, Naphtali, Dan, Asher, and the Transjordan tribes (12:23–27). Thus, the chapter appropriately concludes with a unified description of David's reign (12:38–40).

B. David Brings the Ark to Jerusalem (1 Chronicles 13–16)

While the book of 2 Samuel devotes only a single chapter to David's bringing the ark to Jerusalem (2 Samuel 6), the Chronicler devotes four entire chapters to this subject (chaps. 13–16). Such an extensive treatment is given in order to explain David's **high priority for worship.** His diligence is seen in his preparation of both the Levites (15:1–15) and the singers (15:16–24) for this event. When he eventually brought the ark to Jerusalem, David refused to allow Michal's jealousy to detract him from expressing worship (15:25–29). The significance of national worship is seen in the Chronicler's description of the inauguration of the ark's service at Jerusalem, accompanied by sacrifices and worship (16:1–6), the rehearsal of various psalms (16:7–36; Pss 96:1–13; 105:1–15; 106:1,47–48), and the appointment of the personnel to minister at the tabernacle (16:37–43).

C. Davidic Covenant (1 Chronicles 17–20)

The writer also includes information about the **Davidic covenant** since it reveals David's heart for worship. He sought to build a house for God so that he could worship Him; therefore, the returnees should follow David's lead and continue temple worship.

The Chronicler spends the next three chapters (chaps. 18–20) recording David's various **military victories** over the Philistines, Moabites, Hamath, Edom,

Artist rendition of the Ark of the Covenant.

Ammon, and the Arameans. This section also appropriately observes that these victories affirmed the Davidic rule over all of the land of Israel (18:14–17). Conspicuously missing from this section is David's sin with Bathsheba (20:1). Those events that detract from this literary progress, such as David's adultery and other sins, are dealt with tersely or omitted altogether. The Chronicler omits this event since his purpose is to use David as an example of godly worship. Thus, the writer focuses on David's preparations for the temple.

D. David's Temple Preparations (1 Chronicles 21–29)

The writer seeks to use David's temple preparations to encourage the returnees to realize how important temple worship is (22:2–19), and he includes the events surrounding David's census sin because the conclusion of these events is David's purchase of the **temple site** from Ornan the Jebusite (21:1–22:1). This purchase happened because God told David to erect an altar at this threshing floor in order to stop the plague of pestilence that

A view of the excavations of the City of David.

resulted from his numbering of the troops. David could not go to sacrifice at Gibeon where the tabernacle and altar of burnt offering were located because of the presence of a destroying angel, so God encouraged David to build an altar at this place. Later Solomon would erect the temple on this plot of real estate where David built this altar.

David would not be given the privilege of actually constructing the temple since he was a man of war. His son Solomon would actually build the temple because he was a man of peace. However, the Chronicler identifies David's concern for worship by recording his numerous preparations for the temple's construction and the organization of people who would serve at the temple (22:2–27:34). Six entire chapters are devoted to these **temple preparations**, including David's instructions to Solomon to build the temple (22:2–19), gathering material for the temple (22:2–5), promising Solomon blessings if he builds the temple (22:6–13), and exhorting Israel's leaders to cooperate with Solomon in pursuing this objective (22:17–19). The next five chapters record the personnel that David set in place for the future operation of the temple (chaps. 23–27), including Solomon (23:1), the Levites (23:2–32), the priests (chap. 24), the musicians (chap. 25), the temple servants (chap. 26), and the civil servants whose duties impacted temple activity (chap. 27).

The book of 1 Chronicles concludes with David's final address to the government officials (28:1–29:22) and the **transfer of power** from David to Solomon (29:22–30). Conspicuously absent from these verses is the struggle for power that went on throughout the process of Solomon's accession as recorded in the early chapters of

SOLOMON'S TEMPLE, Exterior View (LOOKING WEST)

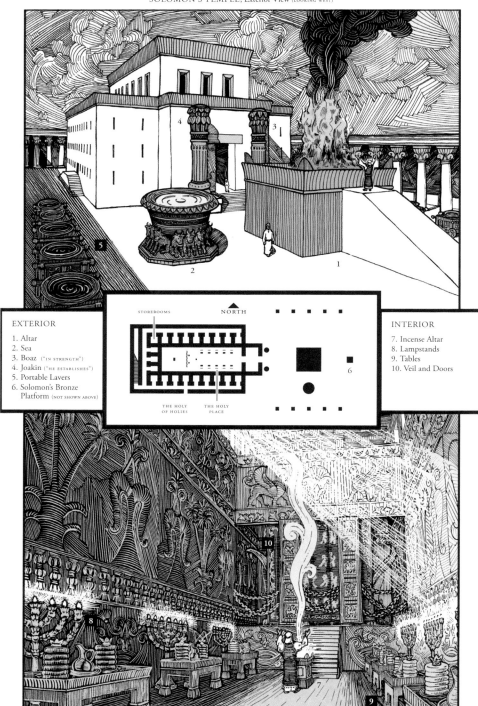

EXTERIOR

1. Altar
2. Sea
3. Boaz ("IN STRENGTH")
4. Joakin ("HE ESTABLISHES")
5. Portable Lavers
6. Solomon's Bronze
   Platform (NOT SHOWN ABOVE)

STOREROOMS

NORTH

THE HOLY
OF HOLIES

THE HOLY
PLACE

INTERIOR

7. Incense Altar
8. Lampstands
9. Tables
10. Veil and Doors

SOLOMON'S TEMPLE, Interior View (LOOKING WEST)

the book of 1 Kings. The writer omits this struggle since it detracts from his purpose of featuring the prosperous, worship-centered reigns of both David and Solomon as a means of encouraging the returnees to devote themselves to temple worship.

III. Solomon's Reign: Building the Temple (2 Chronicles 1–9)

The next major focus in the book is **Solomon's construction of the temple** (chaps. 1–9). This theme fits into the writer's argument in three important ways. First, it reveals Solomon's commitment to faithful worship that the writer hopes his audience will imitate. Second it shows how Israel became the greatest nation on the face of the earth as Solomon made worship in the temple his top priority. Because the writer seeks to emphasize the greatness of Solomon's reign, many of his sins are omitted such as his idolatry, pagan wives, and effort to kill Jeroboam. Third, this section emphasizes God's sovereignty in bringing to pass many of the promises in the Davidic covenant.

A. Solomon's Wisdom (2 Chronicles 1)

This section begins with Solomon offering sacrifices on Moses' bronze altar in Gibeon (1:1–5). This action is included because it shows the solidarity between God's covenant purposes for Solomon and God's covenant program as expressed through Moses. The writer notes that Solomon became the **wisest man that ever lived** since God was pleased to grant his request for wisdom (1:6–13). Thus, the book as a whole relates wisdom with an appetite for worship. The chapter concludes by describing Solomon's prosperous reign (1:14–17).

B. Solomon's Temple (2 Chronicles 2–7)

Second Chronicles devotes six chapters to Solomon's construction and dedication of the temple on **Mount Moriah** (chaps. 2–7). Solomon's heart for worship is seen in the elaborate preparations he made for the coming temple (chap. 2). Solomon's desire for worship is evidenced in how he did not allow his previous prosperity to quench his appetite for achieving his primary goal, which was the temple's construction. No expense was spared as Solomon hired Hiram, the king of Tyre, to provide materials and manpower for the project.

Solomon's heart for worship is also seen in his **transfer of the ark** from David's tabernacle at Zion to the interior of the temple (chap. 5). The ark represented God's presence among His people. Thus, the transfer of the ark to the temple demonstrated Solomon's commitment to the God of Israel. The Chronicler includes Solomon's dedicatory prayer (chap. 6) since it highlights the centrality of God's presence at the temple. According to this prayer, from this point onward, God would hear the prayers offered in this place, which is why the Temple Mount is still sacred to the Jewish people today, even though there is currently no Jewish temple on that site.

C. Solomon's Prosperous Reign (2 Chronicles 8–9)

The Chronicler reminds the reader how Solomon's pursuit of worship contributed to the **greatness of his empire**. The greatness of his empire is made clear based on the cities he built (8:1–6), his many subjects (8:7–11), the number of sacrifices presented (8:12–13), his organization of the priestly and Levitical hierarchy (8:14–16), and his navy at Ezion-geber (8:17–18). He also observes the extent of Solomon's fame, climaxing in the queen of Sheba's journey to Jerusalem to sit at Solomon's feet in hopes of learning from his wisdom (9:1–12).

IV. Judah's Kings: Apostasy and Decline (2 Chronicles 10–36)

In the book's final section (chaps. 10–36), the writer focuses on the **decline of Judah**. Here he emphasizes the blessings on those reforming kings that prioritized worship as well as the withdrawal of divine blessings from those kings that apostatized from temple worship. The reforming kings include Asa (chaps. 14–16), Jehoshaphat (chaps. 17–20), Joash (chap. 24), Hezekiah (chaps. 29–32), and Josiah (chaps. 34–36). In fact, "about 70 percent of chapters 10–36 deals with eight good kings, leaving only 30 percent to cover the twelve evil rulers."[8] This disproportionate treatment shows that the writer sought to encourage the returnees toward resuming temple worship by pointing to the positive example of the good reforming kings.

A. Division of the Kingdom (2 Chronicles 10–13)

Solomon's son Rehoboam's excessive taxation resulted in the split of the northern kingdom of Israel from the southern kingdom of Judah. Since no mercy was shown concerning forced labor from the 10 tribes of Israel, Israel's leader Jeroboam rejected any political and religious association with the house of David. The selfish reactions by both kings reveal the **sinful origin** of the northern kingdom (10–11:4). This partially explains why the Chronicler no longer refers to the northern kingdom except in only a tangential way. Moreover, Rehoboam's covenant violation led to an invasion by Shishak of Egypt who took the temple treasures (12:1–8). Here the author notes the connection between temple defilement and covenant violation. However, the author also observes how Rehoboam's repentance caused Judah to be spared. But in the next chapter the reader discovers that God fought for Judah against Jeroboam because he violated the covenant, rebelled against the Davidic dynasty, and forsook the temple (chap. 13).

B. Kings of Judah (2 Chronicles 14–36)

Because of the author's desire to use **spiritual reforms** as a positive example for his audience to imitate, he devotes three chapters to describing the reign of Asa (chaps. 14–16) and four chapters to describe the reign of Jehoshaphat (chaps. 17–20). These are followed by the apostasy of Jehoram, Ahaziah, and the wicked queen Athaliah, who attempted to eliminate David's seed (and thus the Messianic line) by killing all the royal family except the infant Joash (chaps. 21–23). The Chronicler highlights the sovereignty of God in sparing the life of Joash and keeping the promise to the Davidic covenant.

Next the author deals with **the struggles** of the kings of Judah who started well but did not always finish well. Amaziah began well but was eventually assassinated (chap. 25). Uzziah had a long successful reign but ultimately defiled the temple by usurping priestly prerogatives and died a leper (chap. 26). Jotham also began well but failed in the end (chap. 27). God initially protected Ahaz, but he eventually defiled the temple by using its treasures to bribe the Assyrians for protection (chap. 28).

Because of the author's desire to use the **reforms of Hezekiah** as a positive example for his audience to imitate, he devoted four chapters to his reign (chaps. 29–32) Hezekiah's reforms include the restoration of temple worship (chap. 29), the implementation of the Passover (chap. 30), the eradication of idolatry (31:1), and the establishment of the priests and the Levites in their proper roles (31:2–19). Because of Hezekiah's commitment to God's house, his courage, and his faith (32:5–8), Hezekiah experienced prosperity during his reign (31:20–21), which manifested itself in his defeat of Sennacherib in 701 BC and his resulting international fame (32:1–23).

The author reinforces the lesson that **temple defilement** results in a forfeiture of blessings through the reigns of Manasseh (33:1–20) and Amon (33:21–25). After defiling the temple with pagan images, Manasseh was deported to Babylon by the king of Assyria (Esarhaddon in 681–669 BC or Ashurbanipal in 668–627 BC). However, after he humbled himself and repented, he was able to return to Jerusalem where he pursued orthodox worship. The Chronicler includes Manasseh's captivity, conversion, and return despite the fact that these events are omitted from the book of 2 Kings. Next he deals with the reign of Amon (33:21–25) who defiled the temple just like Manasseh. As a result, his servants conspired against him resulting in his assassination. The people of the land then came and killed Amon's assassins and enthroned Josiah.

The chronicler devotes two chapters toward discussing the religious reforms that took place during Josiah's reign (chaps. 34–35). **Josiah's reforms** took on even greater dimensions when the law (Deuteronomy 28) was discovered, resulting in even more reforms (34:14–33), including the implementation of the celebration of the Passover (35:1–19). The writer's skillful connection of Josiah's reforms to the rediscovered law establishes that Josiah was acting consistently with God's previously articulated covenant principles.

The writer concludes his survey of Judah's kings by surveying the four remaining wicked kings of the southern kingdom (36:1–14). Following Josiah's death, the people of the land enthroned Josiah's son Jehoahaz. However, Pharaoh Neco dethroned him

---

Hebrew Highlight

Kneel. Hebrew ברך (*bârak*). The Hebrew word *Barak* means "to kneel down, to bless God as an **act of adoration**." This word is found many times throughout the pages of the Old Testament (Pss 18:46; 34:1; 95:6; 96:2; 103:1–2). It is used in 1 Chr 29:20 regarding how David led the assembly in worshipping and paying homage to the Lord. The word captures a central theme of the books of Chronicles since the thrust of these books is to stimulate the postexilic community toward orthodox and heartfelt worship. As believers, we must take seriously our calling to worship the true and living God. He is worthy of our praise and adoration since He is both the Creator (Rev 4:11) and the Redeemer (Rev 5:9) of all things.

The Problem of Biased Historiography

Some contend that Chronicles represents a biased historical account. This contention is leveled on the basis of the book's omissions (e.g., David's adultery with Bathsheba) and additions (e.g., Manasseh's repentance). However, these omissions notwithstanding, it should be recognized that the book still often portrays David unfavorably. Examples include his mishandling of the ark (1 Chr 13:9–14), his polygamy (1 Chr 14:3–7), and his premature request to build a temple for God (1 Chronicles 17). Furthermore, these additions and omissions can be explained in terms of the Chronicler selectively using history that is **consistent with his unique purpose** in writing. His readers already would be familiar with the parallel accounts written by the prophets in the books of Samuel and Kings. As a priestly author, the Chronicler focuses on the relation of the kings of Judah to the temple of God.

and enthroned Jehoahaz's older brother Eliakim whom he renamed Jehoiakim. The writer includes the remaining three kings because each of their **covenant rebellions** led to defilement of the temple. Jehoiakim's (36:5–8) and Jehoiachin's (36:9–10) rebellions led to military defeat and the Babylonian defilement of the temple. Zedekiah's rebellion actually led to Jewish defilement of the temple (36:11–14). Thus, the writer closes his treatment of Judah's kings by associating covenant rebellion with temple defilement, which finally resulted in the deportation to Babylon and the destruction of Solomon's temple (36:15–21).

Southeastern corner of the Temple Mount in Jerusalem.

Fortunately the book ends on the optimistic note of **Cyrus's decree** to rebuild the temple (36:22–23). God's call for proper worship continues from the Babylonian era into the Persian era. Thus, the people in Jerusalem should recognize that their calling to worship is part of God's sovereign design as they resume worshipping the Lord in the rebuilt postexilic temple. English Bible readers should note that these verses conclude the Hebrew canon with the words: "let him go up" (Hb. *ya'al*). This is still the desire of religious Jews today to make *aliya* and "go up" to Jerusalem.

THEOLOGICAL SIGNIFICANCE

The major theological theme of Chronicles is the importance of **true worship**. This emphasis explains why the word "heart" is found 32 times in the book. Therefore, the book focuses on those institutions of Judaism that have worship as their focus. These institutions include the priesthood, Levites, the ark, and the temple. The temple is of particular interest to the writer. "As a chronicle of the temple, the book surveys its conception (David), construction and consecration (Solomon), corruption and cleansing (the kings of Judah), and conflagration (Nebuchadnezzar)."[9] The book also focuses on the Davidic covenant and emphasizes the reforms and joyous worship of the Davidic kings. The book is full of references to their reforms, victories, prayers, and prosperous reigns. Not only does Chronicles omit key events covered in Samuel and Kings, but the book also adds key events not covered by those books.[10] Thus, Wilkinson and Boa suggest that "what Deuteronomy is to the rest of the Pentateuch and John is to the synoptic Gospels, Chronicles is to Israel's history in Samuel and Kings."[11] In other words, it complements and completes the earlier accounts.

For Further Study

Hill, Andrew. *1 and 2 Chronicles*. NIVAC. Grand Rapids: Zondervan, 2003.
Merrill, Eugene H. *1, 2 Chronicles*. Grand Rapids: Zondervan, 1988.
Payne, J. Barton. "1 and 2 Chronicles." In *EBC*. Grand Rapids: Zondervan, 1988.
Sailhamer, John. *First and Second Chronicles*. Chicago: Moody, 1983.
Thompson, J. A. *1, 2 Chronicles*. NAC 9. Nashville: B&H, 1994.

Study Questions

1. How does Chronicles differ from the books of Samuel and Kings?
2. Why do many believe that Ezra may have been the author of the Chronicles?
3. What significant roles do David and Solomon play in the history of the Chronicles?
4. How does the author use themes of devotion and apostasy to challenge his postexilic readers?
5. What lessons can we learn from these books about the importance of worship in our own lives?

ENDNOTES

1. R. K. Harrison, *Introduction to the Old Testament* (Grand Rapids: Eerdmans, 1969; reprint, Peabody, MA: Hendrickson, 2004), 1152; Raymond B. Dillard and Tremper Longman III, *An Introduction to the Old Testament* (Grand Rapids: Zondervan, 1994), 169.

2. Andrew E. Hill and John H. Walton, *A Survey of the Old Testament* (Grand Rapids: Zondervan, 1991), 216.

3. C. Dyer and E. Merrill, *Old Testament Explorer* (Nashville: Word, 2001), 293.

4. Other positions on the authorship of Chronicles and Ezra-Nehemiah are possible. H. G. M. Williamson, *Ezra, Nehemiah*, WBC (Waco: Word, 1977), xxii; H. G. M. Williamson, *Israel in the Book of Chronicles* (Cambridge: Cambridge University Press, 1977), 5–70; S. Japhet, "The Supposed Common Authorship of Chronicles and Ezra-Nehemiah Investigated Anew," *VT* 18 (1968): 332–72; R. L. Braun, *1 Chronicles*, WBC (Waco: Word, 1979), 52–54; and J. A. Thompson, *1, 2 Chronicles*, NAC (Nashville: B&H, 1994), 29, all argue that the author of Ezra-Nehemiah is not the Chronicler.

5. Harrison, *Introduction to the Old Testament*, 1153.

6. The 70 years of discipline transpired either in between 605 BC (first deportation) and 535 BC (the people arrived back in the land) or 586 BC (third deportation) and 515 BC (the rebuilding of the temple). Whichever scheme one follows, Kings (550 BC) was written during this time of discipline while Chronicles (400 BC) was written afterward.

7. Adapted from Bruce H. Wilkinson and Kenneth Boa, *Talk Thru the Bible* (Nashville: Thomas Nelson, 2005), 102. Copyright ©2005, Thomas Nelson. Reprinted by permission. All rights reserved.

8. Wilkinson and Boa, *Talk Thru the Bible*, 111–12.

9. Ibid., 111.

10. For a list of some of these omissions and deletions, see J. Carl Laney, *Answers to Tough Questions: A Survey of Problem Passages and Issues from Every Book of the Bible* (Grand Rapids: Kregel, 1997), 91–92.

11. Wilkinson and Boa, *Talk Thru the Bible*, 102.

Chapter 18

EZRA
Rebuilding the Temple

The book of Ezra describes the **resettlement** of the Hebrew people after their 70-year exile in Babylon. The book is named for Ezra, the priest who led a second contingent of Jews back to the Promised Land. Shortly after the Persian king Cyrus II began to rule over Babylon (539 BC), he recorded an account of his conquest on a clay cylinder. It was written in Babylonian cuneiform and is popularly referred to as the Cyrus Cylinder. It declares that he began a campaign to restore various people groups held captive

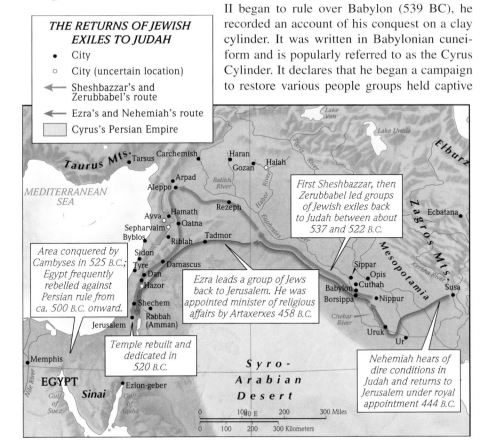

THE RETURNS OF JEWISH EXILES TO JUDAH

- • City
- ○ City (uncertain location)
- ← Sheshbazzar's and Zerubbabel's route
- ← Ezra's and Nehemiah's route
- Cyrus's Persian Empire

First Sheshbazzar, then Zerubbabel led groups of Jewish exiles back to Judah between about 537 and 522 B.C.

Area conquered by Cambyses in 525 B.C.; Egypt frequently rebelled against Persian rule from ca. 500 B.C. onward.

Ezra leads a group of Jews back to Jerusalem. He was appointed minister of religious affairs by Artaxerxes 458 B.C.

Temple rebuilt and dedicated in 520 B.C.

Nehemiah hears of dire conditions in Judah and returns to Jerusalem under royal appointment 444 B.C.

MEDITERRANEAN SEA

Taurus Mts. · Tarsus · Carchemish · Haran · Gozan · Halah

Aleppo · Arpad · Balikh River · Rezeph · Ecbatana

Avva · Hamath · Qatna · Sepharvaim · Byblos · Riblah · Tadmor

Sidon · Damascus · Tyre · Dan · Hazor · Shechem · Rabbah (Amman) · Jerusalem

Sippar · Opis · Babylon · Cuthah · Borsippa · Nippur · Susa

Chebar River · Uruk · Ur

Memphis · EGYPT · Ezion-geber · Sinai · Gulf of Suez · Gulf of Aqaba · Nile River

Syro-Arabian Desert

Zagros Mts. · Mesopotamia · Kerkha Mts. · Elburz · Lake Van · Lake Urmia · Tigris River · Euphrates · Habor River

0   100   200   300 Miles
0   100   200   300 Kilometers

KINGS OF PERSIA			
Persian King	Dates (BC)	Biblical Connections	Events And Accomplishments
Cyrus II (the Great)	559–530	Permitted return of the Jews from exile; facilitated rebuilding of the temple at Jerusalem (Ezr 1:1–4; 6:3–5); the "Anointed One" of Is 45:1	King of Anshan, 559 BC, conquered kingdom of Media (550 BC) and Lydian kingdom (546 BC); conquered Babylon, 539 BC
Cambyses II	530–522	Not mentioned in the Bible	Son of Cyrus the Great; conquered Egypt, 525 BC; his death (suicide?) in 522 BC led to two years of fighting between rival claimants to the throne
Darius I Hystaspes	522–486	Haggai and Zechariah preached during the second year of Darius I (520 BC; temple rebuilt and dedicated 515 BC (cf. Ezr 6:13–15)	Member of a collateral royal line; secured the throne ending the unrest following the death of Cambyses; reorganized the Persian Empire into satrapies; establishing royal postal system; began building Persepolis; invaded Greece and was defeated at Marathon, 490 BC; revolt in Egypt
Xerxes I	486–465	Possibly Ahasuerus of the Book of Esther	Son of Darius I; continued building Persepolis; encountered numerous rebellions at the beginning of his reign (Egypt, Babylon); invaded Greece, sacked Athens (480 BC), but was defeated by the Greeks in a naval engagement (Salamis, 480 BC) and on land (Plataea and Mycale, 479 BC); killed in a palace coup in 465 BC.
Artaxerxes I Longimanus	465–425	Nehemiah, cup bearer to Artaxerxes; came to Judah (444 BC, compare Neh 2:1; 13:6); traditional date of Ezra's mission in the seventh year of his reign (458 BC, cf. Ezr 7:7)	Faced revolt in Egypt; completed major buildings at Persepolis; made peace with the Greeks (Peace of Callias, 449 BC); died of natural causes
Xerxes II	423	Not mentioned in the Bible	Ruled less than two months
Darius II Nothus	423–404	Not mentioned in the Bible; Jews in Egypt (Elephantine) appealed to Samaria and Jerusalem for help in rebuilding their temple about 407 BC	Peloponnesian War, 421–404 BC; Persia recovered several Greek cities in Asia Minor
Artaxerxes II Mmemon	404–359/8	Some scholars place Ezra's mission in the seventh year of Artaxerxes II, about 398 BC	Egypt regained freedom from Persia for a time; revolt of the Satraps, 366–360 BC
Artaxerxes III Ochus	359/8–338/7	Not mentioned in the Bible	Philip II of Macedon; rises to power about 359 BC; Alexander the Great born, 356 BC; Persia reclaims Egypt, 342 BC
Arses		Not mentioned in the Bible	Unknown
Darius III Codomannus	338/7–336 336–330	Alexander subdues the Levant; Tyre and Gaza besieged, 332 BC; conquest of Egypt by Alexander, 332 BC	Philip assassinated, 336 BC; Alexander the Great invades the Persian Empire, 334 BC; Darius III defeated by Alexander at Issus, 33 BC, and Gaugamela, 331 BC; death of Darius, 330 BC

in Babylon, by allowing displaced people to return to their homelands. This decree fulfilled the prophecy of Isa 44:28–45:7 almost 150 years earlier, when God called Cyrus by name and told what he would do for His people. Furthermore, the timing was also predicted by Jeremiah, who foretold the captivity in Babylon would last for 70 years (Jer 25:11).

Although Ezra does not show up until the book's second section (chaps. 7–10; Nehemiah 8), the work derives its **title** from its central character Ezra, whose name seems to be an Aramaic form of the Hebrew *'ezer*, "help." Ezra is a short form of *Azariah*, which means "Yahweh has helped."[1] The name "Esdras" (Ezra) refers to two books in the Septuagint: 1 Esdras (or Esdras A) is an apocryphal book, while 2 Esdras (or Esdras B) includes the canonical books of Ezra and Nehemiah. While Ezra is not overtly called the book's author in the work itself, several lines of evidence point to him as the author because of his role as a postexilic scribe (7:6a,10,21), Jewish tradition indicates that Ezra was a disciple of Baruch, who acted as Jeremiah's scribe (*Megilla* 16b). Second, tradition attributes authorship of the book to Ezra (*Baba Bathra* 15a).

The apocryphal book of 2 Maccabees 2:13–15 indicates that Ezra had access to a **library** created by Nehemiah. Having access to such material was important since the book of Ezra contains documents (4:7–16), genealogies (2:1–70), and memoirs (7:27–9:15). If it is accepted that Ezra wrote the book of Chronicles, then it is likely that the book of Ezra was also written by Ezra as well since the latter seems to pick up where the former left off (2 Chr 36:22–23; Ezra 1:1. Furthermore, they both exhibit a priestly emphasis, common themes or concepts (lists, prominence of the Levites and the temple servants, and descriptions of religious holidays), and many common words and phrases ("singer," "gate keeper," "temple servants," "house of God," "heads of families").[2] While critical scholars attempt to date the book much later, conservative scholars have identified the similarities of the Hebrew to that of Haggai and Chronicles and the Aramaic sections (4:7–6:18; 7:12–26) with fifth century BC royal Aramaic.[3]

BACKGROUND

Following Israel's 70-year captivity, there were three postexilic returns of Jews from Persia to Jerusalem. The first contingent returned under the leadership of Zerubbabel in c. 538 BC, and a second group followed Ezra 80 years later in 458 BC.

	Date	Duration	Persian King	Jewish Leader	Scripture	Purpose	Number of Returnees
1st return	538–515 BC	23 years	Cyrus II to Darius I	Sheshbazzar Zerubbabel	Ezra 1–6; Isa 44:28	Rebuilding the temple	50,000
2nd return	458–457 BC	2 years	Artaxerxes	Ezra	Ezra 7–10	Adorning the temple and reforming the people	2,000
3rd return	444–432 BC	8 years	Artaxerxes	Nehemiah	Nehemiah	Rebuilding the wall	

The book of Ezra centers on the first two returns. The book's first section (chaps. 1–6) concerns the **return under Zerubbabel** to rebuild the temple between 538 and 515 BC. This section lists the people who returned under Sheshbazzar and Zerubbabel, the governors of the Persian province of Judah. The specific details in Ezra 1–2 even list the numbers of the inventory of temple articles that were returned (1:10–11). The book's second section (chaps. 7–10) concerns the **return under Ezra** to adorn the temple and to reform the people by rebuilding them spiritually. In this section the restoration is accomplished by Ezra's prayer (chap. 9) and the people's pledge (chap. 10). Initially, Ezra returns to find the temple rebuilt but the people living in gross covenant violation through mixed marriages. Sandwiched in between these two sections (chaps. 1–6 and chaps. 7–10) is nearly a six-decade period during which the book of Esther transpired (482–473 BC). This entire picture is captured on the following chart.

RETURN OF THE JEWISH EXILES				
Return	*First*	*Intermediate*	*Second*	*Third*
Date	538–515 BC	482–473 BC	458–457 BC	444–424 BC
Jewish Leader	Zerubbabel	Esther	Ezra	Nehemiah
Persian Leader	Cyrus	Xerxes I	Artaxerxes I	Artaxerxes I
Biblical Reference	Ezra 1–6	Esther	Ezra 7–10	Nehemiah

DATE

Ezra probably finished the book between 458 BC (when he arrived in Jerusalem) and 444 BC, when Nehemiah arrived in Jerusalem.[4] Ezra probably did not write the book **after Nehemiah's return** since he does not mention this return. Ezra likely completed the book just prior to Nehemiah's arrival since the book's last recorded event probably transpired around 446 BC (4:21–23; cf. Neh 1:1–3). While some have challenged this early date for the composition of Ezra, the late date theory seems unlikely since Ezra was a contemporary of Nehemiah. Although some date the book in 398 BC or later, its linguistic similarities with the fifth-century Aramaic papyri from the Jewish community at Elephantine, Egypt, argue for an earlier date during the lifetime of Ezra. Kidner notes that proponents of later dates claim nothing more than probability for their suggested reconstructions.[5]

The date of the book (446–444 BC) best harmonizes with the **second return** that took place under Ezra. Zerubbabel's return (538–515 BC) had long since transpired, and the return under Nehemiah was yet to occur (444 BC). This second group of returnees was struggling to adorn the temple, rebuild the city of Jerusalem, avoid syncretism, and defend themselves against foreign aggression. Ezra likely composed the book from Jerusalem in order to minister to this second group of returnees.

Outline

I. Restoration of the Temple (Ezra 1–6)
   A. Return under Sheshbazzar and Zerubbabel (Ezra 1–2)
   B. Rebuilding the Temple under Zerubbabel and Jeshua (Ezra 3–6)
II. Reformation of the People (Ezra 7–10)
   A. Ezra Leads the Second Return from Persia to Jerusalem (Ezra 7–8)
   B. Ezra Leads Reformation among the People (Ezra 9–10)

MESSAGE

In order to preserve the nation from **assimilating** into the surrounding Gentile cultures and in order for it to fulfill God's messianic purposes, God sovereignly worked among the pagan Persian leaders, as well as among His people, to preserve Judah's religious and worship identity. Such preservation was accomplished through the nation's return to the land and the rebuilding of the second temple, despite much Gentile opposition (chaps. 1–6). Preservation was also accomplished through the community's commitment to put away their foreign wives so syncretism could be avoided and covenant standards and distinctives could be maintained (chaps. 7–10).

A unique characteristic of the book is that some of its sections were recorded in **Aramaic** (4:8–6:18; 7:12–26), which was the *lingua franca* of the Persian period. Because 67 of the book's 280 verses are recorded in Aramaic, the Aramaic language makes up almost one-fourth of the book. Fifty-two of these verses are official records or letters Ezra apparently copied and inserted into his work. The rest of the book is composed in late Hebrew. The use of dual languages is only replicated in Daniel where chaps. 2–7 are in Aramaic. The book's other significant features include its emphasis on the fulfillment of prophecy (Jer 25:11; 29:10), its record of postexilic history, and Ezra's command regarding divorce.

I. Restoration of the Temple (Ezra 1–6)

In the book of Ezra, the writer seeks to show how God acted sovereignly in history to **preserve the religious culture** of the nation of Israel so that she could fulfill her covenant destiny. In the book's first major section, Ezra reveals how God providentially acted so that His people could return to their land and rebuild their temple (chaps. 1–6).

A. Return under Zerubbabel (Ezra 1–2)

This section begins with a discussion of the **first return** under Sheshbazzar and Zerubbabel. God's sovereign work on His nation's behalf is evident in the opening chapter where God moves the heart of the pagan, Persian king Cyrus II to issue a decree allowing the Jews to return to their land (1:1–4). This work was consistent with what God had earlier promised through the prophet Jeremiah regarding the termination of the 70-year captivity (Jer 25:11; 29:10). Thus, God's present work was consistent with His previously articulated covenant principles. In other words, the exile in no way abrogated or cancelled Israel's covenant program.

The Wailing Wall where a large crowd gathers during a Jewish holiday.

The notion that the exile did not vitiate the messianic line is reinforced through the list of the various returnees, which identifies them with their **tribal ancestry** (chap. 2). Thus, Joshua records the political leaders (2:1–2), people (2:3–35), religious leaders (2:36–42), and servants (2:43–58) who returned from the exile. He also mentions a number of returnees who had uncertain genealogies (2:59–68), the grand totals of both people and animals returning (2:64–67), the amount of money the returnees worshipfully gave (2:68–69), and the cities to which the returnees eventually settled including Bethlehem (2:23) where the future Messiah would be born (Mic 5:2). Because of the continuation of the Davidic line through the returnees from exile, God would now continue to sovereignly act to protect this line and preserve Israel's worship culture.

B. Rebuilding the Temple under Zerubbabel and Jeshua (Ezra 3–6)

For the Jewish culture to be preserved, God had to revitalize the nation's worship identity. Thus, He sovereignly raised up **two leaders** named Jeshua and Zerubbabel to erect the altar (3:1–2), reestablish the sacrificial system (3:3–6), and lay the temple foundation (3:7–9). However, God's work never occurs without **opposition**. While the first sign of internal opposition occurred in the form of discouragement as recorded in the previous chapter (3:12a), external opposition rose to the forefront in the book's fourth chapter. After Israel's leaders refused to allow the people of the land to assist in the rebuilding effort (4:1–3), the Gentiles living in the land retaliated by discouraging, frustrating, and intimidating the temple builders (4:4–5). Unfortunately, such obstructionism was not an isolated incident but rather represented an ongoing pattern against God's restorative agenda throughout the postexilic era.

Later opponents of the Jews also won a temporary victory by procuring an injunction from Artaxerxes halting the rebuilding of the walls of Jerusalem (4:8–23). Thus, the people of the land caused the cessation of temple work until Darius' second year (4:24). These formidable challenges were met by God's raising up **two prophets**, Haggai and Zechariah, to exhort the people to resume building the temple (5:1–2). In spite of questions about the legitimacy of the rebuilding efforts by local authorities, God caused Darius I to find Cyrus's initial decree in the royal archives (5:3–17) and moved him to authorize the building to continue (6:1–12).

God not only worked through his prophets but also in the hearts of pagan rulers to accomplish His purposes. As a result, the temple was completed on March 12, 515 BC (6:13–15). After it was dedicated (6:16–18), the people celebrated Passover and the Feast of Unleavened Bread on April 21, 515 BC (6:19–22). In sum, in the first half of the book (chaps. 1–6), Ezra records God's sovereign work in overcoming seemingly insurmountable obstacles so the **nation's religious heritage** could be preserved. Such divine preservation was necessary so the nation's future covenant purposes would not be jeopardized and the prophetic promise of a coming Messiah could be preserved.

II. Reformation of the People (Ezra 7–10)

God's sovereign purpose for Judah included confronting the nation regarding her syncretistic tendencies (chaps. 7–10). The pressure of living under Persian rule in the midst of people with vastly different religious beliefs caused some of the Jews to compromise their religious beliefs and spiritual standards. By taking foreign wives, the Jews were also inclined to merge pagan beliefs and practices with the principles of the covenant.

A. Ezra Leads the Second Return (Ezra 7–8)

The genealogy of Ezra is given in 7:1–5 indicating he was of the **priestly line** of Aaron. Like many of the Jews of his time, Ezra had political connections with the Persian government because "the king had granted him everything he requested" (7:6). Also, Ezra enjoyed the presence of God in his life. The fact that "the hand of Yahweh his God was on him" introduces Ezra as a godly man and spiritual leader among the Jews.

Ezra was a **serious scholar** who "determined in his heart to study the law of the LORD, obey it, and teach its statutes" (7:10). His example set a standard for Jewish scribes who took seriously their charge to copy and preserve the Word of God for future generations. Unfortunately, many of the scribes of Jesus' time degenerated into arguing about prescriptions of the law and failed to live by its principles (Matt 23:1–36).

Since there was a need for more priests, Levites, and temple servants in Jerusalem, by faith Ezra led a group of people back to Jerusalem without any military escort (8:21–23), after finding almost 250 more people who could assist in temple worship (8:1–20).

B. Ezra Leads Reformation among the People (Ezra 9–10)

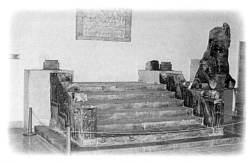

After Judah's sin of intermarriage with the pagans was reported to Ezra (9:1–2), he realized that such behavior posed a threat to the spiritual and cultural survival of Israel (9:3–4). Consequently, he led the people through moral reformation and **covenant renewal**. This reformation began with Ezra's prayer of confession regarding the returnees' sin (9:5–15). This prayer includes Ezra's personal remorse (9:5–7), a recollec-

Remains of the throne of Darius the Great.

tion of God's previous extension of grace to the nation (9:8–9), the confession of the nation's specific sin of intermarrying with pagans (9:10–14), and an acknowledgment of God's right to covenant judgment (9:15). Sensing how the seriousness of this sin threatened the nation's covenant destiny, the returnees also expressed remorse (10:1) and pledged to put away their foreign wives (10:2–5).

Throughout these events God was **preserving the nation** from assimilating into the surrounding Gentile cultures so that her messianic purposes could be accomplished. God sovereignly worked among the pagan Persian leaders as well as among His people to preserve Judah's religious and spiritual identity. Such preservation was accomplished through the nation's return to the land, the rebuilding of the second temple in the midst of much Gentile opposition (chaps. 1–6), and the community's commitment to reject syncretism and maintain covenant standards and distinctives (chaps. 7–10). As a result, Israel's unique identity was preserved, orthodox Judaism was defined, and according to Talmudic tradition, the Hebrew canon was established.

THEOLOGICAL SIGNIFICANCE

The book of Ezra shows how God sovereignly works through human circumstances to restore the remnant of His people to the Promised Land, thus fulfilling part of the covenant God made with Israel. Ezra's theological concern was to restore the Jewish community in Jerusalem to **covenant purity**. Ezra also emphasizes that God preserves His people even when there is great opposition. The genealogies demonstrate the ongoing integrity of these families and the priesthood, for eventually the Messiah would come from the roots of Judah. Ezra also emphasized the reinstitution of true authentic worship of the Lord at the temple site. Beginning with the laying of the temple's foundation, the people gave a "great shout of praise," while others wept loudly and the "sound was heard far away" (3:11,13).

Ezra also describes the **providence of God** who works His will among His people. God used the exile in Babylon to punish His people, and then God used the religious tolerance of Persian kings to allow Israel to return home. Although the Babylonian's fierce nature motivated them to punish Israel, the Persian's kind nature wanted them to occupy their land, pay taxes, have children, and add abundance to the Persian Kingdom. But God's purposes for Judah were far greater as the sovereign Lord of heaven ruled through the actions of men to fulfill His eternal plan.

The Second Temple

The *first temple* is called *Solomon's temple* because it was built by King Solomon (2 Kings 5–8) around 966 BC (1 Kgs 6:1). This temple was plundered (2 Chr 36:7) and eventually destroyed by the Babylonians when the Jews were taken into captivity in 586 BC (2 Kgs 25:9). The *second temple* of Scripture is sometimes referred to as *Zerubabbel's temple* because it was rebuilt under the leadership of Zerubbabel (515 BC) when the Jews returned from the 70 years of Babylonian captivity (Ezra 6:13–15). The ministries of the postexilic prophets Haggai and Zechariah were largely dedicated toward motivating the returnees to rebuild this second temple (Ezra 5:1–2; Hag 1:1–15). This temple was later desecrated by the Seleucid king Antiochus IV Epiphanes during the Intertestamental period (170–164 BC). The desecration and eventual liberation of the temple from Seleucid rule was predicted 400 years in advance by the sixth-century exilic prophet Daniel (Dan 8:9–14; 11:31–32). This Intertestamental liberation also forms the background for the holiday in Judaism known as the Feast of Lights or *Hanukkah*, which means "dedication" (John 10:22).

The second temple was renovated and expanded years later by King Herod (John 2:20) and was standing in the time of Christ in the New Testament. For example, Jesus entered the temple as a youth and confounded the religious leaders with His wisdom (Luke 2:41–50). As an adult He drove the money changers out of the temple (John 2:12–22). Satan took Him to the pinnacle of this temple to be tempted (Matt 4:5). The disciples recalled Christ's attention to the beauty of the temple (Matt 24:1). The early church met in the courts of the temple (Acts 2:46). All of these passages are references to this second Jewish temple which was built under the leadership of Zerubbabel and renovated by Herod. This temple was ultimately **destroyed by the Romans** when they invaded Jerusalem in AD 70. Forty years before this invasion, Jesus predicted that this second temple would be destroyed (Matt 24:2; Luke 19:41–43), reminding us that God is more concerned about the heart of worship than the place of worship.

For Further Reading

Breneman, M. *Ezra, Nehemiah, Esther*. NAC. Nashville: B&H, 1993.
Fensham, F. C. *The Books of Ezra and Nehemiah*. NICOT. Grand Rapids: Eerdmans, 1983.
Kidner, Derek. *Ezra and Nehemiah*. TOTC. Downers Grove, IL: IVP, 1979.
Smith, Gary V. *Ezra-Nehemiah, Esther*. CBC. Carol Stream: Tyndale House, 2010.
Williamson, H. G. M. *Ezra, Nehemiah*. WBC. 16. Waco, TX: Word, 1985.
Yamauchi, Edwin M. "Ezra-Nehemiah." In *EBC*. Grand Rapids: Zondervan, 1988.

Study Questions

1. How did Ezra's love for the Word of God influence his life and ministry?
2. Why was the building of the second temple so important for the Jewish people and religion?
3. How do we see God's providence at work in the events described in the book of Ezra?
4. How did Ezra's reforms set the standards for Orthodox Judaism?
5. How can we keep a proper balance between spiritual devotion and external legalism?

ENDNOTES

1. Gleason L. Archer, *A Survey of Old Testament Introduction* (Chicago: Moody, 1996), 456.

2. For a list of words and constructions showing similarities between Chronicles, Ezra, and Nehemiah, see S. R. Driver, *An Introduction to the Literature of the Old Testament*, 12th ed. (New York: Scribner's Sons, 1906), 535–40.

3. Cf. John C. Whitcomb Jr., "Ezra, Nehemiah, and Esther," in *The Wycliffe Bible Commentary* (Chicago: Moody, 1962), 423; Edwin Yamauchi, *The Stones and the Scriptures* (Grand Rapids: Baker, 1981), 81–91; Stephen R. Miller, *Daniel*, NAC 18 (Nashville: B&H, 1994), 30–32.

4. See detailed discussion in M. Breneman, *Ezra, Nehemiah,* Esther, NAC 10 (Nashville: B&H, 1993), 15–48; and J. S. Wright, *The Date of Ezra's Coming to Jerusalem* (London: Tyndale Press, 1958).

5. D. Kidner, *Ezra and Nehemiah*, TOTC (Downers Grove, IL: IVP, 1979), 146–58.

Chapter 19

NEHEMIAH
Rebuilding the Wall

The book of Nehemiah is the second in the historical sequence that describes the **Jewish return** after the Babylonian captivity to repopulate the land, reestablish temple worship, and rebuild the walls around Jerusalem. The books of Ezra and Nehemiah are one book in the Hebrew Masoretic text and tell a continuous narrative of the Jewish return to the Holy Land.[1] The title of Nehemiah ("comfort of Yahweh") is derived from the central character and the phrase "the words of Nehemiah" (1:1). He was a Jew living in Persia in the fifth century BC. The fact that he was the king's cupbearer indicates that he was a man of character and integrity.

In 445 BC in the twentieth year of King Artaxerxes I Longimanus, Nehemiah learned of the terrible conditions of the people who had returned to Jerusalem (1:2–3). The walls were destroyed and the gates were burned. Nehemiah mourned in prayer and fasting (1:5–11) and appealed to **King Artaxerxes** to allow him to return to Jerusalem to rebuild its walls. The king gave Nehemiah permission to restore the walls, resources to do the job, and even appointed Nehemiah as governor over Jerusalem and Judah. Although there was some opposition, they built the walls in 52 days.

After Nehemiah accomplished the external rebuilding of the walls, a number of **spiritual reforms** were necessary to bring the people back into right relationship with God. This was accomplished by the public reading and explanation of the Word of God. A national fast was held where people confessed their sins and solemnly confirmed a new covenant. The people agreed to avoid marriage with foreigners and to support the temple.

BACKGROUND

The book of Nehemiah was written in the Hebrew language and was connected to Ezra, forming one unbroken history in the original Hebrew. It was probably written by Ezra, with Nehemiah contributing his narrative written in first person (1–7:73; 11–13). Ezra could have included these passages from Nehemiah's personal diary. Interestingly, Neh 7:5–73 is almost identical to Ezra 2:1–70. Chapters 8–10 were written in third person by Ezra because he mentions himself by name numerous times. Ezra could have included information from official documents: (1) a list of Jerusalem residents (11:3–24), (2) a list of residents of farming communities (11:25–36), and (3) a list of priests and Levites (12:1–26). The events of the book cover a 19-year period from Nehemiah's first return in 444 BC and his second return in 425 BC.

Nehemiah's Jerusalem.

While some scholars attempt to treat Nehemiah as fiction, conservative scholars cannot overlook many evidences of historical data that verify its historicity and authentication, i.e., (1) the dating of events; (2) the references to historical and geographical settings, such as the palace at Susa (1:1); and (3) the naming of historical personage, i.e., Artaxerxes, Sanballat, etc. The details of the account fit with the postexilic conditions in Jerusalem, and the archaeological discovery of the remains of Nehemiah's wall confirm this. The general history of the book is also supported by the 1903 discovery of the Elephantine papyri which mention Sanballat, Jehohanan, and Bigvai.[2]

Nehemiah is identified as the son of Hacaliah (1:1), and he had a brother named Hanani (1:2; 7:2). Some have suggested he was also a priest because his name "Nehemiah the governor " (10:1) is mentioned in a paragraph that ends with, "These were the priests" (10:8). This view is supported by the *Syrian Version* that reads, "Nehemiah the elder, the son of Hacaliah, the chief of the priests." The *Latin Vulgate* also called him "Nehemiah the priest," and 2 Macabees 1:8 said, "Nehemiah offered sacrifices."[3]

OUTLINE

The book of Nehemiah consists of **two main units** joined by the hinge of chap. 7. The first major unit (chaps. 1–6) involves the reconstruction of the wall. This section is more political than religious, and it involves physical construction rather than spiritual instruction. This unit concludes with a census or registration of the new inhabitants of Jerusalem that returned with Zerubbabel (chap. 7), which serves as a bridge to the final section. The second major unit (chaps. 8–13) involves the restoration of the people. Unlike the first major unit, this section is religious rather than political. It emphasizes religious instruction rather than physical construction. This unit can be further divided between the people's revival and covenant renewal (chaps. 8–10) and further registration of Jerusalem's inhabitants accompanied by Nehemiah's later reforms (chaps. 11–13).

Outline

I. Rebuilding the Wall (Nehemiah 1–6)
   A. Nehemiah's Concern (Nehemiah 1)
   B. Nehemiah's Commission (Nehemiah 2)
   C. Nehemiah's Conquest (Nehemiah 3–6)
II. Repopulating the City (Nehemiah 7)
III. Renewing the People (Nehemiah 8–13)
   A. Revival and Covenant Renewal (Nehemiah 8–10)
   B. Reforming the Society (Nehemiah 11–13)

MESSAGE

In order to prevent the nation of Israel from **assimilating** into the surrounding cultures so she can fulfill her messianic and covenant destiny, the book of Nehemiah narrates the sovereign work of God among both the Persian rulers and His own people in Jerusalem. This covenant work was accomplished through the covenant obedience and skilled leadership of Nehemiah. This work involved God's separating the remnant unto Himself both politically and spiritually. The political element was accomplished through the restoration of the dilapidated wall around Jerusalem despite much internal and external opposition (chaps. 1–7). The spiritual element was accomplished through covenant renewal and ongoing reforms (chaps. 8–13).

The story of Nehemiah shows the necessity of **courageous leadership** if God's people are to experience God's protection and guidance in accomplishing God's will. Against overwhelming odds Nehemiah was able to motivate the people to "rise up and build" (2:18 NKJV). The rapid completion of the walls was a testimony to the success of his godly, courageous leadership. Nehemiah's story also reveals the importance of prayer by the godly worker to complete any project for God. In the middle of writing his diary, Nehemiah includes the prayer that crossed his lips while doing the work of God, "Remember me" (1:8; 4:14; 5:19; 6:14; 13:14,22,29,31) and "Think upon me my God" (5:19; 6:14, author's translation). He constantly realized "the gracious hand of God upon me" (2:8,18, author's translation). One underlying insight in Nehemiah is the change in the people's perception of God. In the wilderness God went before them as a pillar of cloud by day and a fire by night (Exod 13:21–22). Next God dwelt in the holy of holies in the tabernacle (Exod 40:34) and then in the temple (1 Kgs 8:11). But Nehemiah uses a unique **identification for God**, referring to Him as "the God of heaven" (1:4,5; 2:4,20). God speaks from heaven (9:13) and hears from heaven (9:27), and He delivers His people from heaven (9:28). In essence Nehemiah establishes a new emphasis on the relationship between Israel and the Lord. From Nehemiah's time onward, the Lord will be "the God of heaven."

The book of Nehemiah also includes the "**Ezra story**." Ezra emphasizes the truth that rebuilding the law of God in the hearts of the people is just as important as rebuilding the walls to protect a city. A spiritual defense of the people of God is just as important as a stone wall. Although an enemy could destroy material walls, they could not capture God's people who were protected inwardly by the Word of God.

I. Rebuilding the Wall (Nehemiah 1–6)

The first major section of the book of Nehemiah records how God sovereignly worked through Nehemiah to **restore the nation politically** (chaps. 1–7). He did so through the rebuilding of Jerusalem's walls so that His covenanted nation could be preserved from assimilation into the surrounding Gentile nations. The maintenance of the nation's distinctiveness was necessary for her to fulfill her spiritual destiny. The city of Jerusalem had to be rebuilt before the Messiah could come.

A. Nehemiah's Concern (Nehemiah 1)

The book begins with a recounting of Nehemiah's concern with the **vulnerability of Jerusalem**. After receiving the report from Hanani concerning Jerusalem's vulnerable condition (1:1–3), Nehemiah not only expressed grief (1:4) but also directed a prayer to God regarding Jerusalem's vulnerable condition (1:5–11). In this prayer Nehemiah acknowledged the sins of the nation (1:6–7) and reminded

The Wailing Wall is the only remaining wall of the ancient temple area of Jerusalem.

God of His covenant promises of national restoration (1:8–10). Thus, the stage was now set for God sovereignly to act through His servant Nehemiah to rebuild Jerusalem's walls so that these covenantal promises to Israel could be fulfilled.

B. Nehemiah's Commission (Nehemiah 2)

The **sovereignty of God** in preserving the political and cultural distinction of Israel is evident in the book's second chapter. Such sovereignty is seen in how God strategically placed Nehemiah into the position of cupbearer in Artaxerxes' court so that he in turn could influence Artaxerxes to do something about the vulnerable condition of Jerusalem. The Persian king was the son of Xerxes. Esther would have been his stepmother and may have influenced his appreciation for Nehemiah's concerns. God's sovereignty is also apparent in how He moved Artaxerxes' heart, thereby causing him to issue a decree giving Nehemiah permission to return to the land and rebuild Jerusalem's walls (2:1–8).

Nehemiah returned to Jerusalem in 444 BC and surveyed the condition of the walls, then gathered the leaders of the city to share his vision.[4] "I told them how the gracious hand of my God had been on me, and what the king had said to me. They said, 'Let's start rebuilding,' and they were encouraged to do this good work" (2:18).

C. Nehemiah's Conquest (Nehemiah 3–6)

The next chapter records how various Jewish families began to build the sections of the wall to which they were assigned (chap. 3). Nehemiah's **administrative genius**

The tomb on the right is the tomb of Artaxerxes I. He died in 424 BC of natural causes. His wife is said to have died the same day.

is seen in his ability to delegate responsibilities and check on their progress through accountability. However, God's work is never accomplished without opposition. The next three chapters describe the various threats Nehemiah and his team faced as they sought to rebuild Jerusalem's walls (chaps. 4–6). However, these chapters also record how God sovereignly allowed Nehemiah to overcome each of these challenges so that the nation could be politically insulated from the surrounding nations, thereby giving her the potential of fulfilling her covenant destiny.

First, the writer notes **external threats** Nehemiah and his team faced. Ridicule from Sanballat the governor of Samaria, Tobiah the Ammonite, and Gesham the Arabian was answered through Nehemiah's imprecatory prayer (4:1–6). Nehemiah's harsh tone exhibited in this prayer can be explained by the fact that he saw this attack as an attack on God Himself. The opponents mocked, threatened, spread rumors, and used political intrigue to put fear in the hearts of those working on the wall. In response to these threats, Nehemiah armed the workers with swords and spears to ensure the success of the project (4:16–18).

Second, Nehemiah had to deal with **internal threats**. He had to overcome the threat to the builders' discouragement by reminding his workers of God's sovereignty as well as implementing some strategic defensive planning (4:10–23). He also overcame the threat of dissension and discouragement due to a financial crisis and covenant violations by the workers (5:1–13). In the process Nehemiah set an example to the Jewish workforce by refusing to eat of the king's allowance and by personally participating in the building project (5:14–19). Finally, Nehemiah resisted the temptation to compromise his standards by refusing to meet his enemies on the plain of Ono (6:1–4) or at the temple (6:10–14).

The chapter concludes by noting the **completion of the wall in record time** despite the ongoing subversive efforts of Tobiah (6:15–19). The sovereign hand of God is discernible in all of these events. The wall was rebuilt in a mere 52 days despite the fact that it was in ruin for 94 years following the nation's first return under Zerubbabel. Even Nehemiah's enemies recognized the rapid reconstruction of the wall was nothing less than the sovereign work of God (6:16). In the process Nehemiah's efforts fulfilled Daniel's prophecy that the walls of Jerusalem would be rebuilt "in difficult times" (Dan 9:25).

II. Repopulating the City (Nehemiah 7)

The book's first major section on rebuilding the wall concludes with a transitional record of guarding the city (7:1–3) and a record of the Jews who came back in the first return under Zerubbabel (7:4–73). Perhaps God sovereignly prompted Nehemiah to **record this census** (7:5) to show that God's purpose in allowing the return was partially accomplished through the wall's reconstruction.[5] The nation was spiritually revived through the restoration of its religious system as recorded in the book of Ezra and politically revived through Nehemiah's rebuilding of the Jerusalem wall. Thus, the nation could now protect itself from Gentile attacks and assimilation. Such distinctiveness now placed her in a position to fulfill her future covenant purpose by bringing forth the Jewish Messiah.

III. Renewing the People (Nehemiah 8–13)

A. Revival and Covenant Renewal (Nehemiah 8–10)

This section begins with Ezra reading the law (8:1–4) followed by the people's repentant and reverential reactions to what they heard (8:5–16). This culminated in their repentance and observance of the Feast of Tabernacles (8:17–18). **Ezra's reading** and the **people's response** to the law was necessary for the nation to become culturally and religiously distinct and thus prepared to fulfill her future covenant destiny. Ezra's reading of the law produced its intended effect as the nation repented of its sins (chap. 9) and renewed its commitment to the Mosaic covenant (chap. 10). Such covenant renewal translated into Israel's marital (10:30), commercial (10:31), and religious (10:39) distinction among the nations.

The story of Ezra's preaching illustrates some changes in the process of **religious instruction** after the return from the Babylonian exile. Nehemiah 8:1–9 introduces several new ideas due to changing circumstances. Ezra stands up on a wooden pulpit to read the Scriptures and then interprets them in order to explain their meaning to a mixed audience of men, women, and older children ("those who could understand," 8:3). This interpretation was necessary because Ezra read the Torah in Hebrew, but the people needed it interpreted and explained in Aramaic, the common language of the people at that time. As Ezra preached, the audience responded by lifting up their hands and saying, "Amen!" (8:6).

The Return from Exile

PHASE	DATE	SCRIPTURE REFERENCE	JEWISH LEADER	PERSIAN RULER	EXTENT OF THE RETURN	EVENTS OF THE RETURN
First	538 B.C.	Ezra 1–6	Zerubbabel Jeshua	Cyrus	1) Anyone who wanted to return could go 2) The temple in Jerusalem was to be rebuilt 3) Royal treasury provided funding of the temple rebuilding 4) Gold and silver worship articles taken from temple by Nebuchadnezzar were returned	1) Burnt offerings were made 2) Festival of Booths was celebrated 3) The rebuilding of the temple was begun 4) Persian ruler ordered rebuilding to be ceased 5) Darius, King of Persia, ordered rebuilding to be resumed in 520 B.C. 6) Temple was completed and dedicated in 516 B.C.
Second	458 B.C.	Ezra 7–10	Ezra	Artaxerxes Longimas	1) Anyone who wanted to return could go 2) Royal treasury provided funding 3) Jewish civil magistrates and judges were allowed	Men of Israel intermarried with foreign women
Third	444 B.C.	Nehemiah 1–13	Nehemiah	Artaxerxes Longimas	Rebuilding of Jerusalem was allowed	1) Rebuilding of wall of Jerusalem was opposed by Sanballat the Horonite, Tobiah the Ammonite, and Gesham the Arab 2) Rebuilding of wall was completed in 52 days 3) Walls were dedicated 4) Ezra read the book of the law to the people 5) Nehemiah initiated reforms

B. Reforming the Society (Nehemiah 11–13)

With the wall now rebuilt, the nation was free to begin to repopulate the city. Thus, the writer is careful to record the leaders and the people chosen by lot to reside in the city of Jerusalem (11:1–2). The writer also preserves a record of the heads of the families residing in Jerusalem (11:3–24) as well as the villages occupied by the Jews living outside Jerusalem (11:25–36).

Unfortunately, during the time Nehemiah returned to Persia (13:6), some of the people wandered away from their covenant commitments. Such **covenant neglect** put the nation at risk of being no different from their Gentile counterparts (13:24). Such a lack of distinctiveness jeopardized the nation's future covenant purposes of bringing forth her Jewish Messiah.

In God's providence Nehemiah returned to Jerusalem in order to hold the nation accountable for adhering to its prior covenant commitments. Nehemiah's **covenant enforcement** took the form of excluding foreigners from the assembly (13:1–3), removing Tobiah from the temple (13:4–9), restoring the Levitical tithes (13:10–14), stopping Sabbath breaking (13:15–22), and disciplining those who had intermarried with pagans (13:23–29). Nehemiah was a man of prayer, vision, determination, and administrative skill. The result of his efforts set the stage for the foundation of Orthodox Judaism in the years that followed.

THEOLOGICAL SIGNIFICANCE

Although the book contains no direct messianic prophecies, Nehemiah points to the coming Messiah in several ways. First, Neh 2:1 furnishes the starting point for the 70-weeks prophecy indicating that the Messiah would come forth exactly 483 years later (Dan 9:25; Luke 19:42). Second, in order for messianic prophecies to be fulfilled, Israel had to be back in the land (Mic 5:2). The book of Nehemiah records how the Jews were politically and spiritually restored in the land of Israel in **preparation for the Messiah**. Third, the messianic line had to be intact at the close of the Old Testament era in preparation for the Messiah to come 400 years later. The books of Ezra and Nehemiah record how this messianic line was protected as they narrate how the temple was rebuilt, Jerusalem was reconstructed and repopulated, the covenant was renewed among the Jews, and the people were reformed. Thus, because the temple was built as recorded in the book of Ezra and the wall was rebuilt as recorded in the book of Nehemiah and the race was delivered as recorded in the book of Esther, the postexilic stage was now set for the coming of the Jewish Messiah.

For Further Reading

Fensham, F. C. *The Books of Ezra and Nehemiah*. NICOT. Grand Rapids: Eerdmans, 1982.

Getz, Gene A. "Nehemiah." In *BKC*. Colorado Springs, CO: Chariot Victor, 1983.

Kidner, Derek. *Ezra and Nehemiah*. TOTC. Downers Grove: IVP, 1979.

Laney, J. Carl. *Ezra/Nehemiah*. Chicago: Moody, 1982.

Merrill, Eugene. *Nehemiah*. OTSB. Springfield, MO: World Library, 2000.

Smith, Gary V. *Ezra-Nehemiah, Esther*. CBC. Carol Stream: Tyndale House, 2010.

Williamson, H. G. *Ezra, Nehemiah*. WBC 16. Waco, TX: Word, 1985.

Yamauchi, Edwin M. "Ezra-Nehemiah." In *EBC*. 4. Grand Rapids: Zondervan, 1988, 546–771.

Study Questions

1. Study the principles of leadership exercised by Nehemiah in rebuilding the walls. Make a list of spiritual principles then a list of natural principles that were effective. How did Nehemiah blend these two factors together?

2. What do we know about the godly character of Nehemiah? What does his walk with God say to us about being a leader today?

3. How did Nehemiah overcome the various obstacles that hindered the work he was doing? What can we learn from Nehemiah to overcome barriers that face us today?

4. What can we learn from this book about the role the Word of God has in our walk with God

5. What is God challenging you to do to make a difference in your world today?

ENDNOTES

1. Cf. Talmud (*Baba Bathra* 15a), Josephus (Contra Apion 1.8) and Melito of Sardis (Eusebius, *Ecclesiastical History*, 4.26). See also, R. K. Harrison, *Introduction to the Old Testament: Including a Comprehensive Review of Old Testament Studies and a Special Supplement on the Apocrypha* (Grand Rapids: Eerdmans, 1969 reprint, Peabody, MA: Hendrickson, 2004, 1135.

2. R. K. Harrison, *Introduction to the Old Testament*, 1135.

3. Edwin M. Yamauchi, "Ezra-Nehemiah," in EBC (NIV): *1 & 2 Kings, 1 & 2 Chronicles, Ezra, Nehemiah, Esther, Job*, ed. F. E. Gaebelein (Grand Rapids: Zondervan, 1988), 572.

4. The likely year of Artaxerxes' accession was 464 BC, making 445 BC his nineteenth year. Cf. Harold Hoehner, *Chronological Aspects of the Life of Christ* (Grand Rapids: Zondervan, 1977), 127–28.

5. For an enumeration of the differences between Ezra's list of those involved in the first return and Nehemiah's list of this same group, see Gene Getz, "Nehemiah," *BKC* (Colorado Springs: Chariot Victor, 1983), 688. See also Charles Dyer and Gene Merrill, *Old Testament Explorer: Discovering the Essence, Background, and Meaning of Every Book in the Old Testament* (Nashville: Thomas Nelson, 2001), 357.

Chapter 20

ESTHER
Rescuing the People

The story of Esther is filled with palace intrigue, personal adventure, and anti-Semitic drama. Hill and Walton write, "It would be difficult to find a more riveting, dramatic, and suspenseful plot in the pre-Hellenistic world than the book of Esther."[1] The cast of characters alone would make it a best-seller in today's world: the powerful king, the defiant queen, the diabolical villain, and the courageous Esther. The **anti-Judaic thread** of Gentile animosity runs through nearly every chapter as does the providential hand of the unnamed God of the Jews.

Despite the book's popularity, critics have questioned, criticized, debated, and sometimes excluded Esther as an inspired canonical book.[2] It is the only canonical Old Testament book missing among the documents and fragments of the Dead Sea Scrolls. Esther is also the only Old Testament book in which the **name of God** does not appear.[3] Yet the religious practice of fasting by Esther, Mordecai, and the Jews certainly indicates a

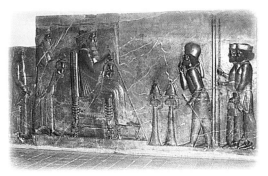

Relief of Darius I giving an audience.

dependence on God's divine intervention (4:16). Despite these challenges Esther has remained a message of hope over the centuries for Jewish and Christian readers alike.

The title of the book is derived from its central character, an obscure Jewish girl who became one of the queens of Persia. Esther's Hebrew name *Hadassah* (2:7) means "myrtle," but it was changed to the pagan name *Ester* derived from the Persian word for "star" (*stara*). **Esther's name** was a form of the Babylonian goddess *Ishtar* or *Ashtar*. The book of Esther is one of the five books the Jews called the *Megilloth* or "Rolls." The other four books are Canticles, Ruth, Lamentations, and Ecclesiastes. These books were read at Israel's various feasts. The book of Esther was read at the

Feast of *Purim*, celebrating the **deliverance and preservation** of the Jews during the Persian period.

The intricately carved wall of the palace of Xerxes of Persia at Persepolis (modern Iran).

BACKGROUND

The book of Esther is an anonymous work by a Jewish writer living in Persia (ancient Iran). His familiarity with Persian culture is frequently revealed, indicating the book did not come from the Hellenistic period. The author knew about the seven royal advisers "who saw the king's face" (1:14 ASV), the well-organized postal system (1:22; 3:13; 8:10; 9:20,30), the practices of showing respect for high officials (3:2), the recording and rewarding of the king's benefactors (2:23; 6:8), the king's signet ring (3:10; 8:8), Persia's irrevocable royal decrees (1:19), the observance of special days (3:7), the king's horse with a royal crown (6:8), the practice of eating while reclining on couches (7:8), and the fact that Persian kings did everything on a grand scale (six-month banquets, displaying wealth).[4] The **author's sources** certainly included writings of Mordecai (9:20), words of Esther (4:16–17), and the books of the Chronicles of Median and Persian kings (2:23; 6:1; 10:2). Therefore many believe Mordecai was probably the original author.

The events in the book of Esther cover a period of **10 years** from 483 to 473 BC. The story begins in the third year of Xerxes (Greek name), called Ahasuerus in Hebrew and Khshayarsh in Persian. Xerxes ruled the Persian Empire from India to Africa (Esth 1:1) from 486 to 464 BC. Thus, the events recorded in the book happened after Zerubbabel's return to Jerusalem in 538 BC and before Nehemiah's return in 444 BC. Conservative scholars generally date the events of this period as the following (see chart on next page):[5]

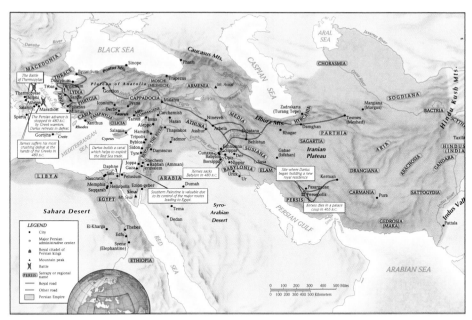

The Persian Empire.

538 BC	Return under Zerubbabel
515 BC	Dedication of Second Temple
483 BC	Xerxes's Military Planning at Susa
482 BC	Deposition of Queen Vashti
481 BC	Xerxes's Invasion of Greece
480 BC	Esther's Arrival in Susa
479 BC	Esther's Coronation in Susa
474 BC	Decree to Exterminate the Jews
473 BC	Esther's Banquets and Feast of Purim
464 BC	Death of Xerxes and Ascension of Artaxerxes
444 BC	Nehemiah Dispatched by Artaxerxes

King Ahasuerus's throne hall or second audience hall, in right of photo.

Although the events of the book of Esther (483–473 BC) transpired during the reign of Xerxes (486–465 BC), the book was likely written after the Xerxes' administration ended. The book indicates that the Feast of *Purim* that was established during his reign had already been in practice for some time (9:28,32), and the writer seems to speak of both Xerxes (1:1) and his administration (10:2–3) in the past tense. However, the book was not written later than 400 BC due to its historical and linguistic characteristics as well as the absence of any Greek influence.

The book of Esther was written to **Jews living outside Israel**. The words "Jew" and "Jews" are mentioned 51 times. While many Jews in Persia may have felt they were separated from God's protective care and love because they no longer had access to the temple or lived in the holy land, the message of Esther is unmistakable: God loves His people and takes care of them no matter where they live and no matter what their circumstances. Esther was a symbol of such Jews.

OUTLINE

The book has **two main parts.** First, it records the threat or the risk to the Jews (chaps. 1–5). This section can be further divided into Esther's ascension to the throne (1:1–2:20) and Haman's plot to destroy the Jews (2:21–5:14). This section features Xerxes's four banquets (1:3,5–8,9; 2:18). In the second main part, the book records the deliverance or rescue of the Jews (chaps. 6–10). This section can be further divided into Mordecai's triumph over Haman (6:1–8:3) and Israel's triumph over her enemies

(8:4–10:3). This section features Esther's second banquet (chap. 7) and the Feast of *Purim* (chap. 9).

Outline

I. Danger to the Jews (Esther 1–5)
  A. Demotion of Queen Vashti (Esther 1)
  B. Destiny of Esther (Esther 2)
  C. Decree Against the Jews (Esther 3)
  D. Decision of Esther (Esther 4–5)
II. Deliverance of the Jews (Esther 6–10)
  A. Valor of Mordecai Rewarded (Esther 6)
  B. Venture of Esther (Esther 7)
  C. Victory of the Jews (Esther 8–9)
  D. Vindication of Mordecai (Esther 10)

Another structural observation made by many is the book's chiastic organization.[6]

A. Prelude: introductory information (Esther 1)
  B. Xerxes's decree to eradicate the Jews (Esther 2–3)
    C. Haman seeks to gain victory over Mordecai (Esther 4–5)
      D. Xerxes's insomnia (Esther 6:1)
    C.′ Mordecai's victory over Haman (Esther 6–7)
  B.′ Xerxes's decree to rescue the Jews (Esther 8–9)
A.′ Epilogue: Mordecai's ascension (Esther 10)

MESSAGE

The book of Esther is a continuous story that contains six banquets and seven decrees. It begins with a crisis when Queen Vashti refused to appear for her husband King Ahasuerus (Xerxes) and embarrassed him before his government leaders. The story tells of Vashti's banishment and how a young Jewish girl was chosen to be queen in her place. A subplot reveals Prime Minister Haman's hatred of the Jews primarily because Mordecai, a noted Jewish leader, would not bow to him. Haman persuaded King Xerxes to order the execution of the Jews. Based on **Esther's wisdom and intercession**, Haman's evil intent was revealed, and he was executed. The king's decree was supplemented with another decree that allowed the Jews to defend themselves against attacks. After this crisis the Jews were allowed to live in peace, and Mordecai took Haman's place as prime minister. In celebration of their victory, the Jews instituted a celebration of the annual Feast of *Purim* ("lots").

I. Danger to the Jews (Esther 1–5)

The book of Esther describes how God sovereignly worked on behalf of the Jewish people in Persia to spare them from **eradication** so that the nation could fulfill her future covenantal and messianic purposes. The first major section of the book describes the threat that developed against the Jews (chaps. 1–5). The first two chapters of this section describe how God sovereignly orchestrated events behind the scenes so that His people would be in place to thwart Haman's future plan to destroy the Jews.

A. Demotion of Vashti (Esther 1)

The first chapter describes how God **providentially** arranged for Vashti's dismissal as Xerxes's queen so that Esther, who would be the divine instrument of Jewish deliverance, could be elevated to the position of queen in Vashti's place. The author notes the extent of Xerxes's Persian Empire from India to Africa (1:1) and his elaborate banquet, which many scholars believe was held for the purpose of planning his invasion of Greece. In the meantime Vashti held her own banquet for the women. Vashti's refusal to follow Xerxes' command to appear at the conclusion of his banquet ultimately led to her dismissal (1:10–20).

B. Destiny of Esther (Esther 2)

The second chapter describes how **Esther was elevated** to the role of queen in the place of Vashti. However, her decision to hide her Jewish identity and take a pagan name was typical of many Jews living in the *diaspora* ("dispersion") outside of Israel. The author also notes that Esther was far from perfect by Jewish standards. Her presumed sexual activity with Xerxes upon entering his harem (2:15–16), her partaking of the food at Xerxes's table (2:9; Dan 1:5), and her eventual marriage to Xerxes (2:17–18) violated God's covenant (Exod 20:12; Deut 7:4). Mordecai, a Benjamite, was Esther's guardian. His work brought him into contact with Persian government officials, and eventually he became the target of anti-Judaic prejudice. As such, he represents Jews everywhere who believed they were unfairly persecuted because of their religious beliefs and national identity. Yet Mordecai is also depicted initially as encouraging Esther's deception (2:10). Nevertheless, God used these imperfect people to accomplish His perfect plan for delivering the Jews from annihilation.

Painted relief of Persian soldier. The Persian Empire had significant influence on biblical history.

This chapter ends with Mordecai overhearing a plot against the king's life. This news was passed on to Esther who reported it to the king. The king executed the perpetrators, but for some mysterious reason Mordecai never was rewarded for his heroic efforts.

C. Decree Against the Jews (Esther 3)

Despite Mordecai's intervention to foil an assassination plot against Xerxes (2:21–23), Haman, the king's advisor, hatched a plot to **eradicate the Jews** (chap. 3). After Xerxes promotion of Haman (3:1), Mordecai refused to bow down to Haman (3:2–4). Consequently, Haman flew into a rage culminating in his ambition to exterminate all of the Jews throughout Persia (3:5–6). Haman's plot was planned with exactness, including great care in determining the exact date of the slaughter (3:7). He deceptively influenced Xerxes to issue a decree calling for the destruction of a people who did "not obey the king's laws," (NIV) though he did not identify them by name as the Jews (3:8–12). Had this "ethnic cleansing" succeeded, they would have exterminated the line of Christ because His ancestors were then living in Judah under the Persian administration (Matt 1:12–13; Luke 3:26).

D. Decision of Esther (Esther 4–5)

As the drama unfolds in chap. 4, the Jews are mourning, fasting, weeping, and lamenting (4:3) because of this threat. While God's name is not mentioned specifically, it is obvious to Jewish readers that they are calling on God to help them. Mordecai used his influence with Esther to convince her that she was the **instrument** God had chosen and strategically placed in a position of power to deliver the Jews during this dark hour. Esther first expressed reluctance to fulfill this role out of a concern for her own life (4:1–11). However, Mordecai explained that her death was inevitable and that God had allowed her to become queen for the purpose of **saving the Jews** (4:12–14). At this point Esther made her courageous decision to risk her life to appeal to the king saying, "If I perish, I perish," and asked the Jews to fast for God's protection (4:15–16). Such fasting probably included praying, though this is not specified.

Esther's poise, grace, and wisdom are shown in a series of **clever choices** she made to present her case to Xerxes. It was unlawful for her, or anyone else, to enter the king's presence without being invited. First, she appeared in her royal robes in the courtyard opposite the throne room. Impressed, Xerxes extended the golden scepter of approval and asked what she wanted. The scene must have stunned the king's male advisors. When offered "half the kingdom" (5:3), Esther cleverly responded that she merely wanted to invite him and Haman to a banquet (5:5). At the banquet she extended another invitation to do it again the next day. In the meantime the arrogant Haman was once again offended by Mordecai so Haman determined to have Mordecai hung from a gallows the next day (5:13–14).

II. Deliverance of the Jews (Esther 6–10)

The book's first major section discussed the developing threat against the survival of the Jews and the sovereign work God accomplished in guiding His **deliverer** into a position of influence (chaps. 1–5). The book's second major section (chaps. 6–10) describes how the Jews were ultimately delivered by Esther's courageous and clever intervention.

The Source of Anti-Semitism

God promised to bless the world through the Jews (Gen 12:3; Isa 42:6; 49:6). Thus, the three greatest blessings God could ever give the world will come through the Jews. These blessings include the Scripture (Rom 3:2), the Savior (Matt 1:1–17; John 4:22; Rom 9:5), and the future kingdom (Isa 2:2–3; Zech 14:16–18). Because of this divine pattern, Satan has a special animosity toward the Jew. His ambition has always been to stop this flow of blessings by prematurely eradicating Israel. Therefore, **Satan** is the ultimate source of anti-Semitism. The book of Esther reveals Satan's policy of preempting the birth of Messiah by attempting to destroy the nation through which He would be born (Rev 12:1–4). Xerxes' decree to eradicate the Jews would not only have affected those Jews living in Persia proper but also those returning to Judah. However, the book of Esther records how the nation was rescued. As the historic books of the Old Testament came to a close, the postexilic stage was now set for the coming of the Jewish Messiah. Yet even today Satan works through fallen people to eradicate the Jew in an attempt to thwart God's promise that the Messiah will ultimately reign over all the earth (Isa 66:15–20; Zech 14:4–11; Rev 5:10; 20:4).

A. Valor of Mordecai Rewarded (Esther 6)

Chapter 6 opens with a servant reading the king's chronicles to the king because he was unable to sleep (6:1). Upon discovering in the king's chronicles that Mordecai's previous good deed on his behalf had gone unrewarded, the king decided to reward Mordecai. Xerxes asked Haman how the king should reward a special person, but Haman thought the king wanted to reward him. Haman's **lavish suggestions** were accepted, and then Haman was instructed to honor Mordecai in a manner he would have preferred for himself. Humiliated, the angry and frustrated Haman expressed his exasperation to his wife and friends, who warned him that he would not prevail against Mordecai because Haman's downfall was certain (6:14).

B. Venture of Esther (Esther 7)

The triumph of the Jews over Haman reaches its climax in chap. 7. These events happen at the second of **Esther's banquets**. When Xerxes asks Esther to state her request (7:1–2), she reveals Haman's plot to eradicate the Jews and asks the king to spare her life and the lives of her people (7:3–6). Xerxes's anger over this revelation was extreme (7:7–8), but it was compounded when he saw Haman "falling on the couch" where Esther was seated. The end result was the hanging of Haman on the gallows he had prepared for Mordecai (7:9–10). These events are included in order to show God's sovereign intervention in history, for many years ago He promised to curse those who curse His chosen nation (Gen 12:3). These events were an encouragement to Jews living outside Israel in the *diaspora* to trust God and rely on His protection.

C. Victory of the Jews (Esther 8–9)

Because of the immutability of Persian law, Esther influenced Xerxes to issue yet **another decree** allowing the Jews to defend themselves against those who might try to attack them based on Xerxes's previous decree (chap. 3). Because the second decree represents God's providential work to spare His people from extinction, many have noted how Xerxes's second decree parallels his first decree.

The gate building of Ahasuerus (Xerxes) at Persepolis that led to a mammoth terrace built by his father, Darius the Great.

XERXES'S FIRST DECREE (ESTHER 3)	XERXES'S SECOND DECREE (ESTHER 8)
Haman's request for the decree (3:8–9)	Esther's request for the decree (8:3–6)
Xerxes authorizes the decree (3:10–11)	Xerxes authorizes the decree (8:7–8)
Scribes compose the decree (3:12)	Scribes compose the decree (8:9)
Decree disseminated (3:13–15)	Decree disseminated (8:10–14)
Susa confused (3:15)	Susa rejoices (8:15)
Jews mourn (4:1–3)	Jews rejoice (8:16–17)

Chapter 9 explains the significance of the **Festival of Purim** ("lots"). Since Haman cast lots to determine when he would execute the Jews, they celebrated their victory over this procedure with feasting, rejoicing, and sending gifts (9:18–19). To this day the Jews celebrate "Esther's Banquet" at the Feast of Purim on the fifteenth of Adar (February–March) in remembrance of God's blessing and protection.

D. Vindication of Mordecai (Esther 10)

The book concludes with a reminder of the blessings or curses individuals experience when they bless or curse God's covenant people. While Haman was hung on his own gallows due to his ambition to destroy the Jews, Mordecai was elevated to second in command (10:3) in the Persian Empire that initially sought Israel's destruction (10:1–3a). He also enjoyed the enduring respect of the Jews (10:3b) on account of his work on their behalf. In conclusion, the book of Esther describes God's sovereign and providential work in **protecting** from eradication **His people** living outside the land of Israel. It also depicts the respective blessings and curses upon both the friends and enemies of the nation. All of this information reveals God's unconditional commitment to the nation's purpose as expressed in the Abrahamic covenant. Esther's courageous intervention and Mordecai's elevation secured the Messianic promise by securing the future of the Jewish people who would give birth to their ultimate Deliverer.

THEOLOGICAL SIGNIFICANCE

The **providence of God** is obvious throughout the book of Esther. While God's name is not specifically mentioned, His providential intervention to rescue His people is unmistakable. In a series of interconnections between the book's six banquets set in the opulence of the Persian Empire, the timing of God is seen over and over again in the details of the story. These are not accidents of timing but divine appointments by which the Jewish reader easily discerns the presence of Israel's unseen and unspoken God. As the Jews fasted, they would naturally pray to God whose name (*ha shem*) was so sacred they would not pronounce it. Thus, the presence of God is clearly demonstrated in His providential actions. Even though God's name does not appear in the book of Esther, God's hand was revealed in the deliverance of His people.

For Further Reading

Baldwin, Joyce. *Esther*. TOTC. Downers Grove, IL: IVP, 1984.

Breneman, M. *Ezra, Nehemiah, Esther*. NAC 10. Nashville: B&H, 1993.

Jobes, Karen. *Esther*. NIVAC. Grand Rapids: Zondervan, 1999.

Tomasino, A. "Esther." In J. Walton, ed., *Zondervan Illustrated Bible Backgrounds Commentary*. 3:468–502.

Whitcomb, John C. *Esther: Triumph of God's Sovereignty*. Everyman's Bible Commentary. Chicago: Moody, 1979.

Study Questions

1. How is God's presence revealed in the book of Esther?
2. What lessons can be learned about pride and humility in the book of Esther?
3. How can we trace God's hand in our lives even when we can't see His face or hear His name?
4. What does Esther's experience tell us about God's working in our own lives?
5. How did God use Esther to protect the messianic line of Christ?

ENDNOTES

1. A. Hill and J. Walton, *A Survey of the Old Testament* (Grand Rapids: Zondervan, 2009), 348.

2. See details in R. Beckwith, *The Old Testament Canon of the New Testament Church* (Grand Rapids: Eerdmans, 1985), 283–91.

3. E. W. Bullinger (*The Companion Bible* [Grand Rapids: Kregel, 1999], appendix 60, 85), suggests the name Yahweh (Jehovah) is hidden in four acrostics (1:20; 5:4; 5:13; 7:7) which Hebrew readers would easily recognize. While this observation is debated by some, it is certainly possible that this was intentional.

4. E. Yamauchi, *Persia and the Bible* (Grand Rapids: Baker, 1990). The linguistic differences between Esther and Ezra-Nehemiah demand a different author who was living in Persia, was an eyewitness of these events, and had access to official court records.

5. Cf. John Whitcomb, *Esther: Triumph of God's Sovereignty* (Chicago: Moody Press, 1979), 12–28; C. Dyer and E. Merrill, *Old Testament Explorer* (Nashville: Word, 2001), 360–65; J. Stafford Wright, "The Historicity of the Book of Esther," in J. Barton Payne, ed. *New Perspectives on the Old Testament* (Waco, TX: Word, 1970), 37–47.

6. For an example, see John D. Levenson, *Esther: A Commentary*, OTL (Louisville, KY: Westminster/John Knox, 1997), 8.

Chapter 21

POETIC BOOKS

Poetry is one of the world's earliest forms of **artistic expression**. While it is not as common today in the Western world, it was a familiar mode of communication in the Middle East. In ancient cultures entire epics were recorded and preserved in poetry. They usually originated in verbal and musical expressions and were later recorded in written form.

The Hebrews were imaginative people. Their poetry and music were closely connected to each other and accompanied domestic and social life in all of its prominent scenes. Not only were poetry and music an important part of weddings, harvests festivals, feasts, and funerals, but they also had a central place in the religious life of Israel. While prose may seem sufficient for recording facts, the Hebrews used poetry to **express the soul**. The religious life of Israel is a record of real human experiences. The poetic portions of the Old Testament therefore portray the emotions and the experiences of God's people.

The English Bible groups **five poetic books** together: Job, Psalms, Proverbs, Ecclesiastes, and Song of Songs. This, however, is not to exclude other portions of Scripture from the poetic genre. The prophetic books rely heavily upon the poetic mode of expression to communicate their timeless message, as do a few portions of the Pentateuch and the historical books.

- Job: Questions of Suffering
- Psalms: Songs of Praise
- Proverbs: Words of Wisdom
- Ecclesiastes: Meaning of Life
- The Song of Songs: Songs of Love

PURPOSES OF HEBREW POETRY

1. To express emotion—Poetry is intended to appeal to the emotions, to evoke feelings rather than propositional thinking, and to stimulate a response on the part of the reader. While it certainly challenges us to think, it does so by eliciting an emotional response. Poetry is the language of the soul, and thus, the Hebrew poems still speak to us today and resonate with the deepest issues of the human heart.

2. To facilitate worship—Poetry is easy to memorize and put to music and often took on the role of lyrical expression in the psalms. Many of the psalms were sung in relation to specific worship services at the temple, and poetic books were read in connection with specific religious festivals:[1]

- Passover: Song of Songs; Hallel Psalms
- Weeks/Pentecost: Ruth; Hallel Psalms
- Feast of Ab: Lamentations
- Hanukkah: Psalm 30
- Tabernacles: Ecclesiastes; Hallel Psalms

3. To instruct in wisdom—Hebrew wisdom literature is a certain kind of poetic literature that was used to instruct the young person in the ways of wisdom. Hebrew wisdom tends to be practical and was meant to be applied to the many aspects of everyday secular life. While wisdom dealt with the practical, it did not leave out the recognition of God in the daily affairs of life. Hebrew wisdom teaches the reader not only how to live a good life but also how to live a *godly* life.

CHARACTERISTICS OF HEBREW POETRY

1. Figurative language—Hebrew poetry is rich in its use of figurative language. Nearly every verse of Old Testament poetry contains figures of speech, and thus the ability to recognize various figures of speech greatly enhances the reader's ability to understand and appreciate the text. Common figures of speech include simile, metaphor, metonymy, personification, anthropomorphism, and hyperbole.

2. Chiasm—A common structural characteristic found in Hebrew poetry is the use of chiasm. Chiasm is a thematic "crisscrossing " between adjacent lines of poetry, sometimes occurring in extended passages of poetic literature. In a chiastic parallelism the second line inverts the elements found in the first line so that you have a pattern of A-B/ B-A or even A-B-C/ C-B-A. We find such a chiastic structure in Ps 91:13:

On lion and snake (a) you tread (b)
You crush (b) lion-cub and serpent (a)

and in Ps 3:7:

You strike (a) all of my enemies (b) on the jaw (c)
The teeth (c) of the wicked (b) you break (a)

3. Acrostics—An acrostic occurs when each line of poetry begins with a successive letter of the alphabet. This stylistic method is much like alliteration in modern-day preaching, a tool used primarily for the sake of memory. While acrostics are found throughout the Old Testament, they are lost to the English reader through the translation from Hebrew to English. An example may be seen in the quoting of the Hebrew alphabet in Psalm 119, where each new stanza begins with a succession of Hebrew letters, following the Hebrew alphabet.

4. Parallelism—The essential characteristic of Hebrew poetry is parallelism. Parallelism is the practice of balancing one thought or phrase by a corresponding thought or phrase containing approximately the same number of words or a correspondence of ideas. Although translation can lose some of the significance of parallelism, most modern English translations seek to retain as much parallelism as possible by arranging each verse in two or three poetic lines instead of a flowing prose sentence.

The most common feature of Hebrew poetry is parallelism, which Longman defines as "the correspondence which occurs between the phrases of poetic lines."[2] Parallelism is repetition for the sake of emphasis or clarification rather than redundancy. There are three basic types of parallelism which are most common:

Synonymous parallelism—The second line expresses the same thought as the first line, though with different but similar words. Psalm 19:1 (NIV) states:

The heavens declare the glory of God;
the skies proclaim the work of his hands.

Though stated slightly differently, both lines are asserting that God has revealed Himself through nature. A similar pattern is seen in Prov 20:1:

Wine is a mocker,
beer is a brawler.

Antithetical parallelism—The second line expresses a thought that is in contrast to the first line. We read in Prov 10:1:

A wise son brings joy to his father,
but a foolish son, heartache to his mother.

And in Prov 10:7:

The remembrance of the righteous is a blessing,
but the name of the wicked will rot.

The lines are not in opposition to each other. Both express the idea that lifestyle choices have consequences, but they express that idea by using contrasting terms and opposite perspectives. This type of parallelism is especially prominent in Proverbs because the contrast between the ways of wisdom and folly were developed in that book.

Synthetic parallelism—The second line completes the thought of the first line in some way. In Ps 2:6 (author's translation), the Lord declares:

I have installed my King,
on Zion, my holy mountain.

The second line completes the thought of the first line by telling where the Lord has installed the king as ruler. There is no repetition in this form of parallelism, but instead the first line would not be complete without the second. An even more developed synthesis is seen in Ps 1:3:

> He is like a tree planted beside streams of water
> that bears its fruit in season
> and whose leaf does not wither.
> Whatever he does prospers.

The older understanding was that parallelism was simply a way of saying the same thing twice. A newer and **more nuanced understanding** recognizes that parallelism is "the art of saying something similar in both cola but with a difference added in the second colon."[3] As Longman explains, the more correct way to explain the relationship between parallel lines is not simply "A = B" but rather "A, what's more B."[4]

The three categories of parallelism listed above provide only a general understanding of the relationship between the poetic lines. Synthetic parallelism seems like more of a catchall category for all the poetic lines that do not reflect synonymous or antithetical parallelism. Deeper study of parallelism requires a more detailed explanation of the precise relationship between the parallel lines. In some cases the second line makes the first line more specific. Psalm 5:12 (NIV) reads:

> For surely, O Lord, you bless the righteous;
> you surround them with your favor as with a shield.

The second line specifies the first by stating how the Lord blesses the righteous—by providing them with protection. In other cases the second line provides an explanation for the first. In Ps 119:9, the psalmist asks a question in the first line: "How can a young man keep his way pure?" He then answers in the second line, "By living according to your word" (NIV). The second line explains how the action of the first line is to be accomplished.

Other forms of parallelism reflect the artistic beauty and literary complexity of poetry. In an **emblematic parallelism** the first line gives the emblem (a simile or metaphor), and the second line gives the reality behind the figure of speech. We read in Ps 42:1 (NIV):

> As the deer longs for streams of water,
>   so I long for you, O God.

This same type of parallelism also appears in Ps 103:13 (NIV):

> As a father has compassion on his children,
>   so the Lord has compassion on those who fear him.

In **staircase parallelism** words from the previous line are repeated and added to in the next line in a step-like progression:

> Ascribe to the LORD, O mighty ones,
> ascribe to the LORD glory and strength,
> ascribe to the LORD the glory due His name (Ps 29:1–2a NIV)

One can sense the verse building to a crescendo as the Lord is worshipped and given the glory and honor He deserves.

A **pivot pattern** is where a statement at the end of the first line can be read as the end of the first parallel line as well as the beginning of the second line. We see this pattern in Ps 98:2 (NIV):

> The LORD has made his salvation known
> and revealed his righteousness to the nations.

The phrase "to the nations" goes with both lines. Similarly, the phrase "tremble, o earth" goes with both lines in Ps 114:7 (NIV):

> Tremble, O earth, at the presence of the Lord,
> At the presence of the God of Jacob.

External-Internal parallels can be seen in Isa 1:10:

> Hear the word of the LORD
>   you rulers of Sodom!
> Listen to the instruction of our God,
>   you people of Gomorrah!

Hebrew poetry was also used to **convey wisdom** (Hb. *chokmah*), and the "beginning" or source of wisdom was viewed as the "fear of the LORD" (Prov 1:7). Rooker notes: "Wisdom literature fits within the framework of a theology of creation. It rests on the belief in the goodness of God's created order."[5] Whereas, Akkadian and Egyptian terms for wisdom often refer to "magic," the Hebrew connotation of wisdom refers to "skillful living" which is rooted in reverence for God.[6]

Forms of wisdom expressions include: proverbs, riddles (Judg 14:13–14), parables (Judg 9:7–15), analogies (Prov 27:17), and songs (Pss 34:11; 119:72). Within wisdom literature two distinct types may be found in the Old Testament: (1) *didactic*, the teaching of practical themes for successful living; and (2) *skeptical*, or philosophical inquiry into the meaning of life (Ecclesiastes), the purpose of pain (Job), or the search for true love (Song of Songs).

For Further Reading

Brueggemann, W. *Israel's Praise: Doxology Against Idolatry and Ideology.* Philadelphia: Fortress, 1988.

Bullock, C. Hassell. *An Introduction to the Old Testament Poetic Books.* Chicago: Moody Press, 1988.

Crenshaw, J. L. *Old Testament Wisdom: An Introduction.* Louisville: Westminster John Knox, 1998.

Estes, Daniel J. *Handbook on the Wisdom Books and Psalms.* Grand Rapids: Baker, 2005.

Longman, Tremper, III. *How to Read the Psalms.* Downers Grove, IL: IVP, 1988.

Murphy, R. E. *Wisdom Literature.* FOTL 13. Grand Rapids: Eerdmans, 1982.

Ryken, Leland. *How to Read the Bible as Literature.* Grand Rapids: Zondervan, 1984.

ENDNOTES

1. See details in Eugene Merrill, Mark Rooker, and Michael Grisanti, *The World and the Word* (Nashville: B&H, 2011), 496.

2. Tremper Longman, *How to Read the Psalms* (Downers Grove, IL: IVP, 1988), 95.

3. Mark D. Futato, *Transformed by Praise: The Purpose and Message of the Psalms* (Phillipsburg, NJ: P&R Publishing, 2002), 36.

4. Longman, *How to Read the Psalms*, 97–98.

5. Mark Rooker, "The Poetic Books," in *The World and the Word: An Introduction to the Old Testament.* Nashville: B&H, 2011, 498. Cf, also W. Zimmerli, "The Place and Limit of Wisdom in the Framework of Old Testament Theology, *SJT* 17 (1964), 148.

6. J. Williams, "Wisdom in the Ancient Near East," *Interpreter's Dictionary of the Bible: Supplementary Volume* (Nashville: Abingdon, 1976), 49.

Chapter 22

JOB
Questions of Suffering

The question of suffering can be especially distressing to believers who know that things do not just happen by chance or accident. When tragedy strikes, some people wonder: Is God unjust? Is He unfair? Or does He simply not care about a person's pain? Suffering has a way of turning the suffering person either toward God or away from God, and thus it is intricately tied to the spiritual life of God's people. Why do **bad things** happen to good people? This is a question for the ages, which every person on earth will face sooner or later. If someone has not had their own experiences in suffering, they know someone who has. As the saying goes, "We all have a story." So when calamity strikes, many are inclined to ask, "Why me, Lord?"

Suffering draws out the deepest **human emotions**, which are best communicated through the literary form of poetry. God has provided the story of a man who suffered more than anyone can even imagine. Through the avenue of poetic expression, the reader is drawn into the heart of Job, to feel his frustration and pain. Furthermore, as wisdom literature, the book of Job deals with some of life's most important philosophical questions. How can an all-powerful God allow the righteous to suffer? Do people always get what they deserve? Are supernatural powers influencing the circumstances of individuals, and to what extent does God permit such activity?

Ultimately, God's sense of justice is called into question, and the book of Job provides a wisdom-based response to these most pressing and relevant questions. The book of Job addresses these questions of human suffering from **five perspectives** to help the reader grapple with these same issues. Norman Geisler summarizes these by the following:

1. Author: Suffering is pernicious (satanic).
2. Job: Suffering is a puzzle (serious).
3. Friends: Suffering is penal (sinful).
4. Elihu: Suffering purifies (shortcomings).
5. God: Suffering is providential (sovereignty).

Geisler adds: "There is some truth in all these views of suffering. But as applied to Job's situation, the friends were wrong. Job was not suffering because of his sins."[1] God's providential purposes were being accomplished by His sovereign permission to allow Job to suffer so that he, his friends, and all who read this amazing story may benefit from it.

AUTHOR

The authorship and date of composition for Job are shrouded in mystery. Significant clues in the book provide evidence of an early setting for the events surrounding the narrative of Job. Some believe that Job lived during the **time of the patriarchs** because of the total lack of Mosaic references within the book. Job was a priest to his family, his age was that of the patriarchs, and there are no references to the tabernacle, temple, feasts, or sacrifices that accompanied the Mosaic law.[2] Additionally, the various places and names within the book reflect a setting prior to the conquest of Canaan.[3] Therefore, the internal evidence supports an early setting for the narrative of Job.

A vineyard worker examining grapes on his vines.

While the events of Job suggest an early date for the person Job, the actual date of composition remains a mystery, as does the identity of the author. The book itself does not identify an author, and the language is ambiguous in identifying a specific period of compositional origin. Jewish tradition has Moses as the author of the book, but little concrete evidence supports such a claim. The similarities in content and structure with other Hebrew wisdom books suggest the possibility of Solomon as the author, but this conclusion has no consensus. Other possible candidates include Elihu, who presumably overheard and had the opportunity to take notes on the conversations between Job and his friends. Perhaps the wisest approach is to leave the authorship of this inspired masterpiece **anonymous**. After all, the lack of authorial identification seems intentional, and perhaps one might speculate that this was meant to heighten the aura and general appeal of the book as it addresses universal questions with widespread application.[4]

STRUCTURE AND STYLE

The book of Job is a literary masterpiece with an unusual structure of poetic dialogue set within a narrative framework. While many Bible readers are familiar with the narrative story line of Job, this only provides the background for the dialogue itself, a dramatic roller coaster of rich lament, forceful accusation, and biting sarcasm. The literary genius of Job is characterized by the unique mixture and wide variety of literary forms employed, including the narrative prologue and epilogue (chaps. 1–2; 42:7–17), Job's initial speech of lament (chap. 3), and a self-contained poem expressing the virtues of wisdom (chap. 28). The poetic dialogue between Job and his three friends contains three cycles of speeches, each using rich examples of metaphor, hyperbole, sarcasm, irony, and a host of word pictures.

As with most ancient Near Eastern wisdom literature, Job deals with the issue of **theodicy** (the attempt to justify God's actions), but it does so from a thoroughly monotheistic perspective.[5] One also notices a thread of "lawsuit drama" that runs throughout the dialogue, and many have viewed this **courtroom motif** as the foundational literary genre of the dialogue.[6] The speech of Elihu wrestles with difficult issues through reasoned logic and wisdom while often digressing into verbose overkill (which Elihu himself seems to notice; 36:2). Finally, the "God speech" (chaps. 38–41) contains more than 70 rhetorical questions aimed at expressing in no uncertain terms God's unfathomable wisdom.[7]

OUTLINE

While a detailed outline is possible, it is not necessary in analyzing the content of the book of Job. However, the changes in genre and style reveal a number of clear structural breaks within the book. These discernible breaks are indicated by clear introductory references to the speakers of the various speeches throughout the book. Based on these indicators, the following outline may be helpful in discerning the flow of the book of Job:[8]

Outline

   I. Prologue: Opening Narrative (Job 1–2)
  II. Dialogue: Job and His Friends (Job 3–27)
 III. Interlude: Poem on Wisdom (Job 28)
 IV. Monologues: Job, Elihu, and God (Job 29–42:6)
     A. Job's Closing Oration (Job 29–31)
     B. Elihu's Speeches (Job 32–37)
     C. God's Response to Job (Job 38–41)
     D. Job's Reply to God (Job 42:1–6)
  V. Epilogue: Closing Narrative (Job 42:7–17)

MESSAGE

I. Prologue: Opening Narrative (Job 1–2)

The opening narrative of Job introduces the circumstances and characters that provide the background for the exploration of wisdom and justice addressed throughout the poetic core of the book. The narrator introduces the reader to Job, a man whose righteous character is affirmed three times in the first two chapters of the book (1:1,8; 2:3). Job is also described as a wealthy man from a distant land, "the greatest man among all the people of the east" (1:3). Taking the reader into the realm of **supernatural conflict**, the narrator sets the stage with the first test as the Lord presents His servant Job as a model of righteousness before Satan. Satan replies with the accusatory challenge, "Does Job fear God for nothing?" (1:9). God then allows Satan to take from Job everything he has but sets limits by not allowing Satan to take his health (1:12). The following verses describe the loss of Job's possessions and all his children, yet in all his loss Job "did not sin by charging God with wrongdoing" (1:22 NIV).

Camels are still used by Bedouins and others as a mode of travel in the Middle East.

With concision and style the narrative transitions the reader into a second cosmic test, with Satan responding to Job's righteous reaction by charging that Job will indeed curse God if his health is taken. The Lord in turn allows Satan to take his health, but he must preserve his life (2:4–6). In the midst of his physical affliction, the response remains the same; Job does not curse God (2:10). **Job's wife's** reaction, "Why don't you curse God and die?" (2:9 GNT) is not necessarily a statement of unbelief. She reflects the realistic agony of a woman who has lost all her children and is about to lose her husband. The opening narrative concludes with the introduction of **Job's three friends**: Eliphaz, Bildad, and Zophar. While these friends came to sympathize with and comfort Job, they would later become adversarial as they accuse Job of heinous sins in the dialogue that follows. Nevertheless, upon their initial sighting of Job, the three friends wept aloud and then remained speechless for seven days to mourn with Job over his circumstances (2:12–13). Their initial reaction reminds us that it is better to share the grief of those suffering than to speak impulsively, foolishly, or improperly.

II. Dialogue: Job and His Friends (Job 3–27)

Job's lament breaks the silence between Job and his three friends and introduces the dialogue that follows (chaps. 4–27). While the prologue states that Job did not

---

HEBREW HIGHLIGHT

Reject or **despise. Hebrew** מאס (*mâ'as*). Mâ'as is a dismissive evaluation that involves contempt. It frequently occurs with synonyms like "abhor" (*ga'al*) or "despise" (*na'ats*). Mâ'as involves rejection that could lead to abandonment. Thus, it means to "renounce," "refuse," or "dismiss" (Job 9:21; 30:1; 31:13). Mâ'as is used 11 times in the book of Job to indicate everything from "giving up" on life (Job 7:16), "taking back" words (Job 42:6), or "despising" one's self (Prov 15:32). This term is employed throughout the story of Job, who goes from despising his life, to questioning God and finally despising himself and "repenting in dust and ashes: (42:6).

---

curse God because of his suffering (1:22; 2:10), Job clearly did not mince words in cursing the day of his birth. As the week of silence allowed a time of reflection, a shift occurs in Job's reaction to his suffering. Job opens his mouth by cursing the day of his birth (3:1–10) and questions why God would allow him to be born if his only plan was to bring him to a place of such intense suffering (3:11–26). While still not accusing God of injustice, Job indicates that he wishes he had died at birth.

Structured around **three cycles of speeches** (first cycle, 4–14; second cycle, 15–21; third cycle, 22–27), the poetic dialogue in chaps. 4–27 is a literary masterpiece that communicates the full range of emotions experienced by the afflicted. Additionally, the dialogue calls into question widely accepted assumptions regarding the reason people suffer, namely, the retribution of a just God against the sinner. Job's friends assume he must have done something terribly wrong, unjust, or unwise to experience such an incredible tragedy.

Each cycle begins with a speech by Eliphaz, which in turn receives a response from Job. Bildad speaks second, followed by Job's reply; and finally Zophar speaks, followed by a response from Job. Each cycle follows the same pattern, with the only variant being the lack of a speech from Zophar in the third cycle. Noticeable **escalation** occurs as the speeches progress, with the intensity of language, accusations, and rebukes building to a climax as the third cycle closes. While the three friends begin their speeches in the first cycle by asking Job to consider if he might have some hidden sin in his life, this plea for consideration evolves into unfounded accusations by the third cycle, and the dialogue breaks down as the war of words reaches a stalemate between Job and his accusers.

Although minor distinctions can be observed between the arguments of each friend, the central message of the three friends is consistent throughout the dialogue: Divine justice demands **retribution** for sin, and thus those who suffer are afflicted due to seen or unseen sin in their lives.[9] Throughout their speeches Eliphaz, Bildad, and Zophar mount various arguments in support of their theological position, ranging from a vision, experience and tradition, or reason and speculation; but in the end they are unable to mount any evidence to prove that Job is suffering because he is a sinner.

As Job responds to each of his friend's speeches, he maintains his **innocence** in the midst of many accusations to the contrary (9:21; 16:17; 23:10). Job knows he has done nothing to deserve the calamities that have befallen him, and in spite of intense pressure to confess, Job never backs away from his claims of innocence (27:1–6). Instead of confessing to a sin that he did not commit, Job calls into question the justice of God, which only heightens the ire of the three friends. While Job never curses God in his speeches, he certainly comes close to questioning whether God has unjustly brought affliction against him (6:4; 16:7–14; 19:6–22).

Another key characteristic in Job's speeches is his **inquisitive plea** to know why he is suffering (7:11–21; 10:2; 13:20–27). Job not only questions God's sense of justice; he also wants to know the reasons for his suffering. What charges does God bring against him, and in what way has Job offended God? Apparently Job is not aware of the heavenly test in which he is a participant, nor is there any indication in the epilogue that Job is ever made aware of the circumstances behind his suffering. Maybe a slight hint of this comes in the vision in 4:17–21 when God indicates that He cannot trust some of His angels because they do evil things.

In keeping with his desire to know what charges God has against him, Job desires an opportunity to have his **day in court** with God, and to a degree the courtroom motif is apparent throughout the dialogue between Job and his three friends (9:32; 13:6–19; 31:35–37). Job is convinced that if he could only have the opportunity to present his case to God, then God would realize He is judging the wrong man, and Job would be proclaimed innocent from any wrongdoing (13:3–27). However, God is not immanently present, and Job's frustration mounts as he longs for an encounter with God but finds no way to approach the Almighty (23:1–17). Nevertheless, Job holds on to his faith, hoping that one day he will be vindicated as he stands before his God (9:33–35; 16:18–22; 19:25–27). In this context Job states his faith in the resurrection when he says: "I know that my Redeemer lives. . . . And after my skin has been destroyed, yet in my flesh I will see God" (19:25–26 NIV).

III. Interlude: Poem on Wisdom (Job 28)

Although at first glance the book of Job may not seem like typical wisdom literature, the book nevertheless deals with one of wisdom's most pressing questions: the apparent inequity of divine justice and retribution. Understanding the issue of **divine justice** as the driving theological question in the book, it is only fitting that a poem praising the virtues of wisdom is included as a self-contained unit within Job's final reply. Comparing the search for wisdom with the difficult endeavor of mining for precious metals and gems under the surface of the earth, the poem suggests that the worth of wisdom far exceeds that of riches, and its gain is far more elusive. Nevertheless, in keeping with Proverbs, the poem concludes that wisdom ultimately rests in the fear of the Lord (28:28), even when man is unable to comprehend the activity of God (Eccl 3:14).

IV. Monologues: Job, Elihu, and God (Job 29–42:6)

A. Job's Closing Oration (Job 29–31)

After the poetic interlude between Job's final reply (chaps. 26–27) and final oration (chap. 29–31), Job concludes his speeches by reflecting on his life prior to his suffering (chap. 29) and contrasting that with the **plague of despair** that now accompanied his every hour (30:1–19). With one last affirmation of his innocence, Job challenges God to judge him honestly, even suggesting appropriate punishments for various sins; and yet in all of this, Job affirms that he is innocent of all such iniquities (31).

B.   Elihu's Speeches (Job 32–37)

Elihu's speeches begin with a short narrative commentary introducing the young man Elihu. Presumably he was with Job and his three friends as they dialogued, but up until this point he remained silent. Elihu was angry at Job for "justifying himself rather than God," and was upset with the three friends "because they had found no way to refute Job, and yet had condemned him" (32:2–3 NIV). His entrance into the dialogue remains somewhat of a mystery, and as quickly as he enters the scene, he exits without further reference in the epilogue. Elihu provides a **new perspective** on the age-old question of human suffering. His wisdom provides an appropriate transition between the clearly wrongheaded thinking of Job's three friends and the call to faith brought about by the Lord's reply (chaps. 38–41).

A view of the beautiful snow-capped peaks of Mount Hermon, one of the wonders of God's creation.

Elihu's speech begins with a lengthy defense of his qualifications to speak wisdom in spite of his youth (chaps. 32–33). He then proceeds to defend the justice of God against the accusations of Job. He makes clear that Job is guilty of sin by "multiplying his words against God" (34:34–37). Elihu then follows by presuming to speak on God's behalf (36:2), defending the justice of God, and calling on Job to consider the wonders of creation (36:22–37:22).

The **justice of God** is clearly affirmed in Elihu's conclusion (37:23), and God's ways are deemed "beyond our understanding" (36:26; 37:5 NIV). Furthermore, within his speech Elihu introduces a "middle ground" in understanding the purposes of God in suffering, suggesting that God may use suffering as a means to keep men from sin (33:29–30), to chastise (33:19), and to maintain a healthy degree of reverence before the Almighty (37:24). In other words, God may permit suffering to mature and grow our faith in spite of our shortcomings.

C. God's Response to Job (Job 38–41)

At long last the Lord replies to Job and brings clarity concerning the misconstrued theology of the three friends and, more particularly, the misconceived accusations of injustice mounted against God by the suffering Job. Although Job looked forward to a day when he would question God and God would answer him, God now questions Job. Through the use of more than 70 rhetorical questions, God appeals to creation as a demonstration of His **unfathomable wisdom**. The main point expressed through God's speech is captured by Job 41:11 (NIV), "Who has a claim against me that I must pay? Everything under heaven belongs to me." God does not explain the rationale or the reason behind Job's suffering, and He reveals no compulsion to justify His actions before Job. God reminds us, as He did Job, that He is God and we are not.

D. Job's Reply to God (Job 42:1–6)

In response to God, **Job repents** of his wrongheaded thinking and the fact that he "spoke of . . . things too wonderful for me to know" (42:3 NIV). There is no indication in Job's response of any awareness regarding why he suffered. Rather, Job simply responds in faith knowing it is enough that God is in control. As a true believer Job submits to God's sovereign will and stops questioning His intentions. In so doing, Job remains a powerful example to all of us who struggle with the seemingly insurmountable questions of life, only to fall in faith, exasperated, into the arms of God.

V. Epilogue: Closing Narrative (Job 42:7–17)

In the narrative epilogue to the book, Job is vindicated, and his health is restored to him. The three friends are condemned as to their false accusations and misguided theology, and Job is called upon to serve as a priest and pray on their behalf (42:7–9). As for **Job's restoration**, God prospered him once again and blessed him with twice the wealth he had prior to Satan's challenge (42:10,12). The fact that he was blessed with 10 more children in place of the 10 he lost possibly indicates that he would have double the number of children in heaven. Finally, Job is said to have lived another 140 years beyond the end of his testing, implying that he lived to the age of 210.[10]

THEOLOGICAL SIGNIFICANCE

As wisdom literature Job functions to address one of wisdom's most perplexing theological challenges: Why do the righteous suffer? While the reader of Job gets a glimpse into the affairs of the supernatural realm, the question of suffering remains one of life's mysteries. Suggestions are made throughout the book to explain human suffering, some with greater merit than others. The Old Testament teaches as a general principle **retribution theology**, the idea that God will exalt the righteous and cut down the sinner (Psalm 1). However, wisdom literature observes many exceptions to this general rule (Eccl 8:14), and as such Hebrew wisdom sought to address the complexities of failed justice in a world governed by an omnipotent God.

The epilogue of Job makes clear that the strict retribution theology of the three friends was wrong in Job's case, and this certainly holds true in many cases of suffering experienced throughout history. Their wrong perspective reminds us not to judge others too quickly else we fall into the same hypocritical trap. Elihu's suggestion that suffering can be used as a **preventative measure** against sin is certainly valid. Scripture clearly affirms that suffering *can* be chastisement for sin (Heb 12:7–11). But it can also be permitted by a loving God as the apostle Paul attests in 2 Cor 12:7–9 when he affirms God's promise that His grace is sufficient for our every need. In the end the main point in the book of Job is that God is just however the circumstances may appear to man. Thus man is called to trust God in spite of his circumstances.

For Further Reading

Alden, R. I. *Job*. NAC. Nashville: B&H, 1993.
Anderson, Francis. *Job*. TOTC. Downers Grove, IL: IVP, 1976.
Ellison, H. L. *Job: From Tragedy to Triumph*. Grand Rapids: Eerdmans, 1977.
Hartley, John. *The Book of Job*. NICOT. Grand Rapids: Eerdmans, 1988.
Smick, Elmer, and Tremper Longman. "Job." *EBC*. Grand Rapids: Zondervan, 2010.
Zuck, Roy. "Job." *BKC: OT*. Colorado Springs: Victor, 2000.

Study Questions

1. Describe the enormity of Job's losses. Why did God allow this to happen to him?
2. How did these tragedies impact Job's wife?
3. What was wrong with the advice of Job's three friends?
4. How was Elihu's perspective different and unique?
5. Is God really the final answer to the problem of suffering? How do you know?
6. What is the most serious challenge you have faced with the issue of personal suffering? How are you handling it?

ENDNOTES

1. Norman L. Geisler, *A Popular Survey of the Old Testament* (Grand Rapids: Baker, 2007), 192.

2. Arguing from a lack of evidence is somewhat precarious, for every writer is selective and may choose not to mention people, places, or things, yet that does not mean they do not exist at that time. Although the prophet Amos does not mention the giant Goliath, this lack of evidence cannot be used to prove that Amos prophesied before David fought Goliath. Nevertheless, when a large amount of evidence is not mentioned, which one might expect to fit into the story, then one can hypothesize evidence for dating a book.

3. Additionally, the geographical location of "Uz" (Job 1:1) reflects a setting outside the region of Canaan, perhaps in Edom or Midian. See Robert L. Alden, *Job*, NAC (Nashville: B&H, 1993), 29.

4. Roy B. Zuck, "Job," *BKC: Old Testament* (Wheaton, IL: Victor Books, 1985), 716.

5 See the helpful discussion in B. Arnold and B. Beyer, *Encountering the Old Testament* (Grand Rapids: Baker, 2008), 200–294.

6. For more options on proposed genre, see W. S. LaSor, D. A. Hubbard, and F. W. Bush, *Old Testament Survey: The Message, Form, and Background of the Old Testament*, 2nd ed. (Grand Rapids: Eerdmans, 1996), 486–87.

7. Note the implied irony in these questions. Throughout the dialogue Job envisions a day when he will stand in court and question God regarding the circumstances of his suffering, but he is frustrated by God's silence—an inapproachable standing. However, in spite of Job's intentions, when God does speak, God questions Job.

8. The main points of the outline are taken from E. H. Merrill, M. Rooker, and M. Grisanti, *The World and the Word* (Nashville: B&H, 2011), 502–3.

9. Grisanti distinguishes the arguments of the three friends as follows: "Eliphaz, an empiricist, based his counsel on experience. Bildad, a traditionalist, grounded his advice on the orthodoxy of the past. Zophar, was a rationalist who carefully avoided any minimizing of Job's sin." See Merrill, Rooker, and Grisanti, *The World and the Word*, 504.

10. This assumes that the "twice than" factor in the Lord's restoration of Job (42:10) would also apply to the years of his life, and based on the 140 years of life given after his testing (42:16), the presumed age of Job at the time of his suffering was 70.

Chapter 23

PSALMS
Songs of Praise

Psalms was the prayer book of ancient Israel, and these 150 songs were collected for use in worship at the temple in Jerusalem. Some psalms were expressions of personal devotion, but many were composed as songs for public worship. The congregation sang them when they gathered for Israel's religious festivals and other times of celebration. Individuals and the people collectively repeated the lament songs during times of personal crisis and national disaster. Because of their spiritual depth and honest portrayals of the life of faith, the Psalms have greatly enriched the prayer life of individual believers and the corporate worship of the Christian church. Psalms reflects the passion of the true worshipper and expresses the full range of human emotions the community of faith experiences as they enter into God's presence and seek His help for daily living. Vernon Whaley observes: "Throughout the Bible's pages, saints of God used music to express both their joy and their sorrow. We read anthems of gladness—and grievance. Ballads were sung to inspire prophets, enthrone kings, celebrate marriages, and lament deaths."[1]

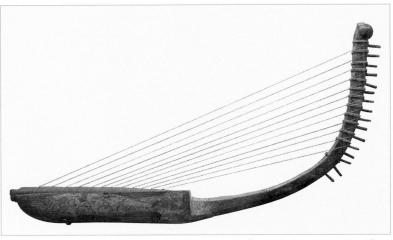

Wooden harp, dating from 1379–1320 BC, that is similar to the instrument David would have played as a young man.

BACKGROUND

The title *Psalms* comes from the name of the book in the Greek Septuagint (*Psalmoi*). The term *psalmos* in Greek refers to a song sung to the accompaniment of a harp. The New Testament also uses the designation "psalms" or the "Book of Psalms" (Luke 20:42; 24:44; Acts 1:20). The **Hebrew title** for the book, *Tehilim*, means "praise" or "songs of praise." This word is derived from the root *halal* ("to praise"), the basis for the English word "hallelujah." Psalms opens the third division of the Hebrew Bible known as the Writings (*kethuvim*) and is grouped with the poetic books in English Bibles.

The individual psalms were composed by many different individuals. Titles (or superscriptions) with various types of information are found in 116 of the 150 psalms. Of these 116 titles, 103 of them connect the psalm to a specific individual:

- David—73 psalms
- Asaph—12 psalms
- Sons of Korah—10 psalms
- Jeduthun—3 psalms
- Solomon—2 psalms
- Ethan the Ezrahite, Heman the Ezrahite, and Moses—1 psalm each

The titles of 13 psalms (Psalms 3; 7; 18; 34; 51; 52; 54; 56; 57; 59; 60; 63; 142) contain historical notations linking them to specific events in David's life. Some **psalm superscriptions** include information regarding the literary genre, liturgical function, or musical performance of the psalms.

Earlier generations of critical scholars rejected Davidic authorship of the Psalms because they believed the poetic features and religious ideas expressed in the psalms were too advanced for the time of David, but the discovery of other **Semitic poetic texts**, like the materials from Ugarit (c. 1400 BC) that preceded David, have weakened these arguments, especially the evolutionary understanding of the development of Israelite religion.

Some scholars attach little value to the reliability of the psalm titles because they view them as late additions. Despite the secondary nature of at least some of the psalm titles, they also reflect the most **ancient traditions** concerning the authorship and composition of the psalms. The superscriptions are found in all of the ancient Hebrew manuscripts and versions of the Old Testament, though some superscriptions in the Greek Septuagint (LXX) differ from what is found in the Hebrew text.

FORMATION OF THE PSALTER

The psalms are divided into **five books**:

Book I	Psalms 1–41
Book II	Psalms 42–72
Book III	Psalms 73–89
Book IV	Psalms 90–106
Book V	Psalms 107–150

The first four books conclude with a doxology or word of praise (Pss 41:13; 72:18–19; 89:52; 106:48), and the praise song in Psalm 150 provides a conclusion for the fifth book and Psalms as a whole. The reason for this fivefold division of Psalms is unclear, though rabbinic sources suggest this arrangement may reflect an attempt to parallel the five books of the Torah.

Book I prefers the name Yahweh (273 times) over Elohim (15 times), while Book II prefers Elohim (164 times) over Yahweh (30 times). Other **smaller collections** making up Psalms include the songs of Asaph (Psalms 50; 73–83), the psalms of the sons of Korah (Psalms 42; 44–49; 84–85; 87), and the "songs of ascent" (Psalms 120–134), which were likely sung by worshippers as they were making their pilgrimage to Jerusalem. Some of the Psalms scrolls from Qumran reflect a different arrangement in Books IV–V, suggesting that these sections were added last to the Psalter and that some Jewish sects had a different order for a few psalms.

More recent scholarship on Psalms, particularly through the influence of Gerald H. Wilson, has suggested the possibility of literary and theological design behind the arrangement of the Psalter.[2] Wilson noted that **royal psalms** focusing on the Davidic king appear at the seams (beginning and end) of the five books of Psalms, and each concludes with a doxology (Psalms 2; 72; 89; and 144). The fact that royal psalms were included in the final postexilic form of the Psalter, when there was no king on the throne, illustrates how Psalms looked back to past history as well as forward to a future Davidic, messianic king. Psalms 1–2, with their emphasis on the wisdom of God's law and the rule of the Lord through the Davidic king, serves as an introduction to the Psalter, while Psalms 145–150, with their emphasis on the kingship of the Lord and the call for Israel to praise Him, provide the conclusion.

A rabbi prepares to read directly from the open Torah in front of the Western Wall in Jerusalem.

LITERARY FORMS OF THE PSALMS

The individual songs in the Psalter can be classified into eight or nine basic literary types or genres. The German scholar Hermann Gunkel was a pioneer of modern study of Psalms in his work identifying the major literary forms in Psalms.[3] Other scholars have refined Gunkel's approach and the ways the psalms are classified.[4] Studying the **psalm genres** provides understanding into the shared literary forms, elements, and themes of the different types of psalms. Modern scholarship has greatly enhanced the understanding of the connection between the psalms and various temple services and rituals (e.g., songs sung at thanksgiving meals, national feasts, enthronement festivals, etc.). Ugaritic studies have provided new insights into the nature of Semitic poetry in general.[5]

Hymns

Hymns are **songs of praise** that focus on the Lord's eternal attributes and His great acts in creation and history. Worship begins with response to the person of God and the desire to honor God for who He is. Reflection on the Lord's incomparable power, holiness, love, mercy, and faithfulness led the people of Israel to celebrative praise as they gathered at the temple. The two basic features of a hymn are the call to praise and the reason for praise. The reason explains why the Lord is worthy of worship.

View of the turbulent waters (Ps 65:7) of the Mediterranean at the ancient harbor of Dor, about eight miles north of Caesarea Maritima.

Psalms 8; 19; 29; and 104 are representative of the hymns that reflect on the perfection of the **Lord as Creator**. Psalm 19 celebrates how God revealed Himself both in creation and in His law. The silent heavens universally declare the glory of the Lord, but the law of the Lord gives an even more perfect revelation that transforms the soul. Psalm 104 is a beautiful hymn of thanksgiving that exalts the Lord for His initial work of bringing the world into existence and for His continuing work of sustaining the creation by providing food and drink for each of His creatures.

Other hymns like Psalms 105; 106; 114; 135; and 136 praise the Lord for His past acts in **Israel's history**. The Lord's saving acts in Psalm 105 include His protection of the patriarchs, the sending of Joseph into Egypt ahead of his family, the rescue out of Egypt through the plagues, the provision of food in the wilderness, and the defeat of Israel's enemies that allowed the Israelites to take possession of the Promised Land. Psalm 106 contrasts the Lord's wondrous deeds for Israel with Israel's long history of rebellion and disobedience toward Him. Each time the worship leader recites one of the Lord's past acts for Israel in Psalm 136, the people respond, "His love endures forever" (NIV). All of Israel's history is testimony to the Lord's covenant faithfulness.

Laments

Laments are prayers offered in **times of trouble**, pleading for God's help, intervention, and deliverance. They are offered by individuals facing personal distress or by the entire community when experiencing national calamity. Laments comprise nearly one-third of the Psalter, making them the largest category of psalms. True worship is not only celebration but also involves approaching God with pain and hurt. The key elements of a lament include: (1) address and introductory petition, (2) lament, (3) confession of trust, (4) petition, (5) praise or vow of praise.

Lament psalms pray for **deliverance** from various types of distress. In Psalm 3, the psalmist prays for the Lord to deliver him from the enemies that have surrounded him on every side. Psalm 6 is the prayer of a sick individual who is about to die and needs God's healing. Psalm 7 is a prayer for vindication from slander and false accusations. In communal laments the people express their anguish and prayers for God's help in times of military defeat (Psalms 44; 60; 80; 85; 94). In Psalm 74, the people lament the destruction of the Lord's sanctuary and ask if the Lord has rejected them forever.

Shepherd leading his sheep.

A special type of lament is the **penitential psalm**, in which the psalmist confesses his sin and prays for the Lord's forgiveness and restoration. The intensity of emotion expressed in these psalms reflects the seriousness of sin and its consequences. In

Messianic Psalms

The book of Psalms is the most frequently quoted Old Testament book in the New Testament Scriptures. At least 25 of the 116 quotations from Psalms **predictively refer to Christ**, the anointed messianic King. After His resurrection Jesus told His disciples that "all things must be fulfilled, which were written in the law of Moses, and in the prophets, and in the psalms, concerning me" (Luke 24:44 KJV). Christ Himself taught the disciples which Old Testament Scriptures predicted His life and ministry. Luke 24:45 says, "Then opened he their understanding, that they might understand the scriptures" (KJV).

The threefold designation—law, prophets, psalms—refers to the three major divisions of the Hebrew Bible. The entire Old Testament was a picture, prophecy, type, and prediction of Christ's life, ministry, death, and resurrection. For the apostles and the early Christians, the life of Christ became a lens through which they read the Old Testament in general and Psalms in particular. Their **Christological perspective** gave a clear understanding to the pictures of the Messiah in the Psalms.[6] These include:

Ps 2:7	God's Son	Matt 3:17
Ps 8:4–5	Made lower than angels	Heb 2:5–9
Ps 16:8–11	Raised from the dead	Acts 2:25–31
Ps 22:1	Forsaken by God	Matt 27:46
Ps 22:16	Pierced hands and feet	John 19:37
Ps 22:18	Casting lots for clothing	Matt 27:35
Ps 40:6–8	Came to do God's will	Heb 10:5–9
Ps 41:9	Betrayed by a friend	John 13:18
Ps 68:18	Ascended to heaven	Eph 4:7–11

Psalm 38, the psalmist acknowledges that he is deserving of the physical and emotional anguish he has received as punishment for his sin, but he prays that God would show mercy and turn from His anger. Psalm 51 is David's prayer of confession after he committed adultery with Bathsheba and tried to cover his sin by having her husband Uriah killed in battle (2 Samuel 11–12). David not only prayed for the blotting out of his sin but also for God to purify His heart so that he would no longer be inclined to sin. In response to his forgiveness, David vowed that he would teach sinners the Lord's ways.

Thanksgiving Psalms

Thanksgiving psalms are prayers expressing thanks to God for specific **answers to prayer** or for deliverance from danger. The lament is offered before the deliverance, and the thanksgiving is offered after. The three basic elements of a thanksgiving song are:

1. The proclamation or resolve to praise ("I will praise . . .")
2. The report of the deliverance
3. Concluding praise or instruction for other worshippers

In Psalm 30, the psalmist recounts how the Lord answered his prayer by healing him of an illness. The Lord rescued the psalmist from going down to the grave and turned his mourning into dancing. In response the psalmist promises to praise the Lord forever. Psalm 32 expresses thanksgiving for the forgiveness of sins. The psalmist had wasted away in his guilt and anguish until he confessed his sin; then he came to know the joy of God's forgiveness. He encouraged others to turn from their wickedness and to trust in the Lord. Psalms 66; 118; and 124 are examples of communal thanksgivings when the Lord delivered His people from their enemies in times of battle.

The thanksgiving psalms represent the fulfillment of the **vow of praise** expressed in the lament when the psalmist was petitioning the Lord for help and deliverance in the midst of adversity (Ps 66:13–15). Sometimes these psalms would be sung at the time a person was presenting a fellowship offering at the sanctuary, in which the worshipper received back part of the sacrificial meat for use in a communal meal (Leviticus 3; 7:11–34). The worshipper would invite family and friends to share in this meal as he recounted the story of how God answered his prayer.

Psalms of Confidence

The psalms of confidence are **expressions of trust** in the Lord and praise to the Lord for the security He provides to those who trust in Him. Psalms 23; 46; 62; 91; and

The modern city of Jerusalem looking south through the Kidron Valley from Mount Scopus.

Hebrew Highlight

Lift up and **Exalt. Hebrew** סלה (*selâh*). The exact meaning of *selâh* is uncertain. It is used 71 times in the psalms, generally occurring with "choir director" or *mizmor* ("psalm"), so it may indicate a musical recitation or pause. It also appears to derive from *salal*, meaning to "lift up" or "exalt," thus, calling worshippers to pause, think about what they are singing, lift their eyes to heaven, and exalt the Lord. In Psalms 46–49, *selâh* appears in the margin after particularly triumphant refrains: "the mountains quake" (46:3); "God . . . is our stronghold" (46:7,11); "Jacob, whom He loves" (47:4); "God will establish it forever" (48:8); "God will redeem my life from . . . Sheol" (49:15). Regardless of its original meaning, *selah*, is a reminder to take our worship seriously.

---

125 are representative examples of the songs of confidence, and metaphors of God's protection and security are especially prominent in these psalms. Psalm 23 presents the Lord as the Shepherd-King who provides for His people, leads them through life, and delivers them from danger. The psalmist rejoices that he is an honored guest in the house of the Lord. Psalm 46 celebrates how the Lord protects His people from the two greatest fears of all—the natural disaster of an earthquake (vv. 1–3) and the attack of an invading army (vv. 8–10). In contrast to the roaring seas and the raging nations, the Lord's protective presence is like a gentle river flowing through the city of Jerusalem. The occasion for this psalm may be connected to the Lord's miraculous deliverance of Jerusalem from the Assyrian army in 701 BC (cf. 2 Kings 19).

Psalms of Ascents

Psalms 120–134 are songs of praise the people sang as they made **pilgrimage to Jerusalem**. These are sometimes called *hallel* psalms. The one who trusts in the Lord is as secure as Zion because the Lord surrounds His people like the mountains that surround Jerusalem. The righteous are confident that the Lord will not allow the wicked to prevail over them forever. These psalms express steplike parallelism emphasizing the verb *aliah*, "go up," in these 15 songs of Zion.

Royal Psalms

The royal psalms are prayers that celebrate the special relationship between the Lord and the house of **the Davidic king**. The Lord chose Israel as His royal-priestly people through whom He would mediate His presence and blessing to all peoples (Exod 19:5–6), and He chose the house of David to rule over Israel. The Lord unconditionally promised that He would establish the throne of David "forever" (2 Samuel 7; Ps 89:28–29,33–37), with the condition that the Lord would bless or punish each Davidic king based on His obedience to the law of God (Ps 89:30–32). The earthly reign of the Davidic monarch was a reflection of the Lord's heavenly rule and the earthly instrument by which the Lord would exercise His sovereignty over the earth. Psalm 20 is a prayer for the king as he prepares to go into battle, as the people petition the Lord to protect the king and give him victory over his enemies. Psalm 21 is the song of thanksgiving for answered prayer as the king returns triumphantly from the battlefield. Psalm 45 was a prayer for the king on his wedding day. Psalm 72 appears to be the coronation prayer for a new king. The people pray for the Lord to enable the king to rule with justice so Israel might enjoy prosperity and dominion over the nations.

Kingship (or Enthronement) Psalms

While the focus of the royal psalms is the human Davidic king, the theme of the kingship (or enthronement) psalms is the **Lord's kingdom rule** over His creation. These psalms include Psalms 47; 93; and 95–99. The expression, "The LORD reigns!" (or "God reigns" in 47:8) appears in 93:1; 96:10; 97:1; and 99:1; and Ps 95:3 declares that "the LORD is a great God, a great King above all gods." The Lord's sovereignty is supreme and absolute. The Lord is sovereign because He is the Creator of all things (Ps 93:3–5) and because He subdued His enemies throughout history (Pss 47:1–3; 96:4–10). In the execution of His kingship, the Lord acts with justice toward all peoples at all times (Pss 96:10,13; 97:2). Some nations brought tribute to Jerusalem and joined with the people of Israel in worship at the temple. They did this in recognition of the Lord's sovereignty, for many nations experienced God's blessings, just as He promised in the Abrahamic covenant (Ps 47:8–9; cf. Gen 12:3).

Wisdom Psalms

The wisdom psalms teach the value of **living a godly life** by focusing on the central importance of the law of God and the contrasting ways of the righteous and the wicked. Psalm 1 is representative of the wisdom psalms and, as the introductory psalm, provides a wisdom orientation for the entire Psalter. The wise individual avoids the influence of the wicked by delighting in the law of the Lord. The wise man flourishes and prospers, but the wicked man has no stability and perishes under God's judgment. Psalm 119 is an extended praise in **acrostic format** of the excellence of God's law. The psalmist loves the word of God more than gold or silver because it keeps him from sin and makes him wise. He expresses his intention always to follow the Lord's commandments but also prays for resolve to obey because he recognizes his inclination to stray from the path of righteousness. Divine discipline and even the persecution of the wicked have increased his resolve to obey the Lord.

Like Proverbs the wisdom psalms often teach **practical lessons** about everyday living. Psalm 49 reflects the deceptiveness of riches in light of the brevity of life. Only a fool puts his trust in wealth because what one possesses can never deliver a person from death. Psalm 112 promises that the righteous person has no fear of calamity and that the Lord rewards those who are generous to others. Psalm 118 teaches that the Lord blesses the one who fears Him with prosperity, children, and long life. As in Proverbs these psalms offer general principles about how life works rather than absolute guarantees of what always happens.

Imprecatory Psalms

The imprecatory psalms are prayers containing elements of extreme emotion and anger calling on God to bring severe judgment on the enemies of God and the psalmist. Psalms belonging to this category include Psalms 35; 55; 58; 59; 69; 79; 109; and 137. David prays in Psalm 58 for his enemies to vanish like stillborn children who never see the light of day. These psalms were certainly honest expressions of what was on the psalmist's heart, but more than that, they were also righteous prayers calling for God to **execute justice** against the wicked for their abuse and persecution of His people. The foes of the king and Israel were ultimately the enemies of the Lord. In times of warfare, the destruction of the enemy was often essential for the survival of the king and the people of Israel. Rather than taking vengeance into their own hands, the psalmists committed their cause to the Lord and petitioned Him to bring retribution on their behalf. In praying for the judgment of the wicked, the psalmists were praying for God to act in accordance with the righteous provisions of His laws and covenants.

Christians also can pray for the **final judgment** of the wicked even as they pray for individual sinners to come to repentance. Paul pronounced a curse on those who preach a false gospel (Gal 1:8–9), and the martyred saints in heaven ask how long it will be before they see the Lord avenge their blood (Rev 6:10–11). Like their Father in heaven, Christians do not rejoice in the death of evil individuals; but they do anticipate the final judgment when God will destroy the wicked and make all things right (2 Thess 1:6–10).

THEOLOGICAL SIGNIFICANCE

Psalms portrays the person and nature of God through the use of metaphor and imagery. The Lord is a Warrior, Shepherd, Redeemer, Rock, Refuge, and Shield for His people; but the prevailing metaphor and unifying theological concept in Psalms is that the Lord is King over all creation. The **Lord's kingship** is eternal and absolute (Pss 135:6; 145:13), and He is worthy of worship and praise because He is the "great King over all the earth" (Ps 47:2). The Lord is sovereign over all because He is the Creator of all things (Pss 24:1–2; 95:3–5). The motif of the Lord controlling or subjugating the sea is a metaphor that represents God's overcoming the powerful forces of evil in the world. This recurring image emphasizes the kingship of the Lord in Psalms (Pss 29:3–10; 65:7; 74:13–15; 89:9; 93:3–4; 104:6–9).

The Lord's kingship demands a response of **praise and worship** from His subjects (Pss 100; 105:1–3; 150). The angels of heaven and all of humanity join in ascribing to God the glory and honor due His exalted person and position (Pss 29:1–2; 148:1–5). Even the creation itself

The thickets of the Jordan River.

declares God's glory and greatness (Pss 19:1–6; 148:4). Praise and worship were communal activities to be participated in at the temple of the Lord in Jerusalem (Pss 84:2–4; 122:1–5). Moral purity was a requirement for entrance into the Lord's presence (Psalms 15; 24). The faithful are careful to meditate on and obey God's law (Pss 1:2; 37:31; 119:1–8,15–16). Love for God's law is an expression of devotion to God (Ps 119:57–58,72). While demanding a life of righteousness from the true worshipper, Psalms also recognizes that human beings are thoroughly sinful (Pss 51:5; 58:3). God is gracious to forgive and restore the righteous when they confess their sins and seek the Lord's enablement for living a life of integrity (Pss 32:1–2; 51:10–12).

For Further Reading

Allen, Leslie. *Psalms 101–150*. WBC. Waco, TX: Word, 1983.
Bullock, Hassell. *Encountering the Book of Psalms*. Grand Rapids: Baker, 2001.
Craigie, Peter C. *Psalms 1–50*. WBC. Waco,TX: Word, 1983.
Kidner, Derek. *Psalms 1–72*. TOTC. Downers Grove, IL: IVP, 1973
_____ *Psalms 73–150*. TOTC. Downers Grove, IL: IVP, 1975.
Longman, Tremper, III. *How to Read the Psalms*. Downers Grove, IL: IVP, 1988.
Westermann, Claus. *The Praise of God in the Psalms*. Richmond, VA: John Knox, 1965.
Wilson, Gerald. *Psalms*, vol. 1. Grand Rapids: Zondervan, 2002.

Study Questions

1. What is the major purpose of Psalms in regard to worship?
2. How do the psalms express the heart of God's people?
3. Why do some of the psalms seem angry, depressed, or even vindictive?
4. What are the messianic psalms, and how are they interpreted in the New Testament?
5. How should the poetic language of the psalms be understood?
6. Which is your favorite psalm and why?

ENDNOTES

1. Vernon Whaley, *Called to Worship* (Nashville: Thomas Nelson, 2009), 149. See his insights on "Worship in the Psalms," 149–79.

2. Gerald Wilson, "Evidence of Editorial Divisions in the Hebrew Psalter," *VT* 34 (1984): 337–52.

3. Hermann Gunkel, *The Psalms: A Form Critical Introduction* (Philadelphia: Fortress Press, 1967).

4. Cf. Claus Westermann, *The Praise of God in the Psalms* (Richmond, VA: John Knox Press, 1965), and S. Mowinckel, *The Psalms in Israel's Worship* (Nashville: Abingdon Press, 1967).

5. See Peter C. Craigie, *Psalms 1–50*, WBC 19 (Waco, TX: Word, 1983): 48–56.

6. See Walter C. Kaiser, *The Messiah in the Old Testament* (Grand Rapids: Zondervan, 1995), 92–135.

Chapter 24

PROVERBS
Words of Wisdom

Life is full of choices. No one can get through life without being faced with choices, and bad decisions can often result in harmful consequences. In ancient society the ability to make wise decisions in all of **life's practical matters** was highly esteemed. Ancient Near Eastern wisdom shares the same basic emphasis on practical matters and success in life that one finds in the wisdom of the Hebrew Bible. However, the Jewish sages infused their literature with an understanding that all wisdom, even things related to everyday practical matters, begins with the fear of the Lord (1:7). Therefore, Hebrew wisdom literature taught people not only how to make good choices in life but also how to make godly choices.[1] Within the Old Testament there is perhaps no better example of the practical side of godly living and success than what is found in the book of Proverbs.

FORM AND FUNCTION

A proverb (Hebrew *mashal*) is a **short poetic sentence** conveying wisdom in a concise and memorable form. Proverbs are typically based on experience and observation and are written in such a way that they produce reflection within the mind of the reader. They encapsulate profound wisdom in simple sentences. Most proverbs take on the form of a two-line unit, with the second line corresponding to the first line through some form of parallelism. Indeed, the key literary characteristic within the individual proverb is parallelism.[2] However, it is possible to observe some variety between individual proverbs even beyond the typical types of parallelism.

Various types of parallelism may be seen in the following examples:

Synonymous
Pride comes before destruction,
and an arrogant spirit before a fall. (16:18)

Antithetical
Genuine righteousness leads to life,
but pursuing evil leads to death. (11:19)

Synthetic
The one who conceals hatred has lying lips,
and whoever spreads slander is a fool. (10:18)

259

Comparative
Good news from a distant land
is like cold water to a parched throat. (25:25)

Absurdity
Why does a fool have money . . . to buy wisdom,
when he is not able to understand it? (17:16, author's translation)

The pylon entrance to the Luxor temple in Egypt.

In a general sense the proverbs can be grouped into two major forms: instructive discourses (1–9; 22:17–24:22; 31:1–9) and pithy sayings (10:1–22:16; 24:23–34; 25–29). Additionally, the book of Proverbs concludes with appendices of the sayings of Agur (chap. 30), Lemuel (31:1–9), and the poem concerning the ideal wife (31:10–31).

Within the instructive discourses one finds a variety of means to communicate instruction and admonition, but the most prominent are **direct address** ("Listen, my son, to your father's instruction," 1:8 NIV) and **imperative command** ("don't reject your mother's teaching," 1:8 NIV). While these discourses contain clear imperatives, they are primarily structured through the means of direct address and therefore are meant to be read in the same manner they were received, that is, as complete speeches communicated in whole and not in part. Therefore, while one may reflect on an individual verse (or "proverb") among the sayings, it is better to read the discourses as complete units.

The sayings tend to be **concise** in form and lack an extended structural arrangement. They are noted for their extensive use of figurative language and consistently employ parallelism as a means to heighten the point they seek to convey. If one were to categorize the sayings, it may be sufficient to recognize the examples listed above as well as the prolific use of antithetical parallelism used to contrast wisdom and folly. For example:

> A wise man is cautious and turns from evil,
> but a fool is easily angered and is careless. (14:16)

> A wise son brings joy to his father,
> but a foolish man despises his mother. (15:20)

Within Proverbs certain distinct **subgenres** reflect variety among the sayings. For instance, among the "Sayings of Agur" (chap. 30), one finds an extensive use of numerical formula, where Proverbs contains a numerical introduction followed by a list of coordinated items. Also, scattered among the proverbs are "better than" sayings, where one thing is esteemed as "better than" another. For example:

> Better a little with the fear of the LORD
> than great treasure with turmoil. (15:16)

> Better a meal of vegetables where there is love
> than a fattened calf with hatred. (15:17)

> Better . . . to meet a bear robbed of her cubs
> than a fool in his foolishness. (17:12)

Repeated warnings (19:13–14; 21:9,19; 27:15–16) are directed at marrying or provoking a contentious spouse ("Better to live on the corner of a roof than to share a house with a nagging wife," 21:9; 25:24). Additional subgenres within Proverbs include "comparative sayings," where the use of simile (translated with "like" or "as") heightens the impact of the point (see Proverbs 25 for an extensive use of comparative sayings) and "abomination sayings," which contrast what the Lord "detests" with what pleases him (15:26; see also 11:1; 15:8–9; 16:5; 20:23). Finally, it is worth noting the use of acrostic in the final poem extolling the characteristics of the virtuous wife (31:10–31).[3]

AUTHORSHIP

Most of the proverbs contained in the book of Proverbs are attributed to King Solomon. Solomon's name appears at three different parts of the book (1:1; 10:1; 25:1), and according to the biblical account, **Solomon's wisdom** was divinely granted and surpassed that of all other sages (1 Kgs 4:29–34). More specifically Solomon "composed 3,000 proverbs" (1 Kgs 4:32); and while the book of Proverbs contains only 915 individual proverbs, it is clear that Solomonic origin for the majority of Proverbs is consistent with the biblical account of Solomon's reign. Jesus accepted the historicity of the biblical account of Solomon's wisdom (Matt 12:42), and thus there is little reason from Scripture to question Solomon as the author/originator of the proverbs attributed to him.

While it is proper to think of the historical Solomon as the sage behind the sayings of Solomon (10:1; 25:1) and the instructive discourses (1:1), it is also important to recognize that the text itself indicates that the final compilation of the book of Proverbs did not occur until the time of Hezekiah (25:1).

OUTLINE

The book of Proverbs is **unique** within Scripture in that it is a collection of collections; that is, individual discourses and sayings were compiled into collections. Then these collections were compiled into the book of Proverbs. Within the text itself the collections are easily recognized by their headings:

Outline
I. The Discourses of Solomon (Proverbs 1–9)
II. Individual Proverbs of Solomon (Proverbs 10:1–22:16)
III. The Sayings of the Wise (Proverbs 22:17–24:34)
IV. Proverbs of Solomon, Copied by the Men of Hezekiah (Proverbs 25–29)
V. Appendixes
A. Sayings of Agur (Proverbs 30)
B. Sayings of Lemuel (Proverbs 31:1–9)
C. Poem of the Ideal Wife (Proverbs 31:10–31)

Further distinctions are recognized by the break between the wisdom introduction (1:2–7) and the instructive discourses (1:8–7:27), which in turn can be distinguished as 10 individual speeches through the repeated addresses from father to son (1:8; 2:1; 3:1,21; 4:1,10; 5:1; 6:1,20; 7:1). The first nine chapters then conclude with the personified invitation from lady "Wisdom" (8:1–9:12) and a warning against "the woman Folly" (9:13–18). Chapters 5–7 give extensive instruction about marriage and warnings against adultery.

Among the collections of sayings, which include the proverbs of Solomon (10:1; 25:1), there is little consistent arrangement verse to verse, with the exception of the sayings of Agur (30:1–33), the oracle of King Lemuel (31:2–9), and the acrostic poem on the virtuous wife (31:10–31). Most proverbs are **capsules of wisdom** that summarize great truths in simple phrases.

INTERPRETATION

Wisdom is meant to be applied, not just studied or memorized. Correct application, however, always depends on accurate interpretation. As with other unique literary forms in Scripture, certain guidelines prove helpful when applied to the reading of Proverbs.

Perhaps most importantly, one must recognize that in regard to **form**, the proverbs are poetry, not prose. Thus one must think in terms of parallel lines as the primary means by which thoughts relate to one another. Additionally, with the rich use of figurative language in Hebrew poetry, it is always necessary to contemplate carefully the point of comparison, substitution, sarcasm, or exaggeration in the figures of speech employed within a proverb. Indeed, nearly every prov-

A young Jewish boy receives his first phylactery during his bar mitzvah.

erb contains at least one example of a discernible figure of speech, so it is helpful to recognize basic figures of speech when reading through Proverbs.

In terms of **function**, proverbs are wisdom literature, and thus certain guidelines prove helpful beyond the mere discernment of poetic features. With this fact in mind, the reader may benefit from some guidelines to help in understanding the book of Proverbs as Hebrew wisdom.

First, Proverbs concentrates primarily on **practical issues**, rather than focusing on theological issues. This is not to suggest that theological questions were not of interest to the wisdom sages in Israel, for books like Job and Ecclesiastes wrestle with significant questions regarding divine justice in this world and the next. Even in the book of Proverbs, the fear of the Lord is prominent in defining wisdom, and reflections on the mysteries of divine sovereignty are present (16:9; 19:21). However, the bulk of content in Proverbs has a decidedly practical orientation and, as such, is meant to be applied to daily life. While the proverbs do not specifically tell the reader how to get to heaven, they do give instructions on how to live until that time.

Second, the book of Proverbs continually presents a **sharp contrast** between the life of wisdom and the life of folly. However, this contrast has little to do with book knowledge or "street smarts" but rather a person's orientation to God. Thus the contrast between wisdom and folly is often a contrast between righteousness and wickedness, a point clearly drawn out in the prologue (1:1–7) and the instructive discourses (1:8–9:18). Furthermore, as the sayings address practical issues ranging from work ethics to the use of the tongue, the various contrasting points are usually emblematic, describing the wise and the fool within various realms of practical interest (e.g., the diligent person is wise while the sluggard is a fool, or the one who holds his tongue is wise while the fool hastens to speak).

Finally, proverbs are **general truths**, not specific promises or guarantees from God. When applied, the general point taught in a proverb is likely to hold true, but in a fallen

FORMS OF WISDOM TEACHING IN PROVERBS

1. Proverb	A proverb is a short, carefully constructed ethical observation (13:7) or teaching (14:1).
2. Admonition	An admonition is a command written either as a short proverb or as part of a long discourse.
3. Numerical Saying	The numerical pattern lists items that have something in common after an introduction like, "Six things the LORD hates; in fact, seven are detestable to Him" (6:16 HCSB).
4. Better	A better saying follows the pattern "A is better than B" saying (21:19).
5. Rhetorical Question	A rhetorical question is a question with an obvious answer that still draws the reader into deeper reflection (30:4).
6. Wisdom Poem	Wisdom poems or songs teach a series of moral lessons (31:10-31). These poems are often acrostic which means that the first letter of the first line begins with the first letter in the Hebrew alphabet. The first letter of the second line is the second letter of the Hebrew alphabet, and so on.
7. Example	An example story is an anecdote meant to drive home a story moral lesson (7:6-27).

Forms of wisdom in Proverbs.

world exceptions will confound even the wisest individuals. Some of these exceptions are considered in detail in the books of Ecclesiastes and Job. The book of Proverbs, however, is not so concerned with the inevitable exceptions. Its concern is with the more likely outcome. Thus, in the classic example of Prov 22:6 (NIV), "Train a child in the way he should go, and when he is old he will not turn from it," the general rule is that parental discipline and instruction will typically result in a positive outcome. However, this is not a guarantee. Almost everyone who reads this book knows of an exception to the rule, a relative or an acquaintance that despite every advantage of a godly upbringing has rejected the teaching and discipline of his or her parents. Nevertheless, the wisdom of Prov 22:6 holds true as a general rule, not an absolute promise.

MESSAGE

Due to the noncontextual arrangement of broad segments within Proverbs 10–29, it is probably best to study Proverbs with a topical approach rather than a contextual approach. By correlating the instruction found within individual proverbs to broader topical themes, it is possible to come to an overall understanding of what Hebrew wisdom teaches regarding various practical topics. Even as one distinguishes between popular topics of practical interest, it is important to remember that the consistent thematic emphasis throughout the book of Proverbs is the **praise of wisdom** in all of its manifestations.

The following list is merely representative of popular topics. Other topical arrangements are certainly possible, although the general teaching of what entails wisdom and folly is consistent and clear.[4]

Marriage and Sexuality

One of the most important choices people can make concerns their potential marriage partner. A spouse can be the greatest asset or the worst liability to one's life and general happiness. The book of Proverbs contains timely advice regarding the value of marriage, its moral responsibility, traits of a good partner, and the quality of true love. The proverbs were originally addressed to young men, but the precepts are easily adapted to both men and women of every age.

- Marital faithfulness comes with wisdom and the benefits of sexuality are a blessing within marriage (5:15–19).
- The folly of infidelity contains many pitfalls and temptations that can lead to the destruction of one's marriage, health, and life (5:20–23; 6:20–35; 7:6–27; 23:26–28).
- Inherent goodness accompanies the blessing of marriage (18:22).
- A spouse has the power to make or break a person's well-being (12:4).
- The character of one's spouse has great impact on the family and household (14:1).
- Great caution ought to accompany one's choice of a spouse as a protection against living unhappily with a contentious person (19:13–14; 21:9,19; 27:15–16).
- It is better to choose a spouse based on character rather than outward appearance (31:10–31).

Wealth and Poverty

Proverbs contains a **balanced view** of wealth and poverty. Some people are poor due to misfortune while others are poor due to their own laziness. Some are rich because of greed and corruption while others are blessed by God and their own diligence.

Hebrew Highlight

Wisdom. Hebrew חכמה (*chokmâh*). This word is a derivative of *chakam*, used 312 times in the Hebrew Bible, most frequently in Job, Proverbs, and Ecclesiastes. It describes prudence in practical matters, skills in the arts, moral sensitivity, and spiritual insight. God, who is holy and wise, expects us to exhibit His character in our lives as well. In addition *chakam*, "wise," refers to those who are skillful in exercising good judgment in managing personal relationships (Prov 20:26). In Proverbs *chakam* carries both intellectual and moral connotations and describes the skill of right living (16:21), with a focus on ethical and spiritual conduct.

- Lazy behavior results in poverty while diligence results in wealth (10:4; 20:13). However, poverty may also result from corruption and injustice (13:23).
- A degree of practical security comes with wealth while poverty results in numerous pitfalls (10:15). However, the security wealth provides is limited (11:4,28). Furthermore, wealth may even become a liability (13:8).
- Mere talk leads to poverty while diligent action brings prosperity (14:23). Furthermore, those who seek the benefit of wealth without working for it will find themselves in poverty (21:17; 28:19).
- In a world where injustice is common, favoritism often benefits the rich (14:20; 19:4).
- Great wealth without the peace of God has little benefit (15:16; 28:6).
- Profit comes not only as a result of hard work but also from wise planning. Meanwhile, haste leads to poverty (21:5).
- Wealth brings power in society while poverty results in servitude (22:7).
- Wealth gained through corruption will eventually be judged (22:16,22–23; 28:8,20).
- Riches are a fleeting entity; the wise will not be consumed by the pursuit of wealth (23:4–5).
- Those who lack generosity will find themselves in poverty (28:22,27).

Bedouin mother and child.

Power of the Tongue

The modern proverb, "Sticks and stones may break my bones, but words will never hurt me," certainly does not reflect biblical wisdom. Most people have felt the power of encouragement as well as the destruction wrought by gossip or hateful words. Indeed, the tongue can be a powerful instrument for good or evil. As with other topics, one finds that Proverbs presents a balanced and realistic perspective on the power and use of the **spoken word**:

- Spoken words have tremendous power to encourage and discourage (12:18,25; 15:4,23; 16:24; 18:21; 25:11). However, even encouragement needs to be measured (25:20).
- Spoken words have power to lessen and to heighten tension and strife (15:1).
- The ability to refrain from speaking is a mark of wisdom, while hasty speech may result in ruin (10:19; 13:3; 15:28; 17:27–28; 18:13). Furthermore, it is better to listen with discernment than speak with haste (10:14).
- The Lord abhors lying and slander, and from the perspective of wisdom, those who speak such are considered fools (6:16–19). Furthermore, false testimony has great power to destroy (25:18).
- Those who gossip and cause dissension among others are judged most negatively through the proverbs (11:9,12–13; 16:28). However, even the book of Proverbs recognizes how tempting it is to participate in gossip (18:8).
- Flattery is destructive for those to whom it is rendered (29:5), while rebuke is beneficial to the wise (25:12; 27:5–6; 28:23).
- The spoken word has a tendency to reflect what is in the heart (10:31–32; 16:23). Words can be used for deception so the wise must be discerning as kind words can mask an evil heart (26:23–26).
- Words are meant to be taken at face value; therefore, to deceive in a careless way is foolish (26:18–19).

Principles on Child-Rearing

The book of Proverbs is especially timely in providing advice on **raising a family**. In Proverbs, child-rearing is a family affair, and discipline begins in the home. The responsibility of raising children is as great today as at any time in history, and Proverbs provides God-given wisdom on a topic relevant to many today.

- Discipline is an act of love, whether from God or from a parent (3:11–12).
- Parents who love their children will discipline them (13:24).
- Children are a heritage to their parents, and thus a wise son or daughter brings joy while a foolish one brings grief (10:1; 15:20; 17:21).
- Parents are responsible to discipline children, not to destroy or overdiscipline them (19:18).
- A child who receives instruction and discipline will retain the benefits for a lifetime (22:6).
- Children naturally disobey, but with discipline comes obedience (22:15).

- Discipline will bring success in life while a lack of discipline results in a child's demise and disgrace to his parents (23:13–14; 29:15).
- The greatest joy parents can experience is to see their children living in wisdom and integrity (23:15–16,22–25; 27:11). When fathers and mothers discipline their children, they will find peace and delight in the results (29:17).

Personal Discipline

The book of Proverbs consistently presents the **sluggard** as a fool and the **diligent** person as wise. Various traits of the diligent and the lazy are explored, as are the rewards of diligence and the consequences of lazy behavior. Some people have the tendency to put things off and make excuses. If these traits are unchecked, people can quickly find themselves in a state of ruin and poverty. Thus, for every person, a choice is presented through the reading of Proverbs between following the lifestyle of diligence or one of lazy indifference. In today's society, where children are often given things without even the thought of working for them, these proverbs are especially relevant.

- A diligent person, like the ant, does not need a taskmaster to find motivation (6:6–8), while the sluggard cannot find enough motivation to rise out of bed (26:14).
- Poverty is quick to overcome the sluggard, while diligence produces wealth (6:9–11; 10:4; 24:30–34).
- A sluggard is an irritant to those who employ him (10:26).
- In an ironic twist, laziness (when young) results in hard labor (as an adult) while the diligent find themselves in positions of leadership (12:24).
- The diligent man prizes what he has earned while the lazy neglect what is given to them (12:27).
- Desire without action produces nothing; the diligent will put their dreams into action and reap the benefits of doing so (13:4; 21:25–26).
- The sluggard always seems to find excuses for not getting things done, and thus, the excuses of the sluggard become a self-fulfilling prophecy (22:13; 26:13).
- A trait of sluggards is to fail to complete a task even when it is to their own benefit to bring it to conclusion (19:24; 26:15).
- The procrastination of the sluggard results in missed opportunity and a lack of accomplishment (20:4).

Friendship

The book of Proverbs places a high value on **friendship and relationships** between neighbors. Knowing how necessary it is to have a good friend by your side in the time of trouble, one may learn from the book of Proverbs how to gain friends and how to be a good friend to others.

- Due to the influence of one's friends, it is important to choose friends wisely (12:26).

- A good friend will quickly forgive, but the reminder of an offense causes disharmony even between friends (17:9).
- It is better to have few friends who are dependable and loyal than many friends who are not (18:24).
- A good friend is dependable during times of adversity, while poor friends are quick to distance themselves when needed most (17:17; 27:10).
- An upright companion encourages one to grow in a positive direction (27:17).
- People tend to become like those they associate with. Therefore, it is foolish to befriend an ill-tempered person (22:24–25).
- The counsel of a wise friend brings great joy and comfort (27:9).

Dealing with Emotions

The book of Proverbs addresses many practical issues, but it also deals with **inner emotions and attitudes** and the power these have in driving the affairs of life. Indeed, powerful emotions have the power to destroy the whole person. Examples of such attitudes include jealousy, envy, anger, and pride.

- Envy has the power to destroy people, and once they are emotionally drained, their physical well-being is affected as well (14:30).
- While anger displays itself in the open, jealousy is often hidden but more potent as it destroys relationships at their core (27:4).
- A quick temper demonstrates one to be a fool (14:17,29), while one who controls his anger demonstrates himself to be wise (29:11). Furthermore, an outburst of anger is usually not a unique occurrence; one who offends in this regard is likely to do it again (19:19).
- The Lord is in favor of the humble but is set against those who are proud in heart (3:34; 11:2; 16:5). Furthermore, pride inherently precedes calamity (16:18; 18:12).
- The proud will not heed advice, and their pride breeds disharmony (13:10).

Proverbs is filled with **practical advice** regarding principles of success (10:4–5), honesty (11:1), humility (11:2), and generosity (11:24). The book also includes warnings against adultery (5:1–23), drunkenness (23:29), and excessive appetite (23:2). In many ways Proverbs serves as a teacher's manual for teaching biblical principles of success, prosperity, and godly living.

THEOLOGICAL SIGNIFICANCE

The book of Proverbs emphasizes the **fear of the Lord** as the key to wisdom and knowledge. While Proverbs focuses on matters of earthly living, it reminds us that the God of heaven is the ultimate source of truth (2:5–6). His storehouse of wisdom is available to those who trust Him and keep His commandments (2:7–10). Hill and Walton note that the theological focus of the Proverbs keeps us balanced between this life and the next. It prevents us from "oversimplifying the complexities of life and offering pat answers to hard questions."[5] Ultimately, Proverbs provides instruction for the ideal life while Job and Ecclesiastes help us struggle with the awful realities of life.

For Further Reading

Atkinson, David. *The Message of Proverbs*. Downers Grove, IL: IVP, 1996.
Garrett, Duane. *Proverbs, Ecclesiastes, Song of Songs*. NAC. Nashville: B&H, 1993.
Kidner, Derek. *The Proverbs: An Introduction and Commentary*. TOTC. London: Tyndale, 1964.
Koptak, Paul. *Proverbs*. NIVAC. Grand Rapids: Zondervan, 2003.
Longman, Tremper, III. *How to Read Proverbs*. Downers Grove, IL: IVP, 2002.
Ross, Allen. "Proverbs." *EBC*. Grand Rapids: Zondervan, 1991.
Waltke, Bruce. *The Book of Proverbs*. NICOT. Grand Rapids: Eerdmans, 2004.

Study Questions

1. In what way does Proverbs exhibit the wisdom of God?
2. Describe the various types of proverbs with biblical examples.
3. What factors are important in interpreting the book of Proverbs?
4. What practical matters are addressed in the book of Proverbs?
5. Why are there so many warnings against wrong choices and wrong behavior in Proverbs?

ENDNOTES

1. Gordon D. Fee and Douglas Stuart, *How to Read the Bible for All Its Worth*, 3rd ed. (Grand Rapids: Zondervan, 2003), 225–32.

2. For a brief introduction to the various kinds of parallelism, see the introduction to Hebrew poetry in this volume.

3. Ronald L. Giese Jr. and Brent Sandy, eds., *Cracking Old Testament Codes: A Guide to Interpreting the Literary Genres of the Old Testament* (Nashville: B&H, 1995), 233–54.

4. For an alternate topical survey, see Daniel J. Estes, *Handbook on the Wisdom Books and Psalms* (Grand Rapids: Baker, 2005), 221–61. Estes comments on the content of Proverbs by analyzing the following themes: cheerfulness, contentment, decisions, diligence, friendship, generosity, humility, kindness, parenting, purity, righteousness, and truthfulness.

5. A. Hill and J. Walton, *A Survey of the Old Testament* (Grand Rapids: Zondervan, 2009), 447.

Chapter 25

ECCLESIASTES
Meaning of Life

Ecclesiastes is written like a postmodern sermon. It begins with the shocking statement "Everything is meaningless" (1:2 NIV) or "futile." The author was frustrated by injustice and the inability of man to straighten that which is crooked (1:15). He was also frustrated by the **transitory nature of life** and the inability of wisdom to provide any sense of guarantee over what tomorrow might bring. He observed oppression and corruption and noted that life does not always play out the way one might expect. Although many things have changed in the past 3,000 years, these same basic observations hold true today regarding life "under the sun."

The book of Ecclesiastes is a wisdom book, and as such, it teaches a **practical message** concerning how the wise should live in a fallen world. While the book fully engages the reader with the realities of the natural world, its overall message is positive, and the wisdom taught throughout the book is readily applicable to our world today. However, reading Ecclesiastes is not without its challenges, and many consider it one of the most perplexing books of the Bible. Taken out of context, many sayings within the book can be construed to teach an overly negative and pessimistic view on life. Furthermore, Ecclesiastes reflects on concepts that require careful consideration to discern between the realities of life "under the sun" and the wisdom-based conclusions that provide a positive basis for making the most of life in a fallen world.

AUTHOR

While the wise sage of Ecclesiastes has traditionally been identified as King Solomon, the name of Solomon is never explicitly referenced within the book. This, however, does not rule out Solomonic authorship. Allusions to **Solomon's wisdom** and lifestyle are clear in chap. 2, and the writer identifies himself by way of introduction as "son of David, king in Jerusalem" (1:1). Furthermore, extensive references to life under a monarch imply a readership living within the context of the United Kingdom Period (tenth century BC) of Israel's history.

Nevertheless, the author identifies himself only as "**Qohelet**," a Hebrew term meaning "one who gathers or assembles." Most English Bibles translate "Qohelet" as either "Teacher" or "Preacher," based on an understanding that the wise sage Qohelet is speaking to an assembly of people. The text itself is clear that the observations and the wisdom within the book ought to be attributed to Qohelet. However, the question of authorship is complicated by references to Qohelet in the third person (1:1; 7:27; 12:9–14) and statements by Qohelet in the first person (1:12–18). Furthermore, the use of the perfect tense in 1:12 seems odd if Solomon were the writer, and the first-person statement, "I have grown and increased in wisdom more than anyone who has ruled over Jerusalem before me" (1:16 NIV) is unusual given that David was the only Israelite king to rule over Jerusalem prior to Solomon, although there were numerous Canaanite and Jebusite kings prior to David.

Ecclesiastes takes its name from the Greek and Latin titles for the "Preacher" (Gk. *ekklesia*). Whereas the Hebrew title Qohelet indicates a teacher of wisdom, the text has clearly sought to conjure up images of Solomonic grandeur, wisdom, and authority. However, the authorship of the book is **technically anonymous**, and it is reasonable to refer to the main character of the book simply as "Qohelet."[1] This of course does not in any way diminish the authority or integrity of this inspired Old Testament book of wisdom. The timeless nature of the book makes it universally applicable to readers of all eras.

OUTLINE

While a firm outline of the structure of Ecclesiastes is difficult to ascertain, the book has **continuity** throughout in reference to content and message. Key words and themes consistently reappear throughout the book, and the overarching observation that all is *hevel* ("futility") introduces and concludes the main body of material through a literary technique that "bookends" the contents (1:2; 12:8).[2] The reader will also recognize the repetition of an "enjoy life" refrain found seven times throughout the book (2:24–25; 3:12–13,22; 5:18–20; 8:15; 9:7–10; 11:9), and the occurrence of familiar phrases such as "chasing after the wind," "under the sun," and "this too is *'hevel.'*" Also, the book is guided by programmatic questions directing the initial quest to find a solution through wisdom for the fallen condition (1:3; 3:9) and then redirecting the question to find "what is good" and "worthwhile" that wisdom might bring in a fallen world (2:3; 6:12).[3]

Modern Orthodox Jews praying at the Wailing Wall of the Temple Mount in Jerusalem.

Outline

I. Prologue (Ecclesiastes 1)
II. Pleasures of Life (Ecclesiastes 2)
III. Plan of God (Ecclesiastes 3–5)
IV. Problems of Life (Ecclesiastes 6–8)
V. Process of Living (Ecclesiastes 9–12:8)
VI. Postscript (Ecclesiastes 12:9–4)

The wisdom and message of Ecclesiastes are expressed through a wide range of **literary forms and techniques**, including autobiographical narrative (1:12–2:11), example story (9:13–16), allegory (12:1–7), reflection speeches (2:12–16; 9:1–6), and poem (3:2–8). Throughout the book one finds a wide variety of proverbs and sayings, most notably in chaps. 7, 10, and 11. Included among the proverbs is a high concentration of "better than" sayings (4:3,6,9,13; 6:3,9; 7:1–3,5,8; 9:4,16,18), along with numerous aphorisms and admonitions. To suggest that Ecclesiastes is anything short of a literary masterpiece is a gross understatement.

Of special note to Ecclesiastes is the **conclusion** in the form of an epilogue (12:9–14). The epilogue first describes Qohelet's accomplishments as a wise sage and affirms that what he wrote was "upright and true" (12:10 NIV). Second, the epilogue states the conclusion of the matter at hand: "Fear God and keep his commandments, for this is the whole duty of man. For God will bring every deed into judgment, including every hidden thing, whether it is good or evil" (12:13–14 NIV). The essential continuity between the epilogue and the main body of the text, especially in reference to the fear of God and His judgment (3:17; 5:1–7; 11:9–12:1), suggests that the epilogue is an integral component of the inspired text of Ecclesiastes and gives its ultimate message: life can only be enjoyed in the context of the fear of God.

Hebrew Highlight

Hevel. Hebrew הבל (*hevel*). The Hebrew word *hevel* is the key word in the book of Ecclesiastes. It is used 38 times in the book and literally means "mist," "vapor," or "breath." In the Old Testament, however, this word is almost always used in a metaphorical sense, usually denoting some characteristic of "breath." Old Testament examples include *hevel* as depicting transience (Job 7:16; Ps 39:5–6,11) and *hevel* emphasizing that which is insubstantial due to being false. In this sense Jeremiah uses the term to describe false idols and their attendant worship (Jer 2:5; 10:3,8). Additionally, throughout the Old Testament the word *hevel* is used to describe vain effort (Isa 30:7; Ps 62:9–10). In Ecclesiastes the term is used to describe the "futility" of life from a human perspective.

MESSAGE

The key to unraveling the mysteries of Ecclesiastes is to recognize the **recurring themes** or motifs found throughout the book, and come to an informed understanding of how those themes relate to one another. The following seven themes represent the content of Ecclesiastes:

1. The Vanity of Life

"Vanity of vanities, saith the Preacher, vanity of vanities; all is vanity" (Eccl 1:2 KJV). Qohelet uses the word translated "vanity," "futility," "meaningless," or "worthless" 38 times in the book. It is the Hebrew word *hevel*, literally meaning "vapor or mist." Qohelet is able to communicate a broad range of ideas through the use as a **metaphor** of the single Hebrew word *hevel*. The metaphor is used throughout Ecclesiastes to describe various aspects of life experienced in a fallen world.[4] Among these aspects, four families of meaning are observed that highlight the dilemma facing Qohelet as he observes the fallen condition of man:

Jewish men dancing during a private ceremony in the Court of the Men at the Wailing Wall in Jerusalem.

- Some contexts highlight the ephemeral and transitory nature of mortal beings, and in these cases the word may best be translated as "fleeting" (6:12; 11:9).
- In reference to attaining a solution to the dilemma of the fallen condition, human effort and wisdom are described as "vanity," usually qualified by the companion phrase "chasing after the wind" (2:11,17,26; 4:4,8 NIV).
- Describing injustices and enigmatic circumstances that plague a fallen world, Qohelet proclaims these things as *hevel,* an affront to reason and justice. In these cases the word may best be translated as "senseless" or "absurd" (8:14).[5]
- Qohelet sometimes describes the fallen world as *hevel*, highlighting his frustration with reality. This sense is clear as qualified by companion phrases such as a "great evil" (2:21), an "evil occupation" (4:8), and a "grievous evil" (6:2) (all author's translation).

The dilemma facing Qohelet is that there seems to be no solution to the fallen condition. And so he searches to find through wisdom a solution to the dilemma of *hevel*, seeking *yitron*, a Hebrew word variously translated as "surplus," "gain," or "profit"

(1:3; 3:9). The pursuit of *yitron* drives Qohelet's quest in the book of Ecclesiastes. Indeed, this wise sage seeks to find if wisdom can provide any solution to the dilemma of *hevel*.

2. Life "Under the Sun"

Used 29 times the expression "life under the sun" refers to the activities of man as observed and experienced from a **human perspective** (1:3,13). As one reads the book of Ecclesiastes, note that Qohelet is not overly pessimistic in his assessment of the fallen world. He is simply realistic in observing life from a human perspective. The phrase "under the sun" indicates an earthly perspective; in other words, life without God. This perspective reveals the random emptiness of life without God. By contrast the name of God (*Elohim*) appears 28 times although the name of Jehovah (*Yahweh*) does not appear at all.

3. The Value of Wisdom

Ecclesiastes is written from a wisdom perspective, and the quest is made through "wise eyes" (1:13; 2:9). Although Qohelet acknowledges the limits of wisdom to provide any lasting solution to the fallen condition, he nevertheless upholds the value of wisdom throughout the book (2:13–14). In finding what is good for a man in the "*hevel*" days of his life (6:12), Qohelet affirms the application of **probabilistic wisdom** to a wide variety of affairs, and in this sense the wisdom of Ecclesiastes suggests ways in which a person might make the most of every opportunity given by God throughout the years of one's life (7:1–29; 10:1–20; 11:1–8).

4. The Sovereignty of God

Throughout the book Qohelet recognizes that a sovereign **God rules** over the affairs of mankind. Coupled with that, he also observes that mortal man has little power over his own fate. Qohelet recognizes man's inability to fathom the ways of God yet in confidence realizes that God "has made everything beautiful in its time" (3:11, NIV). Furthermore, Qohelet acknowledges that God has purposed to keep man from ever fully grasping the mysteries of His sovereign ways, knowing that God "does it so that men will revere him" (3:14). In the end Qohelet notes that wisdom can only plan for contingencies but not guarantee the future (7:13–14; 9:11–12; 11:1–6).

5. The Inevitability of Death

As Qohelet observes life "under the sun," he cannot escape the reality that death is coming (3:18–21; 12:1–7). The inevitability of death highlights the **transitory nature** of mortal life and, due to its prominent voice in the book, adds a somewhat depressing tone to Ecclesiastes. However, the recognition of life's brevity and the unknown day of its reckoning provide the impetus for Qohelet's conclusion to make the most of every opportunity (9:1–10).

6. The Enjoyment of Life

As Qohelet observes all that life is and has to offer, seven times he concludes that life should be enjoyed to its fullest. Altogether, he uses the word "joy" (*simchah*) 17 times. The enjoyment of life is not an incidental or minor aspect to Qohelet's wisdom. Rather, it is a conclusion revealed through structured refrains spaced throughout the book (2:24–26; 3:12–13,22; 5:18–20; 8:15; 9:7–10; 11:9–10). Furthermore, one can observe a **degree of escalation** throughout these refrains, moving from observation (2:24–26; 3:12–13,22; 5:18–20) to commendation (8:15) and then to imperative command (9:7–10; 11:9–10).[6] Indeed, the greatest folly would be for a man not to enjoy the few short years that God has given him as a gift. In light of the brevity of life, man should enjoy the simple things in life while he has the opportunity.

Men winnowing grain in the ancient way with wooden winnowing forks.

7. Remembering God

Although Qohelet comes to realize that wisdom does not have the capacity to explain fully the ways of God, he clearly understands that wisdom demands **reverence for God** (5:1–7). The years of a mortal man are brief, and death and judgment are surely coming (3:17–19; 12:14). In light of eternity, the wise will acknowledge his Creator all of the days of his life; indeed, only a fool would live his few short years without remembering God in all that he does (12:1,13). In one of the author's strongest appeals, he urges: "Remember your Creator in the days of your youth" before you are too old to appreciate what God has given you (12:1).

THEOLOGICAL SIGNIFICANCE

As Qohelet observes and experiences all that life has to offer "under the sun," he sees that it is full of difficulties, calamities, and unfairness. These are the results of the **fallen condition** that makes life "meaningless" without God. In all of this, man seems destined to his lot in life. Though the application of wisdom may prove to be beneficial in life, even wisdom cannot deter the common enemy of both the fool and the wise, that is, death. Qohelet observes that through the good times and the bad, one thing is always constant: life is fleeting. It is a brief vapor vanishing with time. In light of eternity, is there any solution to the fallen condition of the world?

With the inevitability of death so pressing, Qohelet searches to find if anything in this fleeting life has **enduring value**. Qohelet embarks on his quest with great passion, using all his God-given wisdom on his journey. Qohelet soon realizes that man, so far as "life under the sun" is concerned, cannot take anything with him beyond the grave. All of his possessions, pleasures, fame, and fortune, the accomplishments for which he spent many hours in toil and labor, all of these things are like vapor, vanishing away.

Pastor Ed Young refers to the outlook of Ecclesiastes as "flat land living" that results in "going nowhere fast." He suggests that the author deliberately examines the perspectives of party harder, think deeper, study further, and acquire more to show the futility of life without God.[7] Dr. Walter Kaiser observes: "Qoheleth was working on the problem of man's attempt to find meaning in all aspects of God's world without coming to know the world's Creator, Sustainer, and Judge."[8] The concerns raised in Ecclesiastes can also be found in the other Wisdom Books: Job, Proverbs, and the Song of Songs, as well as in some of the Psalms.

Philip Yancey provides an excellent perspective on the brilliance of Ecclesiastes to foresee the quandary of the **postmodern world**: flat emotions, radical indifference, a sense of drifting, and a resigned acceptance of a world gone mad. He views the author as the "first existentialist" and observes that the "bleak despair" of Ecclesiastes rises from the "golden age" of Israel's prosperity, not deprivation. He adds: "Existential despair did not germinate in the hell holes of Auschwitz or Siberia but rather in the cafes of Paris, the coffee shops of Copenhagen, and the luxury palaces of Beverly Hills."[9] Thus, it is the burden of excess that humans cannot handle. All that life offers eludes any sense of meaning and purpose without God.

Qohelet never does find a solution to the dilemma of man's fallen condition through the mere application of wisdom. That is why God has "put eternity in their hearts" (3:11) so we are never satisfied with that which is less than **eternal**. In this sense wisdom alone was insufficient to solve the problems of the curse that Qohelet observed; only the revelation of God in Christ could provide the reconciliation the world so desperately needs.

Although a solution to the dilemma of *hevel* would await future revelation in Christ, the book of Ecclesiastes does function as wisdom literature in providing man with a **paradigm** for making the most of life while here on earth. First, in light of the fact that life is fleeting, death is inevitable, and the circumstances of one's future lie outside the realm of man's control, the wise will enjoy life as a gift from God. Second, in light of the fact that God's enigmatic ways on earth are sure to be followed by an equitable future judgment, the wise will fear God and keep His commandments (12:13).

For Further Reading

Eaton, Michael. *Ecclesiastes*. Downers Grove, IL: IVP, 1983.
Fox, Michael. *A Time to Tear Down and a Time to Build Up*. Grand Rapids: Eerdmans, 1999.
Kaiser, Walter C., Jr. *Ecclesiastes: Total Life*. Chicago: Moody Press, 1979.
Longman, Tremper, III. *Book of Ecclesiastes*. Grand Rapids: Eerdmans, 1998.
Miller, Douglas. *Symbol and Rhetoric in Ecclesiastes*. Atlanta: Society of Biblical Literature, 2002.
Wrybray, R. N. *Ecclesiastes*. NCBC. Grand Rapids: Eerdmans, 1989.
Young, Ed. *Been There. Done That. Now What?* Nashville: B&H, 1994.

Study Questions

1. What is unique about the author's approach in writing Ecclesiastes?
2. What indications does the text give that the writer is Solomon?
3. How is the Hebrew term *hevel* ("meaningless" or "vapor") used throughout the book?
4. Is there any real purpose to life without God?
5. How do the "goads" and "nails" of wisdom help us find the meaning of life?

ENDNOTES

1. Walter Kaiser, *Ecclesiastes: Total Life* (Chicago: Moody, 1979), 7–42.
2. The technical term for this literary technique is "inclusio."
3. Kathleen A. Farmer, *Who Knows What Is Good?* ITC (Grand Rapids: Eerdmans, 1991).
4. While a wide variety of commentators have opined concerning the use of "*hevel*" in Ecclesiastes, perhaps the most comprehensive work espousing a multivalent approach is Douglas B. Miller, *Symbol and Rhetoric in Ecclesiastes* (Atlanta: Society of Biblical Literature, 2002).
5. On the use of the gloss "absurd" as a translation of "*hevel*" in Ecclesiastes, see Michael V. Fox, *A Time to Tear Down and a Time to Build Up* (Grand Rapids: Eerdmans, 1999).
6. R. N. Whybray, "Qohelet, Preacher of Joy," *JSOT* 23 (1982): 87–98.
7. Ed Young, *Been There. Done That. Now What?* (Nashville: B&H, 1994), chaps. 1–5.
8. Kaiser, *Ecclesiastes: Total Life*, 16.
9. Philip Yancey, *The Bible Jesus Read* (Grand Rapids: Zondervan, 199), 143–67.

Chapter 26

THE SONG OF SONGS
Songs of Love

The Song of Songs is a **love song** that is in many ways similar to other love songs from the ancient world. Although the subject matter contained in the song seems out of touch with the religious material found throughout the rest of Scripture, it nevertheless carries an important function within the body of Hebrew wisdom literature. This book teaches people how to make wise choices for earthly living. The ability to make the right choices in the realm of romantic love concerns every one of God's people, whether married or single.

Perhaps the greatest benefit the believer can gain by studying the Song of Songs is the reminder that love is a gift from God and should be enjoyed as a gift. What God has created and declared as good (Gen 1:31) should be enjoyed in the **context of marriage**. The positive presentation of the love relationship in the Song of Songs provides a necessary balance to the prohibitions against illicit sexual expression found throughout the rest of Scripture. This song affirms the strength of true love that is essential to every marriage.

Many people are surprised to find such explicit and openly **erotic lyrics** in the Bible. The lovers show no embarrassment in enjoying each other's love. However, though sensuous, the lyrics are never distasteful. The Song of Songs teaches that love, romance, sex, and marriage were created by God to be enjoyed within marriage between a man and a woman. In this sense the Song of Songs serves as a model for marital relationships for all of God's people.

AUTHOR

The title of the book, "Solomon's Song of Songs" (1:1 NIV), seems to identify **King Solomon** as the author of the Song.[1] The title can literally be translated from the Hebrew "The Greatest Song of Solomon." However, the phrase "of Solomon" does call into question whether this was a song "by Solomon," "about Solomon," or "for Solomon."[2] In support of Solomonic authorship is the fact that 1 Kgs 4:32 credits the king with at least 1,005 songs, so the fact that Solomon was a writer of songs is without question. Therefore, the clear implication in the title is that this is the greatest of Solomon's many songs. Also, a distinction between "by" and "about" is unnecessary, as it is possible that the Song carries an element of autobiographical reflection and thus was written *by* Solomon and yet is also *about* Solomon.

Further evidence supporting Solomonic authorship, or at least a Solomonic context, can be found in the internal references to exotic spices, precious metals, and a political monarchy; all these were a part of Solomon's reign. Furthermore, there are external parallels with Egyptian love poetry predating the united monarchy, so an early date for the song is possible.[3] All considered, the evidence supporting Solomonic authorship is strong.

Enclosed Garden, used as a description in Song 4:12.

Mark Rooker notes that Solomon's name appears seven times in the book (1:1,5; 3:7,9,11; 8:11–12). He also observes that 21 varieties of plant life and 15 species of animals harmonize with Solomon's knowledge of such matters (1 Kgs 4:33). The reference to place-names throughout Israel (from Jerusalem to Carmel and Hermon to Engedi) indicate the geography of the **united monarchy**. Altogether 49 unique terms use the imagery of nature in a premodern world to describe the intricacies of human love.[4]

INTERPRETATION

Historically, the most common method used in interpreting the Song was to treat the Song as an **allegory**. Jewish tradition interpreted the book allegorically, taking verses totally out of context; thus the two breasts were viewed as Moses and Aaron, or the book was seen as a metaphor of the history of Israel's relationship to God. Many church fathers viewed the book typologically as a picture of Christ's love for His bride, the church. While Scripture does use human marriage as a type in describing the relationship between God and Israel, as well as Christ and the church, for many reasons the Song of Songs should not be interpreted allegorically.

First, whenever the relationship between God and Israel is presented as an allegory in the Old Testament, the text clearly indicates that an allegory is being used as a means of communication, and the **figurative expressions** are almost always defined as to their appropriate referent. Furthermore, when this does occur in the Old Testament, the relationship between God and Israel is pictured by allegory in a negative sense, not in the positive sense found in the Song of Songs (Ezekiel 16; 23).

Second, to allegorize the Song leaves much detail without explanation as to its referent and allegorical point of comparison. The history of allegorical interpretation of the Song can be described as "**fantasy unlimited**," and the imposition of theological concepts upon the language of the text has little basis in any natural method of interpretation.[5]

In addition, some have even questioned whether the language of the book can be appropriately applied to the typological relationship between Christ and the church, especially since it is not quoted in the **New Testament**. Furthermore, while Paul had ample opportunity to quote the Song in support of the "profound mystery" of Christ's love for the church, he chose not do so, even while quoting Gen 2:24 in his admonition to husbands and wives in Eph 5:22–33. Since they did not quote it, even when making a conceptual argument depicting the "marriage" of Christ to the church, it seems unlikely that the apostles would have viewed the Song typologically concerning Christ and the church. On the other hand, the fact that the New Testament illustrates Christ's relationship to the church with a marriage metaphor could indicate an allusion to the language of the Song of Songs.

Finally, it is only natural that the Bible would contain an expression of one of life's strongest human emotions, that is, **marital love**. While the topic of love between a man and a woman may seem too secular for the inspired canon, it should be remembered that God "created them male and female," so it would seem fitting for Him to inspire a song that deals with the power of love between the sexes.

IMAGERY AND DRAMA

Assuming an approach that embraces a "literal" understanding of the Song as an inspired love song, one is still faced with **interpretive challenges**. Modern-day love songs with their vivid figurative imagery and idiomatic expressions can be difficult to understand. How much more a song that was written nearly 3,000 years ago! Three major problems hinder today's reader of the Song:

First, the **poetic imagery** of the ancient Near Eastern culture seems strange to modern-day readers. The lovers speak of spices and perfumes and compare each other to agricultural elements that seem less than flattering to the modern ear but nevertheless communicated a level of attraction and a range of emotions that demonstrate the full force and potential of erotic love. The particulars are often difficult to decipher, but the primary message is clear in regard to how the lovers speak to each other.

Second, the **story line** and changeover between speakers within the Song makes it sometimes difficult to follow. The original

The Rhorr gazelle is one species of antelope found in Israel.

text did not reveal whether the man, the woman, or the chorus was speaking (or singing), and as with any lyrical poetry, the story line can be difficult to follow. While the

Song is clearly not a drama meant to be acted on a stage or a romantic novel meant to be read with characters and a plot, the Song appears to move from romantic courtship to marriage and subsequent intimacy. As the lovers sing to each other (as in a romantic duet), they tell a story of unfolding love; however, one should not read the Song as a historical drama piecing the story line together into a detailed plot. Rather, as in a love song, one should seek to understand how the lovers feel about each other and note how the lovers are communicating to each other; this is where the wisdom of the Song is found. Only secondarily does a dramatic tale unfold.

The third problem pertains to the **drama** that seems to underlie the lyrics of the Song. The standard approach is to see the Song as depicting the love between Solomon and his beloved while a less popular approach details a dramatic plot involving a woman, her shepherd lover, and Solomon as a villain who has come to take the woman into his harem. The "three-character" plot, called the "Shepherd Hypothesis," seems unlikely since that means Solomon wrote or accepted a Song where he is depicted as a villainous monarch seeking to steal a bride from the embrace of her true love.

Norman Geisler suggests a reasonable plot for the drama of the Song.[6] He views it as an **antiphonal love song** sung by the bride and groom at their wedding. In a kind of Jewish "Cinderella story," the virgin was sent to the vineyard by her brothers after the death of their parents. While working there, she meets and falls in love with a shepherd who promises to return to her one day. In his absence she dreams of him only to awake and he is not there. Finally, when he returns for her, he is none other than King Solomon, and his royal coach takes her to the palace where they will be married. Later they return to her village where her brothers praise her (she is a "wall" of virtue). While this approach expresses a possible story line, it does not fully explain the intimacy of the language used throughout the songs.

OUTLINE

Although some have argued that the Song is an anthology of shorter love lyrics, the **progression of the lovers' relationship** provides a discernible movement that unifies the Song from beginning to end. Furthermore, a literary consistency in language and motif suggests a single author rather than a collection of songs. However, it is difficult to outline the book according to a detailed plot or linear progression of events. As a song, the individual units function like snapshots in a photo album that provide lyrical glimpses into the progression of the lover's relationship from courtship through marriage and into maturation.

Although some attempt to develop a detailed structural outline following the cycle of individual "scenes," a simpler approach is to follow the broader strokes of discernible movement within the song, recognizing that the lovers alternate with their lyrics of admiration and reflection throughout the song. These cycles of love lyrics are broken only by the interruption of short choruses by the "friends" of the lovers and the repetition of three refrains ("do not stir up or awaken love until the appropriate time") within the song (2:7; 3:5; 8:4). As such, the Song of Songs can be broadly divided into four parts:

I. Romantic Courtship (Song 1:1–3:5)

Following a superscription (1:1), the song immediately begins with the female voice expressing her strong desire for **romantic affection**, "Let him kiss me with the kisses of his mouth" (1:2 NIV), thus setting the tone of lyrical love language that escalates throughout the book. However, while desire for intimacy is clearly communicated throughout this "courtship" section (1:4,16; 2:3–6,10–13; 3:4), the lovers show restraint until the wedding night in fulfilling their physical desires (4:16–5:1).

While the courtship segment of the Song consists of frequent changeover between the male and female voices, **two consistent themes** can be observed in their lyrics. First, the female voice reflects frequent insecurities in her appearance (1:5–6), in her longing for his presence (1:7), and in her fear of losing her lover (3:1–4). Second, the lovers show no restraint in praising each other's appearance (1:10–11,15–16; 2:14), affirming their unique commitment (1:9; 2:2–4,16), and expressing their desire to be together (2:8–13). The word pictures they express about each other's appearance are like mental imprints of each other in an age before photography. They memorize every feature of the other person to enhance their longing while they are apart. By their words of praise, they affirm their love in preparation for the marriage to follow. Clearly the woman's insecurities regarding her appearance and her fear of losing her lover are resolved in full through the affirmation of her lover's praise and presence.

One of the cedars of Lebanon.

II. Marital Intimacy (Song 3:6–5:1)

The shift from courtship to marriage is indicated by the vision of a **great wedding processional** accompanied by all the extravagance of royalty (3:6–11). In this processional account Solomon is identified by name (3:7,9,11), and the indication that this is a wedding processional is clear (3:11).

Following the processional, the Song does not describe the ceremonial aspects of the wedding but rather celebrates the consummation of intimate desire (4:16–5:1). Solomon praises the beauty of his beloved on their wedding night (4:1–7) and expresses the depth of his love for her (4:8–11). He praises her purity (4:12) and the rich satisfaction her love provides (4:13–15).

The **consummation** of the marriage is expressed in delicate metaphor so as to celebrate its sensuous beauty with taste and elegance. There is no hesitation in the invitation of the beloved (4:16) now that the wedding has taken place, and the fulfillment of sexual intimacy is unrestrained and celebrated as a gift from the Creator (5:1).[7]

III. Affirmation of Marital Love (Song 5:2–8:4)

The third segment of the Song opens with another **dream sequence** (as with 3:1–4) where the beloved is separated from her lover (5:2–8). However, she regrets this separation (5:8) and affirms her love for him through renewed praise over his appearance (5:10–16). Through the prompting of the friends (5:9; 6:1), the lovers are reconciled, and the growth of their commitment is reaffirmed in full: "I am my love's and my love is mine" (6:2–3). Following this veiled separation between the lovers, the male voice again affirms his beloved's appearance and his desire for her (6:4–9; 7:1–9) in love language as beautiful and intense as any written by human hands. In song she responds by renewed invitation to intimacy (7:9b–8:3) and affirms the mutual possession of their being together (7:10).

IV. Epilogue (Song 8:5–14)

The affirmation of the couple's love is expressed poetically as a **seal** over the heart and arm, an indication of mutual ownership over the thoughts and actions of each other (8:6a).[8] Then, in climatic fashion, the Song erupts to proclaim love's power and treasure, the ultimate expression in Scripture of the power of romantic love. "Love is as strong as death, its jealousy unyielding as the grave. It burns like blazing fire, like a mighty flame. Many waters cannot quench love; rivers cannot wash it away. If one were to give all the wealth of his house for love, it would be utterly scorned" (8:6b–7).

Although the poem expressing the power and value of love functions as the **climatic conclusion** to the Song (8:6b–7), the Song continues beyond this climax through a flashback affirming the purity of the beloved prior to her relationship with Solomon (8:8–12) and a restatement of the lovers' desire to be possessed by each other in the coming years of their marriage (8:13–14).

THEOLOGICAL SIGNIFICANCE

As lyrical love poetry the Song of Songs exalts the **virtues of love** and evokes the emotions that run deep in the attraction God created between the sexes. As wisdom literature the Song of Songs teaches God's people how to express their love to the one to whom they commit their hearts and bodies in marriage. However, beyond the practical aspects of instruction in communication and intimacy, the Song functions in Scripture to demonstrate the ultimate power of love and its victory over the curse (Gen 3:16–19). Although conflict between the sexes has come as a result of the fall, by God's grace the marriage relationship can still be as fulfilling as intended in creation (Gen 2:18–25). To this end the prayer of single saints the world over ought to be, "Lord, prepare me to have a Song of Songs relationship in Your own time," and for God's people bound in marriage their prayer ought to be, "Lord, instill in me and my spouse the love modeled in the Song, and help me to communicate that in word and deed." While allegorical interpretations of the Song are not based on careful exegesis of the text, the overall typological picture of marital love certainly **illustrates God's love** for His people. Thus, both Old and New Testament writers use marital themes to describe the relationship of God to Israel (Isa 62:4–5; Jer 3:1–11; Hos 2:19–20) and Christ to the Church (Eph 5:21–33; Rev 19:7–9; 20:9–11).

For Further Reading

Carr, G. Lloyd. *The Song of Solomon*. TOTC. Downers Grove, IL: IVP, 1984.
Garrett, Duane. *Proverbs, Ecclesiastes, Song of Songs*. NAC. Nashville: B&H, 1993.
Hess, Richard. *Song of Songs*. BCOT. Grand Rapids: Baker, 2005.
Keel, Othmar. *The Song of Songs*. Translated by F. J. Gaiser. Minneapolis: Fortress Press, 1994.
Longman, Tremper, III. *Song of Songs*. NICOT. Grand Rapids: Eerdmans, 2001.
Provan, Iain. *Ecclesiastes/Song of Songs*. NIVAC. Grand Rapids: Zondervan, 2001.

Study Questions

1. What factors indicate Solomon actually wrote the Song of Songs?
2. What are the challenges of the allegorical interpretation?
3. What are the challenges of the literal interpretation?
4. How does the Song caution the reader?

ENDNOTES

1. The Latin title is "Canticles," from the Vulgate, *canticum canticorum.*

2. The Hebrew syntax is not as clear as the English. The English reader may not see such flexibility in this phrase, but the Hebrew does allow for a variety of uses.

3. Garrett argues that the similar formal elements and literary motifs between the Song of Songs and extant Egyptian love poetry supports "that the biblical work was written by someone who was familiar with Egyptian poetry and who lived when the motifs common to both collections were current and appreciated." Since Solomon married the daughter of an Egyptian Pharaoh, he had the background to know about this kind of poetry. See Duane A. Garrett, *Proverbs, Ecclesiastes, Song of Songs*, NAC (Nashville: B&H, 1993), 350.

4. Mark Rooker, "The Book of the Song of Songs," in Eugene Merrill, Mark Rooker, and Michael Grisanti, *The World and the Word* (Nashville: B&H, 2011), 547.

5. For examples of allegorical excess, see John Gill, *An Exposition of the Song of Solomon* (1724: repr.; London: Longmans, 1854), 211–13. Gill interprets the bushy black head of the bridegroom as the headship of Christ over the church and the locks of his hair as the multitude of believers.

6. Norman L. Geisler, *A Popular Survey of the Old Testament* (Grand Rapids: Baker, 2007), 225–27.

7. Although Bible translations often attribute the final portion of 5:1 to the "friends" of the bride ("Eat, O friends, and drink; drink your fill, O lovers" NIV), some have argued that the speaker was God Himself, celebrating the consummation of the marriage and approving of it as "good." See Daniel J. Estes, *Handbook on the Wisdom Books and Psalms* (Grand Rapids: Baker, 2005), 421.

8. Jack S. Deere, "Song of Songs," *BKC* (Wheaton, IL: Victor Books, 1985), 1024.

Chapter 27

MAJOR PROPHETS

The Major Prophets in the English Bible include the books of Isaiah, Jeremiah, Ezekiel, Daniel, and Jeremiah's poetic Lamentations. They are generally designated as "major" because of their **length and prominence** in the history of God's revelation to Israel and the nations. Isaiah, Jeremiah, and Ezekiel were preaching prophets as well as writing prophets, whereas Daniel was an administrator who received divine revelations from God. He interpreted the dreams of others and recorded his own visions of the future, so it is not surprising that he was recognized as a prophet by Jesus (Matt 24:15).

The Hebrew prophets **spoke for God**. They wrote the books of history ("Former Prophets") and the books of prophecy ("Latter Prophets") in the Old Testament. The prophetic books of history are followed in the Hebrew Bible by the prophetic books of preaching and prediction. The two categories of prophetic books form a unit in the middle of the Hebrew Scriptures under the common term "prophets" (Hebrew, *nebi'im*).

THE PROPHETIC OFFICE

The Hebrew term *nabi'* itself designates the prophet as a spokesman for God. The **twofold aspect** of the prophet's ministry included declaring God's message for people of their day and foretelling God's actions in the future. Thus, the prophet was also called a "seer" (Hebrew, *ro'eh*) because he could see future events before they happened.

The Bible depicts the prophet as one who was admitted into the **divine council chambers** where God "reveals His secret" (Amos 3:7 NASB). The Hebrew text of 1 Sam 9:15 pictures God "uncovering the ear" of the prophet (see KJV). By the process of divine inspiration, God revealed what was hidden (2 Sam 7:27) so the prophet perceived what the Lord said (Jer 23:18). This communion with God was essential for God's truth to be revealed by the process of **prophetic inspiration**. The word of the Lord was communicated to the prophet and mediated to the people by the Holy Spirit with powerful conviction and precise accuracy.

The full picture of prophecy, then, is that it encompasses both a **forthtelling** of God's messages and a **foretelling** of God's actions. Isaiah, for example, was such a man, addressing himself to his own times as he brought God's direction to the kings

The Hebrew Prophets in History
(9th–5th century BC)

PROPHET	APPROX. DATES (B.C.)	LOCATION/ HOME	BASIC BIBLE PASSAGE	CENTRAL TEACHING	KEY VERSE
Elijah	875–850	Tishbe	1Kg 17:1–2Kg 2:18	Yahweh, not Baal, is God	1Kg 18:21
Micaiah	856	Samaria	1Kg 22; 2Ch 18	Judgment on Ahab; proof of prophecy	1Kg 22:28
Elisha	855–800	Abel Meholah	1Kg 19:15–21; 2Kg 2–9; 13	God's miraculous power	2Kg 5:15
Jonah	786–746	Gath Hepher	2Kg 14:25; Jonah	God's universal concern	Jnh 4:11
Hosea	786–746	Israel	Hosea	God's unquenchable love	Hs 11:8–9
Amos	760–750	Tekoa	Amos	God's call for justice and righteousness	Am 5:24
Isaiah	740–698	Jerusalem	2Kg 19–20; Isaiah	Hope through repentance and suffering	Is 1:18; 53:4–6
Micah	735–710	Moresheth Gath/ Jerusalem	Jr 26:18; Micah	Call for humble mercy and justice	Mc 6:8
Oded	733	Samaria	2Ch 28:9–11	Do not go beyond God's command	2Ch 28:9
Nahum	686–612	Elkosh	Nahum	God's jealousy protects His people	Nah 1:2–3
Zephaniah	640–621	?	Zephaniah	Hope for the humble and righteous	Zph 2:3
Jeremiah	626–584	Anathoth/ Jerusalem	2Ch 36:12; Jeremiah	Faithful prophet points to new covenant	Jr 31:33–34
Huldah (the prophetess)	621	Jerusalem	2Kg 22; 2Ch 34	God's book is accurate	2Kg 22:16
Habakkuk	608–598	?	Habakkuk	God calls for faithfulness	Hab 2:4
Ezekiel	593–571	Babylon	Ezekiel	Future hope for new community of worship	Ezk 37:12–13
Obadiah	580	Jerusalem	Obadiah	Doom on Edom to bring God's kingdom	Ob 21
Joel	539–531	Jerusalem	Joel	Call to repent and experience God's Spirit	Jl 2:28–29
Haggai	520	Jerusalem	Ezr 5:1; 6:14; Haggai	The priority of God's house	Hg 2:8–9
Zechariah	520–514	Jerusalem	Ezr 5:1; 6:14; Zechariah	Faithfulness will lead to God's universal rule	Zch 14:9
Malachi	500–450	Jerusalem	Malachi	Honor God and wait for His righteousness	Mal 4:2

of Judah, and also seeing far into the future to explain God's plans for His people in the last days.

THE PROPHETIC MINISTRY

The Hebrew term *nabi'* identifies the prophet as a preacher or proclaimer of God's word, as does the Greek term *prophetes*. Biblical prophets were both preachers of truth and predictors of the future. Prophecy has its roots in **history**, but it also extends into the **future**. In other words, the nature of predictive prophecy arises out of the prophet's historical context as the revelation of God points him toward the future as well as the present. Thus, the prophets speak both to their own generation and to future generations as preachers and predictors.

The Old Testament prophets spoke for God. They believed they were sent by God with a specific message. Whereas the priests represented the people to God, the prophets presented God to the people. Thus, the prophets spoke with **divine authority** and divine enabling. Prophets were called by God, accountable to God, and empowered by God. The people of Israel acknowledged them as "holy men of God" who spoke the word of God (2 Pet 1:21).

PROPHETIC LANGUAGE

The prophets delivered their messages in **three basic ways**: verbally, in writing, and through symbolic acts. They preached it, wrote it, or demonstrated it. Their verbal declarations were "the word of the Lord" (Hebrew, *debhar Yahweh*). The divine origin and inspiration of these declarations were presumed by their nature. God said to Amos (7:14–16 NASB), "'Go prophesy to My people . . .' Now hear the word of the LORD."

Written prophecies were especially poignant because they often employed the Hebrew verbal form known as the **prophetic perfect**. The prophets used this form of speech to describe future events as though they were already happening, bringing the listener or reader into a direct experience with the full impact of their predictions.

PROPHETIC PREDICTIONS

One of the most unique features of the true Old Testament prophets was their ability to **predict future events** with perfect accuracy. God Himself predicted Israel's bondage in Egypt and subsequent deliverance (Gen 15:13–18). Moses predicted the Israelites' successful conquest of the Promised Land under Joshua (Deut 31:23). Samuel predicted the failure of Saul's dynasty (1 Sam 15:28). Nathan predicted the consequences of David's sin and its effects on his own family (2 Sam 12:7–12). Elijah predicted the deaths of Ahab and Jezebel (1 Kgs 21:19–23). Isaiah predicted the deliverance of Jerusalem from the Assyrian invasion of Sennacherib (2 Kgs 19:34–37). Jeremiah predicted the Jew's 70-year captivity in Babylon.

The biblical prophets speak to future events as though they had already occurred. Thus, they foresee things yet to happen as though they were already in the present: The virgin is pregnant (Isa 7:14), the divine child is already born (Isa 9:6), the star of Jacob has already appeared (Num 24:17), Israel has already gone into captivity (Isa 5:13). These are but a few of the hundreds of examples of such language by which the prophet foresees the future and predicts its exact fulfillment with such certainty that he describes it as already having come to pass.

PROPHETIC PATTERN

The prophets were essentially preachers who declared the message of God to their own generation. But their messages also influenced future generations. Hill and Walton observe that the message of the prophets is found in the proclamation of God's word to their contemporary audience, whereas its fulfillment often came later in the unfolding of history they foresaw.[1] In analyzing the pattern of prophetic speech, they suggest four categories of a prophetic oracle:

Indictment	Statement of the Offense
Judgment	Punishment Prescribed
Instruction	Repentant Response
Aftermath	Future Hope

HISTORICAL BACKGROUND

Isaiah dates his ministry from the reign of king Uzziah (c. 740 BC) into the reign of Hezekiah (c. 680 BC), clearly placing himself in the days of the Assyrian threats against Judah. During his lifetime Samaria, the capital of the northern kingdom, fell to

Ahab's palace in Samaria.

the Assyrians in 722 BC. The northern tribes were scattered and replaced by Assyrian settlements in the hills of Galilee and Samaria.

By contrast, Jeremiah, Ezekiel, and Daniel lived during the last days of Judah, the southern kingdom, and witnessed the fall of Jerusalem to the Babylonians in 605 BC (Daniel), 597 BC (Ezekiel), and 586 BC (Jeremiah). Within their lifetimes their beloved Jerusalem was conquered, Solomon's temple was destroyed, the royal line of the "house of David" was removed, and the Jews were deported to Babylon.

MESSAGE OF THE MAJOR PROPHETS

The English Bible includes five books of the Major Prophets. Among these, Isaiah and Jeremiah are the longest. They emphasize the preaching of these two great prophets of Judah. Ezekiel and Daniel both include apocalyptic visions of Israel's future and provide hope to the Jewish exiles that God is still on the throne.

- Isaiah: God Is with Us
- Jeremiah: The Babylonians Are Coming
- Lamentations: Jerusalem Is Burning
- Ezekiel: The Glory Will Return
- Daniel: The Messiah Will Come

The messages of the Major Prophets remind us that God holds all nations accountable for their behavior and policies. He alone is the One who sets up and takes down kings (Dan 4:17). He is the sovereign Lord of the universe before whom the nations are but "a drop in a bucket" (Isa 40:15). But He is also the God who gives us hope even in the most difficult times of our lives (Jer 29:11).

For Further Reading

Bullock, C. Hassell. *Introduction to the Old Testament Prophets*. Chicago: Moody Press, 1986.

Chisholm, Robert B., Jr. *Handbook on the Prophets*. Grand Rapids: Baker, 2002.

Hindson, Ed. "Prophets," *Popular Encyclopedia of Bible Prophecy*. Eugene, OR: Harvest House, 2004.

McConville, J. G. *Exploring the Old Testament: A Guide to the Prophets*. Downers Grove: IVP, 2002.

Smith, Gary V. "Prophet," ISBE. Rev. ed. Grand Rapids: Eerdmans, 1986.

Wood, Leon. *The Prophets of Israel*. Grand Rapids: Baker, 1979.

Young, Edward J. *My Servants the Prophets*. Grand Rapids: Eerdmans, 1965.

ENDNOTE

1. Andrew Hill and John Walton, *A Survey of the Old Testament* (Grand Rapids: Zondervan, 2009), 509 ff.

Chapter 28

ISAIAH
God Is with Us

Isaiah stands at the peak of the Old Testament as the **literary genius** of the Hebrew prophets. This amazing book of prophecy includes Isaiah's unique prophecies about Immanuel (chaps. 7–12) and the suffering servant (chaps. 49–53). The book is set in the tumultuous days of the Assyrian and Babylonian threats to Judah's future and the survival of the messianic line of the "house of David." It combines elements of sublime poetry with preached sermons and prose narratives. It includes extended doublets, arch trajectories, and unique palindromes (sentences beginning and ending with the same words), chiastic parables, and cross alliteration.[1] Thus, Isaiah has often been called the "Shakespeare of Israel" and the "Prince of the Prophets."

One of the copies of the book of Isaiah found among the Dead Sea Scrolls.

Isaiah (*yesha yahu*, "Yahweh is salvation"), the son of Amoz, was a prominent citizen in Jerusalem in the eighth century BC. Jewish tradition in the Talmud (Sota 10b) identifies Isaiah's father as the brother of King Amaziah, making Isaiah a cousin of King Uzziah. Whether this is true or not, Isaiah certainly had **access to the royal**

court and gave advice on personal matters and foreign affairs to the kings of Judah (Isa 7:3–4; 37:5–7; 38:1–8; cf. 2 Kings 19–20). Isaiah was married to a prophetess (Isa 8:1) and had at least two children, Shear-Jashub ("A Remnant Shall Return") and Maher-Shalal-Hash-Baz ("Swift to the Plunder, Swift to the Spoil"). The names of these two sons served as prophetic "signs" illustrating and confirming Isaiah's message (Isa 8:18). Tradition (*The Ascension of Isaiah*) states that the wicked king Manasseh placed Isaiah in a hollow log and sawed it in half, and Heb 11:37 perhaps makes reference to this event.

BACKGROUND

Isaiah ministered in Judah c. 740–686 BC, during a time of great national crisis. The Lord commissioned Isaiah as a prophet in the year of King Uzziah's death after a long and effective reign that brought prosperity and stability to Judah. Isaiah subsequently served during the reigns of **four kings in Judah**—Jotham (750–735 BC), Ahaz (735–715 BC), Hezekiah (715–686 BC), and Manasseh (686–642 BC). Assyria became a major threat to Israel and Judah as they looked to expand their empire westward under the vigorous leadership of Tiglath-pileser III (745–727 BC). After several decades of decline and internal problems, the Assyrians eventually established an empire that extended from present-day Iran in the east to Egypt in the west across the Fertile Crescent.

Pekah of Israel and Rezin of Damascus (Aram) formed an alliance in an attempt to resist Assyrian control over Syria-Israel, but when Ahaz king of Judah refused to join their coalition, the **Syro-Ephraimite** War erupted in 734–732 BC (cf. 2 Kings 16; Isaiah 7–8). Pekah and Rezin invaded Judah and marched on Jerusalem, hoping to

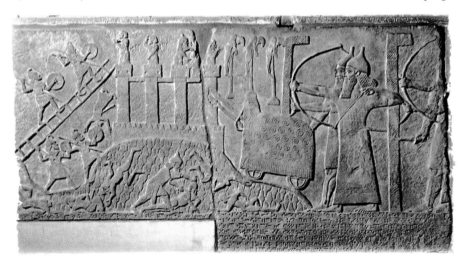

An Assyrian relief from the palace of Tiglath-pileser III at Nineveh showing an Assyrian battering ram at work.

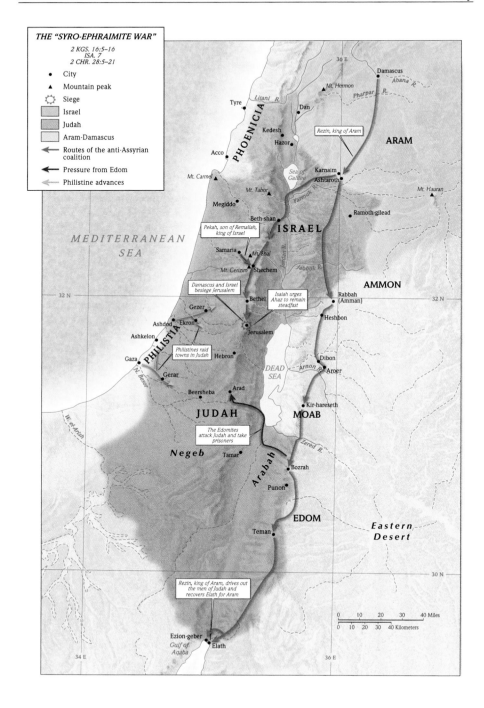

THE "SYRO-EPHRAIMITE WAR"

2 KGS. 16:5–16
ISA. 7
2 CHR. 28:5–21

- City
▲ Mountain peak
✻ Siege
Israel
Judah
Aram-Damascus
◄— Routes of the anti-Assyrian coalition
◄— Pressure from Edom
◄— Philistine advances

Damascus
Abana R.

Mt. Hermon
Pharpar R.

Tyre
Litani R.

Dan

PHOENICIA

Kedesh

Rezin, king of Aram

ARAM

Hazor

Acco

Sea of Galilee

Mt. Carmel ▲

Karnaim
Ashtaroth

Mt. Hauran ▲

Mt. Tabor

Yarmuk R.

Megiddo

Ramoth-gilead

Beth-shan

Pekah, son of Remaliah,
king of Israel

ISRAEL

MEDITERRANEAN
SEA

Samaria

Mt. Ebal

Jabbok R.

Mt. Gerizim Shechem

Damascus and Israel
besiege Jerusalem

Bethel

Isaiah urges
Ahaz to remain
steadfast

Rabbah
(Amman)

AMMON

Gezer

Heshbon

Ashdod Ekron

Ashkelon

PHILISTIA

Jerusalem

Philistines raid
towns in Judah   Hebron

Gaza

Gerar

Dibon

Aroer

DEAD
SEA

Arnon R.

Beersheba   Arad

Kir-hareseth

JUDAH

MOAB

The Edomites
attack Judah and take
prisoners

Negeb   Tamar

Zered R.

Arabah

Bozrah

Punon

EDOM

Eastern
Desert

Teman

30 N

Rezin, king of Aram, drives out
the men of Judah and
recovers Elath for Aram

0   10   20   30   40 Miles
0 10 20 30 40 Kilometers

Ezion-geber

Gulf of
Aqaba   Elath

34 E

36 E

replace Ahaz with a ruler supportive of their coalition. Isaiah counseled Ahaz to trust in the Lord and assured the king the attack on him by Pekah and Rezin would not succeed. Rather than trusting the Lord, Ahaz appealed to Assyria for assistance and paid off Tiglath-pileser to defeat Judah's enemies. The Assyrians destroyed Damascus and decimated Israel as well. Israel and its capital city of Samaria fell to the Assyrians in 722 BC (2 Kings 17). The Assyrians took the people into exile and turned the land of Israel into an Assyrian province.

Judah became an Assyrian vassal during the reign of Ahaz, but Hezekiah rejected his father's pro-Assyrian policies and rebelled against Assyria. The **Assyrian response** was severe, as Sennacherib invaded in 701 BC and captured 46 cities in Judah. Jerusalem was spared when the Lord destroyed the Assyrian army surrounding the city in response to the faith of Hezekiah who prayed for the Lord to deliver the city (2 Kings 18–19; Isaiah 36–37). Having avoided disaster from Assyria, Isaiah next warned Judah of a more fearful invasion in the future from the Babylonians.

AUTHORSHIP

The book of Isaiah presents itself as the "vision" of the eighth-century prophet by that name (Isa 1:1; cf. 2:1; 13:1; 20:2 for specific oracles also attributed to Isaiah), and the traditional view is that Isaiah composed the book c. 700 BC. Critical scholarship has argued for **multiple authorship** of the book and has viewed chapters 40–66 as coming after the time of Isaiah. They propose an unnamed exilic writer referred to as Second Isaiah (Deutero-Isaiah) who composed chapters 40–55 and a postexilic writer referred to as Third Isaiah (Trito-Isaiah) who composed chapters 56–66. More contemporary critical scholarship has moved beyond the three-author view but continues to view the composition of the book as occurring over several centuries from the eighth through the fifth centuries BC. A few evangelical scholars have adopted views on the formation of Isaiah that accommodate multiple authorship, extensive editorial revision, and the growth and development of the book over a long period of time.

Critical scholarship argues for a later date for Isaiah 40–66 because of the shift to a more poetic, theoretical, and conciliatory tone plus an **exilic perspective** reflected in these chapters. The writer(s) identifies Babylon as the place people must flee from (48:20) and reflects familiarity with the destruction of the temple (63:18; 64:10–11). They suggest that the prophet refers to the return from exile (40:9–11) and the fall of Babylon (47:1–3) and even identifies Cyrus the Persian as the ruler whose conquests would make possible the exiles' return (44:28; 45:1,13). All these apparent predictive prophecies are explained either as words expressed just before their fulfillment or as *vaticinia ex eventu* (i.e., prophecies after the event), despite the author's insistence that God declares "the end from the beginning, and from long ago what is not yet done" (46:10). Frequently these interpretations read into the text an exilic setting when it is not expressly stated, interpreting eschatological promises like 40:9–11 as exilic.

Predictive prophecy about a future exile and a later return from exile through the work of Cyrus is not a problem for those who believe the prophetic word is supernatural revelation from God and the inspired prophet spoke and wrote under the influence of the Holy Spirit. Long-range prophecies occur elsewhere in the Old Testament. These include the rise of Josiah in 1 Kgs 13:1–2, the details concerning the rise of the four world empires and the working out of the 70 sevens in Daniel 7–11, and the future rebuilding of the temple in Ezekiel 40–48. If one can accept Isaiah's ability to prophesy concerning the future Messiah 700 years in advance (Isaiah 53), then there is no reason to doubt Isaiah's ability to prophesy concerning Cyrus 150 years ahead of time.

Conservative scholars have pointed out several **unifying factors** in the whole of Isaiah. The use of the title "Holy One of Israel" appears equally in both "halves" of the book. Jesus quoted from both "halves" attributing both to Isaiah the prophet (John 12:38–40; Luke 4:17–21). Several scholars have pointed out that references to vegetation (plants and trees) and geography (locations and topography) in chaps. 40–66 reflect a Judean, not Babylonian, Jewish author. The reference to enemies at war with Israel in 41:10–13 argues against an exilic setting because Israel experienced no wars while they were in exile. Smith comments on several *linguistic connections* between chap. 1 and chaps. 65–66.[2] Some of these include:

Heaven and Earth	1:2	65:17; 66:1,22
I Have No Pleasure	1:11	66:4
Seek	1:12	65:1
Hear the Word of the Lord	1:11	66:5
The Woman Zion	1:21,26	66:7–13
You Have Chosen	1:29	66:4
Fire Not Quenched	1:31	66:24

Motyer argues for a **single author** who both spoke and wrote his words and then edited them to pass on to his disciples.[3] He argues: "There is no external, manuscriptal authority for the separate existence at any time for three supposed divisions of Isaiah."[4] He concludes: "The whole book is a huge mosaic in which totally pre-exilic material is made to serve pre-exilic, exilic, post-exilic and eschatological purposes."[5] In other words, one prophet, Isaiah himself, spoke of events that would happen in the immediate future (deliverance from Assyria), the distant future (Babylonian captivity), the Messianic era (the Anointed One), and the eschatological future (new heavens and new earth).[6]

Isaiah's literary efforts may rightly be termed the classical period of Hebrew literature. The grandeur of style, the liveliness of energy, and the profusion of forceful plays on words, vivid descriptions, and dramatic rhetorical touches undoubtedly make him the "Prince of Prophets."

The canonical witness of the New Testament confirms Isaiah's authorship of all parts of the book. Relevant New Testament references include Matt 3:3 (quoting Isa 40:3); Matt 4:4 (quoting Isa 9:1–2); Luke 4:17 (introducing a quote of Isa 61:1–3); John 12:39 (introducing a quote of Isa 53:1); Acts 8:28–35 (quoting Isa 53:7–8); and Rom 10:20 (quoting Isa 65:1). These New Testament texts attribute Isaianic authorship to passages critical scholars attribute to Second and Third Isaiah. Beyond just using the name Isaiah as a conventional form of citation, various expressions refer to Isaiah's personal involvement in the writing and prophesying of the book's contents. There are citations stating, "Isaiah was right when he prophesied about you" (Matt 15:7 NIV; Mark 7:6 NIV) and, "The Holy Spirit spoke the truth to your forefathers when he said through Isaiah the prophet" (Acts 28:25 NIV). No ancient manuscript evidence supports the division of Isaiah 1–39 and 40–66 as separate works. The oldest complete Hebrew text, the Great Isaiah Scroll from Qumran (1QIsaᵃ), contains no break in the text between chaps. 39 and 40.

The tomb of Cyrus the Great.

Outline

MESSAGE

I. Prophecies Against Judah (Isaiah 1–6)

The book of Isaiah opens with five sermons that we might call "the best of Isaiah." They serve as a **thematic introduction** to the book. The opening chapters present in abbreviated form the message of Isaiah as a whole—the Lord will send a purging judgment against His sinful people, producing a righteous remnant that will enjoy the future blessings of salvation and restoration. Standing over this section and the entire book is Isaiah's vision of the holiness of the Lord in chap. 6. Isaiah recognized both his own sinfulness and that of his people and accepted his commission to become the Lord's messenger of judgment until the cities of Israel and Judah were ruined and destroyed. It seems strange that Isaiah's call as a prophet in Isaiah 6 does not appear as the opening episode in the book, so there is a question if this is his first call or a recommissioning to a new phase of ministry. Clearly these early messages in the book establish the guilt of Israel and Judah that provides the larger context of Isaiah's vision (6:5: "I . . . live among a people of unclean lips"). The holiness of the Lord and the sinfulness of His people stand in stark contrast to each other.

A. Coming Judgment and Blessing (Isaiah 1–5)

The opening message in Isaiah 1 is both a **covenant lawsuit** establishing Israel's guilt and a call to repentance exhorting the people to change their sinful ways. As an unfaithful covenant partner, the Lord's people were like a rebellious child deserving judgment (1:3–4; cf. Deut 21:18–21). Consequently the covenant curse of an invading enemy army left Judah bloody and battered (1:5–6). Even Judah's religious rituals become an offense to God. Yet, if they would repent and become both willing and obedient, they could be forgiven. "Though your sins are like scarlet, they will be as white as snow" (1:18). The people had a choice either to obey God and "eat" (*akal*) the best of the land or to persist in their rebellion and be "devoured" (*ʾakal*) by the sword in judgment (1:19–20).

In the second sermon, Isaiah foresees God coming to Zion to teach His ways to all people and to end all wars in the eschatological future of the "last days" (2:2–4). He will judge the proud so that God alone is exalted on the coming Day of the Lord (2:12). In the third sermon Isaiah indicts Judah's leaders and suggests that they will be replaced by people who act like unstable youths (3:4). Then he denounced the "daughters of Zion" because of their pride and materialism (3:16–26). In chap. 4 Isaiah predicts the coming of the messianic Branch of the Lord and the gathering of everyone who is holy to Jerusalem (4:2–6).

The re-internment funerary inscription discovered in the 19th century of the Jewish King Uzziah. Its Aramaic writing translates "Hither were brought the bones of Uzziah, King of Judah. Do not open."

In chap. 5 Isaiah sings the "**Song of the Vineyard**." The harvest was a time of great celebration, and the vineyard imagery reflects a love song (cf. Song 1:2,14; 3:15; 5:1; 7:8,12), but the marriage between the Lord and Israel is fractured by sin. The Lord's provisions made it possible for Israel to be a fruitful vineyard (cf. Ps 80:8–16), but

Israel as a disobedient people gave the Lord the exact opposite of what He expected in return for His priceless investment. Instead of good grapes (*'anuvim*), they were worthless wild grapes (*be'usim*) (5:4). Instead of standing up for doing justice (*mishpat*), they promoted "bloodshed" (*mishpach*); and instead of "righteousness" (*tsadaqah*), there was an outcry (*tse'aqah*) of distress because of the violence and oppression (5:7). The five "woes" that follow announced the Lord's judgment on the vineyard for its many sins. Jesus used similar imagery in Matt 21:33–42.

B. Call of the Prophet (Isaiah 6)

In chap. 6 Isaiah recounts his **call to the prophetic ministry** undoubtedly many years prior to this writing, although his use of imperfect verbs indicates that he is describing the scene as it happened. He dates his call from the year that King Uzziah died (740 BC). Since Isaiah introduces himself as prophesying during the reign of Uzziah, some view this as a recommissioning to prepare him for a difficult ministry in the reign of Ahaz. The **death of king Uzziah** also left Isaiah concerned about the future of the kingdom. Thus, the vision of Yahweh seated on the throne of heaven reassured him that God was still in control of the destiny of His people. The Hebrew text makes clear that Isaiah saw the Lord (*Adonay*) seated on the throne and that it was the LORD (*Yahweh*) the seraphs ("burning ones") worshipped. This substantiates that *Adonay* and *Yahweh* are One and the same. The triple declaration: Holy (*qadosh*) reflected the glory (*kabod*) of God.

The foundations of the Broad Wall in Jerusalem attributed to the building activities of Hezekiah as he prepared his city for revolt against the Assyrians.

Isaiah's confrontation with God (vv. 1–4) led to his confession: "Woe is me" (v. 5), but this is quickly followed by his consecration (vv. 6–7), call (v. 6), and commission (vv. 9–13). Isaiah recognized that he was "unclean" because he had seen the holy King, the Lord of hosts (*hamelek Yahweh tseba'oth*). This title appears in the book of Isaiah to identify the "King of glory" (also in Ps 24:10). The vision of God radically changed Isaiah. When the Lord asked: "Who will go for Us?" Isaiah replied," "Here I am. Send me" (v. 8). Newly cleansed and commissioned, Isaiah launches on his prophetic ministry even though his audience in the time of Ahaz would close their ears to the messages he would deliver (6:9–10).

II. Promise of Immanuel (Isaiah 7–12)

Ahaz ruled over Judah from 735 to 715 BC, and his refusal to trust in the Lord during the **Syro-Ephraimite** crisis early in his reign had disastrous consequences. In the years 735–732 BC, Syria and Israel formed a military alliance against Assyria as Tiglath-pileser III looked westward to expand his empire. Ahaz wisely refused to join the coalition, recognizing that resistance to Assyria was doomed to failure. In retaliation the armies of Syria and Israel marched south, attempting to force Judah to join their alliance and to replace Ahaz with a king named Tabeel who would support them as an ally. Isaiah encouraged Ahaz to trust the Lord and assured the king that his enemies would not succeed (7:4–5). The prophet even encouraged the king to ask the Lord for a confirming "sign" to strengthen his faith, but the king piously refused, stating that he would not put the Lord to the test.

Because of Ahaz's unbelief, the Lord took the initiative to give a "sign" that portended both salvation and judgment (7:14). The birth of a son named ***Immanuel*** ("God with us") would demonstrate God's presence with His people and His commitment to preserve and protect the house of David. Before this child was old enough to know the difference between right and wrong, the kings of Syria and Israel would be destroyed. However, the child would also serve as a reminder of the foolishness of Ahaz's unbelief. Because Ahaz had appealed to Assyria for military assistance against Syria and Israel rather than trusting in the Lord, the Assyrians would eventually invade the land of Judah.

The **identity** of the promised child in 7:14 is a source of major controversy. While some have suggested it refers to the birth of a child at that time, the extended prophecy points beyond the immediate context to a divine child who is identified in 9:6 as the "Mighty God" (*'el gibbor*). The ultimate fulfillment of the Immanuel prophecy was the virgin birth of Jesus Christ, who was literally God incarnate and who would preserve the line of David forever (Matt 1:21–23).[7] Smith notes: "This ruler was not Ahaz's son or Isaiah's son, but an unknown future king specifically identified in 9:1–7 in clear messianic terms."[8]

The invasion of foreign armies on the immediate horizon would fail, Isaiah promised, "For God is with us" (8:10). The prophet goes on to predict that "a great light" will shine in Galilee (9:2), a verse quoted in Matt 4:16 and Luke 1:79 in relation to

---

Hebrew Highlight

Believe. Hebrew אמן (*'âman*). The Immanuel Prophecy (Isa 7:10–14) was prompted by Ahaz's refusal to "believe," "stand firm," or have "faith" in God. *'Aman* is related to *'emeth* (truth) and *'emunah* (faithfulness). It is the basis of the English "amen" (Neh 8:6). Passive reflexive forms can mean endure, be faithful, or reliable. Participles imply faithful, trustworthy, assured, or certain. Causative verbs signify believe, trust, or rely. Isaiah's challenge to the worried king to "stand firm in your faith" (7:9) emphasizes the significance of true faith or belief as a confident assurance in God's promises.

Jesus' Galilean ministry. Then he announces that a son will be born, given by God Himself (9:6). The **fourfold title** makes clear that this is not a typical human child. He is described as "Wonderful Counselor" (*Pele' yo'ets*), "Mighty God" (*el gibbor*), "Everlasting Father" (*'abî 'ad*), "Prince of Peace" (*sar shalom*). His government is also described in a fourfold manner: (1) peace without end, (2) throne of David, (3) justice and righteousness, (4) reign forever. Again Smith notes these messianic promises, descriptive parameters, titles, and time frames rule out any possible human rulers.[9] God Himself will come in the future to rule the world.

Ahaz epitomized the failed leadership of the past, but the future Messiah would fulfill every ideal the Lord had designed for the Davidic rulers. He would establish His throne with justice and righteousness and deliver His people from their oppressors (9:2–6). He would rule in the power of the Lord, and His kingdom would last forever. Unlike the arrogant Assyrian rulers who are depicted as lofty trees, Messiah would emerge as a tiny **Branch** from the stump of the felled Davidic dynasty (11:1–2). From this humble origin, His kingdom would extend over the nations and bring peace and harmony to the earth, reversing even the effects of the fall and the curse upon humanity and the creation (11:6–11). "In that day" (in the future) the Lord's people will sing for joy because of the blessings of His reign over them (12:1–6). This hymn of thanksgiving ends with the assurance that the "Holy One of Israel is among you" (12:6), again emphasizing the Immanuel ("God is with us") connection throughout these chapters.

III. Prophecies Against the Nations (Isaiah 13–23)

The Lord's judgment would extend beyond Israel and Judah to include all of the nations and people surrounding them. Isaiah's oracles against the **nations** include messages directed against:

- Babylon (13:1–14:23)
- Assyria (14:24–27)
- Philistia (14:28–32)
- Moab (15:1–16:14)
- Syria and Israel (17:1–14)
- Cush and Egypt (18:1–20:6)
- Babylon (21:1–10)
- Dumah (21:11–12)
- Arabia (21:13–17)
- Jerusalem (22:1–25)
- Tyre (23:1–18)

The Lord would judge both the great superpowers and the smaller nation-states that were struggling for survival just like Israel and Judah. These oracles focused primarily on other nations (*goyim*, "Gentiles") but were delivered for the benefit of God's people. These messages served to assert the Lord's sovereignty over the nations. Yahweh was not just a nationalistic deity but the ruler and judge of all peoples. The promise of God's judgment of Israel's enemies offered hope for the future and provided assurance that the Lord had not abandoned His people. The Lord would reverse Israel's fortunes by punishing her oppressors (14:1–3). The nations that attacked Israel were like the raging waters of the sea, but the Lord would drive them away (17:12–14). When the Lord restores Israel, He will place a Davidic king on the throne who will seek justice and righteousness (16:8). For the more immediate future, these oracles were also a warning against Israel's forming political alliances with these nations that stood under God's judgment.

The Lord would judge the nations for their **excessive pride** (13:11,19; 14:11; 16:6; 17:7–11; 23:9), which caused them to practice evil and to put their trust in idols, wealth, and military prowess. The extreme example of pride in this section is the king of Babylon who boasted that he would ascend into heaven and make himself like the Most High (14:12–15). Instead, the Lord would bring the king of Babylon down to the grave, and the kings of the nations he had slain in battle would rejoice when he joined them in the underworld (14:9–11,15–20). In demonstration of His sovereign power, the Lord would bring down both Babylon and its false gods (13:9; 21:9–10).

Isaiah's oracles against the nations contain two especially **surprising elements**. The first surprise element is the inclusion of messages against Israel and Judah in the context of these oracles dealing with the judgment of their enemies (17:1–11; 22:1–14). Their special status as the Lord's chosen people would not exempt them from judgment, and in fact it made them more culpable than the pagan nations around them. The second surprising element is that tucked within these messages of judgment against the nations are grand promises of the inclusion of people from some of these nations in God's glorious future kingdom. The Lord as righteous judge would punish the nations for their sins, but He also had a redemptive concern for these people (19:19–25).

IV. Predictions of Judgment and Blessing (Isaiah 24–27)

Some scholars have called this section "**The Little Apocalypse**" because of its similarities to the book of Revelation. The previous chapters focus on the historical judgment of the nations surrounding Israel and Judah that were involved in the international conflicts and political intrigues of Isaiah's day, but this portion of Isaiah's message looks forward to the final judgment of all nations and the coming of God's eschatological kingdom to earth on the day of the Lord. The recurring phrase "On that day" (24:21; 25:9; 26:1; 27:1) refers to a future day and reflects the eschatological perspective of this section.

The Lord's final judgment of the wicked will usher in the **eschatological kingdom**, in which the righteous will enjoy a lavish banquet on Mount Zion (25:1–13). The ultimate promise for the righteous is that the Lord will destroy and "swallow up" death itself (25:7–8 NIV). While the hope of a personal resurrection is expressed in earlier times (cf. Job 19:25–26; Ps 16:11), the promise of physical resurrection is clearly stated in Isa 26:19. The Lord promises that the "dead will live" and "their bodies will rise" up out of the dust. Isaiah also promises the future resurrection of the Suffering Servant (53:10–12), and Ezekiel employs the image of resurrection to speak of the future restoration of Israel (Ezekiel 37). Daniel adds to the Old Testament

Pictures of Christ in Isaiah	
1. Virgin Birth (7:14)	13. Incarnate God (40:9)
2. Light in Galilee (9:1–2)	14. Servant of the Lord
3. Divine Child (9:6)	(42:1–4)
4. Mighty God (9:6)	15. Redeemer of Israel
5. Wonderful Counselor	(44:6)
(9:6)	16. Light of the Gentiles
6. Prince of Peace (9:6)	(49:6)
7. Branch of Jesse (11:1)	17. Suffering Servant
8. Anointed King (11:2)	(52:13–53:12)
9. Banner of the Nations	18. Resurrected Lord (53:10)
(11:10)	19. Anointed Messiah
10. Holy One of Israel (12:6)	(61:1–3)
11. Angel of the Lord	20. Coming Conqueror
(37:36)	(66:15–16)
12. A Forerunner Prepares	
His Way (40:3)	

understanding of resurrection by revealing that there will be resurrection to life for the righteous and resurrection to judgment for the wicked (Dan 12:1–2).

V. Perilous Woes (Isaiah 28–33)

A series of five **woe oracles** (28:1; 29:1,15; 30:1; 31:1) announced the coming destruction of Israel and Judah, and then a final woe (33:1) announces the doom of Assyria. Israel's leaders were drunkards lacking moral and spiritual sense (28:1–13). Since they have dismissed the prophetic calls to trust in God as simplistic baby talk in contrast to their wise military strategies, the Lord will speak to them through the foreign language of the invading Assyrian army that would sweep through their land. The Lord Himself will wage warfare against the city of Jerusalem (29:1–3) to purge the city of its sin. The issue of trust in man versus trust in God once again comes to the forefront (28:16; 31:1–3). Isaiah dismisses the treaties that they think will keep them safe, calling them a covenant with death (28:14).

The woe against Assyria in chap. 33 offered **hope for Israel's future**—the Lord will establish justice by destroying the "destroyer." The judgment of Assyria prefigures God's judgment of all nations (34:1–7). However, Isaiah warned that the sinners among God's own people should also be terrified because they too would be destroyed by God's fiery judgment (33:14). This purging judgment would be the prelude to Israel's restoration and the future kingdom of peace and prosperity. Israel will finally have a king who will rule over them with justice and righteousness (32:1). As the center of the Lord's earthly kingdom, Zion will become a place of peace and security and will never again be subjected to enemy attack (33:16–20).

VI. Promise of Destruction and Triumph (Isaiah 34–35)

These two prophecies are **apocalyptic** in nature. God will judge all the nations with cataclysmic catastrophes. The mountains will melt, and the heavens will dissolve in the Lord's "day of vengeance" (34:1–10). The "birds of prey" will be gathered by the Lord to the great day of battle (34:16). The language is similar to the description of the battle of Armageddon in Rev 16:14–16. After the "day of vengeance," the desert will "blossom like a rose" and the people "will see the glory of the LORD" (35:1–2). The redeemed will walk on the highway of holiness and "come to Zion with singing" (35:8–10). Thus, this section ends with the promise of triumph in the future.

VII. Prayers for Deliverance (Isaiah 36–39)

These narratives dealing with the reign of Hezekiah, his passionate prayer, and the deliverance of Jerusalem from the Assyrian army in 701 BC function as a **hinge** for the two halves of the book of Isaiah. The story of Hezekiah's faith and the deliverance of Jerusalem in chaps. 36–37 provide closure to the first half of the book as the Lord brings the *Assyrian* crisis to an end. The Lord used Assyria to punish His people, but then He will deliver Judah from their enemy. The story of Hezekiah's healing and the visit of the Babylonian envoys to Jerusalem in chaps. 38–39 introduces the threat of *Babylonian* invasion and exile that will be taken up in the second half of the book (chaps. 40–66). The Lord's deliverance of Jerusalem from Assyria offered assurance that He was willing and able to deliver His people from the power of any foreign nation, even from Babylon.

Hezekiah's faith was not perfect, and he often turned to political intrigue and military alliances in the midst of threatening circumstances (chaps. 30–31; 39), but in the end Hezekiah displayed great faith in the Lord as his sole source of security when the Assyrian army surrounded the city of Jerusalem in 701 BC. In fact, Hezekiah is remembered as the king of incomparable faith in 2 Kgs 18:5. The Assyrian military commander sent a threatening letter demanding the surrender of Jerusalem and warning that the Lord would not be able to thwart the Assyrian army. Hezekiah laid the letter out before the Lord at the temple and prayed for deliverance. Isaiah announced that the Lord heard the king's prayer and He would deliver Jerusalem from its attackers. The angel of the Lord went out in the middle of the night to kill 185,000 Assyrian soldiers, causing Sennacherib to return to his homeland with what was left of his army (37:36–37).

Isaiah 7–8 and 36–39 are the two **narrative portions** in the book, and these sections directly contrast Hezekiah's faith in the Lord with his father Ahaz's lack of faith. The parallels and similarities between the two stories highlight the stark contrast between the two: Ahaz trusts in armies while Hezekiah trusts in God. The choices of these two kings represent the options facing God's people at this time: Will they trust in their man-made gods, political leaders, building projects, and military alliances; or will they look to the Lord as their sole source of security? The prophet Isaiah also has "fear not" messages in the second half of the book (41:10,13,14; 43:1,5; 44:2,8; 51:7; 54:4), for each generation must make the choice to act in faith on the Lord's promises.

The story of **Hezekiah's healing** from a life-threatening illness in chap. 38 further demonstrates the king's faith and the power of prayer. Hezekiah petitioned the Lord after Isaiah announced that he was going to die from his illness, and the Lord graciously extended the king's life for 15 years. The healing of the king also reflected how the Lord would extend the life of Judah as a nation and not bring judgment from Babylon until after the time of Hezekiah. The narrative in Isaiah 39, however, reflects a significant lapse in judgment by Hezekiah. The envoys of Merodach-baladan, the king of Babylon, came to congratulate Hezekiah after his recovery from his illness. However, Hezekiah failed to take advantage of a significant opportunity to honor the greatness of the Lord and instead showed off his temple treasures in an attempt to demonstrate that he was a worthy treaty partner. Isaiah rebuked the king and warned that his actions would lead the Babylonians to return to Jerusalem for these treasures.

Chronologically, the events in chaps. 38–39 occurred before the deliverance of Jerusalem narrated in chaps. 36–37, but these events were placed at the end of the first half of the book to lead into the promise of the return from Babylon in chaps. 40–66. This arrangement also reveals that Hezekiah's prayer for healing strengthened his faith to pray for help in light of the greater crisis of the invasion of Jerusalem.

The Taylor Prism recounting King Sennacherib's third campaign, including his conquests in Judah.

VIII. Prophetic Consolation (Isaiah 40–66)

The section of Isaiah from chap. 40 to 66 forms the "**Book of Consolation**." The second half of the book of Isaiah differs from the first in several key ways. Chapters 1–39 focus primarily on trusting God in the midst of the Assyrian crisis rather than trusting in silver and gold, alliances with pagan nations, or trusting in one's own strength. Chapters 40–66 argue that one should trust God because the idols are nothing; only God has the ability to predict the future. God's Servant will establish justice on earth and suffer for the sins of many. God's people will one day return to their land, and in the end many people from many nations will come to worship God in His glorious kingdom. The first half of the book is primarily a message of judgment, recording preached sermons, while the second half of the book is predominantly a message of salvation and hope written in exquisite poetry. In the first half of the book, the future Messiah is portrayed more as a triumphant King, while in the second half of the book, He assumes the role of a suffering Servant before becoming an Anointed Conqueror. While the future Babylonian captivity is in view in some of these chapters

(44:20–45:13), the prophet's audience is preexilic, and several references in these chapters predate the exile.[10]

A. The Promise of Peace (Isaiah 40–48)

Isaiah was called to proclaim the judgment of Israel and Judah in chap. 6, but here the prophet and the future inhabitants of Jerusalem receive a renewed call to share the **eschatological news** of comfort because their mighty God will come to gather His people and rule the earth like a shepherd takes care of his sheep (40:1–11). The prophet's message was that Israel's days of warfare would be complete, its sins would be forgiven, and the Lord would come to reward His people. Isaiah described this eschatological gathering in terms similar to the Exodus (43:16–21; 51:9–11; 52:10–12; 55:12–13). Ultimately, the Lord would gather His people out of many nations (43:5–7), and all nations would observe the Lord's power to save (52:10–12). Israel would not need to leave the land of bondage in haste as they did from Egypt (52:12), and the wilderness would be transformed into a paradise as the Hebrew people made their way home (41:8–20; 43:19–21).

Isaiah announced that **two figures** would play a key role in Israel's restoration and renewal. The Lord would raise up the Persian ruler Cyrus as His "anointed one" to secure Israel's release from exile (44:28–45:7). Cyrus, who reigned over Persia from 559 to 530 BC, would solve Israel's immediate problem by conquering Babylon and issuing the decree that would allow the Jews to return to their homeland (fulfilled in Ezra 1:1–5). Beyond Israel's military subjugation to Babylon, the larger issue impeding their restoration was the problem of Israel's sin and separation from the Lord. Rather than a conquering king, a Suffering Servant would accomplish Israel's ultimate restoration by giving His own life as a sin offering for the people. The role and mission of this figure are highlighted in a series of four Servant Songs (42:1–7; 49:1–6; 50:4–9; 52:13–53:12).

Isaiah highlighted several key themes in order to show the Israelites why they could trust in the **Lord's promises** to restore them. Isaiah reminded the people of the Lord's power to fulfill His promises as the Creator of the universe (40:12–17). The military power of their enemies was great, but the strength of all of the nations was nothing more than a drop in the bucket when compared to the Lord's power. As Creator, the Lord is also superior to the idols and false gods made of wood and plated with gold (40:18–26). The Lord is not only all-powerful, but He is also able to share His strength with His people so they mount up and fly like eagles even when they are weak and wearied (40:27–31).

One of the common speech forms in this section of Isaiah is the **trial speech** in which the prophet invites his audience into the courtroom as he demonstrates the superiority of the Lord to the gods of other nations. The gods of the nations are mute and silent, but the Lord announces His plans and actions before they come to pass (41:21–26; 42:9; 43:9; 44:7–9; 45:20–21; 48:5–7). The Lord revealed Cyrus as Israel's future deliverer and provided extensive details concerning his conquests so the

Hebrews would know that the Lord had accomplished these things. This section makes an apologetic appeal to God's ability to predict the future (46:10–11).

The prophet also engaged in a **sarcastic polemic** to demonstrate the folly of idol worship. A man may cover a god with gold or silver, but first he must make sure the idol is made of wood that will not rot and is constructed well so it does not topple (40:19–20). The idol worshipper cuts down a tree and uses half of the wood as fuel to cook his food and half to craft the idol as his object of worship (44:6–20). The gods have to be "carried" (*nasa'*) by their devotees (46:1,7), but the Lord has "carried" (*nasa'*) His people throughout their history (46:3–4). Idols have to be "lifted up" (*sabal*) so they can be carried on the shoulders (46:7), while the Lord promises to "sustain" (*sabal*) Israel (46:4). The gods are unable to "rescue" (*malat*) (46:2) and "save" (*yasha*ᶜ) their people as they are taken away into exile, but the Lord promises to "rescue" (*malat*) the exiles (46:4) because He is a God of "salvation" (*yeshuah*) (46:13).

B. Provision of Peace (Isaiah 49–57)

The identity of the **Servant of the Lord** in Isaiah 40–55 is a major source of discussion and controversy because some view the Servant as Israel, others point to the prophet Isaiah, a few think he is Cyrus, but the New Testament claims the Servant is Jesus. The Servant in Isaiah has both corporate and individual features. In some places the Servant is identified as Israel (41:8; 42:1; 43:10; 44:21; 45:4; 49:3). As the Lord's national Servant, Israel was commissioned with the task of reflecting the Lord's greatness to the nations, but Israel failed in its mission by not obeying the Lord (42:18–22). Because of Israel's disobedience, the Lord would commission an individual Servant to restore His people. The individual features of the Servant are especially prominent in the four Servant Songs. This individual would be identified with Israel (49:3) but would also have a ministry to Israel. Unlike unfaithful Israel the individual Servant would be obedient to God's instruction (50:4–5). Israel's as God's Servant was blind and deaf (42:18), but the role of the individual Servant was to open the eyes of the blind (42:7). While Israel suffered for its own sins (40:2; 42:24–25; 43:24–25; 44:21–22; 48:1–8), the Servant would suffer for the sins of others (53:4–6,10–12).

The most detailed and well-known of the Servant Songs in Isaiah 52:13–53:12 prophesies more extensively and specifically concerning the **sacrificial atonement** of the Servant and points ahead to the death and resurrection of Jesus. This song consists of five stanzas (52:13–15; 53:1–3,4–6,7–9,10–12). The opening and closing stanzas portray the Servant's exaltation. After His horrific suffering and disfigurement, the Servant will receive blessing, honor, and vindication from the Lord. Even the kings of the earth will be amazed at this startling reversal (52:13–15; cf. 49:7).

The remaining three stanzas focus on the nature of the **Servant's mission** and the divine purpose behind His suffering. The Servant's obscure origins and suffering would cause Israel not to recognize Him as their deliverer. They would fail to see how the Lord's saving power could be demonstrated through such a weak and despised figure (53:1–3). The Servant would be crushed by God for Israel's sins. His punishment would bring healing and restoration for God's sinful people (53:4–6). The

Servant would be like an innocent lamb led to slaughter, and he would be "cut off from the land of the living" (53:7–9). After the Servant completed His mission, the Lord would vindicate Him and restore Him to a place of honor and blessing because of His willingness to offer His life as a guilt offering for others (53:10–12). This final stanza ultimately implies the resurrection of the Servant to share in the spoils of His victory after His death.

Through His innocent suffering, the Servant would give His life as a sin offering that would make many righteous (53:11) and would restore Israel to its honored status as the Lord's national Servant (54:16–17; 65:18–19). Every use of the word "servant" following the song of the suffering Servant in Isaiah 53 appears in the plural and refers to the collective rather than the individual Servant (54:17; 56:6; 63:17; 65:8–9,13–15; 66:14). This corporate servant would include the **faithful remnant** from Israel as well as those from the nations who would turn to the Lord (56:3–8; 66:18–21). The Servant's role was not only to restore Israel but also to be a light leading the nations to the Lord as well (42:6; 49:6).

The progress of revelation from the Old Testament to the New clearly identifies **Jesus Christ** as the Isaianic Servant. In Acts 8, Philip explains to the Ethiopian eunuch that the innocent lamb led to slaughter in Isaiah 53 refers to Jesus (Acts 8:32–34). In several other passages the New Testament quotes from the Servant Songs and applies these passages to the person and work of Jesus:

1. Matthew 8:17 quotes from Isa 53:4 (*"He took up our infirmities and carried our diseases,"* NIV).
2. Luke 22:37 quotes from Isa 53:12 ("And he was numbered with the transgressors," NIV).

"Like a lamb led to the slaughter . . . He did not open His mouth" (Isa 53:7).

3. John 12:38 quotes from Isa 53:1 ("Lord, who has believed our message and to whom has the arm of the Lord been revealed?" NIV)
4. First Peter 2:21–25 cites and quotes from Isa 53:4–5,9,11–12 ("He committed no sin, and no deceit was found in his mouth," and "by his wounds you have been healed," NIV).

Numerous other allusions and references apply Isaiah's Servant Songs to Jesus in the New Testament. The declaration of Jesus that He came to serve others and *"give his life as a ransom for many"* in Mark 10:45 (NIV) likely alludes back to Isa 53:11–12. The description of Jesus as "the Lamb of God, who takes away the sin of the world!" in John 1:29 likely recalls Isa 53:7. Paul's description of Jesus as a "servant" who experiences death so that He might be ultimately exalted and recognized as Lord over all in Phil 2:6–11 also reflects how Jesus fulfills the role of Isaiah's Suffering Servant.

C. Program of Peace (Isaiah 58–66)

Isaiah 40–57 promises Israel's return, but the **full restoration of Israel** would only occur when the people truly repented of their sinful ways and returned to the Lord (chap. 55). Isaiah saw the sinful patterns of the present carrying over into the time when the people would return to the land. In many ways the return from exile was a disappointment. Israel would continue to live under foreign oppression. The return from Babylon would only be the first stage of Israel's restoration, and their complete salvation would await the future time when God's kingdom would come to earth and the Lord would deliver His people from their sins once for all.

The prophet called for a true fast of repentance and a commitment to righteousness (58). The only cure for Israel's sin was that the Lord would have to arm Himself as an Anointed Warrior and deliver them. The Lord would exact vengeance on Israel's enemies, but the real enemy to be destroyed was sin itself. The Lord's mighty arm would destroy sin, and the gift of the Spirit as part of His **new covenant** with Israel would enable His people to live in righteousness and obedience (59:20–21; cf. Jer 31:31–34; Ezek 36:25–29).

The focus of chaps. 60–62 is the future glories of Zion as the center of the **Lord's earthly kingdom**. The nations will be drawn to Jerusalem and to the light of God's salvation. As in the days of Solomon's empire but on a grander scale, the nations will bring tribute to Zion in honor of the Lord. The inclusion of the Gentiles in the blessings of the future kingdom is a prominent theme in Isaiah. Premillennialists believe these passages describe the future millennial (1,000-year) reign of Christ (Rev 20:1–6).

Isaiah was the Lord's herald to announce Israel's future salvation and their Day of Jubilee (61:1–3). Jesus specifically claimed that this prophecy was fulfilled in Him (cf. Luke 4:16–30). Jesus not only announced the deliverance but also accomplished Israel's salvation through His sacrificial death. The **fulfillment** of Isaiah 61 in the ministry of Jesus demonstrates that the final restoration of Israel points to the kingdom blessings that will be consummated at His Second Coming.

Portions of Isaiah 63–66 reveal that a **tribulation and judgment** will precede the coming of the Lord's earthly kingdom. This judgment will separate sinners from the righteous and purge the earth of its wickedness. The Lord will march out as the Anointed Warrior to exact His vengeance on the Edomites (who represent all God's enemies) and return from battle with the blood of His enemies spattered on His garments. This same imagery appears in Rev 19:11–16, describing the triumphal return of Jesus Christ as the Divine Warrior from heaven who comes to rule as the King of kings.

The book of Isaiah ends much as it began, with a message of both impending doom ("The LORD will come with fire," 66:15) and potential deliverance ("all mankind will come to worship Me," 66:23). The one recurring **theme** is that "God is with us." Jesus Christ (*yeshua hameshiah*) is the virgin's Son, Immanuel, the Branch of the Lord, the Mighty God, the Prince of Peace, the coming Messiah, the Suffering Servant, the Anointed Warrior, the Glorious King! "All the prophets testify about Him" (Acts 10:43).

THEOLOGICAL SIGNIFICANCE

The message of Isaiah has significantly impacted the New Testament presentation of the **person and work of Jesus Christ**. Next to Psalms, Isaiah is the most referenced Old Testament book in the New Testament, with approximately 100 citations and 500 allusions. Some estimate that 1 out of every 17 verses in the New Testament contains material taken from Isaiah. The New Testament announces that the blessings of the eschatological kingdom prophesied by Isaiah are fulfilled in the person of Jesus. The eschatological kingdom of God is inaugurated at the first coming of Jesus and will be consummated at His Second Coming. Jesus is the promised Messiah who will reign over the earth in justice and peace (Isa 9:2–6; 11:1–5). At the synagogue in Nazareth, Jesus declared that He was the fulfillment of Isaiah's promise of a Spirit-anointed messenger proclaiming freedom and deliverance for the people of Israel (Isa 61:1–2; Luke 4:16–21).

In **His sacrificial death** Jesus would take on the role of the Suffering Servant in providing salvation for His people (Matt 8:26–27; Mark 10:45; Acts 8:26–35; 1 Pet 2:22–25). Jesus would die as the sacrificial lamb for the sins of the world (Isa 53:7; John 1:29). More than any other prophet, Isaiah anticipated the inclusion of Gentiles as participants in the blessings of the Lord's future salvation.

In the **future kingdom** established at Christ's Second Coming, Jesus will rule over all and all will bow before Him in recognition of His sovereignty (Phil 2:10–11). Jesus will triumph over death by raising up those who have trusted in Him in fulfillment of Isaiah's promise that the Lord would "swallow up" death forever (Isa 25:6–8; 1 Cor 15:23–28,51–55). In preparation for the eschatological kingdom, the Lord will bring about the national restoration of Israel as the people turn from their unbelief and embrace Jesus as their Messiah (Isa 59:20; Rom 11:26–28). In the millennial kingdom the nations will come to Zion to worship and serve the Lord (Isa 2:1–4; 60:1–9; Rev 20:1–10) in anticipation of the new heavens, new earth, and new Jerusalem where the righteous will dwell with God forever (Revelation 21–22).

For Further Reading

Beyer, Bryan. *Encountering the Book of Isaiah*. Grand Rapids: Baker, 2007.
Hindson, Edward E. "Isaiah." In *KJBC*. Nashville: Thomas Nelson, 1999.
Motyer, J. A. *The Prophecy of Isaiah: An Introduction and Commentary*. Downers Grove, IL: IVP, 1993.
Oswalt, John. *The Book of Isaiah: Chapters 1–39*, NICOT. Grand Rapids: Eerdmans, 1986.
————. *The Book of Isaiah: Chapters 40–66*, NICOT. Grand Rapids: Eerdmans, 1997.
Smith, Gary V. *Isaiah 1–39*. NAC, Nashville: B&H, 2007.
————. *Isaiah 40–66*. NAC, Nashville: B&H, 2009.
Young, Edward J. *The Book of Isaiah*, 3 vols. Grand Rapids: Eerdmans, 1965.

Study Questions

1. What is the major difference between Isaiah 1–39 and 40–66?
2. How would you defend the unity of the authorship of both sections?
3. How does the Immanuel Prophecy (Isaiah 7–12) emphasize the deity of Christ?
4. What does God's judgment of the nations indicate about His sovereignty over the whole world?
5. What lessons in prayer did Hezekiah learn, and how did they affect his life and the city of Jerusalem?
6. How did God use Cyrus the Great to accomplish His sovereign purposes?
7. How did the Suffering Servant Prophecy (Isaiah 52–53) predict the death and resurrection of Christ?

ENDNOTES

1. See the extended discussion and examples cited by J. A. Motyer, *The Prophecy of Isaiah: An Introduction and Commentary* (Downers Grove, IL: IVP, 1993), 13–25.

2. Gary Smith, *Isaiah 40–66*, NAC 15B (Nashville: B&H, 2009), 95–97.

3. J. A. Motyer, *The Prophecy of Isaiah: An Introduction and Commentary* (Downers Grove, IL: IVP, 1993), 13–34.

4. Ibid., 27.

5. Ibid., 31.

6. See the excellent article by G. K. Beale, "A Specific Problem Confronting the Authority of the Bible," in L. Tipton and J. Waddington, eds., *Resurrection and Eschatology* (Phillipsburg, NJ: Presbyterian & Reformed, 2008), 135–76.

7. For an extended discussion see E. Hindson, *Isaiah's Immanuel* (Philadelphia: Presbyterian and Reformed, 1978).

8. Smith, *Isaiah 40–66*, 219.

9. Ibid., 242.

10. See ibid., 26–51. He argues for an Assyrian crisis setting for chaps. 40–66 with an early destruction of Babylon (chaps. 46–47) by Sennacherib in 689 BC.

Chapter 29

JEREMIAH
The Babylonians Are Coming

Jeremiah ("Yahweh lifts up") was one of Judah's greatest prophets. His ministry spanned half a century in the darkest days of Judah's history. In spite of his numerous warnings to the people and kings of Judah, the "weeping prophet" lived to see his beloved Jerusalem destroyed by the Babylonians. In the early days of his ministry, Jeremiah called the people of Judah to repent of their sinful ways and return to the Lord. His early ministry coincided with that of Zephaniah and Habakkuk and the priestly ministry of Hilkiah, all of which cumulated in the great revival of 622 BC under King Josiah.[1]

BACKGROUND

Jeremiah began his prophetic ministry in 626 BC and prophesied during Judah's last days as a nation, warning of the coming Babylonian exile as the Lord's punishment for Judah's sins. Jeremiah prophesied during the reign of **Judah's last five kings**:

Josiah (640–609 BC): Judah's last godly king who carried out significant religious reforms motivated in part by the discovery of the Mosaic book of the law in 622 BC. Josiah was killed in battle against the Egyptians in 609 BC, and his reform movement died with him. Jeremiah composed laments for Josiah when he died.

Jehoahaz (609 BC): Reigned only three months until Pharaoh Necho of Egypt removed him from the throne and took him to Egypt, where he died.

Jehoiakim (609–597 BC): the Egyptians installed him as king over his younger brother. However, he vassilated between Egypt and Babylon. This brought Babylonian reprisals for his attempted rebellions, but he died before Babylonians could take the city in 597 BC. He was a wicked and unjust ruler who was hostile to Jeremiah and burned the scroll of Jeremiah's prophecies in 605 BC.

Jehoiachin (597 BC): Reigned only three months before the Babylonians captured Jerusalem and took him away to Babylon. He was later released from imprisonment but died in Babylon.

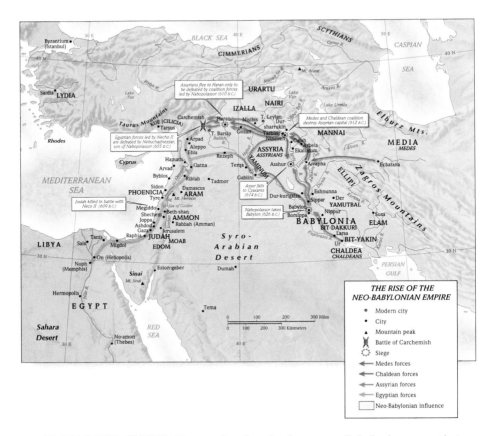

Zedekiah (597–586 BC): He was placed on the throne as a Babylonian puppet but foolishly did not follow Jeremiah's counsel and rebelled against the Babylonians, leading to the capture and destruction of Jerusalem in 586 BC. After the execution of his sons, Zedekiah was blinded and taken as a prisoner to Babylon, where he died.

The **moral failure** of Judah's leadership was largely responsible for the spiritual corruption of the nation. The covenant between the Lord and David promised an eternal dynasty to David, but it also warned that the Lord would punish David's sons if they were disobedient (2 Sam 7:14–16). During the ministry of Jeremiah, the Lord brought the Davidic dynasty to a temporary end, but Jeremiah promised that the Lord would raise up an ideal Davidic ruler (the Messiah) in the future (cf. Jer 23:5–6; 30:8–9,21; 33:15–17).

Jeremiah warned that the Lord was sending the **Babylonians** to punish Judah. In 605 BC, Nebuchadnezzar led the Babylonian army to victory over the Egyptians at Carchemish, establishing his control over Syria and northern Israel. Next, Nebuchadnezzar marched south to Jerusalem and took away the first wave of exiles, including Daniel. Jehoiakim became a vassal to Babylon but rebelled in 602 BC and again in 597 BC. Nebuchadnezzar captured Jerusalem in 597 BC and deported King Jehoiachin and 50,000 more exiles, including Ezekiel. The third stage of the exile occurred when Nebuchadnezzar responded to Zedekiah's rebellion with a siege on Jerusalem that lasted 18 months in 588–586 BC. Jerusalem and the temple were destroyed, and Judah came to an end as a nation. Zedekiah and most of the people in Judah were deported to Babylon in August 586 BC.

The Babylonians allowed Jeremiah to remain in the land of Judah, and he ministered there until he and his scribe Baruch were kidnapped by a faction of Jews and taken away as **hostages to Egypt**. Jeremiah likely continued his prophetic ministry to the Jewish community in Egypt until his death.

AUTHORSHIP

The book of Jeremiah appears to have a long and complex **compositional history**. Jeremiah and his scribe Baruch (cf. 36:4–21; 43:1–7; 45:1–5) were largely responsible for the contents of the book. The Lord commissioned Jeremiah and Baruch to compose a scroll of Jeremiah's prophecies in 605 BC, more than 20 years after the prophet began his ministry. This original scroll likely contained only the oracles and messages found in Jeremiah 1–25. When King Jehoiakim destroyed this scroll, Jeremiah and Baruch composed an expanded version. Baruch likely continued to collect messages and narratives of Jeremiah throughout his ministry, including the reference to the release of Jehoiachin in 562 BC in chap. 52.

Outline

   I. Call of the Prophet: Fire Within (Jeremiah 1)
  II. Concern of the Prophet: Doom of Judah (Jeremiah 2–25)
      A. Judah's Unfaithfulness (Jeremiah 2–6)
      B. Judah's False Hope (Jeremiah 7–10)
      C. Judah's Impending Disaster (Jeremiah 11–20)
      D. Judah's Unfaithful Leaders (Jeremiah 21–25)
 III. Rejection of the Prophet: Personal Illustrations (Jeremiah 26–45)
      A. Problem with Jeremiah's Message (Jeremiah 26–29)
      B. Promise of Restoration (Jeremiah 30–33)
      C. Problem of Judah's Response (Jeremiah 34–45)
  IV. Oracles Against the Nations: Words of the Lord (Jeremiah 46–51)
   V. Epilogue: The Fall of Jerusalem (Jeremiah 52)

MESSAGE

I. Call of the Prophet: Fire Within (Jeremiah 1)

The Lord called Jeremiah in Judah's last days to warn of the impending Babylonian exile and to provide one final opportunity for the people to repent and avoid national destruction. Jeremiah objected that he was too young and did not know what to speak, but the Lord promised to put His words in the prophet's mouth. The call of Jeremiah reflects the same basic elements found in other Old Testament call passages (see chart).

THE CALL OF THE LORD					
	Jeremiah	*Moses*	*Gideon*	*Isaiah*	*Ezekiel*
Vision of God Voice of God	"The word of the Lord came to me."	Burning Bush	Angel of the Lord Appears	Sees the Lord Seated on His Throne	Vision of God on the Chariot Throne
Commission to Task	"I appointed you as a prophet to the nations."	"I am sending you to Pharaoh."	"Go and save Israel out of Midian's hand."	"Go and tell this people."	"Son of man, I am sending you to the Israelites."
Objection of Unworthiness	"I do not know how to speak; I am only a child."	"Who am I?"	"How can I save Israel?"	"Woe is me! I am undone. For I am a man of unclean lips, and I live among a people of unclean lips."	"When I saw it [the glory of God], I fell facedown." "I sat among them for seven days over-whelmed."
Promises of God's Protection and Enablement	"Do not be afraid of them, for I am with you and will res-cue you."	"I will be with you."	"The Lord is with you mighty warrior."	"Your guilt is taken away and your sin is atoned for."	"Do not be afraid, though briers and thorns are all around you and you live among scorpions."

 Despite the enormity of the task, the Lord promised that He would enable His called ones to fulfill their commissions despite their feelings of personal inadequacy. The source of strength for the ministry would be the Lord Himself.

    In addition to narrating the prophet's call, the opening chapter also provides a **summary overview** of the message of the book of Jeremiah as a whole. The Lord had appointed Jeremiah as a prophet to the nations (Hb. *goyim*, Gentiles, 1:10). Jeremiah not only announced judgment against Judah but also announced how God would use Babylon to judge all nations and then would also in turn judge Babylon (Jer 25:12–14; 27:7). The Lord called Jeremiah as a prophet of both judgment and salvation.

Archaeology and the Book of Jeremiah

The archeological evidence for the historical accuracy of Jeremiah is astounding. Several discoveries verify the people and events mentioned in this book. The most prominent discoveries include the **Lachish** and **Arad Ostraca** (ink-inscribed pottery shards) that date from the years just prior to the destruction of Jerusalem. The Lachish letters are from one of the last cities in Judah still standing as the Babylonians were attacking. They refer to requesting reinforcements from Egypt and a warning from a prophet. The name is illegible but ends in *yahu* and may refer to Jeremiah (*Yirme' yahu*) himself. The Arad letters (200 ostraca) written in Hebrew and Aramaic mention the names Pashur (Jer 20:1) and refer to the temple as "the house of Yahweh."

Additional **personal names** from the book of Jeremiah have been confirmed as well. Two seal impressions have been found bearing the name of Jeremiah's scribe Baruch: "Berekyahu, son of Neriyahu, the scribe." One contains the fingerprint of Baruch himself. Another clay seal reads: "Belonging to Gemariah (son of) Shaphan" (Jer 36:12). Another *bulla* (seal) was found at Lachish referring to Gedaliah "overseer of the royal house" (Jer 36:12). Yet another seal reads: "Belonging to Seriah son of Neriah," Baruch's brother (Jer 51:59). And still another seal reads: "Belonging to Jehucal, son of Shelemiah" (Jer 37:3) one of the court officials serving King Zedekiah. A jar handle was found at Ramat Rahel between Jerusalem and Bethlehem which reads: "Belonging to Eliakim, steward of Jehoiachin" (Jer 22:24).

A clay prism dated c. 570 BC found in Babylon during the excavations of Nebuchadnezzar's palace refers to Nebuzaradan as "the chancellor," an appointment received after his military career (Jer 39:9). The account of the Babylonian conquest of Jerusalem refers to their military commanders sitting in the **Middle Gate** of Jerusalem. The remains of this gate were excavated by Nahman Avigad and can be seen today in Jerusalem's Jewish Quarter. Even the most critical scholars have admitted the historical accuracy of the details of Jeremiah's account of the last days of Judah.

The verbs "to uproot," "tear down," "destroy," "overthrow," and "build up" appear as summary statements of the dual nature of the prophet's message throughout the book (1:10; 24:6; 31:4–5; 42:10; 45:5).

The visions of the **almond branch** (1:11–12) and the **boiling pot** from the north (1:13–16) symbolized Jeremiah's message of judgment against Judah. The "almond branch" (*shaqed*) visualized how the Lord was "watching over" (*shoqed*) Judah to bring judgment against His sinful people, and the boiling pot represented the invading army from the north that would conquer Judah. The Lord charged Jeremiah not to be afraid of his enemies and promised that He would deliver him from all dangers. This assurance anticipated the various forms of opposition, persecution, and threats Jeremiah would encounter during his ministry.

II. Concern of the Prophet: Doom of Judah (Jeremiah 2–25)

This first major section of the book focuses on Jeremiah's message of judgment against Judah. The Lord would judge His people for their failure to turn from their sinful ways. Along with Jeremiah's poetic oracles, and laments a series of **prose sermons** provides order and arrangement for this section by serving as reflective summaries on the prophet's message of judgment. These prose sermons particularly focus on Judah's defective understanding of their covenant with the Lord. They believed the Lord would protect them as His covenant people, regardless of their behavior. So the purpose of these sermons was to undermine the people's false confidence in their status as the Lord's chosen people and their misplaced trust in the temple.

A. Judah's Unfaithfulness (Jeremiah 2–6)

The indictment in Jeremiah 2 takes the form of a **covenant lawsuit** or legal dispute. Like a prosecuting attorney Jeremiah presented the Lord's case against His unfaithful people. Though a devoted bride in her early days, Israel had become like an unfaithful wife, prostituting herself by following other gods. The people traded their relationship with the living God for gods who did not exist and would never satisfy their deepest longings. Judah also prostituted itself by making foreign alliances with Egypt and Assyria, so the Lord warned that they would be disappointed by these alliances. Their decision to trust in man rather than God was doomed to failure. Continuing with the marriage metaphor, Jeremiah called for the people "to turn/return" (*shuv*: 3:1,7,10,12,14,22; 4:1) to the Lord and to repent of their sinful ways

Relief figure of a lion from the Ishtar Gate in Babylon.

(3:1–4:4). Thus he supported Josiah's reform movement (3:6). Jeremiah referenced the divorce law in Deut 24:1–4 in order to demonstrate the Lord's grace in giving His people the opportunity to return to Him in spite of their repeated infidelity.

If the nation did not repent, judgment would take the form of a **military invasion** by a powerful enemy from the north. More than giving an inflexible prediction of future events, Jeremiah was attempting to move the people to repentance by graphically portraying the horrific judgment they were facing. If they changed their ways, they still had the opportunity to avoid the coming disaster (4:14). Vivid images of the approaching army dominate this part of Jeremiah's message (4:5–9,13–17; 5:6,14–17; 6:1–8,22–24). This army would be like a ravaging predator, and the Lord Himself would be the warrior leading these troops against Judah. Jeremiah mourned over the destruction the Lord was prepared to bring against His people (4:19–21) and called for the people to take seriously the warnings of judgment (6:24–26).

B. Judah's False Hope (Jeremiah 7–10)

Jeremiah's **temple sermon** (7:1–15) was one of the defining and critical moments in his ministry. This sermon was delivered "early in the reign of Jehoiakim" (c. 609 BC) at a time when Judah could avoid the disaster of the Babylonian invasion if its leaders and people would turn from their sinful ways (7:3–7; cf. 26:3–6). Jeremiah courageously announced that the Lord was prepared to destroy Jerusalem and His temple because the people substituted empty ritual for true obedience. The miraculous deliverance of Jerusalem by the Lord from the Assyrians earlier in 701 BC (Isaiah 37) led to the mistaken belief that the city was inviolable to enemy attack. To remove this mistaken idea, Jeremiah reminded them that God allowed the destruction of the sanctuary at Shiloh during the time of the judges. The Lord did not protect His people then and would not in the future if they did not repent.

Judah would be destroyed because the people chose to believe in the empty promises of the **false prophets** instead of Jeremiah's warnings of coming judgment (8:1–9:26). The people's trust in the prophets' false assurances of "peace, peace" (8:11) allowed them to continue in their sinful behavior, but they would be greatly disappointed when the expected deliverance did not arrive (8:15). The people would wail and mourn over the devastation brought by the invading army. Expressing the Lord's own grief over the destruction of Judah, Jeremiah wished that his head were a fountain of tears so he could weep continuously over the horrible fate awaiting his people (8:18–9:2).

C. Judah's Impending Disaster (Jeremiah 11–20)

The broken covenant demonstrated the fragmented relationship between the Lord and His people. From the time the Lord had formed the covenant with Israel at Sinai after bringing them out of Egypt, the people had failed to keep the covenant commandments (Jeremiah 11). Even though the Lord inflicted the covenant curses, they persisted in their disobedience so the Lord decided to bring upon them the ultimate curse of **expulsion** from the land (cf. Deut. 28:58–68. The people's rejection of Jeremiah as the Lord's spokesman reflected their rejection of the Lord. The people plotted to put Jeremiah to death for speaking God's word to them, but the Lord warned that they and their children would die as a fitting punishment for how they treated the prophet (11:18–25).

In these chapters Jeremiah expresses a series of laments, complaints, and confessions (12:1–6; 15:10–21; 18:19–23; 20:7–18) that are reflections of some of the laments in Psalms. They provide an **autobiographical insight** into the soul of the prophet and remind us that preaching is a difficult business. The prophet was hated by kings, priests, and people alike for his strong preaching. But time revealed that Jeremiah was right and they were wrong.

Jeremiah's two **visits to the potter** in chaps. 18–19 were prophetic sign acts that visualized how the covenantal relationship between the Lord and His people had reached a breaking point. In his first visit Jeremiah observed the potter reshaping a ruined piece of wet clay, representing how the Lord was offering His people the opportunity to repent and be spared from judgment. But, when the prophet called the people to turn from their sinful ways, they stubbornly refused in open defiance of the Lord (18:12–13). In light of this response, there was nothing left but for the Lord to bring destruction upon Judah, which was dramatically portrayed by Jeremiah's smashing a clay jar in front of the people. The two visits to the potter demonstrated Judah's missed opportunity to repent and avoid disaster.

D. Judah's Unfaithful Leaders (Jeremiah 21–25)

The Lord's judgment would especially target Judah's **kings and prophets** because their failed leadership was largely responsible for Judah's spiritual corruption. The Lord chose David and his sons to rule over Israel and to be the earthly representatives of His heavenly rule, but the covenant between the Lord and the house of David required each king to obey the Lord and to administer justice in order to be blessed (22:2–5; cf. 17:24–27). After Josiah's godly rule and religious reforms, the final four kings of Judah were evil and did not follow the Lord. Jeremiah announced the judgment of these four kings and also the end of the Davidic dynasty.

Jehoahaz (609 BC) would die in Egyptian exile (22:10–12). Jehoiakim (609–597 BC) refurbished his palace and ignored the needs of the poor during a time of national crisis, so he would die and not even be given the honor of a proper burial (22:15–19). Jehoiachin (597 BC) would never return from his exile in Babylon, and none of his sons would rule on the throne (22:24–30). As the final king of Judah, Zedekiah (597–586 BC) requested that Jeremiah pray for a miraculous deliverance of Jerusalem from the Babylonians, but the prophet refused his request and warned instead that the city would fall. Zedekiah would be taken away in exile to Babylon as the Lord Himself fought on the side of the Babylonian army (21:1–10; 34:1–5).

Rembrandt's painting of Jeremiah as the weeping prophet.

When Jeremiah announced to King Jehoiachin that the Lord was casting him off as his **signet ring** or symbol of authority, it meant the temporary rejection of the house of David and the end of the Davidic dynasty (22:24). But the Lord also promised He would not abandon His covenant with David or His promise that David's dynasty would endure forever. At a future time the Lord would raise up a Davidic king as a **righteous Branch** who would do what was just and right (23:5–6; 33:15–16), in contrast to the final Davidic king Zedekiah ("the Lord is my righteousness"), who miserably failed to live up to his name. Many years later when the people returned to the land, the Lord announced through the prophet Haggai the reversal of this prophecy and affirmed that He would restore the Davidic dynasty and make the Davidic ruler His "signet ring" once again (Hag 2:20–23).

Chapter 25 concludes Jeremiah's oracles of judgment by providing a **theological explanation** of the Babylonian exile and how the Lord would use Babylon as His instrument of judgment. The Lord would send His people into captivity for 70 years as punishment for their persistent disobedience and idolatry. In carrying out this judgment, Nebuchadnezzar would serve as the Lord's "servant" (25:9:), but this favored status would last for only a short time. After the Lord had used Babylon to judge Judah, the Lord would destroy Babylon as punishment for its own sins. Babylon would cause all nations, including Judah, to drink the wine of God's wrath so they would stagger like drunken men, but Babylon itself would also drink that cup as final retribution for its crimes.

III. Rejection of the Prophet: Personal Illustrations (Jeremiah 26–45)

Jeremiah 26–45 is a narrative story of Jeremiah's ministry, documenting Judah's rejection of the prophet's message and recounting the fall of Jerusalem to the Babylonians. The judgment of exile was due to the fact that the leaders and people of Judah did not "listen to/obey" the word of the Lord (see 26:5; 29:19; 32:33; 34:14,17; 35:14–15,17; 36:31; 37:14; 40:3; 42:13,21; 43:7; 44:16,23). Jeremiah encountered various forms of persecution and opposition because he preached an unpopular message. Even after the fall of Jerusalem in 586 BC, the people persisted in their disobedience, and Jeremiah was eventually kidnapped and taken away to Egypt. However, judgment was not God's final word for His people. The Lord promised to bring the exiles back to the land after 70 years (29:10). Chapters 30–33 contain Jeremiah's **Book of Consolation** that promises the ultimate restoration of Israel. At that time the Lord will establish a new covenant with His people so they will obey Him and consequently enjoy His blessings forever.

With the exception of chaps. 37–44, the narratives and messages of Jeremiah in this section are not arranged chronologically. Chapters 26–45 are framed by four passages (chaps. 25; 35; 36; 45) dated from the time of Jehoiakim. These stories and messages from the reign of Jehoiakim (609–597 BC) highlight this king's rejection of Jeremiah's message as a decisive time in Judah's history. This frame also divides chaps. 26–45 into two smaller blocks of material (26–35 and 36–45), which both demonstrate how Judah missed one final opportunity to repent and avoid judgment. Both sections begin with a call for the people to turn from their "evil" (ra‘ah) so that the

Lord might relent from sending "disaster" (*ra'ah*) against them (26:3; 36:3), but both sections end with the people persisting in their disobedience and bringing judgment upon themselves.

Jeremiah 26–35 and 36–45 both contain a promise of personal salvation to certain individuals that contrasts with the national judgment the Lord would bring against Judah. In Jeremiah 35, the promise to preserve the Rechabite clan for their faithfulness to their godly family traditions contrasts with God's plan to judge Judah for its unfaithfulness. In Jeremiah 45, the promise of deliverance to Jeremiah's faithful scribe Baruch contrasts with God's plans to judge the unfaithful Jews who fled to Egypt in chapter 44.

CONCLUSION OF JEREMIAH 26–35	
National Judgment	*Personal Salvation*
The Lord will judge Zedekiah and the people of Judah. (Jeremiah 34)	The Lord will preserve the faithful Rechabites. (Jeremiah 35)
CONCLUSION OF JEREMIAH 36–45	
National Judgment	*Personal Salvation*
The Lord will judge the Jews in Egypt. (Jeremiah 44)	The Lord will preserve the faithful scribe Baruch. (Jeremiah 45)

This structure reflects that the Lord's salvation was reserved for those who were faithful and obedient to Him, whereas the nation had forfeited the Lord's blessing because of their disobedience.

A. Problem with Jeremiah's Message (Jeremiah 26–29)

Jeremiah primarily experiences **religious opposition** to his message in this section. After warning of the destruction of Jerusalem and the temple in his temple sermon (see 7:1–15), the priests, prophets, and people called for him to be put to death (26:1–15). Any prophet who dared to speak against the temple was viewed as a false prophet deserving of execution (cf. Deut 18:20). In his own defense Jeremiah warned that they would be guilty of innocent blood if they put him to death for speaking the Lord's message to them. Jeremiah was spared when some of the elders recalled the repentant

The circular opening to a cistern at the site of Lachish in Israel.

response of Hezekiah when Micah warned of the destruction of Jerusalem a century before (26:17–19; cf. Mic 3:9–12). While Jeremiah was not put to death, the appended account of King Jehoiakim's execution of the prophet Uriah (26:20–24) demonstrates how unpopular Jeremiah's message of judgment really was and how much it cost to be a true spokesman for the Lord.

The **false prophets** offered empty promises of peace and opposed Jeremiah's message, which called for submission to Babylon and warned of an extended exile (chaps. 27–28). When the leaders of various nations gathered in Jerusalem for a meeting with Zedekiah to discuss an alliance against Babylon (c. 593 BC), Jeremiah wore an animal yoke to picture the impending subjugation of these nations to Babylon. The false prophet Hananiah directly countered Jeremiah's message by declaring that the exile would be over in two years, so he broke Jeremiah's wooden yoke to visualize this promise of impending freedom from Babylonian domination (28:1–11). The people were caught in the conundrum of trying to determine which prophet was telling the truth. The Lord announced that He would replace the wooden yoke Hananiah broke with an iron yoke that could not be broken. In addition, Hananiah would die for his presumption in speaking for the Lord when the Lord had not sent him. As fitting punishment for his promise that the exile would last for only two years, Hananiah died within two months of uttering his false prophecy.

Jeremiah also encountered opposition from false prophets among the exiles in Babylon (chap. 29). Jeremiah wrote a letter to the exiles in Babylon encouraging them to submit to the Babylonians and to build houses and raise their families in Babylon. They were to pray for the peace and prosperity of Babylon because they would be there for **70 years**. Though this judgment would bring the nation of Judah to an end, the Lord promised to restore them when they returned to Him and sought Him with all their hearts (29:12–14; cf. Deut 30:1–10). Thus, God's promise in this section was: "For I know the plans I have for you . . . to give you a future and a hope" (29:11).

B. Promise of Restoration (Jeremiah 30–33)

Jeremiah's message of hope concerning Israel's future restoration is known as the **Book of Consolation**. Jeremiah's message of hope for Israel's future contrasted with the empty promises of the false prophets. Even in his message of judgment, a message of hope and restoration for Israel stands at a prominent position in the center of the book. Salvation and blessing, not doom and destruction, would be the Lord's final word for Israel.

Clay pot.

Despite Israel's unfaithfulness to the Lord as His covenant people, the Lord would remain faithful to His people and would establish a new covenant guaranteeing their future blessing.

The recurring promise in Jeremiah's message of hope is that the Lord would "restore the fortunes" (*shuv shevut*) of His people (30:1,18; 32:44; 33:11,26). The reversal of the present conditions of defeat and exile is the prominent theme in the poetic oracles of salvation in chaps. 30–31. The nation was now in a time of trouble, but later the Lord would deliver His people and break their yoke of bondage. A **new David**, rather than a foreign king, would reign over Israel (30:8–9). Even though Judah had an incurable wound (the destruction of the nation) that would not heal, the Lord's inexplicable grace would one day heal them and restore Israel to health (30:15–16). The exiles would return to rebuild their ruined cities after the Lord had exhausted His anger against them.

The tel of ancient Lachish.

The Lord would restore Israel because He loved His people with an eternal love (31:2–6). The return from exile would be like a second exodus as the Lord redeemed His people from bondage in a foreign land. The weeping and mourning of the Lord's unfaithful wife and daughter would be transformed into the rejoicing of a young woman anticipating her marriage. The second exodus will surpass the first because the Lord will establish a **new covenant** that will be better than the one enacted at Mount Sinai (31:31–34). The New Testament reveals that believers today currently enjoy the blessings of the new covenant through the death of Jesus and the giving of the Spirit (Matt 11:28; 1 Cor 11:25; Heb 8:7–10; 10:15–18), but the complete fulfillment of this new covenant was made originally with the house of Israel, and Judah awaits the future time of restoration when "all Israel will be saved" (Rom 11:26–27).

The Lord encouraged the prophet to trust Him even as Jeremiah remained **imprisoned** in the final days before the fall of Jerusalem (33:1–5). The Lord again confirmed to Jeremiah four key promises concerning the future restoration: (1) the rebuilding of Israel's cities (33:7), (2) the forgiveness of sins (33:8), (3) the renewal of joy (33:9–11), and (4) the repopulation of the land and cities (33:12–13). The promise of restoration was rooted in the Lord's covenantal promises to Israel. Even without a king on the throne, the Davidic line would endure, and the Lord would eventually raise up a

Davidic king who would rule over the people in righteousness and peace (33:15). The Lord would also fulfill His promises concerning an enduring priesthood for the Levites. The roles of enduring king and priest would find their ultimate fulfillment in the person and work of Jesus Christ.

C. Problem of Judah's Response (Jeremiah 34–45)

Judah moved from possible repentance in the reign of Jehoiakim to irrevocable judgment resulting in the fall of Jerusalem. In 605 BC, the scribe Baruch recorded and read a **scroll of Jeremiah's prophecies** warning of the coming judgment. A group of scribes and officials took these warnings seriously and arranged to have the scroll read to Jehoiakim. The king showed his disregard for the prophetic word (just as he had done with the execution of Uriah the prophet in 26:20–24) by cutting up the scroll and throwing it into the fire as it was read to him. The Lord commissioned Jeremiah and Baruch to compose another scroll with additional warnings of judgment and announced that Jehoiakim would die and that, as punishment for his destruction of the scroll, none of his descendants would sit on the throne.

Detail of the siege of Lachish recorded on the walls of the palace of Sennacherib at Nineveh. Assyrian battering rams attack the desperate defenders of the Judean city who attempt to counteract the assault by hurling flaming torches toward the battering rams. At the right captives stream out of the doomed city (courtesy of the British Museum).

While Jehoiakim's unbelief took the form of violent hostility, King Zedekiah demonstrated his unbelief by being fearful and unwilling to follow Jeremiah's counsel (chaps. 37–38). Jeremiah warned that Judah would not be able to resist the Babylonians (37:6–10) and that submission to Babylon was the only way Jerusalem would be spared from destruction (38:2–3,17–18,20–23). But Zedekiah refused to listen because he feared the royal and military officials who wished to continue their resistance against Babylon. Jeremiah was kept in prison and was even thrown into a muddy cistern and left to die. Only the intervention of a foreign court official, a **Cushite named Ebed-melech,** convinced the king to rescue Jeremiah from the cistern and save the prophet's life (38:1–13). Zedekiah protected Jeremiah, hoping for a favorable oracle of deliverance, but such a promise was not forthcoming.

The Babylonians captured Jerusalem in 586 BC, after a siege lasting for a year and a half, in fulfillment of Jeremiah's prophecies of judgment. Zedekiah attempted to

Ebed-melech the Cushite

One of the most touching stories in the narrative section is that of Jeremiah's rescue by an **African court official** named Ebed-melech ("servant of the king"). Under pressure from his own court officials, King Zedekiah permitted them to imprison Jeremiah in a cistern in the guard's courtyard (38:1–6). Sinking into the mud and his own refuse, Jeremiah was left to die. But a "court official" of African descent, a Cushite from Ethiopia, came to the prophet's rescue. Ebed-melech risked his own life, insisting that Jeremiah be released and treated more humanely (38:7–10).

In this story the Ethiopian came to the prophet's rescue and was later himself saved by the prophet's intervention (39:13–18). In a contrasting story in Acts 8:26–39, the prophet/evangelist Philip comes to the aid of the Ethiopian official on the road to Gaza. Philip heard him reading from the text of Isaiah 53 and pointed him to faith in Jesus as the promised Messiah.

flee but was captured by the Babylonian army near Jericho. Nebuchadnezzar executed Zedekiah's sons and then blinded the king before taking him away as a prisoner to Babylon (39:1–7). Because of his refusal to listen to the prophet, the last thing the king saw with his eyes was the death of his sons. The walls of Jerusalem were torn down, and the king and most of the people in the land were taken away as exiles to Babylon. In the meantime **Jeremiah was set free** from prison by the Babylonians.

Jeremiah chose to remain in the land and minister to the poor people left there by the Babylonians (39:11–14; 40:1–6). Gedaliah was the Jewish governor the Babylonians had appointed over the land (40:9–10). The Lord offered the remnant remaining in the land the opportunity to experience peace and blessing if they would follow Jeremiah's counsel of submitting to Babylon. Instead the Jews remaining in the land committed two specific acts of disobedience. The first was that Ishmael, from the family of David, **assassinated Gedaliah**, likely in an attempt to restore the Davidic monarchy (41:1–3). Ishmael also brutally murdered a group

One of the "Lachish Letters" found in the ruins of the city of Lachish destroyed by Nebuchadnezzar. The letter contains a report of a junior military officer to his superior indicating his compliance with orders received by means of a fire signal. The text reads: "Know that we are watching for the signals of Lachish according to all the indications that my lord has given, for we cannot see the signal of Azekah."

Hebrew Highlight

Declare. Hebrew נְאֻם (*ne' ûm*). This term appears 376 times in the Hebrew Bible of which 176 appear in Jeremiah. It is translated "declaration" or "oracle" and is almost always associated with prophetic declarations from the Lord Himself. It occurs only 19 times outside the Prophets. It is also translated "says," as in: "This is what the Lord says." As such, *ne'ûm* opens and closes divine messages in which the prophet claims to be speaking the words of God.

---

of 80 pilgrims who had come to worship at Jerusalem and then took Jewish hostages at Mizpah. A military commander named Johanan rescued the hostages, but Ishmael was able to flee to the land of Ammon. Second, Johanan and his military contingent took **Jeremiah hostage** and fled to Egypt (42:1–43:7) in a reversal of the exodus.

After he was taken away to Egypt, Jeremiah announced that the Lord would destroy the Jewish refugees in Egypt because they persisted in the sinful ways of their fathers and refused to turn from their idolatry (chap. 44). They worshipped the gods of Egypt and made offerings to the "Queen of Heaven" (the fertility goddess Ishtar). They defiantly stated they would not listen to Jeremiah's message (44:16). Their covenantal perspective was so warped that they believed Josiah's reforms, which purged Judah's worship of pagan rituals, were the cause of the fall of Jerusalem (44:17–18). In response to their vow that they would carry on with their pagan rites, the Lord swore that He would destroy the remnant in Egypt and that only a few of them would survive. Nebuchadnezzar's army attacked Egypt, and the rebels fell under God's judgment.

The promise of salvation at the conclusion to this section is extended to two lone individuals, the Cushite Ebed-melech (39:15–18) and Jeremiah's **scribe Baruch** (45:1–5). Baruch had courageously and faithfully served the Lord and Jeremiah. He read the scroll of Jeremiah's prophecies at the temple when it was not safe for Jeremiah to be there (36:8–10), and Baruch was even blamed as the source of Jeremiah's message calling for submission to Babylon (43:3). Baruch shared in Jeremiah's persecution and was taken away with the prophet to Egypt (43:6–7). Because of his faithfulness, the Lord promised that He would protect and preserve Baruch wherever he was taken. The promise to Baruch parallels the earlier promise to Ebed-melech, who had acted to save Jeremiah's life when he was thrown into the cistern (cf. 39:15–18). Obedience to the Lord was a matter of life and death, and only those who followed the Lord would enjoy the blessings of His salvation.

IV. Oracles Against the Nations: Words of the Lord (Jeremiah 46–51)

Israel's restoration would also include the **judgment of its enemies**, so the book of Jeremiah concludes with a series of oracles against nine foreign nations:

- Egypt (46:1–28)
- Philistia (47:1–7)

- Moab (48:1–47)
- Ammon (49:1–6)
- Edom (49:7–22)
- Damascus (49:23–27)
- Kedar and Hazor (49:28–33)
- Elam (49:34–39)
- Babylon (50:1–51:64)

In the Septuagint (LXX) version (which may represent an early edition of Jeremiah), these oracles appear immediately after 25:13 and are in a different order. These judgment oracles refer to the historical judgments carried out against these nations, primarily through the military operations of the Babylonian army. These oracles are bookended by the oracles against the superpowers Egypt and Babylon. They were Israel's first and last oppressors, and they also vied for control of Judah during Jeremiah's ministry.

The Lord's judgment would fall on these nations for their pride in their wealth and military might (46:8; 48:7,26,29–30,42; 49:4), their idolatry (46:26; 48:13,35), and their mistreatment of Israel (48:27; 49:1–2). The most remarkable feature of these oracles against the nations is that the Lord promises a restoration for some of these people. Egypt would again be inhabited as in its former days (46:26), and the Lord promised to "restore the fortunes" (*shuv shevut*) of Moab (48:47), Ammon (49:6), and Elam (49:39), the same expression used in Jeremiah to describe the future restoration of Israel.

Jeremiah's primary focus is on the **judgment of Babylon**. The Lord used Babylon as His "hammer" of judgment against Judah and the nations (50:23; 51:20–23), but He would also hold Babylon accountable for its crimes and violence. The Lord would judge the false gods of Babylon (50:2–3), and He would also execute vengeance against Babylon for the violence it inflicted upon Judah (50:11–14,28–35; 51:5,10–

11,24,34–37,49–53). The Lord would reverse the fortunes of Judah and Babylon by restoring His people at the same time He was bringing an enemy army to destroy Babylon. Jeremiah's earlier oracles of judgment against Judah were reapplied to Babylon. The message concerning the enemy from the north attacking the "Daughter of Babylon" in 50:41–43 duplicates the message against the "Daughter Zion" in 6:22–24. The depiction of Babylon's defeat in 51:27–33 recalls earlier prophecies concerning the fall of Judah and Jerusalem (cf. 4:5–8,16–21; 6:1–8). To represent the coming fall of Babylon,

The seal of Baruch.

the scribe Seraiah read the scroll of Jeremiah's prophecies against the city and then threw the scroll tied to a stone into the Euphrates River (51:61–64).

Babylon in Scripture is also representative of human opposition to God and His people. Babylon was the site of the rebellion that led to the confusion of human language and the division of the nations (Gen 11:1–9). Revelation 17–18 depicts the destruction of the future empire of Antichrist as the fall of Babylon. This reference to Babylon in Revelation appears symbolic rather than geographic. Just like the Babylon of the past, the future empire of Antichrist would oppose God and persecute God's people in an even greater way. Several parallels are obvious:[2]

JEREMIAH	PROPHETIC EVENTS	REVELATION
51:7	Cup of God's Wrath	18:3
51:9	Sins Piled Up to Heaven	18:5
51:22	Judgment as a Harvest	14:14–15
51:22	Babylon as a Volcano	18:20
51:48	Heaven and Earth Rejoice	18:20

V. Epilogue: The Fall of Jerusalem (Jeremiah 52)

The final verse of Jeremiah 51 states, "The words of Jeremiah end here," and the narrative of the fall of Jerusalem in chap. 52 serves as an appendix to the book that was likely added by a later editor. This account closely parallels 2 Kings 25 and serves canonically to connect the book of Jeremiah with the story of the covenant failure of

View of the Valley of Gehenna (Hinnom Valley) looking northeast toward the new city of Jerusalem.

Israel and Judah in the books of Kings. The record of Jerusalem's fall in Jeremiah 39 focuses more on the fate of King Zedekiah, while this chapter emphasizes more the destruction of the temple and the removal of the temple articles to Babylon. King Jehoiachin was deported to Babylon in 597 BC, and his release from prison in Babylon is the last recorded event in the book of Jeremiah (52:27–30). His favorable treatment by the Babylonians provided a glimmer of hope for the restoration of Israel and the Davidic monarchy. Even when the people were in exile, the Lord did not abandon them.

THEOLOGICAL SIGNIFICANCE

Jeremiah's message of "tearing down" and "building up" played a pivotal role in the working out of God's plan of **salvation history**. Jeremiah was a "prophet like Moses" (Deut 18:18) whom the Lord raised up to issue a call for repentance and a warning of coming judgment to the sinful nation of Judah. Jeremiah announced that the Lord would use Babylon as His instrument of judgment and that the Lord's judgment would bring about the fall of Judah, the collapse of the Davidic dynasty, and the destruction of the temple. With the Babylonian exile it appeared that the Lord's covenant relationship with Israel had come to an end.

In the midst of this hopelessness and despair, Jeremiah offered hope and the promise of a **new beginning** for Israel as the people of God. Jeremiah prophesied that the Lord will bring the Jews back to their homeland, restore the Davidic dynasty, and establish a new covenant that would erase the failures of the past and guarantee Israel's obedience and blessing. Judgment would not be the final word because the Lord's love for Israel was everlasting.

Modern Anathoth (1:1), which is a few miles east of Jerusalem.

During His earthly ministry **Jesus** was in many ways a prophet like Jeremiah who denounced the people of His day for turning the temple into a "den of thieves" (Mark 11:17; Jer 7:11) and warned of the coming destruction of Jerusalem and the temple (Matt 24:1–2). Like the prophet Jeremiah, Jesus lamented the destruction that would come upon Jerusalem (Luke 19:41–44). Because of continued unbelief and disobedience, He announced that Israel must endure more judgment before its final restoration.

But, more importantly than His role as a prophet, Jesus is the personal fulfillment of Jeremiah's prophecies of hope. As Messiah, Jesus will restore the throne of David and will rule for all time in fulfillment of Jeremiah's prophecies concerning the future ideal Davidic ruler. Through His death on the cross, Jesus also inaugurates and brings into effect the new covenant promised by Jeremiah. The church presently enjoys the blessings and benefits of the new covenant in anticipation of the final fulfillment of the new covenant promises in the future kingdom and the national restoration of Israel.

For Further Reading

Dearman, J. A. *Jeremiah / Lamentations*. NIVAC. Grand Rapids: Zondervan, 2002.

Feinberg, Charles. *Jeremiah: A Commentary*. Grand Rapids: Zondervan, 1982.

Harrison, R. K. *Jeremiah and Lamentations*. TOTC. Downers Grove: IVP, 1973.

Huey, F. B. *Jeremiah, Lamentations*. NAC 16. Nashville: B&H, 1993.

Ryken, Philip. *Jeremiah and Lamentations*. Wheaton, IL: Crossway, 2001.

Thompson, J. A. *The Book of Jeremiah*. NICOT. Grand Rapids: Eerdmans, 1980.

Study Questions

1. What nation threatened Judah in the days of Jeremiah, and what advice did he give them?
2. How did Jeremiah describe his call to the ministry?
3. What words of hope did the prophet give to the people of Jerusalem?
4. What was the ultimate fulfillment of the prophecy of the new covenant?
5. How do archaeological discoveries help assure the accuracy of the personal and historical references in Jeremiah?
6. Who should we listen to when we are facing a possible crisis in our own lives?

ENDNOTES

1. "Jeremiah," in Walter Elwell, ed., *Baker Encyclopedia of the Bible* (Grand Rapids: Baker, 1988), 2:1110–13.

2. See HCSB Study Bible (Nashville: Holman Bible Publishers, 2010), 1329.

Chapter 30

LAMENTATIONS
Jerusalem Is Burning

The book of Lamentations is a series of **five separate laments** over the fall of Jerusalem to the Babylonians in 586 BC. The intensely emotional nature of the book indicates that the writer experienced these events firsthand. He is among the survivors of the destruction of Jerusalem who continue to endure grief, depravation, and humiliation. The wounds and emotional pain over the fall of Jerusalem are still fresh. There is no evidence of a return to the land or the rebuilding of the temple. The book concludes with the complaint that the Lord appears to have forgotten His people and a cry for their restoration (5:19–22).

Lamentations was most likely composed shortly after 586 BC and long before 538 BC when Cyrus decreed that the Jews could return to their homeland. Commemoration of the destruction of Jerusalem is attested at an early time in the Old Testament (Jer 41:5; Zech 7:3–5; 8:19), and the reading of Lamentations ultimately became part of the ceremonies marking the fall of Jerusalem on the **ninth of Ab**. Lamentations is part of five books in the Hebrew canon known as the *Megilloth* (also including Ecclesiastes, Esther, Ruth, and Song of Solomon) that were associated with specific Hebrew festivals.

BACKGROUND

The poems in the book most closely resemble the **communal laments** in the Psalms. These laments expressed the peoples' sorrow following military defeats (Psalms 44; 60; 74; 79; 80). Lamentations 1, 2, and 4 are introduced by the exclamation "how" (*'ek/'ekah*) and recall similar terminology used in the funeral dirge of David when he learned of the deaths of Saul and Jonathan (2 Sam 1:19–27). Six laments over the destruction of cities are also found in Mesopotamian literature dating from 2000–1500 BC. Like Lamentations these compositions attribute the destruction of a city to divine abandonment and judgment. However, Lamentations is monotheistic in its perspective and also reflects a clearer understanding of the moral violations on the part of the people that prompted the divine judgment. The God of the Old Testament is not capricious but acts in accordance with the covenants He established with His people. His judgments are the result of their deliberate violations of His covenant with them.

Chapters 1–4 in Lamentations are **acrostic poems**. The Hebrew poems in chaps. 1 and 2 consist of 22 verses of three lines each, with each new verse beginning with successive letters of the Hebrew alphabet. Chapter 4 is the same but with each verse having two lines. The acrostic in chap. 3 is the most elaborate, with 66 verses consisting of 22 stanzas of 3 verses. The poem works through the alphabet with each of the three lines in a stanza beginning with the same letter. Chapter 5 is not an acrostic but has 22 verses corresponding to the number of Hebrew letters in the alphabet. The acrostic form may have aided in memorization, but the use of the entire alphabet is also a literary device to suggest that the lament expresses the full range of human grief and the depth of suffering the people of Judah endured.

Another prominent poetic feature is the use of the *qinah*-**meter**, in which the second part of each poetic line is shorter than the first. This meter is typically used in Old Testament laments, and these unbalanced lines may suggest the sobbing speech or halting limp of mourners in a funeral procession. The skillful use of metaphor, particularly the personification of Jerusalem as a woman in chap. 1, reflects the literary quality of Lamentations and helps the reader share the painful emotions of those who lived through the fall of Jerusalem. The length and positioning of chap. 3 make this

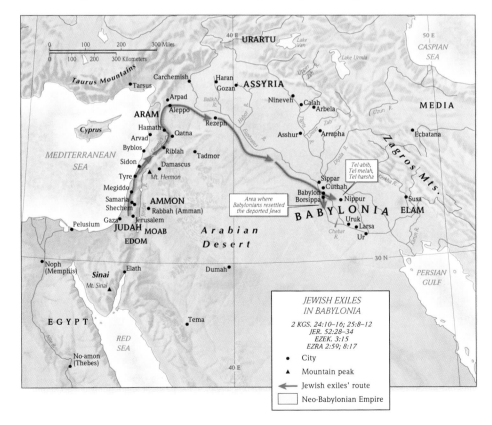

poem the key chapter in the book. In the midst of this disaster, the writer encourages people to trust in the covenant faithfulness (*chêsêd*) of the Lord as their source of hope for the future (3:21–36).

Hebrew Highlight

Faithful Love. Hebrew חסד (*chêsêd*). This word appears 249 times in the Hebrew Bible (129 times in the Psalms). It refers to God's faithful and constant covenant love. This love includes kindness (Gen 19:19), loyalty (Job 6:14), and faithfulness (Isa 40:6). *Chêsêd* also implies favor (Esth 2:9) and grace (Ezra 9:9). Its plural form indicates acts of love (Ps 107:43) or good deeds (Neh 13:14). It reminds us that God loves us even when we don't deserve it.

The book of Lamentations is an anonymous composition that appears in the Hebrew Bible in the Writings section of the canon, but early tradition identifies **Jeremiah** as the author of the book. The first verse of Lamentations in the Greek Septuagint (LXX) attributes the book to Jeremiah, and the Septuagint also placed Lamentations after the book of Jeremiah as does the English Bible. The Aramaic Targum, the Syriac Peshitta, the Latin Vulgate, and the Babylonian Talmud also attribute the book to Jeremiah. With its focus on the fall of Jerusalem to Babylon in 586 BC, the book fits the time frame of Jeremiah's ministry. Second Chronicles 35:25 states that Jeremiah composed laments at the death of Josiah, and the book of Jeremiah often portrays the prophet as weeping over the destruction of his people (Jer 9:1–2; 14:17–22).

Outline[1]

    I. The Grief of Jerusalem: Mourning Widow (Lamentations 1)
   II. The Lord as Warrior: Weeping Daughter (Lamentations 2)
 III. Hope in Suffering: Afflicted Man (Lamentations 3)
 IV. The Ravages of War: Tarnished Gold (Lamentations 4)
  V. Prayer for Restoration: Fatherless Child (Lamentations 5)

MESSAGE

I. The Grief of Jerusalem: Mourning Widow (Lamentations 1)

This poem portrays Jerusalem as a **grieving widow** mourning her destruction. Jerusalem's lovers and friends refer to the nations she depended on through alliances. She trusted in them rather than trusting in the Lord for protection, but suddenly they abandoned her. In her days of former greatness, Jerusalem was a proud princess, but her enemies reduced her to slavery. The recurring refrain that "there was no one to comfort" Jerusalem reflected the city's hopeless condition (1:2,9,16–17,21). Jerusalem acknowledged that her sins were the cause of her misery but also pleaded for the Lord to see her distress and act on her behalf.

II. The Lord as Warrior: Weeping Daughter (Lamentations 2)

The Hebrews celebrated how the Lord protected Jerusalem and defeated the enemies that attacked her (Pss 46:5–11; 48:3–8; 76:1–12), but this lament faces the harsh reality that the Lord Himself brought about the destruction of the daughter of Jerusalem. As the **Divine Warrior**, the Lord poured out His anger and wrath on the city and even abandoned His own sanctuary. The poet wept over the suffering and death all around him and encouraged the people to give full expression of their grief to the Lord. There was hope that their cries would turn away the Lord's anger.

III. Hope in Suffering: Afflicted Man (Lamentations 3)

In the central section of the book, the poet expresses a first-person lament that describes his **intense suffering** with vivid emotion and metaphor. His experiences are representative of the community. The Lord relentlessly attacked him by ravaging his body, confining him in a dark dungeon, mangling him like a wild animal, and shooting him with arrows. Not relenting from His assault, the Lord gave him bitter food and drink, broke his teeth, and then trampled him underfoot. The piling up of metaphors reflected the intensity of his afflictions. Some commentators believe this beleaguered individual is the personified city of Jerusalem.

Despite the suffering of the present, the Lord's covenant **faithfulness** (*chêsêd*) offers hope for the future. The Lord will continue to show mercy and compassion to His people because His love for them is greater than His anger over their disobedience. The writer encourages the people

Beggar at the Damascus gate in Jerusalem.

to return to the Lord and confess their sins. While weeping over the disaster that Jerusalem experienced, he prays for the Lord to exact vengeance on Judah's enemies. The poet's faith is such that he speaks as if God has answered His prayer even as he speaks it.

IV. The Ravages of War: Tarnished Gold (Lamentations 4)

This poem contrasts Zion's glorious past with its deplorable present. Jerusalem was "the perfection of beauty" and "the joy of the whole earth" (2:15; Ps 48:2), but the city was ravaged by war because of the Lord's judgment. Jerusalem's fate was worse than that of Sodom. **Siege warfare** in the ancient Near East was brutal and involved depriving the besieged city of food and water. The Babylonian siege of Jerusalem lasted for a year and a half (2 Kgs 25:1–3), so some of the residents of Jerusalem were reduced to cannibalism because of the severe famine. This was a fulfillment of the covenant curse announced by Moses (Deut 28:53–57). The judgment of Judah was especially the fault of its corrupt prophets and priests that led the people astray.

V. Prayer for Restoration: Fatherless Child (Lamentations 5)

The poet called for the Lord once more to **remember** the pitiful condition of those that survived the fall of Jerusalem and to intervene on their behalf. Judah forfeited the land given to them as an "inheritance" from the Lord (Exod 32:13; Deut 12:9–10; 15:4). The Lord had blessed them with a bountiful land, but now they suffered from famine and starvation. The defeat of Judah's army deprived families of fathers and husbands. Babylonian soldiers committed atrocities by raping women and executing Judah's princes, and their occupation of Judah reduced the population to slavery. The writer confessed that Judah's humiliation was due to the sins of both previous generations and the present one (5:7,18). The people suffered the residual effects of their fathers' sins (Exod 34:7; Deut 34:9) but were equally guilty before God for their own disobedience.

The poet concluded with a **petition** for the Lord to restore His people. While acknowledging God's sovereignty, he also questioned why it appeared that the Lord had forgotten and abandoned His people. Lamentations 3 affirmed that the Lord's covenant faithfulness guaranteed a future for Israel, but this final complaint is an honest expression of what the life of faith is really like. The people of God would struggle between fear and faith as they waited for the Lord's deliverance. Restoration would come but only in the distant future after a long period of exile and foreign oppression. The people of God continue to wait for their final deliverance in the distant future.

THEOLOGICAL SIGNIFICANCE

The time of the fall of Jerusalem and Babylonian exile was a national calamity (Psalm 137) and constituted the greatest theological crisis faced by ancient Israel. The temple where the Lord dwelt among His people was in ruins. The Lord appeared to have abandoned His people, or perhaps His covenant promises to them had failed. The survivors of this disaster were left to wonder if the Lord was able or willing to restore them. Lamentations gives voice to the suffering of these survivors and offers theological reflection to help them through this crisis. The writer openly acknowledges that the fall of Jerusalem is due to the sins of the people (1:5,14,18; 3:42; 4:6,22; 5:7,16). The people rather than the Lord are the ones who have failed to keep the covenant. The message of Lamentations is a vivid reminder of the severe **consequences** of sin and a living illustration of the spiritual principle of reaping what one sows (Gal 6:7). Moses warned that military defeat and exile would be the ultimate covenant curses if Israel failed to obey the Lord's commands (Deut 28:49–57). Thus the Lord inflicted these punishments on Israel and Judah after hundreds of years of disobedience and countless calls for the people to turn from their sinful ways. God's dealings with Israel serve as a serious reminder to us today. If God allowed Israel to come under judgment for her sins, we dare not believe that we will escape if we take His warnings lightly.

Lamentations also informs a proper understanding of **prayer.** Prayer is both an individual and a corporate activity. Confession of sin is essential when entering into the presence of a holy God. The prayers in this book remind readers of the privilege believers have to bring their deepest sorrows and hurts to the Lord. The raw emotion and transparent honesty of Lamentations offer a corrective to the shallow and contrived prayers that are too often a part of private and public worship. While recognizing the sovereignty of God, the poet questioned the Lord's apparent inactivity on behalf of His people and challenged the Lord to act in accordance with His character and promises. Jesus prayed these same types of laments when facing the cross and other hardships in His earthly ministry (Matt 27:46; Luke 22:41–42; Heb 5:7). Jesus is also the sympathetic High Priest who responds to the cries of His people because He has shared in their trials (Heb 4:15–16).

Jewish men praying at the Wailing Wall—a point close to the site of the ancient temple.

For Further Reading

Dearman, J. A. *Jeremiah/Lamentations*. NIVAC. Grand Rapids: Zondervan, 2002.
Ellison, H. L. "Lamentations," *EBC*. Grand Rapids: Zondervan, 1986.
House, Paul R. *Lamentations*. WBC. Nashville: Thomas Nelson, 2003.
Huey, F. B. *Jeremiah and Lamentations*. NAC. Nashville: B&H, 1993.
Provan, Iain. *Lamentations*. NCBC. Grand Rapids: Eerdmans, 1991.

Study Questions

1. What is a "lament," and how does it help us express our deepest feelings?
2. What tragedy prompted the author to write Lamentations?
3. Does the author express hope in the middle of his lament?
4. What are you facing right now that seems overwhelming to you?
5. Who alone can help us overcome our deepest sorrows, disappointments, and grief?

ENDNOTE

1. Outline follows Norman L. Geisler, *A Popular Survey of the Old Testament* (Grand Rapids: Baker, 2006), 275.

Chapter 31

EZEKIEL
The Glory Will Return

The book of Ezekiel is structured around **three visions** of the Lord. In the first vision (Ezekiel 1–3), the Lord appears to Ezekiel and commissions him to be a prophet to his fellow exiles. In Babylon the Lord did not forsake His people and provided a prophetic messenger for the exiles. In the second vision (Ezekiel 8–11), Ezekiel saw the glory of the Lord depart from Jerusalem. The Lord abandoned the city and removed His protective presence because the people defiled the temple with their idolatry and their wickedness. In the final vision (Ezekiel 40–48), Ezekiel saw the glory of the Lord return to Jerusalem (43:7–9; cf. 37:27). This will occur with the rebuilding of the temple in connection with the restoration of Israel in the last days. The judgment of Israel was only temporary, and the Lord would once again dwell among His people and His glory would return.

BACKGROUND

Ezekiel ("God has strengthened") was transported into exile as part of the **second Babylonian deportation** in 597 BC. He was taken along with Jehoiachin and other leading citizens of Judah (2 Kgs 24:10–16). He received his call as a prophet in July 593 BC, on his thirtieth birthday (1:1–3), and ministered among his fellow exiles while living at Tel Abib in southern Mesopotamia near Nippur. Chronological notations in the book indicate that Ezekiel's ministry extended until at least 571 BC. The prophet came from a priestly family, which helps to explain his emphasis on sin as uncleanness and defilement (5:11; 7:20; 20:43; 22:4; 36:29; 43:8) and his interest in the rebuilding of the future temple (chaps. 40–48). Ezekiel experienced some serious personal hardships in fulfilling his prophetic commission. From the time of his call until he heard about the fall of Jerusalem, Ezekiel suffered some type of speech impediment that allowed him to speak only when God wished to speak through him (3:26–27; 24:27; 33:22). Ezekiel's wife also died as a sign to the exiles of the impending fall of Jerusalem (24:25–27).

Outline

I. The Judgment of Judah and Jerusalem (Ezekiel 1–24)
II. The Judgment of the Nations (Ezekiel 25–32)
III. The Future Restoration of Israel (Ezekiel 33–48)

MESSAGE

I. The Judgment of Judah and Jerusalem (Ezekiel 1–24)

Ezekiel 1–3 narrates the details of Ezekiel's prophetic call. This account contrasts the awesome power of the Lord with the frailty of Ezekiel as a human being (a "son of man"). The term "**son of man**" appears as a descriptor for Ezekiel 93 times in the book. Ezekiel needed to know that his strength for ministry came from the Lord and not from himself. The Lord appeared to Ezekiel as a mighty warrior riding out of the clouds on his war chariot. The Lord was present with His people in Babylon; He had not abandoned them.

The four living creatures that helped to propel the chariot with their wings are identified as "*cherubim*" in Ezek 10:20. These angelic creatures serve as the **Lord's royal attendants** around His throne. These types of winged, hybrid creatures appear throughout the ancient Near East in connection with temples and palaces. They had the

Painted relief of a bull from the famous Ishtar Gate in Babylon.

faces and features of humans, eagles, lions, and oxen, testifying to their great strength; and they moved with the speed of flashes of lightning. The Lord appeared seated on a throne above a crystal expanse that looked like the sky. The sovereign Lord of heaven asserted His sovereignty in the land of Babylon, and no human ruler or army would be able to oppose Him. His voice was like the roar of mighty rivers. The flashes of light- ning, flames of fire, glowing metals, and shining jewels reflected the Lord's radiance and majesty. When seeing the greatness of God's glory, Ezekiel fell on his face in awe and worship (1:28).

The Spirit of the Lord would energize Ezekiel as a frail human being (a "son of man") to fulfill his prophetic calling. The Lord warned Ezekiel that his ministry would not be easy. Preaching to the rebellious house of Israel would be like walking among briers and thorns and living with scorpions (2:6). Ezekiel was not to fear the people but to keep preaching whether they believed his message or not. Ezekiel's visionary experience of **eating a scroll** of prophecies symbolized being filled with the word of God and his acceptance of the Lord's call on his life. Though the scroll was filled with words of lament and woe, it tasted sweet to Ezekiel. His experience is repeated later in John's experience of eating the "little scroll" in Rev 10:8–9.

Ezekiel's role as a prophet is compared to the work of a "**watchman**" who stood on the city wall and warned the people of approaching attack from an enemy army (3:17–21). If Ezekiel warned the people of the coming judgment and they refused to believe, then the people were responsible for their own destruction, but if the prophet failed to warn them, then their blood would be on his hands. Ezekiel was only respon- sible for proclaiming the message, not for how the people responded. To make sure the people recognized that Ezekiel's message was coming from God, the prophet was only able to speak when enabled by the Lord.

Ezekiel portrayed the siege of Jerusalem through a series of **four sign acts** in order to show the exiles that the fall of Jerusalem was near (Ezekiel 4–5). The prophet built a model of Jerusalem and raised siege works against it. He placed an iron plate between himself and the city, depicting how the people's sins separated them from God's pres- ence and protection. He lay on his side for 430 days to symbolize the accumulated sin of Israel and Judah. The Lord made the prophet eat bread from an odd assortment of grains cooked over dung and to drink small portions of water in order to illustrate the future famine conditions in the besieged city of Jerusalem. Ezekiel shaved his head and beard and then burned one-third of his hair, cut up another third with a sword, and the last third he scattered into the wind. The small portion the prophet tucked inside his belt represented the tiny remnant that would survive the fall of Jerusalem. Ezekiel was announcing a disaster for Jerusalem and the end of Judah because God would pour out His wrath on His sinful people (chap. 7).

In Ezekiel's second vision of the Lord, the **glory of the Lord departed** from the Jerusalem temple in response to the people's idolatry (Ezekiel 8–11). Ezekiel focused particularly on how the people's worship of idols was an "abomination" that defiled the sanctuary where the Lord lived among His people. The people brought idols into the temple area and engraved images of gods in the form of animals on its walls.

Women practiced the mourning rites associated with the fertility god Tammuz within the temple precincts. Men were worshipping the sun god on the temple steps. The Lord would not share His glory with these false gods, and He would not tolerate the demeaning of His holiness. The Lord would kill the idolaters among His people, sending out a heavenly messenger to put a mark on those appointed to die. His executing angels would pass through the land (9:1–8) in a reversal of the first Passover when the Lord killed the Egyptians and saved the Israelites.

In Ezekiel's second vision the glory of the Lord moves to the door of the temple (9:3; 10:4), then to the east gate of the temple (10:18–19), and then out of the city of Jerusalem completely (11:23–33). The departure of the Lord's presence from the Mount of Olives meant the removal of the Lord's protection when the Babylonian army invaded. The Lord had promised to protect Jerusalem from enemy armies that attacked the city (Pss 46:5–9; 48:4–8; 76:3), but the Lord's blessings and protection were contingent upon the people's obedience. Only those with clean hands and pure hearts could dwell in God's presence (Psalms 15; 24:3–5).

Winged lamassu (face of a man, body of a bull, wings of a bird).

Ezekiel performed another symbolic act to explain the reasons for the coming judgment (Ezekiel 12–14). The prophet packed a bag so he would look like someone heading off for exile, and then he began digging through the city wall so he would look like someone fleeing from an invading army. These **dramatizations** were necessary because the exiles treated the prophet's warnings as empty proverbs or predictions for the distant future, or just good entertainment. Judah's rebellion was largely the fault of its ungodly leadership. Their prophets preached lying messages from their own mind rather than the word of the Lord (chap. 13). Instead of standing in the gap and repairing Judah's broken walls, the prophets with their empty promises merely covered over the nation's problems with whitewash. Women prophetesses had influenced the people not to trust in the Lord by introducing magical rites that were designed to protect the people from danger. The elders of the land were also responsible for leading the people into idolatry.

Along with his symbolic acts, Ezekiel told **three parables** to portray the sinfulness of Judah and the certainty of coming judgment (Ezekiel 15–17). In the first parable the prophet compared Jerusalem to a charred vine that was worthless for producing fruit, so the Lord would completely burn up this useless vine. Second, Ezekiel portrayed Jerusalem as an unfaithful bride (chap. 16). Jerusalem had pagan origins as a Canaanite city, but the Lord took Jerusalem for His own when the city was like an abandoned baby in a field. The Lord raised Jerusalem and then took her as His wife when she became a beautiful young woman. Despite the many blessings the Lord lavished upon her, Jerusalem turned against Him and became a prostitute by worshipping other gods and making alliances with pagan nations.

Ezekiel also illustrated Judah's political situation with a parable about two eagles, a cedar, and a vine (chap. 17). The first eagle lopped off the top part of the cedar tree, took it away, and planted a vine in its place, referring to Nebuchadnezzar's taking Jehoiachin away and putting Zedekiah on the throne when he captured Jerusalem in 597 BC. The lowly vine then turned to another eagle for help, picturing how Zedekiah made an alliance with Egypt for military assistance against the Babylonians. Judah kept looking for political and military solutions when their real need was to turn to the Lord. But even in judgment God promised that He would restore the Davidic line through the future Messiah (17:22–24). At a future time the Lord would turn a tiny sprig from the cedar into a great tree.

Ezekiel 20 gives one of the most **negative assessments** of Israel's history in the entire Old Testament. The prophet Jeremiah pictured Israel's early days with the Lord in the wilderness as a honeymoon when they were devoted to Him (cf. Jer 2:2–3), but Ezekiel saw no such idyllic time in Israel's history. Their idolatry extended back to the time when they were in bondage in Egypt. The Lord rescued Israel out of Egypt for the sake of His own name, only to have the people rebel against Him again in the wilderness. The Lord punished the people but did not destroy them, again for the sake of His own reputation among the nations. Even after entering and enjoying the Promised Land, their entire history was a story of rebellion against the Lord and the worship of false gods. Instead of fulfilling their mission to reflect the Lord as the one true God to the nations, they wanted to be like the nations in worshipping gods of wood and stone. The Lord would bring a purging judgment against His people in order to break this longstanding pattern of judgment and to produce a pure remnant whose restoration would demonstrate the Lord's holiness to all the nations.

The negative assessment of Israel leads into a series of severe **judgment messages** to close the first section of the book (Ezekiel 21–24). The Lord would brandish a sharpened sword against His people that would slash to the left and the right (Ezekiel 21). In Israel's past history the Lord often fought for His people in delivering them from their enemies. Now the Lord would fight against them and would wield the sword that would bring death and terror on the land. The Babylonian king was the Lord's instrument of judgment (cf. Isa 10:5), and the Lord would even direct the king's pagan omens in leading him to attack Jerusalem (21:18–23). The Lord would judge the people for their rebellion and particularly Judah's wicked leaders. The Davidic dynasty would come to an end until its restoration with the future Messiah.

II. The Judgment of the Nations (Ezekiel 25–32)

Like Isaiah (Isaiah 13–23) and Jeremiah (Jeremiah 46–51), Ezekiel's prophecies contain an extended series of **oracles against foreign nations**. The Lord's sovereignty extended beyond Israel and Judah and included all peoples and nations. Judah would receive comfort in knowing that the Lord would ultimately punish the nations that mistreated them. These oracles would also serve as a warning against forming alliances with other nations, for they too would become the objects of God's judgments. In line with the overall message of the book, the purpose of these judgments was to cause all peoples to know that the Lord was the true God.

In 587 BC, Ezekiel delivered an extensive message of **judgment against Tyre**, the capital of Phoenicia and a prosperous commercial trading center. Tyre rejoiced over the fall of Judah because this removed a potential rival. But soon the Lord would bring an enemy army against Tyre that would reduce the city to a bare rock and a place to cast fishing nets. Nebuchadnezzar besieged Tyre for 13 years (585–572 BC), destroying many of its buildings; but many of its citizens escaped to an island fortress. Alexander the Great was finally able to reduce Tyre's island fortress to rubble in 332 BC, literally casting its remains into the sea (26:19).

The **lament over Tyre** in Ezekiel 27 appropriately portrays the city as a stately ship made from the products of its many trading partners. Tyre sailed the seas and accumulated great wealth by exchanging many goods and engaging in slave trade, but a powerful wind would eventually shatter the ship of Tyre in the heart of the seas (vv. 35–36). The peoples of the earth would react with shock and horror over the downfall of Tyre and its vast financial empire.

In Ezekiel 28:1–19, the prophet turns his focus to the judgment of the **king of Tyre**, who in his great hubris believed himself to be a god (28:2). However, the king would die like any other mortal at the hands of a powerful invading army that the Lord would send against Tyre. The king's superior wisdom and the vast wealth of Tyre would

Harbor at Tyre showing ancient Phoenician harbor (facing northwest).

not preserve him from dying an ignominious death. His fall is described in terms that remind some of the fall of Satan. The pride of the king of Tyre that led to his downfall was also the cause of Satan's rebellion and fall (1 Tim 3:6), and other passages mention that Satanic power and influence stand behind evil human rulers who oppose God and His people (see Dan 10:1–21; Matt 4:8–9; Eph 2:2; 1 Jn 5:19).

Ezekiel also delivered a series of **oracles against Egypt** (29:1–32:31). During the Assyrian and Babylonian crises, Judah often trusted in political and military alliances with Egypt rather than the Lord as their source of security (Isa 30:1–3; 31:1–3; Jer 37:4–10; Ezek 17:15–17). Nevertheless, Egypt's promises of help often did not

Ezekiel settled with a group of Jewish exiles near the city of Nippur by the Chebar River.
Shown here are ruins of a temple in Nafur, Iraq (ancient Nippur).

materialize. At best help provided only temporary relief from some pressing threat.
Trusting in Egypt was like using a reed stalk for a walking stick because that stick
would splinter as soon as Judah leaned on it for support (29:6–7; Isa 36:6).

Ezekiel employed **powerful imagery** to portray the downfall of the proud and arrogant Egyptians. Addressing the Pharaoh as a "monster" from the sea (29:2; 32:2), the
prophet depicts the king as a fearsome crocodile in the Nile River. Though the Pharaoh
boasted of his great strength, the Lord would catch him in His net, put hooks in his jaws,
and cast him into an open field to be consumed by the birds of the air (29:1–5; 32:1–3).
This imagery likely recalls Leviathan, the sea monster the Lord subdued at creation (Job
26:12–13; Pss 74:12–17; 89:9–13). The Lord's judgment would ultimately fall not only
on evil human rulers but also on the evil powers that stood behind them.

III. The Future Restoration of Israel (Ezekiel 33–48)

The final section of Ezekiel's prophecy turns to the hope of Israel's future restoration. The Lord would restore His people in spite of their flagrant disobedience for the
sake of His own reputation. He did this so that all peoples from all nations would know
that He was the Lord. The Lord would also bring about Israel's spiritual and national
restoration so they might enjoy His presence and the rich blessings of the promised

Israel In Bible Prophecy

Ezekiel 36 provides the theological ground for the restoration of future Israel to fulfill God's promises and restore His glory. Ezekiel 37 gives the mechanics of the restoration through the vision of the valley of dry bones (vv. 1–14). The whole "house of Israel" will be regathered to the Promised Land prior to their spiritual rebirth. Thus, a two-stage return is promised in the "last days." Stage one is **physical** and portrays the political revival of national Israel (the bones coming together), and stage two is **spiritual** and portrays the regeneration of the nation (breath entering into them). The word "forever" is used five times in vv. 25–28 repeatedly affirming the eternality of God's restoration and requires an eschatological fulfillment. Ezekiel's prophecies predict Israel's victory over Gog and Magog (chaps. 38–39), the conversion of Israel (39:22–29), and the erecting of the restoration temple and the return of the **Shekinah** glory (chaps. 40–48).

land forever. This final section of Ezekiel's messages entails **prophecies of hope** for the people of Israel. They include Israel's regathering, regeneration, and restoration.

Ezekiel 33:21 records the event that all of Ezekiel's warnings of judgment pointed to—the fall of Jerusalem to the Babylonians. Five months after the event (January 586), Ezekiel received word from a Jewish refugee that Jerusalem had indeed fallen. Ezekiel's muteness had allowed him to speak only when he received a message from God (3:22–27), but at this time his inability to speak came to an end. Ezekiel 33:21 functions as a **hinge verse** in the book of Ezekiel. The focus before this verse is centered on judgment and the Lord's wrath against Judah's sins, but the focus from this point forward is on Israel's salvation and restoration.

Israel's restoration would involve the removal of Judah's corrupt leaders. The **shepherd motif** is prominent in this chapter, and it conveys the idea that leaders are expected to care for God's people with the same concern, devotion, and selflessness as a shepherd caring for his flock. In the OT the term "shepherd" primarily refers to kings, princes, royal officials, and civil judges. The metaphor of king as shepherd extended throughout the various cultures of the ancient Near East. When David became king over Israel, the Lord commissioned him to "shepherd" the people (2 Sam 5:2; 1 Chron 11:2), and Ps 78:72 claims that David shepherded the people of Israel with "a pure heart" and "skillful hands." Rather than tending the flock under their care, the shepherds of Ezekiel's day exploited and consumed the people for their own selfish gains. The Lord promised that in the future He would shepherd His people and that He would raise up a new David as the right kind of shepherd for the people.

The restoration of Israel would mean the judgment of her enemies. **Edom** is targeted in 35:1–36:15 and in 25:12–14 (cf. Jer 49, Obad) as the object of God's judgment because the Edomites allied with Babylon in the assault on Judah and Jerusalem. The Edomites arrogantly believed they would not be held accountable for their actions, but the Lord would pour out His wrath on the Edomites for plundering His people.

Edom is also representative of all the evil nations the Lord would destroy in His final judgment (cf. Isa 34; 63:1–6).

The Lord would **restore Israel** by returning the people to the land and causing the land to be fruitful and productive. Israel would rebuild their ruined cities and would enjoy the blessings of the Promised Land they forfeited because of their disobedience. Israel was deserving of judgment because they defiled the land with their sinfulness, but the Lord would save them to regain His own reputation that was profaned by Israel's exile. The Lord would also bring about the spiritual transformation of His people so they would never again need to be punished. The Lord would cleanse them from their past wickedness and would give them a new heart and spirit to follow Him (36:22–36). Ezekiel's prophecy parallels Jeremiah's promise of a new covenant and of God's writing the law on the heart of His people (Jer 31:31–34). The Lord would provide this enablement to obey Him through the imparting of His Spirit. Because of the people's obedience, the land would become like the garden of Eden.

A view from Megiddo of the Valley of Jezreel with the town of Nazareth in the distance.

Ezekiel's **vision of the dry bones** (37:1–14) confirmed the Lord's promise to restore and spiritually renew the people of Israel. The valley is pictured as a battlefield littered with the bones of dead soldiers. The Lord commanded Ezekiel to prophesy to the bones, and then the Lord put flesh on the bones and breathed life into them. Israel's destruction scattered them like dry bones and left them as good as dead. Humanly speaking, there was no hope for the future. But God's "breath" (*ruach*) would bring the dry bones to life, and God's "Spirit" (*ruach*) would bring renewal to Israel as a nation. Israel's restoration would be like a resurrection from the grave.

Ezekiel's object lesson involving the **two sticks** provided a second confirmation of the Lord's promise to restore Israel. Ezekiel wrote the names "Judah" and "Joseph" on the two sticks, representing Judah and Israel, and then joined the sticks together so they became one. This sign act symbolized how the Lord would reunify the northern and southern kingdoms as one nation. The **Davidic Messiah** would reign over the reunified nation and would lead the people to follow the Lord. The stages of Israel's regathering are progressive and sequential with 37:21–22, describing Israel's physical regathering from the nations, and 37:23–25, describing the spiritual rebirth of Israel at the time of Christ's second coming when He would reign as the Davidic Messiah.[1] The Lord would establish a "covenant of peace" with Israel guaranteeing that He would dwell among His people forever.

The vision of **Gog and Magog** in Ezekiel 38–39 concerns an end-time invasion against Israel when Israel is back in the land and dwelling there securely. Just as Babylon invaded Judah in Ezekiel's day, a powerful and arrogant ruler named Gog would form a coalition of seven nations to invade Israel in the distant future. Israel would not need to defend itself because the Lord Himself would destroy these enemies by pouring down upon them torrential rains, hailstones, and burning sulfur. The invading armies in their confusion would even turn against each other. The enemy armies' weapons would provide fuel for Israel for seven years, and it would take Israel seven months to bury the dead. The total destruction of this enemy army would cause the nations to recognize the glory of the Lord and cause Israel to be ashamed of its past sins. This great victory on Israel's behalf would reverse the defeats of the past, and the Lord would establish His people in the land. He would pour out His Spirit on them so they never again need to be punished for their disobedience.[2]

The prophecy of Ezekiel concludes with an extended vision of the **eschatological temple** and the return of the Lord to dwell among His people. This section represents the climax of the book with the return of God's glory on the future temple.[3] Scholars have offered several different interpretations of this vision of the new temple. Some have interpreted the vision symbolically to represent the restoration of the relationship between God and Israel. Others view the passage as an idealized prophecy concerning the rebuilding of the temple in the postexilic period under Zerubbabel, but that temple fell far short of what Ezekiel envisions. Another interpretation is that the passage is fulfilled figuratively in Jesus Christ as the replacement of the temple and in the church as God's spiritual temple. The detailed measurements and specifications concerning the layout and design of this temple strongly suggest that a real physical sanctuary is in view here and that the focus of this prophecy is the temple that will exist in Jerusalem during the earthly millennial kingdom (see Rev 20:1–10). Ezekiel 43:10–11 states that the Lord provided the exact design for the temple so that Israel would be careful to carry out His instructions. Other Old Testament prophets also anticipated the restoration of Jerusalem and the temple in the future kingdom (see Isa 2:2–4; 60:7,13; 62:9; Mic 4:1–3; Zech 14:16–19).

The most important feature of Ezekiel's vision is the promise that the Lord would return to dwell among His people in Jerusalem (43:1–12). The book of Ezekiel is built around three visions of the **glory of the Lord**. First, in Ezekiel 1 the prophet saw the glory of the Lord on His throne chariot in Babylon with His people. Second, Ezekiel observed the glory of the Lord depart from Jerusalem because of Judah's flagrant sin and idolatry (Ezekiel 8–11). Third, in the future temple, the glory of the Lord will enter through the east gate, the place from which it departed (43:4; cf. 10:18–22; 11:23). The Lord will again establish His throne in Jerusalem, and the people will be purged of their sins so they can live in God's presence (43:6–9). Judgment necessitated the Lord's departure from Jerusalem and the removal of His protective presence, but the Lord would not abandon His people, for He promised that He would dwell among them forever. The name of Jerusalem would become "The LORD is there" (48:35 NASB).

The detailed layout for the temple gates, courts, and rooms in Ezek 40:1–43:12 describe the structure that will be rebuilt. The most significant feature of the description of the physical structure of the future temple is its **enormous size**. The temple measures 500 cubits (or 1,500 yards) on a side (42:16–20), which is three times larger than the temple in Jesus' day. The size of the temple suggests its prominence and importance in the future messianic kingdom.

Ezekiel also devotes significant attention to the priests, the Levites, and the services at the temple (43:13–46:14). The priests would offer the regular daily sacrifices and the special offerings during festivals and holy days. The sacrifices would include sin offerings that made atonement for the sins of the people and the leaders (45:17,22). The use of **animal sacrifices** in the future temple appears to present a problem in light of the fact that Jesus offered the perfect and final sacrifice for sin (Heb 10:10–14). Some interpreters have resolved this tension by arguing that these sacrifices will serve as a memorial of Christ's death in the millennium or that they will be required to remove physical impurity so that sinners can enter into the presence of a holy God.[4]

Ezekiel describes a **river** flowing out from the temple that begins as a tiny stream but eventually becomes a mighty river (47:1–12; cf. Zech 14:8). The river brings fertility to the land and even causes the Dead Sea to come to life so that fishermen will cast their nets there. This river recalls the one flowing from the garden of Eden (Gen 2:10).

Hebrew Highlight

Glory. Hebrew כבוד (*kâbôd*). The glory of God is described by the Hebrew term that indicates heaviness. The root and its derivatives occur 376 times in the Hebrew Bible, including 25 times in Ezekiel. It is also used adjectivally 200 times (eg., "King of glory," meaning "glorious king"); 45 times the root form refers to a visible manifestation of God as an objective reality, often having to do with the appearance of God in the tabernacle (Exod 16:10) or the temple (Ezek 9:3). The "heaviness" of the glory indicates the reality of God's presence. It is also on display in Jesus Christ, of whom His disciple John said: "We observed his glory" (John 1:14).

The millennial kingdom of Christ will bring about a reversal of the curse and the return of the earth to Eden-like conditions. The river is connected to the presence of God that will bring blessing and security to Jerusalem and the land of Israel (see Ps 46:4; Isa 33:21). John's vision of the eternal kingdom also envisions the new Jerusalem as a new Eden, with its river flowing from the city and the tree of life providing food and healing for the nations (Rev 22:1–2).

Ezekiel describes how the **land is to be allotted** among the tribes of Israel in the future restoration. The sacred districts around the temple at the center of the land would belong to the Lord; and the prince, the Levites, and the priests would be given adjoining territories (45:1–7). The city of Jerusalem would be located between the tribes of Judah and Benjamin and would be for all the peoples. Oppressive leaders would no longer prevent the people from enjoying their portions of the land (45:8). The boundaries of the land will be essentially the same as during the reigns of David and Solomon. The tribes will receive equal allotments, but the specific boundaries will be different from their historical territories (47:13–48:29). Ezekiel's prophecies concerning the distribution of the land help to inform our understanding that the future restoration of Israel promised in Rom 11:25–27 will include the reconstitution of Israel as a nation in the Promised Land.

Along with the Israelite tribes, **foreigners** living as aliens in the land will receive allotments of land as their inheritance (47:22–23). Foreigners will share in the blessings of the future kingdom as the Lord fulfills His covenant promises to Israel. Ezekiel's prophecy ends with the promise of the restoration of the Zadokite priesthood (48:11), the allotment of the 12 tribes of Israel, and the placing of their names on the gates of the city (48:21–34) which shall be called "The LORD is there" (48:35 NASB).

THEOLOGICAL SIGNIFICANCE

The Lord's judgment and salvation of Israel would cause all peoples to know that He is the true God (5:13; 12:20; 20:42; 37:13,28; 39:28). The expression "know that I am the LORD" appears 72 times in the book of Ezekiel. Judah's sin and subsequent judgment tarnished the Lord's reputation among the nations (36:20; 43:8) so the Lord will act in power to save Israel for the sake of His own name and honor (20:42–44; 36:21–23; 39:7,25). More than return to the land following exile, Israel's restoration would also involve **spiritual transformation**. The Lord would give the people a "new heart" by pouring out His Spirit upon them so they would be obedient to His commandments and never again have to face His judgment (11:18–20; 36:26–28). Ezekiel's warnings and promises to Israel remind us to take God's message seriously or we too may face His judgment and lose His blessings.

For Further Reading

Allen, Leslie C. *Ezekiel*. 2 vols. WBC. Dallas: Word, 1990, 1994.
Block, Daniel I. *Ezekiel*. 2 vols. NICOT. Grand Rapids: Eerdmans, 1997, 1998.
Cooper, Lamar E. *Ezekiel*. NAC. Nashville: B&H, 1994.
Craigie, Peter C. *Ezekiel*. DSB. Philadelphia: Westminster, 1995.
Duguid, Iain M. *Ezekiel*. NIVAC. Grand Rapids: Zondervan, 1999.
Feinberg, Charles L. *The Prophecy of Ezekiel*. Chicago: Moody, 1969.

Study Questions

1. Describe the circumstance of Ezekiel's ministry during the Babylonian captivity.
2. What term was applied to Ezekiel to emphasize his human limitations?
3. How does Ezekiel describe the glory of God departing from the temple? What is the significance of this departure?
4. What did the "vision of the dry bones" signify?
5. What will be the result of the invasion of Israel by Gog and Magog?
6. Why should we be concerned about the glory of God in our lives?

ENDNOTES

1. See comments in Tim LaHaye and Ed Hindson, *The Popular Bible Prophecy Commentary* (Eugene, OR: Harvest House, 2006), 179–89.
2. Ibid., 189–95.
3. Cf. detailed discussion in Randall Price, *The Temple in Bible Prophecy* (Eugene, OR: Harvest House, 2005).
4. See Charles Feinberg, "Millennial Offering and Sacrifices," in *The Prophecy of Ezekiel* (Chicago: Moody Press, 1969), 263–70.

Chapter 32

DANIEL
The Messiah Will Come

The book of Daniel, written in both Hebrew (1:1–2:4a; 8:1–12:13) and Aramaic (2:4b–7:28), combines the **personal histories and prophecies** of Daniel during the Babylonian captivity and the first few years of the Persian era (605–535 BC). It includes detailed prophecies of the fate of the Jewish people under Gentile rule in what it describes as the "time of the end" (Dan 8:19) or what Jesus called the "times of the Gentiles" (Luke 21:24). Daniel foretells the rise and fall of four Gentile empires (chaps. 2; 7), the coming of the Messiah (7:13–14; 9:25–26), the rise of the Antichrist (8:21–25; 9:26–27; 11:36–45), the time of tribulation (12:1–7), the triumph of the kingdom of God (2:44), and the final resurrection (12:13).

BACKGROUND

Daniel ("God is my Judge"), a contemporary of Jeremiah and Ezekiel, went into captivity to Babylon in 605 BC. His book records events and visions dating to 535 BC (10:1), indicating that he lived through the entire 70 years of the **Babylonian captivity**. Nebuchadnezzar, the Babylonian prince, attacked the city of Jerusalem in August 605 BC and removed Jehoiakim the king of Judah sometime after he defeated the Egyptians at the battle of Carchemish in May–June 605 BC. In the meantime his father

An artist's reconstruction of Babylon as it would have appeared in the sixth century BC (courtesy of the University of Chicago).

Nabopolassar died, and Nebuchadnezzar returned to Babylon to receive the kingship officially. The time Nebuchadnezzar ruled extended from 605 to 562 BC.

The **Babylonian setting** of the book is indicated by the constant references to the language, culture, and history of the Neo-Babylonian Empire. The author identifies Babylonian cultural concepts (e.g., trial by ordeal), deities (Bel, Nebo, Marduk), architectural details (plaster walls in the palace), and long forgotten historical information (the co-regency of Belshazzar and Nabonidus). The Persian sections of the book also reflect Persian loan words ("satraps"). Even critical scholars have admitted, "We have here true reminiscence of the elaborate organization and civil service of Persia."[1]

DATE AND AUTHORSHIP

Despite numerous historical references, the book of Daniel has been widely criticized since the eighteenth century as a pseudonymous forgery of the Maccabean period (170–160 BC). The detailed and accurate prophecies in the book of Daniel are the **target of criticism** by those who reject the concept of prophecy that predicts events beyond the immediate setting of the prophet. Many deny that Daniel could predict what would happen in the distant future, so they assert that these "prophetic" statements were made *post-eventu* (after the fact). They suggest that a second-century Jew was writing about the persecution of Antiochus Epiphanes some four centuries after the Babylonian captivity.[2]

The book of Daniel specifically dates its proceedings and prophecies according to the regal years of various Babylonian and Persian monarchs (1:1,21; 2:1; 5:31; 7:1; 8:1; 9:1; 10:1; 11:1). Daniel dates himself repeatedly by describing himself as a Judean exile (1:1–6; 2:25; 5:13; 6:13). **Additional confirmation** for dating the book in this era comes from historical figures associated with Daniel, such as Nebuchadnezzar (1:18), Belshazzar (5:29), and Cyrus (6:28). Literary and archaeological sources confirming these figures support a literal historical setting for the book of Daniel, and the accuracy of the details within the book argues for a date of composition in the sixth century BC, around 535 BC.

Was Daniel a Prophet?

Contemporary critics are quick to point out that Daniel was listed in the section of the "writings" (*kethuvim*) in the Hebrew Bible and not among the "prophets" (*Nevi'im*). Thus, they assert that Daniel was not considered a prophetic book and in some cases even suggest it is apocryphal. However, several key factors weigh against this analysis. First, Daniel served as an **administrator** in a foreign court. He was not a preaching prophet to the nation of Israel. Second, he claimed to receive visions from God that were clearly prophetic in nature. Thus, Daniel's book was later placed among the prophets because he clearly demonstrated the **gift of prophecy**, even if he didn't hold the office of prophet. Jesus specifically called him "the prophet Daniel" (Matt 24:15). Third, there is no clear evidence Daniel was listed in the "writings" prior to the fourth century AD. The second-century BC Septuagint (LXX) lists Daniel among the "prophets" as did Josephus (first century AD), Melito (second century AD), and Origen (third century AD). Finally, several fragments in the Dead Sea Scrolls refer to words that were "written in the book of Daniel the prophet," indicating a pre-Christian acceptance of Daniel as a prophetic book.

The **language** of the book argues for a date much earlier than the second century. Linguistic evidence from the Dead Sea Scrolls, which furnish authentic samples of second-century Hebrew and Aramaic, demonstrate that the Hebrew and Aramaic chapters of Daniel were composed many centuries earlier.[3] The few Persian and Greek terms appearing in the book refer to government officials (chap. 6) or musical instruments (chap. 3) and do not provide ample evidence of a late date for the composition.[4] In addition, careful analysis of the Hebrew text of Daniel compared to the Qumran scrolls indicates the Hebrew of Daniel is much earlier than the second century BC.[5]

The exilic prophet Ezekiel (14:20; 28:3) names Daniel as a model of faith and righteousness to the exilic community. The Septuagint (LXX) includes the book of Daniel among the "prophets" and the first-century Jewish historian Josephus (10.267) notes that the "events under Antiochus IV Epiphanes . . . had been predicted many years in advance by Daniel." The existence of 20 **fragments from Qumran**, which date from the Maccabean period, and nine complete manuscripts of Daniel, make it highly improbable that the book of Daniel was composed during that same period. On the basis of paleography, these 20 fragments are dated around 125 BC. The early semicursive script of 4Q Dan (4 Q 114) is dated to the late second century BC within less than 50 years from the assumed autograph according to the critical theory.

The argument that prophecies cannot predict details in advance is contrary to the evidence, for several of Daniel's prophecies were fulfilled long after the Persian and Maccabean era: the rise of the Roman Empire (2:33; 7:7), the coming of "Messiah the Prince" 483 years after the command to "restore and rebuild Jerusalem" (9:25), the death of the Messiah (9:26), and the destruction of Jerusalem and the second temple (9:26). These cannot easily be explained away as lucky guesses. **Objective evidence**, therefore, appears to exclude the late date hypothesis and indicates sufficient reason to affirm Daniel's authorship in the sixth century BC. The fact that Jesus Himself (Matt 24:15) referred to "Daniel the prophet" is ample testimony to the Savior's belief that Daniel was the author of the book.

Outline

I. Daniel's Personal History (Daniel 1–6)
  A. Four Hebrews (Daniel 1)
  B. Four Empires (Daniel 2)
  C. Furnace of Fire (Daniel 3)
  D. Fate of Nebuchadnezzar (Daniel 4)
  E. Fall of Babylon (Daniel 5)
  F. Fearless Prayer (Daniel 6)
II. Daniel's Prophetic Visions (Daniel 7–12)
  A. Four Beasts (Daniel 7)
  B. The Ram and the Goat (Daniel 8)
  C. Seventy Sevens (Daniel 9)
  D. Israel's Future (Daniel 10–12)

MESSAGE

The overall theme of Daniel is **God's sovereignty** over the people of Israel and the nations of the world. Despite the threats of Gentile powers, the God of Israel is always triumphant. "The Most High God is ruler over the kingdom of men" (5:21). He alone sets up and takes down human authorities who rule by His divine permission (2:21). The book is made up primarily of historical narrative (chaps. 1–6) and apocalyptic prophetic visions (chaps. 7–12). The latter may be defined as symbolic, visionary prophecies that are mainly eschatological in nature. Often composed during oppressive conditions, apocalyptic literature is written to provide encouragement to the people of God by providing a clear revelation of the future.

NAME	DATES (B.C.)	SIGNIFICANT EVENTS
Nabopolassar	626–605	Chaldean chieftain who seized Babylon in 626; established an alliance with Cyaxares the Mede; conquered Nineveh in 612.
Nebuchadnezzar	605–562	Defeated Egypt at Battle of Carchemish in 605; twice besieged Jerusalem (698/97; 587/86).
Evil Merodach (Amel-marduk)	562–560	Son of Nebuchadnezzar; freed Jehoiacahin, king of Judah (2 Kg. 25:27-30).
Neriglissar	560–556	Son-in-law of Nebuchadnezzar; likely the Nergal-sharezer who was present at the final siege of Jerusalem (Jr. 39:3).
Labashi-marduk	556 (3-month reign)	Son of Neriglissar; removed by Nabonidus.
Nabonidus	556–539	Spent considerable time outside of Babylon; Belshazzar served as regent in his absence; Babylon surrendered to Cyrus the Great in 539.

Kings of the Neo-Babylonian Empire.

I. Daniel's Personal History (Daniel 1–6)

A. Four Hebrews (Daniel 1)

The book of Daniel begins with Daniel and his three friends, Hananiah, Mishael, and Azariah (v. 6), being taken captive to Babylon as **intellectual hostages** by Nebuchadnezzar in August 605 BC. The four Hebrews were among a number of young men from the nobility of Judah who were forcibly placed into a three-year training program to learn the language (Akkadian), literature (written in cuneiform script), and the sciences of the Babylonians. Every attempt was made to accommodate them to Babylonian life and culture to prepare them for government service to the Babylonian Empire. Accordingly, their Hebrew names were changed to Babylonian names (Belteshazzar, Shadrach, Meshach, Abednego), and they were allotted a portion of the king's diet. Immediately these young men asked to be exempt from eating the king's food, probably based on a kosher dietary principle, because they determined in their hearts not to defile themselves (v. 8). Ultimately they won the favor of their guards and with God's blessing proved themselves to be "10 times better" than all the other captives (v. 20).

B. Four Empires (Daniel 2)

The second chapter involves Nebuchadnezzar's fantastic dream of a great **metallic statue** and his insistence that the wise men and magicians of Babylon reproduce and interpret his dream. At this point the text of Daniel switches to Aramaic. While the wise men failed to reproduce and interpret the dream, the "mystery was then revealed to Daniel" after much prayer (v. 19). In his explanation Daniel pointed out that God revealed to the king what would happen "in the last days" (v. 28). Daniel proceeded to identify the elements of the metallic statue that was eventually crushed and replaced by a falling stone which he identified as the "kingdom of God" (v. 44). The head of gold symbolized Nebuchadnezzar and the kingdom of Babylon (v. 38), and it would be followed by kingdoms of silver, brass, and iron (vv. 32–33). Finally, the feet of the statue were identified as "iron mixed with clay," indicating the instability of the entire statue (vv. 41–42). Later prophecies in Daniel 7–8 identify the second kingdom as Media-Persia (arms of silver) and the third as Greece (belly of brass). The fourth kingdom is unnamed in Daniel, but many commentators identify it with Rome.

Daniel then explained that in the days of the 10 toes of iron and clay, the God of heaven would destroy the earlier kingdoms, symbolized by the stone falling on the toes of the statue. This would cause the preceding kingdoms to disintegrate; then God replaced them with the **kingdom of God** (v. 44). While commentators differ on how this should be interpreted, premillennialists identify the stone with the second coming of Christ because only then will human governments literally be replaced by the kingdom of God on earth.

Hebrew Highlight

Interpretation. Hebrew פְּשַׁר (*peshar*). The Aramaic noun *peshar* occurs 32 times only in Daniel. It is similar to the Akkadian word for "interpreting" dreams or omens associated with divination. The Aramaic *peshar* is similar to the Hebrew *petar*, which means "interpretation" (in Exodus 40–41). Daniel 2:30 makes clear that true interpretation of hidden things can come only from God through divine revelation. Commentaries among the Dead Sea Scrolls, such as Peshar Habakkuk, use this term for interpretation of biblical teachings.

C. Furnace of Fire (Daniel 3)

Daniel's companions—Shadrach, Meshach, and Abednego—are the subjects of the incident of the golden statue which Nebuchadnezzar required all of his government officials to worship. The musical instruments mentioned included Greek terms for lyre (*kitharis*), harp (*psalterion*), and pipes (*sumphonia*) expressed in Aramaic. Such terms were well known in the Middle East by the sixth century.[6] Daniel's absence in this account is explained in 2:49, for Daniel gave up his role as a political official in order to remain at the king's court in Babylon, serving as chief of the wise men. His political responsibilities were given to Daniel's three friends who were serving in the province (3:1); thus they were required to attend the event described in chap. 3. The names of Daniel's three friends, along with Nebuzaradan (Jer 39:9–13) and Neriglissar (Jer 39:3,13), were found in a Babylonian text from the time of Nebuchadnezzar.[7] The furnace was probably a **brick kiln** used to fire bricks. The fact that the Hebrews did not burn and were released (vv. 25–26) follows the Babylonian legal concept of trial by ordeal, innocence being validated by surviving one's punishment.

D. Fate of Nebuchadnezzar (Daniel 4)

The Babylonian monarch dreamed of a **great tree** being cut down, leaving only the stump wet with the dew for "seven periods of time" (4:14–16). The chapter begins with a firsthand account of the king's desire to express the "miracles and wonders" of God toward him (4:1–2) and reads like the opening of a personal testimony of God's power. In it the king acknowledges that he heard angels ("holy ones") say: "the Most High is ruler over the kingdom of men" (v. 17). After a period of temporary insanity (possibly lycanthropy) afflicted him with animal-like behavior (v. 33), the king's sanity returned when he acknowledged the king of heaven (v. 37).

E. Fall of Babylon (Daniel 5)

Belshazzar served as **co-regent** with his father, Nabonidus from 553 to 539 BC when Babylon fell to the Medes and Persians on October 12, 539 BC. By the time this chapter opens, Nebuchadnezzar has died (562 BC), and so has Amel Marduk (562–560 BC), Neriglissar (560–556 BC), and Labashi Marduk (556 BC). The biblical account skips over several of these monarchs who apparently had little or no contact with Daniel.

Belshazzar's appearance in this chapter was explained as a myth by biblical critics until the discovery of the **Nabonidus Chronicle,** which clarified that Belshazzar, whose name was missing from the ancient Babylonian king list, ruled as co-regent with his father for 14 years while Nabonidus resided in Tema (Arabia). Thirty-seven archival texts now attest to the historicity of Belshazzar as the second ruler in Babylon, thus explaining his offer to make whoever could read the handwriting on the wall the "third ruler" in the kingdom.[8]

During an extravagant and excessive banquet, in which Belshazzar desecrated the temple vessels taken from Jerusalem years earlier, a divine **handwritten message** appeared on the plaster wall of the palace reading:

מנא	MENE	numbered
מנא	MENE	numbered
תקל	TEKEL	weighed
פרס	PERES	divided

When the king could find no one to read or explain it, the queen (probably Amytis, the queen mother and widow of Nebuchadnezzar) suggested that they call for Daniel, now an old man, probably into his eighties. Daniel read the writing and told Belshazzar that God had numbered his kingdom, weighed it on the scales of justice, found it lacking, and would divide it and give it to the **Medes and Persians**. That very night Babylon fell without a battle to Cyrus the Great, and Belshazzar was executed (v. 30).

F. Fearless Prayer (Daniel 6)

The sixth chapter refers to **Darius the Mede** as ruling Babylon on behalf of the Median-Persian coalition, possibly under the authority of Cyrus. As was the case of Belshazzar prior to the twentieth century, there are no extrabiblical references to Darius the Mede. Some have suggested this may be another designation for Cyrus, but others argue that this is unlikely since Cyrus was a Persian. Whitcomb made a strong case for identifying Darius as Gubaru the governor of Babylon, who ruled the city on behalf of the Medes and Persians.[9] When the ruler succumbed to pressure to pass a law against prayer, Daniel, now in his eighties, refused to comply and continued praying with his

Relief of Nabonidus, king of Babylonia (556–539 BC) when Babylon fell to Cyrus. Here Nabonidus stands before emblems of the moon god, sun god, and war/love god.

windows open (v. 10). Despite the attempts of Darius to release him, Daniel was thrown into the lions' den overnight but survived because of his innocence (v. 22).

Median soldiers in the royal Persian guard as shown on a relief made of glazed bricks found at Susa.

II. Daniel's Prophetic Visions (Daniel 7–12)

A. Four Beasts (Daniel 7)

The second half of the book records four prophetic visions of future events that will affect the Jewish people in the years ahead. The vision in chap. 7 is dated from "the first year of Belshazzar" (553 BC). In the vision Daniel saw **four huge beasts,** animals that were comparable to the four elements in the metallic statue in chap. 2. The winged lion was a well-known symbol of ancient Babylon. The bear represented the Medes and Persians; the four-headed leopard symbolized Greece and the four divisions of the Hellenistic Empire. The monster with iron teeth represented the Roman Empire.

Daniel's vision went beyond that of Nebuchadnezzar's dream in focusing on the 10 horns of the fourth beast and a **little horn** which came up afterward (v. 8) and eventually "made war with the holy ones" (v. 21) for three and one-half "times" (v. 25). The book of Revelation calls this individual the Beast (Rev 13:1–11) although he is generally designated as the Antichrist. God the Father is pictured as the "Ancient of Days" who judges the little horn and presents the kingdom to Christ, designated as "a son of man" (vv. 11–14). He, in turn, shares the greatness of the kingdom with the saints of God, who are pictured as true believers (v. 27). Since the beast is the fourth animal, this indicates the Antichrist's connection with Rome.

B. The Ram and the Goat (Daniel 8)

This vision pictures the coming clash between **Persia and Greece**. The ram with two horns symbolizes the Medes and Persians coming from the East, moving westward (vv. 3–4). The goat with one horn represents Alexander the Great of Greece, coming from the West, moving eastward. In this prophecy Daniel predicted the triumph of Greece over Persia 200 years in advance. Alexander defeated the Persians at Issus in 333 BC and Arbela in 331 BC, within three years of his ascension to the throne at age 20. But Alexander died in Babylon in 323 BC at the age of only 32, thus the "great horn" of the goat was "broken" and his kingdom was divided into four sections. One of these four territories (Syria) produced a "little horn" of Greek origin, Antiochus IV Epiphanes (a type of antichrist) who persecuted the Jews and desecrated the temple for "2,300 days" (170–164 BC).

C. Seventy Sevens (Daniel 9)

After reading **Jeremiah's prophecy** of the 70 years' captivity (Jer 25:11; 29:10) during the first years of Darius the Mede (c. 538 BC), Daniel realized the time for his people to return to Jerusalem was near. Knowing they were not ready to return, Daniel poured his heart out in one of the finest prayers recorded in Scripture, confessing his sins and the sins of his people, acknowledging that the curse of their covenant law was still upon them (vv. 3–19).

In response to Daniels' prayer, the angel Gabriel came to him to reveal the prophecy of the **70 "sevens"** (Hb. *shavuah*)—70 sevens ("weeks") of years—decreed about "your people" (the Jews) and "your holy city" (Jerusalem). The 70 x 7 (490 years) would culminate in sealing "up vision and prophecy" and "anoint the most holy place" (v. 24). But after seven sevens and 62 sevens (69 x 7 = 483 years), the Messiah would be "cut off" (killed) and the city (Jerusalem) and the sanctuary (temple) would be destroyed (v. 26). During the final "seven" years (the seventieth seven), the "coming prince" (Antichrist) will break his covenant with the Jews and bring about the "abomination of desolation" (v. 27). Jesus clearly indicated that the "abomination" was still a future event, indicating that this prophecy was not fulfilled by Antiochus Epiphanes (Matt 24:15).

The prophecy indicates that the first 69 sevens (483 years) will begin with the decree to rebuild the city, presumably Artaxerxes's decree to Nehemiah to rebuild the walls of Jerusalem in 444 BC. It will culminate 483 years later (based on a lunar sabbatical calendar) with the death of the Messiah in AD 32. While many evangelicals agree with this interpretation of this amazing prophecy, some debate the fulfillment of the final seventieth seven. Many view this as the seven years of tribulation yet to come in the future which will result in the **eschatological restoration** indicated by the prophetic goals to "seal up vision and prophecy" and "anoint the most holy place."

Alexander the Great fighting Darius III at the Battle of Issus in 333 BC. The scene comes from a first-century mosaic found in Pompeii.

D. Israel's Future (Daniel 10–12)

The final vision is dated in the "third year of Cyrus" (536/535 BC) at the end of the 70 years of the Babylonian captivity. By that time Zerubbabel and nearly 50,000 Jewish captives were returning to Jerusalem. At this time Daniel received his final vision for the Jewish people "in the last days" (10:14). The details of this prophecy in chap. 11 focus on the **Hellenistic Kingdoms** of the intertestamental period (331–160 BC). After the division of Alexander's empire (11:3–4), the prophecy traces the future conflicts of the "king of South" (Egypt) with the "king of the North" (Hellenistic Syria under the Seleucids), culminating in a detailed prophecy about a "vile person" (Antiochus IV Epiphanes) who will rule by "intrigue" (11:21–35).

Daniel 11:36–45 is often regarded as a reference to the **Antichrist** since it does not apply to Antiochus but rather reveals this future ruler as typified by him. Miller states, "Exegetical necessity requires that 11:36–45 be applied to someone other than Antiochus IV." He adds, "He is none other than the 'little horn' of Daniel 7 and the 'ruler who will come' of Daniel 9:26."[10] This section ends with a description of the wars of Antichrist and his final defeat at the "time of the end" (vv. 40–45).

Chapter 12 closes the prophecy with the promise of the **final triumph** of God's people in the future messianic era.[11] A "time of distress" (tribulation) will come in the future, but those whose names are "written in the book [i.e., Book of Life] will escape" (12:1). Then Daniel is told to seal the prophecy "until the time of the end" (v. 9) because he will "rest" (die), then later "rise to your destiny at the end of the days" (v. 13). Thus, the book ends with the promise of a literal bodily resurrection in anticipation of our participation in God's eternal kingdom.

Chapter 2 Nebuchadnezzar's Dream of the Image		History	Chapter 7 Daniel's Vision of the Four Beasts	
Prophecy		*Fulfillment*	*Prophecy*	
Dream 2:31–35	Interpretation 2:36–45	World Empire	Interpretation 7:15–28	Dream 7:1–14
2:32 Head (gold)	2:38 You–Nebuchadnezzar	Babylonian 612–539 B.C.	7:17 King	7:4 Lion with wings of an eagle
2:32 Breasts and arms (silver)	2:39 Inferior kingdom	Medo-Persian 539–331 B.C.	7:17 King	7:5 Bear raised up on one side
2:32 Belly and thighs (bronze)	2:39 Third kingdom	Grecian 331–63 B.C.	7:17 King	7:6 Leopard with four heads and four wings on its back
2:33 Legs (iron) Feet (iron and clay)	2:40 Fourth kingdom	ROME — Ancient Rome 63 B.C.–A.D. 476 / Revived Roman Empire	7:23 Fourth kingdom; 7:24 Ten kings; 7:24 Different king	7:7, 19 Fourth beast with iron teeth and claws of bronze; 7:7–8 Ten horns; 7:8 Little horn uttering great boasts
2:35 Great mountain; 2:44 Kingdom which will never be destroyed		Messianic kingdom	7:27 Everlasting kingdom	7:9 Thrones were set up

Adapted from Thomas Ice. Taken from H. Wayne House and Randall Price, *Charts of Bible Prophecy*, p. 63. Copyright © 2003 by H. Wayne House and World of the Bible Ministries, Inc. Used by permission of Zondervan.

THEOLOGICAL SIGNIFICANCE

Daniel emphasizes the **sovereignty of God** over the nations of the world in general and over the nation of Israel in particular. The book also underscores the importance of faith, hope, character, and endurance. Daniel and his friends are pictured as determined to obey God rather than men, even at the risk of their own lives (chaps. 1, 3, 7). This amazing book of personal narrative and prophetic pronouncement reveals the heart of God for His people and their confidence in Him for their future hope. Jehovah (Yahweh) is the King of heaven and Lord of the universe. He is the Most High (*El elyon*) who rules over Gentiles as well as Jews. He sets up and takes down human kings, limits their authority, reveals His secrets to whomever He chooses, and determines the destiny of people and nations.

God reveals His glory by **predicting the future**. He forecasts four Gentile empires that will rule over the Jewish people and their final downfall when the Son of Man receives the kingdom of God from the "Ancient of Days" and the saints of God come to rule with the Messiah in the "greatness of the kingdom." Thus, Daniel predicts the whole future of Israel: return from captivity, rebuilding the temple, conflicts of the future, coming of Messiah, Messiah's death, the destruction of Jerusalem and the second temple, the rise of Antichrist, the time of tribulation, the triumphal return, the resurrection of the Jewish saints, and the future Messianic kingdom.

For Further Reading

Archer, Gleason. *"Daniel."* EBC, 7. Grand Rapids: Zondervan, 1985.
Culver, Robert D. *Daniel and the Latter Days.* Chicago: Moody Press, 1977.
Miller, Stephen R. *Daniel.* NAC, 18. Nashville: B&H, 1994.
Walvoord, John F. *Daniel: The Key to Prophetic Revelation.* Chicago: Moody Press, 1971.
Whitcomb, John C. *Daniel.* Chicago: Moody Press, 1985.
Wood, Leon. *A Commentary on Daniel.* Grand Rapids: Zondervan, 1973.
Young, Edward J. *The Prophecy of Daniel: A Commentary.* Grand Rapids: Eerdmans, 1977.

Study Questions

1. Why did God elevate Daniel and his friends among the Jewish captives?
2. How do the details of the interpretation of the metallic statue (chap. 2) and the four beasts explain the historical fulfillment of biblical prophecy?
3. What character qualities enabled Daniel (chaps. 1; 6) and his friends to stand for God against the pressure to compromise their convictions?
4. What was the significance of the handwriting on the wall?
5. To what does the prophecy of the 70 "sevens" refer?
6. Why should we have confidence in biblical prophecies?
7. What is the final promise and prophecy of Daniel 12?

ENDNOTES

1. J. A. Montgomery, *A Critical and Exegetical Commentary on the Book of Daniel*, ICC (Edinburgh: T&T Clark, 1964), 269.

2. For a detailed discussion of the critical view, cf. S. R. Driver, *The Book of Daniel* (Cambridge: University Press, 1922) and contrary to Gleason Archer, *A Survey of Old Testament Introduction* (Chicago: Moody Press, 1964), 365–88.

3. K. A. Kitchen, "The Aramaic of Daniel," in D. J. Wiseman, ed., *Notes on Some Problems in the Book of Daniel* (London: Tyndale Press, 1965), 31–79.

4. E. Yamauchi, *Persia and the Bible* (Grand Rapids: Baker, 1990), 380–82.

5. Gleason Archer, "The Hebrew of Daniel Compared with Qumran Sectarian Documents," J. H. Skilton, ed., *The Law and the Prophets* (Nutley, NJ: Presbyterian & Reformed, 1974), 470–81.

6. T. C. Mitchell and R. Joyce, "The Musical Instruments in Nebuchadnezzar's Orchestra," in Wiseman, *Notes on Some Problems*, 19–27.

7. W. H. Shea, "Daniel 3: Extra Biblical Texts and the Convocation on the Plain of Dura," *AUSS* 20 (1982), 37–50.

8. P. A. Beaulieu, *The Reign of Nabonidus, King of Babylon 556–539 BC* (New Haven: Yale University Press, 1989), 156–57.

9. John C. Whitcomb, *Darius the Mede* (Philadelphia: Presbyterian and Reformed, 1963).

10. Stephen Miller, *Daniel* (NAC, 18 (Nashville: B&H, 1994), 305–6. Church fathers such as Chrysostom, Jerome, and Theodorat clearly identify this king as the future Antichrist. Cf. Gleason Archer, trans., *Jerome's Commentary on Daniel* (Grand Rapids: Baker, 1977).

11. J. J. Slotki, *Daniel-Ezra-Nehemiah* (London: Socino Press, 1978), 100–101.

Chapter 33

MINOR PROPHETS

The Minor Prophets cover the books of Hosea to Malachi and form the final section of the Old Testament canon. They follow the Major Prophets in the Hebrew Scriptures. Their present arrangement follows the order of the Latin Vulgate, which in turn follows the order of the Septuagint (LXX) in placing Hosea first as an introduction to the general themes of warning, judgment, repentance, and restoration in the 12 prophets.

Jewish rabbinic tradition held that the men of the Great Synagogue edited the 12 individual books into a single volume in the Hebrew Bible.[1] Their placement of the Minor Prophets in relation to the Major Prophets indicates that these books were revered as inspired Scriptures of equal value to their larger counterparts. In other words, the messages of the Minor Prophets were of major significance for the people of Israel.

These books are 12 separate compositions in our English Bible, but they appear as a single "Book of the 12" in the Hebrew Bible. Along with Isaiah, Jeremiah, and Ezekiel, they form the Latter Prophets. The history of these 12 prophets covered a span of more than three centuries. The first historical reference to these books in the apocryphal Sirach (c. 200 BC) treats them as a single work because these smaller books could all fit on a single scroll. The order of these books is the same in the Hebrew and English canons, and some Jewish traditions viewed these books as arranged chronologically.

Six of the books (Hosea, Amos, Micah, Zephaniah, Haggai, and Zechariah) contain historical headings or superscriptions and are generally arranged chronologically, though many would put the ministry of Amos (760 BC) earlier than Hosea (755–715 BC). The other six (Joel, Obadiah, Jonah, Nahum, Habakkuk, and Malachi) have no headings and are more difficult to date so it is hard to make strong claims about their chronological order. Commentators do not agree on the dates of Jonah, Joel, and Obadiah. Thematic considerations also appear to have influenced the order and arrangement of these books.

In terms of larger themes, Hosea-Micah focused on the sin of covenant breaking; Nahum-Zephaniah emphasized the approaching judgment of the Day of the Lord; and Haggai-Malachi promised the reversal of judgment and the future glory of Israel. Key words and phrases also provided links between the end of one work and the beginning of another. Joel 3:16 and Amos 1:2 refer to the Lord's roaring like a lion. Amos 9:12 prophesies the judgment of Edom, and the fall of Edom is the thematic focus of the book of Obadiah that follows. Altogether the Minor Prophets are a collection of the messages of 12 individual prophets to Israel and Judah that serve both as predictions of judgment and as promises of hope for the future.[2]

HISTORICAL BACKGROUND

The books of the Minor Prophets cover the period from the eighth to the fifth centuries BC. This time began with an era of great prosperity for both Israel (northern kingdom) and Judah (southern kingdom) but ended in disaster for both kingdoms. The early success of Jeroboam II (793–753 BC) would end with the total collapse of the northern kingdom and the destruction of its capital Samaria by the Assyrians in 722 BC. Although Judah would survive a similar assault by the Assyrians in 701 BC, the southern kingdom would fall repeatedly to the Babylonians, and Jerusalem would be totally destroyed in 586 BC.

The earlier Minor Prophets, like their counterparts, the Major Prophets, predicted the fall of both Samaria and Jerusalem to the Assyrians and Babylonians. Then, in turn, they also predicted the fall of Assyria and Babylon and the future restoration of Judah. Thus, the history of the Minor Prophets extends all the way through the Babylonian captivity (605–535 BC) and includes three postexilic prophets (Haggai, Zechariah, and Malachi) who preached to the Jewish people who returned to rebuild Jerusalem from their exile in Babylon.

STRUCTURE AND STYLE

The messages of the Minor Prophets were delivered on separate occasions and later collected and arranged in book form. Robert Chisholm suggests six distinct patterns of prophetic speech that appear in the messages of the prophets.[3]

1. *Inclusio*: the conclusion corresponds to the introduction (see Mic 1:8–16).
2. *Chiasmus*: the center of the literary unit builds toward a climax (see Joel 2:19–27).
3. *Judgment speech*: an accusation is followed by a pronouncement of judgment (see Amos 1:3–5).
4. *Woe oracles*: judgments that presume guilt and begin with the word "woe" (Hb. *hoy*).
5. *Exhortation*: a call to repentance reinforced by a promise of hope (see Joel 2:12–14).
6. *Salvation announcements*: promises of God's deliverance and blessing (see Amos 9:11–15).

The preexilic prophets delivered warnings of judgment in which they predicted that God would implement the curses of the covenant based on Israel's ratification of the covenant stipulations in Deuteronomy 27–30. This same theme can be seen in the postexilic prophets. Therefore, it should not surprise us that the final verse of the Old Testament warns: "Or else I will come and strike the land with a curse" (Mal 4:6 NIV).

FOCUS OF THE PROPHETS

Three of the Minor Prophets (27 chapters in the English Bible) are focused on the northern kingdom of Israel (capital, Samaria):

- Hosea: God's Unquenchable Love
- Amos: God's Ultimate Justice
- Jonah: God's Universal Concern

Six of the Minor Prophets (20 chapters in the English Bible) are focused on the southern kingdom (capital, Jerusalem):

- Joel: Day of the Lord
- Obadiah: Doom of Edom
- Micah: Divine Lawsuit
- Nahum: Destruction of Nineveh
- Habakkuk: Destruction of Babylon
- Zephaniah: Disaster Is Imminent

The last three Minor Prophets (20 chapters in the English Bible) are focused on the Jewish exiles who have returned from Babylon to rebuild the temple and reestablish Jerusalem. They form the final link to the Messianic prophecies, which are fulfilled in Jesus in the New Testament:

- Haggai: Rebuild the Temple
- Zechariah: Restore the King
- Malachi: Repent of Sin

The messages of the Minor Prophets still speak to us today. They remind us that God holds all people responsible for their behavior, especially those who claim to belong to Him. God's warnings to Israel and Judah were meant to turn them away from impending disaster and urge them to be faithful to the One who really loved them. Thus, the call of the prophets echoes down the canyon of time, calling us to repent, return, and experience God's grace and forgiveness resulting in revival, restoration, and hope for the future.

For Further Reading

Bullock, C. Hassell. *An Introduction to the Old Testament Prophetic Books.* Chicago: Moody Press, 1986.

Chisholm, Robert B., Jr. *Interpreting the Minor Prophets.* Grand Rapids: Zondervan, 1990.

Craigie, Peter C. *The Twelve Prophets,* 2 vols. Philadelphia: Westminster Press, 1985.

Feinberg, Charles L. *The Minor Prophets.* Chicago: Moody Press, 1976.

Freeman, Hobart E. *An Introduction to the Old Testament Prophets.* Chicago: Moody Press, 1968.

Hays, J. Daniel. *The Message of the Prophets.* Grand Rapids: Zondervan, 2010.

Smith, Gary V. *The Prophets as Preachers: An Introduction to the Hebrew Prophets.* Nashville: B&H, 1994.

ENDNOTES

1. R. K. Harrison, *Introduction to the Old Testament* (Grand Rapids, MI: Eerdmans, 1969), 858.

2. Paul R. House, *Old Testament Theology* (Downers Grove, IL: IVP, 1998), 348.

3. Robert Chisholm, *Interpreting the Minor Prophets* (Grand Rapids, MI: Zondervan, 1990), 260.

Chapter 34

HOSEA
God's Unquenchable Love

Hosea ("salvation") prophesied from the reign of Jeroboam II (791–750 BC) to the reign of Hezekiah (715–687 BC), and his ministry likely covered a time span of 35–40 years. Most of Hosea's recorded messages focus on the **coming judgment of Israel** and thus occurred before the fall of Samaria in 722 BC. It is unusual that the heading of a book for a prophet who ministered in the northern kingdom mentions four kings of Judah and then only one king of Israel. Hosea prophesied concerning Judah as well as Israel (cf. Hos 1:7,11; 4:15; 5:5,10–14; 6:4,11; 8:14; 10:11; 11:12; 12:2), and the focus of the heading on Judah is likely due to the fact that the written form of Hosea's prophecies were viewed as much as a warning of the future exile of Judah as a historical message about the fall of Israel. The omission of Israel's rulers following Jeroboam II reflects their political and religious insignificance.

The temple platform at Dan used by Jeroboam I. The steps lead up to a large platform made of ashlar masonry.

369

BACKGROUND

Hosea's ministry began at a time of great economic prosperity for Israel that rapidly disintegrated into one of national catastrophe. Both Israel and Judah prospered under the lengthy and effective reigns of Jeroboam II and Uzziah, so the weakness of both Syria and Assyria enabled Jeroboam II to expand Israelite territories (2 Kgs 14:23–29). Israel's political size and economic stability, however, were not indicators of spiritual vitality. Israel turned away from the Lord, worshipped Baal, and engaged in the perverse rites and practices that accompanied such worship. Israel wrongly credited Baal, rather than Yahweh, as the provider of the wealth and economic blessing they enjoyed. The veneration of the golden-calf gods in the sanctuaries at Dan and Bethel and various forms of **religious syncretism** also corrupted their worship of the Lord and blurred important distinctions between Yahweh and the pagan gods.

At the social level Israel's accumulation of wealth led to a wide disparity between the upper and lower classes, and a **climate of injustice** prevailed as the rich used their power and influence to take advantage of the poor. Selfishness, greed, and the pursuit of pleasure characterized Israelite society rather than love for the Lord and one's neighbor.

Following the death of Jeroboam II, Israel had a rapid succession of weak and ungodly leaders over its final 30 years. The assassination of Jeroboam's son, Zechariah, six months into his reign, set in motion a bloody and violent struggle in which four of Israel's final five kings came to the throne by murdering their predecessor (cf. Hos 7:5–7; 8:4–6; 2 Kings 15). The stability that Israel enjoyed in the first half of the eighth century BC quickly turned to chaos.

Jeroboam's death also coincided with the rise of Tiglath-pileser III to the Assyrian throne in 745 BC. Tiglath-pileser III (745–727 BC) restored the power of the central government in Assyria and looked westward to expand his territories and gain much-needed tribute for his kingdom. Israel was no match for the **Assyrian military machine**. Menahem of Israel (749–739 BC) paid tribute to Assyria during his reign (2 Kgs 15:19–20). Pekah (737–732 BC) later attempted to form an alliance with King Rezin of Syria against the Assyrians, but the resultant Syro-Ephraimite War ended with the destruction of Damascus and heavy losses for Israel. The annals of Tiglath-pileser III record that Israel's final king, Hoshea, was installed as an Assyrian puppet. Hoshea later rebelled against the Assyrians by refusing to pay tribute and appealing to Egypt for military assistance (2 Kgs 17:4), and the Assyrian king Sargon II took the city of Samaria in 722 BC after a three-year siege. Hosea's prophecies of judgment against Israel were fulfilled, and Israel became an Assyrian province.

Outline

I. Personal and National Problem: Unfaithfulness (Hosea 1–3)
II. Prospect of Judgment and Salvation (Hosea 4–14)
   A. Judgment for Israel's Rebellion (Hosea 4:1–6:3)
   B. Judgment Results in Israel's Ruin (Hosea 6:4–11:11)
   C. Judgment Turns to Restoration (Hosea 11:12–14:9)

MESSAGE

I. Personal and National Problem: Unfaithfulness (Hosea 1–3)

God commanded Hosea to marry a promiscuous and **unfaithful wife**, who subsequently gave birth to three children with symbolic names. Both the woman and the children were metaphors of Israel's covenant unfaithfulness toward the Lord. Israel had prostituted itself by turning away from the Lord and following other gods. Scholars have interpreted the marriage of Hosea and Gomer in several different ways. Jewish and Christian interpreters alike have struggled with the moral dilemma of how the Lord could direct Hosea as His prophet to marry a promiscuous woman. Some have viewed the marriage as an allegory or parable rather than an actual union. Others have argued that Gomer was a cult prostitute or that she was guilty of spiritual infidelity like many others in the land of Israel. Still others have suggested that she became promiscuous after they were actually married.

The most natural reading of the text is that Hosea and Gomer were actually husband and wife. Desperate times called for desperate measures, and the outrageous act of a prophet marrying an immoral woman graphically demonstrated how the Lord viewed Israel's covenant defection. Without a **real marriage** and all of the moral messiness accompanying such an act, the message of Hosea loses much of its rhetorical impact. Nothing could also more effectively communicate Yahweh's unconditional love and covenant commitment to Israel than a husband showing love to a promiscuous wife.

Did Jesus Fulfill Hosea 11:1?

In Hosea 11:1, Yahweh recalled His past deliverance of Israel at the exodus, "When Israel was a child, I loved him, and out of Egypt I called my son" (NIV). Matthew 2:15 asserts that the return of Jesus from Egypt after his fleeing there with his parents from Herod was the fulfillment of Hosea 11:1. How can a passage referencing Israel in the Old Testament be applied to Jesus in the New Testament? Matthew interpreted the Hosea passage **typologically**, drawing a parallel between the experience of Israel as God's son and Jesus as the incarnate Son of God. God would not allow His son to remain in servitude and obscurity in Egypt.

The Gospels present numerous parallels between the life of Jesus and the experiences of Israel. The hostility of Herod and his slaughter of the infants mirrored Israel's experiences in Egypt. Jesus was tempted in the wilderness like Israel but, unlike Israel, was faithful and obedient when tested. As Moses received the law on Mount Sinai, Jesus expounded the law to His disciples in the Sermon on the Mount. As Israel's Messiah, Jesus completed and fulfilled the story of Israel in the Old Testament. Through His obedience and ultimately His saving death, Jesus would restore Israel as God's people and instrument of blessing to the rest of the world.

Hebrew Highlight

Repent. Hebrew שׁוּב (*shûb*) is used 1,075 times in the Old Testament. It means to "turn" (Josh 19:12), "turn back" (Exod 14:2) or "return" (Gen 3:19). It denotes "repent" (Ps 7:12), or "reconsider" (Job 6:29). Used with other verbs, *shûb* emphasizes decisive and repeated action. It is the strongest Hebrew term to indicate that true repentance involves a change of direction that results in renewal and restoration (Hos 6:1).

Rather than a dream or vision, the Lord's command for Hosea to marry Gomer most closely parallels other texts in which the Lord directs a prophet to communicate His message by performing a **symbolic act**. The Lord commanded Isaiah to preach naked and barefoot for three years (Isa 20:1–3). He instructed Jeremiah to wear an animal yoke as he preached (Jeremiah 27–28) and directed Ezekiel to shave his head and beard (Ezek 5:1–4) as visual demonstrations of their messages of judgment. The Lord commanded Jeremiah not to marry or have children in order to warn the people that the judgment of exile would deprive them of their family members (Jer 16:1–4). Ezekiel's wife also died on the day the Babylonians took the city of Jerusalem, and the Lord commanded the prophet not to mourn so the people would understand they were about to experience a disaster that would leave them too numb to grieve (Ezek 24:15–26).

It is not clear to some if Gomer was **promiscuous** before her marriage to Hosea or only engaged in immoral behavior after the marriage had occurred. Many interpreters have argued that Hosea retrospectively came to realize that the Lord had commanded him to marry an immoral woman after she was unfaithful to him in their marriage. Such a reading is possible and might better reflect the history of the Lord's relationship with Israel. Israel was devoted to the Lord at the beginning of the covenant relationship (Hos 2:15; cf. Jer 2:2) and only later became unfaithful. However, other texts indicate that the people of Israel had worshiped other gods in Egypt and were unfaithful to the Lord from the beginning of their relationship (cf. Exodus 32; Numbers 25; Josh 24:14; Ezek 20:20–21). If the command to marry Gomer was the symbolic act commencing Hosea's ministry, it would seem more likely that she was promiscuous when the prophet took her as his wife. Gomer's unfaithfulness to Hosea was a metaphor of Israel's unfaithfulness to the Lord, and the issue of her purity at the time of her marriage has no real impact on the message behind the metaphor. It was also not necessary for every aspect of the marriage between Hosea and Gomer to correspond to the exact details of the history between the Lord and Israel in order to serve as an illustration to the nation.

The **children** born to Gomer also represented Israel's unfaithfulness, and the names of these children had symbolic significance and warned of the judgment that was coming upon Israel. *Jezreel* ("God sows") was the place where God visited judgment on the house of Ahab (2 Kings 9–10). A name like "Columbine" would carry a similar connotation in a modern American context. The name also signified that the dynasty or house of Jehu, which King Jeroboam II was leading, was about to come to a violent and bloody end. *Lo-Ruhamah* ("not pitied") meant that the Lord would not show mercy as He punished Israel for its sins. *Lo-Ammi* ("not my people") indicated that Yahweh would sever His relationship with Israel as punishment for their covenant unfaithfulness. However, the Lord also promised that after their time of judgment He would restore His people and would bring about a reversal of the negative circumstances reflected by the children's names (1:10–2:1,23).

Instead of a place of violence, Jezreel, which can also mean "God sows," would become a place of **renewal** as God securely planted His people in their land. The Lord would show His love to unloved Israel, and they would once again become His people. The text specifically identifies only Jezreel as the son of Hosea, and scholars have debated if Hosea was the father of the other two children, particularly in light of their names Lo-Ammi and Lo-Ruhamah.

At the beginning of chap. 3, Yahweh instructed Hosea to take back his unfaithful wife. **Gomer** had committed adultery and had degraded herself to the point that she had become the property of another man. Hosea paid the price of both silver and grain that cancelled out any debt she may have owed and that freed her from her servitude. After a time of isolation, Gomer would live with Hosea and be exclusively devoted to her husband. Similarly, the Lord would discipline Israel with a time of deprivation so that she would become devoted to Him. The renewal of Israel would also mean the restoration of the Davidic dynasty through the raising up of a new David in the last days.

II. Prospects of Judgment and Salvation (Hosea 4–14)

The marriage of Hosea and Gomer was a powerful **object lesson** of Israel's unfaithfulness toward the Lord and the Lord's unfailing commitment to His people. Moving beyond the issue of Gomer's infidelity, chaps. 4–14 present a detailed explanation of Israel's covenant infidelity. Like a prosecuting attorney presenting the Lord's case against Israel, Hosea charged Israel with covenant infidelity in three separate indictments:

"The Lord has a charge to bring against you who live in the land." (4:1 NIV)

"They have broken the covenant—they were unfaithful to me there." (6:7 NIV)

"The Lord has a charge to bring against Judah; he will punish Jacob according to his ways and repay him according to his deeds." (12:2 NIV)

Other prophets also presented similar **covenant lawsuits** against Israel (cf. Isa 1:3–20; Mic 6:1–8). Hosea documented that Israel had committed spiritual adultery against the Lord in four specific ways: (1) worship of Baal and other false gods (4:10–14; 8:11; 11:2; 13:1–2), (2) religious syncretism and the worship of the calf god at their sanctuaries (4:17; 8:5–6; 10:5–6; 13:2), (3) violation of Yahweh's commandments (4:1–2; 6:7; 7:1–2), and (4) political alliances with other nations (5:13–14; 7:8,11; 8:9–10; 12:1).

Chapters 4–14 consist of **three cycles** of alternating messages of judgment and salvation:

CYCLE 1	CYCLE 2	CYCLE 3
Judgment (4:1–5:15a)	Judgment (6:4–11:7)	Judgment (11:12–13:16)
Salvation (5:15b–6:3)	Salvation (11:8–11)	Salvation (14:1–9)

This structure reflects that though the Lord would punish Israel severely for its many sins, He would not reject His people forever and would ultimately restore and bless them. The Lord's purging judgment would turn Israel away from its worship of false gods and would cause them to recognize Him alone as their source of security and blessing.

A. Judgment for Israel's Rebellion (Hosea 4:1–6:3)

The prophet charged that Israel was guilty of **disobedience** to Yahweh's covenant commands, specifically calling attention to their violation of six of the Ten Commandments. Ultimate fault lay with Israel's priests and prophets who had failed to teach the word of the Lord. Consequently the people were perishing for their lack of knowledge. Israel's spiritual leaders were greedy and selfish, and the priests loved to feed themselves

A Canaanite altar located at Megiddo in Israel.

on the sacrifices and offerings the people presented to the Lord. Selfish priests had produced a pleasure-seeking people who turned to the worship of false gods and the practice of abhorrent Canaanite fertility rites as a means of satisfying their sinful lusts. Some Israelites were outright polytheists and worshipped other gods; more of the people likely gave into subtle forms of syncretism in which pagan beliefs and practices were integrated into the worship of Yahweh. Such syncretism had begun with the worship of the calf gods at the sanctuaries in Dan and Bethel. Hosea announced that God's judgment would fall on both Israel and Judah for their sin and rebellion. Because they had turned away from the Lord, the Lord would abandon them in their day of distress.

Nevertheless, for now God would wait for a while to see if some would seek Him, desire to return to God, and trust Him for healing and revival. If those individuals were truly determined to know Him, God would surely pour out His blessing on them (5:15–6:3)

B. Judgment Results in Israel's Ruin (Hosea 6:4–11:11)

In the second phase of his covenant lawsuit against Israel, Hosea delivered **two extended indictments** of Israel's sins against the Lord (6:4–7:16 and 10:1–15) and a detailed description between them of how the Lord intended to punish them for their crimes (8:1–9:17). Injustice and violence characterized Israelite society because the people did not think the Lord saw or took notice of their actions. The people defrauded one another in their business dealings, and drunken princes conspired against each other and engaged in bloody conflict for control of the throne. Four of Israel's last six kings came to the throne by murdering their predecessor.

Israel's **military alliances** with other nations were as much a form of spiritual adultery as their worship of false gods. Israel was caught in a vise between two superpowers— Egypt to the south and Assyria to the north, and Israel's officials vacil-

Statue of a lion standing over a bull's head.

lated between the two powers in seeking the assistance of one against the other. They trusted in their treaties with Assyria and Egypt as their ultimate source of security rather than trusting in the Lord. By mixing with other peoples, Israel became like a half-baked cake, raw on one side and burnt on the other. Israel's foolish officials were like doves flitting back and forth between Egypt and Assyria (7:11). By entering these political alliances, Israel sowed the wind of folly, and they would reap the whirlwind of military invasion (8:7).

Hosea employed a series of **four extended metaphors** that contrasted both the Lord's faithfulness to Israel with Israel's unfaithfulness to Him. Israel was compared to spoiled grapes, a wild vine, a trained heifer, and a rebellious son. Even in judgment, however, Yahweh's fatherly love would trump His anger, and He would not completely destroy His people (11:8–11). The Lord would preserve a remnant and restore them to their homeland. His roaring as a lion in judgment would cause the survivors of the exile to come trembling before Him in repentance.

C. Judgment Turns to Restoration (Hosea 11:12–14:9)

In the third segment of his indictment against Israel, Hosea compared the people with their deceptive forefather **Jacob**. Jacob struggled with his brother in the womb, wrestled with God, and earnestly sought His blessing as a man. However, Israel did not seek the Lord and ignored the many messages of the prophets who attempted to call them back to God. Instead of acknowledging the Lord as the source of their blessings, Israel attributed their wealth and prosperity to their idols and their calf gods. Because of her rebellion against Yahweh, the capital city of Samaria would fall in battle, and the pregnant women and small children of the city would be torn to pieces by their vicious attackers.

The final message in the book of Hosea is one of **hope and promise**. The consistent message of the prophets was that Israel's salvation and restoration would follow its time of judgment. In spite of Israel's covenant unfaithfulness, Hosea called on the people to return to the Lord with confession of their sin and repudiation of their trust in military alliances and false gods. When Israel "returned" (*shub*) to the Lord (14:1), then the Lord would "turn" (*shub*) from His anger and would freely love them again (14:4). Hosea employed agricultural imagery to portray the great blessing the Lord would pour out on His repentant people. Like the refreshing dew, Yahweh would be Israel's source of life and vitality. Israel would become fruitful once again, its beauty like the lilies and its strength like the trees of Lebanon. Israel would flourish like the olive tree, the grain, and the vine. Like an evergreen tree the Lord would be a constant source of blessing, and He would provide for Israel everything they had wrongly sought from their false gods.

"They will follow the Lord; He will roar like a lion. When He roars, His children will come trembling from the west" (Hos 11:10).

THEOLOGICAL SIGNIFICANCE

Hosea presented the covenant relationship between the Lord and Israel as a marriage. The **marriage metaphor** communicated the depth of the Lord's love for Israel and the intimacy of their relationship. The portrayal of the covenant between Yahweh and Israel as a marriage also highlighted the treachery and betrayal behind Israel's sin. Israel was to give exclusive love and worship to the Lord as her husband, but they committed spiritual adultery against Him by following after false gods. The prophets employed graphic sexual imagery in order to shock the people into seeing how disgusting and repulsive their behavior was in the eyes of God (cf. Jeremiah 2–3; Ezekiel 16; 23). The sexual nature of this metaphor was also appropriate in light of Israel's involvement in pagan fertility rites (Hos 4:13–14).

Israel did not simply break God's laws; they broke His heart. Adultery was a capital offense in Israel, and the infidelity of the wife also brought shame and dishonor on the husband. The marriage metaphor also conveyed hope for Israel's future because of the Lord's **unfailing love** for His wife. Even in judgment the Lord could not give up His feelings of love for Israel, and He would not destroy them completely (Hos 11:8–9).

The marriage metaphor carried over into the New Testament as a picture of Christ's love for the church. Christ bought the church through His death on the cross so that she could be His pure and holy bride, and husbands are to follow His example of sacrifice in loving their wives (Eph 5:25–27). Paul ministered on behalf of the church so he could present her as a pure virgin to Christ at the time of the Second Coming (2 Cor 11:2), and the second coming of Christ to earth will be the time for the eschatological banquet and the marriage supper of the Lamb when Christ is finally joined to His bride to live with her for all eternity (cf. Matt 22:1–14; Rev 19:6–10).

For Further Reading

Dearman, J. Andrew. *The Book of Hosea*. NICOT. Grand Rapids: Eerdmans, 2010.

Garrett, Duane. *Hosea, Joel*. NAC. Nashville: B&H, 1997.

Kidner, Derek. *Love to the Loveless: The Meaning of Hosea*. Downers Grove, IL: IVP, 1981.

King, Philip J. *Amos, Hosea, Micah—an Archaeological Commentary*. Philadelphia: Westminster, 1988.

McComiskey, T. E. "Hosea," in *The Minor Prophets: An Exegetical and Expository Commentary*, vol. 1: *Hosea, Joel, Amos*. Edited by Thomas Edward McComiskey. Grand Rapids: Baker, 1992.

Smith, Gary V. *Hosea, Amos, Micah*. NIVAC. Grand Rapids: Zondervan, 2001.

Stuart, Douglas. *Hosea-Jonah*. WBC. Waco, TX: Word Books, 1987.

Study Questions

1. Why did God lead Hosea to marry a promiscuous woman?
2. What did the names of her three children signify?
3. How did God use Hosea's personal problems to speak to the people of Israel?
4. Did warnings of divine judgment mean that Israel was beyond hope in the future?
5. What lessons can we learn from Hosea about forgiving those who have wronged us and hurt us?

Chapter 35

JOEL
Day of the Lord

The book of Joel derives its name from its central character. His Hebrew name *yoʻel* combines the names Yahweh and Elohim, meaning "Yahweh is God." Nothing is known today of the prophet Joel except that he was the son of Pethuel. The temple references found throughout the book (1:8–10,13–14; 2:17) have caused some to speculate that he may also have been a priest. The book's multiple references to Zion and the house of the Lord (1:9–14; 2:15–17; 3:1–6,16–21) indicate that he probably lived near Jerusalem.

BACKGROUND

No chronological data is disclosed in the book. Therefore, biblical scholars have to depend on internal factors to date this prophecy. Three completely **different dates** have been suggested for the original composition: (1) early preexilic (835–830 BC), (2) late preexilic (609–585 BC), and (3) postexilic (515–350 BC). The latter view is argued on the basis of the reference to Greeks (3:6) and the assumption that the temple references are to the rebuilt second temple. Conservative scholars have generally preferred either of the preexilic dates, arguing that the reference to the valley of Jehoshaphat (3:12) fits with preexilic times since Jehoshaphat (872– 848 BC) was the last godly king of Judah prior to Joash. Also, the prophet lists Judah's preexilic enemies as Tyre, Sidon, Philistia, Egypt, Edom, and the Sabeans (Joel 3:2–19) while failing to mention Assyria, Babylon, and Persia from exilic and postexilic times.

Valley of Jehoshaphat (Kidron Valley) in Jerusalem.

378

The dating of Joel does not significantly affect its message, for if Joel ministered before or after the exile, his message demonstrates that the people had not fully accepted the warnings and admonitions of earlier prophets. They continued to struggle with spiritual lethargy, misplaced priorities, and outright disobedience to Yahweh's commands. Joel announced that God sent the recent locust plague in order to awaken His people from the spiritual dullness and warned that even greater disaster in the form of yet another **military invasion** would occur if the people did not soon change their ways. The positive and repentant response of the people to Joel's message ultimately transformed this warning of judgment into a promise of blessing.

Locust swarm.

Hebrew Highlight

Locust. Hebrew ארבה (*'arbeh*) is the common Hebrew term for locust, as in the plague against Egypt (Exod 10:4). The unique use of four different Hebrew words for "locusts" in Joel 1:4 emphasizes the totality of their destruction. The *chasil* indicates the caterpillar stage, *yeleq* is a "young locust" that could hop but not fly, *gazam* is the "devouring locust," and *govai* means a "swarm of locusts."

Outline

I. The Locust Plague and a Call to Lament (Joel 1)
II. The Imminent Day of the Lord and Call to Repent (Joel 2:1–17)
III. The Ultimate Day of the Lord (Joel 2:18–32)
IV. The Future Judgment of the Nations (Joel 3:1–21)

MESSAGE

I. The Locust Plague and a Call to Lament (Joel 1)

In the aftermath of an unusually severe **locust plague**, the prophet Joel called the people of Israel to come to the temple and lament. Moses had warned the nation that if Israel was disobedient to Yahweh's commands, the covenant curse of locusts would fall on them (cf. Deut 28:38,42). The Lord sent locusts as one of the plagues

---

What Is the "Day of the Lord"?

The "Day of the Lord" is a prominent motif in the Old Testament prophets and refers to a **day of battle** when Yahweh would dramatically intervene on earth to accomplish His work of judgment and salvation. Kings in the ancient Near East often boasted of their ability to defeat their enemies in a single day, and Yahweh would destroy His foes in the same decisive manner when He came down to earth in His awesome power as the great King and Warrior (cf. Amos 1:2; Hab 3:2–15). The concept of the Day of the Lord was likely rooted in Israel's holy war traditions which celebrated how Yahweh intervened to deliver Israel from her enemies (cf. Exod 15:1–18; Judg 5:4–5). The prophets also emphasized that the Day of the Lord would first be a time of judgment for Israel. The people mistakenly looked forward to this day as a time of God's deliverance and failed to realize that they had become the Lord's enemies through their disobedience and unfaithfulness (Amos 5:18–20). The Lord would first lead the armies that fought against Israel and then would ultimately turn and deliver His people (Isa 29:1–8).

The prophets employed "Day of the Lord" terminology to refer both to the near events of their own day and to Yahweh's work of judgment and salvation in the eschatological last days. Thus, the prophets could warn that the Day of the Lord was "near" as enemy armies prepared to attack Israel and Judah (cf. Joel 1:15; Zeph 1:7), but they also anticipated a final Day of the Lord that would involve all peoples and nations (cf. Isa 2:7–22; Zech 14:1–21). In continuity with the prophets, the writers of the New Testament employ "Day of the Lord" terminology to the judgments and salvation of the last days associated with the second coming of Christ (cf. Matt 24:42; 1 Cor 5:5; 1 Thess 5:2–5; 2 Thess 2:2–3; 1 Pet 3:10–12).

---

against the Egyptians in the exodus (Exod 10:4–19), but now He punished His own people with the destructive insects (cf. Amos 4:9). Joel views the locust like an invading army; wave after wave of locusts had decimated the land. Drunkards awakened to discover they had no more wine. The priests were no longer able to present their grain and drink offerings, and the farmers mourned the destruction of their crops. The prophet mentioned eight specific crops to highlight the extent of the food shortages.

This crisis called for the people to **lament (1:13–14)**. They were to call a public fast and a solemn assembly to cry out to the Lord in lamentation. Although initially there is no call for repentance, we can assume that some of these lamenters would also confess their sins and pray for the Lord's forgiveness and mercy. Joel warned that failure to seek God's mercy might bring more judgment. The "Day of the Lord" was near, and the Lord was about to bring even greater destruction upon Israel. The prophet himself modeled how the people could turn to the Lord. He lamented the devastating effects of the famine in Israel and called for Yahweh to help His people.

II. The Imminent Day of the Lord and Call to Repent (Joel 2:1–17)

The prophet called for the sounding of an alarm and warned of a second locust invasion that would attack the land. These locusts blackened the sky because of their mass numbers and devoured the crops and vegetation of the land like a consuming fire. Israel's defensive walls provided no barrier to this invading enemy. While Joel may have warned of an actual locust plague even greater in scope than the one depicted in the first chapter, the locusts in chap. 2 more likely represent the human army of an enemy nation that would sweep through the land. The Assyrian annals and other ancient Near Eastern literature compared human armies to locusts, and the numbers, movements, and sounds of a locust swarm resembled that of an invading army.[1] Whereas Yahweh had fought with and for the people of Israel at many times in the past, He would now lead this powerful army against Israel. Failure to respond to the locust plague in chap. 1 would lead to the greater judgment of an **enemy invasion** (depicted as a locust swarm).

Joel repeated his call for repentance, fasting, and a solemn assembly (2:12–17), stressing that true repentance not only involved the external wearing of sackcloth but also an internal rending of the heart. The motivation behind the call to repentance was Yahweh's gracious and merciful character, which meant He might turn from the judgment He had threatened to send if the people turned from their sinful ways. Even in judgment the Lord acted graciously in sending the lesser judgment of the locust plague as a wake-up call that He was about to send the greater calamity of military invasion. Although the text does not state it explicitly, between 2:17 and 18 there appears to be a **rare example of obedience** to prophetic preaching. Priests took Joel's warnings of judgment seriously and called a sacred assembly as the prophet instructed. With contrite hearts people prayed that the Lord would spare them from the coming judgment.

III. The Ultimate Day of the Lord (Joel 2:18–32)

At some point Israel's genuine repentance and heartfelt prayers for mercy will mark a turning point, and God's action will change from one of judgment to one of **promise and hope**. In His zeal for Israel, the Lord will restore the crops the locusts destroyed and drive away the army that threatened the land. The people will rejoice in their abundance and prosperity, and the Lord would even repay them for what the locusts had destroyed. Yahweh's covenant faithfulness to Israel will lead them to acknowledge Him as their Lord, and they will never again need to experience judgment if they remained faithful to Him.

Joel anticipated an even **greater future restoration** when the Lord would pour out His Spirit on all peoples in 2:28–32. In past times the Lord primarily gave His Spirit to select leaders, but at this future time He will give His Spirit to all kinds of people—young and old, male and female. The prophets Isaiah (Isa 59:21) and Ezekiel (Ezek 36:26–27) also promised that this age of future blessing would involve the pouring out of God's Spirit in new and fresh ways. This outpouring of the Spirit would occur at a time when cataclysmic signs in the heavens and on the earth warned of the impending arrival of God's final judgment. Even in this terrible time of judgment, those who genuinely call upon the Lord will be saved.

The apostle Peter announced that Joel's prophecy was fulfilled typically and analogically with the outpouring of the Holy Spirit on the day of Pentecost (Acts 2:15–21). Pentecost and the giving of the Spirit to believers today is the initial fulfillment of Joel's prophecy, but the **ultimate fulfillment** of this prophecy awaits the catastrophic events of the end times (Rev 6:12–17) and the full restoration of Israel at the time of Christ's earthly kingdom (cf. Acts 3:19–21; Rom 11:26–27). Joel's original prophecy focused on the giving of the Spirit to all Jews and whoever calls on the name of the Lord, but the fuller revelation in Acts clarifies that the prophecy even includes Gentiles as well. The outpouring of the Spirit on Gentiles is an important focus in the book of Acts (Acts 10:44–48; 11:15–18; 15:8–9).

IV. The Future Judgment of the Nations (Joel 3:1–21)

The future restoration of Israel will also involve the judgment of the nations. Like other prophets Joel prophesied a final assault on Israel by the **armies of the nations** (Ezekiel 38; Zeph 3:1–8; Zechariah 12; 14; cf. Rev 19:11–21), and the Lord will gather these nations to destroy them in retribution for their mistreatment of Israel. The book of Joel begins with the "Day of the Lord" as a time of judgment upon Israel (1:15) and concludes with this day as judgment for the nations. Also in line with the Old Testament prophetic tradition, Joel announced that the Day of the Lord included both the imminent judgment of Israel's historical enemies responsible for her exile and the future enemies of the Lord and His people in the last days (see p. 380). Joel's command for Israel to beat their plowshares into swords and their pruning hooks into spears (3:10) reversed the prophecies of peace and the end of warfare in Isa 2:2–4 and Mic 4:1–4. The warriors of Israel would reap a great harvest when they defeated their enemies and would then enjoy a time of unending peace and prosperity.

THEOLOGICAL SIGNIFICANCE

Joel warned that the devastation of a recent locust plague was merely prelude to the judgment of military invasion if Israel did not turn from its sinful ways. When the people responded to the warning that "the Day of the Lord" was "near," the Lord promised to bless His people and to restore what they had lost in judgment. This blessing foreshadowed the **future restoration of Israel** when the Lord would pour out His Spirit, judge the nations, and enable His people perpetually to enjoy the security and abundance of the Promised Land. Joel's prophecy concerning the outpouring of the Spirit was initially fulfilled with the giving of the Spirit at Pentecost, demonstrating that the last days prophesied by the prophets were inaugurated with the first coming of Christ. The Church presently enjoys a taste of the eschatological blessings promised by God in anticipation of Israel's full and final restoration.

For Further Reading

Allen, Leslie C. *The Books of Joel, Obadiah, Jonah, and Micah*. NICOT. Grand Rapids: Eerdmans, 1976.

Baker, David W. *Joel, Obadiah, Malachi*. NIVAC. Grand Rapids: Zondervan, 2006.

Chisholm, Robert B., Jr. "Joel" in *BKC*. Edited by J. F. Walvoord and Roy B. Zuck. Colorado Springs: Victor, 1983.

Garrett, Duane. *Hosea, Joel*. NAC. Nashville: B&H, 1997.

Finley, Thomas J. *Joel, Amos, Obadiah*. WEC. Chicago: Moody, 1990.

McComiskey, Thomas E., ed. *The Minor Prophets: An Exegetical and Expository Commentary*. Grand Rapids: Baker, 2009.

Stuart, Douglas. *Hosea-Jonah*. WBC. Waco, TX: Word Books, 1987.

Study Questions

1. To what natural disasters did Joel compare the Day of the Lord?
2. In what way were Joel's prophecies of the Day of the Lord both imminent and ultimate?
3. How did Peter use Joel's prophecy in his sermon on the day of Pentecost?
4. In light of Joel's warnings and promises, how should we live our lives today?

ENDNOTE

1. Mark W. Chavalas, "Joel," in *Zondervan Illustrated Bible Backgrounds Commentary*, ed. John H. Walton (Grand Rapids: Zondervan, 2009), 5:45.

Chapter 36

AMOS
God's Ultimate Justice

Amos ("burden bearer") prophesied during the reigns of Uzziah (792–740 BC) of Judah and Jeroboam II (793–753 BC) of Israel. The reign of Jeroboam II was a time of unprecedented prosperity in the northern kingdom, and Israel expanded its territories back to the borders of the Davidic-Solomonic Empire (cf. 2 Kgs 14:23–29). Unfortunately, this economic prosperity also brought **spiritual apathy and moral decline**. The northern kingdom began to worship calf idols shortly after breaking away from Judah and the Jerusalem temple (cf. 1 Kings 12). Another main area of disobedience took the form of social injustice, as the rich and powerful exploited the poor and needy. Wealth, possessions, and pleasure took priority over their relationship with God.

BACKGROUND

Amos prophesied around 760 BC, when the Lord sent Amos to warn northern Israel that their time of **unprecedented prosperity** was about to come to an abrupt halt. It would be replaced by a time of national calamity as the Lord judged the people for their sins. Two years after Amos preached in Israel, the Lord sent an earthquake as demonstration of His displeasure (1:1). Archaeological evidence from Hazor and several other ancient Israelite cities appears to confirm this event. Earthquakes were common because Israel lay on the Jordan Rift fault line. This quake was of such a magnitude that it was remembered by the prophet Zechariah some 200 years later (cf. Zech 14:5).

The larger threat facing Israel was the **Assyrian military invasion** that would lead to the fall of Samaria and the northern kingdom less than 25 years after the reign of Jeroboam II. Israelite kings had paid tribute to the Assyrians as early as the ninth century BC, but military threats and concerns closer to home kept the Assyrians occupied and allowed for Jeroboam's expansion of Israel's territories. These conditions would change with the rise of the Neo-Assyrian Empire under Tiglath-pileser III (745–727 BC). Assyria naturally looked to the West for tribute and the expansion of its territories, and Israel was unable to withstand the onslaught of the Assyrian army. While the Assyrians developed a formidable military machine, Israel's apostasy rather than Assyrian military and political might have led to Israel's fall.

Amos was from the small village of Tekoa in Judah (2 Sam 14:2; 2 Chron 11:6), which was just a few miles south of Bethlehem, but God called him to travel north to Israel. He delivered a scathing message that denounced the sins of the **northern kingdom** and warned of the judgment God was preparing to send. Amos was a shepherd and farmer by occupation when the Lord called him as a prophet (1:1; 7:14). The term for "shepherd" (*noqed*) is not the normal Hebrew word for a common shepherd. This word appears elsewhere in the Hebrew Bible only in 2 Kgs 3:4 to describe Mesha, the king of the Moabites, thus suggesting that Amos was a wealthy herds-

Ruins of a small building, probably dating from post-biblical times, at Tekoa, Israel, Amos's hometown.

man or was employed to care for the sheep of a wealthy herdsman when God called him to prophesy. Amos's assertion, "I was not a prophet or the son of a prophet" in 7:14 reflects his situation when called by God. The unusual circumstances behind Amos's calling reflected the urgency of his message, and Amos was obedient to the Lord's calling even when it meant leaving behind his own business ventures. Ironically the Lord called a man who knew the failures of the prosperous herders and farmers in Judah to condemn the abuses of wealth and prosperity in Israel

Outline

I. Eight Oracles of Judgment Against the Nations (Amos 1–2)
II. Three Sermons of the Coming Judgment of Israel (Amos 3–6)
III. Five Visions of Israel's Coming Judgment (Amos 7:1–9:10)
IV. Five Promises of Israel's Restoration (Amos 9:11–15)

MESSAGE

I. Eight Oracles of Judgment Against the Nations (Amos 1–2)

Amos opened his book of prophecies with the startling images of God as a **roaring lion** and a raging storm.[1] The Israelites who believed that God was obligated to protect them no matter what were being presumptuous, assuming that His grace would always be available. They needed to realize that God could not be trifled with or taken lightly. Rather than protecting them from His temple in Jerusalem, Yahweh would break out in judgment against them. The Lord's powerful voice would melt and wither the land. This judgment would include an earthquake that occurred in Israel two years after

Amos's preaching and would culminate with Israel's military defeat and exile at the hands of the Assyrian army.

This section describes the sins and coming judgment of **eight nations**, six foreign nations as well as Judah and Israel. Each oracle begins with the formula, "For three sins . . . , even for four, I will not turn back my wrath" (NIV), a poetic way of expressing that the sins of these people were many and that God was calling them to account. The indictment of these foreign nations focuses on their violence toward Israel and other

Chasm at Tekoa, Israel, the hometown of Amos the prophet.

peoples as the prime example of their wickedness. Damascus tortured the inhabitants of Gilead, their abuse of these people being compared to a sledge with iron teeth for threshing grain. Gaza and Tyre sold Israelites into slavery to the Edomites after taking them as captives. The Edomites and Ammonites carried out ruthless slaughters that included the killing of pregnant women. The Moabites desecrated the royal tomb of the king of Edom and burned the king's bones as an expression of their contempt.

God's sense of **universal justice** meant that He held these nations accountable not only for how they treated Israel but also for how they acted toward one another. The treachery of international relationships reflected the corruption of the human heart. Edom (through Esau) and Ammon and Moab (through Lot) were blood relatives of Israel, but they showed no kindness or compassion toward Israel in times of warfare. In selling Israelites into slavery, the merchant city of Tyre acted treacherously in disregarding covenant commitments it made to Israel.

The judgment of these peoples reflected that the Lord was God of all nations and not just of Israel. Amos characterized their sins as "transgressions/rebellion" (*pesha`*), indicating that these nations like Judah and Israel were guilty of **covenant unfaithfulness** toward Yahweh (see p. 387). The Mosaic covenant and its statutes and stipulations were only for the people of Israel, but all nations related to God under the terms of the Noahic covenant established after the flood, which stipulated that judgment would fall on those who practiced violence and bloodshed (cf. Gen 9:5–7). Throughout history God has judged wicked nations that violated His standards of judgment and righteousness, and Isa 24:1–5 pictures a final judgment of all nations based on "the everlasting covenant" established between God and all of humanity in the days of Noah.[2]

Amos's **Israelite audience** would have greatly enjoyed and approved of everything the prophet had proclaimed in his first seven oracles. He had announced judgment against the surrounding nations and against their bitter rivals to the south. They were led astray because they rejected God's covenant instructions. Many probably were surprised to hear Amos preaching judgment against his own countrymen.

Hebrew Highlight

Transgression/Rebellion. Hebrew, פֶּשַׁע (*pesha*ʿ) is one of several Old Testament terms for sin, and its noun/verb form appears 12 times in the book of Amos. Amos used this term to characterize the sins of the eight nations that are the objects of Yahweh's judgment in Amos 1–2 (cf. 1:3,6,9,11,13; 2:1,4,6). The prophets commonly used this term to describe Israel's sins because it conveyed the ideas of willful rebellion and violation of covenant standards. At the human level, the verb *pasha*ʿ refers to the breaking of a political alliance or treaty (cf. 1 Kgs 12:19; 2 Kgs 1:1; 3:5,7) or to the breaking of an agreement between two parties (Gen 31:36). This rebellion is comparable to treason. Israel's sin was they had rebelled against Yahweh and had rejected His authority as covenant Lord over their lives (cf. Isa 1:2; Jer 2:8,29). Yahweh warned through the prophets that He would severely punish Israel for their rebellion and disobedience to His commands (cf. Amos 3:14; Hos 8:1), but the Lord would also forgive when sinners turned from their rebellious ways (Ezek 18:30–31).

However, after gaining their approval, Amos turned the tables on his audience by announcing that Yahweh's judgment would also fall on Israel. The prophet reserved the longest list of specific sins for the oracle against Israel, highlighting their excessive oppression of their own people, forgetting God's gracious acts, and rejecting God's word through the prophets. Thus God will destroy Israel's army, for they were no better than the pagan nations who worshipped other gods.

II. Three Sermons of the Coming Judgment of Israel (Amos 3–6)

This section of the book expands on the initial oracle of judgment against Israel in 2:6–16. With incredible bravery Amos left the security of Judah to travel north to call the northern kingdom to repentance. His first three messages are introduced by the call to "Hear this word" in 3:1; 4:1; and 5:1 (NIV) and the last two with the announcement of "woe" upon Israel (5:18; 6:1). The **prophecies of judgment** demanded a response because they were not absolute predictions of what must happen in the future as much as they were warnings of what would happen if Israel did not repent and change its ways. By

Sycamore fig on the shore of the Sea of Galilee. Amos took care of sycamore fig trees.

seeking the Lord and practicing true justice, Israel could avert disaster and experience blessing instead of judgment.

Amos sounded the warning alarm by reminding the people of Israel that their covenantal status did not grant them exemption from God's judgment; in fact, it increased their **responsibility and accountability** (3:1–2). God would judge Israel because He held His chosen people to a higher standard of behavior. With a series of rhetorical questions taken from everyday life, Amos very simply illustrated the principle of cause and effect. Lions roar because they have prey, birds fall when a trap is set, and the Lord would be the cause of the disaster that would fall on the city of Samaria. If the people did not repent, judgment would be severe, and the invasion of a foreign army would leave Israel like a lamb torn out of the mouth of a lion. Ironically, the winged lion (*shedu*) was the national symbol of Assyria, which God would bring against the northern kingdom. God will destroy their temple in Bethel and all their opulent homes if they do not repent (3:14–15).

These human-faced monumental shedu *from Assyria date from the time of Ashurnasirpal II (ninth century BC).*

The theme of warning carries over into chap. 4. With biting sarcasm Amos compared the wealthy **women of Samaria** to well-fed cattle in that they oppressed the poor and were consumed with their own selfish pleasures. While they presently lived in pleasure, a time was coming when they would be led away as captives with hooks in their noses. These disasters were the specific covenant curses Moses had warned the Lord would bring against Israel if they were disobedient to His commandments:

- lack of food (Amos 4:6; cf. Lev 26:20; Deut 28:38–40)
- drought (Amos 4:7–8; cf. Lev 26:19; Deut 28:22–24)
- blight and mildew on their crops (Amos 4:9; cf. Deut 28:22)
- locusts invasions that destroyed their crops (Amos 4:9; cf. Deut 28:38)
- pestilence and disease (Amos 4:10; cf. Lev 26:16,25; Deut 28:21–22,27–28, 58–61)
- military defeat and exile (Amos 4:10–11; cf. Lev 26:17,36–39; Deut 28:49–57)

They were to prepare to meet God, not as their Savior but as their Judge.

The Prophets and Social Justice

In giving the Mosaic law, the Lord provided commandments that would remove the burden of poverty if Israel would obey them (Deut 15:4). The wealthy had a special responsibility to care for the **poor and the needy**. They were to lend money without interest (Deut 23:19–20) and to allow the poor to glean in their fields (Lev 19:9–10; Deut 24:19–22). Judges were not to deny justice to the poor (Exod 23:6) and were to have special regard for the plight of widows and orphans (Deut 10:18). Debts were to be cancelled every seven years (Deut 15:11) and land sold because of debt was to revert to the family of the original owner in the Year of Jubilee (Leviticus 25).

However, by the time of the writing prophets in the eighth century BC, the disparity between the rich and the poor in Israel was shameful because those with wealth and influence increasingly oppressed the disadvantaged. Thus, the call for justice was a recurring theme in the preaching of the prophets as they reminded the people of the uncomfortable truth that there was an inseparable connection between love for God and concern for one's neighbor.

> Hate evil, love good; maintain justice in the courts. Perhaps the LORD God Almighty will have mercy on the remnant of Joseph. (Amos 5:15 NIV)

> He has showed you, O man, what is good. And what does the LORD require of you? To act justly and to love mercy and to walk humbly with your God. (Mic 6:8 NIV)

The prophetic call for social justice carries over into the New Testament. Jesus demonstrated special concern for the outcasts of society (Luke 16:19–30; John 4:7–26) and reminded those who were His true followers to provide for others through simple acts of compassion (Matt 25:31–46). In the early church those who had more than they needed willingly shared with those who did not have enough (Acts 2:45; 4:34–37), and James instructed that concern for widows and orphans was at the heart of true religion (Jas 1:27). Christians today are embracing their responsibility to practice social justice by feeding the hungry, sharing with the poor, standing for the unborn, and caring for the sick as an essential component of gospel ministry.

Continuing to emphasize the severity of the coming judgment, Amos 5 opens with a **funeral lament** over the impending fall of Israel as a nation. Only 10 percent of the people would survive the military defeat, and Israel's only hope of avoiding national destruction and finding life was to "seek" the Lord. More than religious devotion, this seeking the Lord would involve practicing justice toward the poor and needy. As with the lament at the beginning of the chapter, the announcement of "woe" in 5:18–27 conveyed the somber mood of a funeral. They should lament because the people of Israel were deceived about their worship and what would happen on the Day of the Lord. God rejected their worship so the Day of the Lord would bring death, not great joy.

The recurring "**woes**" in 6:1–4 carry forward the message of doom and destruction. Amos contrasted the present luxury of the people of both Judah and Israel with the deprivation they would experience when they were taken away into exile. Amos again challenged Israel's assumption that they were better than the pagan peoples around them. They were not exempt from disaster and would experience military defeat at the hands of the Assyrians, similar to the fate of Calneh in Mesopotamia, Hamath in Syria, and the Philistine city of Gath. The people had become spiritually and morally desensitized as they lounged on their ivory-inlaid couches and pampered themselves with meats, music, and wine. The term for "feasting" (*mirzah*) in v. 7 was used outside of the Bible to refer to pagan religious banquets that included drunken revelry and sexual immorality.[3] Life had become one big party, but those who partied the most would be among the first taken away in exile.

III. Five Visions of Israel's Coming Judgment (Amos 7:1–9:10)

Amos received five visions at the temple in Bethel that initially portray God's grace in delaying the judgment against Israel, but in the end they display His resolve to judge and destroy if the people refuse to repent. In the midst of these visions is the narrative of the confrontation between Amos and the priest of Bethel, reflecting how the prophet's message was ultimately rejected by Israel's corrupt religious leaders in the north. In the first two visions Amos witnessed two natural disasters befalling Israel—a **locust plague** and a **fire** sweeping through the land. The locusts were about to consume all of the vegetation in the land, and the fire was powerful enough to consume both land and water. Amos prayed for God to spare Israel, and God relented from sending these judgments. God's decision to punish Israel was contingent upon human responses to the warnings of judgment, and the Lord was still willing to spare Israel if they repent.

In his third vision Amos saw the Lord measuring a wall with a **plumb line**. The plumb line was a string with a weight attached to it that determined the straightness of a wall. The point of the vision was that Israel did not measure up to God's standards of righteous and that the nation was about to collapse like an unstable wall because of its many sins.

Amos saw a basket of **summer fruit** in his fourth vision, emphasizing that Israel was ripe for

An Arab date vendor.

judgment. The striking word play between "summer fruit" (*qayits*) in 8:1 and "end" (*qets*) (8:2) highlighted that the Lord's patience was exhausted and judgment was near. The harvest of the summer fruits marked the end of Israel's agricultural year, and the judgment would bring an end to Israel as a nation. The joy of their past celebrations in times of prosperity would be turned to mourning.

In the fifth vision Amos once again saw a vision of Yahweh standing (cf. 7:4) and ordering the destruction of Israel's idolatrous **sanctuary at Bethel**. The people of Israel viewed their religious rituals as their protection against calamity, but the site of these rituals would become a place of judgment. Instead of providing protection, the collapsing walls of the sanctuary would fall on those gathered there for worship. To this very day, the ancient ruins of Bethel stand as a witness to the fulfillment of Amos's prophecy.

IV. Five Promises of Israel's Restoration (Amos 9:11–15)

Amos concluded his prophecies of unrelenting judgment with a **message of hope** concerning Israel's future restoration. Critical scholarship has tended to view these hopeful messages as later additions to the prophet's original words. However, Israel's prophetic tradition extending all the way back to the time of Moses was consistent in promising that restoration would follow the judgment of exile (cf. Deut 30:1–10). God promised: (1) to restore the Davidic dynasty, (2) to make Israel victorious over her enemies, (3) agricultural productivity, (4) future prosperity, and (5) permanent settlement in the land. Though the northern kingdom had broken away from the house of David, Amos promised that God would reunite Israel under Davidic rule. Yahweh would **restore the fallen tent** of the Davidic dynasty, and the future Davidic ruler, the Messiah, would lead Israel in triumph over her enemies. The Lord also promised to securely plant Israel in the land so they would never again be taken away into exile. Amos 9:9 foresees the day when Israel will be regathered the second time never to be removed again.

THEOLOGICAL SIGNIFICANCE

Amos warned that Yahweh, like a roaring lion, would bring **judgment** against Judah, Israel, and the nations around them. The Lord would judge the nations for their violence and war crimes and would judge Israel for their false worship and social injustice in violation of His covenant commands. This judgment would bring Israel to the point of national extinction. Despite the Lord's anger, He was patient in providing Israel an opportunity to repent and avoid the impending disaster, but the people refused to turn from their sinful ways.

The Lord would ultimately restore Israel after this time of national judgment. The Lord would restore the Davidic dynasty, a promise that will be fulfilled in the rule of Jesus as the Davidic Messiah. The promises of peace, prosperity, and restoration ultimately will be fulfilled in the messianic kingdom when Jesus rules and reigns on earth for a thousand years (Rev 20:1–6). Amos spoke of the imminent judgment of Israel as the coming "Day of the Lord," and this judgment from past history prefigured the greater judgment of the final Day of the Lord that will fall on all peoples as the prelude for Christ's second coming to establish His kingdom on earth (cf. 1 Thess 5:1–3; 2 Thess 2:3–12; Revelation 7–19).

For Further Reading

Hasel, Gerhard F. *Understanding the Book of Amos*. Grand Rapids: Baker, 1991.

Hubbard, David A. *Joel and Amos: An Introduction and Commentary*. TOTC. Downers Grove: IVP, 1989.

McComiskey, Thomas E., ed. *The Minor Prophets: An Exegetical and Expository Commentary*. Grand Rapids: Baker, 2009.

Motyer, J. A. *The Day of the Lion: The Message of Amos*. Downers Grove: IVP, 1974.

Smith, Billy K. *Amos, Obadiah, Jonah*. NAC. Nashville: B&H, 1995.

Smith, Gary V. *Hosea, Amos, Micah*. NIVAC. Grand Rapids: Zondervan, 2001.

Stuart, Douglas. *Hosea-Jonah*. WBC. Waco, TX: Word, 1987.

Study Questions

1. How did Amos demonstrate his burden to declare God's message?
2. Where did Amos go, risking his life to confront evil?
3. What were the sins of Israel that provoked Amos's preaching?
4. What was the significance of the image of summer fruit?
5. How do acts of social justice demonstrate our faith in God?

ENDNOTES

1. J. A. Motyer, *The Day of the Lion: The Message of Amos* (London: IVP, 1974), 28. Motyer notes that the prophet reverses the normal Hebrew order of words (verb-subject) and places the name of Yahweh first to emphasize the Lord's emphatic displeasure.

2. Robert B. Chisholm Jr., *Handbook on the Prophets* (Grand Rapids: Baker, 2002), 65–66, 381.

3. See Philip J. King and Lawrence E. Stager, *Life in Biblical Israel* (Louisville: WJKP, 2001), 355–57.

Chapter 37

OBADIAH
Doom of Edom

BACKGROUND

Obadiah ("servant of Yahweh") is the **shortest book** in the Old Testament. The short heading of the book of Obadiah provides no details about the prophet or the time of his ministry. Jewish tradition identified the prophet with the Obadiah who served in the court of King Ahab (1 Kgs 18:1–16), but this identification seems unlikely. Some scholars have placed the book in the time of Edom's revolt against Judah in the early part of the ninth century BC (2 Kgs 8:20–22; 2 Chron 21:8–20), but others have suggested Obadiah prophesied in the aftermath of the Babylonian conquest of Judah in 586 BC. Obadiah announced that God would judge Edom (also called Seir in the OT) because of its participation with Judah's enemies in the plundering of Jerusalem.

Other Old Testament texts announce the **downfall of Edom** (Ps 137:7; Isa 34:5–17; Lam 4:21–22; Ezek 25:12–14; 35:1–15), and there are especially close parallels between Obadiah's prophecies and the Edom oracle in Jer 49:7–22. If these texts all refer to the same event, Obadiah appears to be describing what happened shortly after the fall of Jerusalem. Malachi later testified to the fulfillment of the prophecies concerning Edom's downfall (Mal 1:2–4). The Babylonians annexed Edom in 553 BC and brought the Edomite Kingdom to an end. In the fourth century BC, the Nabatean Arabs took control of Edom and established Petra as their capital. The link to the prophecy about Edom in Amos 9:12 perhaps explains the location of Obadiah in the Book of the 12.

The Edomites were **descendants of Esau** and had a stormy relationship with Israel throughout their history. This mirrored the original rivalry between the brothers Jacob and Esau (see Genesis 25–27). During Israel's wilderness wanderings, Edom denied Israel safe passage through their territories (Num 20:14–21). David later conquered Edom and brought it into his empire (2 Sam 8:13–14), and Edom remained under the control of the house of David until its successful revolt during the reign of Jehoram two centuries later (2 Kgs 8:20–22). Over the next 150 years, Judah and Edom had frequent skirmishes over territories and trade routes, and the bitter rivalry culminated with Edom's involvement in the Babylonian destruction of Jerusalem.

A Nabatean temple—"the Khasneh"—carved out of the sandstone cliffs at Petra.

Outline

I. Doom of Edom (Obadiah 1–16)
II. Deliverance of Judah (Obadiah 17–21)

MESSAGE

I. Doom of Edom (Obadiah 1–16)

Edom was lifted up because of **excessive pride**. They trusted in their political and military advisors for their security, and they believed their mountain fortresses made them invulnerable to enemy attack. The narrow canyon leading into Petra insulated them from invasion. However, even though they nested like eagles in a lofty place in the mountains, the rocks and crags would not protect them from the army the Lord was bringing against them. Even their allies would turn against them and plunder their treasures.

The second reason God would judge Edom was their **treatment** of the descendants of their brother when Babylon defeated Jerusalem (vv. 10–14). Instead of helping Judah, the Edomites stood back and watched the Babylonians defeat Jerusalem. Then they went into the city and took whatever they found, laughed, and rejoiced over Judah's defeat. When some Hebrews fled to escape, the Edomites shamefully robbed and imprisoned these helpless refugees. Consequently, God's justice on Edom for violence against Judah on the Day of the Lord will bring God's judgment (vv. 15–16).

II. Deliverance of Judah (Obadiah 17–21)

While the doom of Edom was permanent, judgment was not God's final word for Judah. The Lord would **restore** His people and cause them to triumph over their enemies. Reversing what had happened with the fall of Jerusalem, Judah's exiles would subjugate Edom and rule over their territories. With this restoration of Israel, the kingdom of God would be fully established on earth, indicating an eschatological context for the ultimate fulfillment of Obadiah's prophecies. Ultimately, Mt. Zion will eclipse Mt. Seir. Isaiah 63:1 also predicts the Messiah will march through Edom on His way to establish the kingdom of God on earth.

THEOLOGICAL SIGNIFICANCE

Rather than a nationalistic harangue against a hated enemy, Obadiah's prophecies against Edom are an expression of **God's justice**. The Lord would send a punishment against Edom that was appropriate to its crimes against Judah. Obadiah's prophecies also reflect the working out of God's covenantal promise to Abraham that He would bless those who blessed him and curse those who cursed him (Gen 12:3). Israel was the apple of Yahweh's eye (Zech 2:8), and any nation that attacked Israel would become the target of His wrath. The judgment of the Edomites is also a reminder that God stands opposed to all forms of human arrogance and pride. The Edomites are representative of all of God's enemies, and oracles against Edom appear in eschatological contexts in the Old Testament prophets pointing to the judgment of the last days (cf. Isaiah 34; 63). While judging Edom, God would also restore His people Israel, and the restoration of Israel would be essential to the establishment of God's eschatological kingdom.

For Further Reading

Allen, Leslie C. *The Books of Joel, Obadiah, Jonah, and Micah*. NICOT. Grand Rapids: Eerdmans, 1976.

Baker, David W. *Joel, Obadiah, Malachi*. NIVAC. Grand Rapids: Zondervan, 2006.

McComiskey, Thomas E., ed. *The Minor Prophets: An Exegetical and Expository Commentary*. Grand Rapids: Baker, 2009.

Smith, Billy K. *Amos, Obadiah, Jonah*. NAC. Nashville: B&H, 1995.

Stuart, Douglas. *Hosea-Jonah*. WBC. Waco, TX: Word Books, 1987.

Study Questions

1. What was the connection between Edom and Esau?
2. How did the geography of Edom contribute to their pride and arrogance?
3. Why is the doom of Edom and the deliverance of Judah significant prophetically and eschatologically?
4. What lessons can we learn today from Obadiah's warning and promises?

Chapter 38

JONAH
God's Universal Concern

Jonah ("dove" in Hebrew) was a prophet in Israel from the town of Gath-hepher near Nazareth, who prophesied to **northern Israel** during the reign of Jeroboam II (793–753 BC). Jonah prophesied Jeroboam's military successes in expanding Israel's borders to what they were during the time of the Davidic-Solomonic Empire (2 Kgs 14:25). Jonah's ministry of prophesying blessing and political expansion to Israel certainly stood at odds with his ministry to Nineveh where he provided an opportunity for the Assyrians as Israel's hated enemies to avoid the disaster the Lord planned to bring against them.

Because of the supernatural elements in the story and the implausibility of the people of Nineveh responding to the warnings of a Hebrew prophet, modern critical scholars tend to view the story of Jonah as an allegory, parable, or prophetic legend. The book clearly has a didactic purpose to teach about God's redemptive concern for the Assyrian people, but no literary clues within the book itself suggest that the book of Jonah should be read as anything other than a straightforward historical narrative. The **supernatural elements** are explained by God's involvement in Jonah's life, and similar miraculous events appear in the historical narratives of the lives of Elijah and Elisha (1–2 Kings). Jesus affirmed the historicity of the Jonah narrative on two separate occasions: when He compared His coming burial to Jonah being in the fish for three days and when He spoke of the judgment of Nineveh in connection with the cities of Israel in His own day (Matt 12:39–41; Luke 11:29–30).

Nineveh's repentance does not mean the whole city or the whole Assyrian nation was converted to Yahweh. The city temporarily turned from its wicked and violent ways, and the Lord spared the city from destruction in response to this repentance. However, it is doubtful if these changes were long lasting, for Jonah's warnings only delayed the city's destruction. In the **next century** the prophet Nahum announced the coming judgment of Nineveh for its violence and bloodshed. The Babylonians and Medes captured and destroyed Nineveh in 612 BC. Several incidents appear to have disposed the residents of Nineveh to take seriously Jonah's warnings of divine judgment. A total eclipse of the sun occurred in 763 BC, portending evil for all of the land of Assyria. An earthquake, another sign of divine displeasure, took place during the reign of Ashur-dan III (773–756 BC). Famine and general civil unrest were widespread in Assyria from 765 to 759 BC. The Ninevites might naturally believe the gods were angry with them during such a time of national crisis.

BACKGROUND

Nineveh was a prominent Mesopotamian city located on the Tigris River. Its origin dates back before 3000 BC. The city was an important center for the worship of the goddess Ishtar, and its strategic location enabled the city to control important trade routes by land and river. The narrator portrays Nineveh as a "great city" (1:2; 3:2) and a "very important city" (lit. "a great city to/before God") (3:3 NIV). The statement that "a visit required three days" in 3:3 (NIV) does not refer to how long it took to walk around the city walls. More likely it refers to how long it would take Jonah to communicate his message at the various city gates and public

The ancient seaport of Joppa (1:3).

squares. The statement in Jonah 4:11 that Nineveh had a population of 120,000 likely refers to the entire administrative district of Nineveh rather than to just the city proper.

Critics have pointed to the mention of the "king of Nineveh" in Jonah 3:6 as a historical anachronism because Nineveh did not actually become the capital of Assyria until several decades after the time of Jonah's ministry. However, evidence suggests that Nineveh was at least an alternate **royal residence** when Jonah preached there. The reference to the "king of Nineveh" rather than the "king of Assyria" conforms to Old Testament usage elsewhere in which a king is identified with the capital city or another prominent city in his empire (cf. 1 Kgs 21:1; 2 Chron 24:23). Another possibility is that the "king of Nineveh" in Jonah refers to the governor or noble who ruled over the city and its administrative province.

In the early seventh century BC, the Assyrian king **Sennacherib** made Nineveh his capital. Sennacherib expanded the city so that it covered some 1,800 acres, and he built an impressive palace there. Sennacherib's Nineveh was surrounded by a protective double wall nearly 60 feet thick. The library built by Ashurbanipal (669–627 BC) was one of Nineveh's most important buildings and a significant archaeological discovery from this period.

Outline

I. Jonah Flees from His Prophetic Calling (Jonah 1–2)
  A. Jonah's Disobedience and Its Consequences (Jonah 1)
  B. Jonah's Deliverance and Thanksgiving (Jonah 2)
II. Jonah Fulfills His Prophetic Calling (Jonah 3–4)
  A. Jonah's Obedience and Nineveh's Repentance (Jonah 3)
  B. Jonah's Displeasure at the Lord's Salvation (Jonah 4)

The book of Jonah is a **two-part story**. The first part of the book is about God's mercy to His disobedient prophet. The Lord spared Jonah even when the prophet disobeyed the command to go and preach to Nineveh. The second part of the book is about God's mercy to the wicked people of Nineveh. The Lord spared the city because of their repentant response when Jonah warned of their coming destruction. In this two-part structure, chaps. 1 and 3 parallel one another, as do chaps. 2 and 4. In chaps. 1 and 3, Jonah interacts with two different groups of people who worship pagan gods— the sailors on the ship to Tarshish in chap. 1 and the people of Nineveh in chap. 3. In both of these chapters, these foreigners come to fear the Lord and in many ways present themselves as more spiritually sensitive to the Lord than Jonah.

JONAH 1	JONAH 2	JONAH 3	JONAH 4
Jonah interacts with foreigners: the sailors come to know the true God	Jonah thanks God for his own salvation	Jonah interacts with foreigners: the Ninevites come to know the true God	Jonah complains to God about Nineveh's salvation

This structure demonstrates that Jonah's response to the salvation of the Ninevites is the real key to this story. Jonah confessed that "salvation comes from the LORD" (2:9 NIV) and rejoiced in how the Lord delivered him from drowning in the sea, but the prophet objected when the Ninevites received the same mercy and grace that was extended to him. The story of Jonah contains three great acts of salvation:

Three Great Acts of Salvation in the Book of Jonah

1. God spares the sailors, and the sailors **worship** (Jonah 1:16)
2. God spares Jonah, and Jonah **worships** (Jonah 2:1–9)
3. God spares Nineveh, and Jonah **complains** (Jonah 4:1–8)

The real problem in the story is **Jonah's prejudice** against the Assyrians. Jonah's unresolved anger and the Lord's unanswered question, "Should I not be concerned about that great city?" (Jonah 4:11 NIV) at the end of the book reflect the difference between the Lord's heart and the prophet's. The Lord has a redemptive concern for all peoples, while Jonah believed that the Lord's mercy and grace were only for Israel because of its special status as the chosen people of God. The lack of resolution as the book closes invites the reader to examine if his or her heart is more in line with the angry prophet or the merciful God.

MESSAGE

I. Jonah Flees from His Prophetic Calling (Jonah 1–2)

A. Jonah's Disobedience and Its Consequences (Jonah 1)

Jonah's disobedience to the word of the Lord led the prophet in a dangerous direction. Jonah boarded a **ship for Tarshish** (west) in the opposite direction of Nineveh (east), believing he could flee from the presence of the Lord. Jonah was in fact embarking on a downward path of destruction. The prophet "went down" (*yarad*) to Joppa to board the ship and then "went down" (*yarad*) into the ship itself (1:3 NASB). During the storm at sea, the prophet had "gone down" (*yarad*) to the lower deck of the ship. The sailors eventually threw Jonah down into the sea, and the prophet "went down" (*yarad*) (2:6) toward a watery

Phoenician trader (merchant).

grave until the Lord rescued him from drowning.

When the Lord sent the storm on the sea, the pagan sailors on board the ship with Jonah were far more spiritually aware and sensitive to the involvement of some god than was the wayward prophet. While the storm was raging, the sailors prayed to their gods while Jonah slept. Jonah admitted his guilt to the sailors but not to God (1:10–12), while the sailors prayed for God not to hold them accountable for his death (1:14).

Despite Jonah's direct disobedience, the **Lord remained sovereign**. Throughout the story, the Lord directs and controls the forces of nature to bring Jonah back into conformity with His plan. The Lord "sent" a storm onto the sea (1:4 NIV) and then He "appointed" (*manah*) a fish (1:17), a plant (4:6), a worm (4:7), and a hot wind (4:8) to fulfill His purposes in Jonah's life. The winds, animals, and plants obeyed the Lord, even if His prophet did not. No matter how much Jonah objected, the Lord made sure that His messenger would arrive in Nineveh. By providing the fish, the Lord spared Jonah from drowning and from the death he deserved for disobeying the Lord's command.

B. Jonah's Deliverance and Thanksgiving (Jonah 2)

Jonah's prayer is his response of thanksgiving to the Lord for saving him from death. The prayer closely follows the form of songs of thanksgiving in the Psalms where the worshipper expresses thanks to God for some specific act of deliverance. Hezekiah offered a similar prayer when the Lord healed him from his life-threatening illness and extended his life for 15 years (Isaiah 38). These songs of thanksgiving

Restored gate at the site of the ancient city of Nineveh, located on the left bank of the Tigris River (Iraq today).

accompanied the offering of sacrifices and the payment of vows the petitioner made to the Lord when praying for deliverance. From the belly of the fish, Jonah recalled how he cried out to the Lord as he was drowning at sea. Jonah portrayed himself as descending to the underworld (Sheol) because he was as good as dead. He said: "You raised my life from the Pit" (2:6). Therefore, Jesus referred to His own resurrection as "the sign of . . . Jonah" (Matt 12:39–41; 16:4).

II. Jonah Fulfills His Prophetic Calling (Jonah 3–4)

A.   Jonah's Obedience and Nineveh's Repentance (Jonah 3)

The story turns from the salvation of Jonah to the **salvation of the Ninevites**. Jonah obeyed the second time the Lord commanded him to go to Nineveh, and once there he began to announce that the city would be destroyed in 40 days. The king and people of Nineveh took the warning of destruction seriously and expressed their repentance by fasting from food and drink, wearing sackcloth, crying out to God, and turning from their violent behavior. Because the people of Nineveh turned from their "evil" actions (*ra`ah*), the Lord turned from sending the "destruction" (*ra`ah*) He had planned for the city (3:10 NIV). The Assyrians repented and God relented. When the prophet announced judgment, even in an unqualified and unconditional way, the pronouncement included the possibility that true repentance would lead to the avoidance of the disaster that was threatened (cf. Jer 18:7–10; Joel 2:12–14; Zeph 2:3).

B. Jonah's Displeasure at the Lord's Salvation (Jonah 4)

Rather than rejoicing in his successful preaching mission and the salvation of the Ninevites, **Jonah was angered** that the Lord spared the city. The possibility that the Lord might show mercy to the Assyrians was why Jonah refused to go to the city in the first place. Jonah's statement about the Lord's grace and compassion appears elsewhere in the Old Testament with reference to the Lord's treatment of Israel (cf. Exod 34:6–7; Num 14:18–19; Joel 2:13), but Jonah is scandalized that the Lord would show the same grace to the people of Nineveh. Jonah hated the Assyrians as the enemy of his people and wanted the Lord to give them justice, not mercy. Jonah preferred death over going to Nineveh, and he asked the Lord once again to take his life. The Lord then used a vine, a worm, and a scorching east wind to show the prophet Jonah his misplaced priorities. If Jonah was absorbed in his own comfort and concerned about an insignificant plant that provided shade from the heat, should not the Lord be concerned about the welfare of the 120,000 inhabitants of Nineveh?

THEOLOGICAL SIGNIFICANCE

The story of Jonah is a reminder that the Lord's plan of salvation extends beyond Israel to include **all the nations**, even those who were Israel's greatest enemies. The Lord promised Abraham that he would become a blessing to all peoples (Gen 12:3), and foreigners like Rahab, Ruth, and the queen of Sheba came to know the Lord as the true God. God even demonstrated His grace to the hated Assyrians. The promise of the Old Testament is that the salvation of Israel would extend to nations and that all peoples (Isa 49:6) would come to know and worship the God of Israel (Pss 22:27–30; 47:9; 145:10–13; Isa 2:1–5; Zeph 3:9–10; Zech 14:16). The prophet Isaiah even promised that Israel, Egypt, and Assyria would be the three peoples of God in the future kingdom (Isa 19:19–25).

The Lord demonstrates the wideness of **His mercy** by granting forgiveness to the worst of sinners. God's mercy to the Assyrians also provided hope to the Israelites. If the Lord was willing to forgive the people of Nineveh when they repented, then He would certainly forgive His own people if they turned from their sinful ways. Unfortunately, the Lord sent Israel and Judah away into exile because they did not respond to the warnings of the prophets.

Hebrew Highlight

Sackcloth. Hebrew שׂק (s´aq) comes into English from the Hebrew through Greek and Latin. Sackcloth was a rough, dark-colored, inexpensive cloth made of goat or camel hair (cf. Isa 50:3; Matt 3:4). It was used for storage bags but was also worn as a sign of mourning and repentance (Neh 9:1). Middle Eastern peoples often expressed grief by tearing their clothes and covering themselves with dust or ashes, but wearing sackcloth was an act of humiliation to indicate true repentance (Jer 4:8).

For Further Reading

Baker, David W., T. Desmond Alexander, and Bruce K. Waltke. *Obadiah, Jonah, Micah*. TOTC. Downers Grove, IL: IVP, 1988.

Bruckner, James. *Jonah, Nahum, Habakkuk, Zephaniah*. The NIVAC. Grand Rapids: Zondervan, 2004.

McComiskey, Thomas E., ed. *The Minor Prophets: An Exegetical and Expository Commentary*. Grand Rapids: Baker, 2009.

Stuart, Douglas. *Hosea-Jonah*. WBC. Waco, TX: Word, 1987.

Study Questions

1. What was Jonah's real problem: fear or prejudice?
2. Does everyone get a second chance to obey God?
3. What did Jonah do when the people of Nineveh repented?
4. What was God's real concern for the people and the prophet?
5. How should we express God's mercy to our enemies?

Chapter 39

MICAH
Divine Lawsuit

Micah was a prophet in Judah during the reigns of Jotham, Ahaz, and Hezekiah (750–687 BC). Therefore, he was a contemporary of the prophet Isaiah. He prophesied concerning both the northern and southern kingdoms at the height of the Assyrian crisis. Micah and Isaiah shared a common belief that the Lord would **restore** Zion as the center of His worldwide kingdom of peace and righteousness (Isa 2:1–5; Mic 4:1–5). Micah's name means "Who is like Yahweh?" After the Lord revealed His plans of judgment and then salvation for Israel, the prophet himself exclaimed, "Who is a God like You?" (Mic 7:18).

BACKGROUND

During Micah's ministry Samaria fell to the Assyrians in 722 BC, and Judah became an **Assyrian vassal**. The Assyrian king Sennacherib invaded Judah and captured 46 cities. Jerusalem was spared in 701 BC when the angel of the Lord destroyed the Assyrian army that surrounded the city in response to Hezekiah's faith and prayer for the Lord's help (Isaiah 36–37). Micah was from the village of Moresheth (Mic 1:1) and even had the courage to announce the impending judgment of his own hometown (Mic 1:14). Micah and Isaiah made an interesting tandem. Micah was an outsider from a small village whose preaching influenced Hezekiah's repentant response when the Assyrians invaded his land (Jer 26:17–19). Isaiah, on the other hand, was an insider with access to the royal court who counseled Hezekiah to trust in the Lord during the Assyrian crisis (Isaiah 36–39).

Outline

I. Message of Judgment: "Hear All People" (Micah 1–2)
II. Message of Hope: "Hear, Heads of Jacob" (Micah 3–5)
III. Message of Pardon: "Hear, O Mountains" (Micah 6–7)

The command to "**hear**" (*shema*) introduces the three major sections of the book (1:1; 3:1; 6:1), and each section contains a message of judgment and salvation. The call to "hear" or "listen" reminded his Jewish audience of Deut 6:4 ("Hear, O Israel:

The LORD our God, the LORD is one," NIV). This basic statement of the Jewish faith is known as the *Shema* and would have immediately come to their minds as a call from God Himself.

MICAH 1:1–2:13	MICAH 3:1–5:15	MICAH 6:1–7:20
Judgment (1:1–2:11)	Judgment (3:1–12)	Judgment (6:1–7:6)
Salvation (2:12–13)	Salvation (4:1–5:15)	Salvation (7:7–20)

MESSAGE

The extended message of salvation at the center of the book, as well as the emphasis on salvation at the end of each section, reflects Micah's focus on the hope of Israel's future salvation. In each section the message of hope directly reverses the preceding message of judgment. In the first section Micah warned that Judah would go into exile (1:16; 2:4,10), and then God promised that a **remnant** would return from exile (2:12–13). In the middle section the temple would be reduced to a heap of ruins (3:12), but the next verse promises that Zion will become the most exalted place on earth. In the final section, Micah initially laments over the present ruin of Israel and Judah (7:1–6), but then he ends the chapter with a praise song in anticipation of the future deliverance (7:18–20). The Lord's grace and covenant faithfulness would triumph over Israel's sin and infidelity.

I. Message of Judgment: "Hear All People" (Micah 1–2)

Micah portrayed the Lord marching out from His holy temple as a warrior and the earth crumbling and melting at His presence. The object of the Lord's anger was Israel and Judah, His own people. The Lord would first judge Samaria for its idolatry, and then the same fate awaited Jerusalem. Seeing the destiny that awaited his homeland, Micah composed a **lament** for the towns in Judah that would lie in the path of the invading Assyrian army. Word plays on the names of these cities made this lament

The Problem of Social Injustice

"Perhaps, after the fall of Samaria, the social injustices of **elite classes** are exacerbated by a flood of refugees into Jerusalem from the North. The swollen numbers of refugees into Jerusalem increase the demand for food and lower the price of labor. Moreover, in times of drought or other misfortunes, the rich, contrary to the Law, loan money to the poor at exorbitant interests, leading to foreclosures on the property, thereby forcing the free landholder into indentured slavery (cf. 2 Kings 4:1; Neh 5:1–5; Amos 2:6). In other words, by adding field to field the rich cannibalized the poor (Mic 3:1–5; cf. Ezek 34:2–3; Pss 14:4; 53:5; Hab 3:14)."[1]

particularly vivid and would make the inhabitants of these towns take notice as the prophet announced their downfall:

- *Beth Le`aphrah* would roll in the "dust" (`apar*) as a rite of mourning.
- The residents of *Shaphir* ("Beautiful town") would pass by in nakedness and humiliation.
- The residents of *Maroth* (sounds like *mara*, "bitter") would vainly hope for something "good."
- Disaster would come to *Jerusalem* (the city of *shalom*).
- Residents of *Lachish* would hitch up the "horses" (*rakesh*) to their chariots to flee from the enemy, not to fight against them.
- The town of *Moresheth* (sounds like "betrothed") would be given away as a dowry to the invading army.
- A "conqueror" (*yoresh*) would take possession of *Mareshah*.

The invasion would bring a time of disaster to Judah, like when David commanded that news of Saul's death not be broadcast in the Philistine city of Gath or when David himself fled from Saul to caves in Adullam. In his campaign against Judah, Sennacherib captured 46 cities in Judah and surrounded the city of Jerusalem with his troops.

The Lord was angry that **social injustice** became common in Israel and Judah. Through various legal and illegal means, the wealthy and the powerful conspired to steal the land of needy families (2:1–11). In ancient Israel, the land belonged to the Lord, but He gave this land to His people Israel as a special gift. God gave every tribe, clan, and family their property as an allotment from the Lord (Joshua 14). For this reason property in Israel was not permanently to change hands. Land sold because of debt was to be redeemed by the individual or family, and all land reverted to its original owners in the Year of Jubilee, every fiftieth year (Leviticus 25).

Assyrian kings were known for their exceptional cruelty.

To steal family property, as Ahab and Jezebel did with Naboth's vineyard, was to steal the family's inheritance from the Lord, and that was considered a serious crime (1 Kings 21). Because this practice was common, Micah announced that a foreign army would take possession of the land as Israel went away into exile. Because the rich deprived the poor of their land, the Lord would now do the same to them.

The people wanted nothing of Micah's words of judgment. Because of their **mistaken belief** that their covenant with the Lord guaranteed their blessings apart from their responsibility to obey the covenant, they believed it was the prophet's job to announce only good things from the Lord. Micah sarcastically responded that the perfect prophet for them would be one who promised them more beer and wine.

When the Lord finishes His work of judgment, He will restore the remnant of Israel (2:12–13). Like a shepherd He will gather the remnant into His fold so they will be safe and secure from enemy attack. Like a conquering king He will lead His people into battle. The surviving remnant will once again become a powerful nation.

II. Message of Hope: "Hear, Heads of Jacob" (Micah 3–5)

Micah laid the blame for the spiritual and moral corruption of Israel and Judah with their **sinful leaders**. With their greed and disregard for the poor, their rulers had become like cannibals who chopped the people up and made them into stew. The prophets misled the people with their empty promises of "peace" for their own financial gain when the people needed to hear of the Lord's coming judgment. When judgment fell, the Lord would not respond to these corrupt leaders. When they cried out to Him, the Lord would give no answer to those who had failed to show mercy to others, and there would be no revelation from God to guide them through their darkest hour.

Unlike the false prophets of peace, Micah was empowered by the Spirit of God to proclaim the sins of Israel and Judah and to announce that Jerusalem would be destroyed and reduced to a heap of ruins (3:8). In the next century an elder in Jerusalem reflected on how Micah's message prompted the repentance of King Hezekiah (Jer 26:17–19). When Hezekiah heard Micah's warnings, he feared the Lord and sought His face, leading the Lord to relent from destroying Jerusalem. A prophet's words of judgment were not set in stone. If the people repented, there was always the possibility that judgment could be avoided (cf. Jer 18:7–10). Unfortunately, Hezekiah's obedient response to the Lord only delayed the judgment Micah predicted. Subsequent generations turned away from following the Lord, and Micah's prophecies concerning the fall of Jerusalem were ultimately fulfilled.

An extended promise of **Israel's future salvation** stands at the center of the book of Micah in 4:1–5:15. The prophet contrasted the present pitiful condition of Israel with the glories of the future messianic kingdom. Zion soon would be trampled down, but eventually it will be exalted as the center of the Lord's future kingdom. The nations will stream to Zion to worship the Lord and learn His ways. The Lord's rule will bring international peace, and the nations will turn their weapons of warfare into farming

Tel Sandahannah, Old Testament Moresheth-Gath, home of Micah the prophet.

implements. But before this happens, Jerusalem will find itself like a woman in labor, experiencing the pain of exile and having no king. But then the Lord will redeem His people and destroy the enemy armies that will attack Jerusalem. Israel would

Stairs up to Ahab's palace at Samaria.

experience the humiliation of defeat until the Lord raised up for His people a new David who would shepherd the people in the strength of the Lord and gain international renown. The Assyrians, who attacked Israel in the days of Micah, prefigured the enemy nations that would attack Israel in the last days when the Lord would ultimately deliver Israel from all enemies. The rule of Messiah and His people would even extend over the nations that were Israel's oppressors. In the future kingdom Israel would become a powerful nation and a source of blessing to all peoples.

This section includes Micah's famous prophecy of the future **birth of the Messiah** at **Bethlehem** (5:2). God promised to raise up another "ruler over Israel" who would come from Bethlehem, David's hometown. Matthew 2:3–6 quotes this passage on the lips of the chief priests and scribes in response to Herod's question about where the Messiah would be born. Matthew, in turn, sees the fulfillment of Micah's prediction of a future Davidic king whose "origin is from eternity" in the birth of Jesus at Bethlehem.

III. Message of Pardon: "Hear, O Mountains" (Micah 6–7)

In the final judgment section of the book, Micah called the people into the courtroom as the Lord brought a **lawsuit** against His people. The mountains and heavens were called as witnesses to hear the Lord's indictment against Israel because they witnessed the formal sealing of the covenant between the Lord and Israel in the days of Moses (Deut 4:26; 30:19; 31:18). In His indictment the Lord contrasted His past faithfulness to Israel's unfaithfulness and reminded the people of what He expected from them as His covenant partner. The Lord was not primarily interested in Israel's

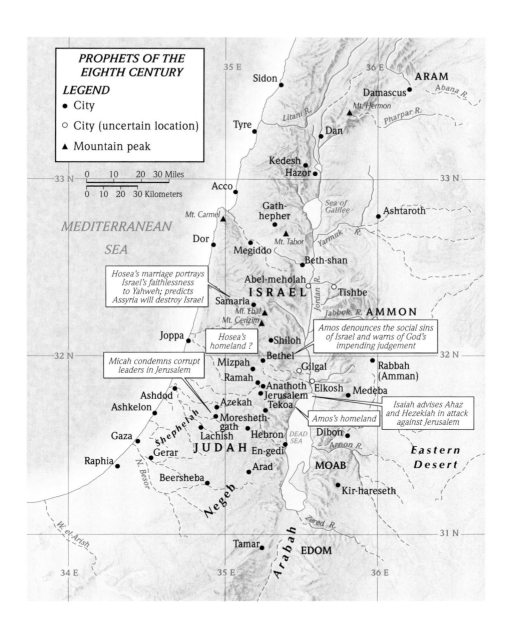

PROPHETS OF THE EIGHTH CENTURY

LEGEND

- City
- ○ City (uncertain location)
- ▲ Mountain peak

0   10   20   30 Miles
0   10   20   30 Kilometers

MEDITERRANEAN SEA

Hosea's marriage portrays Israel's faithlessness to Yahweh; predicts Assyria will destroy Israel

Hosea's homeland ?

Micah condemns corrupt leaders in Jerusalem

Amos denounces the social sins of Israel and warns of God's impending judgement

Amos's homeland

Isaiah advises Ahaz and Hezekiah in attack against Jerusalem

Sidon
Damascus
ARAM
Abana R.
Mt. Hermon
Pharpar R.
Tyre
Litani R.
Dan
Kedesh
Hazor
Acco
Sea of Galilee
Ashtaroth
Gath-hepher
Mt. Carmel
Dor
Mt. Tabor
Yarmuk R.
Megiddo
Beth-shan
Abel-meholah
Jordan R.
Tishbe
ISRAEL
Samaria
Mt. Ebal
Mt. Gerizim
Jabbok R.
AMMON
Joppa
Shiloh
Bethel
Mizpah
Gilgal
Rabbah (Amman)
Ramah
Anathoth
Elkosh
Medeba
Ashdod
Azekah
Jerusalem
Tekoa
Ashkelon
Moresheth-gath
Dibon
Gaza
Shephelah
Lachish
Hebron
DEAD SEA
Arnon R.
En-gedi
JUDAH
Gerar
Eastern Desert
Raphia
N. Besor
Arad
MOAB
Beersheba
Negeb
Kir-hareseth
Zered R.
W. el-Arish
Tamar
Arabah
EDOM

33 N   33 N
32 N   32 N
31 N

35 E   36 E
34 E   35 E   36 E

Hebrew Highlight

Remnant. Hebrew שְׁאֵרִית **(she'erit)** The noun "remnant" (she'erit) is related to the verb "to remain/to be left over" (sha'ar) and is used five times in Micah to refer to the survivors of the Lord's judgment who would become the objects of His blessing and favor when God restored Israel (Mic 2:12; 4:7; 5:7–8; 7:18). Other prophets made similar promises of a blessed and restored remnant. In spite of pervasive unbelief, a few true believers (a remnant) would survive.

The promise of blessed survivors in no way diminished the severity of the prophets' warnings of judgment. The term "remnant" implied that a great destruction would leave Israel small and few in number (Isa 10:22). Isaiah pictured Israel following the judgment as a few olives left over in the top of the tree (Isa 17:6). Amos warned that 90 percent of the people would die in the coming judgment (Amos 5:3) and that what was left of Israel would be like pieces of a lamb torn out of the mouth of a ravaging lion (Amos 3:12).

---

sacrifices and offerings, no matter how extravagant they might be, but rather in their humble obedience to Him reflected in a lifestyle of mercy and justice toward others.

The Lord would judge those who oppressed others by taking away the wealth they gained through their dishonest business practices. The wicked would never enjoy the ill-gotten treasures they stole from others.

The prophet concluded his words of judgment by lamenting the corruption of his people (7:1–6). Violence and injustice were running rampant, and the godly perished from the land. Even when it became difficult to trust family members and neighbors, Micah confessed that he would trust in the Lord and wait for His salvation.

The concluding word of hope in Micah is a **song of praise** to the Lord for His promised deliverance (7:18–20). The righteous would endure the time of God's discipline for Israel, knowing deliverance and vindication were on the other side of judgment. Israel would enjoy a second exodus when the Lord brought them home from their exile and rebuilt the walls of Jerusalem. The nations of the earth would submit to the Lord with trembling in recognition of His sovereign power. The greatest blessing promised to Israel was the forgiveness of their past sins. In the same way the Lord would destroy Israel's enemies (7:10), He would also trample down their sins and cast them into the sea (7:19). The Lord's anger over Israel's sin would give way to His mercy and covenant love.

THEOLOGICAL SIGNIFICANCE

Micah announced that the Lord's plans for Israel and Judah involved **judgment and salvation**. Israel and Judah were deserving of judgment because they worshipped idols and abandoned the practice of social justice. Following the judgment, the Lord would preserve a remnant and would restore Israel. The future Messiah would come from the line of David, would be born in Bethlehem, and would reign over a kingdom of peace and righteousness. The Lord would deliver Israel from its enemies, and the nations would come to Zion to learn the ways of the Lord.

The Lord revealed to Micah that the salvation of Israel would follow His work of judgment, but the exact timing of those events was not made clear to the Old Testament prophets. Micah's prophecies merge together promises of deliverance from the Assyrian and Babylonian exiles with promises of the future kingdom of God (4:9–10; 5:4–5). There is no indication of a time gap between these events or between the first and second comings of Christ (5:1–5). The first coming of Christ and the additional revelation of the New Testament clarified the working out of God's prophetic timetable and His plans for the church and Israel. Like the Old Testament prophets Jesus also warned that the judgment of Jerusalem would take place in the near future and that there would be a future renewal and restoration at His second coming (Matthew 24).

For Further Reading

Baker, David W., T. Desmond Alexander, and Bruce K. Waltke. *Obadiah, Jonah, Micah*. TOTC. Downers Grove, IL: IVP, 1988.

Barker, Kenneth L., and Waylon Bailey. *Micah, Nahum, Habakkuk, Zephaniah*. NAC. Nashville: B&H, 1998.

McComiskey, Thomas E., ed. *The Minor Prophets: An Exegetical and Expository Commentary*. Grand Rapids: Baker, 2009.

Smith, Ralph L. *Micah-Malachi*. WBC. Waco, TX: Word, 1984.

Waltke, Bruce K. *A Commentary on Micah*. Grand Rapids: Eerdmans, 2007.

Study Questions

1. What key word did Micah use to address his listeners?
2. How do social injustices reveal the depth of human sinfulness?
3. What aspects of social injustice concern you in society?
4. Why is the prophecy of a future king born in Bethlehem significant in light of the Messianic promise?

ENDNOTE

1. Bruce K. Waltke, *An Old Testament Theology* (Grand Rapids: Zondervan, 2007), 830.

Chapter 40

NAHUM
Destruction of Nineveh

We know nothing about Nahum beyond his name and that his hometown was Elkosh. Nahum means "comfort," and his message of the coming judgment on Nineveh gave hope and encouragement to the people of Judah who were living under Assyrian oppression at the time of his ministry. The message of Nahum provides the **counterpart** to the book of Jonah in the Minor Prophets. In the previous century, the Lord spared Nineveh from threatened judgment because of their repentant response to the preaching of Jonah. The book of Jonah testified to the Lord's redemptive concern even for the hated Assyrians. However, a generation later, the Assyrians were again brutalizing Judah and the surrounding nations in the Middle East, so God decided to destroy this violent nation.

Both Jonah and Nahum end with a **question**, and both reference the Mosaic confession that the Lord was both gracious and slow to anger as well as just and unwilling to excuse the guilty (Exod 34:6–7; Jonah 4:2; Nah 1:3). These attributes of the Lord applied to His dealings with the nations as well as His treatment of His chosen people, Israel. The Lord in His compassion delayed the judgment of Nineveh, but His justice also demanded that the Assyrians be held accountable for their violence and atrocities.

BACKGROUND

Nahum delivered his message against Nineveh and the Assyrians sometime between 663 and 612 BC. The fall of the Egyptian city Thebes (No-amon) referenced in Nah 3:8 occurred in 663 BC, and Nineveh fell to the Babylonians in 612 BC. The **fall of Nineveh** appears imminent (2:1; 3:14,19), and so it seems likely that Nahum delivered his messages during the reign of Josiah around the same time that Jeremiah commenced his prophetic ministry (c. 627 BC). Babylon and Assyria were longtime rivals; and Babylon, under the leadership of Nabopolassar, gained its independence from the Assyrians. The Medes captured the Assyrian capital of Ashur in 614 BC so the Assyrians transferred their capital to Nineveh. Nineveh was a magnificent city of impressive architecture with temples and palaces. The Medes and Babylonians joined together in the capture and destruction of Nineveh in 612 BC. The Babylonian Chronicles provided an account of the fall of Nineveh, which still remains in ruins today.

MESSAGE

I. Destruction of Nineveh Decreed (Nahum 1)

Nahum began his prophecy with a portrayal of Yahweh as the **Divine Warrior**. As a holy God who is rightly jealous for His honor and reputation, the Lord exacted vengeance on His enemies. At His approach the earth trembled, the sea and rivers dried up, and the mountains melted. The Lord's attributes combined absolute power with perfect righteousness so that He is both a refuge for those who humbly trust in Him and the destroyer of those who arrogantly oppose Him. Metaphors are prominent in this book, and the Lord's enemies were like thorns quickly consumed by the fire of His judgment and like drunkards who staggered after drinking the wine of His wrath. Yahweh's destruction of His proud and idolatrous enemy would bring deliverance for Judah, His oppressed people.

II. Destruction of Nineveh Described (Nahum 2)

Nahum's second oracle turned more directly to the destruction of Nineveh. Assyria had perfected the brutal techniques of siege warfare but would now become

A colossal stylized bull with human face from the time of Sargon II of Assyria.

Does the Lord Endorse the Abuse of Women?

Nahum 3:5–6 depicts the Lord as punishing Nineveh the prostitute by publicly exposing her nakedness and pelting her with filth, a common punishment of unfaithful wives in the ancient Near East. In light of these verses, some feminist critics have labeled Yahweh as a divine rapist, but this imagery does not legitimize spousal abuse or the rape of women taken as prisoners of war. Nahum and other prophets used this type of imagery for theological and **rhetorical impact**, not as a guide for the treatment of women or a model for human relationships. The Old Testament reveals Yahweh as a God who has a special concern for oppressed and needy women (cf. Gen 21:14–19; Deut 10:18; Ps 146:9). The Mosaic law limited Israel in its normal practice of warfare from acts of violence against noncombatants (Deut 20:13–15). A captive woman taken in battle was to be treated with dignity (Deut 21:10–14). Amos condemned the nation, particularly their abuse of women (cf. Amos 1:3,6,9–10,13; 2:7), and the larger message of Nahum was that Nineveh was the object of God's judgment because it also practiced such atrocities.

the victims of an invading army led by the Lord Himself. The prophet dramatically portrayed the **chaos** that would engulf the city of Nineveh in the present tense as if these events were occurring before his eyes, enabling the reader to sense the terror of the residents of Nineveh. The shields and uniforms of the enemy soldiers are scarlet because they are covered in blood. Their chariots dart through the city like torches and flashing lightning. The results of the attack is like the opening of the floodgates that protect Nineveh from the waters of the Tigris River. The inhabitants of the city are seen being taken away into exile, and the treasures of the city are being plundered.

III. Destruction of Nineveh Defended (Nahum 3)

Nahum's woe oracle pronounced a **death sentence** on Nineveh and explained more fully the reasons for the Lord's judgment of the city. God's justice demanded that the Assyrians experience the suffering and degradation they inflicted on others. Assyrian armies had slaughtered its enemies, but now the corpses of the dead Assyrians would be piled high in Nineveh. Like a prostitute Nineveh had seduced other nations into alliances and then had betrayed them because of her greed and lust for wealth. As punishment for her prostitution, the Lord would expose her nakedness and pelt her with filth. Other peoples would flee in horror when they observed what happened to Nineveh, but none would grieve or feel sympathy for her because of what she had done to others.

Nahum warned that the city was no better than the Egyptian city of **Thebes** (No-amon) that the Assyrians themselves plundered in 663 BC. Thebes fell even though it appeared invulnerable because of its strategic location on the Nile, and the same thing would now happen to Nineveh. Nineveh's fortresses would collapse like early figs easily shaken from the tree, and the mighty Assyrian warriors would become like frightened women. Nahum sarcastically ordered the residents of the city to prepare for the coming siege, but nothing would be able to save them. Disaster would consume them like a sweeping fire and a swarm of locusts.

THEOLOGICAL SIGNIFICANCE

Nahum's message against Nineveh and all of the oracles against the nations reflect that Yahweh is the Sovereign King and Judge over **all peoples** and not just the God of Israel. God is just in His judgment. He punished the Assyrians according to their crimes of violence and cruelty toward all the nations she plundered and not just Israel and Judah. The Lord used Assyria as His instrument of judgment against Israel and Judah (Isa 10:7–9), but Assyria was held accountable for going beyond the Lord's intent and plundering Israel and Judah for their own selfish reasons. The Assyrians were guilty of pride and blasphemy in believing that their gods were superior to Yahweh. The judgment of Assyria would bring about the salvation and restoration of God's people (Nah 1:13–15; 2:2).

The Lord's judgment of Assyria in history is a **preview** of His final eschatological judgment of all nations and peoples. As with Assyria in the past, all peoples will be judged according to the Noahic covenant and its prohibition of violence and the shedding of blood (Gen 9:5–6; Isa 24:1–5; Amos 1:3–2:3). The Noahic covenant was the basis for judgment of Nazi Germany and the Soviet Empire as much as it was for ancient Assyria, and the Lord will judge America and all other nations in the future on the basis of this covenant as well. In the Old Testament the Lord came down to earth as the Divine Warrior and destroyed the wicked in His day of judgment; in the New

---

The Cruelty of Assyria

Assyrian artwork reflects how much the Assyrians **glamorized** the **violence** of warfare and used such violence to intimidate other peoples into submission. Assyrian depictions of their conquests include the flaying of enemy soldiers, victims impaled on wooden poles, dismembered bodies, and severed heads stacked in front of city walls. The inscriptions of Assyrian kings also detail their brutal treatment of conquered foes:

> "Like fat steers . . . I speedily cut them down and defeated them. I cut their throats like lambs. I cut off their lives as one cuts a string." *Sennacherib*

> "I flayed as many nobles as had rebelled against me [and draped] their skins over the pile [of corpses]; some I spread out within the pile, some I erected on statues upon the pile. . . . I flayed many right through my land [and] draped their skins over the walls." *Ashurbanipal*

> "Their dismembered bodies I fed to the dogs, swine, wolves, and eagles, to the birds of the heaven and the fish in the deep." *Ashurbanipal*

Testament Christ will come to earth as the Divine Warrior and strike the nations that oppose Him with the sword of His mouth (Rev 19:11–21). As with Nineveh in the book of Nahum, the final Babylon of the end times is also portrayed as a prostitute because of its materialism, idolatry, and evil influence on other peoples (Revelation 18).

At the same time, the work of Christ provides a **new perspective** on Nahum, and we must read this prophet like all others in the Old Testament from the perspective of the cross. On the cross Jesus as the Divine Warrior waged war on Satan, the enemy who is the cause of all evil in the world. He triumphed in His battle over sin, death, and Satan by laying down His life. Because of the cross God extends His offer of grace and forgiveness to all, and Christ calls on His church to spread this good news to all peoples and nations. Even in the Old Testament the Lord demonstrated His redemptive concern for all peoples by sending the prophet Jonah so the people of Nineveh might avoid judgment and destruction. God was not willing that even the cruel and wicked Assyrians perish without the opportunity to repent.

For Further Reading

Armerding, Carl. "Nahum," in *EBC*, vol. 7. Grand Rapids: Zondervan, 1985.
Baker, David. *Nahum, Habakkuk, Zephaniah*. TOTC. Downers Grove, IL: IVP, 1988.
Longman, Tremper, III. "Nahum," in *The Minor Prophets: An Exegetical and Expository Commentary*, vol. 2. Edited by Thomas McComiskey. Grand Rapids: Baker, 1993.
Maier, Walter. *The Book of Nahum*. Grand Rapids: Baker, 1959.
Robertson, O. Palmer. *The Books of Nahum, Habakkuk and Zephaniah*. NICOT. Grand Rapids, 1990.

Study Questions

1. What city in Assyria was the focus of Nahum's prophecy?
2. What other Hebrew prophet dealt with Assyria and ended his book with a question?
3. What does God's judgment of Assyria tell us about God's universal justice?
4. How did Jesus function as a Divine Warrior?

Chapter 41

HABAKKUK
Destruction of Babylon

Habakkuk ("embrace") prophesied in Judah prior to the Babylonian invasion and warned that the Lord would send the Babylonians to punish His people (1:6). Habakkuk was a contemporary of Jeremiah and Zephaniah as well as Daniel and Ezekiel. Even in this time of national judgment, the Lord would not leave His people without a prophetic voice, and even in its final days as a nation, Judah could have turned to the Lord in repentance. Habakkuk's message is a personal one in which the prophet **laments** and **dialogues** with the Lord over the justice of His ways in using the Babylonians to punish Judah's sins.

BACKGROUND

At the end of the seventh century BC, the **Babylonians** replaced the Assyrians as the dominant power in the ancient Near East. The Babylonians under Nabopolassar declared their independence from Assyria in 626 BC and then won a series of military victories over the Assyrians. The Medes and Babylonians captured the cities of Ashur in 614 BC and Nineveh in 612 BC and then finished off what was left of the Assyrian army at Haran in 609 BC and Carchemish in 605 BC. Nebuchadnezzar's victory over the Egyptians and Assyrians at Carchemish brought Syria and Judah under Babylonian control. Nebuchadnezzar marched south from Carchemish and took away the first wave of exiles (including Daniel) from Judah in 605 BC. Judah remained under Babylonian control until the fall of Jerusalem in 586 BC. Nebuchadnezzar would take away two more groups of exiles in 597 and 586 BC. Habakkuk appears to have prophesied just prior to the first Babylonian invasion in 605 BC when Egypt was controlling Judah and Jehoiakim was king over Judah (2 Kgs 23:31–24:16).

Outline
I. Faith Tested (Habakkuk 1)
II. Faith Taught (Habakkuk 2)
III. Faith Triumphant (Habakkuk 3)

417

I. Faith Tested (Habakkuk 1)

Habakkuk's first question was, Why does the Lord not **punish injustice** in Judah? (1:1–4).

Habakkuk complained that the Lord had not answered his prayers to judge violence and injustice in the land. The Lord often delays judgment in order to show mercy, but the prophet believed that the Lord's inactivity only made the problem of injustice worse. The law of Moses no longer had any impact on people's lives, and the wicked outnumbered and took advantage of the righteous. The wicked become emboldened in their sin because the Lord had not punished them for their crimes. How can a person continue to have faith in God when He does nothing to stop these evil people?

The Lord explained that He was not ignoring Habakkuk's prayer or the violence in Judah but was in fact answering his prayer in a manner that was even beyond the prophet's understanding. The Lord was raising up the **Babylonians** (Chaldeans) to punish the wicked people in Judah for their sin. The Lord is the sovereign Lord over the nations and will accomplish His purposes through them. Earlier Isaiah explained how God used the empires of the ancient Near East to punish Israel and Judah for their sins and then to restore them to their homeland. The Assyrians were the "rod" of the Lord's anger (Isa 10:5), the Babylonian king Nebuchadnezzar was His "servant" (Jer 25:9; 27:6), and the Persian king Cyrus was "His anointed" (Isa 45:1). While the Lord worked out His purposes through these nations, He in no way approved of all of their evil actions. When the Babylonians came, they did not attack Judah to do the Lord's bidding but rather to satisfy their own greed and lust for violence. Rather than acknowledging the Lord, the Babylonians in their arrogance made a god of their own military strength.

II. Faith Taught (Habakkuk 2)

Habakkuk's second question was, How can God use the Babylonians to punish Judah?

Habakkuk did not understand how a holy God, too pure even to look on evil, could use the **evil Babylonians** to punish Judah when the Babylonians were even more wicked and violent than Judah. The prophet compared the Babylonians to fishermen who trapped their enemies like helpless fish in nets and destroyed other peoples so they could live in luxury. It again appeared to the prophet as if the Lord was promoting injustice in the world by failing to punish the wicked.

The Lord's response was that His **sovereign purposes** were beyond human understanding and could not be reduced to Habakkuk's simplistic formulas regarding who was most deserving of judgment. The Lord would ultimately punish sinners but in His time and His way. He would first judge Judah and then would judge Babylon. The Lord commanded Habakkuk to record the vision of His future plans in order to encourage the righteous as they waited for the Lord to execute justice and fulfill His promises.

The righteous should trust in God's promise, while the wicked, represented by the Babylonians, would proudly trust in their own violence to satisfy their greed and lust. The promise in 2:4 that "the righteous one will live by his faith," actually reads in Hebrew "the righteous will live by his faithfulness." Because of their promised deliverance, the righteous should remain faithful to the Lord and maintain their integrity and godliness **by faith**. Habakkuk questioned the ways of God's justice, but the Lord promised that He would protect and preserve the faithful even as He accomplished His work of judgment against the wicked. In the New Testament, Paul applied Habakkuk 2:4 to argue that justification (a right standing with God) was by "faith" in Christ alone rather than by the Mosaic law and works of righteousness (Rom 1:17; Gal 3:11). Both the original context of Hab 2:4 and Paul's later usage of the verse stress the importance of trust in God's promise. The believer today trusts in the work of Christ as the basis of salvation in the same way that the faithful in Habakkuk's day trusted the Lord's promise for their ultimate deliverance. The writer of Hebrews also quoted Hab 2:4 to encourage faithfulness to the Lord in the midst of the difficult circumstances that his readers were encountering (Heb 10:38).

Though the Lord had delayed in executing judgment, the **five woe oracles** in 2:6–20 guaranteed the final destruction of the Babylonian Empire. The Babylonians violated the Noahic covenant through their violence and bloodshed (Gen 9:5–6), and they would now experience the violence they inflicted upon others as fitting retribution for their crimes. Former victims would celebrate Babylon's demise with taunts and ridicule. The nations would plunder Babylon as Babylon once plundered them. Babylon made other nations drunk and humiliated them; Babylon would now be exposed and shamed as they became intoxicated with the wine of God's wrath. The Lord would even hold the Babylonians accountable for their wanton destruction of the animals and forests of Lebanon. Babylon's idols and false gods would not be able to deliver them

The site of the ancient city of Babylon in modern Iraq.

in their time of disaster. Two statements about God in 2:14 and 2:20 break up these five woes against Babylon and contrast the greatness of the Lord with the shame of Babylon. The Babylonians would go down to destruction as the nations mocked and taunted them, but the glory of the Lord would fill the earth. The idols of Babylon were worthless and speechless gods, but the Lord was the sovereign ruler over all before whom the whole earth was speechless.

III. Faith Triumphant (Habakkuk 3)

Habakkuk's third question was, Will the Lord have mercy?

After hearing the Lord's responses to his complaints, Habakkuk concludes with a **prayer** for deliverance and a **confession** of trust in the Lord to do what was right in the midst of Judah's national crisis. This prayer was a hymn to be sung to the accompaniment of stringed instruments. Habakkuk heard of the Lord's great works in the past and prayed for the Lord to act once again in a powerful way on behalf of His people and to temper His anger against Judah with mercy.

In answer to this prayer (3:3–15), the Lord appeared to Habakkuk in a **theophany** and revealed to him that when God comes to earth He shakes the earth and causes the mountains to disintegrate when He marches out in His glory as a warrior to fight on Israel's behalf. He terrifies His enemies with lightning bolts, plagues, and torrential storms. Long ago the Lord subjugated the seas, demonstrating His power over everything that stood in opposition to Him (cf. Pss 65:6–7; 74:12–17; 89:9–10). He even used the sea to defeat the Egyptians in the exodus (Exod 15:1–18). God's ultimate purpose on earth is always to destroy evil and bring forth salvation to His people (3:12–13). Even though the Babylonians had supreme confidence in their military might, they would be no match for the Lord.

Habakkuk longed for the Lord's deliverance even as he feared what the day of the Lord's anger would mean for Judah. In one of the greatest confessions of faith in all of Scripture (3:16–19), the prophet affirmed that he would rejoice in the Lord and would wait for His deliverance even in the darkest hour of judgment when Judah was deprived of crops and food. Habakkuk was confident that judgment would turn to salvation.

THEOLOGICAL SIGNIFICANCE

Habakkuk asserts the **Lord's absolute sovereignty** over the nations. The Lord uses nations and their rulers to accomplish His purposes but also holds them morally accountable for their own actions. Though the working out of God's plan and His administration of justice are often mysterious and incomprehensible, He will ultimately punish the wicked and reward the righteous. On the basis of the Noahic covenant, the Lord judges nations for their violence and bloodshed. The judgment of the Babylonian Empire in history is confirmation of God's final judgment of all wicked and oppressive nations. In the commentary on Habakkuk in the Dead Sea Scrolls, the Qumran community applied the promises that God would judge His enemies to the Romans. In the book of Revelation, the empire of Antichrist that will stand in opposition to God and His kingdom in the last days is presented as a second Babylon (Revelation 18).

Habakkuk's interaction with God is also a reminder that the life of faith often involves lament, complaint, and the pouring out of one's honest emotions and feelings to God. **Questioning God** and His ways, when done with the right attitude, can lead to a deeper faith and a greater understanding of God's ways. The Lord does not rebuke or turn away the person that comes to Him with honest questions. Though God spoke in special revelatory ways to Habakkuk as a prophet, true prayer is a dialogue with God and involves waiting on God and listening for Him to speak. God is more than a cosmic force and the dispenser of divine blessings, so vibrant prayer is personal communication with God that involves our intellect, will, and emotions. Believers not only have the right to petition God passionately but also to present the reasons and arguments for why God should answer their prayers. True faith leads to boldness before God but also humbly submits to God's sovereignty even when His ways are not fully understood. After his dialogue with God, Habakkuk confidently trusted in the Lord's promise to deliver His people and patiently waited on God's timing. Even in the most adverse circumstances, Habakkuk resolved to trust in the Lord and to rejoice in the Lord's goodness.

For Further Reading

Baker, David W. *Nahum, Habakkuk, Zephaniah: An Introduction and Commentary.* TOTC. Downers Grove, IL: IVP, 1988.

Bruckner, James. *Jonah, Nahum, Habakkuk, Zephaniah.* NIVAC. Grand Rapids: Zondervan, 2004.

McComiskey, Thomas E., ed. *The Minor Prophets: An Exegetical and Expository Commentary.* Grand Rapids: Baker, 2009.

Robertson, O. Palmer. *The Books of Nahum, Habakkuk, and Zephaniah.* NICOT. Grand Rapids: Zondervan, 1990.

Smith, Ralph. *Micah-Malachi.* WBC. Waco, TX: Word, 1984.

Study Questions

1. What did Habakkuk's questions reveal about his personal struggle with his faith?
2. Why was God's answer difficult for the prophet to comprehend?
3. What questions do you have about God's righteousness and justice in today's world?
4. How is God growing your faith in response to those questions?

Chapter 42

ZEPHANIAH
Disaster Is Imminent

According to the book's heading, Zephaniah ("hidden") was of **royal descent**, the great-great grandson of Hezekiah who ruled in Judah from 715 to 686 BC. Zephaniah's ancestor is not specifically identified as the king, but this connection provides the best explanation for the extended listing of four generations of the prophet's genealogy. The superscription also informs us that Zephaniah prophesied during the reign of the godly king Josiah (640–609 BC). The evil reigns of Manasseh and Amon had plunged Judah into apostasy, but Josiah carried out a series of reforms in response to the discovery of the Book of the Law in the eighteenth year of his reign. Then he sought to purge the land of idolatry and to bring the people back to the Lord (2 Kings 22–23).

BACKGROUND

Zephaniah's condemnation of **Judah's idolatry** in his opening message (1:4–6) indicates that he likely began his ministry prior to Josiah's major reform. Zephaniah's preaching thus helped influence perhaps the greatest revival in Judah's history. Zephaniah began his ministry at approximately the same time as Jeremiah, who began to prophesy in Josiah's thirteenth year (627 BC). Unfortunately, after Josiah's death, Judah quickly returned to its sinful ways. They did not follow the Lord, and the Lord punished His disobedient people by sending them away into exile. Zephaniah ministered during an important transition time as the Assyrian Empire was coming to an end and the Babylonians were rising to power in the Middle East.

Outline

I. Judgment of Judah (Zephaniah 1:1–2:3)
II. Judgment of the Nations (Zephaniah 2:4–15)
III. Justification of the Remnant (Zephaniah 3:1–20)

MESSAGE

I. Judgment of Judah (Zephaniah 1:1–2:3)

The **Day of the Lord** is the central theme of the book of Zephaniah. The prophet warned that the Day of the Lord was "near" (1:7,14) and made repeated references to the "day" of God's wrath. The Lord's judgment would fall on the entire earth. Reversing His work of creation, the Lord would destroy all living things. After warning of this worldwide catastrophe, Zephaniah focused his message on Yahweh's impending judgment of Judah. The Lord would judge Judah because they had worshipped Baal, Molech, and the astral deities of the peoples around them (1:4–6). They were violating their central covenantal responsibility to give the Lord alone their loyalty, worship, and service (Exod 20:3; Deut 6:4–5). The people presumptuously believed that no harm would come to them because they were the Lord's chosen people, but the Lord would in fact search the city of Jerusalem with a lamp to make sure every evildoer and idol worshipper was punished. The people of Judah would wail over the loss of their houses, fields, and wealth.

With these warnings Zephaniah supported **Josiah's reform** movement by calling the people of Judah to humble themselves and gather together at the temple to seek God's mercy before the Day of the Lord arrives. Only those who truly turn to the Lord will be spared from the devastation (2:1–3).

A representation of the god Baal on a relief from Ugarit.

II. Judgment of the Nations (Zephaniah 2:4–15)

The Lord is sovereign over **all peoples** and would also judge the nations for their wickedness and evil. Zephaniah referenced nations from all points of the compass—Philistia to the west, Moab and Ammon to the east, Cush to the south, and Assyria to the north—to demonstrate the encompassing nature of God's judgment.[1] Although the surrounding nations will arrogantly taunt the people of Judah, the remnant of Judah will possess these nations when the Lord restores His people. Judgment would fall not only on the smaller nations surrounding Judah but also on the imperial power of Assyria. Despite their military prowess, they would not be able to stand against the

---

Hebrew Highlight

Remnant. Hebrew שׁאֵרִית (she'erit). The remnant is the "remaining portion" or "residue." The noun emphasizes the basic root idea of sha 'ar, and "speaks of that which has survived after a previous elimination process or catastrophes" (TWOT, 2, 894–95). It is often used as a prophetic technical term for the final future righteous remnant of Israel.

Lord. The Lord would destroy Assyria and turn the great city of Nineveh into a barren wasteland.

III. Justification of the Remnant (Zephaniah 3:1–20)

Zephaniah warned that the day of the Lord's judgment was coming against Judah and the nations, but the prophet also viewed these near events as providing a pattern for the Lord's work of judgment and salvation for Israel and the nations in the eschatological Day of the Lord. Jerusalem stood under a **death sentence** because its people no longer trusted and followed Yahweh. The city's corrupt officials perverted justice, and the prophets and priests who were to provide spiritual leadership were concerned only for their own selfish interests (3:1–4). The rebellious city of Jerusalem will be destroyed because the people in it refused to accept correction from the Lord. The prophet blurred the distinction between near and far events in expanding the judgment of Jerusalem to include all nations. The Lord will pour out His burning anger on all peoples, and the earth will be consumed.

Judgment, however, was not the final word for Judah or the nations. In the last days the Lord would purify the speech of all peoples so they might worship and serve Him (3:9–10). He would purge evildoers from His own people and form a pure and **holy remnant** that would no longer practice injustice and deceit. Zephaniah stressed that the Lord's blessings were for the "humble" who put their trust in Him (3:11–12; cf. 2:3). The Lord would dwell among His people, and an enemy army would never subjugate them again. Those who trusted in the Lord could rest in the promise that He would deliver the afflicted and the oppressed.

THEOLOGICAL SIGNIFICANCE

Zephaniah affirmed that the Lord was king and judge over all nations and that the Day of the Lord would come as a **day of judgment** on Judah and all peoples. The Day of the Lord was both near and far. In the *immediate* future Yahweh would judge Judah and the surrounding nations. In the *eschatological* future the Lord's purifying of the nations would lead to the salvation of Israel and believers from the nations. The purifying of the lips of the nations (3:9) would reverse the curse placed on rebellious humanity at the tower of Babel (Genesis 11). The ultimate fulfillment of this prophecy would come when people from every nation gather to worship in the Lord's future kingdom (cf. Ps 145:10–13; Rev 5:9–10). The Lord would also restore His people

Israel, and they would enjoy the blessings of His kingdom rule as He reigned over them from Mt. Zion.

For Further Reading

Baker, David W. Nahum, *Habakkuk, Zephaniah: An Introduction and Commentary*. TOTC. Downers Grove/Leicester: IVP, 1988.

Bruckner, James. *Jonah, Nahum, Habakkuk, and Zephaniah*. NIVAC. Grand Rapids: Zondervan, 2004.

McComiskey, Thomas E., ed. *The Minor Prophets: An Exegetical and Expository Commentary*. Grand Rapids: Baker, 2009.

Robertson, O. Palmer. *The Books of Nahum, Habakkuk, and Zephaniah*. NICOT. Grand Rapids: Eerdmans, 1990.

Smith, Ralph L. *Micah-Malachi*. WBC. Waco, TX: Word Books, 1984.

Study Questions

1. What did Zephaniah's preaching result in for the people of Judah?
2. What was the prophet's relationship to King Josiah?
3. What key discovery led to the revival in Josiah and Zephaniah's time?
4. In what way was the Day of the Lord both near and far?
5. What will it take to see a great spiritual revival in our own day?

ENDNOTE

1. J. Daniel Hays, *The Message of the Prophets: A Survey of the Prophetic and Apocalyptic Books of the Old Testament* (Grand Rapids: Zondervan, 2010), 337.

Chapter 43

HAGGAI
Rebuild the Temple

The name *Haggai* means "festal" and perhaps indicates that he was born during one of Israel's feasts. In light of his message, the name also points forward to the resumption of Israel's **cycle of feasts** after the temple was rebuilt. Haggai in tandem with Zechariah challenged the postexilic community to resume the work of rebuilding the temple and delivered four different messages in a 15-week period from August to December 520 BC in the second year of Darius's reign over Persia.

First Message (1:1–15)	Sixth month, first day (August 29)
Second Message (2:1–9)	Seventh month, twenty-first day (October 17)
Third Message (2:10–19)	Ninth month, twenty-fourth day (December 18)
Fourth Message (2:20–23)	Ninth month, twenty-fourth day (December 18)

BACKGROUND

Cyrus's decree in 538 BC granted both permission and resources for **rebuilding the temple** (Ezra 3:7; 5:13–15) so the returnees and their leaders began the project with urgency and enthusiasm (Ezra 3:8–13; 5:16). The prophets Haggai and Zechariah returned to Jerusalem with a 50,000-member Jewish remnant in the first return under Zerubbabel (Ezra 2:64–65). Once they arrived, they built an altar and reinstated the Levitical sacrifice; then they began to lay the foundation for the temple in 536 BC (Ezra 3:1–13). However, the enormity of the rebuilding process, economic hardships, and opposition from the surrounding peoples stalled the project for 16 years. When Haggai came to challenge the nation, the people were discouraged and disillusioned and had given up on finishing the Lord's house.

While the temple as an architectural structure was not an automatic guarantee of God's blessing and protection, the temple was necessary for the people to fulfill their calling as a **worshipping community**. The temple in Jerusalem was also essential to the relationship between the Lord and Israel because it was the place where the Lord chose to dwell among His people. To fail to build the temple implied that the people did not see the need for the Lord to dwell among them. Haggai promised that the Lord would bless His people for their obedience to Him and that He would empower them to complete the work on the temple. The Lord also promised that He would elevate Israel and the house of David to a position of prominence and authority over the nations.

Outline

I. First Message: Rebuking (Haggai 1:1–15)
II. Second Message: Recharging (Haggai 2:1–9)
III. Third Message: Ruling (Haggai 2:10–19)
IV. Fourth Message: Reigning (Haggai 2:20–33)

MESSAGE

I. First Message: Rebuking (Haggai 1:1–15)

The people believed they were too poor and that it was not time to rebuild the temple, but Haggai countered that they were in poverty because of their failure to rebuild it. In their **misplaced priorities**, the people had devoted themselves to building their own homes rather than the Lord's house. The exact meaning of the reference to the people living in "paneled houses" in 1:4 is disputed. Paneling is only associated

Stonework showing examples of carpenters with their tools.

with the palace and temple elsewhere in the Old Testament (1 Kgs 6:9; 2 Kgs 7:3,7), so it seems unlikely that a people struggling to survive economically would have such luxuries in their own houses. This description may simply contrast the finished state of their homes with the unfinished condition of God's dwelling place. More likely, since this oracle is addressed to Zerubbabel and Joshua as leaders of the people (1:2), it describes the opulence of the houses in which they were living.

The Persian king Darius I seated upon his throne.

Haggai challenged the people to "consider" (lit. "set your heart") their ways and the consequences of their selfishness and greed (1:5,7). Because the Lord's house remained a "ruin" (*chārēb*, 1:4), the Lord had brought "drought" (*chōreb*, 1:11) upon them. The people were experiencing the **curses** of the Mosaic covenant that included the ruin of crops and famine because of their disobedience (Lev 26:19–20; Deut 28:22–24,38–40). The Lord's curse reduced their labor and economic endeavors to futility, and it was as if the people were putting their wages into money bags with holes in the bottom.

Haggai's challenge had its desired effect because they desired to glorify God. The leaders and people made the necessary preparations and **resumed their efforts** to build the temple on the twenty-fourth day of the same month. By not rebuilding, the people had failed to honor the Lord properly, but now they "feared" Him and took His word seriously. The Lord used the preaching of Haggai to "stir up" the hearts of His people to rebuild the temple in the same way He prompted Cyrus to issue the initial decree for its rebuilding (2 Chron 36:22–23). The Lord initiated this project, but the people's choice to obey the Lord was a necessary part of the process. There is a perfect balance here between divine sovereignty and human responsibility. In response to the people's obedience, the Lord promised that His empowering presence would enable them to complete their task.

II. Second Message: Recharging (Haggai 2:1–9)

The **three oracles** in Haggai 2 focus on the blessings the Lord had in store for His people as they resumed the work of temple reconstruction in Jerusalem. The postexilic community was a poor and struggling people with limited economic resources, so it was naturally discouraging to compare the modest structure they were building with the glories of Solomon's first temple. The temple had been in ruins for 66 years, but some of the older people still remembered the first temple. They felt like giving up when they considered the inferiority of the new temple when compared with the greatness of the former one. The Lord recharged the people with the challenge to be strong, to rejoice, and to remember His presence among them. The enablement of the Spirit would help them complete their task. The Lord would soon do a powerful work of overthrowing the nations and kingdoms of the earth so that they would bring their wealth and treasures as **tribute** to the Lord at Jerusalem. The "desire of all nations" in 2:7 (KJV) is a reference to this tribute rather than to the future Messiah, as some have interpreted this passage, and other prophets made similar promises concerning the nations bringing their tribute to Zion in the future restoration (Isa 60:5–7,10–14; Zech 14:14–16; cf. Rev 21:24–26). Ezra 6:8 indicates that shortly after this prophecy God fulfilled this promise by causing the Persian king Darius to order his officials to pay for the full cost of the temple out of the royal treasury. The Lord even promised that the glory of the new temple would surpass that of the first built by Solomon.

When Was Haggai's Prophecy Fulfilled?

The major issue with Haggai's prophecy about the temple is determining how and when this prophecy was or will be fulfilled. The expression "in a little while" in 2:6 suggests that the Lord would fulfill this prophecy to shake up the nations in the near future. But Israel never experienced anything like what is promised here in the postexilic period, unless the shaking up simply refers to the Persians changing policies and supporting instead of opposing the rebuilding of the temple. This prophecy appears to have "near" elements that were to be fulfilled in the immediate future, plus "far" elements related to the final and complete fulfillment in the **eschatological kingdom** of God. The Lord would enable the postexilic community to complete their rebuilding of the temple because the community feared God and worked, plus the Persians provided the needed money. However, these blessings were merely anticipatory of the final restoration of Israel when the Lord would completely deliver Israel from their enemies after the "times of the Gentiles" were fulfilled.

III. Third Message: Ruling (Haggai 2:10–19)

In this message the Lord promised to reverse Israel's defilement as a people and to bring agricultural blessing and prosperity. Haggai inquired of the priests for a ruling on issues of **ceremonial purity** in order to illustrate Israel's spiritual condition and to explain why Israel had lived under a curse because of its refusal to rebuild the temple. The Mosaic law taught that consecrated meat offered as a sacrifice transferred its holiness to the garment in which it was carried but that the garment could not then transfer holiness to any other objects (Lev 6:27). On the other hand, anyone coming in contact with a corpse became unclean and transferred that defilement to anything he touched (Lev 22:1–9; Num 19:22). The point was that Israel's greed and materialism had defiled them and the sacrifices and offerings they presented to the Lord. Israel could only become a holy people through their obedience to the Lord.

Echoing the original message delivered in 1:5,7, Haggai's **threefold encouragement was for the people** to "give careful thought" (2:15,18 NIV) to their ways, to realize that they and their offerings were unclean, and to observe closely how their punishment would soon turn into a blessing. Until this time the postexilic community had experienced poor harvests and economic deprivation, but from this day forward the Lord promised that He would provide abundant harvests. The people would now

---

Hebrew Highlight

Signet. Hebrew חותם (*chôthâm*). A seal or ring impressed in clay or wax to authenticate a document. Stamp seals worn on the fingers of kings and dignitaries were common in the Middle East. Signet rings were used to indicate royal or official status. The act of "sealing" with a signet designated the security of the item sealed.

---

experience the blessings of the Mosaic covenant rather than the curses if they continued to seek the Lord.

IV. Fourth Message: Reigning (Haggai 2:20–33)

In Haggai's final message the Lord promised to bless **Zerubbabel**, the governor of Judah. Zerubbabel was a member of the house of David and the grandson of Jehoiachin, the king of Judah taken away to Babylon in 597 BC (2 Chron 36:8–10). The Lord would reestablish the primacy of the Davidic throne by shaking the earth and overthrowing the nations and their armies.

The Lord would execute His sovereign rule through Zerubbabel as His "signet ring" and "servant." The Lord's promise to make Zerubbabel "like a signet ring" reversed the curse the prophet Jeremiah had announced against Jehoiachin as the representative of the house of David (Jer 22:24–25). The **signet ring** was a visible symbol of the king's authority. The Lord had temporarily rejected the line of David, but He would once again restore the Davidic king as His human vice regent and earthly representative of His heavenly rule. This prophecy clearly foretold messianic qualities, but Zerubbabel's authority as the governor over a tiny province under the Persians never matched anything like what is envisioned in this prophecy. Zerubbabel in fact merely anticipated the ideal Davidic ruler of the future who would reign over the nations. Zerubbabel's role as governor over Judah was confirmation that the Lord was not finished with the house of David. His present rule pointed to the future reign of his descendant Jesus Christ (see Matt 1:12; Luke 3:27) who ultimately will fulfill the magnitude of this prophecy in His millennial reign.

THEOLOGICAL SIGNIFICANCE

The prophecies of Haggai were both sermons to provoke the Israelites to action and predictions to encourage the success of their efforts. His main concerns were to explain the theological significance of the **temple** as a symbol of God's presence and the promise of the restoration of a Davidic King through the line of Zerubbabel. Haggai was preaching at a time when the future of the nation of Israel was still at great risk. The rebuilding of the temple and the perpetuity of the messianic line were both vital to Israel's hopes and dreams of the future blessing of God.

For Further Reading

Baldwin, Joyce. *Haggai, Zechariah, Malachi*. TOTC. London: Tyndale Press, 1972.

Boda, M. J. *Haggai, Zechariah*. NIVAC. Grand Rapids: Zondervan, 2004.

Lindsey, F. Duane. "Haggai." *BKC*. Edited by John Walvoord and Roy Zuck. Colorado Springs: Victor, 1982.

Merrill, E. H. *An Exegetical Commentary: Haggai, Zechariah, Malachi*. Richardson, TX: Biblical Studies Press, 2003.

Verhoef, P. A. *The Books of Haggai and Malachi*. NICOT. Grand Rapids: Eerdmans, 1987.

Study Questions

1. What kept the Jews from rebuilding the temple after they returned to Jerusalem?
2. How did Haggai's preaching provoke them to action?
3. Why is the temple so important to the Jews?
4. What is the significance of the prophecy about Zerubbabel and the signet ring?
5. How can we better demonstrate our commitment to God's house today?

Chapter 44

ZECHARIAH
Restore the King

Zechariah ("the Lord remembers") was a postexilic prophet who foretold the coming of Israel's true and final King. He reminded the people of Jerusalem that God would remember them and come to their rescue when they called upon the Lord in the last days. His book outlines God's future prophetic program for Israel from the first coming through the second coming of the Messiah.

BACKGROUND

The first part of the book of Zechariah covers the period of the prophet's ministry in Jerusalem from 520 BC until the completion of the second temple in 515 BC. Some conservative scholars date portions toward the end of the book as late as 470 BC at the end of Zechariah's life. His immediate focus in the early chapters is one of encouragement to the postexilic community to build the temple, restore the priesthood, and cleanse the city. His ultimate purpose in the closing chapters focuses on the promise of the **coming Messiah** and His reign over Jerusalem as both King and Priest.

Outline
I. Introduction and Call to Repentance (Zechariah 1:1–6)
II. Eight Night Visions (Zechariah 1:7–6:15)
III. Questions About Fasting and the Call for Justice (Zechariah 7:1–8:23)
IV. Two Burdens (Zech 9:1–14:21)
A. First Burden: God and False Shepherds (Zechariah 9:1–11:17)
B. Second Burden: The King Is Coming (Zechariah 12:1–14:21)

MESSAGE

I. Introduction and the Call to Repentance (Zechariah 1:1–6)

Less than two months after Haggai had successfully challenged the postexilic community to resume building the temple in Jerusalem, Zechariah called the people to repent and return to the Lord in October–November 520 BC. Without true **spiritual**

renewal on the people's part, rebuilding the temple was useless. The Lord promised that He would "return" (*shub*) to His people if they would "return" to Him (1:3). The people responded positively to the prophetic charge and "returned" (*shub*) to the Lord, unlike previous generations that persisted in their sinful ways (1:6). The people's obedient response set in motion the Lord's promise to bless them and to bring about Jerusalem's restoration.

II. Eight Night Visions (Zechariah 1:7–6:15)

Zechariah delivered his next message on February 15, 519 BC. Zechariah received a series of **eight visions** with an angelic interpretation of each. These visions reflect the Lord's gracious response to the people's repentance in 1:6. Because they "returned" (*shub*) to Him, the Lord promised that He would "return" (*shub*) to Jerusalem and enable them to rebuild the temple (1:16). Even though they were a poor and struggling community, the Lord would empower them to complete what seemed like an impossible task. The blessings of the community in the immediate future also foreshadowed the final restoration of Israel and Zion that would occur in the more distant future.

In his first vision Zechariah saw **four horsemen**. He saw a man on a red horse among some myrtle trees with three other horsemen behind him (1:7–16). The "man" on the red horse was the angel of the Lord, and the other horsemen were angelic messengers. After patrolling the whole earth, the messengers reported that they found the whole world at peace. In response to Jeremiah's earlier prophecy that the judgment of exile would last for 70 years (Jer 25:11–12; 29:10), the angel of the Lord asked how long it would be before the Lord would show mercy to Jerusalem. The Lord replied

Sunset over the Judean hills.

that He was stirred with jealousy for Jerusalem and that He would soon pour out His wrath on the nations. The Lord used the nations to punish Judah, but He would now punish the nations for how they treated Judah. This restoration began with the fall of Assyria and Babylon and would continue as the Lord carried out His work of judgment on other nations.

A stand of old olive trees in the traditional garden of Gethsemane.

Zechariah next saw a vision of **four horns** that represented the powerful nations that had destroyed Israel and Judah and taken them away into exile (1:18–21). The number four could refer to Egypt, Assyria, Babylon, and Medo-Persia but more likely denoted the four points of the compass and all of the enemy nations that had opposed the Lord's people. The horn was a common symbol of strength and power in the Old Testament and the ancient Near East (1 Kgs 22:11; Pss 18:2; 89:17; Dan 7:7–8; 8:20–21). Just as these horns had destroyed Israel and Judah, the Lord would raise up four craftsmen to destroy the horns. These craftsmen would construct tools or weapons for the destruction of the enemy nations (Isa 54:16–17). The Lord would reverse Israel's fate by judging her enemies.

In the third vision Zechariah saw a man with a **measuring rod**, surveying Jerusalem in preparation for the rebuilding of its walls. Zechariah's angelic interpreter then sent another angel to announce to this man that his work was unnecessary because Jerusalem would be a city without walls. The Lord Himself would dwell among His people and would be like a protective wall of fire for His people. The imagery here is figurative and hyperbolic because it would become important for Nehemiah in the fifth century BC to rebuild the protective walls that surrounded the city. Jerusalem could not be a viable city without such defensive measures, but the imagery here highlighted the absolute security that Zion would enjoy because of the Lord's protective presence. Jerusalem would become a city of great joy as more of the exiles returned from Babylon and other lands.

Zechariah's fourth vision refers to the restoration of the **high priest Joshua** for service at the temple (3:1–10). As the people rebuilt the temple, they needed to know that the Lord would once again accept the high priest as their mediator and representative. Satan reminded the Lord of Joshua's unworthiness, but the Lord extended His grace to both priest and people. The Lord had plucked them from the fire of exile and spared them from destruction. The Lord replaced Joshua's filth-splattered clothing with clean garments to symbolize that he had purified him for service. The Lord also promised that He would send His servant, "the Branch," to remove Israel's sin and to bring prosperity to the people, referencing Jeremiah's earlier prophecy concerning the Davidic "Branch" (Jer 23:5–6; 33:15). As with Haggai's "signet ring" prophecy (Hag 2:20–23), this promise had both a near and a far referent. The near referent was to Zerubbael, the Davidic descendant and governor of Judah who led the rebuilding of the temple (4:6–12; 6:9–15). The far referent is the Davidic Messiah who would reign as King at the time when the Lord would bring about Israel's full and complete restoration, as envisioned in Jeremiah's original prophecy.

In his fifth vision Zechariah saw **two olive trees** and a **lampstand** with seven lamps (4:1–14). The golden lampstand (menorah) was one of the articles in the holy place of the tabernacle and temple, and the seven lamps on the lampstand in this vision represent the presence of the Lord at the rebuilt temple. From the temple the Lord would exercise His sovereignty over the whole earth. The two olive trees provided oil for the lamps and appear to represent Joshua the high priest and Zerubbabel the governor. No matter how great the obstacles that stood in their way, the Spirit of the Lord would empower and enable them to complete the temple. Joshua and Zerubbabel were the Lord's "anointed ones," and the Lord would bless their work as His representatives. The book of Revelation uses these same symbols to represent the two witnesses (11:1–12) and the seven churches (1:20).

Though the people had returned to the Lord, sin remained a problem to be dealt with. In the sixth vision Zechariah saw a **flying scroll** that

The Jerusalem mercy gate.

measured 30 feet by 15 feet and was covered with writing (5:1–4). The scroll contained God's curse against those who had broken His commandments. The enormity of the scroll reflects the degree of Israel's sin and guilt. Through this curse on sin, the Lord would remove evildoers from the covenant community. Zechariah's seventh vision included a **woman** in a measuring basket (5:5–11). The woman represented wickedness in the land, and a female figure was likely used because the Hebrew word for "wickedness" (*rish`ah*) was feminine. This figure might also be associated with the goddess Ishtar or Asherah. The angel sealed the woman in the basket with a lead cover to make sure she could not escape, and then two winged creatures flew her away to Babylon. Wickedness belonged in the land of false gods rather than among the Lord and His people.

The eighth vision of the four horse-drawn **chariots** resembles and resolves the opening vision of the four horsemen in 1:7–17. The riders in the first vision asked the Lord to deliver Jerusalem from its enemies, and this vision brings the answer to that request. These chariots represent the four winds that will go out from the Lord's presence to execute His judgments and to establish justice in all the earth. Babylon in the north country was the prime target of the Lord's wrath. This vision looks back to the Persian defeat of Babylon that occurred 20 years prior, enabling the Jews to return to their homeland and to rebuild the temple. The historical defeat of Babylon and the return from exile also anticipated the final judgment of all of God's enemies and Israel's ultimate restoration when the Lord would establish His kingdom on earth.

The night visions concluded with a **symbolic** act confirming the Lord's promise to bless Joshua the high priest and Zerubbabel the governor as they led the rebuilding of the temple (6:9–15). The Lord commanded Zechariah to place a crown on the head of Joshua, reflecting how Joshua would be both a priest and a ruler over the people and ultimately anticipating how the offices of priest and king would be fulfilled in the person of Jesus Christ. Zechariah 3:8–10 and 4:6–10 demonstrate that the promises concerning the Branch refer to Zerubbabel, not Joshua. The cooperation between Joshua as high priest and Zerubbabel as representative of the house of David also foreshadowed Jesus' fulfillment of both royal and priestly roles. Jesus was the Son of David, but He also offered the perfect sacrifice for sin and intercedes for believers as their high priest (Heb 4:14–16; 7:24–28; 9:11–14).

III. Questions About Fasting and the Call for Justice (Zechariah 7:1–8:23)

Zechariah delivered his next message in 518 BC in response to questions from a delegation from Bethel regarding whether they should continue fasting and mourning over the fall of Jerusalem since they were no longer in exile. The people fasted in the fifth month to commemorate the fall of Jerusalem (2 Kgs 25:8) and observed other feasts in the fourth, seventh, and twelfth months (Zech 8:19). The only fast commanded in the Mosaic law was on the Day of Atonement (Lev 16:29–31). Zechariah responded that the Lord was more concerned with their practice of justice than their observance of ritual fasts. The exile had occurred in the first place because previous generations had turned a deaf ear to the Lord's commandments.

After looking backward to the lessons learned from the exile, Zechariah pointed forward to the **future hope** for Jerusalem. The Lord promised to dwell once again among His people and to bring all of the exiles back to the land. Jerusalem would once again become a great city and their rituals of mourning would become festive celebrations. The restored remnant of Israel would become so prosperous that the nations would recognize them as a blessed people. Despite the judgment of exile, the promises of the Abrahamic covenant remained in effect, and the prophet anticipated the Lord's blessing Israel so they might become a blessing to all peoples (Gen 12:1–3).

IV. Two Burdens (Zechariah 9:1–14:21)

Zechariah 9–14 has a more **eschatological focus** and portrays the coming of the Messiah, the final restoration of Israel, and the future kingdom of God. Many scholars date this section later than the previous chapters and refer to a second Zechariah, but the shared themes and motifs justify reading this book as a literary unity. The headings in 9:1 and 12:1 divide this last section of the book into two units. The focus in the first section is on the judgment of Israel's "shepherds" (10:1–3; 11:1–17; 13:7–9), which contrasts the corrupt leadership of the postexilic community with the promised transformation of the house of David and the future Davidic Messiah who would rule over Israel in peace and humility (9:9–10; 12:7–8; 13:1).

As already noted, the return from exile foreshadowed **Israel's ultimate salvation**. In response to the people's initial repentance (1:6), the Lord would bless their efforts to rebuild Jerusalem and the temple, but the blessing was only partial because

The Mount of Olives viewed from the Temple Mount.

Zechariah's Messianic Prophecies

Zechariah predicted both the first coming and the second coming of the Messiah; he pictures **Israel's future king** as both rejected and yet ruling. His prophecies ultimately focus on the future triumph of the coming King when God Himself in the person of Jesus Christ fulfills these incredible prophecies. The Messiah will be:

1. The Branch which sprouts from the Davidic line of kings (3:8; 6:12)
2. The King-Priest who combines both offices in one person (6:13)
3. The Lowly King who rides into Jerusalem on a donkey (9:9)
4. One who is betrayed for 30 pieces of silver (11:12–13)
5. One who is pierced in crucifixion (12:10)
6. The Good Shepherd who is smitten (13:7–9)
7. One who opens a fountain of cleansing for the House of David and the inhabitants of Jerusalem (13:1)
8. One who is Yahweh Himself (13:9)
9. God who comes to split the Mount of Olives and defend Jerusalem (14:1–4)
10. The King who rules the holy city of Jerusalem (14:16)

the people's return to the Lord was short-lived. They would soon return to their old sinful ways. Until the end of the Old Testament era, the sins of disobedience to the Lord's commands, social injustice, intermarriage with pagans, spiritual apathy, and indifferent worship would characterize the postexilic community. Israel would only experience their full salvation when they completely returned to the Lord (3:7; 6:15; 8:16–17).The Lord would have to do an even greater work of grace in His people to make such repentance possible (12:10–13:1).

A. First Burden: God and False Shepherds (Zechariah 9:1–11:17)

In Israel's future restoration the Lord promised that He would march out as the **heavenly warrior** and defeat Israel's enemies in Syria, Phoenicia, and Philistia. Most surprisingly, after this judgment the Lord would preserve a remnant from the Philistines to worship Him and to be like one of the tribes in Israel. In connection with Israel's great victory, Israel's future king (Messiah) would come as a humble man of peace, riding on a donkey instead of a horse or war chariot. Jesus fulfilled this prophecy with His triumphal entry into Jerusalem on Palm Sunday (Matt 21:1–11; Mark 11:1–10; Luke 19:28–38; John 12:12–15); but the Jews rejected Jesus as their king and conspired with the Romans to have Him crucified. The complete and final fulfillment of this prophecy will occur only when Jesus returns at His Second Coming. He will then rule over the nations and bring peace to all peoples. The Lord will also bring about the full return of His people from many lands. He will set them free from "the waterless pit," just as He rescued the patriarch Joseph (9:11 NIV; Gen 37:24).

The Lord would make Israel a powerful people and would use them as His weapons to **defeat the Greeks** (9:13). Many scholars have understood this reference to the

Hebrew Highlight

Holy. Hebrew קֹדֶשׁ (*qôdesh*). The noun often functions adjectivally as "holy," "scared," "dedicated," or "consecrated." It may also designate a holy place or sanctuary. The plural usage signifies "holy things" as dedicated to the Lord and deserving of respect or awe. The objects themselves are not to be worshipped, but they are to be respected as reflecting God's glory and holiness. In Zech 14:20–21 even common, everyday pots and pans will become holy objects in the house of the Lord.

Greeks (Hb., "sons of Javan") to indicate a later date for this section or to be a gloss that was later inserted into the book. However, the Persians and Greeks were enemies during Zechariah's day, and the reference to Greece may simply indicate Israel's future superiority over all foreign nations. There may be near and far elements to this prophecy as well. Israel would win its independence in the second century BC from the Seleucids, who were part of the Greek Empire. This victory in turn would prefigure Israel's ultimate triumph over all future oppressors as the Lord fights on their behalf.

In the first half of Zechariah, the Lord had commended the leadership of Joshua as the high priest and Zerubbabel as the governor, but the Lord was not pleased with the corruption of Israel's "shepherds" who succeeded them. They led the people astray with their pagan practices. The Lord promised that He Himself would replace these unfit leaders and become Israel's ruler. He would be like a cornerstone, a tent peg, and a bow in providing Israel with strength and stability. The Lord would bring His people back from captivity in distant lands, and their return would be like a **second exodus**. The Lord would empower Israel to overthrow the powerful nations that subjugated them in the past, with Egypt in the south and Assyria in the north being representative of all of Israel's enemies.

Despite the great promises the Lord made to them, the people in their sinful condition preferred the leadership of the **corrupt shepherds** who took advantage of them rather than the Lord who wanted to bless them. The Lord instructed Zechariah to perform a sign act or drama to demonstrate the people's rejection of the Lord as their shepherd. For one month Zechariah acted as a shepherd over a flock destined for slaughter and shared these duties with other shepherds who were only concerned with how they could profit from the sale of the flock for slaughter. Reflecting God's love for His people, Zechariah tended the flock with staffs called "Favor" and "Union" and removed three of the worthless and greedy shepherds.

Surprisingly, the flock grew weary of the shepherd who loved them by removing the evil shepherds. Zechariah announced that he would no longer shepherd the flock and that he would allow them to die, symbolizing how the Lord would give His people over to judgment and destruction in the future. Zechariah broke the staffs he used to shepherd the flock, and to show their disrespect the owners of the flock paid Zechariah 30 pieces of silver, the wages of a slave. This **act of betrayal** prefigured

Israel's rejection of the Good Shepherd when Judas betrayed Jesus for 30 pieces of silver (Matt 27:9–10).

B. Second Burden: The King Is Coming (Zechariah 12:1–14:21)

This second oracle also promised the **future restoration** of Israel but warned that this salvation would come only after the Lord had once again cleansed and purged His people through judgment. In his final message Zechariah portrays Israel's eschatological future from the time of the nation's recognition of her true Messiah until the establishment of the future Messianic kingdom. Enemy armies would again besiege Jerusalem, but the Lord would intervene on behalf of His people and destroy their attackers. The Lord would make all of Israel as powerful as David and would restore the former glory of David's house by giving it supernatural enablement for battle. This great act of deliverance would cause Israel to mourn over how it had rejected the Lord as their shepherd. Previously the people were incapable of returning fully to the Lord, so the Lord will pour out a spirit of grace that will enable the people to renounce their sinful ways.

The Lord's cleansing of Israel would be a painful process, however. He would cut off the **wicked shepherd** He had raised up in order to punish Israel, and two-thirds of the people would also perish. Of the third that remained, only a portion of them would ultimately survive to form the chosen remnant that would enjoy the blessings of the Lord's covenant renewal with Israel. Since these prophecies have never been fulfilled, they point to a final fulfillment in the future.

The last chapter of Zechariah portrays the final assault on Jerusalem to occur in the **last days**. This fact is highlighted by the repetitious use of the phrase "on that day," meaning that future day. The details differ from 12:1–9 where the Lord appears to destroy the nations while here Jerusalem suffers heavy casualties. However, both passages may describe the same event, with this second portrayal providing more detail. The preceding section already clarified that a purging judgment of Jerusalem would precede its final deliverance. With varying details and perspectives, other prophets also spoke of this final assault on Jerusalem (Ezekiel 38–39; Joel 3:9–16). In Zechariah's final message (14:1–21), the enemy armies will capture Jerusalem and take away half its residents into exile, but then the Lord will come down to fight on behalf of His people. The Lord's arrival would split the Mount of Olives in two and destroy the enemy forces. He would also provide a way of escape for His people. With this victory the Lord's kingdom would come to earth as a time of unprecedented blessing and peace. Life-giving waters, representing the presence of God, would flow from Jerusalem and bring fertility and abundant harvests to all of the land of Israel. The Lord's rule over the earth would be absolute. Jerusalem would finally become a city of holiness. Revelation 19–20 adds to this portrayal of the future kingdom by revealing that Christ Himself will return as the conquering warrior to defeat His enemies. Then He will rule from Jerusalem as King over all the earth.

THEOLOGICAL SIGNIFICANCE

Zechariah presents a theology of **holiness**. He was concerned that the postexilic Jewish community should properly prepare their hearts for the Lord's blessing. They could do this by establishing a holy worship, holy priesthood, holy temple, and holy city. But in the end he recognized that these ideals would only be realized when God Himself came to rescue Jerusalem and rule the world in the person of the Messiah. Only a Holy God could bring true holiness from heaven itself to an earthly kingdom. Thus, the prophet foresaw the coming Messianic kingdom as an era of divine peace, prosperity, and purity.

For Further Reading

Baldwin, Joyce. *Haggai, Zechariah, Malachi*. TOTC. Downers Grove, IL: IVP, 1972.

Barker, Kenneth. "Zechariah," in *EBC*, 7. Grand Rapids: Zondervan, 1985, 595–697.

Boda, M. J. *Haggai, Zechariah*. NIVAC. Grand Rapids: Zondervan, 2004.

Feinberg, Charles L. "Zechariah," in *The Minor Prophets*. Chicago: Moody Press, 1976.

Merrill, Eugene. *Haggai, Zechariah, Malachi: An Exegetical Commentary*. Chicago: Moody Press, 1994.

Unger, Merrill. *Zechariah*. Grand Rapids: Zondervan, 1963.

Study Questions

1. Summarize the significance of Zechariah's eight night visions.
2. How does the book of Revelation reflect some of the elements of these visions?
3. How did Zechariah answer the question about continuing to mourn the destruction of the first temple?
4. How did the prophet contrast Israel's good name and false leaders?
5. List Zechariah's messianic prophecies that are fulfilled in Jesus Christ?
6. Why is holiness such an important theme in the Old Testament?
7. In what ways should we reflect respect for items that have been dedicated to the Lord's use?

Chapter 45

MALACHI
Repent of Sin

The ancient versions are divided on whether Malachi ("my messenger") is a personal name or a title. The use of personal names in the headings for other prophetic books would suggest the same here. Malachi's name is a reminder of his role as God's prophet and connects his ministry to a future prophet ("my messenger") the Lord promised to send in preparation for the future day of the Lord (3:1).

BACKGROUND

The heading of the book contains no specific details concerning the date of Malachi's ministry. He prophesied in the **postexilic** period after the rebuilding of the temple and the reinstitution of the sacrifices and rituals associated with the temple. The term "governor" in 1:8 fits with the Persian period. Malachi was most likely a contemporary of Ezra and Nehemiah. Like Ezra and Nehemiah, Malachi dealt with the problems of intermarriage, corrupt priests, failure to pay tithes, and social injustice. Malachi's ministry can be dated then c. 430 BC. He represents the last of the classical prophets, and his message closes the Old Testament canon with a final call to repentance.

Outline
I. God's Love Announced (Malachi 1:1–5)
II. God's People Denounced (Malachi 1:6–4:3)
A. Question of Worship (Malachi 1:6–2:9)
B. Question of Divorce (Malachi 2:10–16)
C. Question of Justice (Malachi 2:17–3:5)
D. Question of Tithing (Malachi 3:6–12)
E. Question of Rewards (Malachi 3:13–4:3)
III. God's Messenger Promised (Malachi 4:4–6)

The book of Malachi is structured around disputations in which the Lord dialogues with His people in a series of **questions and answers**. Altogether the book raises 23 questions, following the pattern of: (1) accusation, (2) interrogation, (3) refutation, and (4) conclusion. This literary form is effective in that it reflects the people's spiritual condition. The recurring expression "but you say" on the part of the people reflects how they have responded to God in an argumentative and disrespectful manner. The people question God's love, dispute the charges the Lord brings against them, and believe that God is unjust because He was not blessing them in the way that they believed He should. Malachi, as Israel's last prophet, ministers to a people who resemble the grumbling and complaining generation that Moses, as Israel's first prophet, led through the wilderness.

MESSAGE

I. God's Love Announced (Malachi 1:1–5)

In the opening disputation the people questioned the Lord's love for them. Their struggles as an impoverished remnant living under foreign oppression led them to doubt God's care and concern for them (cf. Isa 40:27; 49:14). The Lord reminded them of His **election of Jacob** over Esau. "Love" and "hate" were covenantal terms in the ancient Near East, and the Lord made a covenant with Jacob (Gen 28:12–17) but not with Esau. The Lord chose Jacob and his descendants to be the object

The hills of Edom between Petra and Bozrah toward the Wadi Arabah.

of His favor and to have a key role in salvation history as the instrument of divine blessing to the whole world.

Mosaic Law prohibited the Israelites from showing animosity to the Edomites (Deut 23:7), but the Lord's **opposition to Edom** was a holy hatred of their pride, violence, and moral corruption. Israel's return to the land was demonstration of the Lord's love and faithfulness, but there would be no such restoration from judgment for the Edomites. Earlier prophets had predicted the downfall of Edom (Isa 34:5–15; Jer 49:7–22; Ezek 35:1–15; Obad 3–8,15–18), and Malachi confirmed the fulfillment of these prophecies. Between the years 550 and 400 BC, the Nabatean Arabs forced the Edomites from their homeland, and they eventually faded from history.

II. God's People Denounced (Malachi 1:6–4:3)

A. Question of Worship (Malachi 1:6–2:9)

The Lord demanded that Israel honor Him with worship that was worthy of His name, but the corrupt priests allowed the people to offer **defective sacrifices** to the Lord. In violation of Mosaic law, they let the people offer blind, lame, and sick

---

Hebrew Highlight

Curse. Hebrew חרם (*hêrem*). The Hebrew word actually refers to "devoted things." These were things "set aside" or devoted for God's use. When that devotion was violated, the *hêrem* became a curse, "devoted to destruction." This was the last word and final warning of the text of the Prophets (Mal 4:6). The prophets warned Israel that, as a people devoted to God, they were subject to both His blessing and His curse.

---

animals that were not appropriate for sacrifice (Lev 9:2–3; Deut 15:21). They would vow unblemished animals to the Lord and then offer cheap substitutes that would be unacceptable to their human governor. A day will come when all nations worship the Lord, but the Lord's own people viewed worship as a wearisome duty and obligation. Since their worship was little more than going through the motions, the Lord would prefer that they stop presenting sacrifices and offerings altogether.

Since the priests did not correct the people, the Lord decided to bring a **curse** on the priests who offered these defiled sacrifices. He would dishonor the priests because they dishonored Him. They offered defiled sacrifices, so the Lord would defile them by having the dung of these sacrificial animals spread on their faces. The Lord had conferred a special privilege on the tribe of Levi by choosing them to serve as His priests, but the priests did not take seriously their covenantal responsibilities to the Lord. The priests were especially guilty because it was their duty to teach the law of God and to instruct the people on how properly to worship Him.

B. Question of Divorce (Malachi 2:10–16)

The Lord instituted **marriage** as a **sacred covenant** relationship, but the men in the community dishonored the Lord in their marriages in two specific ways. The first issue was that they intermarried with foreign women who worshipped other gods. The Lord prohibited such marriages because they would lead the people away into idolatry (Exod 34:15–16; Deut 7:3–4; Josh 23:12–13; Judg 3:6–7; 1 Kgs 11:1–6). The problem with these marriages was spiritual rather than racial. Economic issues were probably involved here as well because marriage fostered a relationship with foreigners who owned significant amounts of land. Nevertheless, God knew it was especially important at this time for this struggling remnant of Jews to maintain their spiritual identity. The Lord threatened to cut off those who married pagan women. Ezra and Nehemiah, who were contemporaries of Malachi, also confronted the problem of intermarriage with pagans (Ezra 9–10; Neh 13:23–29).

The second issue was that **divorce** had become a **common occurrence** in the community, perhaps with the men divorcing their wives so they could marry these foreign women whose families owned land and had a higher economic status. The Lord's intent from the beginning was for marriage to be a lifelong commitment between one man and one woman (Gen 2:21–25). Mosaic law allowed for divorce, but it was regulated and restricted in Israel (Deut 24:1–4). Jesus confirmed in His teaching that marriage was for a lifetime, although the New Testament appears to allow for divorce in cases of adultery or when an unbeliever abandons a believing spouse (Matt 5:31–32; 19:3–9; 1 Corinthians 7). The Lord hates divorce and equates it to practicing violence. Because of the covenantal nature of marriage, faithlessness toward one's spouse is also viewed as faithlessness toward the Lord.

C. The Question of Justice (Malachi 2:17–3:5)

The people had wearied the Lord by questioning His justice and whether He was committed to punishing wickedness and rewarding righteousness. At this time they did not see God judging their enemies or blessing them. The Lord promised that He would decisively intervene at a future time to purge evil from His people. The people were anticipating the Lord's acting in justice but will actually be overwhelmed when the judgment happens.

The Lord would send a **"messenger"** to prepare the way for His coming, and the fact that Malachi's name means "my messenger" indicates that his ministry prefigures the role of this future spokesman for God. The New Testament identifies this messenger as John the Baptist, who as the messianic forerunner prepared the people for the coming of Jesus (Matt 11:10; Mark 1:2; Luke 7:27). When the Lord comes to His temple, His judgment will be like cleansing soap and refining fire in purging evil from the priests and purifying Israel's worship. The Lord will judge all those who commit the religious sin of sorcery, the social sin of divorce, and the violent sin of oppression of the poor.

The preexilic prophets preached against **social injustice**, and this was still an issue in the postexilic community. As the governor of Judah at this time, Nehemiah had to take steps to deal with oppressing the poor and charging exorbitant interest during a time of famine (Neh 5:1–11). The people complained that they were not receiving justice from the Lord, but in reality they were not practicing justice toward one another.

D. Question of Tithing (Malachi 3:6–12)

Returning to the problem of Israel's corrupt worship, the Lord charged that the people were **robbing Him** by failing to give their tithes as set forth in Mosaic law. Tithing was a reminder to the people that everything they owned came from the Lord and belonged to Him. Their tithes provided for the Levites who served at the temple (Num 18:21–32), for the poor and needy (Deut 14:28–29; 22:21–29; 26:12–13), and even for their own festive celebrations before the Lord (Deut 14:22–26). The Lord invited the people to test Him and see how He would bless their crops and provide for their needs if they were faithful in giving their tithes. If this would actually happen, then the Lord would be honored as other nations came to recognize Israel as a blessed people.

E. Question of Rewards (Malachi 3:13–4:3)

The people again challenged the Lord's justice by asking if there was any **reward or benefit** in serving Him. It appeared to them as if the wicked prospered and got away with their sins. The Lord responded that there were two fates awaiting the righteous and the wicked. The Lord knew the righteous and had recorded their names in His "scroll of remembrance" (NIV). They would be spared on the future day of judgment while the wicked would be burned up like useless chaff thrown into the furnace. The Lord's salvation would be like the bright light and healing warmth of the sun. The light of God's salvation would dispel the darkness of the present gloom in which Israel lived under foreign oppression and injustice seemed to prevail.

III. God's Messenger Promised (Malachi 4:4–6)

The people had turned away from the Lord in their worship practices and daily living (3:7), so Malachi concluded his prophecies by calling the people back to their covenantal responsibility to obey God's commandments. The Lord promised that He would send the **prophet Elijah** prior to the future Day of the Lord to restore His people, and this promise clarifies and expands on the earlier prophecy that the Lord would send His "messenger" to prepare for His coming (3:1). Elijah would call the people to repentance as he had done at an earlier time of national apostasy.

As noted earlier, the New Testament explains that John the Baptist is the fulfillment of this prophecy. John the Baptist resembled Elijah in his appearance and diet (cf. Matt 3:4 and 2 Kgs 1:8) and ministered in the spirit of Elijah by calling the people

The Chapel of Elijah on Mount Horeb, commemorating the traditional site to which Elijah fled after his confrontation with the prophets of Baal on Mount Carmel. Malachi prophesied that Elijah would precede the Day of the Lord.

of his day to repent of their sinful ways (Matt 11:10–14). His ministry would turn the hearts of fathers and sons to each other as they returned to the Lord, reversing the present situation where sons suffered for the sins of their fathers and perpetuated the sinful behavior of previous generations (Exod 20:5–6). Ironically, the last book of the Old Testament ends with both a call to repentance and a threat of a curse, following the prophetic pattern of the Hebrew prophets.

The book of Malachi forms an important **bridge** between the Old and New Testaments. The final prophetic word in the Old Testament canon anticipates and looks forward to the ministry of John the Baptist as the prophetic forerunner to Jesus Christ. The Lord is the "sun of righteousness" as the source of salvation, and Jesus would come as "the light of the world" to make that salvation possible (John 8:12).

THEOLOGICAL SIGNIFICANCE

Malachi teaches that honor for God involves both **worship and lifestyle**. The prophets often condemned empty ritual as a useless substitute for a lifestyle of obedience and justice (Isa 1:10–17; Amos 5:21–24; Mic 6:1–8). The Lord established the rituals and ceremonies of worship as a means for His people to express their love and devotion to Him, but the people of Malachi's day failed in both ritual and lifestyle. Their failure to give the Lord their best in worship reflected their lack of love and reverence for Him.

The experiences of the Jews following their return from exile hardly matched the promises of the earlier prophets concerning their restoration. The struggling province of Judah remained under foreign domination, but the real issue was that the people returned to the land without truly returning to the Lord. Though the exile largely cured the Jews of their worship of foreign gods, the people continued to struggle with some of the same sins that had necessitated the judgment of exile in the first place—false worship, social injustice, and disobedience to Mosaic law. Malachi and the other postexilic prophets revealed that Israel's ultimate restoration belonged to the still **distant future** and would require an even greater act of salvation on the Lord's part. The purging judgment of the future day of the Lord would remove Israel's sin and make them a truly holy people.

For Further Reading

Baker, D. W. *Joel, Obadiah, Malachi*. NIVAC. Grand Rapids: Zondervan, 2006.
Blaising, Craig. "Malachi," in *BKC*. Colorado Springs: Victor, 1983.
Kaiser, Walter C. *Malachi: God's Unchanging Love*. Grand Rapids: Baker, 1984.
Verhoef, P. A. *The Books of Haggai and Malachi*. NICOT. Grand Rapids: Eerdmans, 1987.
Wolf, Herbert. *Haggai and Malachi*. Chicago: Moody Press, 1976.

Study Questions

1. What unique pattern appears in the message of Malachi?
2. How do the responses of the people reveal the true attitude of their hearts?
3. What do our complaints reveal about our own spiritual condition?
4. What was the actual fulfillment of the promise to send Elijah before the Day of the Lord?
5. Why does Malachi end with both the promise of blessing and the threat of a curse?

Chapter 46

EPILOGUE
The Prophetic Promise

IT'S ALL ABOUT HIM!

The prophetic promise of God runs throughout the Bible. Walter Kaiser calls it the single best **principle** for understanding the Old Testament revelation. "God's revealed promise," he writes, "is not that of a fideistic imposition on the text of a later Christian faith. . . . It is rather the claim of the canon itself."[1] The Old Testament authors describe the God-like characteristics of a coming Messiah, compelling the reader to see one who is more than a mere man. The Hebrew Bible refers to Him as the "seed of the woman" (Gen 3:15), a descendant of the tribe of Judah (Gen 49:10), through the line of David (2 Sam 7:16). He will come as a king and every knee will bow before him (Isa 45:23). But He will also be a suffering servant who will be despised and rejected (Isa 53:1–9).

"I am God, and no one is like Me. I declare the end from the beginning," the Lord announces. "Yes, I have spoken, so I will also bring it about. I have planned it; I will also do it" (Isa 46:9,11). The Old Testament contains more than 100 prophecies about a **person** who is coming in the future to fulfill God's promises to His people. Nonetheless, the Old Testament came to a close; and no one came to fulfill the hopes, dreams, pictures, types, and predictions of the ancient biblical writers. No one came, that is, until He came—Jesus of Nazareth who dared to say: "Everything written about Me in the Law of Moses, the Prophets, and the Psalms must be fulfilled" (Luke 24:44).

It's all about Him? Who does Jesus think He is—the **Promised One**, the Messiah, the Savior, and the King of Israel? Yes, a thousand times yes! When He spoke in the synagogue at Nazareth, His hometown, He read from the prophet Isaiah: "The Spirit of the Lord is on Me, because He has anointed Me to preach good news to the poor . . . to proclaim the year of the Lord's favor" (Luke 4:18–19). When He finished reading the prophetic text from Isa 61:1–2, He said: "Today, as you listen, this Scripture has been fulfilled" (Luke 4:21). Jesus told Peter and the other disciples that His Father in heaven revealed to them that He was the Messiah, the Son of the living God (Matt 16:16–17). At His trial the high priest asked Jesus, "Are You the Messiah, the Son of the Blessed One?" to which Jesus replied, "I am" (Mark 14:61–62).

The Old Testament was written by numerous authors from Moses to Malachi over a period of 1,000 years. Yet, from beginning to end, the Hebrew sages predicted the coming of Christ.[2] Consider just a few examples of their **predictions**:

Genesis 22:18	Born of the seed of Abraham
Genesis 49:10	Born of the Tribe of Judah
Jeremiah 23:5	Born of the House of David
Isaiah 7:14	Born of a virgin
Micah 5:2	Born in the town of Bethlehem
Isaiah 9:7	Heir to the throne of David
Isaiah 53:3	Rejected by His own people
Zechariah 11:12	Betrayed for 30 pieces of silver
Isaiah 53:12	Executed with criminals
Psalm 22:16	Pierced through the hands and feet
Zechariah 12:10	Crucified
Isaiah 53:9	Buried with the rich
Isaiah 53:5	Atonement for our sins
Psalm 16:10	Raised from the dead

It is highly unlikely that Jesus could have fulfilled all these prophecies by chance. The Old Testament has more than 100 messianic prophecies about the first coming of Christ. All of them were fulfilled by Jesus of Nazareth. All of these fulfilled prophecies cannot be mere coincidence. The **messianic prophecies** are not merely a "scarlet thread" that runs indiscernibly throughout the Old Testament. They are the main theme that underlies its history, poetry, worship, and prophetic preaching. The entire Old Testament is the record of God's promises, and the New Testament is the record of their fulfillment.

Within days of Jesus' resurrection, the early Christians proclaimed that the events in Jesus' life fulfilled the prophecies of the Hebrew Scriptures. In the first sermon of the Christian era, Peter announced: "This is what was spoken through the prophet Joel. . . . For David says of Him . . . Seeing this in advance, he spoke concerning the resurrection of the Messiah" (Acts 2:16,25,31). Days later Peter proclaimed: "But what God predicted through the mouth of all the prophets—that His Messiah would suffer—He has fulfilled. . . . Therefore repent and turn back, so that your sins may be wiped out" (Acts 3:18–19). The **purpose** of the messianic prophecies was to make the Messiah known because He fulfilled the events foretold. They served as a preparatory indication to signal His arrival. Thus, the New Testament authors recognized the value of these predictive prophecies and their fulfillment as apologetic evidence to prove the Scripture's credibility and supernatural nature of the Christian message.

Bible prophecies were not written to entertain someone's curiosity but to call everyone to **faith**. These prophecies are an expression of God's love in the Old Testament. Despite humanity's fallen nature and its global consequences, God continued deliberately to intervene in the ancient world. He constantly stepped into the darkness of the times, breaking His silence and affirming His promises. Someone will come to set the people free. Someone is going to die for their sins and yet rule as their King. That someone is Jesus of Nazareth, the King of the Jews, the Lord of the Church, the Lamb of God, and the Savior of the world.

Without Jesus the Old Testament remains **silent and unfulfilled** like the dull thud of Joseph's coffin lid at the end of Genesis (50:26). The Hebrew canon closes with the admonition to "go up" to Jerusalem and start all over again (2 Chron 36:23). The Christian canon of the Old Testament closes with a call to restoration and repentance, "Otherwise, I will come and strike the land with a curse" (Mal 4:6). Without Jesus the promises of God remain unfulfilled. Without the Messiah these predictions are but silent echoes of a long-forgotten past, quickly dismissed by critical scholars as nothing more than the wishful thinking of Jewish mythology. But for the Christian believer, they are "very great and precious promises" based on "the prophetic word strongly confirmed" from men who "spoke from God as they were moved by the Holy Spirit" (1 Pet 1:4,19,21).

The Old Testament propels its readers to look beyond its pages for its **final answers**. It betrays what Philip Yancey calls "a gradual but certain movement toward grace."[3] Without the Old Testament one cannot fully understand the New Testament. Within the laws, history, poetry, and prophecies of the Hebrew Scriptures, one discovers in the Old Testament a God who loves and leads those who will believe, trust, and follow Him. He is a God who establishes principles of social order and justice. He sets up and takes down kings and rulers. He judges human behavior and holds people accountable for their choices. Yet, in the darkest moments of human failure, God intervenes with grace beyond comprehension.

That **grace** (Hb., *hen*) and **unfailing love** (Hb., *chesed*) energize the old covenant. God's contract with the people and nation of Israel was never meant to be limited to them alone. The blessings of the Abrahamic, Mosaic, and Davidic covenants were meant ultimately to bless the whole world (Gen 12:2–3), and indeed they have. For all that was promised to the patriarchs, and confirmed by the prophets, was fulfilled in "Jesus Christ, the Son of David, the Son of Abraham" (Matt 1:1). It is no wonder Jesus said they rejoiced to see His day (John 8:56).

The **story of the Bible** begins in the garden of Eden and ends in the eternal city, the new Jerusalem. In between stand the person of Jesus Christ, the cross, and the empty tomb. These make all the difference. These New Testament events bring many of the Old Testament promises to their fulfillment, but the New Testament writers also point forward to a final day in the future when there will be a decisive fulfillment of the rest of the Old Testament prophecies when Christ will reign as King in the new Jerusalem. The Bible makes some bold claims about Jesus. It presents Him as the promised Messiah, the Son of God, the Savior of the world, and the Lord of the universe. The New Testament even goes so far as to insist that our eternal destiny depends on our faith in Him alone.

ENDNOTES

1. Walter Kaiser, *Toward an Old Testament Theology* (Grand Rapids: Zondervan, 1978), 41–42.

2. For an examination of these prophecies, see Walter Kaiser, *The Messiah in the Old Testament* (Grand Rapids: Zondervan, 1995).

3. Philip Yancey, *The Bible Jesus Read* (Grand Rapids: Zondervan, 1999), 12.

Name Index

453

Subject Index

Scripture Index

IMAGE CREDITS

National Geographic: www.news.nationalgeographic.com: 379

Scofield Collection, E.C. Dargan Research Library, LifeWay Christian Resources, Nashville, Tennessee: pp. 14 (top), 16, 31 (bottom), 43, 146, 166, 192, 208, 221, 222, 239, 241, 251, 276, 280, 283, 390

Shohami, David, http://Israelstorms.netfirms.com: p. 11

Southwestern Baptist Theological Seminary, A. Webb Roberts Library, Fort Worth, Texas: p. 400

Statliche Museen zu Berlin, Berlin, Germany: p. 388

Stephens, Bill: pp. 11, 142, 281, 361, 376, 378, 386

Tolar, William B.: pp. 7, 15, 48, 64, 78, 138, 347, 358, 401, 419, 443

Wikipedia Commons, http://en.wikipedia.org: pp. 18 (top) (Golf Bravo, photographer), 18 (bottom) (public domain, drawn by Faucher-Gudin, from a photograph by Insinger), 19 (public domain, Szilas, photographer), 30 (public domain, BabelStone, photographer), 31, (public domain, photographer unknown), 33 (public domain, Yoav Dothan, photographer), 37 (ChrisO, photographer), 39 (public domain, photographer unknown), 40 (Ronia Harari, photographer), 81 (Lancastermerrin88, photographer), 266 (public domain, Garrigues, photographer), 305 (public domain, David Castor, photographer), 318 (public domain, photographer unknown), 320 (public domain, reproduction of Rembrandt art), 328 (public domain, Berachyahu ben Neriah, photographer), 345 (public domain, Jasmine N. Walthall, US Army), 435 (public domain, Photoglob AG, Zurich, Switzerland or Detroit Publishing Company, Detroit, MI)

ILLUSTRATIONS AND RECONSTRUCTIONS

Biblical Illustrator (Linden Artists, London, England): p. 89

Goolsby, Abe, Principal, Officina Abrahae, Nashville, Tennessee: pp. 100, 194

Latta, Bill, Latta Art Services, Mt. Juliet, Tennessee: pp. 58, 80, 168, 180